GAMES NATIONS PLAY

SEVENTH EDITION

GAMES NATIONS PLAY

SEVENTH EDITION

John Spanier

University of Florida

CQ PRESS

A Division of Congressional Quarterly Inc.

Excerpt on pages 231-232: From *The Great Ascent: The Struggle for Economic Development in Our Time* by Robert L. Heilbroner, 33-36. Copyright © 1963 by Robert L. Heilbroner. Reprinted by permission of Harper & Row, Publishers, Inc.

Illustration acknowledgments: Figure 2-2, reprinted with permission of *The Encyclopedia Americana,* © 1986 by Grolier Inc.; Figure 7-1, Department of State Bulletin, "World Population: The Silent Explosion," Fall 1978, 353; Figure 12-1, Center for Defense, *The Defense Monitor,* February 1979; Figure 12-2, Center for Defense Information, "U.S.-Soviet Military Facts," *The Defense Monitor,* vol. 17, no. 5 (1988): 2-3; Figure 18-1, U.S. Arms Control and Disarmament Agency, *World Military Expenditures and Arms Transfers,* 1985, 9.

Library of Congress Cataloging-in-Publication Data

Spanier, John W.
    Games nations play / John Spanier.— 7th ed.
      p.   cm.
    Includes bibliographical references.
    ISBN 0-87187-531-4
    1. International relations.   I. Title.
JX1391.S7   1990

For Suzanne

Contents

Preface   xv

Part One

THE STUDY AND ANALYSIS OF INTERNATIONAL POLITICS

CHAPTER 1

War and Thinking about International Politics   3

Shock of World War I   4
Games Nations Play   7
Theorizing about Interstate Relations   8

CHAPTER 2

The Three Levels of Analysis: A Framework for the Study of International Politics   19

A State-System Level   19
Nation-State Level   27
Decision-making Level   32
Combining the Three Levels   36

Part Two

THE STATE SYSTEM

CHAPTER 3

The Players: States and Other Actors 45

Characteristics of States 45
Classification of States 53
Nonstate Actors 60

CHAPTER 4

The Stakes: The Objectives of States 74

Power Politics 74
Security, Welfare, and Other Aims 75
Competition among Objectives 86
What Price Security? 90

CHAPTER 5

The Security Game 92

Differences Between Domestic and International Politics 92
International Politics and the 'Security Dilemma' 96
Balance of Power as a System 102
International Politics as a 'Mixed' Game 105
Characteristics of the First Level of Analysis 112
A Reminder: Analysis and Approval 114

CHAPTER 6

Same Game, Different Players 118

Unipolarity (Stable) 118
Bipolarity (Unstable) 119
Multipolarity (Stable) 121
Or Is Bipolarity Stable and Multipolarity Unstable? 122
Bipolar Structure and the Cold War 124

CHAPTER 7

The Ability to Play:
Power and the Rise and Fall of Nations 135

Perception of Power   135
Power: Carrots and Sticks   137
Calculating Power   139
War and Power   157
The Critical Importance of Economic Power   160

Part Three

THE SECOND AND THIRD LEVELS

CHAPTER 8

National and Elite Styles in Foreign Policy:
American and Soviet Perceptions and Behavior   177

Concept of Style: Insular and Continental States   177
American National Style   180
American Policy after World War II   186
Soviet Elite Style   196
Do Styles Change? Détentes I and II   210

CHAPTER 9

The Developing Countries:
The Primacy of Domestic Concerns   225

Foreign Policy as a Continuation of Domestic Politics   225
National Self-determination and Poverty   230
'Westernization' of the Developing Countries   233
Obstacles to Development   235
Nation Building and Civilian and Military Authoritarianism   254
Foreign Policy in the Bipolar Era   257
Characteristics of Nonalignment   260
Failure of Development: Internal or External Causes?   261
Changing the International Economy: Revolution or Reform?   265

CHAPTER 10

The Games Policy Makers Play 274

A Focus on Decision Makers 274
Crisis Decisions 277
Decision Making as a Pluralistic Power Struggle 281
Politics of Strategic Defense 289
American Political Process and Foreign Policy Decision Making 300
Other Systems, Different Decision Making 304
Decision Making and International Negotiations 306

CHAPTER 11

Foreign Policy: A Conclusion 310

Focus on Perception 310
Back to the Levels of Analysis 319

Part Four

HOW TO PLAY—POLITICALLY, MILITARILY, ECONOMICALLY

CHAPTER 12

The Balance of Terror 329

Bargaining and Conflict Resolution 329
Nuclear Revolution and Balance of Power 333
U.S. Arms Control Doctrine 340
Arms Race and Nuclear Peace 352

CHAPTER 13

The Use of Force 364

Limited Warfare in the Nuclear Age 364
Revolutionary Warfare 368
United States in Vietnam and Soviet Union in Afghanistan 373
War By Proxy 378
A Decline in the Use of Force? 379

CHAPTER 14

The International Political
Economy and Statecraft   389

Past Separation of Politics and Economics   389
National Independence and Self-sufficiency   390
Superpowers and Their Allies: Aid and Trade   393
Superpowers and Secondary Adversaries: Quotas,
   Boycotts, and Embargoes   397
Superpowers and the Third World   402
Economics and Power   417

CHAPTER 15

The Multinational Corporate
Revolution and Interdependence   425

Going Global   425
Free Trade and the International Economy   437
Mercantilism and 'Even Playing Fields'   438
Erosion of Hierarchy   445

Part Five

FROM STATE SYSTEM TO GLOBAL SYSTEM

CHAPTER 16

Preserving Peace in the State System   453

United Nations   453
International Law   478
Morality of Nations   483

CHAPTER 17

Peace Through Transformation
of the State System   494

From Micro- to Macropolitics: From Doom to Salvation   494

World Government Through Federalism: The American Example   496
Supranational Community Building Through Functionalism   499
Interdependence and a More Harmonious World   510
Interdepedence and American Norms   513

CHAPTER 18

Violence in a Multipolar Future   520

New Prominence of Economic Issues   523
New Strategic Environment: Proliferation of Nuclear Arms   524
Diffusion of Conventional Arms   533
Terrorism as Warfare   538
Superpowers and Regional Conflicts   547
Obsolescence of War?   551

CHAPTER 19

The Primacy of Realism   557

First Level Revisited   557
American Experience and the Elimination of War   559
Continuing Need for Realism   564

GLOSSARY   569

SELECT BIBLIOGRAPHY OF BOOKS   579

INDEX   591

TABLES

3-1 The Great Powers   54

3-2 A Select Group of Intergovernmental Organizations   63

5-1 The State System   113

6-1 Two Types of Nonnuclear State System   123

7-1 Population of Major European Powers, 1870-1914   142

7-2 Countries with Populations over 50 Million, 1988   144

7-3 Key Minerals for Which the United States Is More Than 80 Percent Import Dependent, 1980-1983   146

7-4 Ranking of Economic Capacity Among Great Powers, 1988   149

7-5 Comparative Military Strength, 1988-1989   151

9-1 Economies Classified According to Income Group   228-229

9-2 Per Capita Income of the Ten Wealthiest Nations   231

9-3 Population Estimations, 1950 and 1980, and Projections, 2000-2100   240

9-4 Population and Economic Growth Rates of Selected Developing Countries   243

9-5 One-Commodity Countries   248

9-6 Profile of Eight Newly Industrialized Countries, 1988   250

9-7 Profile of Nine Typical Developing Countries, 1988   251

10-1 Policy Characteristics   283

11-1 Two Foreign Policy Belief Systems   323-324

12-1 U.S. and Soviet Strategic Launchers (and Warheads), Summer 1988   344

12-2 Provisions of SALT I and II   348

12-3 Objectives of Arms Control and Relevant Agreements   350

12-4 Outline of a Probable START Agreement   356

15-1 Comparison of Free-Trade and Mercantilist Ideas about the International Economy   439

16-1 United Nations Membership, 1946-1985   458

16-2 Selected UN Peace-Keeping Operations, 1948-Present   462

16-3 UN Member Countries, 1945-1985   470-471

16-4 Recent U.S.-Soviet Regional Settlements or Efforts at Resolution   474

17-1 Distinctions Between Power Politics and Interdependence   514

FIGURES

2-1 Soviet Expansion in Europe Since 1939   23

2-2 German Expansion, 1935-1939   25

2-3 Different Policies, Different Actor Participation   37

7-1 The Population Explosion: Where the People Are Likely to Be in the
    Year 2000   145

9-1 Developing and Least-Developed Countries   226-227

12-1 American and Soviet Deaths in Past Wars and in a Projected Nuclear
    War   338

12-2 Breakdown of Strategic Nuclear Weapons, Soviet Union and United
    States, 1988   345

13-1 Eastern Asia   369

14-1 The Middle East and Northeastern Africa   413

17-1 European Economic Community   501

18-1 Shares of World Arms Exports, 1985   535

Preface

Since the last edition of *Games Nations Play* in 1987, world politics have undergone a startling array of changes. This new edition takes these changes into account while maintaining one of the enduring and chief purposes of the book: to teach the reader, primarily the undergraduate student, how to think about international politics in the late twentieth century. Many students are interested in learning more about particular events and issues, such as the cold war, détente, Central America, reforms under Soviet leader Mikhail Gorbachev, the Strategic Defense Initiative, terrorism, the possible reunification of the two Germanies, and the movements to "de-Communize" in Eastern Europe. But what is to be made of this information once it is acquired? In this book I try to provide the intellectual tools needed to analyze events and to gain a deeper understanding of some of the external and internal forces that states confront and the reasons they act as they do, whether they are capitalist or Communist, highly industrialized or economically underdeveloped. I also maintain a strong historical emphasis in the belief that analytical frameworks and concepts do not exist in a vacuum; they are based on events that have had the most profound and far-reaching effects.

One constant throughout the many editions of *Games Nations Play* has been its realist philosophical underpinnings. As fashionable as it has become among some academicians to criticize realism, no satisfactory substitute for its explanation of the continuities and changes in international politics has yet been found. Although other approaches have been useful, realism remains central to the study of international politics, and the reasons for this are spelled out in the concluding chapter of this book.

This edition also continues to focus on the "games nations play"—that is, the strategies and tactics states devise to achieve their security and other objectives. Although there are many ways to understand this subject, I employ three levels of analysis. The first focuses on the state system and emphasizes the balance of power among nations. The second focuses on nation-states themselves, emphasizing their domestic character. And the third level deals with decision making: policy makers' perceptions of reality and the institutions that formulate and execute policy. This three-dimensional approach, which is a modification of Kenneth Waltz's "three images" and David Singer's "levels of analysis," enables students to view a single policy or set of policies from three different—and often conflicting—perspectives.

This threefold scheme reflects my view that international events must be analyzed in the context of the state system, the environment in which they occur. This is basic. But the analyst must also pay attention to the goals of nations and their general behavior patterns, as these patterns are shaped by their societies and specific policy makers. The environment has a powerful effect upon states—for example, upon their objectives and their degrees of choice among alternative policies—but their internal character and politics also exert major influences. To borrow Carl von Clausewitz's observation that war is the continuation of politics by other means, one could also say that foreign policy often is the conduct of domestic politics by other means.

Nothing illustrates the significance of the second and third levels more than the current changes in the Soviet Union and Eastern Europe. The Communist totalitarian systems and ideologies that, together with the bipolar division of power at the end of World War II, had precipitated the cold war are being replaced by political pluralism and elements of free market economies. Above all else, the coming into power of Gorbachev—who in response to the ailing Soviet economy was willing to risk major structural reforms and was able to carry them out despite considerable resistance—made it possible to talk of a post–cold war era.

The state system has endured, and states have been the primary international actors for more than three hundred years. My emphasis on the nation-state, however, does not imply a neglect of nonstate actors, transnational forces, or analysis of "world order" politics. The economic, technological, and other forces of change in the contemporary world are discussed at length. Nevertheless, I contend that the state-centered system not only has survived but also is in some respects stronger than ever.

This seventh edition of *Games Nations Play* has undergone a number of major changes. The one that will immediately strike previous users of this book is its reorganization. Part One again provides the framework for study, and Part Two presents the first level of analysis, which is the state system; but Part Three now addresses the second and third levels of analysis—the domestic character of nation-states and decision making, respectively. The military and economic instruments of power, previously integrated into the first level, now stand as a separate section, Part Four. This rearrangement allows a more balanced, logical treatment of the three levels and an uninterrupted analysis of state behavior before proceeding to the means that states use to achieve their objectives.

This edition also reflects the increasing attention given to domestic and international economics during the past decade. Chapter 7, on power, includes a new section on economics as the most important component of power and introduces two themes that establish the basis for the later, more detailed analysis of economics. The first theme is the relationship between industrial strength and the rise and fall of the great powers since the nineteenth-century Industrial Revolution. The second is the relative industrial declines of both superpowers and the rise of Japan, China, the European Economic Community, and the newly industrialized countries (NICs), with the obvious implications these trends have for the shift away from the postwar bipolar structure to a more multipolar arrangement. Chapter 14, on the economic tools states have used historically to further their aims, is now followed by a new chapter that describes the impact of multinational corporations on the growing interdependence of Western industrial economies (including Japan), as well as the rapidly modernizing economies of the NICs, especially in Asia. The effects of this interdependence, the need for cooperation among the Western states, and the opposing trend toward economic rivalry and mercantilist policies are fully examined at the end of this new chapter.

Another change in this edition is the material on the impact of Gorbachev and his policies of *glasnost* and *perestroika* within the Soviet Union. These have done much to reduce cold war tensions. As Moscow, to everyone's surprise, tolerated the increasing de-Communization of Eastern Europe, and German reunification became a possibility, the end of the cold war seemed near. The contrast between Soviet ideology and behavior in the seven pre-Gorbachev decades and in the Gorbachev era (presented in Chapter 8) is startling.

The speed of the change in the U.S.-Soviet rivalry was also surprising. In the early 1980s the United States had launched a huge rearmament program in response to the prior Soviet one; among the U.S. proposals was President Ronald Reagan's ambitious plan for a space-based defense of the nation's population. In the related area of the politics of strategic defense, Chapter 10, on decision making, includes a new section on this Strategic Defense Initiative. Chapters 12 and 13, an analysis of the effect of nuclear weapons on the threat of force and the actual use of force in the contemporary world, have been revised extensively, with new sections on the strategic arms control regime and the achievements and failures in this critical area.

An author is indebted to many people. I am grateful to the undergraduates at the University of Florida, who over the years have taken my introductory international politics course, who have been exposed to different ways of organizing this material, and who have been kind and gentle in suggesting helpful improvements. Special thanks is also due to Timothy Lomperis of Duke University, whose detailed criticisms of the draft of this, as well as the last, edition were very insightful and helpful; to Joseph Nogee of the University of Houston, who has never failed to let me know what improvements I should make; and to CQ Press director Joanne Daniels, who wanted this book and has done everything she could to make it an even better one; and not least, to Sabra Bissette Ledent, for her careful editing of this edition.

J. S.

Part One

THE STUDY AND ANALYSIS OF INTERNATIONAL POLITICS

CHAPTER 1

War and Thinking About International Politics

Conflict and war historically have been the chief characteristics of international politics and now threaten the end of civilization. In fact, the destructiveness of war has grown so enormously as a result of nationalism, industrialization, and technological innovation that the world may be living in the Indian summer of its existence, to be followed by a "nuclear winter," which will end the history of the human race.[1] This possibility was apparent as early as World War I. When the carnage of that war ended in 1918, Winston Churchill, who was later to become Great Britain's prime minister, wrote,

> Mankind has got into its hands for the first time the tools by which it can unfailingly accomplish its own extermination. . . . Death stands at attention, obedient, expectant, . . . ready, if called on, to pulverise, without hope of repair, what is left of civilisation. He awaits only the word of command. He awaits it from a frail, bewildered being, long his victim, now—for one occasion only—his Master.[2]

Although war, not surprisingly, is often regarded as somehow abnormal—at best an awful error, at worst a criminal undertaking—the fact is that the history of war is as old as human history. In this century the brutality of war has greatly influenced thinking about international politics. This is why this chapter will look first at the impact of war in this century and then at some of the principal schools of thought about international conflict and war. That examination will place the discipline, as well as the approaches in this book, in perspective.

3

SHOCK OF WORLD WAR I

World War I was a cataclysmic experience for Europe. With the exception of the French Revolution, World War I was the first total war Europe had experienced since the Treaty of Westphalia (1648) ended the slaughter of the Thirty Years' War. To be sure, Europe had witnessed a number of wars during the nineteenth century, but these had been minor and of brief duration. World War I also was expected to last only a few months, and casualties were expected to be no heavier than in past wars. But, after the almost one hundred years of relative peace that followed the Congress of Vienna in 1815, which brought the war with Napoleon to a close, Europe suffered the shock of a four-year total war and a terrible bloodletting. Once Germany's initial offensive into France was halted, the war on the western front bogged down in trenches. First one side, then the other tried to break through the opponent's lines, but neither could do so. Successive lines of barbed wire protected each side's trenches. The murderous machine-gun and rapid rifle fire mowed down row after row of advancing infantry. Breakthroughs became impossible.

Yet the offensives continued. The generals had learned, after all, that the only defense was the offense. Thus, headquarters continued to hurl their armies into battles. The artillery first laid down a barrage, sometimes lasting a week or longer, on the opponent's trenches. This tactic was supposed to pulverize the enemy's position and shatter the morale of the troops. It was a simple idea that should have worked but never did. Killing became the objective. If enemy lines could not be ruptured, at least the enemy could be worn down by the various offensives. Sooner or later, these constant blows would wear down troop reserves, and morale would collapse. World War I was not a war of mobility and maneuver but a war of attrition—an organized, four-year-long attempt by both sides to gain victory simply by bleeding each other to death. It was an unsophisticated strategy.

The French lost 955,000 men in five months of 1914; in 1915, 1,430,000 men; and in 1916, 900,000 men. The losses for single battles were staggering. The 1916 German attempt to bleed the French at Verdun led to a ten-month battle that cost France 535,000 casualties and Germany 427,000—almost a million men altogether. A British attempt to pierce German lines in the same year resulted in the five-month Battle of the Somme. Although they pounded the German lines with artillery for eight days before sending troops into battle, the British gained only 120 square miles, at the cost of 420,000 men, or 3,500 per square mile. The Germans lost 445,000 men. Some estimates place the total Somme casualties at 1.2 million, the highest of any battle in history. At Ypres in 1917 the British bombardment lasted nineteen days; 321 trainloads of shells were fired, the equivalent of a year's production by 55,000 war workers. This time the English forces captured forty-five square miles, at the cost of 370,000 men, or 8,222 per square mile. By comparison, total British Empire casualties during the six years of World

War II were almost 1.25 million, including 350,000 dead and 91,000 missing. Approximately 9 million men in uniform were killed during the four years of the Great War, as World War I was called, and the number of dead civilians totaled an additional several million.[3]

But the impact of war cannot be measured merely by citing statistics of the dead. The real impact also must be understood psychologically. Losses are not just quantitative; they are qualitative as well. A nation can ill afford to lose millions of men, nor can it afford to lose almost an entire generation. Is it any wonder that the nations of Europe, which lost so many of their young men who would have fathered children, also lost their self-confidence and their hope for the future? Those who would have supplied this vigor and optimism, had they grown up and become the leaders of government, business, labor, and science, lay dead in Flanders Field.

For Europe, then, the Great War was the Great Divide. The nineteenth century had been one of confidence. Democracy was spreading in Europe and was expected to spread to all other continents too, as soon as colonialism had prepared the natives of Asia and Africa for self-government. The future would belong to the common people; their rights and freedom would supplant the traditional privileges of the few. For the first time in history, people would join together across national boundaries in a new world of mutual understanding and good will. Peace would be both inevitable and permanent. Science and technology would improve everyone's standard of living; the age-old economics of scarcity would be transformed into an economics of abundance and affluence. Poverty and misery would be ended forever. This optimism and faith in progress was aptly voiced by an American, Andrew Carnegie, in his instructions to the trustees of the Carnegie Endowment for International Peace: "When . . . war is discarded as disgraceful to civilized man, the trustees will please then consider what is the next most degrading evil or evils whose banishment . . . would most advance the progress, elevation and happiness of man." [4] It was just a matter of time then until war would be eliminated. It would have been contrary to the spirit of the age to ask whether this abolition of war could indeed be achieved.

The Great War changed this optimism to pessimism, this confidence to doubt and fear. The West's utter certainty of its own greatness and future lay shattered on the battlefields among the decaying corpses. For the first time, Western scholars talked about the "decline of the West." Europe's imperial control was weakened abroad, and at home the expected trend toward democracy was halted, if not reversed. Fascism took over in Italy, nazism gained power in Germany, and Benito Mussolini and Adolf Hitler together helped Francisco Franco seize control of Spain. In eastern Europe, only Czechoslovakia could be considered a democratic country. The nineteenth century had believed in the supremacy of reason and its ability to make the world a safer and better place in which to live. In the interwar period, demagoguery and the manipulation of hysterical crowds, totalitarianism and its warlike spirit, seemed the wave of the future.

As the structure and hopes of the previous one hundred years began to crash all around them, the leaders of France and England became concerned above all with avoiding another war. "No more war, no more war" became their cry. And who could blame them? These leaders were concerned not merely with their personal survival. They were men of honorable intentions and decent motives, greatly concerned about the welfare of their citizens and repelled by the horror and senselessness of modern war. It is easy today to sneer at the appeasement of Hitler, but to the survivors of World War I another war could only mean the slaughter and seemingly wasteful sacrifices of Verdun and the Somme. They still heard the "soldiers marching, all to die." And they remembered that the strain of that war had collapsed four of Europe's great empires: Austria-Hungary, Ottoman Turkey, Imperial Russia, and Imperial Germany. They also recalled that, despite Germany's grievous losses, its European opponents had suffered twice as many losses—and their populations were smaller than Germany's. If fighting another war involved another such blood bath, surely they would be signing their nations' death warrants. Their social structures and morale could not absorb such losses for the second time in two generations. To most people who had lived through the tragic war years, peace became a supreme value. The appeasement of Hitler during the 1930s was to them not just the only policy—it was an absolute necessity. Surely it was saner to resolve differences with reason than with guns. Would it not be better to understand each other's legitimate grievances and settle differences in a spirit of good will rather than by war? Was it not preferable to make mutual concessions, thereby diminishing distrust and fear, and build the mutual confidence that could be the only basis of a firm peace? To ask these questions was to answer them for most of the survivors of World War I. Between the alternatives of appeasement and war, no one of good will and humanity had a choice.

Long before the atom bomb, then, war had already become so costly that questions about its usability were widespread. Instead of the short and not very costly conflict that the diplomats, soldiers, and others had expected, the long and extremely costly Great War was the first modern war to raise the issue of the legitimacy and rationality of warfare as an instrument for advancing a nation's purposes. After 1945 and six years of fighting in which the loss of life, military and civilian, exceeded that of the First World War, the futility of another total war became obvious to all. World War II had ended with the dropping of two atomic bombs, each of which had caused a heavy loss of life and widespread destruction. The bomb was quickly called the "absolute weapon." What was the point of defending one's way of life if, in the process, that way of life was utterly destroyed? In the nuclear age total war had become irrational; the costs of such a war completely exceeded any conceivable gains. One knew that without even having to fight. Had the leaders of Europe, who went to war in 1914, been able to look into a crystal ball and foresee what the costs would be, they might have chosen a different course. Today, we have that crystal ball.[5]

GAMES NATIONS PLAY

The problem is that war cannot be isolated from international conflict in general. To be specific, states have long used war to transact their business. Despite the growing costs of war in the twentieth century, the "games nations play" continue. The games analogy is used because the principal players—states—reject any higher authority.[6] Each state, like any player in a competitive game, seeks to advance its own interests in conflict with those of other states. In this pursuit of its national interests, a state will resort to the use of force if it cannot achieve or defend its goals in any other way. States play this game, of course, with different capabilities; the main players historically have been the most powerful states. The stakes or payoffs are critical: survival, a degree of security, influence, and status, as well as wealth, are some of the principal ones.

Because each state looks at the world from its particular perspective and must plan its moves—its strategy—to enhance its security and other objectives, the games analogy is an apt one. Each state is a player, and each plays to win in a game in which it competes with almost 170 other nations. And although the great powers have in the past been the chief players, today other countries—such as Egypt, Iran, Israel, Libya, Syria, and many other less influential nations—are active participants in the game. Each must therefore concern itself with competing effectively, especially with those states that are its immediate rivals. In this context, the term *strategy* is not defined in its usual narrow military sense, referring to winning a war. Instead, it is defined as a set of calculated moves, a set of decisions, in a competitive and conflictual situation in which the outcome is not governed by pure chance.[7] In other words, the idea of strategy is used as it would be when speaking of chess or football, games that are governed by known formal rules, or politics or dating, activities governed mainly by informal rules. In international politics, as political scientist John Lovell has said, each state seeks to advance its "national interests" in conflict with those of other states in a game whose rules are largely informal and unwritten, evolving mainly through the behavior of the strongest players.[8] A state may advance its interests offensively or it may do so defensively, but in either case, the players must weigh carefully the alternative means of achieving their objectives and then choose the option that will maximize their gains and minimize their losses, as well as their risks and costs.

Thus, there are lots of games going on, such as *adversary games,* in which two or more states are engaged in conflict, and *alignment games,* in which states seek help from other states or seek to attract allies away from their adversaries either in a straight de-alignment or a realignment toward themselves. Just as the alignment game is subsidiary to the adversary game, so too is the arms competition or *preparedness (arms race) game,* in which adversaries seek at a minimum to stay even with their opponents' strengths or at maximum to gain superiority.[9] Another is the *economic game,* played because to maintain its well-being, a state usually must import goods and materials, as well as export the same, and, ideally, maintain a balance between the two. The basic game, however, which historically has constituted the essence of international politics, is the great-power adversary *political-military game*. In a decentralized system of sovereign states, the lack of a superior and legitimate world government—to allocate political, military, and economic goods peacefully and manage the political and economic relations among states peacefully—ensures the survival of the state system, "the womb in which war develops."[10] Thus, international politics focuses on the relations or interactions among states, although states are not the only players. The "games nations play" is therefore basically about *who gets what, when, and how* (see Chapter 5).

Now that the essence of international politics has been defined, how can one better understand it? The answer depends on how it is studied. What follows is a brief examination of some of the principal ways this has been done.

THEORIZING ABOUT INTERSTATE RELATIONS

Historical Approach

The years before World War I were, as already noted, a time of optimism. To be sure, there were wars, but they were limited in objectives and duration. The three wars of German unification of 1862, 1866, and 1870 (against Denmark, Austria-Hungary, and France, respectively) were seen as models for future wars. When the European powers went to war in August 1914, they expected that the "boys" would be home by the time the leaves fell from the trees.

Before the outbreak of World War I, not much attention was given to a theory of international politics. Indeed, international politics was never a preoccupation of Western political thought, which focused primarily on domestic issues. Thinking about conflict among states was largely intermittent and fragmentary. By contrast, Western thinking about order, justice, and liberty within Western states has been continuous and well developed; these subjects are found in the works of Plato and Aristotle. Before the twentieth century, however, only a handful of writers produced works on interstate politics that have become classics: Thucydides, who wrote about the war between Athens and Sparta in ancient Greece; Niccolò Machiavelli, who sought to advise a prince on how to unify Italy; and Thomas Hobbes, an English philosopher who speculated about the life of man in a state of nature. One could even add a few names like Polybius, who wrote about the war between Rome and Carthage; David Hume, who wrote on the balance of power; and Hugo Grotius, who wrote extensively about international law.

If there was a focus at all, it was diplomatic history. In a sense, this was international politics because it recounted what had transpired between nations in the past. But in another sense, diplomatic history cannot be equated with a theory of international politics. Discovering what happened in the years immediately before 1914 can yield an enormous amount of information on specific political and military leaders, the political climate and social and economic conditions within specific countries, their planned military strategies and armaments, and how all these interacted to produce World War I. But this is not to say that some of the issues, such as why the war occurred or who was most responsible for it, will ever be settled; historians in each generation tend to reinterpret earlier events. Nevertheless, diplomatic history can tell us much about such events.

That is precisely its shortcoming. Historians focus on the descriptions of specific events, which are unique to those times and places. While they can tell us how and why a specific war happened, they do not tell us why wars occur more generally. A *theory* of international politics would attempt to answer this question. Such a theory would not look at each war as unique, but would analyze many wars. It would then specify from the data exactly which conditions seem repeatedly to result in war. For example, if the study of half a dozen wars showed that the victors four times out of six fell out with each other, leading to a new struggle and possibly war, one could generalize and state: if, at the end of hostilities, the victors cannot agree on peace terms—or, more crudely, a division of the spoils—a new war may result. Of course, war may not break out each time this situation occurs, but, if it happened sufficiently often in the past, it is likely to occur in the future.

Other conditions that have led to war also can be identified. It took the trauma of World War I, however, to bring about a more sustained search for a theory of international politics. As a discipline, international politics is a product of the twentieth century and, to a large extent, a product of American scholarship.

Utopianism

World War I was a shock for Europe, the worse for not having been expected. Why had it occurred? How could such a senseless slaughter have gone on? Alliances, arms races, and secret diplomacy frequently were cited as the causes. Power politics was blamed; it was alleged that all the great powers had recklessly pursued their national interests. Not surprisingly then the beginning of thinking about international politics started with utopian aspirations: there must be no recurrence of world war. Thus, the motive spurring on the initial theorizing was the passionate desire to avoid another war.[11] War was a disease infecting the body politic; it had to be cut out. But wishing prevailed over careful analysis, and the focus was on the end to be achieved. President Woodrow Wilson typified this mood. On his way to Paris to attend the postwar peace conference, Wilson was asked whether his plan for a League of

Nations to keep the peace would work. He replied, "If it won't work, it must be made to work." [12]

The resulting study of international politics concentrated on three different approaches. First, there was the emphasis on the League of Nations, in which the nations of the world would be represented. In this forum negotiations and debates could be observed by the publics of all countries, making it impossible for secret diplomacy to produce another war. The assumption was that national leaders, unrestrained by public opinion, might intrigue again in the future. Ordinary people, who did the fighting and dying, were believed to be peaceful and would thus watch for and prevent agreements secretly made; agreements or covenants were to be arrived at openly. It was hoped therefore that nations would cooperate within the league's framework, de-emphasizing their nations' egotisms and selfish interests. Second, there were disarmament conferences that aimed to reduce, if not eliminate, the number of arms possessed by the great powers. Examples include German disarmament in the Treaty of Versailles (1919) and the Washington Naval Conference (1921-1922), limiting naval rivalry in the Pacific. Third, there were legal efforts to decrease the likelihood of war. A specific American contribution was the Kellogg-Briand Pact (1928), which for the first time outlawed war as an instrument of state policy—except, of course, wars conducted in "self-defense." Collectively, the twenty years between the two world wars were a time when thinking about international politics, both academically and popularly, in the English-speaking world was characterized by the almost complete neglect of the reality of power.

The search for an end to war was accompanied by a political shift in the domestic policies of the Western democracies, especially Britain and France, which, until World War I, had often been belligerents. This political change was to have a profound impact on the conduct of foreign policy. Before 1914, the conduct of foreign policy had been left basically to the diplomats and soldiers. Foreign policy was usually regarded not as a matter for popular opinion and party politics, but as a matter for experts. This was as true for the democracies as for the more autocratic states such as Germany or czarist Russia. But after the slaughter of World War I, the people of the Western democracies, who had suffered so much, wanted control over foreign policy as they had over domestic policy. Georges Clemenceau, France's premier, uttered a line that was to become famous: "War!" he said, "it is much too serious a matter to be entrusted to the military," and foreign policy, he implied, to the diplomats. In short, foreign policy was now, like domestic politics, to be subjected to popular accountability. The result was twofold. First, a vengeful public opinion in Britain and France was a major reason for the punitive peace treaty imposed on Germany in 1919. And, second, during the 1930s a fearful public opinion was the reason for the appeasement of Hitler; it made a policy of opposition to Germany—as well as to Italy and Japan—impossible. Ironically, the public yearning for peace produced the same result that the soldiers and diplomats had produced earlier.

Realism

Just as World War I was blamed on power politics, it was widely believed that World War II stemmed from the neglect of power politics. If an arms race and close alliances were thought to be responsible for the hostilities of 1914-1918, the failure of the British and French to match German arms and to stand together against Hitler precipitated what Churchill was to call the "unnecessary war." [13] Realism was the reaction to interwar idealism. If war was to be prevented, more than wishful thinking was needed. The reality was that there were ambitious and warlike states that were unappeasable and had to be opposed, and that this required, among other things, a willingness to risk war and strong military forces to support a policy of deterrence. To fear risking war left the states that most desired peace at the mercy of the more ruthless states. Not to build the required strength to avoid provoking a potential aggressor left a state with no choice but to submit to an aggressor's demands and to become a victim.

Realism was to become the dominant school of thinking in postwar America, now the West's chief defender against the Soviet Union. Realism resurrected traditional ideas: that states were the primary actors in international politics; that the environment or state system in which states lived was essentially anarchical; that conflict in this system could at best be managed to reduce the likelihood of war, but war could not be abolished. The central point was that there was no final solution to the problem of war. Appeals to humanity's common interest in survival, appeals to replace the state system with some form of world government, were all in vain. Management of the system had to be rooted in every state's "national interest," and the best way of preserving peace was to maintain the balance of power. The key to the conduct of foreign policy was prudence: states needed to be cautious, not launch crusades against one another. They also had to be flexible and accommodating in their diplomacy. The key figures in the realist revolution were Hans Morgenthau, a German refugee scholar; George Kennan, a U.S. diplomat and historian of Russia; and Reinhold Niebuhr, a Protestant minister.

Realism, however, soon came under attack. For one thing, realism became identified with Morgenthau, whose book *Politics Among Nations* had a profound influence upon American academia.[14] The works of more sophisticated analysts, such as Arnold Wolfers, John Herz, Kennan, and Niebuhr, were largely overlooked at first.[15] One frequent criticism of Morgenthau and, therefore, of realism in general, was that, although it claimed to describe international politics as it was and not in utopian terms, its frequent advice to policy makers on the conduct of foreign policy suggested that states did not in fact behave as the realists described. A second criticism was that, despite their common outlook, realists often disagreed with one another. For example, Morgenthau surprisingly came out early against U.S. intervention in Vietnam, but others supported that policy. Such disagreements raised questions about the value of realism as a guide to making the "correct" foreign policy. A third criticism was that if governments continued to cling to realism in their conduct of foreign policy, nuclear war would be inevitable, an unacceptable result. Most of all, perhaps, the realist outlook was alien to the American outlook. The emphasis on power and the acceptance of conflict and war as natural rather than abnormal and transitory were "un-American" (see Chapters 8 and 19). Realism was especially offensive because it appeared at best amoral, if not downright immoral, in a country that prides itself on being a morally superior nation and that often feels guilty when its foreign policy is not—or does not appear to be—moral.

Behavioralism

Both idealism and realism supplied a unifying focus. What followed in the 1960s and 1970s had no such focus. Instead, what displaced realism—or attempted to do so—was a host of different approaches, some of which were called theories, and others, more cautiously, pretheories. Most were characterized by their way of investigating international politics. The word *investigating* is a clue to this new approach. Utopianism had posited a purpose that had to be achieved. "The wish is father to the thought" was its origin, and its aim was to cure a "sick" international body politic. The actual behavior of states was not a matter for investigation; that behavior was all too clear and it had to be changed! Realism, by contrast, asserted that the twenty years from 1919 to 1939 demonstrated conclusively that the Western democracies' neglect of the reality of power led to the very result their behavior sought to avoid; that those states willing to resort to power—all antidemocratic states—threatened to become dominant; and that those states who believed in reason, mutual good will, and accommodation, but who were not backed by sufficient power, had to retreat and, in the final analysis, had to go to war anyway to save themselves. But the fact that realists had to advise states about how they should behave to better protect themselves suggested realism's weakness—states often acted in ways seemingly contradictory to their best interests.

This is where behaviorism entered. Rejecting both an end to be achieved and *a priori* assumptions about how states behaved, its advocates stated that their purpose was to investigate international politics without any reformist desires or biased preconceptions.[16] Their analyses would be *value free* or *empirical.* They intended to observe the many forms of state behavior, collect the necessary data, and carefully draw conclusions from their studies. In opposition to earlier researchers, who were then almost scornfully called *traditionalists* for their reliance on the study of history, diplomatic memories, and experiences, the behaviorists claimed to be political *scientists.* Obviously, political scientists interested in international politics were part of a larger group of analysts looking at other fields, such as American and comparative politics, as well as novel areas, such as political methodology. Methodology was in fact the heart of the behavioral approach: how to study a particular type of human activity. And the change in the technique for studying political science was only part of a far larger movement spreading across all American social sciences.

The scientific method claimed not only an unbiased approach to research—that investigators could separate their own values from "the facts" and the manner in which they organized these facts—but also, as already suggested, an ability to generalize about the behavior of states and other political actors in the international arena. The political scientists looked for patterns of behavior such as the one mentioned earlier: when one of the victors of a war perceives that its interests are not satisfied at the postwar peace conference—or, at least, that its gains are not as great as those of some of its fellow victors—conflict results and war may occur. Or, if the defeated state harbors grievances against the victors because of the harshness of the settlement they have imposed upon it, the loser may seek to remedy this matter militarily, as well as to avenge its previous humiliation. These generalizations about the conditions under which past wars have erupted allow theorists to hypothesize that *if* the above conditions exist, *then* war results.

What especially characterized much of the behavioral inquiry during the 1950s, 1960s, and 1970s was its use of aggregate data, quantitative techniques, computers, formal models, and the general "laws" of behavior, as well as its rather arrogant attitude toward earlier methods of research.[17] Often implicit in behaviorists' attitudes was the claim that if it could not be quantified, it was not worth saying. Earlier analyses of international politics tended to be dismissed as not only traditional but impressionistic, if not poetic. Only quantitative methods, it was asserted, could be free from bias and produce accurate and verifiable empirical studies of the behavior of international actors. Despite this strong, and occasionally dogmatic, point of view, it is fair to say that even nonquantitative scholars were deeply influenced by the behavioral approach. For whatever its claims to being scientific, let alone holding the only correct approach to the truth, its essence was an emphasis on careful scholarship and analytical precision. Its goals, as two of its proponents have suggested, were to substitute verifiable knowledge for subjective belief, testable evidence for intuitive explanations, and data for appeals to "expert" or "authoritative" opinion.[18] Traditional scholars, probably feeling defensive, and also wishing to avoid being considered outside the mainstream of American political science, reacted by demonstrating greater care in their research activities.

The intensity of the battle between the traditional and scientific or empirical approaches therefore diminished over time. Traditional scholars showed more precision in their analyses, and at least some of the behaviorists interested in international politics were ready to admit that several charges leveled by the traditionalists were not totally unjustified. These charges included a preoccupation with what sometimes appeared to be methodology for the sake of methodology; a focus on issues to which their methods could be applied, frequently issues of a secondary or even lesser significance, if not irrelevant; and a disregard of a world of nuclear weapons, widespread poverty, and injustice.

Even more basic, every study, no matter how carefully carried out, starts out with some assumptions. They may be implicit and the investigators unaware of their influence. Nevertheless, researchers' selection of facts and how the facts are organized and interpreted are hardly value free. Every social scientist starts with a purpose, perhaps to eliminate war or make a better world. "It is the purpose of promoting health which creates medical science. . . . Desire to cure the sickness of the body politic has given its impulse and its inspiration to political science. . . . Purpose and analysis became part and parcel of single process." [19]

Contemporary Approaches

Currently, there are basically two schools of thought that receive much attention. Both shift the focus of analysis from politics to economics, and both are essentially nineteenth-century analyses, brought up-to-date and applied to contemporary conditions. One school of thought can trace its heritage to the classical liberal tradition of free trade, which was supposed to create a common interest in peace by bringing all nations a higher standard of living. But war would disrupt free trade and was therefore counterproductive. In its modernized twentieth-century form, interdependence—the close linking of states to one another—also focuses on the formation of transnational economic, social, and technological bonds. Functionalism, a form of this thesis current during the 1950s, emphasized the almost automatic nature of growing ties between nations, a process that was supposed to lead to the United States of Europe.[20] In its 1970s version, the emphasis shifted from regional interdependence to global interdependence.[21] The claim remained the same: the growing ties between countries will increasingly shift state behavior from one marked by conflict and the use of force to one characterized by cooperation based on common interests. A principal indicator of this shift from realism to interdependence is the *regimes* that states establish, incorporating the rules governing their cooperation or decision-making procedures. These rules are used to resolve disputes over various issues, whether military or economic.[22] Disputes occur between adversaries as in arms control regimes or among friendly states as in trade regimes.

The other school of thought, somewhat alien to the other American approaches, is a contemporary version of the nineteenth-century Marxist approach; it is called "dependency."[23] Marxism—actually, Marxism-Leninism—asserted a causal relationship between Western capitalism and imperial expansion. Dependency shares with interdependence a global outlook, but, unlike interdependence, it postulates that an international capitalist economy holds the developing countries, the former colonies, in a dependency relationship as in the old colonial period. Although these nations have gained political independence, the claim is that they remain tied economically to the Western industrial and capitalist states, especially the United States, for markets, capital, and technology. This relationship is viewed as an unequal one and fundamentally an exploitive one. That is why, years after achieving independence, the developing countries remain economically backward. According to the dependency theory, development will come if capitalism is overthrown within the Western states—an unlikely prospect—or if the developing countries liberate themselves by throwing off their capitalist chains. Besides its radical approach to international politics, this school differs from interdependence in emphasizing conflict, revolution, and violence to gain true "national liberation." This radical analysis also differs from the utopian and realist approaches by arguing that the cause of international conflict and war lies in the existence of a particular economic system. Thus the struggle for power is neither the cause of war nor its abolition the solution for peace.

Another Approach: Three Levels of Analysis

Theories of international politics thus are intended to help us organize, interpret, and even predict "reality." To make any sense at all of international politics, one must start by learning how to cope with enormous amounts of fragmented information. Each person perceives reality by abstracting from the totality of experience those parts that he or she considers relevant. And such perceptions are selective. They are bound to be, for obviously no one sees every aspect of reality; the world is so complex and perplexing that simplification is necessary even to begin to understand it. These perceptions of reality are called *theories*. Other words, often used interchangeably with theory, are *approach, paradigm,* or *analytical framework*. Whatever the words, they are a way of looking at a subject from a particular perspective—such as those described earlier. One looks to them for help in organizing much of that random information, selecting the relevant facts or data, arranging them in some intelligible order, and, thereby, interpreting and understanding reality or "what's going on" a bit better. If the perspective is that of the state system, with a focus on the relationships between states and the balance of power, we will see the world quite differently from those with a Marxist perspective, with its emphasis on class struggle, international capitalism, economic dominance, and dependency among states.

Each theory or approach organizes the facts differently; indeed, each is likely to pick out quite different facts. Inherent in each are certain assumptions about what features are important and what events and other factors need to be described and analyzed. Such theories may be informed and sophisticated, producing carefully formulated hypotheses as a result of precise and dispassionate observation and analysis, or they may be simple and intuitive, realizing rather crude generalizations. Indeed, some of these theories are based on *a priori* assumptions that the researcher assumes exist, never proves, and then illustrates them with many examples. Marxism is one such approach with its doctrinaire insistence that war is the result of economic conditions, specifically the result of capitalists searching for foreign markets.

Whatever it is, a theory helps us organize and interpret the reality called international politics. In theorizing, as already noted, we first simplify this reality because we cannot possibly describe all aspects of international politics; we must be selective. We isolate and emphasize certain aspects of this reality and throw them into bold relief, enabling us to make a "conceptual blueprint" of the political life among states. In a sense, we act as an artist would when viewing a panorama. Artists cannot include every detail in their paintings; instead, they select and highlight certain parts of the view, relegate others to the background, and omit still others. The finished painting will be the landscape as seen by the artist's eyes, from a particular physical position and mental perspective. The painting is, in this respect, a partial representation of actuality, emphasizing those features that the artist most wanted to communicate.

We too paint a picture; indeed, to get as complete a picture of the international political landscape as possible, we view that landscape from different perspectives, or "levels of analysis." The problem is one of scope and emphasis. The view is three-dimensional, including the state system, the nation-state, and decision making.[24] At the first level one considers the behavior of states as shaped by the international system and the rules they must respect if they are to survive and be secure. The focus is the environment in which states live, where their concern is with the balance of power or equilibrium. The system, it is assumed, imposes its own logic on each member state. Neglect of the balance threatens the security of states and upsets the system's equilibrium. States therefore ought to act to preserve the balance.

At the second level state behavior is explained not as the outcome of the external environment, but as a reflection of the state's nature (whether capitalist or socialist, democratic or totalitarian, developed or undeveloped). The focus here is on the individual member states rather than the system in which they all live. The concern is with the kind of economic or political system a state possesses, its degree of development, as well as such factors as its class structures, character of its elites, and "national style." The assumption is that there is a relationship between a state's domestic character and its foreign policy.

At the third level foreign policy is explained as a product of the domestic system, but the focus is not on social, economic, political, and cultural characteristics. Instead, it is on the people involved in making and executing foreign policy decisions. Similar states—for example, two capitalist countries or two Communist countries—often pursue quite different policies. Therefore, it is necessary to look at the people making foreign policy, the institutions involved, and the processes of decision making to understand why specific states do what they do.

Together, these three levels of analysis give a comprehensive picture of the "games nations play"—particularly, why and how and for what purposes they play these games. No one level by itself presents the complete picture. The focus on individual states parallels the psychologist's concentration on the individual's personality and character. But, obviously, an individual's behavior can be understood properly only if it is related to the social environment—family, peer groups, and society in general—of that individual. Rather than continue in this abstract fashion, the next chapter takes a preliminary look at case studies at each level of analysis before each level is studied later in greater detail.

For Review

1. What kinds of games are played by nations?
2. Based on these games, what then is international politics?
3. How has war in this century, particularly World War I, influenced the study of international politics?
4. What were some of the "isms" influencing the past study of international politics?
5. What are the two schools of thought currently receiving much attention?

Notes

1. Gwynne Dyer, *War* (Homewood, Ill.: Dorsey Press, 1985), xi.
2. Winston S. Churchill, *The Gathering Storm,* vol. 1 of *The Second World War* (Boston: Houghton Mifflin, 1948), 40.
3. On the slaughter of World War I, see Theodore Ropp, *War in the Modern World,* rev. ed. (New York: Collier, 1962); Hanson W. Baldwin, *World War I: An Outline History* (New York: Harper & Row, 1962); Leon Wolff, *In Flanders Field* (New York: Viking, 1958); and, particularly, Alistair Horne, *The Price of Glory: Verdun 1916* (New York: St. Martin's Press, 1962).
4. Quoted in *Political Realism and the Crisis of World Politics* by Kenneth W. Thompson (Princeton, N.J.: Princeton University Press, 1960), 18.
5. Harvard Nuclear Study Group, *Living with Nuclear Weapons* (New York: Bantam Books, 1983), 43-44.
6. On games and the strategies employed, whether formal ones as in football or baseball, or informal ones as in courting, see Eric Berne, *Games People Play* (New York: Grove Press, 1964). The title of this book obviously was influenced by Berne's. Also see John P. Lovell, *Foreign Policy in Perspective* (New York: Holt, Rinehart & Winston, 1970), part 2.
7. Lovell, *Foreign Policy in Perspective,* 65.
8. Ibid.
9. Glenn H. Snyder and Paul Diesing, *Conflict Among Nations* (Princeton, N.J.: Princeton University Press, 1977), 429.
10. Carl von Clausewitz, *On War,* ed. and trans. Michael Howard and Peter Paret (Princeton, N.J.: Princeton University Press, 1976).
11. Edward H. Carr, *The Twenty Years' Crisis, 1919-1939* (London: Macmillan, 1951), 8.
12. Ibid.
13. Churchill, *Gathering Storm,* iv.
14. Hans J. Morgenthau, *Politics among Nations* (New York: Knopf, 1950).

15. Arnold Wolfers, *Discord and Collaboration* (Baltimore: Johns Hopkins University Press, 1962); John Herz, *Political Realism and Political Idealism* (Chicago: University of Chicago Press, 1951); George F. Kennan, *American Diplomacy 1900-1950* (Chicago: University of Chicago Press, 1951); and Reinhold Niebuhr, *Moral Man and Immoral Society* (New York: Scribner's, 1952). Henry Kissinger was one of the younger realists. For his memoirs as the president's national security assistant and secretary of state during the years 1969-1976, see *White House Years* and *Years of Upheaval* (Boston: Little, Brown, 1979 and 1982, respectively).
    For a thoughtful critique, see Michael Joseph Smith, *Realist Thought from Weber to Kissinger* (Baton Rouge: Louisiana State University Press, 1987).

16. Klaus Knorr and James N. Rosenau, eds., *Contending Approaches to International Politics* (Princeton, N.J.: Princeton University Press, 1969); Morton Kaplan, *Systems and Process in International Politics* (New York: Wiley, 1957); James N. Rosenau, ed., *International Politics and Foreign Policy*, 2d ed. (New York: Free Press, 1969); and Rosenau, *The Scientific Study of Foreign Policy* (New York: Free Press, 1971).

17. Rosenau, *International Politics and Foreign Policy*; J. David Singer, ed., *Quantitative International Politics* (New York: Free Press, 1968); Dina A. Zinnes, *Contemporary Research in International Relations* (New York: Free Press, 1976); and Herbert C. Kelman, ed., *International Behavior* (New York: Holt, Rinehart & Winston, 1965).

18. Charles W. Kegley, Jr., and Eugene R. Wittkopf, *World Politics*, 2d ed. (New York: St. Martin's Press, 1985), 21.

19. Carr, *Twenty Years' Crisis*, 3. Also see Yale H. Ferguson and Richard W. Mansbac, *The Elusive Guest* (Columbia: University of South Carolina Press, 1988), 32-34.

20. Ernst B. Haas, *The Uniting of Europe* (Stanford, Calif.: Stanford University Press, 1958).

21. Seyom Brown, *New Forces in World Politics* (Washington, D.C.: Brookings, 1974); and Robert O. Keohane and Joseph S. Nye, *Power and Interdependence* (Boston: Little, Brown, 1977).

22. Stephen D. Krasner, "Structural Causes and Regime Consequences," *International Organization* (Spring 1982): 185-206. The entire issue is devoted to regimes.

23. James Caporaso, ed., "Dependence and Dependency in the Global System," *International Organization* (Winter 1978); and Howard Wiarda, ed., *New Directions in Comparative Politics* (Boulder, Colo.: Westview Press, 1985).

24. The basic organization of this book was suggested by Kenneth N. Waltz's notion of "three images," introduced in *Man, the State and War* (New York: Columbia University Press, 1959). Also see J. David Singer, "The Level-of-Analysis Problem in International Relations," *World Politics*, October 1961, 78-80. Only two changes have been introduced here: the order of the three images or levels of analysis has been reversed, and Waltz's first image (the third level here), based on the traditional and behavioral analysis of man, has been replaced by emphasis on official policy makers and decision making.

C H A P T E R 2

The Three Levels of Analysis: A Framework for the Study of International Politics

A STATE-SYSTEM LEVEL

International politics can be analyzed on three levels: the state-system level, the nation-state level, and the decision-making level. The term *state system* refers to the international system that comprises all existing political units that interact with one another according to some regular and observable pattern of relations. The term *system* is used for two reasons. First, it encompasses all the sovereign states and therefore possesses the virtue of being *comprehensive*. Second, it helps place the focus on the relations or *interactions* among the component units. The behavior of each state depends upon the behavior of other states.* In gamesmanship, each player's move or "strategy"—the set of moves he or she makes in the expectation of winning—is influenced by the moves of every other player.

---

* Michael Mandelbaum has offered a twofold scheme for analyzing state behavior: The "inside-out" and "outside-in" approaches. According to the "inside-out" approach, a nation's behavior is the product of its policy makers or of its own particular character. For example, Iran pursued the policies it did during the 1980s because its rulers were religious, anti-Western zealots; or Soviet behavior has been expansionist because of its Communist totalitarian system.

In contrast to the "inside-out" explanation with its suggestion that foreign policy is the outward expression of a state's internal rules or character, the "outside-in" approach emphasizes the constraints placed on all states. For example, because there is no world government to protect states from other states and each must guard itself against attack, every state's security policy is a product of the international or state system, not of the state itself. It is this "outside-in" explanation that is focused on above. See Michael Mandelbaum, *The Fate of Nations* (New York: Cambridge University Press, 1988), 1-7.

A system then is simply an abstract but convenient way of defining some part of reality for purposes of analysis. One speaks, for example, of a human being's circulatory system, the parts of which—veins, arteries, organs, and cells—must all work properly if the larger system is to give peak performance or to run at all. Similarly, a car has a cooling system, ignition system, electrical system, and exhaust system. Each system, in turn, has sub-systems—for example, the electrical system includes a battery, alternator, and spark plugs. Each system also may be considered a subsystem of the larger system, the car. All the subsystems must work together if the car is to run properly; the failure of one affects all the others.

In international politics each state is part of the system, and each is the guardian of its own security and independence. Each regards other states as potential enemies that may threaten fundamental interests. Consequently, states generally feel insecure, regard one another with apprehension and distrust. All become very concerned about their strength, or power. To prevent an attack, a state must be as powerful as potential aggressors, for a disproportion of power may tempt another state. A "balance of power," or equilibrium, is therefore desirable to deter an assault. "Equilibrium is balanced power, and balanced power is neutralized power."[1] A balance of power is a prerequisite for each nation's security, if not for its survival, as well as for the preservation of the system itself. Any attempt by any nation to expand its power and attain dominance or hegemony, which would allow it to impose its will upon the other states, will be resisted. When the balance is disturbed, the tendency will be to take responsive action to return to a position of equilibrium. If states disregard this operational rule that power must be counterbalanced, they place their own security in jeopardy. *The balance of power is therefore an empirical description of how states do act (or, more cautiously, how most of them, especially the great powers, act most of the time). It is also a recommendation for the way states should act.* In political scientist Inis Claude's words: "When any state or bloc becomes powerful, or threatens to become inordinately powerful, other states *should* recognize this as a threat to their security and respond by taking equivalent measures, individually or jointly, to enhance their power."[2] In short, the foreign policy of a state reflects the distribution of power within the state system; as that distribution changes, so does that state's foreign policy.

Balance of Power and U.S. Intervention in Two World Wars

The impact of a shift in the distribution of power is well demonstrated in the involvement of the United States in the two world wars of this century. The country's historical isolation from European "power politics" during most of the nineteenth century and the early twentieth century was the product of a balance of power on the European continent. A threat to this isolationism arose from the possibility that one state or a coalition of states might conquer most of Europe, organize its vast human and industrial resources, and use those resources to menace the United States. Britain, to protect its own security, had long opposed any state's hegemony and thereby had made it possible for the United States to maintain its isolationism. But in 1870, during its war with France, Prussia united Germany, and the new Germany became the country with the largest population in Europe, except for Russia. Germany then launched a massive program of industrialization, and it was only a matter of time until its power overtook Britain's. Unlike previous occasions, British power, even when added to that of France and Russia, was not sufficiently great to defeat Germany in World War I. When czarist Russia collapsed in 1917, the transfer of German soldiers from the eastern front to the western front raised the distinct possibility of a German victory. It was at that point that Germany's unrestricted submarine warfare, which included attacks on U.S. shipping, precipitated American intervention. This intervention made it possible to contain the German spring offensive of 1918 and to bring about Germany's defeat.[3]

A little more than two decades later, the United States, which had retreated into isolationism again, was compelled once more to concern itself with the European balance of power. Germany's victory over France in 1940 brought the United States once again face to face with the specter of an invasion and the defeat of Britain, despite the latter's large navy. President Franklin D. Roosevelt thus set out to strengthen Britain to withstand any Nazi assault.[4] He sent fifty old destroyers to help defend the English Channel, and he set up the Lend-Lease program to supply Britain with arms and ammunition. By the time of the Japanese attack on Pearl Harbor in December 1941, the United States was already engaged in an undeclared naval war with Germany in the Atlantic. American warships escorted British merchant ships filled with war supplies as far as Iceland, where the British navy took over escort duty. American merchant ships were later permitted to sail to British harbors. The American navy even reported the positions of German submarines to British warships and shot at the submarines when they allegedly shot first. The balance of power had made this larger U.S. commitment to Britain necessary, even though such actions increased the risk of war with Germany. In fact, war with Germany was merely a matter of time; German submarines sooner or later would start sinking American ships to force Britain to surrender. The German invasion of the Soviet Union in 1941 briefly postponed the Battle for the Atlantic, and when the battle did take place, the United States was already at war. But had Adolf Hitler, before Pearl Harbor, given the order to sink all ships bound for Britain, Roosevelt, like President Woodrow Wilson before him, would have had to ask Congress for a declaration of war.

Beginning of the U.S.-Soviet Cold War

Nowhere are the continuity of a policy and the degree to which the distribution of power narrows a nation's range of choices in its foreign policy revealed more clearly than in the eruption of the cold war. During World War II the United States, allied to the Soviet Union, believed it had established the basis for a postwar era of harmony and peace.[5] American policy makers recognized that the Soviet rulers had reasons for being suspicious of the West: for example, Western intervention in the civil war that broke out when the Communists seized power, and the Western appeasement of Hitler, especially in the Munich agreement, which gave the Nazi dictator the Sudetenland in Czechoslovakia—and eventually the rest of the country—and which the Kremlin might well have viewed as a Western attempt to "open the gates to the East." But Roosevelt believed that four years of wartime cooperation with the United States and Britain had dissolved Soviet suspicion of Western intentions and had replaced it with sufficient mutual respect and confidence to ensure that possible conflicts between the Soviets and the Western nations could be resolved amicably.

American policy makers apparently were unable to conceive that the Soviet Union, which they acknowledged would emerge as the new dominant power in Europe, would replace Germany as the gravest threat to the European and global balance of power.[6] During the war, the American government therefore did not aim at reestablishing a European balance of power to safeguard the United States. It expected such security to result from a new era of Soviet-American cooperation. Of a wartime conference with Soviet leader Joseph Stalin held at the Black Sea port of Yalta in February 1945, Roosevelt's closest adviser, Harry Hopkins, later recounted:

> We really believed in our hearts that this was the dawn of the new day we had all been praying for and talking about for so many years. We were absolutely certain that we had won the first great victory of the peace—and, by "we," I mean *all* of us, the whole civilized human race. The Russians had proved that they could be reasonable and farseeing, and there wasn't any doubt in the minds of the President or any of us that we could live with them peacefully for as far into the future as any of us could imagine.[7]

The American secretary of state, Cordell Hull, was even more optimistic: "There will no longer be need for spheres of influence, for alliances, balance of power, or any other of the special arrangements through which, in the unhappy past, the nations strove to safeguard their security or promote their interests."[8]

Unlike the United States, with its isolationist tradition, the Soviet Union had been a longtime player of power politics. It was therefore bound to feel fearful. Russia had, after all, capitulated to Germany during World War I and had come close to defeat during World War II. And more than a century earlier, Napoleon had invaded and almost defeated it. In fact, Russia had a long history of invasions and frequent defeat. As World War II was ending, therefore, the Soviet Union could foresee the possibility of conflict with another Western power, whose population was almost as large as its own, whose industrial strength was far greater, and whose enormous military power had been further increased in the closing days of the war by the atomic bomb.

Thus, as the Red Army was driving the German armies backward, Soviet actions were typical of a great power, regardless of its ideology, trying to

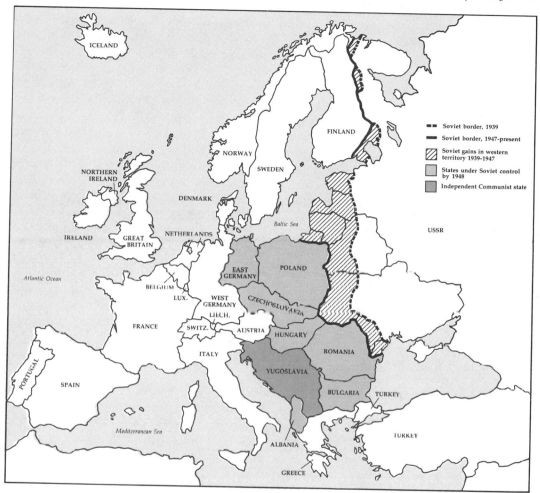

Figure 2-1   Soviet Expansion in Europe Since 1939

provide for its security. It imposed Soviet control over all of Eastern Europe—Poland, Hungary, Bulgaria, Romania, and, after Germany's defeat, East Germany—and it turned the states there into satellites. Yugoslavia was already under the control of Marshal Tito, a Stalin favorite. Czechoslovakia, although under the Red Army's shadow, was not transformed into a Soviet satellite until 1948, several years later. Soviet power thus stood in the center of Europe. But this expansion also led Stalin to try to dominate Iran and to turn Turkey into another satellite in an effort to gain control of the Dardanelles and gain access to the Mediterranean. And he appeared to back Tito's support of the Communists in the civil war in Greece (see Figure 2-1).

These actions led to the U.S. policy of containment. As weary and devastated as the Soviet Union was by the war, it emerged as a major power in the

Eurasian land mass. Its armed forces were reduced—according to Nikita Khrushchev's report in 1960—from 12 million to 3 million; Western estimates in the late 1940s were 1 million to 2 million higher, exclusive of approximately half a million security troops.[9] Still, all the other former major powers in Europe had collapsed. Germany was in ruins, France had not recovered from its defeat and occupation, and Britain foundered soon after victory. Nowhere in Europe was there any countervailing power; the only such power lay outside of Europe. The United States may have wanted to turn its back on the international scene and to concentrate once more on domestic affairs. It had demobilized psychologically and militarily. American armed forces had been reduced from just over 12 million to 1.5 million, and the military budget had been cut from the 1945 high of $81 billion to a low of $11 billion in 1948—a full year after the announcement of the containment policy.[10] But the distribution of power in the state system left the United States no choice. It was not what the government wished to do that was to matter; it was what it *had* to do. A new balance had to be established.

According to the logic of the state system, even had the Soviet Union in 1945 been a capitalist state like the United States (or vice versa), the emerging bipolar balance, the division of power between the two great powers, would have brought on their conflict. The two nations became enemies because, as the only two powerful states left, each had the ability to inflict enormous damage on the other. As political scientist Paul Seabury has noted, bipolarity was "a contradiction in which two powers—America and Russia—were by historical circumstances thrown into a posture of confrontation which neither had actually 'willed,' yet one from which extrication was difficult."[11] Or, as historian Louis Halle has pointed out, the historical circumstances of 1945 "had an ineluctable quality that left the Russians little choice but to move as they did. Moving as they did, they compelled the United States and its allies to move in response. And so the Cold War was joined."[12]

Price of Ignoring the Balance

Britain in the 1930s. The price of failure to heed the operational rule of balancing the power of a potential opponent is a loss of security and probably war. World War II, which fathered the cold war, could have been prevented if Britain and France had remobilized sufficient forces to contain Germany's various moves over a six-year period to upset the European balance.[13] Not until after Hitler had rearmed, reoccupied the Rhineland, and gobbled up Austria, the Sudentenland part of Czechoslovakia, followed by the rest of that country a few months later, did Britain's leaders decide that he could not be allowed to go any farther (see Figure 2-2). Hitler, however, believing that Britain's announced support of Poland was meaningless and that his latest challenge would go unmet as before, attacked Poland. Britain then declared war on Germany, as did France. World War II thus began under the worst of all possible circumstances for the Western powers, because Germany was no

Figure 2-2 German Expansion, 1935-1939

longer the weak power it had been at the time of Hitler's first expansionist moves in the mid-1930s.

The outbreak of World War II, therefore, stands as a monument to a single lesson: decent personal motives, like those of Prime Minister Neville Chamberlain, who wanted nothing more than to spare Britain the horror of another war, do not necessarily produce successful policies. At the very least, they require an understanding of the nature of the state system, its demands upon national leaders, and the rules of its operation. The American conduct of World War II was to underscore the importance of such understanding. U.S. leaders did not expect the Western coalition with the Soviet Union to collapse after Germany's defeat. They did not understand that once the common purpose had been achieved, the partners would have to concern themselves with securing their own protection in a new balance of power. They did not recognize that, even during the war, each alliance member had to take precautionary steps, in anticipation of possible future conflict and perhaps even war, to ensure itself a strong postwar position.

United States and China in the 1950s and 1960s.   The most obvious case of postwar neglect followed the 1949 collapse of Nationalist China and the control of mainland China by a Communist government. The new Chinese People's Republic quickly formed an alliance with Russia, which in the United States was immediately referred to as the "Sino (Chinese)-Soviet bloc," as if it were a single actor.

Yet historically, China and Russia had been antagonists. As the Manchu dynasty was collapsing in China at the end of the nineteenth century and the European powers began to carve China into spheres of influence, czarist Russia, China's neighbor to the north, became a prime carver. Russian influence expanded to northern China, especially Manchuria. (It was Russian expansion from Manchuria to Korea that provoked the Japanese to attack Russia in 1904.) Even Stalin's Russia was hardly considered a friend of the Chinese Communists in their civil war with the Nationalist government. Stalin's advice to the Chinese Communists to cooperate with the Nationalists during the 1920s resulted in the Communists being slaughtered by the Nationalists. This was the first of several blunders and betrayals. In 1945, for example, Stalin signed a treaty of friendship with the Nationalists, pledging support for the government the Communists were trying to overthrow. Thus, the memories of poor relations fed continuing differences between the Soviets and the Chinese Communists, both before and after they acquired power. Moreover, despite sharing a common ideology, Russia and China were highly nationalistic countries. Stalin had reclaimed Manchuria during World War II and held on to it until his death in 1953—so much for ideological friendship!

What is amazing is that the United States did not attempt to play a "divide and rule" game. As late as the early 1960s, when President John Kennedy initially intervened in Vietnam, American policy makers continued to talk of the "Sino-Soviet bloc," although differences between Russia and China had increased since 1956. The Sino-Soviet conflict was already well advanced and quite visible. But it was not until 1972 that an American president, Richard Nixon, exploited this growing split between the two Communist giants. During the 1960s and early 1970s, Soviet military power had grown enormously; in 1969 came the first of a number of border clashes. Fearing for their security, the Chinese Communists were looking for a way to deter a possible Soviet attack. Simultaneously, the United States, weary of international involvement after the Vietnam War, was looking for help in containing the increasingly powerful Soviet Union. The Sino-American reconciliation was a natural result. Putting aside ideological differences, China and the United States acted in a way that preserved the balance of power.

This belated reconciliation had one cost, however. Had the reconciliation taken place earlier, the Vietnam War might not have occurred. In the early 1960s the United States thought not only that Russia and China were still close allies but also that China was the far more militant of the two, that North Vietnam was China's satellite, and that China was responsible for the strategy of guerrilla warfare in South Vietnam. Had the United States recognized the Communist government early and had diplomatic representatives in China, the United States might have known that North Vietnam was independent, that a North Vietnamese victory would not have enhanced Chinese power and certainly not Sino-Soviet power, and, therefore, that it would not have affected the central balance between the United States and Russia, or Russia and China.

Aside from avoiding U.S. intervention in Vietnam, the American failure to exploit Sino-Soviet differences represented an even more profound mistake. In any conflict between major powers, prudence would suggest that no power should face more opponents than it needs to; if it faces two or more adversaries, it should concentrate on the most powerful opponent and try to isolate that power by drawing the others away from it. Why confront two strong states when it is unnecessary? This common sense and logical rule has been called the principle of the "conservation of enemies." [14] The United States ignored that rule from 1949 to 1972—and paid a heavy price.

Why did Britain in the 1930s and the United States during the cold war years follow the wrong course of action? The second and third levels of analysis will give the answer.

NATION-STATE LEVEL

While the state-system level of analysis emphasizes the *external* determinants of state behavior, the nation-state level attributes such behavior to *internal* characteristics: political system, historical experience, nature of the economy, or social structure. The emphasis is not on the likeness of states, the similarity of their motives, or the insignificant impact of domestic attributes. Instead, the emphasis is on differences in motivation, attitudes, and internal composition or domestic structure among states. States are therefore categorized as democratic, revolutionary, capitalist, developing, and so forth— the democratic and revolutionary states are described below. Political scientists and diplomatic historians frequently have attributed certain characteristic patterns of behavior to such categories.

Democratic States

Allegedly, democratic states behave differently than nondemocratic states. For example, it has been hypothesized that democracies are basically peaceful. One reason for this hypothesis is the accountability of the rulers of democratic states to those they govern. Thus, given regular elections, it is not surprising that successive British governments were sensitive to public opinion and a mood that throughout the period between the two world wars was overwhelmingly influenced by memories of World War I. There was a widespread popular demand that another bloodletting be avoided if at all possible. British leaders thought they had no choice. The antiwar mood was far too pervasive. In 1933 the students of the Oxford Union passed a resolution refusing "to fight for King and country." In 1935 there was a general election in which Prime Minister Chamberlain, knowing that Britain should rearm, pledged not to do so because he felt certain that favoring rearmament would lose the election for the Conservatives. In 1938 cheering British crowds welcomed Chamberlain back from Munich, assured that he had brought them "peace in our time." And in 1939, a few months before the outbreak of war and several months after news of Munich and Hitler's violation of the agreements reached England, the Labour party—which had been pacifist throughout the 1930s—was still opposing military conscription.[15]

A second and more fundamental reason for democracies' alleged peaceful behavior is that the increasing mass participation in voting and political decision making has resulted in these countries being primarily oriented inward, concerned with social programs to improve the electorate's lives and standard of living. Democracies have become welfare states. In the absence of clearly visible and recognizable threats to their security, they will not spend much money on arms. Popular interest in foreign affairs is at best sporadic, responding to specific crises; only then will money for arms be allocated.[16] Modern democratic societies, moreover, emphasize values—such as health, education, and welfare—that are in conflict with the conduct of foreign policies that emphasize force and killing.

These generalizations help to explain Britain's policies during the 1930s. The British propensity to look inward was enforced by the need to do something about the economy—an economy, that even before the Great Depression was suffering large-scale unemployment. Foreign policy became a secondary matter. Memories of the war of 1914-1918 only reinforced this ordering of priorities. It was not until Hitler's immense threat to Britain's security became *unambiguously clear* to both the public and its leaders that foreign policy became more important than domestic policy. Then Britain took a firm stand opposing further German expansion, and the result was World War II.

The war that broke out in September 1939 was the second in twenty years to have been precipitated by Germany. It was also the twentieth century's second total war, a war fought for the total destruction and unconditional surrender of the enemy. Again, the democratic typology can be used to analyze what happened. George Kennan, American diplomat and scholar, has noted that, when democracies turn from their inward, peaceful preoccupations toward the external arena and are compelled to fight, they become ferocious:

> A democracy is peace-loving. It does not like to go to war. It is slow to rise to provocation. When it has once been provoked to the point where it must grasp the sword, it does not easily forgive its adversary for having produced this situation. The fact of the provocation then becomes itself the issue. Democracy fights in anger—it fights for the very reason that it was forced to go to war. It fights to punish the power that was rash enough and hostile enough to provoke

it—to teach that power a lesson it will not forget, to prevent the thing from happening again. Such a war must be carried to the bitter end.[17]

Various reasons have been adduced to support this hypothesis about the warlike nature of democracy once it is engaged in military conflict. If war and violence are considered evil—the very denial of democracy's humanitarian ideals—their use demands a moral stance; when it becomes necessary to resort to force, it must be for defensive and noble reasons. The complete destruction of the aggressor regime—particularly if its way of life is authoritarian (as was that of Germany) and therefore by democratic standards inferior, immoral, and warlike—becomes a spiritually uplifting cause. Once destroyed, the vanquished nation can be sent to democratic reform school and transformed into a peaceful state. But beyond this general need for moral justification lies the reality of war. War disturbs the scale of social priorities in an individualistic and materialistic culture. It separates families, it kills and wounds, it demands economic sacrifice, and it imposes regimentation and discipline. If a society that emphasizes personal dignity and the development of individual, family, and social welfare must go to war, the sacrifices demanded must be commensurate with some wholesome, ennobling, and morally transcending goal. Total victory, in this context, becomes the minimum aim.

The consequences of such an attitude in this century have been disastrous. For example, Kennan has attributed the Communist seizure of power in Russia to the drive for total victory by the Allies in World War I.[18] After the collapse of the czarist state during that war, the February Revolution of 1917 established a provisional government composed of liberals and moderate conservatives. If the war had been concluded immediately, the new government might have been able to consolidate its position by, among other things, starting a land-reform program to satisfy the peasantry, the majority in Russia. But the Western allies insisted that Russia stay in the war because they needed its help to achieve the victory. Lenin exploited these circumstances, promising that when the Communists assumed power they would end hostilities and grant a piece of land to every peasant. In November 1917 the Communist party seized power in a second revolution.

If the Western powers' predilection for total war resulted in the collapse of Russia, leaving it in the hands of a regime that was to become openly hostile to the West, it also made World War II inevitable, and for three reasons.[19] The first one was the exhausting experience of World War I, which had gravely weakened Britain and France. The second was the collapse of Austria-Hungary and the birth of a small number of unstable eastern European states that could not contribute to the Continent's equilibrium. And the final consequence of the complete defeat of Germany was the fall of the German monarchy. Its democratic successor accepted the punitive terms imposed on Germany by the victors. As a result, the German people equated the new, democratic republic with humiliation and defeat. Amid the great social unrest that followed the runaway inflation of the early 1920s and the

Great Depression a few years later, Germany had no traditional institutions to cling to as it sought to weather the crisis. These conditions offered fertile ground for Hitler, who gained power by exploiting nationalist frustration, impoverishment, and uncertainty.

This democratic crusading style shows itself, however, not only in wartime, but even in "peacetime," as it did during the cold war (see Chapter 8). Here it is useful to recall the example of U.S. policy toward Communist China and the inability of the United States, until the Vietnam War was coming to an end, to exploit Sino-Soviet differences. The principal reason for this was American anti-Communist fervor, aroused by Soviet behavior after World War II. This crusade reached a fever pitch after the Chinese Communists defeated the pro-American Nationalist government in the Chinese civil war and then in 1950 intervened militarily in the Korean War as U.S. forces were marching toward the Chinese-North Korean frontier. The United States had long considered itself to be both China's friend and benefactor. The anti-Communist emotions, initially aroused by the Soviet Union, were now intensified and directed toward China as well. In these circumstances, recognition of China, let alone exploitation of Sino-Soviet differences, became impossible, especially because the Republican party, having accused the Democrats of having "lost China" and being "soft on Communism," made it too politically costly for the Democrats to recognize China, which the Republicans, of course, would not do either. Recognition of China came only in 1979, thirty years after the Communists took over its government and seven years after Nixon had begun the process of Sino-American reconciliation.

Yet, had the United States recognized the Chinese government after the civil war, it might have ended the Korean War sooner, avoiding many casualties. North Korea attacked South Korea in June 1950, and the United States came to the latter's rescue. By October, the status quo had been restored. At that point, the United States decided to unify Korea. Because the United States had opposed North Korea's attempt at unification, it was not surprising that China reacted the same way and intervened with its forces. The U.S. government had known there were Chinese forces in Manchuria, but it did not know whether the Chinese would intervene. The United States obviously did not think so, although the Chinese had repeatedly warned against sending American forces into North Korea. Had the United States recognized China's new government and sent diplomats to Peking (now Beijing), U.S. intelligence might have been better. The American government might have taken Chinese warnings seriously and avoided a miscalculation that resulted in a war that lasted until 1953. In short, the United States might have been able to avoid hostilities with China in Korea, as well as the Vietnam War.

Revolutionary States

Whether democratic France in aristocratic Europe in the late eighteenth and early nineteenth centuries or the Soviet Union in the twentieth century, the revolutionary state (a term coined by Henry Kissinger) presents a total challenge to the international order.[20] Unlike traditional states that recognize one another's right to live and accept the principle of live and let live, the revolutionary state repudiates the existing order because it does not accept the legitimacy of the other states in the system because of their different socioeconomic systems; it rejects their domestic structures. The revolutionary state's leaders pose two questions: Why do the masses live in poverty, ill health, and ignorance? Why is the human race constantly cursed by war? The revolutionaries point to the *ancien régime*. The majority of people are destitute because they are exploited by a privileged minority. Wars are fought because they pay dividends in the form of enhanced prestige, territorial acquisition, and economic gains. Although the few profit, it is the masses who are compelled to do most of the fighting and dying. People can be freed from economic exploitation, political subjugation, and international violence only by the destruction of the existing system and the overthrow of the ruling classes. In short, the revolutionary state condemns the existing order as unjust and assumes the duty of bringing *justice* to humanity.

By the very nature of its belief, the revolutionary state is thus committed to universal goals—that is, to transforming the prevailing political, economic, and cultural system that has condemned humanity to eternal slavery and to creating a "new order" in which, for the first time in history, people will be truly free from oppression and need. The proclamation issued by the National Convention of the Republic after the French Revolution is characteristic of the revolutionary state as a missionary power engaged in a "just war" to establish eternal domestic social justice and international peace:

> The French Nation declares that it will treat as enemies every people who, refusing liberty and equality or renouncing them, may wish to maintain, recall, or treat with the prince and the privileged classes; on the other hand, it engages not to subscribe to any treaty and not to lay down its arms until the sovereignty and independence of the people whose territory the troops of the Republic shall have entered shall be established, and until the people shall have adopted the principles of equality and founded a free and democratic government.[21]

If this typology of the revolutionary state is valid, Stalinist Russia, in the years immediately after World War II, would have viewed the United States not as just another state trapped by the same security problem, but as a capitalist state that had to be eliminated. And, in fact, Moscow rejected the notion that national insecurity and international conflict were the result *only*—or even primarily—of the state system. Kremlin leaders believed that international antagonism and hostility, as well as domestic poverty, unemployment, ill health, and ignorance, were caused by the internal nature of the leading states in the system. Capitalism was viewed as the cause of all social evil. Only in a political system in which the Communist party, representing the exploited majority, the proletariat, has control and in which all the forces of production are removed from private ownership so that they may be used for the benefit of all people, instead of for the profit of the privileged few, can human beings finally live free from social injustice, deprivation, and war. As a total critique of capitalist society and a promise to deliver the masses from evil and bring them domestic justice and external peace, communism in fact constituted a secular religion of damnation and salvation. It conferred upon the Soviet Union the messianic duty of converting all people to the "true faith." (See Chapter 8.)

Consequently, according to this interpretation of the foreign policy behavior of a revolutionary state, the Soviet Union was engaged in an irreconcilable struggle with non-Communist states, seeking hegemony in the state system. Soviet hostility toward the West predated 1945 because it was to a large degree ideological and preconceived.[22] V. I. Lenin and Stalin had felt it even before they seized power and before Western governments had adopted anti-Soviet policies. It was an enmity deduced from first principles and based not on what Western governments did but on what they were alleged to be; Western actions were almost irrelevant. Once non-Communist states were declared hostile and official declarations and policies were formulated upon that assumption, it was hardly astounding that the West became less friendly and that the Soviet leaders reaped the fruits of the policies that they had sown. Communist ideology, in short, raised the level of mutual fear and suspicion resulting from the state system and caused Stalin's Russia to undertake both "defensive expansionism" (because of its enhanced apprehension of capitalist attack) and "offensive expansionism" (because of its determination to expand the socialist world).

Any modus vivendi like the one finally worked out between czarist Russia and the monarchies of Britain, France, and Austria-Hungary in 1815 was, in the circumstances of 1945, therefore excluded. According to the second level of analysis, the cold war would have erupted regardless of the emergence of bipolarity, because Russia had become *Soviet* Russia, and its aims and objectives extended far beyond those historically entertained by the czars.

DECISION-MAKING LEVEL

Who actually makes foreign policy decisions? Common sense says that "the United States" does not make these decisions; the people who occupy the official political positions responsible for foreign policy do. It is this decision-making level of analysis that is probably the most familiar to many people. At election time Americans debate the virtues of the leading candidates, their expressed and implied views, their alleged values, and groups to which they may be beholden. Citizens watch how candidates handle themselves on television—whether or not they have "substance," are sincere, and remain cool under pressure. Apparently, who is president matters. It affects the priorities between domestic and foreign policies, the kinds of foreign policies that will be adopted, the extensiveness of foreign commitments, and the weapons to be produced.

Three aspects of decision making are emphasized here: the policy maker's perceptions of the world, the different kinds of decisions made, and the corresponding decision-making processes. The central point of the decision-making approach is that it allows an observer to understand and analyze individual decisions in some detail. This approach is particularly revealing when a state's actions do not seem consistent with first- or second-level expectations. How does one explain a state's policy that appears to ignore the balance of power? If a certain category of state—for example, revolutionary— is supposed to produce a particular type of behavior, but two states of that type act quite differently, how does one account for that? A look at the leaders who made the decisions, their responsibilities and perspectives, and the way their decisions were arrived at is likely to reveal the answers.

Policy Makers and Their Perceptions

The first aspect of decision making, the policy makers' perceptions of the world, is very important for the obvious reason that it is the link between the external environment and policy decisions: the real world is the world perceived, whether correctly or not. The emergence of World War II provides a good illustration.

In the 1930s British prime minister Chamberlain not only shared his fellow citizens' desire to avoid another total war, but also thought his policy of appeasing Hitler's demands would achieve that end. He thought this because he saw Hitler as one of his own kind, a statesman who had been born and bred in a system founded upon nationalism. He could even cite a supporting precedent, for Otto von Bismarck, after Germany's unification in 1870, had declared that Germany was satisfied and would thereafter support the new European status quo. Hitler talked in terms of national self-determination, and why should Chamberlain not believe that the new German leader was merely a cruder version of the Prussian aristocrat and German chancellor; that he, too, would be sated once he had achieved his apparently nationalistic aims. If Nazi Germany had, in fact, been merely a nationalist state, the differences between it and France and Britain could probably have been resolved without precipitating a war. But Hitler harbored aims beyond restoring Germany's 1914 frontiers.

Churchill, from his understanding of British history, knew that Britain's foreign policy had long been one of opposition to any power seeking to dominate Europe, whether Philip II of Spain, Louis XIV or Napoleon of France, or the German kaiser. He perceived each of Hitler's limited demands and moves as part of a larger pattern that would lead to Germany's destruction of the European equilibrium. For this reason, he counseled opposition, condemned the Munich agreement, and ridiculed Chamberlain's claim that he had brought back "peace in our time." Instead, Churchill said bluntly, "We have sustained a total and unmitigated defeat." [23] As Churchill himself intimated, had he been prime minister in the late 1930s, World War II might have been avoided. Churchill's perception of Hitler and Nazi objectives was correct, Chamberlain's perception mistaken. Possibly Churchill could have convinced the British public of the true nature of the Nazi regime, placed the German dictator's repeated demands in their proper perspective, and led Britain to oppose *his* moves and speed up rearmament.

Vietnam illustrates the issue of perception even more poignantly. American participation in the Vietnam War, which ranks as one of the most unpopular wars in American history, has often been cited as an instance of misperception by the administrations of John Kennedy and Lyndon Johnson. Kennedy's inaugural address, it is said, was permeated with a sense of the bipolar conflict and confrontation of the 1940s and 1950s.[24] He pledged that the United States was "unwilling to witness or permit the slow undoing of those human rights to which this nation has always been committed, and to which we are committed today at home and around the world. . . . We shall pay any price, bear any burden, meet any hardship, support any friend, oppose any foe, in order to assure the survival and the success of liberty." His conviction that the nation confronted a united and aggressive Communist bloc was reinforced by the Soviet Union's announcement that it would support wars of national liberation. Not surprisingly, therefore, when such a war broke out in South Vietnam, the administration thought that the Soviets or Chinese had instigated it and, starting in 1961, sent in more than 16,000 military "advisers."[25] A few weeks before his death, Kennedy declared that, if South Vietnam fell, it would "give the impression that the wave of the future in Southeast Asia was China and the Communists."[26] Johnson, who relied principally upon his predecessor's counselors for his policy advice, certainly saw the issue that way and in 1965 began massive U.S. intervention.

Critics of the war claim that the commitment of military advisers by Kennedy and of half a million troops by Johnson was based upon the "old myths" of the cold war instead of the "new realities" that had begun to emerge in the mid-1960s.[27] One of these new realities was that the Communist bloc was badly fragmented along nationalistic lines. An extension of Hanoi's control to South Vietnam, therefore, did not mean parallel extension of Soviet or Chinese power. Indeed, it was argued, a nationalistic Communist Vietnam would be a barrier to an extension of Chinese power. Nor would the loss of Saigon mean the collapse of neighboring nations; whether successful guerrilla wars occurred in those countries would depend on their indigenous conditions. In short, had the perceptions of the policy makers during the Kennedy-Johnson period more accurately reflected the changing nature of the international system, the United States could have avoided becoming involved in South Vietnam.

Different Policies, Different Policy Processes

Policy makers make, of course, different kinds of decisions, the second aspect of decision making, and they arrive at them by different means, the third aspect of decision making. Three kinds of decisions and policies—crisis, security, and domestic—are described here. (The distinctions, although discussed here specifically in the context of American foreign policy, are broadly applicable to other democracies, if not most states.)

The first, crisis policy, is related primarily to great-power confrontations, especially direct U.S.-Soviet confrontations. They are considered crises because of the possibility of escalation to nuclear war. The frequent cold war crises over Berlin always posed this danger, although the most serious remains the Cuban missile confrontation in 1962. In crises, decision making "rises to the top." [28] Relatively few policy makers participate: the president, the principal presidential foreign policy advisers, and other selected officials and advisers. The bureaucracy is largely bypassed in the making of a crisis policy, although it plays the primary role in carrying it out. Congress too plays virtually no role. Time is too short for major opposition to be heard and have an impact; in a crisis Congress essentially rallies around the flag.

Security policy refers to the more normal noncrisis foreign and defense policies. Such policies range from foreign-aid bills and defense budgets to arms control policies, arms transfers to allies and other friendly nations, organization and operation of the government's intelligence apparatus, and, not least, conduct of limited wars. In contrast to a crisis policy, these policies involve a far larger number of policy makers and much more time is needed to arrive at decisions. The executive branch continues to act as initiator of the policy and, usually, to play the central role. In addition to the president and White House staff concerned with national security affairs, all the bureaucracies, such as the State Department and Defense Department, officially responsible for the conduct of foreign policy are involved. Other actors might be the Congress, interest groups, and the public. Before the Vietnam War, these latter had usually supported presidential policy; since Vietnam, they have often been more critical and opposed. Nevertheless, the initiative and responsibility for foreign policy remain primarily with the executive branch.

Domestic policy and intermestic policy (stemming from the telescoping of the words *international* and *domestic*, and denoting erosion of the traditional distinction between foreign and domestic policies) revolve largely, although not exclusively, around the objective of welfare or prosperity. In most nations of the world, especially democratic ones, people have increasingly expected governments to provide economic growth, rising incomes, and many social programs. For most citizens, these pocketbook issues are more important than most foreign policies. In recent years, however, many domestic issues have become entangled with foreign policy as the economic health of nations has grown more and more dependent on importing raw materials or exporting manufactured goods or food items. In the United States, these domestic/intermestic issues involve by far the largest number of actors. The jurisdictions of most executive departments are domestic, even if they have an increasing interest in foreign policy and economic issues. Congress, which considers its expertise in domestic affairs far greater than its skill in foreign ones, therefore plays a much larger role in domestic/intermestic policy and often takes the initiative. Interest groups and the various "publics" concerned with domestic/intermestic issues also are active and assertive.

Presidential leadership is the most dramatically visible in crisis policy, the least in domestic and intermestic policies. The more bureaucrats, legislators, and interest groups involved in the policy process, and the more time available to reach decisions, the more constrained the presidential leadership will be (see Figure 2-3).

COMBINING THE THREE LEVELS

One question remains: Which level of analysis should be used in understanding international politics? In this book all three are used. Although the state-system level is fundamental, it cannot by itself explain the world politics of the postwar era. One final look at the three different and previously mentioned historical experiences that have molded the present-day world may help one understand why.

British Policy After World War I

As stressed in the earlier discussion of British policy toward Germany in the late 1930s, the first-level or state-system analysis will reveal that Britain did not adopt the policies it should have after World War I, largely because of the pacifist mood of the British public and Prime Minister Chamberlain's misperception of Hitler's intentions. The second-level (nation-state) and third-level (decision-making) analyses explain why Chamberlain pursued the policies he did. If Churchill had been prime minister, war might have been avoided, for he perceived Hitler's aims correctly. Had a British leader been able to explain to the public the dire threat to the nation's security with Churchill's eloquence and persuasiveness, Britain might have stood up to Hitler.

But is this analysis of what would have happened an accurate one? It is doubtful. Memories of World War I were too vivid, the desire to avoid its repetition too strong. Chamberlain's policy of appeasement was quite representative of British opinion. How horrible, he had said in a radio address when war with Germany over Czechoslovakia loomed, that the British should be digging trenches and trying on gas masks because of a quarrel in a faraway country between people of whom they knew nothing.[29] When Hitler's message that he would see Chamberlain at Munich arrived, the prime minister was addressing the House of Commons. Interrupting his speech with the news, he was cheered by the Commons. "At once pandemonium broke forth. Everyone was on his feet, cheering, tossing his order papers in the air, some members in tears. It was an unprecedented and most unparliamentary outburst of mass hysteria and relief, in which a few did not join."[30] Upon return from Germany, Chamberlain was met by a jubilant crowd.

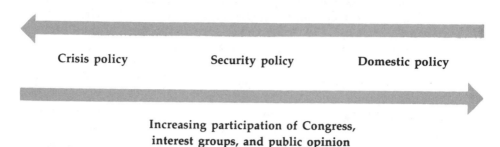

Increasing degree of presidential leadership

Crisis policy   Security policy   Domestic policy

**Increasing participation of Congress,
interest groups, and public opinion**

Figure 2-3 Different Policies, Different Actor Participation

Perhaps the most significant and symbolic aspect of Churchill's career during the late 1930s was precisely that he was not a member of the government. Like Cassandra, he stood with a small group warning of "the gathering storm" over Europe. But Britain did not want to hear him. Churchill was widely condemned as a warmonger in the 1930s. Even when war erupted, Churchill did not take over the prime ministry from the man whose policies had failed so dismally. Chamberlain did not fall until after Germany's unexpected takeover of Denmark and the defeat of British forces in Norway in the spring of 1940. It took both the outbreak of war and a disaster to make Churchill prime minister.

Although the state-system level of analysis can suggest what Britain should have done, the nation-state and decision-making levels can best explain what actually happened. The state-system level correctly predicted that failure to play by the rules of the game would mean loss of security and the necessity to fight a war to recover it. But the climate of British democracy ruled out doing what should have been done. As this example shows, one must be careful not to exaggerate the importance of a nation's leader. Foreign policy is not simply a reflection of his or her preferences and perceptions. The leader makes policy within the confines of a state system, a national political system, and a specific policy process.

U.S. Policy After World War II

The immediate postwar policy in the United States is a striking example of the mutually reinforcing nature of all three levels of analysis. "Rarely has freedom been more clearly the recognition of necessity," observed Harvard political scientist, Stanley Hoffmann, "and statesmanship the imaginative exploitation of necessity. America rushed to those gates at which Soviet power was knocking."[31] At the nation-state and decision-making levels, policy makers ended up doing what they had to do. After the surrender of Japan, eighteen months passed before the official declaration of the containment policy. The American desire for peace, symbolized by a massive postwar demobilization, was intense. Hostile Soviet acts were necessary to erode the widespread admiration for the Soviet Union, the result of the latter's heroic wartime resistance. Not until Britain's support for Greece and Turkey was withdrawn in early 1947 did the United States face the fact that only it possessed the power to establish a new balance of power that would secure both Europe and America while preserving the peace.[32]

President Harry Truman was keenly aware of the strategic significance of the eastern Mediterranean and went before a joint session of Congress to explain to the whole country the new situation facing the United States. American expectations for postwar cooperation with Moscow had by now vanished. Truman was therefore able to mobilize both congressional and popular support for an anti-Soviet policy.[33] Thus, in this example, the state-system level is of primary importance in explaining U.S. policy. The nation-state and decision-making levels reveal how accurately the policy makers perceived "reality" and how they were able in a democratic society to mobilize popular support for the new containment policy.

The United States and China in the 1970s

In the 1930s the British public's mood of appeasement meant that Churchill's warnings about Hitler were ignored, and Britain failed to do what it needed to do to preserve the balance of power in Europe. In the 1940s after World War II, Truman was able to arouse support to contain Soviet power after an initial military demobilization, an attempt to withdraw once more to the concerns of the Western Hemisphere, and a brief period of thinking that it was America's task to mediate between Britain and the Soviet Union. (The British, as usual, had begun to organize European opposition to Moscow.) Years later, President Richard Nixon, together with Henry Kissinger, his national security assistant, were, like Truman earlier, also the right men at the right place at the right time. Even before he became president, Nixon favored exploiting the split between the two largest Communist states and attracting China into a Sino-American coalition against the Soviet Union. Kissinger was assigned the task of "opening the door" to the new China. They were able to pursue this policy because they were Republicans and because of the war in Vietnam. From 1950 until that time, the Republicans had made it impossible for any Democratic administration to recognize China by accusing the Democrats of being "appeasers" and "soft on communism." But a Republican president, who had been one of the chief accusers and had always taken a tough anti-Communist stance, could hardly be accused of being an appeaser. Furthermore, Vietnam had largely disillusioned the nation with anti-communism, which appeared to be the chief reason the United States had become involved in the war. Thus, Nixon and

Kissinger could do in 1972 what they could not have done earlier. Even as Republicans, opposition within their own party would have been too strong, and anti-Chinese feelings still would have been widespread.

In the remainder of this book the three levels of analysis are discussed in three sections. Part Two focuses on the state system; Part Three concentrates on the second and third levels; and Part Four analyzes the means that states use to achieve their aims. Part Five then deals with the possible transformation of the state system to a global system. But, in fact, the division is not quite that neat. An analysis of the state system cannot be separated, for example, from the policy makers' perceptions of the system or from crisis decision making. And, in analyzing the second and third levels, it is not always possible to keep the specific political system separate from decision-making institutions and processes. Nevertheless, the broad distinction between the external environment in which states exist and the internal characteristics of the specific actors remains paramount.

For Review

1. At the first level of analysis, what special insights into how states behave are gained by focusing on how states interact?
2. What role does "balance of power" play in international politics?
3. How do the first-level explanations of international politics differ from those at the second level of analysis?
4. At the second level, what are the alleged relationships between the different types of states and their foreign policies?
5. How does the third-level focus on policy makers and governmental decision-making institutions help explain state behavior?

Notes

1. Nicholas J. Spykman, *America's Strategy in World Politics* (New York: Harcourt, 1942), 21. Also see Raymond Aron, *Peace and War* (Garden City, N.Y.: Doubleday, 1966); and Stanley Hoffmann, *The State of War* (New York: Holt, Rinehart & Winston, 1965). For a more extensive discussion of the various ways in which analysts use the term *balance of power*, see Ernst B. Haas, "The Balance of Power: Prescription, Concept, or Propaganda," *World Politics*, July 1953, 442-477; and Inis L. Claude, Jr., *Power and International Relations* (New York: Random House, 1962), 11-39.
2. Claude, *Power and International Relations*, 43 (emphasis added).
3. Edward H. Buehrig, *Woodrow Wilson and the Balance of Power* (Bloomington: Indiana University Press, 1955); and Arthur S. Link, *Wilson the Diplomatist* (Baltimore: Johns Hopkins University Press, 1957), passim, esp. 61-90.

4. For the period 1937-1941, the most detailed analysis is found in *The Challenge to Isolation* by William L. Langer and S. Everett Gleason (New York: Harper & Row, 1952); and Langer and Gleason, *The Undeclared War* (New York: Harper & Row, 1953). A briefer study is *The Reluctant Belligerent* by Robert A. Divine (New York: Wiley & Son, 1965).

5. William H. McNeill, *America, Britain and Russia—Their Cooperation and Conflict, 1941-1946* (London: Oxford University Press, 1953), written for the Royal Institute of International Affairs; and Herbert Feis, *Churchill-Roosevelt-Stalin: The War They Waged and the Peace They Sought* (Princeton, N.J.: Princeton University Press, 1957). A shorter study is *American Diplomacy During the Second World War, 1941-1945* by Gaddis Smith (New York: Wiley, 1966).

6. Robert E. Sherwood, *Roosevelt and Hopkins: An Intimate History* (New York: Harper & Row, 1948), 748.

7. Ibid., 70.

8. Cordell Hull, *The Memoirs of Cordell Hull* (New York: Macmillan, 1948), 2: 1314-1315.

9. Thomas W. Wolfe, *Soviet Power and Europe, 1945-1970* (Baltimore: Johns Hopkins University Press, 1970), 10.

10. Ibid., 11; and Samuel P. Huntington, *The Common Defense* (New York: Columbia University Press, 1961), 33-39.

11. Paul E. Seabury, *The Rise and Decline of the Cold War* (New York: Basic Books, 1967), 59.

12. Louis J. Halle, *The Cold War as History* (New York: Harper & Row, 1967), xiii.

13. William J. Newman, *The Balance of Power in the Interwar Years, 1919-1939* (New York: Random House, 1968); Arnold Wolfers, *Britain and France Between Two Wars* (New York: Norton, 1966); and Winston S. Churchill, *The Gathering Storm*, vol. 1 of *The Second World War* (Boston: Houghton Mifflin, 1948), 90.

14. Frederick H. Hartmann, *The Relations of Nations*, 6th ed. (New York: Macmillan, 1983), 18.

15. Among other sources on this period, see Churchill, *Gathering Storm*; Charles L. Mowat, *Britain Between the Wars 1918-1940* (Chicago: University of Chicago Press, 1955); and A. J. P. Taylor, *English History, 1914-1945* (New York: Oxford University Press, 1965).

16. Walter Lippmann has defined the role of democratic public opinion negatively. Precisely because of its emphasis on wealth and welfare, Lippmann argues, democratic opinion makes it difficult to take the necessary preparations to avoid war:

    The rule to which there are few exceptions . . . is that at the critical junctures, when the stakes are high, the prevailing mass opinion will impose what amounts to a veto upon changing the course on which the government is at the time proceeding. Prepare for war in time of peace? No. It is bad to raise taxes, to unbalance the budget, to take men away from their schools or their jobs, to provoke the enemy.

    Walter Lippmann, *The Public Philosophy* (Boston: Little, Brown, 1955), 19-20.

17. George F. Kennan, *American Diplomacy 1900-1950* (Chicago: University of Chicago Press, 1951), 65-66.

18. George F. Kennan, *Russia and the West Under Lenin and Stalin* (Boston: Little, Brown, 1961), 33-36.

19. Kennan, *American Diplomacy*, 55-57, 68-69.

20. Henry A. Kissinger, *Nuclear Weapons and Foreign Policy* (New York: Harper & Row, 1957), 326; and Kissinger, *A World Restored* (New York: Grosset & Dunlap, 1964).

21. Quoted from Carlton J. H. Hayes, *The Historical Evolution of Modern Nationalism* (New York: Macmillan, 1950), 40.

22. Kennan, *Russia and the West*, 181.

23. The drama of Munich is captured by John Wheeler-Bennett in *Munich: Prologue to Tragedy* (London: Macmillan, 1948).

24. Townsend Hoopes, *The Limits of Intervention* (New York: McKay, 1969), 7-13.

25. Ibid., 13-16.

26. Tom Wicker, *JFK and LBJ: The Influence of Personality upon Politics* (Baltimore: Penguin, 1969), 192.

27. See J. William Fulbright, *The Arrogance of Power* (New York: Vintage, 1967), pt. 2; Arthur M. Schlesinger, Jr., *The Bitter Heritage* (New York: Fawcett, 1967); and Theodore Draper, *Abuse of Power* (New York: Viking, 1966).

28. Ole Holsti, "The 1914 Case," *American Political Science Review* (June 1965): 365-378; and Glen D. Paige, *The Korean Decision* (New York: Free Press, 1968), 273ff.

29. *Times* (London), Sept. 28, 1938; and Wheeler-Bennett, *Munich: Prologue to Tragedy*, 157-158.

30. Mowat, *Britain Between the Wars*, 617.

31. Hoffmann, *State of War*, 163.

32. Joseph M. Jones, *The Fifteen Weeks* (New York: Viking, 1955).

33. Ibid., 63-64.

Part Two

THE STATE SYSTEM

The Players: States and Other Actors

Characteristics of States

Since the Peace of Westphalia in 1648 the primary political actor in the state system has been the sovereign *state*. The number of states has more than doubled since 1945, when there were fifty-one members of the United Nations—nineteen from Europe and related areas, twenty from Latin America, and only twelve from Asia and Africa. Twenty-five years later, the developing countries of Asia and Africa alone constituted more than half of the 154 United Nations members. If the developing countries of Latin America are included, these states constitute a sizable majority. Altogether there are almost 170 states today, including a few that are not members of the United Nations. Some forecasters predict 200 states by the year 2000. As different as these states are in size, human and natural resources, and political and economic systems, they share certain characteristics: sovereignty, territory, population and nationalism, and recognition by other states.

Sovereignty

Each state is considered sovereign. Sovereignty refers to a state's government—not that of any other state—deciding how it will manage its own affairs. This may mean, as in the words of the U.S. Constitution, that the state's government will "insure domestic tranquility, provide for the common defense, promote the general welfare. . . ." All governments are concerned with maintaining domestic peace and national defense; how capable they are of doing so varies. Colombia is essentially run by the Medellin drug cartel, which controls about 80 percent of the cocaine entering the United States and earns about $4 billion a year. The drug czars use corruption, intimidation and assassination against those fighting it, be they judges, politicians, or journalists. After the country's judges had gone on strike, seeking better government protection against Medellin's army of assassins, and an antidrug presidential candidate had been shot, the government, which had so often been impotent but now feared for the survival of Colombian society, set out in the summer of 1989 to bypass its own court system. It reactivated a policy of extraditing drug traffickers wanted abroad, hoping that U.S. courts (since the traffickers were wanted mainly in the United States) might be able to do what Colombian justice was unable to do: try them, sentence them, and either execute or jail them. In response, the drug lords declared "a total and absolute war" on the government, threatening the lives of ten judges for each extradited person. Colombian society itself was at stake. An even worse case of the disappearance of governmental authority occurred in Lebanon, where armed factions, representing the Christian, Sunni and Shiite Muslim, and Druse populations, have been engaged in a civil war for fourteen years. With additional external interventions by the Palestine Liberation Organization; the Israelis, who invaded in 1982; and the Syrians, who with their troops sought to incorporate Lebanon into a greater Syria—all supporting different domestic factions and adding to the bloodshed—the capital city of Beirut, once considered the Paris of the Middle East, was destroyed. One Druse leader reportedly said that things were so bad in Beirut that not even the laws of the jungle were respected any longer! It was amid this anarchy that American and Western hostages were seized and held by pro-Iranian terrorists.

Governments are also concerned with providing their citizens with general welfare. But again, their concern varies. In democracies, elections not only have provided an extension of freedom but also have created broadly based welfare states. In the case of undemocratic states, however, sovereignty can mean the brutal treatment of their own population. In Cambodia, for example, from 1975 to 1979, the Pol Pot regime killed an estimated 2 million to 3 million of its 8 million people, and 600,000 fled into exile. After it had unified Vietnam in 1973, the victorious North treated the southern population, especially the ethnic Chinese, so harshly that 900,000 fled in rickety boats, and many drowned in the process. At least 10,000 Vietnamese were imprisoned because they worked for the Americans. Hitler slaughtered the German Jews during World War II. And Stalin killed an estimated 12 million to 15 million people in the forced collectivization of the peasantry and the elimination of the class of small landholders during the 1920s, allowed 5 million to die during the 1933 famine while he increased grain exports, and killed several million more during the Great Purges in the later 1930s.

All governments, regardless of how they treat their citizens, however, reject foreign interference in their domestic affairs. The Soviets, for example, have repeatedly dismissed Western human rights campaigns in behalf of Soviet dissidents. But this does not stop governments from interfering frequently in one another's affairs. President Ronald Reagan talked of human rights publicly during his summit visit to Moscow in 1988, much to the annoyance of his host. The United States has also condemned the South African government for its treatment of its black population; Congress even imposed punitive economic sanctions in support of its condemnation of South Africa's racism. When in 1988 the United States tried to remove Panama's ruler, General Manuel Noriega, a drug runner indicted by two U.S. grand juries, no Latin American country was willing to recognize its right to intervene in the domestic affairs of the region—even if, as in this case, it was reportedly to restore democracy in Panama.[1] This reaction was not out of sympathy for Noriega but from long memories and the recent examples of Grenada and Nicaragua. By defending the principle of sovereignty, the Latin American countries were defending themselves and denying the right of an outside power to decide which country's government it wished to remove. More specifically, for these mainly weak countries, the claim of sovereignty was a principal means of fending off the United States' claim to being the regional policeman.

Nevertheless, the sovereignty of smaller states is normally constrained by their dependence on the good will and tolerance of the great powers, both neighboring and far off, upon whom they depend for their security or markets in which to sell their goods. The states of Eastern Europe, for example, used to be referred to as *satellites* because their governments, although nominally sovereign, were in fact under Moscow's control. Over the years, these states have become more independent, mainly in domestic affairs. But in the decades before Mikhail Gorbachev became general secretary and president in 1985, the Soviets intervened directly in 1953, 1956, and 1968, and indirectly (via the Polish army in Poland) in 1981, to ensure these nations' loyalty to the Soviet Union, the Soviet bloc, and the military alliance known as the Warsaw Treaty Organization. Even today as such countries as Poland and Hungary are liberalizing domestically, if not repudiating communism, they remain by necessity sensitive to Soviet security concerns. As the first postwar non-Communist-led coalition government took power in Poland in 1989, the Communists retained control of the military and the police, and Poland's membership in WTO was reaffirmed.

Thus, although sovereignty acknowledges each government's exclusive jurisdiction over its nation's territory and people, in practice that concept cannot always be fully exercised. This is even true for more powerful countries. How sovereign are Italy or West Germany, whose independence depends on the U.S. nuclear deterrent? How sovereign is the United States as it becomes increasingly dependent on Japan for vital technologies for its industries and military hardware? How much control over its economy does the United States, the world's largest debtor nation at the end of the eight years of the Reagan administration, have as foreigners buy up American businesses and real estate? Whether an individual, corporation, or nation, being in debt means loss of control over one's affairs. World power and influence historically have been associated with creditor nations. America emerged as a world power as a creditor supplying investment capital to the rest of the world; now as a debtor, America's role in the world will need to be reexamined and Western Europe and Japan will either have to assume a greater part of the burden sharing or American commitments will have to be reduced. Sovereignty is never absolute. The 1970s have already demonstrated painfully that the Western industrial countries were unable to fully control their own economies as world oil prices escalated and Western inflation and unemployment followed. In an age of increasing interdependence, in which goods and capital flow freely across borders, and economic integration, as in Western Europe, sovereignty is relative. Economies are becoming so intertwined that governments no longer fully control their own. Among the Western industrial states, where interdependence is the most advanced, annual summit conferences of the political and economic leaders seeking greater coordination of economic policies have become more and more critical.

Territory

Another characteristic of a state is its territory. Frontiers separate one state from another. When crossing a border or flying from one country to another, travelers normally have to show immigration officials some sort of identification and proof of their citizenship and have their luggage searched, if customs officials deem it necessary. Sometimes crossing a border can be a grim business, as it used to be in going through the Berlin Wall. The frontier dividing East Germany from West Germany was marked by barbed wire, watchtowers, and armed guards. One may, of course, be forbidden entry into some countries, and sometimes citizens can leave their countries only by escape. Most frontiers, admittedly, are not like that. Nor does the existence of borders mean that they are not, on occasion, contested.

In any event, all states possess territory; without territory there would be no state. When a state relinquishes control of a piece of territory, as the colonial countries of Europe did after World War II, another state is established and exercises authority over the territory. In this way the British gave up their colony in India and transferred its control to a sovereign native government. India defined her frontiers as those established by the British and defended them against Chinese territorial claims. When Austria-Hungary completely disintegrated after World War I, the separate states of Austria, Hungary, Yugoslavia, and Czechoslovakia governed the areas each inherited. It is this association of a state with land that is central to a state's conception of itself, and it is for the preservation of this territorial integrity that states go to war.

Population and Nationalism

States possess not just land; they have populations, ranging from the more than 1 billion people in the People's Republic of China to the fewer than

100,000 people in the island of Dominica. The fact that the terms *state* and *nation-state* are often used interchangeably also suggests one additional characteristic of modern states: the national loyalty that populations feel for their countries. Before 1789 and the French Revolution, most states were ruled by kings, and most people living within the territorial confines of such dynastic states did not really identify with them. At times, kings traded people and lands. But the nationalism born in France and then stirred up in the rest of Europe in reaction to French conquest led people increasingly to identify with their nations.

It is difficult to define a nation exactly, but it can be said that it is a collective identity shared by people living within certain frontiers as a result of their common history (plus a good deal of mythology dramatizing the past), expectations of remaining together in the future, and usually a common language that allows them to communicate more easily with one another than with the inhabitants of neighboring nations who speak different languages. Ernest Renan, a Frenchman, characterized a nation as "a daily plebiscite," a continual emotional commitment to a group of people distinct from every other segment of humanity, celebrating their "nationhood" with anthems, poetry, statues of heroes who have defended it, and other symbols.

But nationality and geographical boundaries do not always coincide in real life. The Soviet Union is a multinational state in which the Great Russians, who historically have controlled Russia, finally ceased constituting the majority of the Soviet people. This shrinking of their minority status will grow because "the battle of the bedroom" has been won by the other nationalities, especially the Moslems of Central Asia who now constitute 14 percent of the total Soviet population. Often hated by the many other nationalities that comprise the contemporary Soviet Union, the Great Russians must be concerned about their future control and dominance of a nation that sprawls over one-sixth of the world's land surface. Textbooks are published in fifty-two languages, and the state radio broadcasts in sixty-seven languages.[2]

Since Gorbachev's reforms began, this conflict has broadened from that between the Russians and non-Russian nationalities to include conflicts among the non-Russian nationalities themselves. Widespread civil unrest occurred in Armenia to press its claims to some territory of its neighboring republic, Azerbaijan. Armenia's capital was paralyzed by massive street demonstrations, general strikes, and rioting as Armenians made the issue one of justice and national pride. Troops and armored vehicles had to be deployed throughout Armenia to contain this ethnic unrest at several points. But for Moscow to accede to demands for territorial changes not only would inflame feelings in mainly Islamic Azerbaijan but would encourage nationalists in other republics as well. In the three Baltic republics (Latvia, Lithuania, and Estonia) annexed by Stalin in 1940, anti-Soviet feelings have also remained high. All these nationalities seek greater autonomy, virtually amounting to independence from the Soviet Union. These demands include establishing a free-enterprise economy, producing their own currency, and using their native language; they would send Moscow part of the tax money to compensate it for their defense! At one point, Estonia declared its sovereignty—that is, its right to reject Soviet laws. Russians actually went on strike in 1989 when Estonia made Estonian the official language and used residency requirements to disenfranchise them. Lithuania raised its own flag over its parliament building and declared Lithuanian the official language (which Moscow, of course, rejected). Even in Georgia, Stalin's birthplace, there were demands for greater autonomy, if not independence, which also led to troop deployments and deaths, including by poison gas. Nationalism, in short, had struck behind the rusting iron curtain, creating enormous problems for Moscow's control over its "domestic empire" and Eastern Europe in the age of national self-determination.

Israel provides another illustration of the conflicts spurred by nationalism. Having conquered the Arab West Bank and Gaza Strip in 1967 after it was attacked by Egypt, Syria and Jordan, Israel found no Arab leader with whom to negotiate a "peace for land" deal. Thus, these territories have become virtually part of Israel. Israel's right-wing Likud party, claiming biblical inheritance, has said that the West Bank, especially, is part of Israel. The party calls this territory by its Hebrew names of Judea and Samaria and appears unwilling to trade peace for territory. Yet in 1985 Israel had 3.5 million Jews and 750,000 Israeli Arabs; the West Bank, however, was home to over 800,000 Arabs and the Gaza Strip to over 500,000. These over 2 million Arabs had a birth rate more than double that of Israeli Jews. In short, in the "demographic war" the Arab population already constitutes over half the population, and some day will be the majority. The longer Israel holds the land and tries to consolidate its hold by allowing Jews to settle on it, the more frustrated and nationalistic will the Palestinians—especially the youth—in the West Bank and Gaza become. Israel therefore faces a growing internal security problem, an example of which was visible globally on television in 1988 as for several months Arab youth, in what became known as the "Uprising," stoned Israeli soldiers, who often with quite brutal beatings tried to suppress their attackers. As a result, the Jewish and Arab populations, including Israeli Arabs, became even more divided. As an increasingly binational rather than Jewish state, Israel faces a fundamental question: Can Israel exist with any degree of harmony and coherence if it exercises permanent rule over a foreign population that is not linked to it by language, faith, historical experience, nationalistic feelings, or common loyalty? Most nations' security problems are external, stemming from other states; Israel's is external as well as internal.

Such a potentially divisive nationalism, leading ultimately to disintegration and possible civil war, occurs more frequently among developing countries than among the older, more cohesive nation-states of Europe. Maintaining national unity remains a primary problem for many of these new states because they are composed of various ethnic or tribal groups, often with different religious beliefs, different languages, and little else in common except the shared experience of colonial rule. Thus, some states, such as Nigeria, Zaire, and India, experienced civil wars upon becoming independent; others, such as Pakistan, which emerged out of India, broke into even smaller sovereign states.

Yet nationalism remains the principal force in the world today. For the developing nations, as for developed nations, Communist or non-Communist, Islamic or not, the nation is the largest political organization with which most people can identify; they may give their loyalty to the family, tribe, religion, or region, but it is generally the nation that commands the ultimate loyalty and for which most have in the past been willing to sacrifice their lives if necessary. This is less a matter of blind patriotism than a recognition that the nation is the largest secular community in which a meaningful life can be lived. It may be that the nation as the fundamental actor in international politics may cause much danger and, in the atomic age, constitute a threat to survival itself; nevertheless, there is as yet no viable substitute for it.

Recognition by Other States

Generally, a state is officially recognized by other states when it is perceived as having established control over the people within its boundaries. At that point it is customary to exchange ambassadors and undertake agreements. In reality, however, matters are not always so straightforward. For example, the state of Israel has existed since 1948, but, of the Arab states, only Egypt has recognized it, taking thirty years to do so; the others still refuse, even though they have fought four wars with Israel. Recognition means acceptance of a state as a legitimate political entity. Even without recognition, however, diplomatic relations can exist. The United States did not recognize mainland China until 1979, but, just as the Arab states have negotiated ceasefires and prisoner exchanges with Israel, the United States negotiated with China to end the Korean War, attended the great-power conference ending the first Indochina war in 1954, and occasionally met with Chinese officials to explore certain issues. Similarly, North Vietnam and the United States negotiated an end to that war, even though neither recognized the other officially. The disadvantage of such relations is that they are intermittent and do not easily permit mutual and accurate assessment of intentions and capabilities.

The basic practice is to extend *de facto* recognition when a new state is born; the fact of its existence is the key. But some states will extend recognition only *de jure*—that is, when they approve of the new government. The United States was slow to officially recognize both the Soviet and the Communist Chinese governments, taking sixteen years and thirty years, respectively. Sometimes the situation becomes an awkward one. The United States recognizes the Sandinista government in Nicaragua, but President Ronald Reagan's administration was committed to its overthrow. Or different states recognize rival governments of another state. Moscow and Washington have at times recognized rival governments in: East and West Germany, North and South Korea, North and South Vietnam, and Communist and Nationalist China. Both now recognize each of the Germanies. South Vietnam no longer exists, but the United States has not recognized the new unified Communist People's Republic of Vietnam. Washington has withdrawn recognition from the Nationalists on Taiwan and opened official diplomatic relations with Communist China. It continues, however, to supply arms to Taiwan. Because both the Communists and Nationalists agree that there is only one China, the United States is supplying weapons to a province that is in rebellion against the government that Washington recognizes as the legitimate ruler of China!

Even more bizarre is the situation of Hong Kong, a British colony leased from China for ninety-nine years until 1997. Adjoining the Chinese mainland, Hong Kong is a thriving capitalist society whose inhabitants enjoy Western-style freedoms. China and Britain have agreed to resolve Hong Kong's future status by a solution known as "one country, two systems." The Chinese Communist flag will wave over Hong Kong as it again becomes part of (Communist) China, but for fifty more years Hong Kong will be an autonomous administrative region of China with its own capitalist social and economic system and a Western way of life. Why does Beijing not just demand the Crown Colony's return or take it, as it could easily do? The reasons are twofold: one, Hong Kong's position as a trading and international financial center is economically beneficial to mainland China; and two, Beijing would like to tempt the Nationalist Chinese on Taiwan to make the same kind of agreement. China could thus be reunited as a single country, while Taiwan, like Hong Kong, enjoyed self-government, its higher standard of living, different economic and political systems, and its own army (supplied with weapons by the United States). Whether, of course, Beijing will tolerate free trade and free speech in Hong Kong when the British lease expires and whether an arrangement similar to Hong Kong's will be acceptable to Taiwan is widely questioned after the brutal suppression of the pro-domocracy movement in Beijing in 1989.

Perhaps the most bizarre situation occurred in late 1988. Before that date the Palestinian Liberation Organization (PLO), the self-proclaimed representative of the Palestinian people, had been committed to the destruction of Israel by the use of terrorism in its pursuit of a Palestinian state encompassing the former British mandate of Palestine. Then, in 1988, the PLO declared the establishment of an independent Palestinian state limited to the West Bank and the Gaza Strip (with PLO leader Yasir Arafat serving as president). Yet these territories captured by Israel in the 1967 war are still controlled by it. Implicit in this act was a recognition of Israel's right to exist, a precondition for any negotiations, but the PLO still refused to make that recognition explicit. Despite the fact that the Palestinian state was unborn, numerous states, especially Arab ones, extended recognition to the nonexisting state, which all Israeli political parties opposed as a mortal threat to Israel's survival.

CLASSIFICATION OF STATES

Great Powers and Small Powers

The most widespread and traditional means of distinguishing among states is in terms of the power they possess. The components of power include geographic location, size, population, industry, and wealth (see Chapter 7). Most observers have long distinguished between "great powers" and "small powers." Almost by definition, the great powers, with their significant military capacity, have been considered the primary actors in the state system because they play the leading role in security issues in international politics. Indeed, according to one student of war, Jack Levy, from 1480 to 1940 there were about 2,600 important battles involving European states.[3] During these 460 years, France participated in 47 percent of the battles, Austria-Hungary in 34 percent, Prussia (Germany) in 25 percent and Britain and Russia in approximately 22 percent. Thus, at least one great power participated in about two-thirds of the wars during these almost five centuries, leading Levy to denote them "the most frequent fighters."[4] Also according to Levy,

> The Great Powers constitute an interdependent system of power and security relations. . . . This is an open rather than closed system, for it is affected to some extent by the larger world system of which it is a part. The primary influences on the Great Powers, however, derive from within the Great Power system, and their patterns of interaction can be explained largely by the internal dynamics of that system. . . . The Great Power system may be a subsystem of the larger international system, but in fundamental respects it is a dominant subsystem.[5]

Primacy of Great Powers.   Particularly striking is the remarkable stability in the ranking of great powers, despite vast geographic, industrial, and social changes in Europe during the nineteenth century. This is revealed in a list of the great powers since the French Revolution and the Napoleonic Wars (see Table 3-1).

Stability in these rankings does not mean that changes in individual positions have not occurred. Prussia, which made its mark against Napoleon, became part of an enlarged and united Germany in 1870 after the defeat of France. Germany then replaced France as the Continent's preeminent power and became a rival to Britain, at that time the leading power in the world. Austria-Hungary, by contrast, declined after the Napoleonic Wars, lost its place as the primary power in central Europe to Prussia in 1866, and collapsed in World War I, which also exhausted France and Britain. It was American power that was critical in both world wars in defeating

Table 3-1 The Great Powers

	Napoleonic Wars	World War I	World War II	Cold War and Détente
Austria-Hungary	x	x	—	—
Britain	x	x	x	x
France	x	x	x	x
Italy	—	x	x	x
Japan	—	x	x	x
Prussia-Germany	x	x	x	x
Russia/Soviet Union	x	x	x	x
United States	—	x	x	x

Germany as was Soviet power in World War II. As continental powers with populations and resources to match, dwarfing the great powers of the past, the United States and Soviet Union emerged as *superpowers* after 1945.

The international system has always granted a special place to the great powers. During the nineteenth century, the Concert of Europe was composed exclusively of the great powers. They were the self-appointed board of directors of the European "corporation," meeting from time to time to deal with significant political problems that affected the peace of Europe. This special great-power status and responsibility was reflected in the 1920 League of Nations Covenant, which gave such powers permanent membership on the league's Council; the Assembly, composed of the smaller nations, was expected to meet only every four or five years. In those days, "the world seemed to be the oyster of the great powers." [6] After Germany's second defeat, their privileged status and obligations were again recognized in the United Nations Charter provision that conferred upon the United States, Soviet Union, Britain, France, and China (which at the time was still controlled by the Nationalists) permanent membership on the United Nations Security Council. The General Assembly was not expected to play a major role in preserving the peace. Interestingly enough, these same five states were, by 1971, when Communist China was admitted to the United Nations, also the only countries to have nuclear weapons. Great powers, in short, not only possess great military power, are recognized as great powers by other states, but they also are accorded formal recognition of their status by their participation in concerts and congresses and permanent membership in the U.N. Security Council. As one example of this status, in 1989, when the celebration of the two hundredth birthday of the French Revolution coincided with the economic summit meeting of the Western industrial states in Paris, the great powers' dinners were even held separately from the dinners of the developing countries invited by France to celebrate their revolution.

Small Powers as Victims. In contrast to great powers, small powers have often acted less than they have been acted upon. Their security frequently depends on the great powers. Even a state like Israel, which has fought its own wars, is very conscious of its dependence on the United States for modern weapons and money. Israel is also constantly concerned about U.S. diplomatic pressure to make concessions that it believes are not in Israel's interest but that Washington perceives as necessary to achieve an overall settlement in the Middle East. Even greater limits are felt by the states of Eastern Europe. Although they are no longer subservient to the Soviet Union, Moscow has repeatedly intervened in their affairs politically and militarily.

The United States under the Monroe Doctrine has also intervened frequently in Latin America. Especially since the failure of the 1961 U.S.-sponsored invasion of Cuba, the United States has intervened either overtly or covertly on several occasions to prevent "another Cuba" and to contain Cuban and Soviet influence in the Western Hemisphere: in the Dominican Republic during the Johnson presidency, in Chile during the Nixon presidency, and in Grenada and Nicaragua during the Reagan presidency—although unsuccessfully in the latter case, suggesting a sharply declining U.S. dominance. Nevertheless, the general proposition remains true: a small country, if it lies close to a great power, must be very careful. It had better not give offense, and it must be especially aware of and sensitive to the great power's interests. Panama's former ruler, General Omar Torrijos Herara, summed up cold bloodedly how great powers have historically treated smaller countries. Commenting on the fall from power of the shah of Iran to the Ayatollah Ruhollah Khomeini and the refusal initially of Britain and the United States to give the shah asylum, Torrijos said, "This is what happens to a man squeezed by the great nations. After all the juice is gone, they throw him away." [7]

Hierarchy of States. Actually, the division of countries into great and small powers, although useful, is rather unsophisticated. It is useful because it simplifies the analysis and conduct of international politics by allowing the scholar and diplomat to focus on the demands of the great powers and the interaction among them. And it does tell the essential story. The needs of the weak have in the past been either ignored or received negligible attention. While oversimplified, the old axiom that the strong do as they please and the weak suffer as they must expresses a simple truth about the relations among nations. But the international hierarchy of states is in reality far more complex than the simple hierarchy of great and small powers.

At the top of the hierarchy since World War II are the United States and the Soviet Union. As *superpowers* they are in a category all by themselves. Usually their status is equated with their vast nuclear forces; the small forces of other nuclear nations are not yet comparable. But, even if nuclear arms had never been invented, these two countries would still be superpowers. As countries with populations of more than 200 million people and sizable industries, they also have been able to afford large conventional forces and to use their wealth and technology to advance their aims. One of the paradoxes of the post-World War II state system has been that it has witnessed simultaneously a massive expansion of states but a significant contraction of primary actors, such as the superpowers, in the system.

After these two powers are the second-rank powers—Britain, France, West Germany, China, and Japan—whose capacities to act in one or more of the regions beyond their own are relatively limited. The first three, pre-World War II members of the great-power club, have recovered from their post-1945 collapse, but only by uniting can the second-rank European states regain the confidence needed to play a role proportionate to their population, wealth, and military experience. Individually, these nations will continue to feel vulnerable in a superpower world.

From there on down nations can be divided into middle-rank powers such as Italy and Spain in Europe, India in Asia, and Brazil in Latin America (the latter two potential superpowers); minor powers such as Colombia, Hungary, Norway, and South Korea; and microstates such as Brunei (population 316,000), Cape Verde (354,000), Djibouti (320,000), Grenada (84,000), the Seychelles (68,000), and St. Kitts and Nevis (37,000). Most of these micro-states are not economically viable and are dependent on other states: their sovereignty is in name only.

Projection of Global, Regional, and Local Power

A closely related criterion for classifying states according to their power is the extent of their interest in and capacity for intervening in affairs beyond their own frontiers. Power "makes ambitious projects feasible and increases . . . their chances of success; weakness constrains, restrains and limits choice and independence."[8] The superpowers have the capacity to project their power throughout the entire state system. The United States, with its sealift and airlift ability, has long had a global reach. It could intervene overnight in Lebanon and fight a long war in Vietnam at the end of ten thousand miles of supply lines. (The generals in Moscow must have been envious.) The Soviet Union was initially a Eurasian power, but control of foreign Communist parties extended its reach. An enormous military buildup, including a blue-sea fleet and airlift capacity, has given Moscow a systemwide capability as well. Under both czars and commissars, Soviet expansion was concentrated around the nation's periphery. In the 1970s, for the first time, the Soviet Union expanded its influence beyond Eurasia to Angola, Ethiopia, and South Yemen.

The second-rank states are essentially regional powers. The former colonial powers have largely limited their roles to Europe. Britain's last foreign intervention came during the war over the Suez Canal in 1956; it was a dismal failure, ending in the collapse of the British government. It was 1982 before Britain again acted far outside Europe. When Argentina seized the Falkland Islands located off its coast, Britain sent a large naval unit to restore British sovereignty and wipe out the humiliation of the seizure. France, which had joined with Britain in 1956 to intervene in Egypt, reacted to the Suez defeat by developing a nuclear bomb in order to recoup its prestige and to play an active role in Europe. In the 1970s, France increasingly used troops to support its interests, largely in former French Africa. In 1978 it intervened with small forces in Zaire, but it needed American planes to carry them. Middle-rank and minor powers have even less capacity to act beyond their regions or even their frontiers. Many of the smaller states have virtually no individual influence.

It is important to recognize that much of international politics occurs in these regional systems or subsystems of the global system.[9] Within each system—Western Europe and Eastern Europe, Middle East, Latin America, Asia, and sub-Saharan Africa—the member states are driven by concerns peculiar to their areas. These often intersect with the global U.S.-Soviet rivalry or broader North-South issues. But within the different subsystems, actors and issues vary, so that while the superpowers may cooperate globally on arms control, they may be in conflict in the Middle East or elsewhere.

Nevertheless, if it were this easy to calculate power and predict who will influence whom and, in war, who will beat whom, it would have been difficult—if not impossible—to predict North Vietnam's victory over the United States, or the quaking of the West European industrial countries before their former colonies in OPEC (Organization of Petroleum Exporting Countries), most of whose member countries have tiny populations, no industry, and no military muscle; or the defeat of the Soviet Union by the Afghan resistance. Equally difficult to foresee was Israel's ability to defy American pressures for more conciliatory behavior, despite its almost complete dependence politically, economically, and militarily upon the United States, or the substantial sums of economic and military aid that have to be paid by the United States to small countries for establishing military bases (for example, the Philippines). Indeed, if power calculations alone could accurately forecast how events would turn out, why have a contest of power, especially a war?

A ranking of states by power may give an initial quick impression of which states are likely to achieve their aims and which are not, but though such a ranking is useful, even necessary, it is clearly not sufficient. States may be classified according to amounts of power, but power relations among states may be quite complex. The components of power, as repeatedly emphasized here, are not automatically translated into equivalent influence or ability to achieve desired goals. It is even difficult to establish rankings below the level of the secondary powers. Is Cuba, which in 1978 and 1979 had more than twice the number of troops in Africa than France, a minor power or a secondary power? Cuba had a population of almost 10 million but a military of 200,000 (for the American population, the equivalent would be 4 million to 5 million, twice the size of current U.S. forces); in 1988 50,000 Cuban troops were reportedly serving in Angola and another large contingent in Ethiopia. Together with its two hundred jet fighters and fifty naval ships, Cuba had by the mid-1970s passed Brazil as Latin America's leading military power. By the late 1980s, Cuba had become "a world class military power."[10] And what about Saudi Arabia, a country even the United States feared to offend in the 1970s and 1980s? Was it a superpower, a secondary power, or on a level even lower than the minor powers such as Israel, Pakistan, and Yugoslavia? Rankings are not necessarily very accurate guides in a world in which arms may not confer more political leverage, economically advanced countries appear politically vulnerable and weak, and states with neither military nor economic strength often appear to dictate events.

Status Quo States Versus Revisionist States

States can also be classified according to their aims in the state system: Are they generally willing to accept things as they are, or do they seek to change them? If they are largely willing to accept the existing situations, they are "status quo powers." The status quo can therefore be identified with such words as *satisfied, defense,* and *preserve.* Revisionist powers are not content with things as they are, and revisionism is associated with such words as *expansion, offense,* and *change.* These terms were particularly useful in the past, when they were associated with peace treaties concluded at the ends of wars. As territorial settlements were usually involved, the victors sought to preserve the status quo, which generally benefited them; the vanquished states wished to arrange changes to alleviate some of the grievances outstanding from the war. At the end of World War I, for example, the Versailles peace treaty included a number of provisions about Germany's frontiers with the new Poland and Czechoslovakia that most Germans disliked. France arranged for alliances with the countries to the east of Germany to contain German power, and it was thus committed to these countries and their frontiers with Germany. There were also other provisions, such as limitations on the size of the German army and the kinds of weapons it could have. Germany, wanting changes in the territorial and political *status quo* even before the rise of Adolf Hitler, was the revisionist state.

Designation of a state as status quo or revisionist looks straightforward, but it often is not. During World War II, the United States thought the Soviet Union was basically a status quo power. After the war, the Soviet Union was redefined as revisionist. Is the Soviet Union today still a revisionist state? Or has it become a status quo power seeking primarily to protect its postwar security in Eastern Europe, embodied in the Warsaw Treaty Organization, and along its frontier with China? Do Moscow's rulers still seek to fulfill their ideological objective of world revolution? Or have they become more and more conservative as their revolutionary fervor of an earlier day has evaporated, and as the Soviet Union—over seventy years after the revolution—has become a highly bureaucratic and industrialized nation with much to lose in a nuclear war? Is its present emphasis on domestic reform an indicator of its shift from a revisionist to a status quo power, or does it represent only a tactical change while the Soviet Union recovers its economic strength?

In short, the questions of how revisionist a state is and on what issues, and to what extent it has become *in practice* a status quo nation even though it may still articulate revisionist purposes and slogans, are not easy to decide and become matters of controversy, if not confusion. What are the criteria of judgment—declaratory statements or acts? If so, what kind? How especially does the observer decide when a status quo power has become revisionist or the reverse? Despite all of the ambiguities and difficulties involved in classifying states in this manner, such a classification can be useful in analysis if applied with care and with awareness of the complexities involved.

West, East, and Nonaligned States (First, Second, and Third Worlds)

A tripartite classification of states, unlike those already given, is more contemporary. It is not based on power or goals but on states' relations with the superpowers—alignment with the United States (the West), with the Soviet Union (the East), or with neither (states termed *nonaligned*). The three divisions are also known as the First, Second, and Third Worlds. This categorization was especially useful during the cold war years, when the Western alliance (the North Atlantic Treaty Organization, or NATO) confronted the Soviet Union and its allies in Eastern Europe, as well as China, in two solid blocs, often called in the West the Free World and the Communist World. The third bloc incorporated the new nations. What united them was their former colonial history, their economically underdeveloped state or poverty, their sharing of the "revolution of rising expectations," and a foreign policy of nonalignment.

This threefold division is no longer quite so applicable. NATO can no longer be called a bloc, as if it were a cohesive unit with a single policy. Differences among the Western allies mean that one must also speak of French or West German policies, for example. Divisions also exist among the Soviet Union's allies in Eastern Europe. And the Sino-Soviet alliance split too: China now aligns itself with the United States, Europe, and Japan. China even briefly invaded Vietnam, after Vietnam had attacked Communist Cambodia to overthrow its pro-Chinese regime and replace it with a pro-Vietnamese and pro-Soviet government. Although in 1989 China and the Soviet Union improved their relationship, China does not consider itself aligned with either superpower. Instead, it publicly identifies itself as a Third World state.

The nonaligned states, too, have become increasingly divided. Composed as they are of more than one hundred nations of varying sizes, histories, ideologies, and political and economic systems, and divided as they are between pro-American and pro-Soviet sentiments, they can no longer be considered a bloc. Rather, the Third World can be split into the oil-exporting countries; the newly industrialized countries (NICs), sometimes referred to as "export platforms" (Hong Kong, Singapore, South Korea, Taiwan); and the many developing countries with an average per capita income of $500 or less. Moreover, not all states are nonaligned. Some, such as Cuba, are aligned with the Soviet Union; others, such as Somalia—formerly aligned with Moscow—

have military ties to the United States; and still others, such as India, have links to both.

North-South States (Rich Nations and Poor Nations)

Another way of looking at the world is to divide it into North and South or rich and poor. These terms, like West and East, are handy tags, even though also oversimplified. *North* refers to all the industrialized, higher-income states, both West and East. *South* includes the former colonial countries that had been governed from London, Paris, Brussels, and other Western capitals. During the cold war, these poorer or economically developing nations used their status between the West and East to enhance their bargaining strength and attract economic assistance from both for their own development; in other words, they learned to play both ends against the middle. But during détente, as their leverage declined, the poorer countries increasingly focused their attention on the richer Western states, which supposedly dominated the international economy and exploited them. The developing countries demanded a new international economic order.

Since 1973 and OPEC's quadrupling of oil prices and the oil embargo against the United States, the conflict between rich and poor has shared center stage in the world arena with the older adversary relationship between East and West. The problems of overpopulation, hunger, and poverty faced by the nations of the South are now very much part of the international agenda, and they are voiced especially in the United Nations Conference on Trade and Development (UNCTAD), which has been called a "trade union of the poor." [11]

NONSTATE ACTORS

Individual nation-states are complemented by other actors. Some are groups of states—intergovernmental organizations (IGOs), or, as they were more commonly called in the past, international organizations. Others are nongovernmental organizations (NGOs).

Intergovernmental Actors

Intergovernmental organizations are voluntary associations of sovereign states, organized to pursue the many different purposes for which states wish to cooperate through some sort of formal and often long-term structure. Decisions made by such IGOs are the product of negotiations among the governmental representatives assigned to them, including foreign and defense ministers, who attend specified meetings. The day-to-day business of each IGO is carried out by its bureaucracy, and its institutional machinery may be relatively small or large and complex, as in the European Economic Community (EEC).

During the nineteenth century, in the wake of the twenty-five years of war that followed the French Revolution, the great powers met repeatedly in the Concert of Europe, a series of multilateral summit conferences designed to deal collectively with potentially troublesome issues ranging from the division of Africa to the regulation of international traffic on Europe's rivers to the admission of new states to the European system.[12] Indeed, in 1899 the states, mainly European, convened in The Hague in the Netherlands to discuss the causes, control, and prevention of war itself, producing, among other things, institutions for the peaceful settlement of disputes. Just as significant, if not more so, than these intermittent, *ad hoc*, high-level meetings of Europe's political leaders were the public international unions that dealt with the increasing number of transnational nonpolitical issues resulting from the proliferating technological, socioeconomic, and cultural "interdependence." In response to the

> unprecedented international flow of commerce in goods, services, people, ideas, germs, and social evils . . . [the] process of international organization . . . quickly resulted in the establishment of a profusion of agencies whose terms of reference touched upon such diverse fields as health, agriculture, tariffs, railroads, standards of weight and measurement, patents and copyrights, narcotic drugs, and prison conditions." [13]

The first of these agencies was the International Telegraphic Union and the Universal Postal Union. The evolution of these types of IGOs testified to the existence of "an area of international affairs within which sovereign states have a common interest in cooperative endeavor." [14] Moreover, such cooperation was the result of need, not idealism.

It is this need that has resulted in the rapid growth of IGOs, from fewer than two hundred in the first decade of this century to well over four thousand by the late 1980s. IGOs may be classified by scope and function. First, the organization may be global or regional. The United Nations includes most existing states and strives for universal membership. The International Bank for Reconstruction and Development or World Bank, International Monetary Fund, and General Agreement on Tariffs and Trade (GATT) have broad membership, although not universal; Western states, especially the United States, are the most prominent members. The developing countries, believing that GATT's promotion of free trade was counter to their interests, started UNCTAD, in which they organized the Group of 77 (now over 100 members) to enhance their bargaining power. By contrast, organizations like the Commonwealth (no longer preceded by *British* because all of its members are regarded as equals) comprises states in almost every area of the world; far short of universal membership, it is nevertheless a global organization. Similarly, OPEC, the nucleus of which is Arab (Saudi Arabia, Algeria, Qatar, Kuwait, Libya, Iraq, and the United Arab Emirates), has other members in the Middle East (Iran), Africa (Nigeria and Gabon), southeast Asia (Indonesia), and Latin America (Venezuela and Ecuador). Mexico accepted "observer" status in OPEC in 1982. Other producer cartels also have multiregional or global membership.

Most IGOs, however, are regional. Many areas have organizations through which member states may promote regional cooperation or resolve common political problems or internal quarrels. The Organization of American States

(OAS), the Organization for African Unity (OAU), and the Arab League are three examples. There are as well military alliances such as NATO and its Soviet counterpart, the Warsaw Treaty Organization (also known as the Warsaw Pact in Europe), and the (Persian) Gulf Cooperation Council (composed of Saudi Arabia, Kuwait, Bahrain, Oman, Qatar, and the United Arab Emirates), a regional IGO organized by developing countries to defend themselves against Iran. As with global organizations, regional organizations are not always completely regional. NATO, for example, has members ranging from North America (Canada and the United States) to the eastern Mediterranean (Greece and Turkey), but the bulk of its membership is European.

A second method of classification is by function: political, military, economic, or social. The United Nations and the OAU are basically political organizations, but they may carry out other tasks as well. NATO and WTO obviously have a primarily military purpose. The European Coal and Steel Community (ECSC) was established in 1950 to integrate these two sectors of the economies of West Germany, France, Italy, and the Benelux countries (Belgium, the Netherlands, and Luxembourg). The ECSC's success led to the formation in 1958 of the European Economic Community, whose purpose was to integrate the economies of the six different countries into one single economy by eliminating trade barriers and other obstacles to the economic foundation of a United States of Europe (by 1986 the EEC had doubled its membership). The Soviet Union, Bulgaria, Hungary, Romania, Czechoslovakia, Poland, East Germany, Cuba, Mongolia, and Vietnam constitute the Council for Mutual Economic Assistance or COMECON, whose stated purpose has been to create a more rational division of labor among the Soviet bloc countries in Eastern Europe, but whose real purpose always has been to give Moscow greater control over these countries. Organizations dealing with health, education, communications, and food, such as the World Health Organization (WHO) and the United Nations Educational, Scientific, and Cultural Organization (UNESCO), focus on social purposes. It should be noted that few regional IGOs are concerned with issues of peace and security; most have economic or social functions (see Table 3-2).

From IGO to Subregional Groupings

In recent years some regional organizations have become more and more divided and unable to act with a united front. For example, in 1982, when Argentina forcibly seized the British-owned Falkland Islands, most of Spanish- and Portuguese-speaking Latin America, from democratic Venezuela to Communist Cuba, supported Argentina. Although the depth of this support for Argentina's aggression was questionable, there was a surface solidarity constituting a majority. The United States supported Britain and helped its military efforts to retake the islands. Because its English-speaking members, mainly Caribbean, refused to support Argentina, the Organization of American States was splintered into eighteen Latin and thirteen English-speaking countries. Indeed, the initial diplomatic efforts to resolve the conflict focused

Table 3-2 A Select Group of Intergovernmental Organizations

Purpose	*Global*	*Regional*
Political	United Nations Commonwealth	Organization of American States (OAS) Organization of African Unity (OAU) Arab League Organization of the Islamic Conference
Military		North Atlantic Treaty Organization (NATO) Warsaw Treaty Organization (WTO)
Economic	Organization of Petroleum Export- ing Countries (OPEC) International Labor Organization (ILO)	Organization of Arab Petroleum Exporting Countries (OAPEC) European Economic Community (EEC) (includes European Coal and Steel Community, or ECSC) Association of Southeast Asian Nations (ASEAN) African Development Bank
Social/ scientific	World Health Organization (WHO) United Nations Educational, Scien- tific and Cultural Organization (UNESCO)	European Space Agency

on the United Nations. The OAS also was not involved in efforts to resolve differences between the United States and Nicaragua resulting from the 1979 Sandinista revolution. Instead, this endeavor fell to the Contadora countries composed of Mexico, Venezuela, Colombia, and Panama. When these efforts failed, the Central American presidents, organized by Costa Rica's president Oscar Arias Sanchez, took the initiative in devising a peace plan, which became the basis for efforts to find a solution after 1987. In 1989, over U.S. protests, they called for the disbandment of the "contras" (the opponents of the government) by the end of the year, thereby ending the contra war. In 1962 the OAS supported the United States during the Cuban missile crisis. But in 1983 the OAS did not approve the U.S. intervention on the island of Grenada; Washington therefore sought legitimation for its action from a previously little-known alliance of small Caribbean islands, the Association of East Caribbean States. In 1987 the presidents of six Latin American states (Colombia, Mexico, Panama, Peru, Uruguay, and Venezuela) met for the first time ever without the United States and agreed that Cuba should be invited to rejoin all regional organizations. And not only did Latin America oppose U.S. intervention against Panama's General Noriega, but the OAS also refused to take a collective strong stand, as desired by the United States, after Noriega stole the election from the opposition parties in 1989. Washington had wanted the OAS to help negotiate a transition from Noriega to a more democratic Panama before the canal is turned over to the Panamanians by the end of the next decade.

Other IGOs have similarly broken down into smaller, more workable groups. Leading examples are: in the Middle East, the Gulf Cooperative Council, the Arab Cooperation Council (Egypt, Iraq, Jordan, and Yemen), and the Maghreb Union (Algeria, Libya, Mauritania, Morocco and Tunisia);[15] in Africa, the Organization of Front-Line States (Angola, Botswana, Mozambique, Tanzania, and since 1980, Zimbabwe), initially formed to help Zimbabwe become independent and more recently involved with South Africa's racial turmoil and independence for Namibia; and in Asia, ASEAN, the Association of Southeast Asian Nations (Indonesia, Malaysia, the Philippines, Singapore, Thailand, and, since 1984, Brunei), which deals mainly with members' common economic issues, although the association has also become concerned with security issues.

Supranational Actor

There is one significant exception to the rule that in intergovernmental organizations the participating members maintain their autonomy. Since 1950 in Western Europe there has been a revolutionary attempt to move beyond the nation-state toward a supranational actor. The six members of the European Coal and Steel Community had joined in an IGO to transfer the authority of their governments in specified economic sectors to a new federal authority, which was to be established above them. Decisions were to be made by this higher authority; they would no longer be arrived at by negotiations among the member governments. By 1958 the ECSC had been succeeded by the European Economic Community. This six-member organization was joined later by Britain, Denmark, Ireland, Greece, Spain, and Portugal. The EEC and the European Atomic Energy Community (Euratom), formed in 1958, together constitute the European Communities (EC). But the EC has not made the progress originally expected in moving toward political union. In 1992, however, in an attempt to reinvigorate the European movement, the twelve member states will take a major step forward by removing the last barriers to economic union in the expectation of making European corporations more competitive in the global economy and turning Europe into an economic superpower. The EEC is also planning to move toward a single European currency to help this process along.

One thing is clear already: The EEC, now usually referred to just as the EC, has moved beyond the more traditional IGO in its decision-making procedures. While the eventual EC goal remains a politically, as well as economically, unified United States of Europe, at least one observant journalist has said that even now the EC is acting less like a well-meaning but ineffective trade association and more like a central government of this continent. Already, steps toward 1992 have entailed unprecedented ceding of national sovereignty from 10 Downing, the Elysees, the Bundeshaus, and other power centers to EC headquarters at the Berlaymont in Brussels. Already, all trade policy emanates from Brussels.[16]

Nongovernmental or Transnational Actors

Increasingly visible since World War II has been the transnational actor, the nongovernmental organization. It is characterized by a headquarters in one country and centrally directed operations in two or more countries. The term *transnational* is appropriate because the NGO performs its functions not only across national frontiers but also often in disregard of them. The increase in the number, size, scope, and variety of NGOs since World War II has led observers to speak of a transnational organizational revolution in world politics.[17] NGOs differ from IGOs in a number of significant ways. The latter are composed of nation-states, and their actions depend upon their members' common interests; conflicting interests must first be reconciled through negotiations, which may not always be successful or rapid. The transnational organization represents its own interests and pursues them in many nations.

> The international organization requires *accord* among nations; the transnational organization requires *access* to nations.... The restraints on an international organization are largely internal, stemming from the need to produce consensus among its members. The restraints on a transnational organization are largely external, stemming from its need to gain operating authority in different sovereign states. International organizations embody the principle of nationality; transnational organizations try to ignore it. [18]

Multinational Corporations.   The most prominent contemporary NGO is the multinational corporation (MNC), the usually huge firm that owns and controls plants and offices in many countries and sells its goods and services there. MNCs may be classified according to the kind of business activities they pursue[19]:

Extractive (resources)
   oil (Mobil)
   copper (Kennecott)

Agriculture (Standard Brands)

Industrial
   capital equipment (Navistar)
   automobiles (General Motors)
   consumer goods (Colgate-Palmolive)

Service
   tourism (Hilton Hotels, Holiday Inns)
   retail (Sears)
   transportation (Hertz)
   public utilities (General Telephone and Electronics)

Banking (Chase Manhattan)

Conglomerates (International Telephone and Telegraph)

The sheer size of these MNCs is one of the reasons they are now often listed as actors of increasing importance internationally. Lester Brown, a self-styled world watcher, in ranking nations and MNCs according to gross national product (GNP, the total worth of goods and services produced) and gross annual sales, found that in the early 1970s the first twenty-two entries were the twenty-two largest nations, ranging from the United States to Argentina.[20] The twenty-third was General Motors, followed by Switzerland and Pakistan; Standard Oil of New Jersey and Ford ranked twenty-seventh and twenty-ninth, respectively; Royal Dutch Shell was thirty-sixth, ahead of Iran and Venezuela; and General Electric and International Business Machines were forty-third and forty-fifth, respectively, ahead of Egypt, Nigeria, and Israel. Of the top fifty, forty-one were nations, and nine were MNCs; of the second fifty, eighteen were nations, and thirty-two were MNCs. Clearly, many MNCs have resources much greater than those of most members of the United Nations, and many operate on a geographical scale exceeding that of the great empires of the past. Oil has enhanced these trends. After the 1973 oil crisis, Exxon overtook General Motors as the world's largest corporation. The oil companies all profited enormously; so, of course, did the oil-producing states, raising them in the ranking. After the collapse of oil prices in the early 1980s, General Motors again became the largest MNC. But Exxon, Mobil, Texaco, Royal Dutch Shell and British Petroleum remain among the leading MNCs. By the late 1980s, more than half of the world's nations had smaller GNPs than the annual sales of any of the leading forty MNCs listed in a ranking of the top one hundred nations and MNCs.

Regardless of the actual rankings, the implications are obvious. One is the strength of MNCs compared to that of the weaker countries, and the influence they can presumably exert within nations. An early fear was that these "new sovereigns" might become more powerful than the governments of many countries, gain control of their economies, and thus dictate their futures. Another fear, of even greater significance, was their possible effects on the state system itself. Because of the MNCs' multinational production, distribution, and service—and the trend is toward attaining global reach but with planning still centralized—some observers have argued that the MNCs would make the nation-state obsolete. The MNCs have already ushered in a global economy, increasingly tying the industrial nations together in an interdependent relationship (see Chapter 15). Their role in helping the developing countries advance has also gained importance. Since many of the government-run economies of developing countries have been unable to induce sufficient economic growth and make their industries profitable, a number of these countries reassessed the potential threat the large MNCs posed to their independence and welcomed American, European, and Asian MNCs to invest in their countries during the 1980s.

Religious, Humanitarian, and Professional Actors. One of the oldest and most visible NGOs is the Roman Catholic church, with a membership of half a billion people in the 1980s. To do its work, the church has learned over the centuries to coexist with all manner of governments, including fascist ones. The political influence of the church can hardly be doubted. Even Communist governments treat the church with caution. In Poland the church played a key role in mediating the quarrel between the government and Solidarity, the independent labor union that in the early 1980s sought to improve economic conditions and create more freedom for Poles and in 1989 formed its first non-Communist government. In late 1989 a first-ever meeting took place between an antheist, Soviet leader and the pope.

The church's influence is worldwide. In 1985 at a Synod of Bishops in Rome, the church welcomed representatives from thirty-four African countries, seventeen Asian countries, and twenty-two Latin American and the Caribbean countries. "Their voices were varied, but their message was clear: This is the new Catholic church, the church of the third world, and it is the church of the future." [21] Almost 50 percent of the world's 800 million Catholics live in the Third World. Despite its best efforts, the church is not always united. Disagreement exists over the use of artificial birth control, celibacy for the priesthood, and the admission of women to the priesthood. Moreover, a growing number of priests in Latin America and in the Philippines are following "liberation theology." Because of their work with the poor, they claim that Christ led them to Marx. They believe that American capitalism is the cause of poverty and that only through social revolution can economic injustice and political oppression end. These priests support Marxist guerrillas, as in El Salvador, or Marxist governments, as in Nicaragua, and, when opposed by the formal church, some have proclaimed themselves to be members of "the people's church." The pope has denounced liberation theology, but the church—conservative, liberal, as well as radical—is deeply entangled in poverty, hunger, oppression, and human rights in the developing countries. It is also involved in social issues in the developed world. In the United States, Catholic bishops have opposed as immoral the use of nuclear weapons, even for retaliation, and have called for a greater governmental role to help the poor.

Other well-known NGOs are Communist International, through which the Soviet Union used to exert its control over foreign Communist parties; the International Red Cross, whose concern in wartime is with prisoners of war and in peacetime with natural and manmade disasters; and Amnesty International, an organization that has gained prominence because of its monitoring of the abuses of human rights in many countries. Other representatives of the multifold professional and social NGOs, are such organizations as the International Political Science Organization; the International Studies Association (which includes many of the "famous" textbook writers students so enjoy reading!); the International Skeletal Society, whose members are radiologists, orthopedists, and pathologists; and the better-known Rotary Club. Their main function is to link human beings in different countries. Most have little influence on the conduct of their nations' foreign policies, but they do foster many international friendships as well as advance professional knowledge. Some, though nonpolitical, have become politicized. The Olympic games, for example, organized by the International Olympic Committee, overlap with the East-West competition, notwithstanding national protestations to the contrary.

'National Liberation' Groups.   An actor of increasing importance in the state system is the self-styled "national liberation" organization. Perhaps the best known of these since the 1960s is the Palestine Liberation Organization. Even before it declared the existence of a Palestinian state, it had been recognized as the legitimate representative of the Palestinians by the Arab states, had been granted observer status at the United Nations, and had been represented at meetings of the nonaligned countries as a full-fledged member. PLO leader Arafat had been received by the political leaders of Europe and Japan, usually with the honors reserved for a visiting head of state. Even the pope received him in 1982. Despite subsequent attempts by President Hafez al-Assad of Syria to wrest control of the PLO from Arafat, the PLO was represented diplomatically in more than one hundred nations, many more than recognized Israel!

Other national liberation organizations include the Patriotic Front, which fought a guerrilla war against the white-dominated government of Rhodesia, claiming that it represented the interests of the majority of black Rhodesians (it later won power in a free election and now controls the new state of Zimbabwe); the Southwest African People's Organization (SWAPO), which sought power in Namibia, a former German colony that was administered by South Africa since the end of World War I to 1989, when it became independent; the Mau Mau in Kenya, which brought British colonialism to an end; the Polisario, which is fighting Morocco for control of the Western Sahara; and the Farabundo Marti Liberation Front, which is seeking to capture power in El Salvador.

Obviously, the PLO and some of these national liberation movements have exerted considerable leverage in international politics—more than many states—in their efforts to found states of their own. They may well be called "states-in-waiting." A key means of achieving this goal has been the waging of guerrilla warfare against the government in power. Communist national liberation groups have been particularly successful in this latter regard: the liberation of Yugoslavia from German occupation in World War II; the long Chinese Communist civil war against the Nationalist Chinese government, which ended with China becoming a Communist nation; Fidel Castro's campaign against the Batista regime in Cuba, which turned Cuba into a Communist nation; the Viet Cong's battle against the pro-American government in South Vietnam, which led to American military intervention; and the Sandinista campaign against the Somoza dictatorship in Nicaragua.

Note the names of some of their leaders: Tito, Mao Zedong, Castro, and Ho Chi Minh. All were charismatic leaders who became famous during their military struggles, which they won. These feats testify not only to their skill as military leaders but also to their ability to organize political discontent in their nations. They were, above all, astute and ruthless politicians and "nation-builders," who, after acquiring power, governed their nations. By contrast, no terrorist leader has successfully overthrown an established government and become a successful "father of his country."

Terrorists

Although national liberation movements do resort to terror, the features that distinguish them from terrorist groups are several. While the former organize the masses (for example, peasants who do not own their own land), the latter tend to be narrowly based. National liberation groups tend to originate in rural areas; terrorists in cities. The former are usually led by renowned individuals who have great appeal, but the latter are normally anonymous. One tends to carve out rural areas as "liberated territory"; the other hides among the multitudes in an urban environment. One wages a protracted conflict or guerrilla war, the other engages in sporadic violence. Both claim to be motivated by a good cause, and both start out from positions of weakness. The national liberation group, however, hopes to isolate the government by neutralizing public opinion while defeating government forces; the terrorist group expects to frighten its enemies into making concessions or surrendering.

A national liberation movement is a serious threat because it may defeat the government, but terrorism constitutes essentially a set of irritating pinpricks not likely to succeed. Nevertheless, given the multiplicity of causes, terrorism is increasingly resorted to by desperate or angry individuals and groups anxious to publicize their grievances and aspirations, whether the Party of God (the Iranian-sponsored Islamic fundamentalists whose favorite targets are Americans), or the Red Brigade in Italy. Hijackings, assassinations, kidnappings, attacks on embassies, and other acts of terror have drawn the world's attention to the demands of these groups and have compelled governments to take notice and in some instances even to negotiate with them.

The Principal Actor

Clearly, then, states are not the only actors on the world scene. Indeed, the proliferation of nonstate actors has led some observers to conclude that states are of declining importance and that nonstate actors are gaining in status and influence. Note, for example, what two writers have said about the multinational corporation: "The rise of the planetary multinational enterprise is producing an organizational revolution as profound in its implications for modern man as the Industrial Revolution and the rise of the nation-state itself." The MNC or planetary corporation is ushering in a world economy, and the corporation itself is "the first institution in human history dedicated to centralized planning on a world scale." Whereas men like Napoleon and Hitler failed in their conquest of much of the world, the managers of the corporate giants "proclaim their faith that where conquest has failed, business can succeed." [22] Even now, these managers make daily business decisions that have more impact upon our daily lives in terms of what we wear, eat, and drink, what work we do, and where we live than do governments.

More broadly, the rise of MNCs and the vast growth of so many other kinds of nonstate actors are said to challenge and weaken, if not actually undermine, the "state-centric" concept of international politics and replace it with a "transnational" world in which relationships are considerably more numerous and complex than just traditional state-to-state ones. There are in fact three sets of relationships. In the first, states deal with one another directly or as members of IGOs (for example, when the United States and the Soviet Union negotiate an arms control agreement, the Indian prime minister visits England, or a Brazilian official talks to the World Bank about a loan). States also deal increasingly with NGOs (for example, when the United States negotiates with Shiite Amal militia in Lebanon for the release of hostages seized on a TWA plane, or a US environmental group, the Natural Resource Defense Council, negotiates with the Soviet government about verifying a low-threshold Soviet nuclear test, or a developing country negotiates with an MNC to set up a factory within its borders). Finally, NGOs deal with one another (for example, when Shiite, Druse, and Christian militia fight one another in Lebanon, when Ford and Mazda produce cars for the U.S. market, or, in a more pleasurable way, when the Montreal Expos play the Houston Astros).

Despite the proliferation of nongovernmental organizations, the state remains—as it has remained for three hundred years—the primary actor in the state system. The birthrate of new states has been high; it has increased fourfold since World War II. Nationalism seems especially rife in the developing countries. People can, of course, be loyal to more than one organization, but the nation-state remains for most people the object of their most intense loyalty. For the millions who have finally achieved the much desired and long sought-after national statehood, it is a new and exhilarating experience. Even transnational loyalties, such as communism, Zionism, or Islamic fundamentalism, have become identified with specific nation-states such as the Soviet Union, Israel, and Iran, respectively.

States also remain unique because of their control of territory. The MNCs need access to territory to make profits; the Roman Catholic church needs access to it to reach people and save souls; terrorists and national liberation groups need access to bases from which to pursue their campaigns. During the 1970s and early 1980s the PLO operated from its base in Lebanon; the former Patriotic Front conducted its war from the countries surrounding Zimbabwe. Such liberation groups cannot survive without at least the acquiescence of the states in which they are based and without the active support of other states, such as Libya, who supply them with weapons, training, and money. Finally, the state remains the principal user of *legitimate* force. It can enforce decisions at home and can decide whether to go to war and when.

Some observers regard the multinational corporation as the strongest competitor of the state, if not indeed a threat to the future viability of the state system. According to two authors,

> The MNCs lack a fundamental characteristic which will quite probably not permit them to challenge the nation-state. And this characteristic is "territoriality." Whether a multi-national corporation executive works for IBM, Singer, Unilever, Volkswagen, or Hitachi, he lives in a nation-state which possesses some sovereignty, greater authority, and even greater control capacity over its environment. MNCs have no jails, no courts and executioners, no passports, no armies, and very, very few weapons. In the last analysis, national governments control an overwhelming concentration of power and authority that would allow them to break up any MNC, provided there were adequate cause for such an operation.[23]

The state has survived since the Peace of Westphalia in 1648, but throughout this period it has never been the sole actor in the system. There have always been significant nongovernmental organizations, such as the Catholic church, the large European trading companies such as the British East India Company, which had its own armed forces and controlled territory, something no modern MNC does; and antislavery societies and great financial houses such as the Rothschilds'.[24] Moreover, these organizations have deeply affected domestic and foreign policies. But the state remains the principal actor and the system has long been defined by its major actors, not by all the types of actors within it.[25]

This does not mean that nonstate actors and transnational activities are unimportant. It only means that they have not yet rendered the state system obsolete. As long as states remain the major actors, the structure of international politics remains state-centric. States continue to dictate the terms of coexistence for themselves and other actors in the system. Kenneth Waltz, a political scientist, has remarked that a theory of international politics that denies the central role of states will be needed only if nongovernmental actors rival or surpass the influence of the great powers, not just a few of the lesser ones, on issues of war and peace. This is most unlikely. Despite the profusion of nonstate actors, the structure and processes of international politics remain basically the same; a new kind of international politics is not yet evident.[26] Moreover, states have a strong record of survival; few ever die. But business organizations do go out of existence. Who is more likely to be around in a hundred years, the United States or IBM? Given the longevity of the state as the principal actor, any analysis of international politics must start with the state, its motivations, objectives, and interaction with other states. Only then shall we also understand the role and impact of other actors.

For Review

1. What is a *sovereign state*, and what are some of its chief characteristics?
2. Is there a difference between *nationality* and *nationalism*?
3. What are the various classifications used for states?
4. Of the nonstate actors in international politics, what is an *intergovernmental organization* (IGO)? A *supernational organization*?
5. What is a *nongovernmental organization* (NGO), and how does it differ from an IGO?

Notes

1. Alan Riding, "In Latin America, Noriega Is a Principle," *New York Times*, Apr. 24, 1987.
2. Bill Keller, "Demographics Puts Strain on Soviet Ethnic Seams," *New York Times*, Dec. 28, 1987; and Philip Taubman, "Estonia Asserts a Right of Veto on Soviet Laws, *New York Times*, Nov. 17, 1988.
3. Jack S. Levy, *War in the Modern Great Power System, 1495-1975* (Lexington: University Press of Kentucky, 1983).
4. Ibid., 53.
5. Ibid., 9-10.
6. Inis L. Claude, Jr., *Swords into Plowshares* (New York: Random House, 1956), 53.
7. Quoted by William Shawcross, *The Shah's Last Ride* (New York: Simon & Schuster, 1988), 317.
8. David O. Wilkinson, *Comparative Foreign Relations* (Belmont, Calif.: Dickensen, 1969), 27.
9. Oran R. Young, "Political Discontinuities in the International System," *World Politics*, April 1968, pp. 369-392.
10. Joseph Treaster, "Soviet Tactics Faulted in Angola War," *New York Times*, July 28, 1988.
11. Robert L. Rothstein, *The Weak in the World of the Strong* (New York: Columbia University Press, 1977), 127.
12. Seyom Brown, *New Forces, Old Forces and the Future of World Politics* (Boston: Scott/Foresman, 1988), 25. Also see Claude, *Swords into Plowshares*, 23-26.
13. Claude, *Swords into Plowshares*, 35.
14. Ibid., 40; and Brown, *New Forces, Old Forces*, 25-26.
15. Alan Cowell, "Arabs Forming 2 Economic Blocs," *New York Times*, Feb. 17, 1989.
16. John Yemma, "Setting Sights Boldly on Unity," *Christian Science Monitor*, June 27, 1988.
17. Samuel P. Huntington, "Transnational Organizations in World Politics," *World Politics*, April 1973, 333; and Richard W. Mansbach et al., *The Web of World Politics* (Englewood Cliffs, N.J.: Prentice-Hall, 1976).
18. Huntington, "Transnational Organizations," 338.
19. The following classification is based on the table in *The Politics of Global Economic Relations* (3d ed.) by David H. Blake and Robert S. Walters (Englewood Cliffs, N.J.: Prentice-Hall, 1987), 97.
20. Lester R. Brown, *World Without Borders* (New York: Vintage, 1973), 213-215; *1983*

World Bank Development Report (New York: Oxford University Press, 1983), 148-149; and *Fortune 500,* May 1983.

21. Quoted in the *New York Times,* Dec. 6, 1985.

22. Richard J. Barnet and Ronald E. Müller, *Global Reach* (New York: Simon & Schuster, 1975), 13-15.

23. Theodore A. Couloumbis and Elias P. Georgiades, "The Impact of the Multinational Corporations on the International System," in *The New Sovereigns,* ed. Abdul A. Said and Luiz R. Simmons (Englewood Cliffs, N.J.: Prentice-Hall, 1975), 164. Also see Hedley Bull, *The Anarchical Society* (New York: Columbia University Press, 1977), 272-273.

24. Bull, *Anarchical Society,* 271; and K. J. Holsti, *The Dividing* (Boston: Allen & Unwin, 1985), 137.

25. Kenneth N. Waltz, *Theory of International Politics* (Reading, Mass.: Addison-Wesley, 1979), 93-94.

26. Holsti, *Dividing Discipline,* 137-138.

CHAPTER 4

The Stakes:
The Objectives
of States

POWER POLITICS

The sovereign state is the heart of the state system, and the first and most fundamental prerequisite for any state to survive and remain independent is power. A state may have extensive power or relatively little, but if it is to stay independent, it must have a sufficient amount to ward off potential threats. It may mobilize enough power by itself, or it can join together with other states in alliances. It is because of the pervasive nature of power in international politics that the term *power politics* often is used. Indeed, international politics cannot be anything but power politics.

Strictly speaking, as often as this term is used, it is misused. Power politics is a tautology—that is, it combines two words having the same meanings. Politics is inseparable from power. Whatever a state's objectives or goals, power provides a means to achieve them. Thus, to say power politics is repetitious and unnecessary. But one point about the term must be stressed: power is a means to an end; it is not an end in itself. Some analysts claim, however, that the accumulation of power is a continual concern of states. Whatever the ultimate aim, the immediate goal is power. In this view, power is seen as desirable in itself and may be pursued for its own sake. "Whatever preserves and enhances power must be cherished. Whatever leads to the enfeeblement of power must be avoided." [1] Yet to treat power as an end in itself is analogous to discussing the accumulation of money without any reference to the purposes for which it is spent. An analysis of power must therefore start with a "theory of end." [2] States are not always preoccupied with enhancing power; sometimes they are satisfied with the power they have, and sometimes they will even reduce it. It depends on the objectives they seek and how intensely these are pursued. Given the priority states attach to their security, for example, it would be better to substitute the term *security politics.*

SECURITY, WELFARE, AND OTHER AIMS

National Security

What are the most common objectives states seek? The first and most basic is *security* against possible external military threats. But a state can expect to realize only some of what it wants. A state can expect a *degree* of security, not absolute security; it can feel only *relatively* safe, not completely safe. There is no such thing as absolute security in a state system composed of many national actors; a state could achieve such security only by universal conquest and the destruction of all other independent states—an unlikely possibility. All states, then, "live dangerously." The only question is how much or how little security does a state feel is enough? Although all states, even great powers, feel some degree of vulnerability, some have more control over their destiny than others. No state, however, is the absolute master of its fate.

The term *security* can be broken down into several categories. At the very least, security means simply *physical survival.* Israel, born in 1948, was surrounded by states that, at least until 1973, were sworn to its extinction; Arabs refused to recognize Israel's right to exist. Only one state, Egypt, has made peace with Israel (in 1979). No other Arab state has yet formally recognized Israel. Neither Jordan nor Syria, Israel's neighbors, nor the Palestine Liberation Organization have explored through direct negotiations whether mutually satisfactory peace treaties could be arranged; the PLO is seeking to use the United States as an intermediary.

A second and more common meaning of security refers to the preservation of a state's *territorial integrity.* Because frontiers may change over time, states may redefine the meaning of this term. Poland, for example, has shifted its eastern and western frontiers westward since World War II. By the same token, the Soviet frontier has also moved westward. Communist China, on the other hand, frequently refers publicly to the Chinese territories seized by the Russian czars during the last century and wants the Soviets to acknowledge that these "unequal treaties" were imposed upon earlier Chinese rulers. The Soviet Union, however, has refused to do so. It considers its frontiers sacrosanct. Gorbachev has told the various nationalities, especially in the Baltic Republics, that are seeking greater autonomy, if not independence, that none will be allowed to secede. The issue of frontiers is particularly troublesome among the developing countries, for their territorial integrity may not always correspond to ethnic and linguistic divisions. The new nations inherited their boundaries from colonial rulers, and it is this territorial integrity that some developing countries seek to defend. Other states, however, claim pieces of their territory on the basis of reuniting ethnic groups. Somalia, for example, had claims against Ethiopia that led to fighting in 1978 and to Soviet-Cuban intervention to defend Ethiopia's territorial integrity. Frontiers are part of a nation's identity and dignity. During the peace negotiations after the 1973 war, Egypt demanded the return of the entire Sinai desert in exchange for peace with Israel. During the 1967 war, Israel seized Syria's Golan Heights to improve its security, but Syria considers the area an integral part of its territory.

A third meaning of security is *political independence*, which refers, negatively, to a state's freedom from foreign control and, positively, to the preservation of its domestic political and economic system. Security involves more than a state's physical survival and territorial security; it also includes the perpetuation of the values, patterns of social relations, lifestyles, and varied other elements that make up a nation's way of life. The threats to the United States in this century were not related to physical danger, for neither Germany during either world war nor the Soviet Union immediately after 1945 had the air power to reach and destroy the United States, or even to invade it across three thousand miles of ocean. The United States intervened on each occasion because its leaders saw the domination of Europe by a nondemocratic—indeed, *antidemocratic*—great power as a threat to the security of the United States and to the kind of world environment in which the United States could most comfortably exist.

President Franklin Roosevelt explained his decision to aid Britain in 1940 and 1941 by stating that the United States should not become a lone democratic island surrounded by totalitarian seas to its east and west (Roosevelt included Japan's threat in the Pacific in this statement). He meant that, as a *democratic* state, the nation had to preserve an international order in which democracy could flourish. Thus, the United States could not stand by and watch one democracy after another snuffed out by antidemocratic regimes. The result would be a hostile external environment, incompatible with American conceptions of what is just and unjust. That is why the United States today, fifty years later, remains committed to the defense of Western Europe.

If Germany was twice an external threat and the Soviet Union took its place after Germany's second defeat, drugs have increasingly become an internal threat. Indeed, in 1984 the U.S. Joint Chiefs of Staff declared drugs a threat to the national security because they were undermining the country's social fabric and the discipline of the military services. In 1986, the year U.S. troops were deployed briefly to Bolivia to cut its cocaine production and exports to the United States, President Reagan also issued a secret directive labeling drug trafficking as a national security threat. (In 1988, while on a visit to Bolivia, Secretary of State George Shultz and his motorcade were the target of a bomb attack, allegedly by drug traffickers.) A "war on drugs" has been officially declared because these imports affect everything from the workplace to lifestyles, from crime to public health. The United States in 1988 spent $3 billion on the war on drugs, and even this sum remains insufficient. This is a "war" that is not likely to end soon. The same year the State Department reported that in most drug-producing countries the production of coca, marijuana, and opium poppy crops has grown substantially and that no single government can control the flood of imports.[3] (The principal sources of coca, from which cocaine is derived, are Bolivia, Colombia, and Peru, and of majrijuana, Colombia, Jamaica, and Mexico.) The report is hardly surprising: as long as demand remains high, there will be supplies. In the meantime, drugs will continue to eat away at the very fabric of American society, a reminder that security needs to be defined in terms broader than military ones.

Also in 1988 drugs were rated a major threat by the American people. Congress called for the appointment of a drug czar, who was appointed by President George Bush, and more money for the war on drugs. The Senate during this time approved a bill calling for the death sentence for "drug kingpins." The military too has become involved in surveillance and intelligence gathering. None of these measures have sufficed against this murderous industry worth tens of billions of dollars a year. Yet all candidates for office, continue to insist that they would be tough on drugs. But what they can do to reduce the demand for drugs at home remains unknown—would they sanction military intervention against supplier countries because drugs are claimed to be a national security threat? Will they spend the far larger sums needed and, if necessary, raise taxes to do so? If the answers to these questions remain unknown, there does seem to be general agreement that narcotics, above all crack cocaine, do constitute a serious threat to the nation's security—and, at a time of renewed détente, perhaps a greater threat to that security than the Soviet Union.

National Prestige

A second objective important to many states is *prestige*. Precisely because prestige is closely related to power, especially military power, it may be defined as a nation's *reputation for power* among its fellow states. In a sense prestige is subjective and intangible because it depends on the perception of other states. Prestige, like love, is in the eye of the beholder. It is, to be sure, acquired as the result of past action. Victory on the battlefield or the successful use of economic power gains prestige for a state. Other states note that a state is powerful, that it is willing to use its power to gain its aims, and that it has used its power effectively to achieve what it set out to do. In short, the state's power has credibility. This reputation for power, given the nature of the state system, is not to be sneered at and shrugged off as "mere prestige," however, for a nation's reputation for power may mean it will not be challenged and will thus avoid war. Or a nation may gain compliance with its demands, again without having to threaten or fight. In other words, prestige is a critical possession for a state.

Because the United States was unwilling to suffer the loss of prestige that Washington thought would accompany the defeat of South Vietnam—a loss it believed would erode the credibility of American power and commitments in other countries, perhaps more significant than Vietnam—it intervened in that country. The subsequent American defeat was an obvious setback and meant loss of prestige. It emboldened the Soviet Union to extend its influence as its Cuban proxies intervened in several places, among them Angola and Ethiopia. Even Iran, a much smaller power, which is as anti-American as it is anti-Communist, was bold enough to seize the U.S. embassy and its personnel in Tehran in 1979. This was a completely unprecedented act, the seizure of what is considered "foreign territory," something not even Adolf Hitler or Joseph Stalin had tried against their opponents. It was this series of setbacks that heavily influenced the administration of the newly elected Ronald Reagan to "get tough," perhaps more than it otherwise might have done; to denounce the Soviets vigorously and thereby alert Moscow that America's post-Vietnam psychosis was over; to remobilize American public opinion for the task of containing Soviet power; to launch a major arms program, including the modernization of U.S. strategic deterrent forces; and even to use conventional force to liberate the tiny Caribbean island of Grenada from "Soviet-Cuban domination" and to punish Libya for its alleged involvement in several anti-American terrorist incidents. The aim was to restore the credibility of U.S. power.

Great powers historically have associated prestige with military power and the successful use of force. Indeed, the Soviet Union's status in the world since 1945 has stemmed largely from its military power, especially more recently its strategic nuclear capability. The Soviet Union's victory in World War II and expansion into eastern Europe transformed the Soviet Union into a superpower, even though it did not at the time have an atomic bomb. Over the past forty years, however, the Soviet Union has performed poorly in feeding and providing consumer goods for its people and has been unable to keep up with the new industrial revolution in electronics and petrochemicals. It has lost its appeal as a model of development for Third World states and has been unable to provide much foreign aid. In addition, Communist ideology has been regarded with increasing skepticism and boredom by the Soviet population. Consequently, the Soviet Union's prestige has increasingly depended upon its military strength:

> By far the most likely source of Soviet agitation over SDI [President Reagan's Strategic Defense Initiative] has to do with high-level concerns that continued progress of the US program may undermine worldwide appreciation of Soviet military prowess, irrespective of any technical problems SDI may encounter along the way. Military power is the sine qua non of the Soviet state. It has singularly bestowed upon the USSR its claim to "equivalence" with the United States. Toward that end the Soviets have invested heavily in their strategic nuclear posture over the past two decades. Insofar as SDI aims, in President Reagan's expression, to render nuclear weapons "impotent and obsolete," it

threatens—at least from the Kremlin's vantage point—to render worthless the very foundation of the USSR's superpower status.[4]

The United States, by contrast, even without nuclear arms, would maintain its superpower status because of its economy, technology, system of government, and cultural attraction.

It is not only the superpowers that are concerned with prestige. Such countries as Britain and France, former great powers reluctant to accept their secondary status, and such countries as China and India, striving to establish their status, have all become nuclear powers. Possession of the bomb is—and seems likely to remain—as much a symbol of prestige as empires were in an earlier age. Even smaller countries that do not have memories of past glory or entertain thoughts of future greatness are concerned about prestige. For them, it is not power but simple dignity that is at stake; they wish to be treated with respect even though they are not strong countries. Even the smallest of them want to have the symbols of nationhood. Tiny island-states in the Pacific feel they need their own airlines, even when they run at a loss. Thus, Kiribati has Air Tungaru; Vanuatu, Air Vanuatu; Western Samoa, Polynesian Airlines; Papua New Guinea, Air Niugini; Fiji, Air Pacific; and the Solomon Islands, Solair.[5]

A last point is worth noting: a nation's prestige may outlast its power. The latter may be declining relative to that of other nations, but its reputation may save it from challenge for a while. When that challenge comes, however, from a state whose power is increasing, prestige vanishes if, as is likely, the waning state suffers a setback. The challenger now acquires prestige.

Economic Security

So far this discussion of security and prestige has focused basically on the military context within which security is traditionally defined. But, in fact, can security be defined only in terms of the most visible and most obvious threat? What about a healthy economy and—as already suggested in the section on drugs—society? Is a nation "secure" if its economic base is declining? Specifically, how "strong" was the United States during the first half of the 1980s as the Reagan administration's domestic policies transformed it into the world's largest debtor nation? Coming into office committed to a substantial increase in defense spending as well as a tax reduction to stimulate the economy, the fiscally conservative Reagan administration ran up the highest deficit of the nation's history. Income taxes and revenues were cut sharply, while defense received almost $2 trillion over eight years.

The competition for money between the private sector looking for investment capital and the government looking for money to finance the deficit kept the nation's interest rates high. These interest rates attracted foreign capital, about half from Europe, sending the value of the dollar soaring upward by about 30 percent against foreign currencies from 1981 to 1985.

Billions in pounds, francs, yen, and other currencies were invested in the United States. As a result, American export prices rose steeply, making them too expensive in a competitive market, and, conversely, the price of imports dropped by 30 percent, undercutting U.S. firms. While all this was a bonanza for American consumers and tourists, American farmers were deeply hurt as overseas sales dropped sharply; thousands of farms were foreclosed or were on the brink of foreclosure. Imports devastated the automobile, steel, and electrical machinery industries, for example, which could not meet the competition. The resulting loss of earnings also meant a loss of capital to invest in their modernization. The nation's unemployed stood at 8 million, between 2 million and 3 million jobs lost in industries that exported and competed with imports. This huge indebtedness also had the effect of accelerating the fight of American corporations overseas where labor costs were less, so that they could stay competitive in an increasingly international economy *(see Chapter 15)*.

In April 1985 the United States became a debtor nation for the first time since World War I. In 1986 the U.S. debt exceeded those of Brazil and Mexico, the world's two largest debtor nations. The entire federal debt in 1980, accumulated since the founding of the Republic, was three-quarters of a trillion dollars. By the end of eight years of the Reagan administration, this figure was almost $3 trillion (while the budget deficit amounted to $155 billion). American prosperity and the sense of well-being that helped elect President Bush was in fact based on borrowed money and borrowed time. Currently, this debt is greater than the total owed by all of the developing countries collectively!

Thus, the manner in which the defense buildup was undertaken hurt the American economy, contributing to its declining influence and uncompetitiveness in world markets *(see Chapters 8 and 15)*.[6] Related to this decline was the deterioration of the American labor force, in turn a symptom of lower educational standards (reportedly among the lowest in the industrial world). The United States was graduating fewer engineers and scientists than Japan, which has less than half its population. American children attend school an average of 180 days per year, Japanese children 240 days, and the average in Europe is 220 days. Moreover, American children go to school for six and a half hours per day, while the rest of the industrial world requires eight hours. It is hardly surprising in an increasingly technological world in which mathematics represents the cutting edge of research and development—a subject in which American children place lower than children of other industrial countries—that the United States also has difficulties competing in the new high-technology industries. Japanese and West German children simply learn more mathematics and science than American children because they are at school longer and do not have a 25 percent high school dropout rate and a 20 percent functional illiteracy rate among high school graduates. Yet knowledge is the key to future economic competitiveness. Even among the brightest products of the U.S. educational system, most are not drawn to science and engineering but to corporate law, investment houses, and management consultant firms—that is, to the manipulation of data and money, not the invention or development of new technologies.

Perhaps symbolic of this American economic decline and the country's new sense of vulnerability was what has been called the "buying into America" or, more aptly, "the selling of America" to the British, Japanese, and Dutch (in that order), as well as to others.[7] The money drawn to the United States by high interest rates declined in value as the United States deliberately devalued the dollar to boost exports and cut imports—and, although never officially stated, to reduce deliberately the amount the U.S. owed foreign investors. Given the cheap dollar, however, and the low stock prices after concerns over the budget and trade deficits had led to a stock market crash on October 19, 1987, foreigners began to convert their IOUs to ownership of real assets such as land, buildings, corporations, and financial institutions. Since 1974, foreign investments have increased from under $20 million to $1.3 trillion or more than sixfold in 1988. This has raised fears about the future control of the "American" economy—a fear that, when expressed by Europeans in the 1960s and developing countries in the 1970s as multinational corporations invested billions of dollars in their economies, had been discounted. Ironically, the individual states and communities seeking to attract Japanese business helped this process of "selling America" along. It is not surprising that U.S. public opinion polls taken in 1988 placed economic security ahead of military security and regarded Japan and other economic competitors as a greater threat than the Soviet Union.[8] In 1988, Democratic vice-presidential candidate Lloyd Bentsen observed that foreigners have "bought 10 percent of the manufacturing base of this country. They bought 20 percent of the banks. They own 46 percent of the commercial real estate in Los Angeles. They're buying America on the cheap."[9] Bentsen could have added Houston and Washington, D.C., Bloomingdale's in New York, Pillsbury, RCA and CBS Records, and Hollywood's United Artists/MGM and Columbia Pictures, among many. Does this selling of America constitute a security threat, especially since foreigners are increasingly taking over military-related industries?[10] Whatever the answer, there can be little doubt that economic security is basic to the issue of economic welfare.

National Welfare

Since the French Revolution, which mobilized the masses, and the Industrial Revolution, which introduced mass production, states with sizable populations and industrial capacities have ranked at the top of the power hierarchy. But industry and technology involve more than power; they also involve welfare, the desire of people in all societies for a better material life. Therefore governments—even dictatorial ones—must respond to their citizens' demands. The "revolution of rising expectations" is universal; if it is usually thought of in connection with underdeveloped countries, that is only because they are copying the large Western states, which, as the first to industrialize, have provided their people with the world's highest standard of living.

Until the recent concern with environmental problems, mostly the byproducts of industrialization, economic growth was the chief, if not the sole, criterion for social policy in the West. Raising everyone's living standards was at the heart of the social policies of all modern Western welfare states, including those of the United States. Attempts to redistribute existing or only slowly growing wealth among different classes or segments of society would have precipitated intense social conflict because one class would have gained at the expense of another. Rapidly expanding the "economic pie" so that everyone could have a larger slice of it made it possible to avoid such conflict and any possible political instability while satisfying the vast majority of groups and people. The 1973-1974 oil embargo by OPEC and its quadrupling of prices demonstrated the vulnerability of Western industrial societies to interruptions in supply and price increases and the degree to which the prosperity of Western economies—income, economic growth, employment, ability to afford social services—was entwined with the fortunes of the international economy and international politics. The 1980s, with America's exposure to the global economy, has reinforced this lesson.

The desire for the "good life" is not limited to Western states. The drive for even higher economic growth rates and gross national product is shared by the Soviet Union as well. Every few years during the 1950s and 1960s, Soviet leaders promised their long-suffering compatriots that, at the end of this or that five-year plan or decade, their standard of living would be comparable to that of the United States, the nation whose economic and social system they never fail to denounce as exploitative and inhumane. But in the 1970s, because the Soviet Union was falling behind in the second industrial revolution of electronics, especially computers, and because this lag affected all areas of its economy, and not just the sector devoted to consumer goods production, the Soviets needed access to Western trade and technology as a "fix" for their own overcentralized, overbureaucratized, and often ideologically hamstrung economy. Otherwise, the Soviet Union might have suffered social unrest; worse, its military capability and its international prestige might have been affected. Thus, détente was partly the political price the Soviet Union was willing to pay to improve both its industrial and its agricultural economies. The second détente, starting in the late 1980s, was caused by conditions similar to those fostering the earlier détente. Indeed, Moscow needs détente even more now, and probably for a longer period, because the economy's stagnation has grown, and Gorbachev realizes that to achieve economic reform he must restructure the political and economic system. Simply tinkering with the economy, as his predecessors did, will no longer do.

But, among all nations, it is the developing countries that have been most bent on modernizing—industrializing and urbanizing—themselves. To attract assistance from the competing superpowers, most of the formerly colonial states have pursued a policy of nonalignment. When the cold war turned into détente, they began to press their demands more assertively. OPEC's aggressiveness, attempts to organize other producer cartels to control supplies and prices of resources, and demands in the United Nations for a "new international economic order" all were aimed at changing the distribution of wealth, status, and power between the First and Third Worlds. They resulted in confrontation between the "haves" and "have-nots" but failed to reduce the gap between the rich and poor nations. Thus, the "revolution of rising expectations" in much of the Third World may turn into a "revolution of rising frustration" with all that it implies for the future stability of the international system.

Ideology

A final goal of states, which some pursue more than others, is the protection or promotion of ideology. An *ideology* is a set of beliefs that purports to explain reality and prescribes a desirable future existence for society and the world in general. It also defines the role of the believing nation in bringing about this future condition. Revolutionary ideologies in particular, which condemn the present state of existence as evil and intolerable, are expressed in terms of long-range goals that amount to a universal transformation of the state system (see Chapter 2). Each ideology tends to impart to the revolutionary state a strong sense of mission and commitment to the achievement of humanity's secular salvation. Each, in the name of justice, wishes to create the new Jerusalem here on earth.

By contrast, in the nineteenth century, protected by the balance of power in Europe, the United States regarded itself as the New World with a political system morally superior to the regimes of the Old World. The United States chose to isolate itself from possible contamination by the European nations. In the twentieth century, however, it has been increasingly drawn into the Old World's quarrels as Britain's power has weakened. The United States has engaged Germany twice in hot wars and the Soviet Union in a cold war.

In all these struggles the United States has justified its participation by a set of universalist goals. For President Woodrow Wilson in World War I, the aim of the hostilities was to make the world "safe for democracy." President Harry Truman at the beginning of the cold war portrayed the conflict as one between democracy and totalitarianism. And so has every president since that time. Once it felt itself to be provoked, the United States launched crusades to destroy the aggressor. But short of such provocation, it remained aloof.

By contrast, regimes like that of France after 1789 and that of the Soviet Union after 1917 have energetically sought to expand their influence and power in the international system to advance their respective faiths. The initial expectation after revolution is that it will spread from one country to another by means of "spontaneous combustion." Leon Trotsky, the first Soviet people's commissar for foreign affairs, did not expect his job to last long. "I will issue a few revolutionary proclamations to the peoples of the world and then shut up shop," he declared.[11] But the proclamations did not spark a global revolutionary fire. Later Soviet leaders preferred to rely on the threat or use of force to ensure that history would march their way.

Ideological passions, however, spend themselves. Seventy years after the Bolshevik Revolution of 1917, the Soviet state has become highly bureaucratized, and cynicism, disillusionment, and materialism are widespread. Food and the simple necessities of life are becoming harder to find as the economic situation deteriorates. And while the Communist party elite still largely sees the world through Marxist-Leninist lenses, the current generation of younger leaders is the first not to remember the revolution, to have experienced Stalin's long and bloody reign, and to have fought in World War II. And this generation confronts a multitude of domestic problems, especially economic ones, that require solutions; if these solutions are unavailing, the Soviet Union may not be one of the world's leading powers in the twenty-first century. Thus, the Soviet Union's ultimate aim of a Communist world becomes further and further postponed into a long-distant future.

Indeed, does Soviet leader Gorbachev's emphasis on "democratization" and "restructuring" of the Soviet economy foreshadow ideological de-emphasis and a loosening of controls within the Soviet Union, the emergence of a more pluralistic society and market economy, and a greater willingness to give up revolutionary aims and accept the principle of live and let live? If so, this would constitute a significant change in Soviet foreign policy.

Since the French Revolution, states have primarily promoted secular ideologies. But Iran, under the Ayatollah Ruhollah Khomeini from 1979 to 1989, advocated an Islamic fundamentalist revolution.[12] Basically a reaction to the Westernization of Iran, which, among other things, displaced the clergy from its prominent role in society, Islamic fundamentalism aims to restore traditional religious values throughout the Islamic world and to eliminate secular Western, especially American, values and power throughout the Middle East and West Asian areas. Much of this drive has become associated with Iranian-sponsored terrorism in Lebanon and other Middle Eastern countries against Western targets, as well as with the Iran-Iraq war, which Iran has fought with great zealousness and willingness to sacrifice life for eight years. In 1988, as casualties mounted, oil prices stayed low, and the economy went into debt, the ayatollah finally was forced to call the war off. Iran was exhausted. It too may lose its ardor to export its revolution.

The ayatollah died in 1989, and his successors face a new situation: Iran is financially drained and politically isolated in the world. During the war with Iraq, Iran faced the opposition of most Arabs states, as well as a Western naval armada in the Persian Gulf; the Iranians also found that the Islamic fundamentalist message has little appeal in the Arab world, even among fellow Shiites, who identified with Arab nationalism rather than assume an Islamic identity that transcended nationalism. Iran therefore needs to turn inward, rebuild its economy, and improve its relationship with the West, which may also bring about a release of American and other Western hostages held by terrorist groups.

Nevertheless, the impact of ideologies upon international politics generally has been to enlarge the scope and intensity of conflict between nations with opposing belief systems. It is difficult enough to resolve differences of interest; it becomes infinitely more difficult to reconcile nations with different ideological outlooks. Each nation sees itself as the representative of truth and morality and sees opposing states as wrong and immoral. Compromise among states in these circumstances is difficult because it is viewed as treason. How can a state claiming to possess a monopoly of wisdom and morality compromise with the "devil"? A nation believing itself to have a moral mission cannot violate its own principles.

'High Politics' and 'Low Politics'

It has become commonplace in recent years to distinguish between the objectives of "high politics" and "low politics." High politics refers to political-security or strategic issues, and low politics to welfare or social-economic issues. The proponents of this distinction argue that the process of modernization is transforming the character of foreign policy and the means by which it is carried out. They claim that modernization has elevated low-politics issues to a higher priority than high-politics issues. According to this hypothesis, the increasing popular participation in modern societies means that people are concerned mainly about their standard of living. Since few, if any, societies are economically self-sufficient, fulfilling people's expectations of more jobs, higher pay, and a constantly improving way of life requires nations to cooperate with one another rather than fight. Anarchy and force therefore will be replaced by economic interdependence and cooperation. Inherent in this high-politics/low-politics distinction is the usually unstated maxim "Politics bad, economics good." Politics is concerned with conflict and war and destruction, economics with humans and their welfare—a more positive and obviously more moral area of concern.

But the issue is not whether economic interdependence exists in the contemporary world. It exists to a high degree (see Chapter 15). The issue is whether the wrong conclusions have been drawn—namely, that modernization is gradually reducing the former priority of security objectives and the role of force in international politics. There is little evidence to support this proposition.

The distinction between security and welfare goals assumes that states place priority on one or the other. States may give primacy to security, for without security, they cannot enjoy other objectives. But the pursuit of security is not without cost. Guns cost money, possibly requiring the sacrifice of other socially desirable goals. Conversely, granting primacy to welfare may require the sacrifice of some degree of security. No country, however prosperous, can maximize both; budgets are finite. Countries have multiple objectives, and in a world of limited resources these objectives compete with one another. What governments must decide is what mix of objectives they seek.

COMPETITION AMONG OBJECTIVES

These then are some, though by no means all, of the principal objectives states seek. The resulting conflict among objectives suggests that *the acquisition of one objective often comes at the cost of another. Objectives are frequently incompatible, and trade-offs must be made.*

Guns Versus Butter

One such conflict is between security and welfare or, in more colloquial language, guns and butter. Realistically, the more a state spends on maintaining military forces, the less it can spend on foreign aid; on the construction of schools, hospitals, and roads; and on education, vocational training, and a "war on poverty." The more taxes it needs to buy bombs, the less the taxpayer has left to buy a new house or car, purchase family insurance, take a vacation, or send the children to college. Nations have limited resources, and they must make choices. The choice is not usually *either* guns *or* butter but how much of each a nation can afford.

A rapidly growing economy could afford a lot of guns and butter. But the slowdown of all Western economies has resulted in a sharper conflict between military spending and social welfare. Already committed to cutting back the government's role in social policies, President Reagan spent almost $2 trillion on defense over eight years (which amounted to $743 million/day, $31 million/hour, $514,000/minute or $9,000/second) while cutting funds for welfare spending. From the late 1940s to the early 1970s, the U.S. economy grew rapidly enough to afford high wages, a rising standard of living, extensive welfare programs, and large outlays for defense and economic aid. Indeed, President Lyndon Johnson during the 1960s waged the War on Poverty and the war in Vietnam simultaneously (but he soon faced a deficit and had to impose a special tax to pay for the war). Since the late 1960s, however, the increasing "deindustrialization" of America—high U.S. wages have led industry to invest overseas where labor is cheaper—plus high oil prices in the 1970s and the decreasing competitiveness of the economy in the 1980s, have resulted in lower rates of economic growth and, in the absence of increased taxes, sharpened the choice between guns and butter.

Between 1950 and 1969 congressional cuts in the defense budget averaged only $1.7 billion compared with $9.2 billion for nondefense expenditures. For the next six years the balance was reversed, with defense being cut $5 billion while nondefense expenditures were raised an average of $4.7 billion. Defense spending sank to 5 percent of the gross national product, the lowest since before the Korean War. The Nixon-Ford years saw the most sizable reduction in American military strength relative to that of the Soviet Union since the cold war began.[13] President Carter began to increase the size of the defense budgets once more by the late 1970s, as congressional post-Vietnam antimilitary sentiment began to weaken in light of the Soviet military buildup. Reagan accelerated the U.S. rearmament effort. But in a democracy, voters do not like to have their benefits cut too much, and so there are limits to how much the butter can be cut without electoral risk. Before the end of the first Reagan administration, support for further increases had waned; by the end of the second term, the defense budget was declining. In 1989 the incoming Bush administration was therefore confronted with the reexamination of America's military budget and alliances. The rising costs of the nation's weapons systems and commitments to approximately sixty countries in the absence of more burden-sharing by the allies may be too great.

In the Soviet Union, because its rulers are unaccountable to public opinion, this choice has in the past been easier to make. After the Cuban missile crisis, Moscow began a program of sustained military growth, both nuclear and conventional, but this program came at the cost of a better life for Soviet citizens. Now it has become clear that the stagnant economy cannot continue to channel, according to Central Intelligence Agency estimates, as much as 16 percent of a GNP less than half that of the United States (whose defense spending is 6 percent of GNP) into the military. The drawing off of so much capital, skilled labor, and scarce materials from the civilian economy is a key reason for the stagnating Soviet economy. More investment is desperately needed to revive the latter.

Thus, Gorbachev must, at least for the time being, reduce the Soviet Union's international ambitions if he wants arms reductions and arms control agreements to shift funds from the military to the civilian economy and a relaxation of international tensions to attract Western credit, technology, and trade.

Security Versus Democracy

Domestic Dilemma. Security may be necessary to protect a nation's way of life, but this does not mean that states impose no limits on what they will do to accumulate power and thereby raise their sense of security. This is especially true for democratic states for whom the conduct of foreign policy raises both domestic and foreign policy questions. The most important question is: Will security come at the cost of democratic values? During the cold war, the balance between defending the United States against antidemocratic threats abroad and preserving democracy at home was generally kept. Nevertheless, U.S. involvement in world affairs since World War II led to the charge in the 1960s and 1970s that, in trying to ensure the external safety of American democracy, the government had endangered democratic values domestically. The constitutional balance had been upset as the presidency had become "imperial," going to war either without congressional support or with support purportedly elicited by deceiving and lying to the legislature. The authority of Congress had been emasculated. The Central Intelligence Agency (CIA), among its other questionable activities, had helped to overthrow a legitimately elected government in Chile and planned a number of assassinations of leaders in other countries. The CIA and the Federal Bureau of Investigation, in carrying out domestic surveillance, had repeatedly broken various laws forbidding such activities. Indeed, it was charged that a "military-industrial complex" had come to dominate the American political process and had distorted the purposes of American society, benefiting Big Business, Big Military, and Big Politicians while neglecting the poor and ignoring the nation's urban, environmental, and educational problems.

Whatever the validity of these charges, it remains true that one possible danger that a democracy faces in fighting an undemocratic adversary is that it may become more like its enemy. In Nicaragua, the Reagan administration's effort to overthrow its Marxist, pro-Cuban, pro-Soviet government and bring democracy to that country by neglecting democratic processes at home—that is, by bypassing Congress, which opposed its efforts—is one of the most blatant examples.[14] The administration was determined to achieve its goals despite a congressional cutoff of funding for arms for the Nicaraguan contras. Constitutionally, the executive cannot pursue policies that Congress refuses to fund. The Reagan administration therefore decided to do an end run around the Constitution and Congress. It collected funds from governments overseas such as Saudi Arabia and Kuwait and from wealthy Americans at home. It even violated its own prescription against trading for American hostages held in Lebanon by pro-Iranian groups. When even the offer of arms did not gain the release of all the hostages (two were released but two new ones were seized), the administration continued the sale of arms to gain funds for the support of the contras. And in order not to violate the congressional mandate that the administration not use the State Department, Defense Department, or Central Intelligence Agency to help conduct the contra war, it transformed the White House's National Security Council—intended by Congress to serve as a presidential advisory and managerial organ in the conduct of foreign policy—into an operational center for what was supposed to be a covert war in Nicaragua (but in fact was on television and in newspaper headlines every day).

Thus, without congressional approval or funding from 1984 to 1986, the administration continued its war. Indeed, it deliberately deceived the Congress, continually denying American involvement when legislative suspicions were aroused. It also organized a "vast psychological warfare operation" to reshape American opinion on Central America. These efforts have been compared to "what the CIA (Central Intelligence Agency) conducts against hostile forces abroad. Only this time they were turned against the three key institutions of American democracy: Congress, the press, and an informed electorate."[15]

Yet the fact that this story became public, that the Congress held long televised hearings on the so-called Iran-contra affair, and that President Reagan's political reputation and status suffered great harm, suggests that American democracy is very much alive and continues to weigh carefully the trade-offs between violations of democratic norms at home and protecting the country against antidemocratic threats from abroad.

External Dilemma.   The external consequences of the clash between security and democracy become starkly apparent when a democracy allies itself with undemocratic states. Can a democracy associate itself with dictatorial states without undermining its own cause? Or should it confine itself only to allies sharing the same political values, even to the point of jeopardizing its security by failing to take advantage of the strategic position, economic benefits, and added military strength that can be gained from alliance with certain undemocratic states? During World War II, Winston Churchill welcomed the Soviet Union as an ally after Hitler became the common enemy. The Soviet Union might not be a democracy, the prime minister said, but to beat Hitler he would eat supper with the devil—though he did admit that he would use a long spoon. But this alliance had been brought about by Germany's attack on the Soviet Union. Indeed, World War II broke out when Britain, a democracy, went to the rescue of Poland, an undemocratic country. Britain apparently did so because it saw its own security linked to that of Poland, regardless of that country's form of government.

After 1945 and the outbreak of the cold war, the United States made alliances with many undemocratic regimes—Turkey, Greece, Spain, Nationalist China, Brazil, and Portugal, to name some of the more prominent—in the pursuit of the containment of Soviet- and Chinese-Communist power. Indeed, containment began with the 1947 Truman Doctrine, which somewhat ironically pictured the threat to Turkey and Greece from the Soviet Union as a conflict between democracy and totalitarianism. The Turkish and Greek regimes were hardly models of democratic purity. Were Truman's declaration and American policy hypocritical because they were inconsistent with the values of American democracy, or was the United States acting as the distribution of power after World War II obliged it to act? Truman's action demonstrated clearly that he believed that a democracy can align itself with undemocratic governments in strategically located areas at moments of perceived danger to American security.

The trade-off between security and democracy is debated frequently. The Congress, the media, and private human rights organizations vigilantly watch the executive when it seeks to align the United States with authoritarian regimes, especially right-wing ones. Or, if aligned already, they report gross violations of democratic norms such as the arrest of opposition leaders or torture. Such publicity limits the flexibility of the president. On the whole, however, the U.S. government has supported movements toward democracy, as in Greece, Turkey, Portugal, Spain, the Philippines, Chile, and South Korea, because it remains in its self-interest that democratic values flourish in the international system.[16]

WHAT PRICE SECURITY?

The central question raised by all these examples of conflicting goals is: *What price security?* Even the means of securing a nation's territorial integrity may be incompatible with the values by which it lives. Should a nation root out all possible "security" risks and dissidents at home, even though innocent people may well be hurt, even though the fear of expressing any criticism of governmental actions may stifle free speech, perhaps even leading to the censorship of books and the banning of debates on "controversial" topics (as occurred in the United States during the 1950s)? Is a democratic nation, in allying itself with patently undemocratic countries, augmenting its own security? Or is it weakening itself by staining its own reputation and impairing the credibility of its claim to be a champion of democracy? Should a democracy committed to holding free elections and abiding by the results help to overthrow a freely elected government elsewhere, as the United States helped to do in Chile in the early 1970s? Should a democracy intervene in the affairs of a major NATO member, financing anti-Communist political parties to prevent the Communist party from being included in a coalition government, thus weakening the alliance? Can a democracy launch a preventive war, firing the first shot? Obviously, security and other objectives may clash; so may the objectives and the methods by which states pursue their ends. For policy makers, deciding on the exact mix of goals the nation ought to pursue, the means by which to achieve them, and the level of commitment to them is controversial and difficult.

For Review

1. What are the principal objectives of states?
2. Why is a definition of *national security*—one objective—in military terms not sufficient?
3. What arguments are advanced by proponents of the recent distinction made between the security, or "high-politics," objectives of states and welfare, or "low-politics," objectives?
4. Do states give priority to high-politics objectives over low-politics objectives?
5. What are the trade-offs between the different kinds of objectives that states pursue?

Notes

1. Frederick L. Schuman, *The Commonwealth of Man* (New York: Knopf, 1952), 38.
2. Arnold Wolfers, *Discord and Collaboration* (Baltimore: Johns Hopkins University Press, 1962), 89-90.
3. Elaine Sciolino, "U.S. Finds Output of Drugs in World Growing Sharply," *New York Times*, Mar. 2, 1988. Also see Susan F. Rasky, "For Its War, Congress Is Brimming With Combative Ideas," *New York Times* (The Week in Review), July 10, 1988. For more on the "war on drugs," see Paul Eddy, *The Cocaine War* (New York: Norton, 1988); and Guy Gugliotta and Jeff Leen, *King of Cocaine* (New York: Simon & Schuster, 1988).
4. Benjamin Lambeth and Kevin Lewis, "The Kremlin and SDI," *Foreign Affairs* (Spring 1988): 759.
5. *New York Times*, Oct. 24, 1981.
6. For an early but devastating critique of American economic policy by a leading European statesman of the time, see Helmut Schmidt, *A Grand Strategy for the West* (New Haven, Conn.: Yale University Press, 1985).
7. Martin and Susan Tolchin, *Buying Into America* (New York: Times Books, 1988).
8. Daniel Yankelovich and Richard Smoke, "America's 'New Thinking,'" *Foreign Affairs* (Fall 1988): 13.
9. Leonard Silk, "Buying America 'On the Cheap,'" *New York Times*, Oct. 7, 1988.
10. Martin Tolchin, "Tracking a Foreign Presence in U.S. Military Contracting," *New York Times* (The Week in Review), Jan. 1, 1989.
11. Quoted in E. H. Carr, *The Bolshevik Revolution 1917-1923* (London: Macmillan, 1953), 16.
12. Said Amir Arjomand, *The Turban for the Crown* (New York: Oxford University Press, 1988).
13. John Lewis Gaddis, *Strategies of Containment* (New York: Oxford University Press, 1982), 320-322. Also see the articles by Melvin R. Laird, by coauthors Colin S. Gray and Jeffrey G. Barlow, and by Robert W. Komer all appearing in "The 'Decade of Neglect' Controversy," *International Security*, Fall 1985, 3-83.
14. William S. Cohen and George J. Mitchell, *Men of Zeal* (New York: Viking, 1988); and Jane Mayer and Doyle McManus, *Landslide* (Boston: Houghton Mifflin, 1988).
15. Robert Parry and Peter Kornblub, "Iran-Contra's Untold Story," *Foreign Policy*, Fall 1988, 4.
16. Joshua Muravchik, *The Uncertain Crusade* (Lanham, Md.: Hamilton Press, 1986) deals with the Carter administration and the dilemmas it confronted over its pursuit of human rights.

CHAPTER 5

The Security Game

DIFFERENCES BETWEEN DOMESTIC AND INTERNATIONAL POLITICS

The adversary game that nations play is the product of an anarchical international or state system. This does not mean anarchy in the sense of disorder and chaos; instead, it means the absence of legitimate governmental institutions with superior authority. Each state is responsible for its own security and other objectives; no world government exists to provide for each member state's security, prestige, influence, prosperity, or fulfillment of ideological goals. The state system is therefore based fundamentally on the principle of self-help; that is, each state decides for itself how to pursue these objectives, including when and over what issues to resort to force. Thus, the system is always in a state of potential war. The seventeenth-century English philosopher Thomas Hobbes caught the essence of interstate politics and of the adversary game when he wrote:

> Though there had never been any time, wherein particular men were in a condition of war one against another; yet in all times, kings, and persons of sovereign authority, because of their independency, are in continual jealousies, and in the state and posture of gladiators; having their weapons pointing, and their eyes fixed on one another; that is, their forts, garrisons and guns, upon the frontiers of their kingdoms; and continual spies upon their neighbours; which is a posture of war.[1]

It is often said that international conflicts are settled with bullets, and domestic differences are settled with ballots. In international conflicts there is no legitimate central government whose policy decisions are accepted as binding, backed by a common political culture (rules or norms that govern the way a society resolves conflicts peacefully). Admittedly, this distinction between international and domestic conflicts is oversimplified. Not all quarrels between states result in war; most are settled without even invoking the threat of violence. Nor are all domestic clashes of interest settled without force or violent disturbance, even within contemporary Western democracies. Of the 278 European wars fought between 1480 and 1941, 28 percent were civil wars.[2] And the incidence of civil war has risen since World War II. The large number of new states that have arisen out of the ashes of colonial empires is one major reason for this increasing frequency of internal violence within nations. Many of the developing countries are deeply divided by religious, ethnic, class, and racial differences, often resulting in civil wars and the disintegration of the new states. The frequency with which governments have been overthrown and the recurrence of civil wars and revolutions suggest that, where legitimate governmental institutions and commonly shared political cultures have not yet been achieved, domestic politics tends to resemble international politics. The distinction between domestic and international politics is then not in the use or nonuse of force, but in the fact that national governments normally provide protection for their citizens. Unlike the international system, domestic systems are not usually based on self-help. Central governments that are legitimate have the authority or right to ensure that the law is obeyed by its citizens and to use force against any private use of violence.

Role of Governmental Institutions

Nevertheless, in some nations, especially the older, more settled Western nations, the role of violence in resolving disputes is considerably less important than the role of international war in the state system. Why? What conditions and processes of conflict resolution exist within these nations to account for their greater capacity to solve inevitable domestic problems?

Executive Branch.   One factor is the presence of executive branches of government to enforce the law and keep order. In Western systems the executive normally holds a preponderance, if not a monopoly, of organized force with which it can legitimately enforce the law, protect society, and discourage potential rebels. The executive controls the armed forces and the national police, and it controls the citizens of the nation by regulating the ownership of arms and forbidding the existence of private or party paramilitary forces. Domestic peace is therefore always armed. If the executive ever loses this superiority of power, either because all or part of the army refuses to support it—as in Weimar Germany or Spain before the rule of General Francisco Franco—or because of the rise of political parties that possess their own armed forces—as did the Nazis in Germany, the Communist Chinese, the Viet

Cong in South Vietnam, and the Sandinistas in Nicaragua—the government may be challenged and the nation plunged into civil war.

Legislative Process.   A second factor is that Western political systems also have institutionalized legislative processes through which conflicts of interests within society, articulated by political parties and interest groups, are channeled and peacefully resolved. The term *legislative process* is used instead of *legislative branch* because the latter does not legislate by itself. In any Western political system, it is the leader of the majority party who, as president or prime minister, draws up the legislative program to be submitted for approval to the congress or parliament. In legislation, too, the executive plays the leading role. The significance of the process of legislation, however, is that law making is essentially synonymous with the issue of domestic war and peace. The most controversial, significant, and bitter conflicts in society revolve around questions of what the law should be. The legislative process is focused on the basic issue of politics, which—as political scientist Harold Lasswell once summed it up—is "who gets what, when, and how."

Politics, therefore, is a series of conflicts over the distribution of "goods" such as wealth, status, and power in society. Other political scientists have used more formal terms, such as *allocation of values*. The more usual term is *justice*. Although various groups and classes in society define that term differently, they all are concerned with attaining justice—realizing group aspirations and redressing grievances. Should there be a redistribution of wealth? Should minorities be granted full equality in American society, and should discrimination in interstate travel, housing, and employment be banned? Should the poor, the unemployed, the aged, the sick, and the hungry receive assistance? What kind and how much? Should labor be permitted to bargain collectively? Should farmers be subsidized or rely on the free market? Should the country have a national health-insurance plan, and, if so, what type and at what cost?

These questions constitute major social issues and arouse strong passions. Yet they are unavoidable; in a pluralistic society new demands are continually being advanced, and people differ on how to resolve the many problems confronting society. A political system that is not very responsive to demands for change and does not provide for sufficient peaceful change will sooner or later erupt in revolution, the domestic equivalent of international war. A political system must either meet the important aspirations of rising and discontented new social groups with sensitivity and sufficient speed or confront violent upheaval. If discontent is widespread enough, the executive's superior power cannot prevent the government's fall because the army and police are recruited from the population. In the ultimate breakdown of society, many soldiers will refuse to fire on their own people; units of the armed forces will instead join the rebellion, as in Russia in 1917, in Iran in 1978-1979, and in Afghanistan after the 1979 Soviet invasion, when soldiers defected from the Soviet-imposed government and joined the rebels. The ordinary soldier-citizen will have no more vested interest in maintaining the system than will most other citizens.

Judiciary.   The final factor is that a judiciary, together with the executive and legislative institutions, helps to maintain expectations of individual and social justice. Violence, domestic or international, is normally an instrument of last resort. While hope remains that peaceful change is possible through existing political processes, rebellion can usually be avoided. But, just as there is no international executive with a monopoly of organized force and no international legislative process to provide for peaceful change, the state system lacks an international judiciary with the authority to ensure this sense of justice and bring about peaceful change.

Role of Political Culture

The state system lacks not only effective central political institutions for preserving peace and regulating the behavior of its members but also an international political culture or consensus of political values comparable to those existing within most Western states. A state's political culture includes the shared political values and attitudes of its people related to the general purposes for which society exists and, even more important, the rules or norms by which the domestic "game" is played. The consensus thus comprises both substantive values (agreement on what the country stands for) and procedural values (agreement on how government should be conducted—for example, majority rule and the supremacy of law). Nondemocratic states can proclaim the same substantive goals as democracies (as, in fact, the Soviet Union does in its constitution). Therefore, it is the way of governing or making political decisions that is critical. If policies were not made according to rules, they would be disregarded and disobeyed; they would lack moral sanction or legitimacy. People obey the law because they agree that the government has the right to govern, not because the government has at its command superior power and the individual is fearful of punishment. "For, if force creates right," the French philosopher Jean Jacques Rousseau wrote in the eighteenth century, "the effect changes with the cause: Every force that is greater than the first succeeds to its right. As soon as it is possible to disobey with impunity, disobedience is legitimate and the strongest being always in the right, the only thing that matters is to act so as to become the strongest." But, Rousseau continued, "the strongest is never strong enough to be always the master, unless he transforms strength into right and obedience to duty." [3] If a government is considered legitimate, even people who disagree with the content of a law normally obey it because they acknowledge that the government has the authority to decide policies for the entire society.

Politics, to sum up, deals with conflicts among groups whose objectives clash. The peaceful resolution of such differences depends on several conditions. First, there must be an executive with superior power, which discourages potentially violent challenges and allows the government to enforce legitimate decisions (according to the apt phrase of another teacher of international politics, Vernon Van Dyke. "A peaceful country is a policeful country"). Second, there must be a set of governing institutions—executive, legislative, and judicial—that provide for peaceful resolution of conflict and allow most people and organizations to attain justice or what they themselves regard as fair shares of what society has to offer. Third, and, perhaps most important, there must be widespread agreement on common purposes and rules of the game so that, even in major disputes, the differing views and needs can be expressed through acceptable political channels and not lead to confrontation and violence. Fourth, this consensus, which serves to legitimize the government, must be reinforced by a deep emotional commitment embodied in nationalism and its various symbols: the flag, national monuments, the national anthem, national institutions, and national celebrations of key events in a nation's history. Such symbols are reminders of national history and the common beliefs and loyalty of a people, as well as of the supremacy of society and the common good.

Instead of such broad agreement, which can buffer and limit areas of conflict so that they do not shred the whole social fabric, the only common agreement on what might be called a minimal "international political culture" is the commitment to the existence of nation-states, their independence, and their security. But this commitment *maximizes* divisions and conflict among nations. The primary loyalty of the nation-state is to itself. The absence of the conditions for peaceful change and accommodation internationally means that the basic condition of the state system is one of potential warfare among its members; at least, there is a higher expectation of violence than in national political systems.[4]

INTERNATIONAL POLITICS AND THE 'SECURITY DILEMMA'

Self-Help and the Drive for Power

The primary distinguishing characteristic of the state system follows from the system's decentralized or anarchical nature. *Each state, as part of this external environment, must rely upon itself, and only upon itself, for the protection of its political independence, territorial integrity, and prosperity.* In what might also be called "politics without government"—perhaps the shortest way of summing up the distinction between international and domestic politics—the issue of who receives what, when, and how is decided, not by a national government recognized as legitimate, but by the interactions of states in a system whose basic rule is "every state for itself." Because a human being's highest secular loyalty is to the nation, policy makers of all states are intensely committed to the maintenance of national security, the prerequisite for enjoyment of the nation's other values—its way or life. If it is further correct that the external environment is anarchical, posing a constant danger to this way of life, policy makers responsible for protecting the nation react fearfully to perceived threats to their country.

More specifically, states living in an environment in which none can acquire absolute security are bound to feel insecure and are therefore driven to reduce their sense of insecurity by enhancing their power. As with human beings in the Hobbesian state of nature, so with states in the state system: they are haunted continually by a fear of violent death.[5] It is the resulting mutual fear and suspicion among states that produce "power politics." When a nation sees its neighbor as a potential foe, it tries to deter potential attack by becoming a little stronger than the neighbor. The latter, in turn, also fears an attack and therefore feels that it too must be strong enough to deter an attack or, if deterrence should fail, to win the resulting conflict. *The insecurity of all states in the system compels each to acquire greater security by engaging in a constant scramble for increased power.* But as each state watches its neighbor's power grow, its own sense of insecurity recurs: it then tries all the harder to gain even greater strength. The result is that each state is continually faced with a "security dilemma."[6]

This is a central problem of international politics. It is not a question of whether one state has aggressive ambitions or not; *both* states can be oriented defensively. Yet this commitment to the status quo is not enough to eliminate the security dilemma. Even if state A explains its increase in arms by saying that it does so only to give itself the added insurance it needs to deter state B, the latter will react by increasing its strength. A will then attribute that reaction to B's offensive intentions, even if the latter also professes status quo aims. After all, did A not declare it was interested only in self-protection? The problem is that B cannot take A's declarations at face value; it is more likely to perceive A's acquisition of new arms as an indication of A's desire to gain military superiority to achieve revisionist goals. Thus, the nature of the system tends to enhance mutual suspicions and distrust, exacerbating already existing conflicts of interests. Even status quo states are compelled to behave like expansionist states because the former cannot afford to allow even states denying revisionist objectives to gain an advantage—just in case they are what they deny they are but are suspected of being. To put it another way, because one state often enhances its security by measures that make other states feel less secure, the assumption that the relations between states that accept the status quo are necessarily peaceful is wrong.[7]

Thus, nations seek power not because simple maximization of power is their goal; they seek it because they wish to guard the security of their "core values," their territorial integrity, and their political independence, as well as their prosperity. And they act aggressively because the system gives rise to mutual fear and suspicion—each state regards its neighboring state as a potential Cain.[8] The dilemma inherent in the state system is essentially kill or be killed, strike first or risk destruction. In this context, it does not take much for one state to arouse and confirm another state's apprehensions and thus to stimulate the development of reciprocal images of hostility, each of which will be validated by the adversary's behavior. Conversely, these images will be hard to dispel even by friendly acts; indeed, such acts may be construed as indications of weakness and may therefore be exploited.

Role of Military Power

Perhaps a more apt way of defining this almost compulsive concern with power that is shared by all states is in terms of the high potential for violence in the anarchical state system. Threats of violence or actual use of violence are in the end the principal means used by states to impose their demands on other states or, conversely, to resist demands imposed on them by others. It is for this reason that the international system frequently has been characterized as being in a state of potential war; it is war, or the constant possibility of war, that all too often determines who receives what and when. In an environment of conflicting demands in which there are no universally accepted supranational institutions to provide for the nonviolent resolution of differences, the power of the respective adversaries—the power to win a war should it erupt—settles who gains what and who loses what. The actual strength of each party will be clear from the outcome: defeat, stalemate, compromise, peace, or victory. This is not to say that wars are common or even the principal expression of power. War is the instrument of last resort, the ultimate test.

More frequently than war, states use the *threat* of force or coercion. The military power not used may be more potent than the power used. Lord Horatio Nelson, England's famous admiral, reportedly said to a diplomat: "I hate your pen-and-ink men; a fleet of British ships of war are the best negotiators in Europe." [9] And Frederick the Great, Prussia's remarkable ruler and soldier, likened diplomacy without armaments to music without instruments.[10] With force a nation takes what it wants from another state; with diplomacy, supported by the threat of using that force, a nation may persuade another state to make concessions to its demands.

The characterization of international politics as a state of potential war does not therefore seem incorrect historically. Even had there been far fewer wars, it remains true, as Hobbes suggested, that war consists

> not in battle only, or the act of fighting, but in a tract of time . . . as it is in the nature of weather. For as the nature of foul weather lies not in a shower or two of rain, but in an inclination thereto of many days together, so the nature of war consists not in actual fighting, but in the known disposition thereto.[11]

Coercion, or the threat of force, generally stands in the background, affecting negotiations among conflicting states, just as the threat of a strike always affects the bargaining between labor and management. The desire to avoid a strike—a long one, anyway—is thus an incentive for both sides to compromise. Similarly, the possibility of violence does not mean that it will occur. States do not go to war lightly, for the costs are high, and in the "fog of war" the outcome among evenly matched opponents can rarely be certain, no matter how carefully each has calculated its power and that of its adversary. The knowledge that war is a possibility is more likely to moderate demands and provide a stimulus for other means of conflict resolution such as persuasion, rewards, and coercion. Renunciation of force, in contrast, eliminates the penalty for an uncompromising attitude and gives the advantage to the party willing to invoke violence.

If a nation has prestige, of course, it is less likely to be pressured or attacked and more likely to gain compliance with its demands. Its reputation for power, based on its past effective use of power—especially military power—enhances the possibility of the peaceful resolution of conflicts. Thus, the actual use of violence or explicit threats of violence are not the everyday fare of diplomacy. It is worth emphasizing in this context that there is no one-to-one relationship between military power and success in achieving a state's objectives. The United States, as pointed out earlier, did not defeat North Vietnam. American military power could not prevent Iran from seizing U.S. officials as hostages in Tehran in 1979, or terrorist groups loyal to Iran from seizing American and other Western hostages in the 1980s. In Nicaragua, the U.S. government used covert war tactics because public opinion was opposed to the use of America's armed forces. Thus, the possession of military power does not guarantee the fulfillment of foreign policy aims; indeed, there are clearly situations in which it may not even be applicable.

Nevertheless, military power plays a key role in interstate bargaining in peacetime as well as in wartime. It follows that the tendency to think of war and peace as mutually exclusive is wrong. To cite one observation among many, "War means that diplomacy failed, that persuasion did not work, and that bargaining was unsuccessful." [12] It is more accurate to think of war and peace as existing on a continuum along which states have conflicting interests of increasing scope and intensity. Some of these conflicts will be resolvable by peaceful negotiations, but at some point one side will feel that the demands made upon it are excessive, that it can no longer offer concessions without endangering its own security. It may calculate that the distribution of power is sufficiently equitable so that it can reject the adversary's demands without war resulting. But the opponent may not be willing to accept this rejection, estimating that the ratio of power favors it. The opponent therefore attempts to intimidate the adversary and, when intimidation proves ineffective, resorts to force; or, if the opponent does not initiate the use of force, the side faced with the demands may declare war rather than accept them.

In either case, the outbreak of war does not mean that diplomacy has failed or that negotiations are discontinued until one of the sides has won the war and imposes its terms on the other. War *is* bargaining. As Carl von Clausewitz argues in *On War*, still the definitive book on the subject after a century and a half, war is the continuation of diplomacy or bargaining by other means—that is, force. War does not suspend the political relationship among sovereign states. "How could it be otherwise? Do political relations between peoples and between their governments stop when diplomatic notes are no longer exchanged? Is war not just another expression of their thoughts, another form of speech and writing?" Its grammar—the fighting—may be its own, Clausewitz said, but "not its own logic." [13] The logic is that of politics: war erupts because states have conflicts of political objectives that they cannot resolve by persuasion or pressures short of war; they therefore seek to achieve these objectives by combat. The fighting will decide who is the stronger and whether the side demanding a revision of the status quo or the other trying to defend it will achieve its goal.

Peace, in short, is not absolute but conditional. If a state can preserve its security in peacetime, it will do so, but, if it cannot, it will invoke force as the instrument of last resort, as Britain finally did when Hitler attacked Poland in 1939. Once fighting erupts it will always continue until one side surrenders conditionally or unconditionally or, more frequently since 1945, until both sides reach a new set of mutually acceptable terms and end the war, an event often symbolized by an official peace conference during which the new postwar balance of power is reached. After the cessation of World War II hostilities, the conflict over this new balance began so quickly that no formal conference was even held. Negotiations between North Vietnam and the United States from 1965 to 1973, for example, could have led to peace at any time, but neither side was willing to accept the other side's terms of peace. The fighting, and the bargaining, thus continued, for they held out the promise to each side of better or more acceptable terms later. *The price of peace was of greater concern than peace itself.*

The axiom "when diplomacy stops, war starts" is therefore untrue. Despite the widespread belief in the United States that war is an alternative to negotiations, it is not; in fact, it is a violent continuation of them. Power, especially military power, is always present. In so-called peaceful negotiations, power stands in the background—"on guard"—and, when needed, is brought to the fore. It is invoked as a threat, and, if that is insufficient, it will be used openly. Power is omnipresent. Peace and war therefore have much in common. As Hobbes said, "Covenants without the sword are but words."

Role of Nonmilitary Power

Although the structure of the state system encourages states to be constantly concerned about the ratio of power between themselves and other states, coercion does not always mean the threat of violence. It may mean the use of nonmilitary, especially economic, sanctions that can sometimes be more effective than the threat of force. In the 1970s members of the Organization of Petroleum Exporting Countries dramatically demonstrated this point to the world. In a system in which, according to all conventional calculations, great powers should be influencing small powers, the reverse seemed to be happening. *One principal characteristic of power is the capacity to hurt.* A state that makes demands on another says, in fact, "Give me what I want, or I will hurt you worse than compliance will hurt." If the other state agrees that compliance will hurt less than resistance, it is likely to submit. If it calculates that the cost of resistance will be less than yielding what is demanded, it is likely to defy the demands made upon it. The threat of force is an obvious example of coercion matched by the "reward" of withholding it and not hurting the adversary. The threat of withholding resources vital to a nation's industry or of greatly raising the prices of these resources is also an effective form of coercion. Infliction of violent pain or deprivation of needed resources are just two of the many strategies that can hurt an adversary. The late Chinese leader Mao Zedong was often quoted as saying that power grows out of the barrel of a gun; OPEC expected power to grow out of a barrel of oil. The military weapon can be replaced by the economic weapon—what Karl Marx called the replacement of the cannon by capital.

Economic means are used not only to achieve national security or high-politics objectives but also for economic or low-politics purposes. Trade is a principal way of obtaining the goods, services, and other resources that a country needs for economic growth, high employment, and a satisfactory standard of living. Oil, for example, can be bought on the international market. If oil-producing countries wish to earn more money, they can organize themselves into a cartel and withhold oil or cut back production. This creates shortages and raises prices, which may then create higher unemployment and inflation in oil-consuming industrial countries, threatening them with economic disaster. States pursue their own economic interests as they do their political interests. The state system's lack of a legitimate government to allocate economic goods peacefully and manage economic relations among the member states means that states pursue low-politics goals as they do high-politics goals.

The very language of international politics—such expressions as economic warfare and aggression, diplomatic fronts, cold wars, crusades for peace—is indicative of the contentious nature of the state system and its susceptibility to coercion. And, in the wake of OPEC actions during the 1970s and early 1980s, many Americans, recognizing that the United States had become the food basket of a hungry world, began to speak of "food as a weapon." In politics among nations, almost anything—oil, food, investments, technology, trade—can become a weapon, a means by which one state can seek leverage over other states. Hobbes would have understood the use of food exports as a weapon in the self-help system that is the state system; he also would not have been surprised by such terms as "investment wars" and "trade wars."

BALANCE OF POWER AS A SYSTEM

Power as a Neutralizer of Power

If states wish to deter potential attackers and ensure their own independence and their ways of life, they will pursue balance-of-power policies. The balance of power is sought because of fear that if one nation gains predominant power, it may impose its will upon other states, either by the threat or actual use of violence. In political scientist Arnold Wolfers's words:

> Under these conditions of anarchy the expectation of violence and even of annihilation is ever-present. To forget this and thus fail in the concern for enhanced power spells the doom of a state. This does not mean constant open warfare; expansion of power at the expense of others will not take place if there is enough counterpower to deter or to stop states from undertaking it. Although no state is interested in a mere balance of power, the efforts of all states to maximize power may lead to equilibrium. If and when that happens, there is "peace" or, more exactly, a condition of stalemate or truce. Under the conditions described here, this balancing of power process is the only available "peace" strategy.[14]

The term *balance of power* is often used in loose and contradictory ways. It may refer, for example, to any existing distribution of power between two states, whether it is at an equilibrium, an approximate balance, or an imbalance (meaning either superiority or inferiority of power, as in "the balance has shifted toward Syria" and "the balance has shifted away from Israel").[15] As the term is used here, however, it refers to a *balance-of-power system* in which any shift away from equilibrium in the state system leads to countershifts through mobilization of countervailing power. This definition suggests a mechanism, like the "invisible hand" in the classical free market, that preserves the equilibrium. The systemic nature of the balance of power is further explained by Wolfers:

> While it makes little sense to use the term "automatic" literally, as if human choices and errors were irrelevant to the establishment, preservation, or destruction of a state of equilibrium, there nevertheless is a significant element of truth in the theory of "automatism" which is valid even today. If one may assume that any government in its senses will be deeply concerned with the relative power position of hostile countries, then one may conclude that efforts to keep in step in the competition for power with such opponents, or even to outdo them, will almost certainly be forthcoming. If most nations react in this way, a tendency towards equilibrium will follow it; will come into play whether both sides aim at equilibrium or whether the more aggressive side strives for superiority. In the latter case, the opposite side is likely to be provoked into matching these aggressive moves. Forces appear therefore to be working "behind the backs" of the human actors, pushing them in the direction of balanced power irrespective of their preferences.[16]

In short, states cannot be trusted with power, for they will be tempted to abuse it. *Unrestrained power in the system constitutes a menace to all other member states. Power is therefore the best antidote to power.* The fundamental assumption, of course, is that power will not be abolished, that it is inherent in a system characterized by competition and rivalry, and therefore that the principal task of the international system is thus the management of power.[17] This is not to say that in "real life" all states—especially the great powers—have sought always and everywhere to expand their power. They have not, as demonstrated by the United States' return to isolationism after World War I and Japan's unwillingness to play a major and active political role even in Asia since World War II. Nevertheless, states have sought to enhance their power often enough so that one can say that not doing so is the exception and often a cause of wonderment to other states, which may be tempted to exploit the situation. For this reason, even a state wishing to act with restraint usually acts preemptively, knowing that potential adversaries may seek such advantage and that it will then be compelled to react.

Purposes of the Balance

Power thus begets countervailing power. But consider the two aims of countervailing power. The first aim is the *protection of the security of each state*, not the preservation of peace. As noted earlier, most states normally feel secure when they are at peace, but peace is the product of a balance that is acceptable to the leading powers because it ensures their individual security. Peace may be desirable in itself, but it is also only one of several objectives that states pursue. States historically have sacrificed peace to achieve any of these objectives, especially their security. "Peace at any price" has rarely been the aim. To put it simply, peace is the cart, security the horse. To place the cart before the horse is to court disaster. This is easier to conceptualize than to practice, for peace is obviously a desirable value. Most states are reluctant to sacrifice peace, and the difficulty arises in deciding exactly at what point preserving a nation's security is worth the costs of war. If the balance of power is kept, however, the motivation for any state to risk launching an attack may be reduced, if not eliminated.

The second aim of countervailing power is the *protection of the state system as a whole*. The rationale underlying the balance of power is that each state has the right to exist. The way to ensure each state's security and independence is to prevent the emergence of any preponderant state. States are rarely eliminated by other states. To destroy the right of another state to exist is to undermine one's own claim to that right. Thus, at the end of the Napoleonic Wars, despite twenty-five years of fighting, France was neither eliminated nor punished. A lenient peace treaty was signed so that France could once more take its place in the family of European states and contribute to the preservation of the system. A vengeful France might have started another war instead of contributing to the European system's peace and stability.

By contrast, the Treaty of Versailles ending World War I was harsh. Germany considered it punitive, and many regard it as a central reason why Germany remained a threat to the stability and peace of post-1918 Europe.

Had Britain and France signed a treaty of reconciliation or modified the Versailles pact in the 1920s when Germany was still weak, the German Republic might have weathered the Great Depression and become a pillar of support for the European settlement. Instead, Adolf Hitler was able to exploit German nationalism to help him achieve power, mobilize support for his regime, and proceed to destroy the Europe of Versailles. Ironically, it was only when Germany threatened to use force that the Western powers sought to appease Hitler—that is, ratify Germany's stated grievances in the hope that this would gain Germany's support for a stable European system. But by then German ambitions and power had outgrown any possibility of being satisfied, and war became unavoidable.

The United States learned from this interwar experience. It signed a generous peace treaty with Japan after World War II and treated West Germany in a spirit of reconciliation. In the subsequent postwar containment policy, in which its former enemies figured prominently, the United States accepted the premise that the Soviet Union is a permanent player on the international chessboard. The aim of containment was not to eliminate the Soviet Union. There was no reason to believe that eliminating it would end the United States' international involvements, any more than had the earlier elimination of Hitler's Germany. The aim of containment was merely to prevent further Soviet expansion. The expectation was that the Soviet Union would "mellow," that the Soviet leaders would accept the international system and coexist peacefully with other states, regardless of their domestic complexion. In short, the Soviet Union's revolutionary ambitions would be subordinated to preserving the state system.

Rules of the Game: Capabilities and Intentions

In a decentralized system, the rules of the balance of power remain the basic norms for states.[18] These rules of the game may be ignored or forgotten only at a nation's peril. They are usually so internalized that those who conduct foreign policy think almost "automatically," as Wolfers has put it, in balance-of-power terms. Policy makers become "socialized" by the system; even revolutionary leaders learn to follow the logic of the balance of power. While behavior patterns vary with the structure of the system—that is, with the number of principal actors or great powers (see Chapter 6) these rules can be stated in general terms:

1. Watch a potential adversary's power and match it.
2. Ally oneself with a weaker state to restore the balance of power.
3. Abandon such alliances when the balance has been restored and the common danger has passed.
4. Regard national security interests as permanent; alliances must therefore change as new threats arise.
5. Do not treat defeated states harshly through punitive peace treaties. (Today's adversary may be tomorrow's ally.)

The emphasis on the power a state has mobilized, or its capability, is deliberate. In theory, intentions are quickly changeable and a peaceful state today can become a warlike state tomorrow, as leaders' views change or as the leaders themselves change. Capabilities may also vary, but they are not as likely to fluctuate dramatically from one day to the next. The underlying tangible components, such as the number of weapons the armed forces have do not usually alter overnight; it takes time to produce arms. "Playing it safe"—and what else should a state in the international environment do?—therefore suggests that keeping up with a potential adversary's capabilities, even to anticipating a buildup in order not to be caught napping, is the safest course. While this may aggravate the security dilemma, states have found it better to be safe than sorry. Conversely, it seems wise to play down intentions as unreliable. Capabilities, however, can be measured.

But in real political life, policy makers do make judgments about intentions. Implicit in their concern with capabilities may be an unspoken estimate of the adversary's intentions as unfriendly and that the buildup had better be matched to serve as a deterrent. American policy makers worry when the Soviets build up military but not when Britain does so. Capability analysis cannot really be divorced from some sort of view of intentions. For example, today what should the United States make of Soviet leader Gorbachev and his reforms? According to former Secretaries of State Henry Kissinger and Cyrus Vance:

> No American President can base his policies for dealing with the U.S.S.R. on the presumed intentions of a Soviet general secretary. We cannot predict whether his intentions may radically change under domestic political pressure. A successor may change policies, as has happened before. Nor can we pretend to understand the inner workings of the Kremlin well enough to know whether Gorbachev will succeed or survive.[19]

INTERNATIONAL POLITICS AS A 'MIXED' GAME

Conflict

If in the state system the struggle for security is basic, and states perceive one another as adversaries, then as Wolfers points out, "the insecurity of an anarchical system of multiple sovereignty places the actors under compulsion to seek maximum power even though this may run counter to their real desires."[20] The inherent fears and suspicions of states would be reflected even in a situation of general disarmament. States might well be better off if none was armed. But then one state might calculate that, if it armed, it would be able to gain an advantage; it could coerce unarmed opponents or go to war to impose its demands. Precisely because most states fear such a possibility, they not only refuse to disarm but also make sure that they are as

strong as potential adversaries, either by being strong themselves or forming alliances with other states. States are potential enemies, then, not because they are necessarily aggressive or have ideological differences, but
because they see that they can harm one another and, being cautious, they
view one another as possible enemies.

According to former U.S. secretary of defense Robert McNamara,

> In 1961 ... the Soviet Union possessed a very small operational arsenal of
> intercontinental missiles. However, they did possess the technological and
> industrial capacity to enlarge that arsenal very substantially over the succeeding
> several years. Now, we had no evidence that the Soviets did in fact plan to fully
> use that capability. But as I have pointed out, a strategic planner must be
> "conservative" in his calculations; that is, he must prepare the worst plausible
> case and not be content to hope and prepare merely for the most probable. ...
>
> Since we could not be certain of Soviet intentions—since we could not be sure
> that they would not undertake a massive buildup—we had to insure against
> such an eventuality by undertaking ourselves a major buildup of the Minute-
> man and Polaris [missile] forces. ...
>
> Clearly, the [subsequent] Soviet buildup is in part a reaction to our own
> buildup since the beginning of this decade. Soviet strategic planners undoubt-
> edly reasoned that if our buildup were to continue at its accelerated pace, we
> might conceivably reach, in time, a credible first-strike capability against the
> Soviet Union. This was not in fact our intention. ...
>
> But they could not read our intentions with any greater accuracy than we could
> read theirs. And thus the result has been that we have both built up our forces to a
> point that far exceeds a credible second-strike capability against the forces we each
> started with.[21]

Competition

States engage not only in conflict but also in competition. Great powers are
particularly prone to compete with one another, even if they are not at the
time in conflict with one another. They are very conscious of their prestige.
When possession of an empire was a sign of great-power status, states aspiring
to that rank sought colonies. At the turn of the century, Alfred Thayer Mahan,
an American naval captain, published a book claiming that a nation's greatness was linked to its possession of a large fleet of battleships—a claim he
based on the experience of Britain, an island power and the world's first
nation to industrialize. The other powers of Europe, as well as Japan *and* the
United States, decided to build navies. But Germany's acquisition of a large
battle fleet was seen as a security threat by Britain. Germany was already the
Continent's strongest land power, and the kaiser had announced that Germany was about to embark upon a world policy beyond Europe. The German
navy was therefore a major contributory factor to the increasing tensions
between Germany and Britain preceding World War I.[22] Ironically, the battle-
ship was already passé. It played virtually no role in deciding the outcome of
World War I. Had the Germans focused on building more submarines, they
might have won the war; in any case, German submarines almost succeeded

in starving England into submission. But the battleship remained a symbol of great power until World War II.

The atom bomb has become a contemporary symbol. Whatever its deterrent value, its acquisition is required for great powers seeking to maintain their rank—for example, Britain and France—or for nations such as India and China seeking to acquire such rank. It is not accidental that all the great powers represented on the United Nations Security Council—the United States, the Soviet Union, Britain, France, and China—are nuclear powers.

When states are in conflict, competition between them increases. Perhaps the most notable contemporary example is the competition in space. It is, in a sense, a natural extension of competition on land, sea, and air, for space is the next area of strategic significance. The real importance of President Ronald Reagan's Strategic Defense Initiative is probably not whether it will defend the population of the United States or partially defend the increasingly vulnerable land-based missiles against a Soviet first strike, or even whether it will serve as a bargaining chip to trade against drastic Soviet cuts of their missiles. Instead, it may give the United States the capability to deny the Soviet Union, which has been interested in space for some time, a technological lead that might translate into military and political advantages. Space, according to Zbigniew Brzezinski, Carter's national security assistant, is becoming the new arena for superpower competition, just as the oceans were at the turn of the century:

> Space control is likely to become tantamount to Earth control. There are striking parallels between the role of the navy in the emergence of American global power and today's incipient competition for a dominant position in space. The earlier competition among the Great Powers for maritime primacy involved rivalry for effective control over strategic space between the key continents. Control over such space was central to territorial preponderance. That is why the United States, in the phase of its geostrategic expansion, placed such an emphasis on the acquisition of dominant Atlantic and Pacific fleets, linked through direct U.S. control over the Panama Canal.
>
> Today the equivalent of that naval rivalry is the competition in space. At the very minimum it must be the U.S. strategic objective to make certain that no hostile power can deny the United States, while retaining for itself, the means for using space for intelligence, early warning, reconnaissance, targeting, and command and control. Modern military operations are highly dependent on space assets performing these functions, and U.S. vulnerability in this area could be crippling. Thus, even short of seeking to exploit space control for offensive purposes against an enemy (e.g., by the use of weaponry deployed in space), the capacity to protect its nonlethal military space assets, or to inflict a denial of the use of space to the enemy, has become essential to an effective U.S. military posture.[23]

Cooperation

If, on the one hand, the structure of the system traps states in adversary relationships, states do, on the other hand, cooperate with one another. In their conflicts, states frequently form alliances. Enemies also cooperate; arms control negotiations between the United States and the Soviet Union have become almost routine since the 1960s. Even while a war is ongoing, states may cooperate. Prisoners, for example, get mail and food packages via the Red Cross. In the nuclear era, "limited wars" and confrontations that result in crises will be kept from escalating only if the superpowers work together despite their simultaneous rivalry.

International politics is thus a mixture of conflict, competition, and cooperation, but much of this cooperation occurs within the context of adversary relations. A state wants to attract the strength of allies to enhance its power and competitive stance. An arms control agreement with an opponent may reduce the level of armaments, ease international tensions, and make the world a slightly safer place, but such agreements are signed, after all, by such states as the United States and the Soviet Union, whose weapons are aimed at each other because they are political rivals. This is true even when states are no longer potential adversaries. Today, the major EEC states, such as France and West Germany, are unlikely to go to war with one another, even though not long ago some of them were bitter enemies. When these Continental states, which were the original members of the EEC, decided to move toward what they hoped would one day be a powerful United States of Europe, they did so, however, within the broader context of the rivalry between the United States and the Soviet Union.

Limits of Cooperation

The structure of the state system limits cooperation among states in two significant ways.[24] First, states concerned about their security or wealth cannot let themselves become too dependent on other states, for then they might become vulnerable to threats to reduce or eliminate any ongoing exchange of goods and services. For example, the 1973 Arab oil embargo—and price increases—led the Western oil-consuming nations to seek non-OPEC oil, develop alternative energy sources, and practice greater conservation. Since the 1970s, the Soviet Union has become increasingly dependent on the United States for large amounts of grain and desirous of all sorts of U.S. technology—and the United States has encouraged this dependency—but the Soviet Union also has been careful to maintain alternative sources of supply.

If a state becomes too dependent for any of its critical needs on another state, it can avoid a reduction or cutoff of supplies only by submitting to the demands made upon it. A preferable strategy therefore is to import critical resources or goods from several countries or to find several markets rather than a single one for any products it must export to earn foreign currencies to pay for imports. Smaller or more poorly endowed states long ago learned that the price of dependence is a restriction of national freedom, and a vulnerability to foreign demands.

Second, even when states cooperate on critical issues such as arms control because both expect to gain from such cooperation, each worries about the distribution of benefits and the sharing of costs. Who will come out ahead? Allowing another nation to gain an advantage might be potentially damaging. Even if President Jimmy Carter had not withdrawn the SALT II (Strategic Arms Limitation Talks) treaty after the Soviet invasion of Afghanistan in 1979, the United States Senate might have defeated it. Many senators thought it an unequal treaty that benefited the Soviet Union more than the United States. Even among EEC countries, which have grown close during two decades of economic cooperation, there have been setbacks, delays, and bitter disputes over the distribution of benefits. Is French agriculture benefiting more than West German agriculture? Are the Continental states gaining more from Britain's annual contribution to the EEC than Britain receives from the community?

Most remarkably, given the collective benefits it receives from high oil prices, OPEC weakened itself in the 1980s because of the inability of its members' to decide how much wealth each was to earn. Most of them sought to enhance their national earnings by selling more oil than allowed under OPEC's allotment; the results were a surplus of oil over international demand and lower oil prices. In 1986, to retain its share of the market, Saudi Arabia flooded the market, leading to precipitous drops in the price of oil. This in turn has led to renewed efforts to agree on production limits in order to raise the price of oil again, but these efforts have been only partially successful.

Anarchy and the Search for Order

The anarchical nature of the state system, in which each state is concerned about its own national security and welfare, should by now be clear.[25] But, as the preceding emphasis on cooperation makes plain, states also seek a degree of order. Not only are they concerned with their survival and safety, but they are also fated—or condemned?—to live together in the state system and therefore, by necessity, to seek a degree of regularity in their relationships. To minimize the unexpected and undesirable, states have established informal, as well as formal, rules and institutions to guide their interactions. For example, despite their intense rivalry and mutual hostility, the United States and the Soviet Union have over the years arrived at certain "rules" to avoid potentially explosive confrontations and make their relationship safer. These range from their mutual acceptance of the division of Europe into opposing spheres of influence (which led, for example, to U.S. nonintervention in the 1950s and 1960s when the Soviet satellites in Eastern Europe attempted to throw off the Soviet yoke) to specific agreements such as those aimed at preventing accidents at seas between warships and limiting or reducing nuclear weapons.

More broadly, states need to know what their rights and obligations are with regard to the oceans, airspace, wartime (as belligerents or neutrals), and the exchange of diplomats. International law incorporates the rules that govern the everyday coexistence of states in peace and wartime, and states have agreed to these rules by either consent or custom. Because nations also trade with each other, some degree of predictable order must govern economic exchanges as well. Many states since World War II, mainly Western industrial ones, have subscribed to the General Agreement on Tariffs and Trade to avoid the kind of chaos that followed the Great Depression and the resulting economic nationalism of the 1930s which only worsened everyone's lot. Several Communist states, including Poland, Hungary, and Yugoslavia, are members of the ninety-five-nation organization. China has applied for membership, and the Soviet Union has expressed its interest in joining GATT as well.

The first institutional efforts to curb the results of unrestrained sovereignty, as already noted, began in the nineteenth century. As war has become more destructive and costly, these efforts to manage inter-nation relations in ways that avoid extreme violence have increased. The Concert of Europe followed the defeat of Napoleon and peace treaty with France in 1815, the League of Nations the surrender of monarchical Germany in 1918, and the United Nations the collapse of Hitler's Germany in 1945. Even if these efforts eroded after a few years as differences among the victors grew, as memories of the wartime collaboration against the enemy faded, and as the laws, rules, and institutions to control violence were disregarded when they stood in the way of some nations' ambitions and determination, international politics is clearly not characterized by just conflict and the drive for national power. States, especially the great powers, may enjoy substantial freedom of action, but they are also subject to constraints.

It is precisely because the state system is basically anarchical that order is such a critical issue in international politics—unlike in domestic systems, where order is usually assumed and, as a result, social justice becomes the key issue, as suggested by the modern welfare state.* This does not mean, of course, that the need to preserve international order is necessarily incompatible with just changes.[26] The decolonization of the European empires in the name of national self-determination, a basic Western principle, is proof that order and justice can be reconciled to some degree. Decolonization took place largely because the Western powers, weakened by World War II and recognizing the justice of the colonies' claims to independence, were willing to grant most of them statehood. A few colonies had to fight for independence, but even in those cases, segments of domestic opinion in the Western colonial country favored the "war of liberation" because self-government is a democratic principle.

The cry of revolutionary groups is "Let justice be done," and sometimes they add "though the earth perish," since in their judgment the world is so

---

* When that order begins to break down, and people begin to feel insecure, they demand "law and order," tougher enforcement of the law, and arms to guard themselves, ranging from home security systems to large dogs to mace. And the resemblance to the international system in which each nation has no option but to protect itself becomes greater.

unjust it deserves to be destroyed if it refuses to change. In fact, revolution-aries do not really expect that the earth will perish, but that they will be successful, capture power, and then consolidate the gains of the revolution in a "new order." This is as true for the Palestine Liberation Organization, seeking the establishment of a Palestinian state, as it was for the Bolsheviks who captured power in Russia in 1917.

And it is not only revolutionary groups that seek justice. States do as well. As suggested earlier, France in 1789 and Russia in 1917 considered themselves to be "revolutionary" powers, states that were going to transform the old regimes (monarchy and aristocracy in one case, capitalism in the other) to new orders in the name of justice. Because the old regimes were alleged to be the cause of poverty domestically and war internationally, their replacement would usher in an era in which people would no longer exploit each other as commodities; instead, they would live together in liberty, equality, and frater-nity at home and in peace abroad.

Nevertheless, justice takes a subsidiary place to order internationally for two reasons. The first is the anarchical nature of the state system. Order, meaning the survival and safety of its member states, must be ranked as a basic need. It is, as domestic politics amply demonstrates, the precondition for the realization of justice. The second and closely related reason is that there is no agreed-upon moral code among the peoples and governments of the world. Within a nation, the moral code may well be imposed upon those who disagree—for example, when laws sanctioning child labor or racial discrimi-nation or the absence of a livable minimum wage are changed by a political process that is recognized as legitimate, and the government enforces the new laws which reflect the nation's conception of justice. Internationally, there is neither an acceptable common moral code (although such norms as national self-determination have received wide acceptance) nor a set of higher institu-tions that possesses the authority to impose such a code upon recalcitrant states.

Thus, with the decentralized nature of the state system also compelling states to seek order, one has come full circle. It is the great powers, as noted in the classification of states (Chapter 3), that historically have been the prime players of the international political game, and each state system has reflected the interests of the dominant powers at that particular time. This primacy of the great power oligarchy has long been recognized not just informally by other states but formally by the status accorded great powers at international congresses and institutions such as the League of Nations and the United Nations. In short, the earlier classification of states ranging from superpowers to minipowers, can be restated: all international systems have international hierarchies or "structures of dominance" of the weak by the strong.[27] Those at the top of the hierarchy are mainly responsible for maintaining some degree of order in the anarchical system in which states live. Because anarchy coexists with the rules that govern the coexistence of states and the common institutions serving them, analysts have used such terms as "anarchical society" and "mitigated anarchy" to underline the point that while the system remains essentially anarchical, it is a qualified anarchy.[28]

CHARACTERISTICS OF THE FIRST LEVEL OF ANALYSIS

Balance of Power

Analysis of the security games that nations play on the level of the state system reveals certain very specific notions of the behavior of states. (See Table 5-1.) *First, the interactions of states revolve around the axle of the balance of power.* Systemic change affects the behavior of all member states. Whenever the system becomes unbalanced, trouble follows. When Britain weakens and can no longer contain a Continental power seeking European hegemony, a previously isolationist power, the United States, must step in to play Britain's role. When Germany, in the center of Europe, is defeated, a conflict erupts between two previous allies, both superpowers on the periphery of Europe. Elimination of a troublesome member does not guarantee, therefore, the end of trouble and conflict. Nor can it. To alter the structure of the system is to change everyone's behavior; the new distribution of power merely leads to new alignments. But competition among states continues.

Uniformity of Behavior

Second, the system imposes a high degree of uniformity of behavior upon states, regardless of their domestic complexion. The same basic interests and motivations are ascribed to all members. The behavior required by their existence in an anarchical state system overrides different national attributes such as political culture, economic organization, or class structure—or, at least, it is supposed to. The systems analyst will examine internal variables only if they seem to have interfered with how a state should have behaved.

In this connection, note again that the systemic model tends to minimize the importance of ideologies, which are generally used to justify whatever states do. States are motivated by their security interests and are therefore concerned with preserving or enhancing their power. Ideology is viewed as a function of this interest.[29] For example, despite its anticapitalist and antifascist ideology, communism did not prevent the Soviet Union from aligning itself with France in 1935, with Nazi Germany in 1939, and with the United States and Britain in 1941 against its previous ally. And after World War II the Soviet Union acted very much like czarist Russia: it expanded into eastern Europe and attempted to extend its power into the eastern Mediterranean area. Ideology did not prevent Moscow from behaving in typical balance-of-power terms.

This de-emphasis of ideology suggests that the analyst of world politics need pay little attention to what policy makers *say* about their policies. Clearly, they will say whatever will make their actions look good. They will

Table 5-1 The State System

Primary actors	Nation-states
	Intergovernmental organizations
	    Universal: United Nations
	    Regional: Organization of African Unity
	    Special-interest: producer cartel: OPEC, "Group of 77"
	      (representing Third World countries)
	Supranational organization
	    Regional: EEC
	Nongovernmental or transnational organizations
	    Multinational corporations; religious, humanitarian groups;
	      national liberation groups; terrorists

Characteristics	Decentralized—composed mainly of sovereign and independent states Anarchical—absence of commonly accepted political institutions and legitimate rules of the game for allocation of values and enforcement of decisions High expectation of violence—coercion and force as the ultimate allocative mechanism or substitute for government Balance of power—principal mechanism that provides systemic stability and individual national restraint
General rules	1. Protect and guard oneself. 2. Be concerned with systemic power distribution. 3. Calculate self-interest rationally on the basis of power, not ideology.

talk about freedom, national self-determination, liberating peoples from Communist or capitalist slavery, and bringing about a world of peace, law, order, and justice. But such concepts should not be confused with the concrete interests that are the real, underlying reasons for the state's behavior. Indeed, the analyst who assumes that state behavior is the product of an ever-changing distribution of power can, according to Hans Morgenthau,

> retrace and anticipate, as it were, the steps a statesman—past, present, or future—has taken or will take on the political scene. We can look over his shoulder when he writes his dispatches; we listen in on his conversation with other statesmen; we read and anticipate his very thoughts.... We think as he does, and as disinterested observers we understand his thoughts and actions perhaps better than he, the actor in the political scene, does himself.[30]

Whether or not Morgenthau is correct, less emphasis on ideologies and statements of intentions does tend to reduce the probability that international politics will be viewed as a morality tale, a conflict between good and evil, and it refocuses attention on the security dilemma shared by all states living in an anarchical environment in which they see other states as potential enemies and are therefore bound to be concerned with their power vis-à-vis one another.

Limitation of Choice

Third, the system places limits on the policy choices of states. Some observers refer to *system-determined behavior.* Although this term may understate the degree of a state's "free will" or the actual range of its choices, it is a healthy reminder that for states, as for individuals, the available options depend on external realities—in this instance, the distribution of power. As political scientist Hedley Bull has noted, "The choice with which governments are in fact confronted is not that between opting for the present structure of the world, and opting for some other structure, but between attempting to maintain a balance of power and failing to do so." [31] The United States again is a perfect example. Each time in this century that the European balance has been upset, the United States has had but two options: to intervene and prevent the Continental powers from achieving hegemony or to remain isolationist. The latter course might have been preferable to the American public, but it might also have jeopardized future U.S. security. Three times, therefore, different administrations have rejected isolationism. The United States really had no choice.

Continuity

Finally, and closely related, continuity of policy is a characteristic of many nations. The political complexion of a great power—such as czarist Russia/Soviet Union—may change, as may its perception of its role in the world and its definition of objectives, but it still lives in a system in which neighbors to the east and west remain the same. And so therefore does the Soviet Union's need to secure Eastern Europe. Czarist or Communist, Russia has no natural protective barriers, such as the English Channel for Britain or mountain ranges for Italy and Spain. Instead Russia, regardless of regime, historically has sought greater security by expanding westward beyond its frontiers. Similarly, two U.S. interventions against Germany and one against Soviet Russia after World War II have demonstrated the remarkable continuity of U.S. policy.

A REMINDER: ANALYSIS AND APPROVAL

All the above observations about state behavior have been deduced from the state-system or balance-of-power framework. While in practice—in "real life"—there will be varying degrees of deviation, construction of such a framework and the deduction of behavior patterns for states is a useful exercise; the conclusions can, after all, be checked empirically. If this method of analysis improves the observer's capacity to understand state behavior, it justifies itself.

Whether the observer personally approves of the "logic of behavior" that a particular framework seems to suggest is not the point. It is one thing to say, as done here, that the state system condemns each state to be continually concerned with its power relative to that of other states, which, in an anarchical system, it regards as potential aggressors. It is quite another thing to approve morally of power politics. The utility of the state-system framework is simply that it points to the "essence" of state behavior. It does not pretend to account for all factors, such as moral norms, that motivate states. As a necessarily simplified version of reality, it clarifies what most basically concerns and drives states and what kinds of behavior can be expected. We, as observers, may deplore that behavior and the anarchical system that produces it and we may wish that international politics were not as conflictual and violent as the twentieth century has already amply demonstrated. We may prefer a system other than one in which states are so committed to advancing their own national interests and protecting their sovereignty. Nevertheless, however much we may deplore the current system and prefer a more peaceful and harmonious world, we must first understand the contemporary one if we are to learn how to "manage" it and avoid the catastrophe of a nuclear war.

For Review

1. Why is anarchy one of the distinctive features of international politics?
2. Why are the balance of power and the "security dilemma" central to understanding the behavior of states?
3. How are war and peace related?
4. What are the rules of the security game that nations play?
5. If anarchy is a principal characteristic of international politics, how can order and hierarchy also be important characteristics?

Notes

1. Thomas Hobbes, *Leviathan* (New York: Collier Books, 1962), 101.
2. Hans J. Morgenthau, *Politics among Nations*, 4th ed. (New York: Knopf, 1967), 490.
3. Jean Jacques Rousseau, *The Social Contract* (New York: Dutton, 1947), 6.
4. The domestic system in the United States assumes people will generally obey the law voluntarily. This is clearly shown by the limited number of police (national, state, and local)—certainly not enough to deal with massive resistance to the law and far, far fewer than the number of men and women in the armed forces

employed to defend the United States against external aggression. For an interesting analysis in which the willingness of governments to use force against other governments is contrasted with their reluctance, if not un-willingness, to use it against their own populations, see E. E. Schattschneider, *Two Hundred Million Americans in Search of a Government* (New York: Holt, Rinehart & Winston, 1969), 17-22.

5. Hobbes, *Leviathan*, 104.

6. John H. Herz, *International Politics in the Atomic Age* (New York: Columbia University Press 1959), 231-232.

7. Robert Jervis, "Cooperation Under the Security Dilemma," *World Politics*, January 1978, 167-214.

8. John Herz characterizes the effects of such suspicion as follows:

> [The] very realization that his own brother may play the role of a Cain makes his fellow men appear to him as potential foes. Realization of this fact by others, in turn, makes him appear to them as their potential mortal enemy. Thus there arises a fundamental social constellation, a mutual suspicion and a mutual dilemma: the dilemma of "kill or perish," of attacking first or running the risk of being destroyed. There is apparently no escape from this vicious circle. Whether a man is "by nature" peaceful and cooperative, or aggressive and domineering, is not the question.

> John H. Herz, *Political Realism and Political Idealism* (Chicago: University of Chicago Press, 1951), 2-3.

9. Quoted in Geoffrey Till, *Maritime Strategy in the Nuclear Age* (New York: St. Martin's Press, 1982), 210.

10. Quoted by Geoffrey Blainey, *The Causes of War* (New York: Free Press, 1973), 108.

11. Hobbes, *Leviathan*, 100. Also see the important book by Robert Gilpin, *War and Change in World Politics* (New York: Cambridge University Press, 1981).

12. Charles W. Kegley and Eugene R. Wittkopf, *World Politics* (New York: St. Martin's Press, 1985), 417.

13. Carl von Clausewitz, *On War*, ed. and trans. Michael Howard and Peter Paret (Princeton, N.J.: Princeton University Press, 1976), 605.

14. Arnold Wolfers, *Discord and Collaboration*, Baltimore: Johns Hopkins University Press 1962), 83. For contrary interpretations correlating peace with a superiority of power and war with a balance, see A. F. K. Organski, *World Politics* (New York: Knopf, 1956), 325-333; and Blainey, *Causes of War*, 112-114.

15. Discussions of the different meanings of "balance of power" can be found in Morgenthau, *Politics among Nations*, 161-163; Ernst B. Haas, "The Balance of Power: Prescription, Concept, or Propaganda?" *World Politics*, July 1953, 442-447; and Inis L. Claude, Jr., *Power and International Relations* (New York: Random House, 1962), pt. I.

16. Wolfers, *Discord and Collaboration*, 123.

17. Claude, *Power and International Relations*, 6.

18. Ibid., 91.

19. Henry Kissinger and Cyrus Vance, "Bipartisan Objectives for Foreign Policy," *Foreign Affairs* (Summer 1988); 903.

20. Wolfers, *Discord and Collaboration*, 84.

21. Robert McNamara, "Address to the United Press International, San Francisco," *New York Times*, Sept. 19, 1967.

22. Paul Kennedy, *Strategy and Diplomacy 1870-1945* (London: Fontana Paperbacks, 1984), 109ff.

23. Zbigniew Brzezinski, "America's New Geostrategy," *Foreign Affairs* (Spring 1988): 684.

24. Kenneth Waltz, *Theory of International Politics* (Reading, Mass.: Addison-Wesley, 1979), 105-106.

25. Roger D. Masters, "World Politics as a Primitive Political System," *World Politics*, July 1964, 595-619.

26. Hedley Bull, *The Anarchical Society* (New York: Columbia University Press, 1977), 77-98.

27. Bruce Russett and Harvey Starr, *World Politics* (San Francisco: W. H. Freeman, 1981), 82.

28. Bull, *Anarchical Society*; and Robert J. Lieber, *No Common Power* (Glenview, Ill.: Scott, Foresman/Little, Brown), 331-332.

29. Morgenthau, *Politics among Nations*, 83-86.

30. Ibid., 5 (emphasis added).

31. Hedley Bull, *The Control of the Arms Race* (New York: Holt, Rinehart & Winston, 1961), 49.

CHAPTER 6

Same Game, Different Players

Distribution of power is the key to understanding the behavior of states. The first-level (state-system) analysis is based on the assumption that the *structure* of the system conditions this behavior. The structure of the state system is defined by the number of major actors, or *poles,* present and the distribution of power among them. A pole is what is popularly known as a "great power," and the measure of that greatness has usually been military strength.

Moreover, there is a relationship between the structure of the international system and its *stability.* Stability is defined as the absence of any nation's predominance, the survival of most member states, and the absence of a major war. The concept of balance of power is based on the assumption that war may have to be invoked as a last resort to preserve systemic equilibrium or to restore it once it has been upset. War, then, is not destabilizing per se, especially if it is infrequent or limited. Major violence, such as a war among superpowers, however, is destabilizing. Therefore, a stable system is said to be characterized by minimal violence, the generally peaceful settlement of differences, and a desire to retain the principal features of the system. An unstable system is prone to major violence that may result in the hegemony of one pole; such hegemony will be a threat to the survival of the other major actors.[1]

UNIPOLARITY (STABLE)

Unipolarity requires one state to be dominant and capable of imposing its will on other states. World conquest by one state or a close alliance of states would produce a unipolar system. Obviously, such a system would be stable even if its members were unhappy to be governed by a foreign power and had little say about how they were ruled. The Roman Empire has probably been the closest thing to a unipolar system. Rome—a city-state—ruled more than 100 million people and much of the known world. To the Romans, *empire* meant the inequality of states; those who rebelled against Roman rule were brutally crushed. Relations existed between the empire and the barbarian tribes whom Rome eventually intended to bring within its sphere of military control.

Some analysts have asserted that the immediate post-World War II period was also a unipolar one.[2] That suggestion is dubious. To be sure, France and Britain collapsed after Germany and Japan were defeated, but the Soviet Union was hardly impotent, even though it had been hurt badly and did not yet possess the atomic bomb. Indeed, it was the Soviet Union's transformation of the states of Eastern Europe into satellites that ended its wartime alliance with the United States and Britain, and the Soviet attempts to expand beyond the lines where the Red Army stood at the end of the war that led to the cold war. If the postwar system had been unipolar, with the United States playing the role of Rome, it is hard to understand why Moscow was not more accommodating on the issue of free elections in Eastern Europe and did not refrain from its expansionist efforts. The fact is that the system after 1945 was bipolar, not unipolar.

These analysts, moreover, remain unconvinced of the uniqueness of unipolarity. They see "long cycles" of about a hundred years' duration, each of which is dominated by a world power. Having won a "global war," such a world power possesses a virtual monopoly of naval power and therefore a global reach and control over world trade. These powers since the fifteenth century have been Portugal, the Netherlands, Britain (which maintained its dominant position for two hundred years), and the United States. Each in turn has structured the international political and economic system and maintained order. This dominance or hegemony has maintained the peace. As each hegemony has weakened because the costs and debts it has accumulated in maintaining its dominant global position have risen faster than its economic capability to support this hegemony, forcing it to cut its naval strength to save money, it has been challenged by a newly rising power, resulting in a series of wars of succession. The next war will erupt, according to the long cycle's founder and chief advocate, George Modelski, in approximately 2030—unless the historic precedent is broken by the presence of nuclear weapons.[3] Clearly, the proponents of this theory reject the anarchical nature of the state system and the focus on self-help. Analysts who accept the latter characterization of the state system believe that the balance of power phenomenon has, with perhaps rare exception, prevented any single state from achieving systemic hegemony.

BIPOLARITY (UNSTABLE)

In a *bipolar* structure, two opposing states or coalitions preserve the balance of power.[4] More specifically, a bipolar system is distinguished by the presence of two actors whose power is so far superior to that of other states that they are called *superpowers*. Secondary powers and a host of lesser states may align themselves with these superpowers, but it is the interactions of the superpowers that are central. In such a bipolar system, conflict is unavoidable, for each superpower regards the other as an adversary—none of the other states can threaten their security. In short, in a two-pole structure *conflict is structurally determined*, and friend and foe are clearly distinguished. Last, and very critical, *bipolarity intensifies international conflict because each of the antagonists tends to see any gain of power and security for the other as a loss of power and security for itself and is determined to prevent this consequence.* Each feels such a high degree of insecurity that each may be said to be driven or compelled to react against the perceived potential threat from the other pole. The balance of power is continuously seen to be at stake. Each side fears that it will be upset, that the adversary will achieve hegemony, and that such hegemony will be irreversible—in short, that the game will be over. Both poles are thus hypersensitive to the slightest shifts of power. Even moves in areas not normally considered of vital interest to the other superpower will be opposed for symbolic and psychological reasons. Each superpower fears a *domino effect*: if one of its allies, friends, protégés, or satellites falls, others will follow and upset the equilibrium.

It is not then so much the single loss that is feared, for in itself it may not create a large deficit in the balance. What is feared instead is a series of small losses over a longer period, for together they could cause a sizable deficit. *When one power pushes, the other therefore feels compelled to push back.* Each constantly watches the other, and both are "trapped," in a real sense prisoners of the system. Neither can advance or retreat; positions must be held. Thus, *bipolar politics is the politics of confrontation.* When one side challenges the other at some spot, it is testing its adversary's will to maintain its own position. If the adversary reacts, a crisis results. Serious threats of violence are forthcoming, possibly even the use of limited violence, with all its inherent potential for escalation into total war. Such crises recur frequently. Furthermore, the possibility of a surprise attack by one side to eliminate the other can never be excluded. Indeed, a bipolar division of power places a premium on such an attack. If done successfully, it leaves one side the clear winner because the only threat to its security has been eliminated. The ancient Greek historian Thucydides, in describing why war had erupted between Athens and Sparta, explained bipolar war in general. The Spartans, he said, attacked Athens because of its growing power and the fear this caused in Sparta. The Spartans, therefore, launched a preventive war.[5]

Is a bipolar system that is both *simple* (because there are only two adversaries) and *rigid* (because most of the allies and friends of the two poles are tied to them and do not shift from one side to the other) stable or unstable? The answer seems clear from the basic rule for behavior in a bipolar structure: oppose any unilateral attempt by the adversary to upset the balance of power. If the opponent pushes, push back. The constant search for allies and friends, the attempts to undermine the opposing "camp" while preventing defections from one's own, the attendant arms race spurred by the constant fear that the opponent may achieve an irreversible power advantage—and end the game—mean frequent crises, occasional limited wars, and a mutually reinforcing fear. It is because of these characteristics that bipolar systems have usually been judged unstable systems. By definition, the two superpowers are far stronger than any of their allies or friends and therefore cannot be restrained by them.

MULTIPOLARITY (STABLE)

A *multipolar* system, according to most theorists, is composed of at least five approximately equal great powers.[6] Such a system is characterized by more restrained national behavior and is generally more conducive to preserving the peace because, compared with the *simple* and *rigid* bipolar division, multipolarity is *complex* and *flexible*. When the division is simple and the major actors are aligned on one side or the other, friend and foe are easy to determine; this division is rigid because no realignment is possible. But a multipolar structure does not by itself distinguish between friend and foe. Each pole views all other major actors as potential adversaries—and potential allies. *Among a larger number of great powers, each state has the mobility to align and realign itself.* Alliances are created as specific conflicts arise, and they usually last for only short periods, as the equilibrium shifts and alignments change. In contrast to bipolarity's confrontations and crises in which antagonisms are constantly reinforced, *the greater opportunity for shifting combinations under multipolarity reduces the risk of mutually reinforcing hostilities between various "players."* Allies of today may be tomorrow's adversaries—and allies again the day after. Since a state may need its present opponent as an ally in the future, hostilities cannot be allowed to become too intense. Individual states have changing relations with so many other states that inevitably their loyalties will cut across one another.[7] A member of one alliance will have interests in common, as well as in conflict, with those of its partners, but some interests are also likely to overlap with the interests of members in the opposing coalition. When the enemy of today may become the ally of tomorrow, it is a bit more difficult to become aroused about any specific state or cause.

In a particular dispute, for instance, it is claimed that the possibility that an ally may defect acts as a restraint on the other members of the alliance. The reason is that in a multipolar system, an alliance has the meaning that most people give that term: a collection of states, most of approximately equal power, who by joining together strengthen themselves in the face of a potential common enemy. The loss of one partner is therefore a serious matter because it weakens the alliance. If one member of a defensive alliance should try to persuade its associates to seek a change in the status quo, another member's threat of "dealignment" is likely to block that effort. For the alliance cannot afford such a loss. Because the state threatening to defect might move into a nonaligned position or even join the opposition, members of the alliance bring collective pressure to bear on the dissenter to moderate its aims. Restraint is thus built into multipolar alliances. Or if one alliance member should enhance its power by increasing its armed forces, a previously unaligned state may throw its weight onto the scales by joining the weaker side. Thus, in a multipolar structure, with its inherent flexibility, friends and foes are clearly more difficult to distinguish than in a bipolar structure. Moreover, because imbalances can be remedied a multipolar system is inherently more stable than a bipolar one. The contrast is striking. If one of the two superpowers in a bipolar system wishes to act in a manner not supported by its allies, they cannot inhibit it. Because of the enormous difference in power between the superpower and its allies, the threat of defection cannot work; defection will not appreciably reduce the superpower's power. In fact, the situation is quite the reverse: the far weaker allies need the superpower's protection more than the superpower needs their support. Bipolar alliances are not, therefore, restrained from within.

One additional argument has been advanced to explain the restraining and peace-preserving characteristics of multipolarity. The more numerous the actors, it has been claimed, the less attention any single actor can give to any other. This is beneficial because "the average share of available attention for any one conflict drops sharply as soon as there are more than three power centers in the system, and more gently after there are more than five such centers." More specifically, if a conflict requires at least 10 percent of a government's critical attention before armed conflict can result, then the "minimal attention ratio for an escalating conflict would have to be 1:9 since it does not seem likely that any country could be provoked very far into an escalating conflict with less than 10 percent of the foreign policy attention of its government devoted to the matter." [8] Whereas in a bipolar system the contestants watch each other unceasingly and are able to devote themselves fully to their quarrels, in a multipolar system, with as many as eleven approximately equal great powers, it is possible to avoid major conflicts. Thus, bipolar systems are said to be prone to crises and the eruption of war; multipolar systems, because of their flexibility, are more likely to maintain peace (see Table 6-1).

OR IS BIPOLARITY STABLE AND MULTIPOLARITY UNSTABLE?

The preceding evaluations of bipolarity and multipolarity have not gone unchallenged. Kenneth Waltz has argued persuasively that bipolarity is stable and multipolarity unstable. [9] His major reason for this conclusion is

Table 6-1 Two Types of Nonnuclear State System

	Bipolar System	*Multipolar System*
Number of powers	Two superior states	Many (usually cited as five to ten) approximately equal states
Nature of system	Simple and rigid	Complex and flexible
Principal characteristics	Unstable: confrontation, crisis, arms competition, preoccupation with adversary's preemptive or first-strike capability, search for allies	Stable: self-restraint and emphasis on negotiating major political differences
Alliance relationship	Cohesive	Rapidly changing

that in a bipolar system each state needs to watch only the other one and counter its moves. Both poles may have allies, but, because their allies have far less power, the two major actors need pay little attention to their wishes and complaints. The allies are so dependent on their poles' protection that, however disgruntled they may be with the bipolar system, they are unlikely to defect.

To be sure, a two-pole system means confrontation that can lead to crises. But such crises also suggest that the balance is being kept. War would be much more likely if one power did not respond to the other's challenge, for that would mean that the opponent had succeeded in enhancing its power. When power confronts power there may be danger, but when power confronts weakness the danger is far greater. Avoiding trouble when challenged does not mean that war has been prevented, only that it is very likely to come later.

Consistent with this logic, Waltz has argued that multipolarity is unstable. Multipolarity's flexibility does not make it stable because fluidity in relationships, with states shifting back and forth among alliances and counteralliances and nonalignment, renders every state's calculations uncertain. Will one's current allies defect? If so, when and under what circumstances? If one member of an alliance is determined to change the status quo, will other members of the alliance threaten to defect and, if necessary, do so to moderate this demand? Or will that power drag everyone with it into a dangerous situation that risks war because, in an alliance of equals, no state can afford to lose the assistance of the other members? Instead of moderating the arms race, will not the uncertainty of future relationships intensify the sense of insecurity of all states', thereby fueling the arms race? Was it not the multipolarity of 1914 that helped precipitate World War I because Austria-Hungary was determined to squash Serbia in the Balkans, and Germany, unwilling to lose Austria-Hungary as an ally, was pulled into the war (admittedly, not at all reluctantly)? When czarist Russia opposed Austria-Hungary, did France, unable to face Germany alone, have any choice but to support its Russian ally? In short, neither Germany nor France felt they could defect, thereby restraining their respective partners.[10] It was the weakest member of each alliance that dragged its stronger partner into what was to escalate into a European-wide war: by pulling in Germany and France, Austria-Hungary and Russia made it impossible to confine the hostilities to the Balkans. Ironically, after the war some German leaders claimed that they would not have gone to war had they known that Britain—which did not have alliances with France and Russia, only ententes—would come into the war (that is, had the system possessed the clarity of a bipolar system).

Are the conventional wisdoms about multipolarity and the stability of the state system and bipolarity and instability then correct or not? Presumably, these causal relationships would not have become conventional wisdoms unless there were a good deal of evidence to support them. Or is Waltz correct? The immediate impression is that he is. Forty-five years have passed since World War II. The peace, if it can be called that, has already lasted twice as long as the period from the end of World War I (1918) to the beginning of World War II (1939). The absence of another world war certainly suggests that the system has been stable. A quick look at the cold war may reveal what structural reasons if any, there may be for that stability.

BIPOLAR STRUCTURE AND THE COLD WAR

Action and Reaction

The bipolar balance is one of challenge and response and therefore virtually maintains itself.[11] Bipolar politics is a zero-sum game—that is, any gain for one is a loss for the other. Thus, the pattern of the cold war was one in which one power sought to improve its position and expand its influence and the other reacted.[12] When after World War II the Soviets sought to turn Iran into a satellite, the United States and Britain countered the effort. And when the Soviets later put pressure on Turkey, Britain initially lent that country its support as well. In the winter of 1946-1947, Britain however, collapsed from the exhaustion of two world wars, leaving the United States to take over Britain's role and become Moscow's chief adversary. The symbol of America's new role was the 1947 Truman Doctrine in which the president committed the nation to the political independence and territorial integrity of both Turkey and Greece. In the civil war in Greece, the Communists received support from Communist Yugoslavia and Bulgaria.

From the eastern Mediterranean, the United States shifted to Western Europe, where both the victors and vanquished were in a state of utter economic and psychological collapse. Fear of the Red Army and of the powerful Communist-led unions in France and Italy loyal to Moscow led in 1948 to the Marshall Plan, a four-year economic aid plan for the economic revival of Western Europe, named after Secretary of State George C. Marshall. Soviet pressure on West Berlin, the western half of Germany's former capital which lay surrounded by Soviet-occupied East Germany, was met by an airlift to feed the city. The Soviets were attempting to force out the Western allies, there by right of occupation, and collapse the morale of West Germany, whose economic recovery was essential to the recovery of all of Western Europe. But European uncertainty about American protection while Europe sought to rebuild itself economically and politically prompted the United States for the first time in its history to commit itself in peacetime to an alliance, the North Atlantic Treaty Organization, to safeguard Western Europe's security. Greece and Turkey were later incorporated into the alliance (1952), as was West Germany (1955). The Soviet Union, which already controlled Eastern Europe, formalized that control in the Warsaw Treaty Organization, shortly after the Western allies admitted West Germany into their alliance. By 1950, Europe's split into two opposing camps was readily apparent.

No sooner had the European situation stabilized than Nationalist China collapsed in Asia as the remnants of the Nationalist Chinese government fled to the island of Taiwan, one hundred miles off the Chinese coast. The United States was now intent on balancing this loss with Japan. Just as in Europe, where West Germany, the former enemy, was to become an ally while the Soviet Union, the former ally, became the United States' chief adversary; in Asia, Japan, the recent enemy, became a desirable ally as Nationalist China, an ally in World War II, became Communist China. Japan signed a mutual security treaty with the United States in 1951. The desire to attract Japan was a key reason why in June 1950 the United States engaged in its first "limited war" when Communist North Korea invaded South Korea, whose security was intimately linked to that of Japan. When U.S. forces advanced into North Korea, however, Communist China intervened to prevent the elimination of North Korea and protect its own security. The war ended in 1953 back at the thirty-eighth parallel, and to guarantee South Korea against another possible attack, the United States signed an alliance with South Korea the same year.

This pattern of action and reaction continued through the 1950s. Once Korea was over, the United States reacted to the Sino-Soviet alliance of 1950 by seeking to encircle it with additional alliances. In the Middle East, on the Soviet Union's southern border, the United States sponsored the British-led Middle East Treaty Organization (METO). (By staying formally out, the

United States hoped that Egypt would be attracted to the West despite its conflict with Israel.) And in southeast Asia, the United States organized the Southeast Asia Treaty Organization (SEATO) to defend South Vietnam after the French defeat in Indochina in 1954. Neither alliance had much support among the countries in these areas and, unlike NATO, were not worth the paper they were written on. In reaction, Egypt and the Soviet Union, both opposed to METO for their own reasons, joined together in an alliance in all but name, leapfrogging and rendering the Western alliance useless. SEATO's main claim to fame was that it dragged the United States into the defense of South Vietnam in 1965 and a losing war, whose principal result— besides loss of life and money and the fall of South Vietnam in 1975—was a weakening of the anti-Communist public consensus in the United States which for two decades had supported the government's international role.

Indeed, Soviet actions revived U.S. policy and led to the further expansion of U.S. commitments. Soviet-Cuban expansionist efforts in Angola in 1975 and in Ethiopia in 1977 and the Soviet invasion of Afghanistan in 1979 resulted in the Carter Doctrine to protect the vital oil sheikdoms of the Persian Gulf. President Reagan expanded this commitment to the survival of the Saudi royal family, Saudi Arabia being the non-Communist world's largest oil producer. In 1987, in part reacting to the fear of an expanded Soviet role in the Persian Gulf, Reagan sent the U.S. Navy to protect U.S.-reflagged Kuwaiti oil tankers, which were being attacked by Iran because Kuwait was a virtual ally of Iraq with whom Iran was at war.

Central America also became involved in the superpower rivalry. Prior to 1979, the United States had intervened intermittently in Latin America to overthrow governments it believed were aligning with the Soviet Union such as Guatemala in 1954, Cuba in 1961 (an unsuccessful operation), and the Dominican Republic in 1965. But, on the whole, the hemisphere to the south suffered from inattention and neglect. America's attention and resources were focused elsewhere: Europe, Asia, and the Middle East. The main thing it wanted in Latin America was peace and quiet. Such "stability" was assured largely by supporting right-wing, often military, regimes. But the collapse of one of these pro-American governments in Nicaragua, stemming from a popular revolution, the consolidation of power by the Marxist Sandinistas after they had displaced their more moderate and democratic allies who had helped them make the revolution, and the prospects of a "second Cuba" in this hemisphere—and the first on the mainland—led the Carter and then the Reagan administration to oppose the Sandinistas. Indeed, Reagan wanted to overthrow the regime, which he claimed also supported the Marxist guerrillas in neighboring El Salvador where the United States supported the government. Regional conflicts and civil wars in the Third World were rarely seen in either Washington or Moscow as having indigenous roots, unrelated to the superpower competition. Consequently, their bipolar competition more often than not was superimposed upon these regional and domestic rivalries in the ex-colonial and underdeveloped areas of the world.

In summary, in the bipolar structure characterizing the cold war both powers watched each other constantly. In a multipolar world, their attention would have been diffused. Alliance partners would have to pay as much, if not more, attention to one another in efforts to hold the alliance together as to the opposing alliance. Thus, it was easier in a bipolar system to ensure that the balance was being kept. A principal means of doing so was alliance formation.

Role of Alliances

Alliances in a bipolar division serve different purposes than those in a multipolar system.[13] In the latter, composed of a half dozen or more powers of approximately equal strength, the chief purpose of the alliance is to add the power of other states to one's own. Mutual obligations of defense are critical; defections would weaken the alliance against the adversary. Continuous attention is therefore directed inward to holding the alliance together.

Alliances in a bipolar structure, by contrast, first draw lines or frontiers around areas considered vital. By incorporating such areas in alliances, each superpower is drawing attention to their importance and warning the opponent not to invade them if it wishes to avoid war. Not all of the United States' alliances, however, have been of equal importance; nor have all survived. METO died the year it was born, although officially it was not interred until after the Iranian revolution of 1979 toppled the pro-American shah. SEATO was buried quietly after the Vietnam War. America's non-European anti-Communist alliances fell victim to the powerful forces of nationalism and social revolution. Even the Latin-American Rio Pact, a symbol of America's former hegemony in the Western Hemisphere, has lost any operational significance as nationalism in Latin America has shrunk American influence. Similarly, the Soviet alliance with China ended as the two became enemies. Nevertheless, in Europe, *the area of the two superpowers' principal interests and of direct U.S.-Soviet confrontation,* the alliances survived. It was clear to each one which area the other considered to be a vital sphere of influence, against which an intervention would run the very great risk of war. NATO and WTO proved to be significant means of communicating to the opponent which area the other intended to protect even if it meant going to war. The result has been forty years of peace, Europe's longest in this century.

Outside of Europe, the interests at stake, while important, were secondary and the lines less clear. The Cairo-Moscow axis negated METO, and SEATO drew a line through Vietnam—one that Washington, and apparently Beijing and Moscow as well, regarded as part of the line running around the then Sino-Soviet bloc—but that North Vietnam's leader, Ho Chi Minh, did not. As a nationalist, not just a Communist, he believed that he and his party were the legitimate heirs to French colonial rule. Thus, the civil war resumed, with the United States defending South Vietnam because it regarded the area as much a part of its sphere of influence as South Korea and West Germany.

At least as important as line-drawing in a bipolar division is the power differential between each superpower and its allies. Each superpower is the producer of security; its partners are the consumers of that security. Thus, an alliance, within the bipolar structure, with its unequal internal power distribution, is in effect a unilateral guarantee extended by the superpower to its allies, which are really its protectorates. This implies that the United States and Soviet Union needed only keep their eyes mainly on each other and make policy accordingly, instead of becoming absorbed with holding their respective alliances together and making policy responsive to their allies' interests. On the one hand, such an arrangement allowed the two adversaries to concentrate fully on the management of crises when they occurred so that war could be avoided; this is particularly important in this nuclear era. On the other hand, if their allies acted in ways that might draw them into a dangerous confrontation, the superpowers could restrain their partners. In an alliance in which each superpower is so much stronger than its allies, who are in effect its dependents, the latter are in no position to exercise much restraint upon the superpower. But the superpower can compel them to restrain themselves. Thus, once the United States decided to oppose the installation of Soviet missiles in Cuba in 1962, its NATO partners could do little but give the United States verbal support while praying that a nuclear clash would not result. They could have protested, but it would not have done much good. Conversely, when Britain and France attacked Egypt in 1956, or the Nationalist Chinese wanted to attempt an invasion of the mainland in the 1950s, U.S. opposition stopped both. But no one defected; neither Britain and France nor Nationalist China had anywhere to go. Similarly, in 1958 when Communist China wished to invade Taiwan, unite China, and destroy its Nationalist rival, the Soviet Union, unwilling to risk war with the United States, refused to support Beijing. This caused friction, however, and eventually proved to be the key exception to the rule that alliances within the bipolar division are rigid, not flexible.

While in the key area of Europe the cold war alliances held, there were exceptions in the Third World. The major exception to bipolarity's simplicity and rigidity was the People's Republic of China. It was one thing to prevent the defection of a Hungary or a Guatemala, but China's defection could not have been prevented without a major and costly intervention whose outcome was uncertain. China, in fact, switched sides twice—once from the United States to the Soviet Union and then back again. It was far more normal for Third World states, wooed by the two superpowers to shift from one to the other. While most remained nonaligned during the cold war, some did align themselves but eventually switched allegiances—for example, Egypt, Ethiopia, Indonesia, and Somalia.

While, as noted, bipolarity accentuates what has been called the zero-sum character of international politics and the self-feeding growth of mutual distrust and fear, these reversals in alignments have tended to dampen the adversary relationship. One need but recall that before the Sino-Soviet alliance in 1950, U.S. foreign policy was strictly anti-Soviet, limited to responding to Soviet expansionist moves. After 1950 the United States launched an anti-Communist crusade. Fearful of facing the two largest Communist states together, it forgot to make critical distinctions between primary and secondary opponents or between areas of vital and lesser interest. Erroneously assuming a monolithic Communist bloc, the United States overreacted, especially in Vietnam, where it assumed that the North Vietnamese were Chinese puppets who, if allowed to conquer South Vietnam, would enhance both Chinese and Soviet power. Thus, the United States intervened militarily to prevent a shift in the regional and central U.S.-Soviet balance. Since the Sino-American reconciliation, the United States has reverted to an anti-Soviet policy, which, despite occasional rhetorical excesses, has, on the whole, been restrained.

One reason that Moscow sought a détente in the 1970s was to slow Sino-American reconciliation. It also warned against too close a relationship and the shipment of U.S. arms to China. Although Secretary of State Alexander Haig once referred to China as NATO's sixteenth member, the United States does sell China nonlethal military equipment, and Chinese ties to the United States are not likely to be reversed again in the future, the United States has not been anxious to provoke the Soviets by signing a military alliance with China (unlikely anyway while Washington continues to support the Nationalists on Taiwan). Moreover, in the 1980s, China, to enhance its influence, took advantage of its pivotal position between the United States and the Soviet Union to move toward a more equidistant position between the two as Gorbachev made efforts to eliminate past differences.

The effect, on the whole, has been beneficial. Indeed, one analyst has talked of the "salutory role of the smaller powers" in bipolar systems:

> If one of these, say Ethiopia, decides to draw closer to the Eastern bloc, another Somalia, can approach the West. . . . Chile can cease being governed by a Marxist party while South Vietnam moves steadily towards incorporation with communist North Vietnam. None of these are zero sum conflicts, *for each side gains something in the end.* More generally, with the rise of the new nations in the postwar era, both superpowers sought to gain new adherents with simultaneous gains for both, principally in the Middle East, Asia and Africa. Without the existence of these smaller powers, *it is possible that a more direct confrontation could have occurred.*[14]

Thus, despite the fear in a bipolar system that any loss of even a small country may lead to further losses, and that such a "domino effect" may result in a major shift of power affecting one or the other of the superpowers, this analysis suggests that this concern has been exaggerated. The foundations of their respective power will not erode as they "exchange" countries such as Ethiopia for Egypt, or if one suffers the loss of a country such as Iran but the other does not pick it up as a gain, or worse, it does "add" it but the burden becomes a drain on its resources. Thus, Moscow did not, as it had in Cuba whose shift from the United States to the Soviet Union in 1960 was a plus for the latter, provide large-scale economic aid for Chile in the 1970s or Nicaragua in the 1980s; the Soviets provided the latter mainly with military equipment which it had in abundance. In Afghanistan the drain was so great that after eight years of fighting, Moscow withdrew.

Intrabloc Divisions and Interbloc Links

This dampening effect of bipolarity's zero-sum characteristic has been strengthened by two other occurrences. The first is the increased "loosening" of both WTO and NATO. Despite past Soviet interventions, the countries of Eastern Europe can hardly be called satellites as they once were. Moscow repeatedly demonstrated until 1989 that it would not tolerate the loss of Communist party control, nor power-sharing arrangements, nor withdrawal from WTO. But within these broad parameters, the reemerging nationalism in Eastern Europe has meant that governments must be responsive to popular sentiment to a degree. The pattern ranges considerably from Romania, which is domestically orthodox but has taken independent positions on foreign policy (for example, good relations with China when Sino-Soviet relations were bitter, opposition to Soviet intervention in Poland in the early 1980s, a friendly attitude toward Israel, and a refusal to participate in WTO military exercises), to Hungary, which has been loyal to Moscow on foreign policy while liberalizing at home (for example, dismantling collective farms and permitting a degree of entrepreneurship). Most East European countries have improved their relationship with the West and especially seek a closer relationship with Western Europe. In the past, one reason for the large number of Soviet troops in Eastern Europe was to ensure the security of the area, but there was always a question of how loyal the Eastern European forces would be and how well they would fight in a war with NATO. This question is even more pertinent now that Poland in 1989 organized its first non-Communist-led coalition government (in which the Communist party retains control of the police and military, however). Will other East European governments follow the Polish example of non-Communist regimes in power with the Communist party mainly in opposition (although the bureaucracy remains in Communist hands)? Will Moscow accept them as long as they call themselves socialist, leave the police and military in Communist control, and swear to remain in WTO even as its bonds of unity erode? What happens if a non-Communist government is unwilling to accept any or all of these conditions?

The Western alliance, NATO, has also witnessed more frequent internal disagreements, particularly between Europe and the United States.[15] The reasons are multiple: differences in attitudes toward the Soviet Union with the West Europeans more inclined toward détente than hard-line policies; fear, on the one hand, of being entrapped in war stemming from what are often seen as unwise American policies in the Third World; and concern, on the other hand, about being abandoned by the United States as the American security guarantee has grown less credible with the emergence of strategic parity and the pressure to reduce the huge U.S. budget deficit; questions about the quality of U.S. presidential leadership, and whether U.S. priorities are shifting from Europe to Asia; and the economic rivalry between the two parts of the alliance. These differences mean that the united front that NATO often showed toward the Soviet Union during the earlier cold war is no longer as cohesive. Indeed, as the United States criticism of Europeans has grown, ranging from unfair trade practices, to the "softer" policies toward Moscow, to the more basic issue of why the allies with a larger population and gross national product than the Soviet Union still rely so heavily on the United States for protection against a country that also has to worry about China as a possible enemy to its back.

While intra-alliance differences have presumably placed some restraints upon U.S. and Soviet policies—especially in the Western alliance composed of democratic states—the two alliance leaders have also dampened their zero-sum relationship by complementing its adversarial character with coopera-tion. The resulting "adversary partnership" has had its ups and downs, the conflictual nature of the relationship sometimes coming to the fore, the cooperative nature at other times, usually referred to as periods of détente. Arms control has been the central issue in this adversary partnership because both powers want to avoid a nuclear war; both also have an interest in preventing, or at least slowing down, nuclear proliferation. In addition, since the 1970s the Soviets have shown an increasing interest in trade, from wheat to high technology, and the United States, with its bountiful harvests, has been keen to increase agricultural exports but is more cautious on technology and machinery. And efforts to resolve regional problems—such as those in Afghanistan (where the Soviets withdrew in 1989), Angola and Cambodia, also brought nearer to solutions in 1989—have diminished the American-Soviet rivalry. With both superpowers facing growing economic domestic problems, the 1990s and perhaps beyond may well be another period of détente, although not necessarily a complete end to their rivalry.

For all the simplicity of the bipolar structure and its characteristic action-reaction pattern, the ability to clearly define areas of vital interest, the duration of key alliances, the hierarchical structure of its alliances, and the role that Third World states play, we will never completely know whether Waltz is right in claiming that bipolar structures are more stable. There is much to be said for the traditional position that bipolarity is an unstable distribution of power. The zero-sum nature of a two-power conflict, of contin-ual challenge and response, and of each pole seeing even defensive moves as offensive, creates tension, mutual suspicion, and fear, and intensifies feelings of hostility. Ever wary of shifts in the balance and always alert to the possibility of a first strike by the opponent (or the need to beat the latter to the punch), both powers must think not only of the risks and costs of such an initial blow but also of the risks and costs of *not* doing so.

Yet we do know that in the specific circumstances of a divided postwar Western Europe, bipolarity produced a high degree of order and predictabil-ity in spite of the risks created by a series of Berlin crises. And, more broadly, bipolarity kept the peace. As the cold war abates in the 1990s, as both NATO and WTO erode further (especially the latter, as Poland, Hungary, and other members try to shed Soviet-imposed socialism), and as the issue of German reunification surfaces once more, there is in fact great uncertainty. Thus, while the prospective conclusion of the cold war is welcome, the end of the old bipolarity is accompanied by concern about changes whose consequences are unknown, but not all of which may be benign and peaceful.

What makes Waltz's conclusion persuasive is the post-World War II presence of nuclear weapons and the possibility that stability may be principally related to the number of major *nuclear* actors. If a major nuclear actor is defined as a power capable of destroying its opponent's society, Waltz's conclusion is acceptable, but with a major difference: *nuclear bipolarity will be a stable system; nuclear multipolarity will be an unstable system.*

Nuclear bipolarity is more stable for two reasons. First, unlike war during the prenuclear age, war among nuclear powers now includes the very real possibility that those who fight it will be committing suicide. Second, because the confrontation is between only two powers and they watch only each other, they learn about each other's behavior patterns. Long acquaintanceship results in their becoming more familiar with each other's ways of "crisis management"; there is definitely an upward learning curve. Not that major mistakes and misassessments cannot occur; but fewer miscalculations are likely between two warriors who have faced each other before.[16]

Conversely, nuclear multipolarity will be unstable, and nuclear proliferation, therefore, must be prevented or slowed down to keep the number of nuclear powers at a minimum (generally agreed to be the United States, Soviet Union, Britain, France, Communist China, and India, as well as possibly three or four more undeclared states). The reason for this conclusion is also twofold. First, in a multipolar system the larger number of states means that conflicts among them are likely to be far more numerous than if there were only two powers. Second, the greater the number of conflicts, the greater the chance that at least one conflict will erupt into war. The fewer fingers on the nuclear trigger, the better, sums up this position.

For Review

1. What are some of the principal distributions of power in the state system?
2. How do these different systemic structures affect state behavior?
3. Which state-system structure is the most stable or least likely to erupt into a major war?
4. How can one use concepts like "bipolarity" and "multipolarity" to explain the actual conduct of states in the real world, as in the cold war?
5. What is the role of alliances in bipolar and multipolar systems?

Notes

1. Joseph L. Nogee, "Polarity: An Ambiguous Concept," *Orbis,* Winter 1975, 1211-1212.

2. George Modelski, "The Long Cycle of Global Politics and the Nation-State," *Comparative Studies in Society and History* (April 1978): 214-235; Modelski, ed., *Long Cycles in World Politics* (Seattle: University of Washington Press, 1986); William R. Thompson, "Polarity, the Long Cycle, and Global Warfare," *International Studies Quarterly* (December 1986): 587-615; and Thompson, *On Global War* (Columbia: University of South Carolina Press, 1988). A summary of past works may be found in Joshua Goldstein, *Long Cycles* (New Haven, Conn.: Yale University Press, 1988), 21-147.

3. George Modelski, ed., *Exploring Long Cycles* (Boulder, Colo.: Lynne Rienner, 1987), 1-15, 218-248. A critique of this theory may be found in Richard Rosencrance, "Long Cycle Theory and International Relations," *International Organization* (Spring 1987): 297-301.

4. There is considerable disagreement about the dangers and virtues of bipolarity. On the dangers, see Hans Morgenthau, *Politics among Nations,* 5th ed. (New York: Knopf, 1972), 346-347; and on the virtues, see Kenneth H. Waltz, "The Stability of a Bipolar World," *Daedalus,* Summer 1964, 881-909; Waltz, "International Structure, National Force, and the Balance of World Power," *Journal of International Affairs* 21 (June 1967): 215-231; and Waltz, *Theory of International Politics* (Reading, Mass.: Addison-Wesley, 1979), 163-176. For a comparative study of the bipolar struggle between Athens and Sparta, see Peter J. Fliess, *Thucydides and the Politics of Bipolarity* (Baton Rouge: Louisiana State University Press, 1966). My own analysis throughout this chapter is heavily indebted to Glen H. Snyder and Paul Diesing, *Conflict Among Nations* (Princeton, N.J.: Princeton University Press, 1977), 419-450.

5. Thucydides, *History of the Peloponnesian War* (New York: Oxford University Press, 1960), 46.

6. Morton Kaplan, *System and Process in International Politics* (New York: Wiley, 1957).

7. Karl W. Deutsch and J. David Singer, "Multipolar Power Systems and International Stability," *World Politics,* April 1964, 392-396.

8. Ibid., 396-400.

9. Waltz, "The Stability of a Bipolar World," 163-170.

10. Snyder and Diesing, *Conflict Among Nations,* 441.

11. On the general phenomenon of alliance balancing and security cooperation, see Stephen M. Walt, *The Origins of Alliances* (Ithaca, N.Y.: Cornell University Press, 1987).

12. For broad analyses of the beginning of the cold war and American foreign policy during the cold war period, see Louis J. Halle, *The Cold War as History* (New York: Harper & Row, 1967); John Spanier, *American Foreign Policy Since World War II,* 11th ed. (Washington D.C.: CQ Press, 1988); and Joseph L. Nogee and John Spanier, *Peace Impossible—War Unlikely* (Boston: Scott/Foresman, 1988).

13. Snyder and Diesing, *Conflict Among Nations,* 419-429.

14. Manus I. Midlarsky, *The Disintegration of Political Systems* (Columbia: University of South Carolina Press, 1986), 118ff.; and Midlarsky, *The Onset of World War* (Boston: Unwin Hyman, 1988), 28-29.

15. Josef Joffe, "Europe's American Pacifier," *Foreign Policy,* Spring 1984, 64-82 (emphasis added); and Joffe, *The Limited Partnership* (Cambridge, Mass.: Ballinger,

1987).

16. John Lewis Gaddis, "The Long Peace; Elements of Stability in the Postwar International System," *International Security* (Spring 1986): 99-142.

The Ability to Play: Power and the Rise and Fall of Nations

PERCEPTION OF POWER

Power, great power, superpower, balance of power—these terms have been used here repeatedly, but at no point has the nature of power been described. In one sense, there hardly seems reason to do so, for *power* is a term with which most people are familiar; it seems so obvious what power is. Everyone knows that some nations are more powerful than others and that international politics generally has been the story of the games played by the stronger members of the state system.[1] Such adjectives as *more powerful* and *stronger*, usually refer to military capacity. No one thinks of Belgium or Burma as powers; their military strength, by either conventional or nuclear standards, is puny. The label *power* historically has been awarded to those states that have won significant military victories. Without a demonstration, a state's power is undetermined, but military victory confers a reputation for power or prestige. Conversely, a military defeat jeopardizes a nation's reputation for power. There may not even have to be a defeat; the mere fact that a great power is unable to win a conflict with a lesser power hurts its prestige. Perhaps the great power should not have indulged in such a conflict in the first place, but, once it has done so, its ability to exercise power effectively is one of the issues at stake.

There are, of course, variations on this theme of victory and defeat. During the 1960s, when all-out war was no longer viewed as a true test of a nation's power, the "space race" replaced the test of battle. The launch of the first manned Soviet satellite to orbit the earth in April of President John Kennedy's first year in office convinced him that a second-rate effort was not consistent with his country's role as a world leader and a great power, whose reputation was based largely on its industrial-technological capabilities. Prowess in space had come to symbolize power. Kennedy immediately ordered a review of various space projects in which the United States could surpass the Soviet Union.[2] The most promising was the landing of a man on the moon, and in May 1961 the president announced that this objective would be achieved before the end of the decade. Indeed, in July 1969 the first men stood on the moon, and, although they talked of having come on behalf of all "mankind," their shoulder patches read *U.S.A.*

Three points about power are very important. The first, generally shared by many citizens and policy makers, is that *power is identified with military capacity*, regardless of whether the estimate of that capacity is based on power overtly applied, peacefully demonstrated (as in parades, maneuvers, and space shots), or held in check during bargaining. When books are written on power, they bear such titles as *The War Potential of Nations*.[3] Because war has been the *ultima ratio* of power in interstate politics, the emphasis on military strength is hardly surprising. The Prussian general Carl von Clausewitz's classic definition of war is the continuation of political relations by other means. Turning this phrase around, peace may be called the continuation of the last war by other means. Earlier it was suggested that the state system, unlike most modern domestic political systems in the West, is characterized by a condition of potential warfare. Each state's continuing concern with its military power thus has been very understandable. Today it is that military power, because of its enormous destructive ability, that must be controlled and managed most. To be sure, there are other ways of exercising power, especially by economic means. But coercion and the use of violence to achieve state ends in a system of politics without government has long substituted for governmental allocation of values.

The second point is that *power is what people think it is.* A distinction thus must be drawn between subjective (perceived) power and objective (actual) power. If power is in the eyes of the beholder, simple calculation of a nation's power is insufficient. If one country believes it is strong enough to deter an enemy, but the latter perceives it otherwise, it may still go to war. Thus, policy makers must concern themselves not only with what the actual balance of power is, but also with how that balance is seen in other capitals. This is a difficult task because access to another state's assessments are not usually available; therefore the best that one can do is guess. Nevertheless, it is a task that must be done.

The third point is that *a reputation for power will confer power*, whether others' estimates of a nation's power are correct or not. If a nation or its leadership has prestige, it is less likely to be challenged; if its prestige is declining, challenges are likely, not only from powers of equal strength but also from less powerful states. These challengers will think that they can defy that nation's policies with impunity. After Britain's appeasement of Adolf Hitler at Munich in 1938 over the issue of the Sudetenland, Benito Mussolini, Italy's dictator, said: "These men [the British leaders] are not made of the same stuff as Francis Drake and the other magnificent adventurers who created the Empire. They are after all the tired sons of a long line of rich men." [4] Shortly afterward, Hitler seized the rest of Czechoslovakia and began to look hungrily at Poland.

POWER: CARROTS AND STICKS

Power thus may often be identified with military power and may exist only in the mind. But what is power? Probably the most common definition is the capacity to influence the behavior of other states in accordance with one's own objectives. Implicit in this definition is the understanding that, without the exercise of power, other states will not accede to demands made upon them. Power, then, is several things. It is something that a state has; the exact quantity depends on measurement of each of the various components of power (as seen later in this chapter). It is also a means of achieving a state's various ends, or goals. Finally, and most important, power is a relationship. China may be strong relative to India or Pakistan, but it is weak compared to the United States and the Soviet Union. What matters is not a nation's absolute power but its relative power.

It has been argued that power relationships exist when four factors are present. [5] First, *there must be a conflict of values or interests.* If states A and B agree on objectives, B consents freely to A's demands or proposed course of action. Power is not used. One state may be stronger than the other, but, as there is agreement on what to do, power remains latent. Even when there are relatively small differences among states, as perceived by the parties to a dispute, persuasion is very likely all that is necessary to resolve the differences. There is an appeal to common interests, principles, and values; there may be attempts to introduce facts new to one party or interpretations of the situation that have not yet been considered; and the consequences of different courses of action may be pointed out.

Second, for a power relationship to exist, state *B must comply, however unwillingly, with state A's demands.* Compliance is necessary because, though the two states may have a conflict of interest, B may simply stand its ground and not offer any concessions. Then A must either give up its demands or resort to force.

Third, in a power relationship *one of the parties must invoke sanctions that the other regards as likely to inflict "severe deprivation" or pain upon itself.* The cost for state B of not accepting state A's demands must be greater than the cost of compliance. B must believe that A's threat of sanctions is credible and not a bluff—that is, that A has both the power or capability, as well as the will, to apply military or economic sanctions. Indeed, and especially between stronger and weaker states, B's knowledge that A possesses both the power and the will often suffices; an actual verbalization of a threat should not even be necessary.

This emphasis on sanctions is not meant to imply neglect of promises of *rewards* that A may offer B to promote resolution of their differences. When these differences are too large to be settled by persuasion but not of such magnitude that sanctions must be invoked, holding out rewards and granting them if B complies may be the most effective way to exercise power. A reward might take the form of economic aid, lowered tariff barriers, the sale of high-technology products, or simply the nonuse of force. But a conflict involving deep disagreement may lead one party to invoke first the threat of sanctions against the other, and in the case of noncompliance, to apply them. There are a wide variety of ways to punish or coerce an adversary: reduce imports, impose embargoes, raise prices, withhold arms (in peace or war), break off diplomatic relations, threaten the use of force, mobilize military forces. U.S.-Soviet relations during much of the cold war included little economic intercourse, but they were characterized by the very visible presence of the military and frequent threats of its deployment.

Fourth, when differences between states cannot be resolved peacefully, *force may be used.* If state B complies when state A exercises coercion, the use of force is, of course, unnecessary; A resorts to force only if state B does not comply with A's demands. But the use of force does not guarantee the attainment of A's objectives. American intervention in Vietnam did not prevent the loss of South Vietnam. *Thus, the use of force may at times result in the loss of one's reputation for power* (see Chapter 13). If the sanctions, once applied, do not inflict as severe a deprivation as A's threat had implied, B's future compliance with A's demands is even less likely. Other states also may not comply with A's demands. Thus, the likelihood that the unsuccessful use of force will be very costly to a nation's prestige, means that state A should exercise extra caution in its use. (War is always a risky enterprise, despite the most careful power calculation. Murphy's Law that "if things can go wrong, they will" is especially applicable in wartime when states with smaller armies have beaten those with larger armies.)

The same caution applies to use of economic coercion. To use economic pressure on a country, as the United States did on Panama in 1988 to get rid of its military chief General Manuel Noriega, who in effect ran the country, and to fail was not only humiliating but also a sign of impotency. Such an event encourages other states, including small ones, not to comply with U.S. demands but to defy them. The general rule is—or ought to be—that it is better not to invoke sanctions than use power, whether it is military or economic, ineffectively.

The different degrees of disagreement that lead states to use persuasion, rewards, coercion, and force depend on the parties involved, their demands, their disinclination to comply, and their perceptions of the stakes. Furthermore, these methods of exercising influence may in practice be mixed. If persuasion cannot quite resolve differences, rewards may be held out. Rewards may be enticing, but hints of threats for noncompliance also are useful. A threat may well be more effective if the belief is strong that force will be forthcoming unless agreement is reached. Combinations of carrots *and* sticks may be more useful in resolving differences than either carrots *or* sticks. Carrying a "big stick" but "speaking softly" may be more fruitful than swinging the stick. Finally, coercion and force are more likely to be used against adversaries than against friendly states, but rewards may also accompany such threats if the adversary complies with the demands.

CALCULATING POWER

Most readers have an idea of the principal components of power. They probably would include: geography, population, natural resources, economic capacity, military strength, political systems and leadership, and national morale. Several points must be made, however, before taking a brief look at each of these elements. First, any calculation of a nation's power and the power balance must include a mix of *tangible components* such as population, uniformed personnel, and tanks and missiles, and *intangible components* such as morale, efficiency and effectiveness of political systems, and quality of political leadership. The intangible components do not lend themselves to accurate calculations; they are matters of judgment.

Second, when doing such calculations, one must always remain aware of the distinction between *potential power* and *actual capability*—that is, power that has been mobilized. Except for periods of total war, states do not completely transform their economies into war economies or maximize their military strength. There is always a gap between potential and actual power.

Third, an accurate assessment of even the tangible elements is not at all easy. Population figures for different states, for example, can be readily compared, and the rule of thumb "the bigger, the better" tends to be true for the more powerful states such as the United States and the Soviet Union. Sometimes, however a large population is a liability rather than an asset. In India, for example, its huge population is making economic development difficult. Progress is eaten up by the need to feed, clothe, and educate millions of new people.

For all countries, other factors also must be taken into account: age distribution, educational and skill patterns, and ethnic composition, for example. Any one of these factors can complicate the calculation of a single component. For countries deeply divided by various nationalities, religions, and races, a "subtraction" from the calculation may be necessary because in a crisis or war such states may demonstrate low morale or even disintegrate. The developing countries are particularly subject to political fragmentation because of such problems.

Fourth, calculations of any single component of power make sense only when linked with those of other components. Large populations can ensure great-power status only when an industrialized economy is present as well;

the marriage of these two elements constitutes power. The power rating is certain to be low in a nation characterized by poverty, a largely agrarian and unskilled population, a high birthrate, and great difficulties in urbanizing and industrializing.

Finally, the balance of power is dynamic, not static. Because various components are always changing, the balance needs frequent recalculation. This makes it particularly difficult to project into the future. Policy makers are obviously concerned about the current balance, but they must also look at the balance five or ten years in the future to be prepared for new relationships with other states, especially adversaries.

Geography

The location and physical size of a nation are clearly very important. The United States and Britain have long been protected from invasion by bodies of water too wide for their enemies to cross easily. The United States was even able to isolate itself from the international political system for more than a century. Similarly, such states as Italy and Spain have been well protected by high mountain ranges—the Alps and the Pyrenees, respectively. Indeed, little of Western Europe's modern culture seems to have crossed the Pyrenees until late in the twentieth century! But little Belgium, not well protected and lying between great powers, was not so fortunate during the two world wars. Switzerland, by contrast, also lying between great powers but very well protected, has remained untouched. The countries on the axis from France to the Soviet Union all lie on a plain. The Rhine River, separating Germany and France, was of little help, however, in halting repeated German invasions of France. Russia historically has had no natural protection at all and has been invaded repeatedly from the west. But the same lack of barriers that permitted invasions also allowed Russian expansion into Western Europe, the Middle East, and northern Asia. While Russia has suffered defeats, invaders have found it difficult to conquer because it has used its vast interior space to neutralize invasions. By drawing the enemy—such as Napoleon or Hitler—in, the Russians have forced invaders to exhaust themselves trying to conquer such a vast territory, maintain long supply lines, control a large and hostile population, and survive the severe winter weather.

Note the correlation between the world's leading democracies and geographic protection: the United States, Britain, and the northern Scandinavian countries lie off the axis of repeated invasions. The states lying on the axis—France, Prussia/Germany, and Russia/Soviet Union—know war well, and not surprisingly they have developed large bureaucracies and standing armies to guard themselves. For these countries, notions of individual freedom, rights of opposition, and criticism, were luxuries that were subordinated to security and physical survival. Highly centralized governments and authoritarian politics have become the pattern. Even in France, the westernmost of these states, bounded by both the Atlantic Ocean and the Mediterranean Sea, and the home of nationalism and democracy since the revolution of 1789, democracy continued to face challenges from the authoritarian tradition until World War II. But democracy was foreign to Prussia and Germany (after Prussia unified Germany in 1870) until after World War II, when it was imposed upon West Germany by its conquerors; it was also foreign to czarist and Soviet Russia. And, although there is no suggestion that geography is the primary reason these countries have long been authoritarian, geography surely has been a major contributing factor. The farther east one goes in Europe, the more authoritarian it becomes; the farther west, the more democratic.

The United States, the western most power of all, had plenty of time to nurture its democratic roots and no need for large military forces. When drawn into Europe's wars in the twentieth century, the United States was unprepared each time. But, because it was far from the battlefields, it paid no penalty for this lack of readiness; it mobilized its power after war had been declared. The disadvantage of this geographic location and the century-long protection it afforded was that, to come to grips with its enemies, the United States had to project its power over vast distances. Not surprisingly, America's allies and friends often had the jitters because, knowing they were far from the United States, they feared the possibility of being either insufficiently protected or abandoned.

Today, technology has reduced the significance of geography. The United States no longer has the time it had in World Wars I and II to decide whether its security interests are involved. The United States is now vulnerable to attack and cannot afford long indecision; nor can it wait until after it has been challenged to prepare itself militarily. That is why the nation has defined many of its interests around the world, signed alliances to communicate these interests to its principal adversary, and maintained large military forces. Yet obviously geography still profoundly affects the foreign policies of many states, whether it is Germany or Israel or the Soviet Union.

Population

Population figures are good initial indicators of a nation's power ranking and of possible changes in its ranking. Table 7-1 shows immediately how Prussia's unification of Germany in 1870 changed the map of Europe and finally brought the United States out of its isolation. Except for Russia in the east, the Continent's traditional great powers, Austria-Hungary and France, were displaced by Germany. France, which had the largest population (36 million) in 1850, was by 1910 just ahead of Italy, the least populous of the major powers in Europe. Germany's top ranking was underscored by its large-scale industrialization but, Britain had become the world's greatest power by the nineteenth century. Steel production was usually the major indicator of industrial strength because of its association with the production of modern arms. In the first decade of the twentieth century, Germany overtook Britain in steel production (and, by using much of that steel to

Table 7-1 Population of Major European Powers, 1870-1914 (in millions)

Year	Austria-Hungary	France	Germany	Britain	Italy	Russia
1870	36	36	40	31	27	82
1890	41	38	49	38	30	110
1900	45	39	56	41	32	133
1910	50	39	64	45	35	163
1914	52	39	65	45	37	171

SOURCE: Adapted from *A Study of War*, I, 670-671, by Quincy Wright, by permission of The University of Chicago Press, copyright 1942 by The University of Chicago Press; and A. J. P. Taylor, *The Struggle for Mastery in Europe* (London: Oxford University Press, 1954), xxv.

build a sizable navy, challenged the British navy and drove Britain into closer relations with France and Russia).

Only the United States was a match for Germany. With a population of 76 million in 1900 and 92 million in 1910 and with steel production more than twice that of Germany, the United States clearly would be compelled eventually to abandon its isolationism. In the words of historian A. J. P. Taylor: "By 1914 she was not merely an economic Power on the European level; she was a rival continent. Her coal production equalled that of Great Britain and Germany put together; her iron and steel production surpassed that of all Europe. This was the writing on the wall: economically Europe no longer had a monopoly—she was not even the centre of the world." [6] In Europe, however, Germany was becoming too powerful for its neighbors. It was acquiring the capability to become the dominant power and a threat to the independence of the other European great powers. World War I and the U.S. participation in it were predictable from population and industrial figures alone. It was also clear that even after Germany's defeat no lasting peace in Europe was feasible without continued American political involvement. A unified Germany remained potentially Europe's most powerful state, despite some restrictions on its armed forces. The United States' return to isolationism was certainly one factor responsible for World War II, which again required American intervention.

But population figures can be deceptive. Before 1914, Germany's ally, Austria-Hungary, had a population larger than that of either France or Britain. Composed of a multitude of feuding nationalities who were beginning to demand self-determination, Austria-Hungary was on the brink of dissolution. That is why it was determined to crush Serbia, a Slav state that was fanning the flames of nationalism. Vienna decided that it could avoid death only by risking suicide in a war to eliminate Serbia. Because Russia supported Serbia, Germany supported Austria, and France backed

Russia, the result of Austria-Hungary's ethnic composition was World War I.

The coming of World War I illustrates the value of changing population figures, as well as the limitations of looking only at such figures. Nonetheless, it remains true that a large population in a *developed* nation clearly confers an advantage. There are several reasons for this. First, a large population translates into a big army, especially if the age distribution is such that the country has a sizable percentage of youth. Second, the industries that develop to serve so many consumers tend to be large-scale, and the country is likely to be very productive. This translates into large numbers of guns, as well as a lot of butter. Third, a large economy with many consumers means that many nations will want access to that nation's economy to sell their products. This circumstance may give that nation leverage. And fourth, the nation can use its wealth as an instrument of foreign policy—foreign aid, for example. Because a large population with many scientists and engineers is also likely to produce high technology, this too can be employed to advance the nation's purposes internationally. Few nations have populations over 50 million, and many of these—eight, including China—are already classified as the major actors or potential great powers of the future. Indeed, China's population already exceeds 1 billion; by the year 2000 its population may reach 1.5 billion, with India following at 1 billion (see Table 7-2).

National population figures reveal that Europe and the United States collectively already contain a minority of the world's population (see Figure 7-1). When these figures are combined with productivity data, the trend toward a *division of the world* between a minority of states that are rich and a growing majority that are poor becomes clear. This trend is potentially very dangerous and is one reason for growing concern about the North-South confrontation. By the year 2000 the population of the West (including the Soviet Union) will constitute less than 20 percent of the world's population.* The developing nations will have more than 80 percent of the world's population, about half of which will be under twenty years of age.

Natural Resources

Industrialization married to population gives birth to power, but industrialization cannot produce a nation's goods without natural resources. In the past Britain, Germany, and the United States were able to industrialize because of plentiful supplies of coal. Today the United States still has enormous reserves of coal, far more than Saudi Arabia has of oil. The index of economic development in the earlier stage of industrialization was steel, which was

---

* The U.S. Census Bureau has forecast that the U.S. population will peak in 2038 at 302 million and then gradually decline (Richard Berke, "Census Predicts Population Drop in Next Century," *New York Times*, Feb. 1, 1989).

Table 7-2 Countries with Populations over 50 Million, 1988 (in millions)

Country	Population
China	1,088
India	817
Soviet Union	286
United States	246
Indonesia	184
Brazil	151
Japan	122
Nigeria	112
Bangladesh	109
Pakistan	107
Mexico	83
Vietnam	65
Germany (West)	61
Philippines	58
Italy	57
Britain	57
France	56

SOURCE: Central Intelligence Agency, *The World Factbook, 1988* (Washington, D.C.: Central Intelligence Agency, 1988).

used for everything from railroad tracks to cannons to machinery. Iron and coal were key resources. Coal remains a major substitute for oil in the production of electricity, but its use is harmful to the environment.

After World War II, oil replaced coal because oil was cheap. Had oil been more expensive, especially in the United States, the industrial nations might have kept a better balance between oil and coal and become less vulnerable to the Organization of Petroleum Exporting Countries and its continual price increases from 1973 to the early 1980s. Not only bombers and tanks but also the whole Western industrial structure and high standard of living have been based on oil. (Would such southern cities as Houston and Atlanta have become great commercial and cultural centers without oil and air conditioning?) The United States, once an oil exporter, now imports much of its oil, as do the other members of the North Atlantic Treaty Organization (although Britain is becoming self-sufficient thanks to its North Sea reserves); Japan imports almost all of the oil it needs.

Table 7-3 shows other imported resources on which the United States is becoming increasingly dependent. Note the higher than 90 percent import levels of cobalt, manganese, and other metals, many of which are used in manufacturing jet engines, computers, machine tools, tanks, and missiles. The availability of oil and of these and other resources obviously depends on

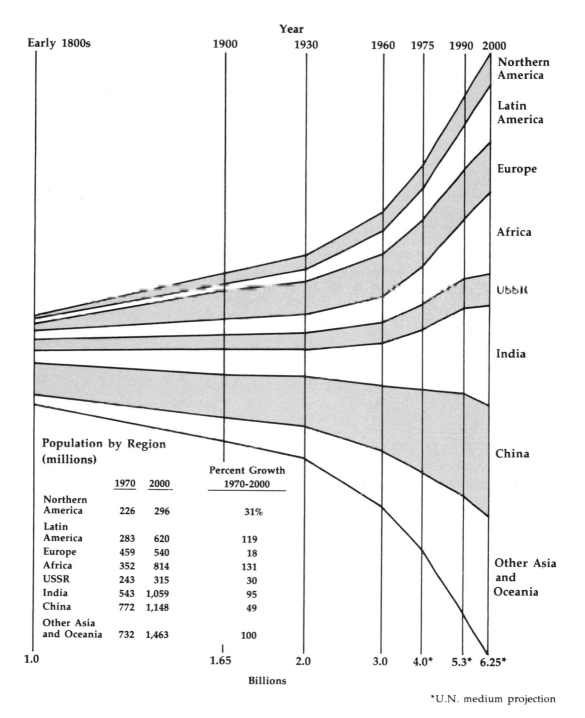

Year

Early 1800s   1900   1930   1960   1975   1990   2000

Northern America

Latin America

Europe

Africa

USSR

India

China

Other Asia and Oceania

Population by Region (millions)

	1970	2000	Percent Growth 1970-2000
Northern America	226	296	31%
Latin America	283	620	119
Europe	459	540	18
Africa	352	814	131
USSR	243	315	30
India	543	1,059	95
China	772	1,148	49
Other Asia and Oceania	732	1,463	100

1.0   1.65   2.0   3.0   4.0*   5.3* 6.25*

Billions

*U.N. medium projection

Figure 7-1 The Population Explosion: Where the People Are Likely to Be in the Year 2000

Table 7-3 Key Minerals for Which the United States Is More than 80 Percent Import Dependent, 1980-1983 (average percent of apparent U.S. consumption)

	Bauxite 95%	Chromium 86%	Cobalt 94%	Manganese 99%	Platinum group 86%
Key Minerals Critical to High Quality in the Production of:					
Basic steel					x
Stainless, tool, alloy steels		x	x	x	
Basic aluminum	x				
Aluminum alloys	x			x	
Nickel-based and cobalt-based superalloys	x	x	x	x	
Items Made Using Key Minerals:					
Ordnance (tanks, fighters, bombers, missiles)	x	x	x	x	x
Power generating (turbines, controls, transmission)	x	x	x	x	
Electric motors, equipment (locomotives to mixers)	x		x	x	
All electronics (appliances, computers, phones, TV, navigation, controls, telecommunications	x	x	x	x	x
Nuclear application	x	x	x		
Jet engines, gas turbines (hot parts)		x	x		x
Batteries, fuel cells				x	x
Aerospace (airframes, hulls, rocket engines)	x	x	x		x
Projectiles, gun barrels, machine parts, crankshafts, axles, gears, machine tools		x	x	x	
Mining, drilling (valve stems and systems, drill bits)		x	x	x	
High-tech medical (cryogenics, heart-lung, scanners)	x	x	x		x
Petroleum processing, drilling		x	x	x	x
Chemical processing		x	x	x	x
Glass products			x		x
Pharmaceutical production					x
Food processing, enrichment		x	x	x	x
Synfuel production		x	x	x	x

SOURCES: Adapted from Uri Ra'anan and Charles M. Perry, *Strategic Minerals and International Security* (McLean, Va.: Pergamon-Brassey International Defense Publishers, 1985), p. 4; 1980-1983 figures taken from Department of State, Bureau of Public Affairs, *Atlas of United States Foreign Relations*, 2d ed. (Washington, D.C.: Department of State, 1985).

NOTE: Because effective military technology requires highest possible performance, substitutes are not desirable. Substitutes for purely commercial and civilian items, however, are possible on a mixed basis—recognizing that lower quality and performance would occur.

many factors, including the friendliness or unfriendliness of specific regimes. That is why President Jimmy Carter committed the United States to the defense of the oil sheikdoms on the Persian Gulf after the Soviet invasion of Afghanistan and why President Reagan strengthened this commitment to Saudi Arabia.

The Reagan administration was also concerned about the racial situation in South Africa, a country in which fewer than 5 million whites rule about 1 million Asians and more than 17 million blacks in a system of rigid separation called apartheid. In this potentially explosive situation the United States tried unsuccessfully to promote gradual, peaceful change and thereby keep a friendly government in power. The reason was obvious. In the early 1980s South Africa supplied the United States with 61 percent of its cobalt, 55 percent of its chromium, 49 percent of its platinum, 44 percent of its vanadium (used as an alloy in making steel and a key component in aircraft bodies and engines), and 39 percent of its manganese. The United States was thus quite dependent on South Africa for some key industrial metals. South Africa, according to the U.S. Commerce Department, has more than 80 percent of the world's chromium and platinum, 70 percent of its manganese, and 47 percent of its vanadium.[7] For these reasons, President Reagan opposed economic sanctions against South Africa in 1986.

Western Europe and Japan, America's principal allies, are even more dependent on imported raw materials. Japan, for example, imports virtually 100 percent of its petroleum, bauxite, wool, and cotton; 95 percent of its wheat; 90 percent of its coal and copper ore; and 70 percent of its timber and grain.

Still, Western industry is not as dependent upon Third World natural resources as the above suggests for two reasons. First, the industrial states can adjust in several ways if access to one or more supplies were cut off: (1) use substitutes; (2) develop synthetic substitutes; (3) seek alternative Third World resources; (4) develop sources of supply in the industrial states; or (5) conserve resources. Listing the resources Western countries import then is not equivalent to dependence.

Second, some nations have developed great wealth or power without possessing all the necessary raw materials. Japan and the newly industrialized countries (NICs) have experienced rapid economic growth; other Southeast Asian countries have undergone somewhat slower growth. Yet none of them has been blessed with an abundance of resources.

Economic Capacity

A common standard for comparison of national power, probably more reliable than population in this industrial age, is wealth or degree of economic development. Wealth is clearly related to military power, for the richest states presumably can afford to buy the most military power. Indeed, wealth can buy power of all kinds, which remains important for distinguishing the superpowers from the secondary powers. The United States and the Soviet Union can mobilize both large nuclear and conventional forces, as well as other kinds of power, such as economic and technical assistance, that could serve as diplomatic tools; their allies cannot. A nation's gross national product (GNP)—the total value of its production and services measured in currency—thus has been used frequently as a relatively accurate and measurable standard for comparing the power of states.

A glance at Table 7-4 shows three things: the clear-cut distinction between the superpowers and the secondary powers; the rankings of the principal and secondary actors listed, which are pretty much as most observers would guess without knowing the GNP figures; and the wide gap between the Soviet Union and the United States. Japan is second to the United States.

Still, the GNP, figure is not completely reliable. In the United States, at least, it reflects the production not only of automobiles but also of about nineteen different brands of cat food and billions of hamburgers sold through fast-food chains. In the mid-1960s, the Soviet Union, with a GNP of less than half that of the United States launched a massive arms program; it was able to compete with the United States in arms and aerospace manufacturing because it devoted less of its wealth to consumer goods. Soviet cats, no doubt, did not eat as well as American cats. In the 1970s, American military spending was about 5 percent of GNP (and 6-7 percent in the 1980s), but Moscow was spending a minimum of 15 percent of a GNP, about half that of the United States, on arms (some estimates range up to 25 percent of a GNP figure more like one-third that U.S. figure!).

GNP also does not reflect total production and services. The U.S. figure would be even higher if it included Mafia activities and the billions of dollars earned in the drug business. Moreover, the GNP does not reflect volunteer work or women's household duties, for which wages are not paid. More broadly, GNP reveals little about a nation's unity, the stability of its government, its political leadership, its popular morale, its military doctrine, and the quality of its diplomacy, which are relevant to an analysis of a nation's power and foreign policy. At best, then, economic productivity—like population and military power—remains a crude indicator of power and a convenient shorthand means of comparison.

Per capita incomes are used sometimes as a standard of wealth. Again, the assumption is that individual income is highest in the most economically advanced nations. The figures for the United States, Western Europe, and Japan are indeed the highest worldwide, but that for the United States—which long enjoyed the highest standard of living in the world—has slipped below the figures for Sweden, Switzerland, and West Germany. Britain has dropped to a level below Italy, which for a long time had the lowest per capita income of the larger European states. In a way, per capita income figures are more accurate indicators of wealth than GNP figures. The Soviet GNP was second to that of the United States until recently when Japan overtook the Soviet Union (see Table 7-4), but Soviet per capita income is below that of any major Western country, indicating a much lower standard of living. The per capita incomes of the developing countries are the lowest. Actually, these

Table 7-4 Ranking of Economic Capacity Among
Great Powers, 1988 (in billions of dollars)

Country	Estimated 1988 GNP
United States	4,486
Japan	2,664
Soviet Union	2,356
Germany (West)	908
Italy	743
France	724
Britain	557
China	286

SOURCE: Figures taken from Central Intelligence Agency, *The World Fact-book 1988* (Washington, D.C.: Central Intelligence Agency, 1988).

figures also can be misleading on occasion. In the early 1980s Kuwait's annual per capita income was more than $20,000, about 60 percent higher than that of the United States. This high figure reflects Kuwait's enormous income from oil in the 1970s, but the income is not equally distributed.

Finally two points must be emphasized about economic capacity. First, a nation's economic capacity is enhanced if it possesses strength in the scientific and technological arenas. American technology has been sought widely throughout the world—as have European and Japanese technologies—not only by the developing countries but also by the Soviet Union and China. China is looking to the United States and Japan for economic assistance and to Europe for military hardware. As political scientist Robert Gilpin has noted: "Whereas, beginning in the latter part of the nineteenth century, control over petroleum resources became essential once naval ships shifted from sail to diesel, so today an independent aerospace and electronics industry, along with the supporting sciences, has become crucial for a nation to enjoy diplomatic and military freedom of action." [8] This is why it is so worrisome that the United States is falling behind Japan in key areas of the new technologies.

Second, the importance of agriculture is often underrated. Even a country such as Britain, which neglected agriculture while it industrialized, confronted the possibility of starvation during wars in this century. Germany almost succeeded twice in blockading the British Isles during the world wars. For much of the post-war period, the developing countries in their eagerness to modernize—by which they mean industrialize—have tended to neglect agriculture, with the devastating results of widespread malnutrition and even starvation for their rapidly growing populations. Although most of the people in these countries live on the land, agricultural production is inefficient and unscientific. By contrast, the United States, with less than 5 percent of its population employed in agriculture, has for much of the postwar period been the breadbasket for the world. A balance between the agricultural and industrial sectors of the economy is clearly desirable and indeed necessary for economic growth and modernization. A move toward a more balanced growth now appears to be occurring.

Military Strength

Because international politics resembles a state of potential war, military power has become a recognized standard of measurement. In the past every new great power proclaimed its appearance by a feat of arms. The decline of a great power was signaled equally by a defeat at arms, or what other states perceived as a defeat.

A nation's military power is usually measured by the number of people in uniform and by the number of different weapons it has. As might be expected, the countries with the largest populations have the largest armed forces, though not necessarily in proportion to their populations. Table 7-5 shows the military strength of the world's sixteen largest countries and the size of their armed forces in 1988. These figures do not include reserves, nor do they say much about the combat training, morale, and discipline of these forces. The American army in Europe during the 1970s, for example, was often reported to be suffering from a lack of discipline, widespread drug use, and racial strife. In the 1980s, however, with higher educational levels, a volunteer force, and better pay plus improved training, morale was up. Israel, with its population of slightly fewer than 4 million, is obviously not in the same league with the countries listed in Table 7-5. Yet in twenty-four hours it can mobilize 400,000 soldiers to supplement its permanent army of 164,000, and these forces are highly trained and well led, as four victories in four wars have shown. Switzerland, with slightly more than 8 million people, can mobilize 625,000 troops in forty-eight hours; Swiss reservists train three weeks each summer. Sweden, with roughly the same population, can mobilize 750,000 troops within seventy-two hours. Thus, these countries can almost overnight raise forces as large as the standing armies of Britain, France, or West Germany!

The heavily populated industrial powers also have the largest nuclear arsenals. The United States and the Soviet Union are, of course, in a class by themselves, for they can wipe each other, as well as any other country, off the face of the earth. It is significant that the first five nuclear states (the United States, the Soviet Union, Britain, France, and China) were the five great powers whose status was reflected in their permanent UN Security Council membership when the organization was established after World War II. India has since joined this nuclear club.

The two superpowers are also producers of huge quantities of conventional arms, as are the Western allies. The adjective *conventional* hardly does these weapons justice. For one thing, they are becoming very accurate; their chance of hitting and destroying the target in one shot has increased to more than 50 percent. One result has been that opposing forces use war material at an ever-

Table 7-5 Comparative Military Strength, 1988-1989 (in thousands)

Country (in order of population)	Size of Armed Forces (in thousands)
China	3,200[a]
India	1,300[a]
Soviet Union	5,100[a]
United States	2,200[a]
Indonesia	284
Brazil	319
Japan	245
Nigeria	94
Bangladesh	101
Pakistan	480
Vietnam	1,252
Mexico	254
Germany (West)	488
Italy	386
Britain	317
France	457

SOURCE: Figures from International Institute for Strategic Studies, *The Military Balance, 1988-1989* (Letchworth, England: Garden City Press, 1985).
[a] Numbers are rounded to the nearest ten thousand.

faster clip. A war can last only a few days under these conditions; a steady stream of new supplies is needed to continue hostilities. In such circumstances, a superpower's client state cannot be defeated. If defeat appears likely, the allied superpower sends more arms to avert it. As the Soviet Union poured in arms for the Arabs in the 1973 Yom Kippur War, the United States poured in even more arms for the Israelis, who were badly mauled in the opening phase of the war. Only countries with no superpower friends can still win wars! "Wars between small countries with big friends are likely to be inconclusive and interminable; hence, decisive war in our time has become the privilege of the impotent." [9]

Weapons balances are not easy to calculate. For example, how does one compare an intercontinental ballistic missile (ICBM) with a single warhead to one with multiple independently targeted reentry vehicles (MIRVs) or several warheads; or a missile with a megaton (million-ton) warhead to one with a 200,000-ton warhead but with extreme accuracy? How does one compare bombers having quite different characteristics or tanks with antitank guns? It is also difficult to compare divisions of different sizes and compositions. In every war Israel's enemies have had more soldiers, guns, tanks, and fighter planes, but the smaller Israeli forces have consistently outfought their enemies. Better leadership, training, discipline, motivation, and tactics have helped them to beat numerically superior forces. In 1940 the stunning German defeat of France was accomplished not by a much larger German army, as has usually been thought, but by forces of about the same size as those of the Allies. The German army won because of its better leadership, its mobility, and its unique tactical combination of tanks and fighter planes.

Moreover, what is really important is that the soldiers and their political superiors know what kind of war they are entering. "No one starts a war—or rather, no one in his senses ought to do so—without first being clear in his mind what he intends to achieve by that war and how he intends to conduct it." [10] This common-sense advice from Clausewitz is too often ignored. In the 1960s, a proud American army of half a million, provided with all the latest equipment that American technology could invent, was unable to defeat the Viet Cong and the North Vietnamese army. American military leaders thought that they were fighting a miniature World War II and used essentially orthodox military tactics. The North Vietnamese military leaders, however, were fighting an unorthodox war (see Chapter 13).

Political Systems and Leadership

It is one thing for nations to "have" power, but how that power is used and for what purposes are decided by the leaders of political systems. A nation must ask itself what role it wants to play in the world. What are its objectives and priorities among them? Can its leaders make decisions with reasonable speed, gain popular approval for their policies, and then carry them out with reasonable effectiveness? Are their policies appropriate to the circumstances? What methods are used to achieve the nation's various aims, and are they compatible with its values? Is the overall foreign policy steady, or does it change from one administration to the next? Are governments stable, or do they fall frequently, to be replaced by new ones?

These questions can be asked about any political system, but there is no attempt to deal with all of them here. Often the issue of the effectiveness of different types of governments in dealing with the outside world is presented as an issue between dictatorship, authoritarianism, or totalitarianism, on one hand, and democracy, on the other. Frequently the superior effectiveness of a dictatorship is assumed. The reasons are clear-cut: first, decisions can be taken relatively quickly; second, there are no leaks or attempts to head off or dilute policy while it is being formulated; and third, once a decision has been taken by the top officials, it can be executed immediately. There are no independent parliaments, parties, or interest groups and no free press or organized public opinion to question, criticize, or oppose. By contrast, making foreign policy in a democracy is like running an obstacle course without any certainty of reaching the end. The policy process is usually slow, and the result almost always embodies a compromise among many conflicting points of view, which may weaken the policy's effectiveness in alleviating the problem at which it is aimed. And, given ultimate dependence on public opinion and support, a democratic foreign policy may—as George Kennan pointed out—be either too little or too much for the issues the nation confronts.

But are totalitarian governments in fact more effective in making policy on issues of war and peace? Not necessarily. Neither Hitler nor Mussolini nor the Japanese militarists who were responsible for World War II succeeded; their regimes were all defeated. This point raises a fundamental doubt about the wisdom of their policies. They start wars that they did not win. Miscalculation, admittedly, is not a vice peculiar to undemocratic regimes; democratic governments miscalculate as well, but perhaps in systems in which policy is debated and criticism must be answered, the substance of policy may more often be wiser and more balanced.

Actually, the dichotomy between democracy and totalitarianism is probably exaggerated. Both types of governments at times have acted successfully, at other times with folly. Even undemocratic regimes, unrestrained by consensus politics, can act slowly and hesitantly, and democratic governments on occasion can act speedily with the full support of public opinion. The Truman Doctrine in support of Greece and Turkey, as well as the Marshall Plan for the economic recovery of Europe, were produced in only fifteen weeks in 1946-1947. The decision to demand the withdrawal of Soviet missiles from Cuba in 1962 took less than a week; the entire crisis lasted only thirteen days.

Whatever the differences in effectiveness between democracies and totalitarian regimes, there are also differences among democratic governments. After 1945, as the United States became a world power, American political scientists worried that the constitutional separation of powers would make it very difficult to conduct a coherent, responsible, and steady foreign policy. Quarrels between the president and Congress, lack of party loyalty, and the influence of pressure groups exploiting this political fragmentation were expected to result in a paralysis of policy or at best slow decision making, a change of policies with every administration, and constant pressure reflecting electioneering and the disproportionate influence of all types of interests seeking to impose their narrow demands. The British parliamentary system, with its unity of executive and legislative branch and its strong party discipline, appeared more likely to meet the requirements of the cold war. But the structure of the U.S. government could not be transformed. Friction between the president and Congress has occurred frequently, especially in the years since the Vietnam War. Often the United States has spoken to the world with (at least) two voices. Executive policies have been weakened, undermined, or rejected by Congress, especially the Senate, and interest group pressures, especially from ethnic groups (Jewish, Greek, black, and so on), have been effective in constraining the president's freedom in negotiations and the conduct of foreign policy. Conflicts over priorities have often remained unresolved because administrations could not make up their minds about exactly what to do. Whether the conduct of U.S. foreign policy would have been more effective under a parliamentary system is unclear, however. Britain's record in postwar foreign policy has hardly been outstanding. It has been characterized by indecision, procrastination, and mistaken choices (such as its slowness to join the European Community and its maintenance of an "independent" nuclear force at the expense of conventional forces).[11]

By contrast, after 1945 the Soviet Union built unprecedented military power and attained global status. But by the 1980s, its policies had driven virtually all the world's great powers—the United States, Europe, China, Japan—together in an anti-Soviet alliance. Soviet industry has lagged technologically, and its agriculture remains troublesome. After seven decades of communism, the Soviets' principal achievement has been the relatively efficient and massive production of arms. The proletariat and peasantry in whose name the revolution had been made in 1917 have remained without political or civil rights until Gorbachev, and the sufficient food and consumer goods that they have been promised for so long are still only promises. In terms of its standard of living, the Soviet Union is frequently these days classified as an advanced third world state, not an advanced industrial state.

The wisdom of policy or lack of it can surely be attributed as much to the intelligence, ability, and drive of specific national leaders as to governmental structures and processes. One need only recall the names of some of the twentieth-century leaders whose special qualities have shaped history: V. I. Lenin, Joseph Stalin, Adolf Hitler, Woodrow Wilson, Franklin Roosevelt, Winston Churchill, and Charles de Gaulle. Others, perhaps not quite of the same stature, are Harry Truman and John Kennedy, who did not have sufficient time to demonstrate great leadership. These men had an impact because they could articulate their nations' purposes, make significant domestic and foreign policy decisions—sometimes drastically changing their nations' directions—pursue their goals with vigor and flair, mobilize support for their courses of action at home, and even inspire their peoples to sacrifice and discipline. How can one compare contemporary leaders in the West to the giants of yesteryear such as Roosevelt, Churchill, and de Gaulle? Only one thing is clear: all nations, democratic and otherwise, require leadership.

Perhaps Soviet leader Gorbachev is one of those extraordinary leaders or will become one if he survives. In power only since 1985, he has already had a significant impact both domestically and internationally. He has instituted a process of significant reforms at home because the Soviet economy was stagnating and the Soviet Union's status as a superpower was threatened.[12] He has talked of unpleasant realities that have long been suppressed; subjects long taboo are now open to discussion. For example, even Lenin, the founding father of the Soviet Union, has been implicated in creating the secret police, terror, and a totalitarian dictatorship. Gorbachev has also withdrawn Soviet troops from Afghanistan and signed an arms control agreement with the United States that allows the foreign inspectors who will verify that agreement to be based in the Soviet Union. Gorbachev's youthfulness when compared to past Soviet leaders, his charm, his many pronouncements on peace and nuclear disarmament, his travels in the West, and his willingness to meet with the Western media and great crowds have made him a formidable opponent and perhaps for the first time have made the Soviet Union as much a diplomatic rival as a military one. For Gorbachev, the appellation "great communicator" is as apt as it was for Reagan. Of course, if he succeeds and the Soviet economy becomes modern, up to date technologically, productive, and efficient, will the Soviet Union not become a *more* formidable rival? Or will it become less concerned with the global expansion of its influence—not necessarily the spread of communism—if by this process of modernization Soviet society becomes more open and focuses more on domestic affairs? Whatever the result, there can be no doubt of Gorbachev's considerable leadership capability, his efforts to restructure the home front, the new Soviet tone in foreign policy, and his credibility in the West. In the late 1980s, polls in Western Europe, showed that people gave him more credit than President Reagan for the new relaxation of tensions. Even in the United States, public opinion showed that most Americans thought that the United States could do business with him.

Nevertheless, the focus on personality and leadership should not divorce analysis from the political system in which the leader operates. For example, could Egypt's president Anwar Sadat have held out the hand of peace and accepted the legitimacy of Israel's existence had Egypt been a democracy? Despite popular yearnings for peace, would not opposition party leaders (possibly in Sadat's own party), newspapers, and segments of Egyptian society have opposed his moves, perhaps successfully? If Israel, by contrast, were an authoritarian state, would it not be easier for an Israeli leader to make concessions on the West Bank and Gaza Strip to resolve the Palestinian problem—an important element if a comprehensive peace in that area is ever to be established? Quite apart from Israel's genuine fears of a Palestinian state governed by the PLO, how can a government, which is composed of a coalition of two equally strong parties, give up the West Bank, when one party believes deeply that the West Bank belongs rightfully to Israel by biblical inheritance and that Jews should be settled there? How can these parties work out security arrangements that would enable Israel and a Palestinian state to live without constant fear of each other? These questions are not meant to suggest that democracies are obstacles to peace—probably because of their nature they find it harder to go to war than do undemocratic states—but only to observe that differences in political regimes do matter. Clearly, some institutional arrangements are more effective than others in permitting policy making and execution.

National Morale

National morale—also often called *national will*—is perhaps best defined as popular dedication to the nation and support for its policies, even when that support requires sacrifice. Examples abound—most occurring in wartime— when identification with one's country is intense. The government, even in undemocratic states, cannot do without mass support, and a people's acceptance of military service, separation of families, and deaths measures its commitment to the nation. Indeed, whether morale in democracies is higher, more intense, or longer lasting than that in undemocratic states is debatable. The German armies fought very well in two wars, despite the Allied blockade of World War I and the heavy bombing of World War II; widespread support for Germany's government lasted until near the end in each instance. Japanese soldiers demonstrated a tenacious fanaticism during World War II, which led them to fight hard for every inch of territory, to sacrifice their own lives freely in the process, and to impose heavy casualties on American marines.

Bombing, which is frequently favored as a way of beating an enemy into submission, appears to be a positive factor in preserving, even raising, morale. Before World War II it was widely believed that bombing cities not only would destroy the war industries supporting the front-line soldiers but also would break civilian morale. Civilians were not expected to be as tough as soldiers. The Battle of Britain after the German defeat of France in 1940 proved otherwise. The German bombing of Britain probably did more to raise British morale than any other single factor. Likewise, the American bombing of North Vietnam probably helped to maintain support for the Hanoi government. North Vietnamese general Vo Nguyen Giap, the mastermind behind his nation's strategy, predicted victory against the United States because he believed that democracies lose patience in long, drawn-out wars and will finally quit. As Giap had forecast, the war caused immense domestic turmoil in the United States, which in the end had no choice but to disengage from the conflict.

It is difficult to make definitive statements about American morale. The two world wars were fought far away, there was no physical damage to the homeland through invasion or sustained bombing, and civilians were not endangered. The loss of American life was very small compared with that of the other combatants. Standards of living were maintained at a fairly high level at home. Sacrifices were minimal and lasted for just over a year in the first war and a bit over three and a half years in the second—compared with four years for Britain and France in World War I and six years for Britain in World War II. The Vietnam War, because it was considered a "limited war" in response to a limited threat, was never popularly perceived to pose much danger to American security, and life went on pretty much as usual in the United States. There was little willingness to sacrifice butter for guns, as during the world wars. The draft of college students was resented, and there was widespread resistance to it; many youths emigrated to Canada and elsewhere. Perhaps it was the nature of that particular war only. There is still no record on how the national morale will hold up when sacrifice is demanded in a real crisis. The peacetime domestic gas crisis of the 1970s demonstrated that Americans do not like to do with less. The overall twentieth-century evidence remains fragmentary and ambiguous. American society has not really been tested yet.

What seem to be critical components in upholding national morale are patriotic feelings that can be rallied when the nation is attacked or insulted, even when the government may not be particularly popular (as in the Soviet Union during World War II), and a belief that the government places the nation's welfare first and pursues policies compatible with the nation's historic role. In the early 1980s, President Reagan was able to mobilize Americans' patriotism and their pride in their country, both of which had suffered during the 1970s and the Vietnam era. The country supported his use of force in Grenada (1983), Libya (1981 and 1986), and even in Lebanon (1982-1983). In Lebanon, however, the president was forced to withdraw U.S. forces shortly after 241 marines were killed in a suicide terrorist attack on their barracks. He refrained from direct military intervention in Nicaragua because of widespread fears of "another Vietnam."

In this context, three problems deserve a brief mention. One is that it is now clear that in any past war with NATO, Moscow could not have counted on Eastern European armies. The number of Warsaw Pact divisions therefore exaggerated the threat from the East. Another problem is that the Europe of the ECC, with its 325 million people and a combined GNP larger than that of the Soviet Union and its allies, has remained unable to defend itself since World War II without 300,000 American forces to help it against a nation of 276 million Soviet citizens, which also has more than 1 billion Chinese to its rear. This has been due to a lack of will, not material strength. A third, more general contemporary problem is the deep internal divisions of many nations, rent by quarrels among ethnic, tribal, racial, or religious groups who do not see each other as "countrymen" but only as enemies and rivals. This phenomenon of strong ethnic loyalties in competition with national loyalties has been remarkably widespread, especially among the developing countries. It is present even in Western nations such as Belgium, Canada, and Spain; and, as noted, it has become a potentially very divisive force in the Soviet Union.

WAR AND POWER

Overestimating One's Power

A war begins when the contestants disagree on their relative power; it ends only when they agree on their relative strength.[13] That is, war erupts because one of the nations in an adversary relationship has miscalculated the distribution of power. The fighting will clarify the actual ratio of power, making war a bitter teacher of "reality." More specifically, power calculations—by either underestimating or overestimating the power of the adversary—have influenced decisions to go to war in two ways. The state that has underestimated its opponent's power may be emboldened to make reckless decisions leading to war. The state that has overestimated its opponent's power may become so fearful or cautious that it makes unnecessary concessions or, to avoid later disaster, strikes preventively before the enemy has grown too strong.

Examples are unfortunately plentiful. The German kaiser risked World War I in the summer of 1914 because he believed that the war would be over by the time the fall leaves fell. Hitler believed that the Soviet Union would collapse quickly and, confident of German power, invaded it before he had eliminated Britain, thus creating a two-front situation for Germany. Then, after Japan had attacked Pearl Harbor, the Nazi dictator declared war on the United States as well. He had contempt for the United States, a racially mixed society.

In Vietnam, the Joint Chiefs of Staff failed President Johnson badly when they predicted that 200,000 troops could win that conflict in a reasonable amount of time—about two years. Few Americans rated North Vietnam's military strength highly. Before the 1965 American military intervention in South Vietnam, who would have doubted that it was but a matter of weeks, at most months, before the world's greatest military power would clobber North Vietnam, one of the world's smallest powers, a "half-country" with a population less than 10 percent of that of the United States and virtually no industry. Moscow probably had a similar sense of its superior power before it invaded Afghanistan in 1979.

In all of these examples, the power initiating the war not only overestimated its own power and therefore expected to win the war but also expected a *quick* victory. With the exception of the North Vietnamese, none of the states even won the war they had started. The lesson: miscalculation of the power distribution is easy; in particular, as one would suspect, confidence in one's own strength and high hopes of a quick victory can lead to an underestimation of the opponent's power.

Underestimating One's Power

Quite the contrary phenomenon occurred just before World War II. The French and the British, remembering German military prowess in World War I and impressed by Hitler's aggressive speeches and bold international moves, consistently exaggerated German power on land and in the air and were therefore never sure that they could resist him without risking defeat in a war. Thus, they appeased him, only to find that appeasement did not avoid the war they dreaded either.

Israeli policy makers too have consistently overestimated Arab power. Given the history of persecution of Jews, in particular Hitler's policy of extermination, the leaders of the new Jewish state in 1948 felt highly insecure among hostile neighbors who had tried to strangle Israel at birth. In 1956 and 1967, when these neighbors were forming joint commands, talking of war and of "driving the Jews into the sea," boasting of their imminent victories, and parading their Soviet weapons, Israel struck preemptively. Power seemed to be shifting to its enemies. Why leave them the initiative to strike? Why not hit them before they were completely ready? Overestimating an opponent's power can also result in war.

Threat and Vulnerability Analyses

In calculating a nation's power, one problem deserves special mention: the tendency to emphasize heavily the military factor—the number of troops in uniform, the quality and number of arms, and so forth—in what is often called a *threat analysis*. Using this analysis, Soviet military power with its plentiful missiles and warheads, its immense army, its new surface navy and airlift capability, looks awesome.[14] But a concentration on military power overlooks Soviet weaknesses such as its stagnating industrial economy, the agriculture sector unable to feed its people, intra-ethnic differences and demands for greater antonomy by some nationalities, as well as such problems as the questionable loyalty of the states of Eastern Europe. For a careful calculation of the power of another state, it becomes critical that a threat analysis be balanced with what, for want of a better term, might be called a *vulnerability analysis*. It is all too easy to add up the number of soldiers and tanks and not look underneath such figures.

A brief example: one reason the Germans felt 1914 was the right time for a war was that the German General Staff, looking strictly at Russia's population figures and men under arms, was becoming alarmed by the growth of "Russian might." Indeed, some German generals had been advocating a preventive war for several years. If such a war were not undertaken, they felt, Germany would be crushed.[15] Incredibly, this threat analysis totally overlooked the fact that Russia, while always possessing forces larger than those of other European states, had just lost a war to Japan (1904-1905) and had not done well in preceding conflicts. After its defeat by Japan, Russia had suffered widespread peasant unrest, a harbinger of the revolution to come. A vulnerability analysis would have shown that Russia's outer strength was matched by internal weakness and that this alleged "military colossus" was an "economic pygmy."

A focus on military power and lack of a vulnerability analysis may cause a state to be successful in achieving some objectives but unsuccessful in achieving others.[16] The usual reason it fails to attain its declared objectives is that it did not try hard enough or was not sufficiently skillful, even if it did mobilize greater strength. For example, it has been claimed that the United States did not win the war in Vietnam because political restraints were placed on the military. Had the United States bombed North Vietnam very hard from the beginning and made the war unbearably painful for the North Vietnamese, they would have had reason to sue for peace. No doubt there are occasions when such explanations of failure are correct, and it may be that Vietnam is one such case, but more often such explanations are misleading and prevent one from drawing the correct lessons from the experience.

A better explanation of why a state may achieve success in one situation and encounter failure in another is that the state may have the right kind of power for one but not the other. The variables are the *kind* of power being used or not used, the *purposes* for which it is used, and the *situations* in which it is used. These three factors account for the American failure to win in Vietnam and for its helplessness in preventing OPEC from raising oil prices, a feat that damaged the United States far more seriously than the loss of South Vietnam ever did. A gross assessment of American power cannot explain why a superpower could not avoid a defeat at the hands of an inferior power, or prevent a group of small countries, many dependent on U.S. protection, to raise oil prices drastically. Only an analysis of the *specific context* in which the relationship of the United States and Vietnam or the United States and OPEC occurred can do so.

This difference between power as a *possession*—involving the quantitative measurement of the components of national power—and power as a *relationship* among states has been aptly explained by political scientist James Rosenau in this way:

> For reasons having to do with the structure of language, the concept of "power" does not lend itself to comprehension in relational terms. Without undue violation of language, the word "power" cannot be used as a verb. It is rather a noun, highlighting "things" possessed instead of processes of interaction. Nations influence each other; they exercise control over each other; they alter, maintain, subvert, enhance, deter, or otherwise affect each other, but they do not "powerize" each other. Hence, no matter how sensitive analysts may be to the question of how the resources used by one actor serve to modify or preserve the behavior of another, once they cast their assessment in terms of the "power" employed, they are led—if not inevitably, then almost invariably—to focus on the resources themselves rather than on the relationship they may or may not underlie.[17]

THE CRITICAL IMPORTANCE OF ECONOMIC POWER

Which of all the components of power is the most important? Undoubtedly, it is the economic. While, as emphasized, a gross calculation of power may not help forecast the outcome of a specific power relationship, assessments of the overall power of the larger states have been accurate indicators of the decline of some great powers and the rise of others. The key component of power in modern times has been industry. Britain, the first nation to industrialize, was the nineteenth century's preeminent power, keeping the balance in Europe while directing most of its energy to its colonial empire. The unification of Germany and its subsequent rapid industrialization changed European politics forever. Traditional great powers such as Austria-Hungary and France, although also industrializing, fell behind Britain and

Germany. Russia, despite very rapid economic growth toward the end of the century, was particularly weak as a modern industrial-military power. Germany had become Europe's preeminent power. By early in this century, its steel production was greater than that of Britain, France, and Russia put together.

This transformation of the power equation compelled France and Russia to ally themselves with Britain, their rival in the colonial world. The three countries signed ententes (just short of formal alliances) to form an anti-German coalition. But World War I demonstrated that it was no longer enough for Britain to add its power on the side of the weaker coalition to prevent a Continental challenger from establishing hegemony over Europe. After Germany defeated Russia in 1917, it was questionable whether France and Britain alone could have staved off defeat. It was at this point (as described in Chapter 2), that the United States entered the war and became Europe's balancer, for "its economic growth during the preceding two or three decades was probably *the single most decisive shift in the long-term global balances.* . . . [The United States] was growing so fast that it was on the point of outproducing *all* of the European states combined!" [18] Its population was almost 100 million.

Thus, when the United States, after the victory over Germany, withdrew into isolationism, the containment of Germany was left largely to France and Britain. It was a task that proved to be beyond their collective efforts once the appeasement policy had allowed Germany to recover its economic and military strength. Only an American commitment to the defense of the two Western powers—an interwar NATO—might have been able to deter Hitler's Germany. In its absence, war erupted. Germany defeated France quickly, and Britain was saved from the same fate only by the English Channel. Hitler's division of his armies when he invaded the Soviet Union, as well as the severe Russian winter, saved that country. It took the combined power of the Soviet Union and the United States, with the help of Britain as a junior power, to finally bring Germany down in defeat after six years of fighting. With the U.S. army moving eastward and the Soviet army advancing westward, the two met in the center of Europe—where they still are forty-five years later. A bipolar world had emerged.

Decline of the Superpowers

In the years after World War II the United States was the supreme Western power; U.S. technology and productivity were immense. With much of Europe's and Japan's industries destroyed, the United States produced almost half the world's goods and services. The U.S. economy, which from 1940-1945 had produced 207,000 aircraft, 86,000 tanks, 15,400,000 small arms, 64,500 landing vessels, and 5,200 larger ships (of almost 53 million tons), now made it possible for the United States to make foreign policy commitments worldwide, build and support powerful nuclear and conventional forces, and vastly expand the domestic welfare state while affording steady increases in wages through the late 1960s and early 1970s.[19] By the 1980s, however, this economy was floundering.[20] Such traditional smokestack industries as steel were especially hard hit because they had become increasingly uncompetitive internationally and had declined. There were many reasons for this decline: U.S. underinvestment in the American economy because of high U.S. wages, the desire of U.S. industry to be nearer overseas markets, and the EEC's tariff barriers against imports. American industry was going overseas where it could save transportation costs and especially where wages were lower, particularly in Third World countries. American manufacturers also found that they could avoid the EEC's tariff wall by building factories in Western Europe. Industry considered its actions rational: goods could be produced more cheaply outside of the United States, where large-scale markets and opportunities were also opening up. Goods for consumers both abroad and at home, U.S. industry argued, would be less expensive and more competitive with foreign goods while also increasing corporate earnings.

Another reason was that America's allies and friends, whom it had helped to rebuild or build following World War II, had by the 1970s become major industrial competitors. In some countries, older industries such as the textile, steel, shipbuilding, and automobile (in Europe) were rebuilt, and in other countries new industries such as the automobile (Japan) and electronics (Japan, South Korea, and Taiwan) were started. Because U.S. industries were accustomed to having the enormous domestic market virtually to themselves, they had not made the necessary investments in research and development. The U.S. textile, steel, shipbuilding, automobile, even electronics industries became successively unable to compete with goods produced elsewhere by newer technology and at lower wages. Europe and the Far East found new markets in the United States, as American consumers were eager to buy less expensive and better-made products from abroad. Even the high-technology sector of the U.S. economy (computers, machine tools, robotics, and aerospace technology), often acclaimed to be the basis for future economic growth and prosperity, experienced difficulties.

In 1987 the U.S. trade deficit—the gap between exports and imports—with Japan in electronics was almost as large as in cars, the $22 billion 1983 deficit had tripled by 1987. The total trade deficit, $25 billion in 1980, had risen to $161 billion seven years later, a sixfold increase. According to the Council on Competitiveness, composed of 150 of the nation's industrial, labor, and educational leaders, "In field after field . . . foreign competitors have moved into markets pioneered and once dominated by American firms. . . . Often their success was built on exploiting inventions made in American laboratories by American scientists."[21] In the 1980s, as well as the prior decade, American capital investments were among the lowest in the Western industrial world (Canada, Japan, and Western Europe), and the American labor force was declining qualitatively, a reflection of lower educational standards, especially in mathematics and the sciences. And while the United States did spend on research and development, the bulk of it was military; Japan's focus was civilian. Today, as the United States slips downward in its ability to compete with other nations in high-technology sales, so too does its dependence on foreign nationals. In U.S. engineering schools in the late 1980s, 40 percent of the students and one-third of the faculty were foreign-born (but most of those earning an engineering doctorate will return to their countries).

In short, the decline of the American economy—not an absolute decline but a relative decline—was inevitable to a degree as the economies of its allies recovered and grew. Some of this decline, however, was caused by complacency and lack of industrial competitiveness because business and labor had for so long had the huge U.S. market largely to themselves and had been protected from foreign competition. The result was a growing gap between the nation's foreign policy commitments and the capabilities to sustain them. Yet while its power base was shrinking, the United States had further extended its commitments after 1979, first to the Persian Gulf, then to Central America. It is as though the nation's leaders were unaware of its so-called imperial overstretch.[22] Since the early 1970s, the United States had tried to close the gap between ends and means in a number of ways.[23] First it reduced the non-Soviet threats to its interests, principally by reconciling with China and, to a lesser extent, by transforming Egypt from a hostile to a friendly state. Second, the United States improved relations with the Soviet Union, primarily by arms-control agreements to lower the costs and risks of the nuclear arms race and the Soviet willingness and capability to threaten the United States. Third, the United States sought greater defense contributions from its NATO allies and Japan. But the gap remains. The waning of the cold war and the Soviet threat may save the United States from the more chaotic cuts that would otherwise have been required, especially because in the 1980s the Reagan administration, by cutting taxes while greatly increasing defense spending, turned the United States into the world's largest debtor nation and left it broke in the absence of a tax increase.[24] Gorbachev came along at just the right time.

The reason is that the Soviet economy is in even greater trouble.[25] While American agriculture is so bountiful that it has become dependent on exports, the Soviet Union, under the czars a major grain exporter, now imports grain to feed its people. But a balanced diet that includes more meat remains a goal. Industrially, economic growth, after rapid advances in the 1950s and early 1960s, was down to 2 percent by the 1980s. While the Soviet Union is still the world's leading producer of steel, cement, and many types of chemicals and machinery, and its economy is not devastated by foreign competition, its economic decline was particularly notable in the new industrial revolution areas of computers, microelectronics, and petrochemicals.

In short, the Soviet Union, which had long presented itself to the Third World as a model for development, was falling further and further behind in those industries that were critical for future economic growth. Not only was its industrial sector unable to meet consumer needs, but the Soviet leadership had to confront the unpleasant fact that the Soviet economy had already fallen from second to third in GNP, behind Japan, and behind other newly industrialized countries, such as South Korea, in per capita production and rate of economic growth. This threatens the Soviet Union's ranking as a world power. In fact, the Soviet Union has been called the world's most advanced developing country—an "Upper Volta with nuclear weapons.". Communism was clearly not a model for other developing countries.

Even the economic growth it had achieved evident mainly in the outpouring of weapons instead of consumer goods, had been gained by the enormous sacrifices of the population over several generations. Each had been promised that its sacrifices were necessary so that future generations could live better. Yet food shortages, even rationing, and lack of consumer goods have been the lot of Soviet citizens. As former White House security adviser Zbigniew Brzezinski has pointed out, perhaps never before in history has such a gifted people, with such an abundance of resources, worked so hard for so long to produce so little.[26]

Gorbachev, very much aware of the Soviet economic decline, therefore launched a desperate program of *glasnost* (openness) and *perestroika* (restructuring) to revitalize the Soviet society and economy not too long after he assumed power in 1985.[27] Gorbachev realized that the two were intimately related: without more openness in Soviet society and the harnessing of the energies of the Soviet people, long used to suppression and obedience, the Soviet economy would not recover from its stagnation. Thus, Gorbachev advocated strengthening civil liberties; allowing more openness in the press, literature, and the arts; encouraging scholarship; and even re-examining the darker side of Soviet history, hitherto generally kept secret. The Soviet leader also took such measures as decentralizing the economy, cutting back the pervasive role of the Moscow-based planning bureaucracy, and encouraging the profit motive and market forces in stimulating production, including a degree of private ownership and entrepreneurship. To raise food production, farmers were allowed to lease state-owned land for a lifetime and then pass it on to their children—a fundamental reversal of the collective farm policy.

But it quickly became clear that *glasnost* and *perestroika* would not succeed unless accompanied by a restructuring of the political system. At the nineteenth Communist party conference in 1988, Gorbachev called for the removal of the party from the daily management of the economy and other sectors of Soviet life, multiple candidacies and secret ballots, in party and legislative elections; fixed terms of no more than two five-year periods for party, government, and legislative officials; a powerful new post of president of the Soviet Union (which he soon made himself); and a partial transfer of power from the Communist party to the popularly elected governmental bodies while still preserving the party's overall authority to determine national policy and its role as the "vanguard" of communism. What it all amounts to, in the final analysis, is an effort to entice Soviet workers, long plagued by indifference, inertia, drunkenness, and absenteeism, to work harder in a system that has been inefficient because of its overly centralized, bureaucratic, politicized character.

But despite Soviet leader Gorbachev's entreaties and reform efforts, there is strong resistance from those with a strong vested interest in the *status quo*. They fear change because it threatens their jobs and privileges. The Soviet Union has an army of 19 million party and government bureaucrats. The political system that Gorbachev wants to change might well be described as a system of the bureaucrats, by the bureaucrats, and for the bureaucrats. Many of Gorbachev's more conservative critics are concerned that decentralization and more autonomy for factory managers will threaten the party's monopoly of political power. Moreover, these opponents fear that any loosening of central controls would be harmful, if not fatal, in another way. The Russian portion of the population, which controls the levers of power, is particularly fearful that such a devolution of power from Moscow would result in greater political self-determination by the non-Russian nationalities. Economic decentralization might spill over into political decentralization. In other words, the fear is that the fundamental structural reforms that the Soviet Union needs might threaten Moscow's imperial control over its own vast country. Quite contrary to Marxist analysis then, the political substructure determines the fate of the economy rather than the other way around; the political system is the greatest obstacle to economic modernization.

This situation confronts the Soviet leadership with a genuine dilemma. Can it risk basic reform and yet not lose control over the consequences (assuming it can get the various bureaucracies to go along)? To stimulate the economy, it must open up society, including reexamining Soviet history (as is indeed occurring), while preserving the party's control of power. The Soviet Union really has no choice, if only because without reforms it cannot sustain its superpower status and enhance its global role. Gorbachev's leadership is intimately tied to the success of the Soviet economy *and* success in Soviet foreign policy. The Soviet Union has achieved a superpower status and equality with the United States; it belongs to a club of two. It is proud of that achievement, and no Soviet leader who would reduce, let alone abandon, that status could survive. All these considerations suggest that the Soviet leadership will require a prolonged period of *détente* and arms-control agreements to carry out its domestic changes and to shift resources from the military to the civilian sector. But in cutting military spending, Gorbachev will be endangering the basis of the Soviet Union's superpower status. Unlike Britain or its challengers, France and Germany, the Soviet Union is a one dimensional power.[28] It is neither an example of a modern economy nor a financial center; its ideological appeal as a model for economic development is fading. Nor does it possess the cultural attractions of American rock, pop art, and jeans; things American are desired even in the land of ballet, Tchaikovsky, and Tolstoy. The Soviet Union's power and status in the world depend almost exclusively on its military power.

Rise of the 'Others'

Notwithstanding its relative decline, the United States remains the non-Communist world's strongest military power. The dollar is still the international currency, weakened as it is, and English remains the international language. Still, unlike right after World War II, no European or Japanese today is likely to utter the following prayer:

> Sam be thy name.
> Thy navy come,
> Thy will be done,
> in London, as it is in Washington.

Yet, as Brzezinski has emphasized, "The change in America's global economic position is neither the consequence of an antagonistic competition nor the result of a hostile rival for global primacy gradually displacing America. Instead it is the outcome of a cooperative policy initiated and sustained by the United States itself." [29] Brzezinski is saying that the rise of the "others" is the result of the postwar American programs of reconstruction. One of those helped was Europe, and today the European Economic Community's economic potential is enormous. In Hedley Bull's words: "The countries of Western Europe are superior to the Soviet Union in population, wealth, technology, and military potential, and the idea that Russia is the naturally dominant power in Europe, against which Europe itself can construct no counter balance without importing outside [U.S.] help, is a rather recent one." [30] The question confronting Western Europe is whether its member-states nations can complete their economic and financial union after 1992, remain in step with technology, and move toward greater foreign and defense policy coordination. Without greater political unity, Europe cannot play a great-power role, especially in the midst of the current changes in Eastern Europe.

But the real economic dynamism at present is in Asia. China appears to be set on its path of agricultural growth and industrial development. In 1984, for example, the growth in China's GNP exceeded the total GNP of one of Asia's fastest growing economies, South Korea. [31] Can China continue its current modernization program and economic liberalization in conjunction with the United States and other Western economies, thereby joining the world's most powerful countries sometime in the twenty-first century? [32] This is the big question. China has undergone a significant economic *perestroika* but no *glasnost*, precipitating widespread popular dissatisfaction and vehement student protests in the late 1980s against widespread corruption, the privileges of the Chinese leadership, and major inflation. This contrasts to the Soviet Union, which has growing *glasnost* but a *perestroika* so lagging that in 1989 Moscow began importing such basic items as soap, razor blades, and pantyhose to pacify consumers increasingly angered by the growing short-ages of the necessities of life. In short, in China the question is whether the economic miracle of the past decade can continue without an opening up of the political system—a process already set back by the 1989 crushing of the students' pro-democracy movement—while in the Soviet Union the question is whether Gorbachev can survive the growing public discontent as *perestroika* fails to stock the store shelves while *glasnost* allows this discontent to be voiced. In 1989 hundreds of thousands of coal miners even went out on strike, demanding better apartments, more food, and soap to wash off their grime. There are shortages of everything including salt and matches. There may be a popular revolt if in the next few years the declining Soviet living standard is not arrested.

The current Asian economic dynamo is, of course, Japan. Its economy, together with those of Singapore, Hong Kong, South Korea, and Taiwan is the reason why the future has been called by some the Pacific Century. These "little Japans," two of which are city-states, are all major economic actors. South Korea and Taiwan, "now world-class industrial and manufacturing centres, need to be thought of not so much as the 'new Japans,' but as the 'new Frances' or the 'new Italys.' " [33] Export-led development has transformed backward, agrarian countries into modern, dynamic ones. Japan may in fact of course become the world's number one economic power.[34] It has already overtaken the Soviet Union, and the gap between the Japanese and U.S. GNPs is closing gradually (see Table 7-4). Japan not only has made its mark in such areas as textiles, steel, shipbuilding, automobiles, and electronic products (from calculators, cameras, stereos, televisions, and microwave ovens for consumers to office equipment), but it also finds itself competing in some of these areas with the other newly industrialized Asian countries and China, whose labor costs are lower than Japan's. Japan is thus moving persistently toward gaining the lead in the sectors that will be prominent in the twenty-first century: computers, especially the supercomputers, and computer soft-ware, as well as robotics. It is investing as well in biotechnology, pharma-ceuticals, and telecommunications, and may move into aerospace.[35] Where Japan will not be number one, it is likely to be number two.

In 1951 Japan's total GNP was one-third that of Britain and one-twentieth that of the United States. Three decades later, Japan's GNP is twice that of Britain and half that of the United States.[36] Complementing this miraculous achievement, since 1985 Japan has also been the world's chief financial power (and America's leading creditor nation), a position until recently occupied by the United States, now the world's largest debtor nation. The world's ten largest banks are all Japanese.[37] Citibank, America's largest bank, ranked twenty-fourth worldwide at the end of 1988. In 1986 Japan's capital outflow was more than twice that of all the OPEC nations combined at the height of their wealth.[38] Among the world's largest insurance companies, Japanese companies are number one, four, and five; Prudential Life and State Farm are numbers two and three, respectively. The largest stock brokerage firm in the world is Japanese, and Japan is a major presence on Wall Street. The Japanese have been charged with pursuing the goal of economic domination and doing so with the same zeal that they made war in World War II; indeed, that their approach to economic competition is that of war.[39]

How can the United States—and Western Europe—cope with this "economic attack" on the traditional industrial, high-technology, and service sectors? The Soviet competition was, in a sense, easier to deal with, for there was a political and military threat that included weapons and troops, but the Japanese competition reveals no visible threat or loss of blood. Nevertheless, it represents a challenge to the very organization of the societies, values, work habits, and educational practices of the older democracies. It is not merely a matter of more U.S. research and development, better business management, and closer management-labor practices. The Japanese challenge is more fundamental. Indeed, increasingly, it will be an Asian challenge as the other newly industrialized countries progress as well. If the Pacific Rim countries continue to grow at current rates of 5 percent per year until the year 2000, they may exceed the combined GNP of the United States and Europe, possess the world's most modern stock of capital, and become the world's largest source of credit and technological innovation. According to the *New York Times*, "Japan may achieve a clear lead in four key technologies (semiconductors, advanced structural materials, manufacturing technology, and biotechnology), rough parity in two (telecommunications and data processing) while lagging in three (aircraft, space, and nuclear power)." [40] Perhaps symbolic of this broader U.S. loss of technological and industrial competitiveness is the decimation of the U.S. semiconductor industry.*

Having in fact caught up technologically with the United States in two decades, Japan appears assured of going into the lead. In the new area of high definition television (HDTV), for example, the Japanese, having invested seventeen years and $700 million in research as U.S. industries quit the

---

* The United States is so worried by the prospect that American weapons, satellites, and supercomputers will become dependent on foreign corporations for microchips that the Defense Department is planning to invest several billion dollars to help the U.S. electronic industry recover (Andrew Pollack, "U.S. Sees Peril in Japan's Dominance in Chips," *New York Times*, Jan. 5, 1988). Indeed, the worry about U.S. technological leadership is so great that the Defense Department has been advised by experts in and out of government to take a more assertive role in setting economic policy, not just in stimulating advances in specific military technologies. The lack of U.S. competitiveness, inadequate research and development, and increasing foreign ownership of U.S. companies, which affect the whole economy, also affect the weapons manufacturers (John H. Cushman, Jr., "Pentagon Is Urged to be More Active in Economic Policy," *New York Times*, Oct. 19, 1988). The critical high technologies for national security, listed by the U.S. government, may be found in Martin Tolchin's "Crucial Technologies: 22 Make the U.S. List," *New York Times*, Mar. 7, 1989. But the Bush administration reportedly is reconsidering government support to maintain U.S. high-technology industries.

television business, are clearly in the lead, followed by the Europeans. At stake are not only the $50 billion a year that is expected to be spent by the end of the 1990s on a new generation of televisions and videocassette recorders, but the loss of American international sales for personal computers, automated manufacturing equipment, and semiconductors. HDTV will provide the basis for future technologies, including the electronics that will constitute 30 percent of the cost of automobiles by the year 2000. Ceding HDTV development, therefore, will help the Japanese and Europeans monopolize the next generation of electronic components. In that case, America, whose workers are already losing critical skills as industry moves offshore, may well become a second-rate manufacturing nation.[41] "In short, the United States already faces a formidable industrial, financial, and technological challenge from the nations of East Asia. That challenge will continue to grow."[42] In 1987 the East Asian and Pacific economies (including Malaysia and Thailand) accounted for 60 percent of the record U.S. trade deficit ($60 billion with Japan, $19 billion with Taiwan, and $10 billion with Korea).[43] Of the 110 countries with which it trades, America runs a trade deficit with 71.

From Bipolarity to Multipolarity?

If, as in the past, the economy remains an indicator of power relations, a geopolitical shift in the state system is all but certain. Brzezinski has speculated that if the Kremlin cannot substantially reduce its military commitment, it is quite probable that over the next two or three decades the Soviet Union will fade even further. As a result the global economic hierarchy by the year 2010 might be the following: first, the United States (with a GNP just under $8 trillion); second, the European Economic Community (with a similar or perhaps even larger GNP but lacking the attributes of a single political power); third, China (with a GNP of just under $4 trillion); fourth, Japan (with roughly the same GNP); and then only fifth in rank, the Soviet Union (with a GNP of just under $3 trillion).[44]

Europe's future remains more of a question mark, largely because it is uncertain whether the EEC nations will integrate economically and politically after 1992. In 1989 China underwent an internal upheaval and appears to be returning, at least-partially, to ideological and economic orthodoxy. Only Japan's course appears to be onward and upward. What all this means politically and militarily is even harder to say. If China becomes a modern industrial technological society, its military power will obviously be enhanced to support a more active foreign policy role in both Asia and elsewhere; but this is some time off. Japan's military capacity, by contrast is relatively small, 1 percent of GNP. Japan has basically relied on the United States for its defense, and the fact that Japan has invested so few resources and scientific engineering talent in the arms competition has undoubtedly contributed toward its economic successes in the nonmilitary sector. Indeed, Japan is often referred to as Sony Inc., suggesting that Japan is a huge trading company. Japan's interest is trade, and its foreign policy is one of not alienating anyone, lest it lose any customers. How much longer Japan can continue this orientation depends in large part on the United States, reassessments of its global commitments, and the future of U.S.-Japanese relations as Japan becomes more nationalistic and resentful of what it calls America's "Japan-bashing" over economic issues. But sooner or later, given the relative decline of the U.S. economy, Japan, like Western Europe, will have to do considerably more for its own defense, instead of leaving this responsibility mainly to the United States. After all, the United States was an economic power long before it began to play a foreign policy role and transformed some plowshares into swords. The same may be true for Japan.[45]

Using what has become known as "burden sharing," the United States is seeking to cope with the growing gap between its commitments and economic means, not only to balance Soviet power but to compete more effectively economically with its allies. According to Brzezinski, "The relative decline in American global economic preeminence occurred not in spite of America but because of America."[46] The United States, for strategic reasons, deliberately initiated and pursued a policy of economic revival for Europe and Japan. Neither is a hostile rival for primacy among the Western states nor seeks to displace the United States. But given the redistribution of world economic power, the management of the East-West relationship must become a more collective affair, if that will still be required in the future.[47] A closer relationship between Europe, Japan, and the United States, as well as fairer burden sharing among them, will thus be important. The increasing economic rivalry between them, however, may also produce a number of trade wars that will seriously harm these alliance links and have a profoundly negative impact despite their need for one another (Chapter 15).

To sum up, the postwar bipolar pattern will become less so. Its passing, however, is not likely to produce genuine multipolarity. The current in-between system might best be called *bipolycentric*. As awkward as that term is, it aptly represents the two elements of the contemporary international system. The *bi* refers to the continuing primary political-military roles of the United States and Soviet Union over the next decade or so, despite their relative economic declines and fading of the cold war. Their relationship remains critical. Given the stark alternatives of coexistence or nonexistence and the recognition that their fate is inextricably bound together, continued negotiations between the two countries to reduce tensions is obvious. The two powers have long been locked in an "adversary partnership," combining a changing mix of competition and accommodation over time. Their domestic economic needs are likely to reinforce the current trend toward greater cooperation and away from cold war confrontation.

The *polycentric* in bipolycentric refers primarily to the many new state actors or centers of foreign policy. A multipolar system has a number of roughly equal great powers; a polycentric system, has numerous actors whose power varies considerably. None of them, however, is the equal of the superpowers, who remain at the top of the state hierarchy. But weak or relatively strong compared to neighboring states, the states in the polycentric system affect events in the international system, whether it is Iran seizing American hostages, or Iraq going to war with Iran, or Saudi Arabia (or OPEC) raising oil prices, or foreigners exchanging their IOUs for pieces of the U.S. economy, ceding to non-Americans an increasing ability to make decisions that affect all Americans. The world is no longer dominated by the superpowers as in the bipolar days. Even their allies who continue to rely upon them for security have regained a considerable measure of diplomatic freedom. In a sense, it is precisely because the superpowers are stalemated while continuing to be the producers of their allies' security, that the allies, who are growing stronger economically, have been able to take advantage of this stalemate to pursue more independent foreign policies. International politics, in short, has become more complex as the number of actors and issues have increased, and "power politics" is increasingly being supplemented by economic cooperation, as well as conflict, over markets and money.

For Review

1. What are the principal components of power?
2. How does one calculate a nation's power?
3. How can such calculations help prevent or precipitate war?
4. Is any one of the components of power more important than others and why?
5. What do power calculations reveal about the contemporary changing distribution of power among the principal states?

Notes

1. Only recently have some analysts questioned the assumption that the great states are the primary actors. See Stanley Hoffmann, *Gulliver's Troubles or the Setting of American Foreign Policy* (New York: McGraw-Hill, 1968), 26-43. For a response to Hoffmann, see Kenneth N. Waltz, "International Structure, National Force, and the Balance of World Power," *Journal of International Affairs* 21 (June 1967): 161-193.
2. Theodore C. Sorensen, *Kennedy* (New York: Bantam Books, 1966), 589-592.
3. Klaus Knorr, *The War Potential of Nations* (Lexington, Mass.: D.C. Heath, 1970).
4. Quoted by Winston S. Churchill, *The Gathering Storm*, Vol. 1 of *The Second World War* (Boston: Houghton Mifflin, 1948), 341.
5. Peter Bachrach and Morton S. Baratz, *Power and Poverty* (New York: Oxford University Press, 1970), 17-38. Also see Charles A. McClelland, *Theory and the International System* (New York: Macmillan, 1966), 68-88; and K. J. Holsti, *International Politics: A Framework for Analysis* (Englewood Cliffs, N.J.: Prentice-Hall, 1967), 191-209.

6. A. J. P. Taylor, *The Struggle for Mastery in Europe* (London: Oxford University Press, 1954), xxxi; and Paul M. Kennedy, "The First World War and the International Power System," *International Security* (Summer 1984): 23.

7. *New York Times*, Aug. 25, 1985. Also see President Reagan's speech on sanctions against South Africa, *New York Times*, July 23, 1986; and L. Harold Bullis and James E. Mielke, *Strategic and Critical Materials* (Boulder, Colo.: Westview Press, 1984).

8. Robert Gilpin, *France in the Age of the Scientific State* (Princeton, N.J.: Princeton University Press, 1968), 76.

9. John G. Stoessinger, *Why Nations Go to War* (New York: St. Martin's Press, 1974), 220.

10. Carl von Clausewitz, *On War*, ed. and trans. Michael Howard and Peter Paret (Princeton, N.J.: Princeton University Press, 1976), 579.

11. Kenneth N. Waltz, *Foreign Policy and Democratic Politics* (Boston: Little, Brown, 1967).

12. Mikhail Gorbachev, *Perestroika* (New York: Harper & Row, 1987).

13. Geoffrey Blainey, *The Causes of War* (New York: Free Press, 1973), 115-119, 122. Also Jack S. Levy, "This Perception and the Causes of War: Theoretical Linkages and Analytical Problems," *World Politics*, October 1983, 76-99.

14. Andrew Cockburn, *The Threat* (New York: Random House, 1983).

15. Stephen Van Evera, "The Cult of the Offensive and the Origins of World War I," *International Security*, Summer 1984, 58-107; and Paul M. Kennedy, "The First World War and the International Power System," *International Security*, Summer 1984, 7-40.

16. David A. Baldwin, "Power Analysis and World Politics: New Trends Versus Old Tendencies," *World Politics*, January 1979, 163-164.

17. James N. Rosenau, "Capabilities and Control in an Interdependent World," *International Security*, Fall 1976, 34.

18. Paul M. Kennedy, "The First World War," 23. On Britain's decline, see Aaron L. Friedberg, *The Weary Titan* (Princeton, N.J.: Princeton University Press, 1988).

19. Paul M. Kennedy, *The Rise and Fall of British Naval Mastery* (Malabar, Fla.: Robert E. Krieger, 1982), 309-310.

20. Among other works, see Paul M. Kennedy, *The Rise and Fall of the Great Powers* (New York: Random House, 1987), 413 ff. For a briefer analysis, see the section entitled "The Pacific Century" in *Newsweek*, February 28, 1988, 42-63.

21. Martin Grutsinger, "U.S. Edge in Technology is Slipping," *Gainesville Sun*, Sept. 8, 1988. For Japan may be taking the lead in technology, see Clyde V. Prestowitz, *Trading Places* (New York: Basic Books, 1988).

22. Paul M. Kennedy, "The (Relative) Decline of America," *Atlantic Monthly*, August 1987, 29-37.

23. Samuel P. Huntington, "Coping with the Lippmann Gap," *Foreign Affairs* (America and the World, 1987/88 issue): 456-458.

24. *Newsweek*, 62.

25. Marshall I. Goldman, *Gorbachev's Challenge* (New York: Norton, 1987); and Edward A. Hewett, *Reforming the Soviet Economy* (Washington, D.C.: Brookings, 1987).

26. Zbigniew Brzezinski, *Game Plan* (Boston: Atlantic Monthly Press, 1986), 123.

27. Mikhail Gorbachev, *Perestroika* (New York: Harper & Row, 1987). Also see Timothy J. Colton, *The Dilemma of Reform in the Soviet Union*, rev. ed. (New York: Council on Foreign Relations, 1986); and Bill Keller, "Soviets to Allow Private Farmers to Lease State Land for a Lifetime," *New York Times*, Mar. 17, 1989.

28. Brzezinski, *op. cit.,* 99-144.
29. Zbigniew Brzezinski, "America's New Geostrategy," *Foreign Affairs* (Spring 1988): 693.
30. Hedley Bull, "Europe's Self-Reliance," *Foreign Affairs* (Spring 1983): 878.
31. *Newsweek*, 45. Also see the speeches by Under Secretary of State for Political Affairs Michael H. Armacost, "China and the U.S.: Present and Future," June 1, 1988, and "The United States in the Changing Asia of the 1990s," June 6, 1988, *Current Policy*, nos. 1078 and 1079, respectively, published by the Bureau of Public Affairs, Department of State.
32. Goldman, in *Gorbachev's Challenge*, 174-226, thought China was more likely to succeed than the Soviet Union. Also see Zbigniew Brzezinski, *The Grand Failure* (New York: Scribner's, 1989), 177-182 for a similar evaluation of China's future development. Both books were written before the 1989 crackdown.
33. Bernard K. Gordon, *Politics and Protectionism in the Pacific* (London: International Institute of Strategic Studies, 1988), 10.
34. Erza Vogel, "Pax Nipponica?" *Foreign Affairs* (Spring 1986): 752-767; and Kennedy, *Rise and Fall of the Great Powers*, 458-471. For a case study of the rise of Nissan (Datsun) and decline of Ford as examples of efficiency of the Japanese automobile industry and inefficiency of its American competitor, see David Halberstam, *The Reckoning* (New York: Morrow, 1986). Ironically, right after the book was published, Ford made a major comeback while Nissan slumped. Only in 1989 with new models is Nissan seeking a reverse of its fortunes.
35. Wiliam J. Broad, "Novel Technique Shows Japanese Outpace Americans in Innovation," *New York Times*, Mar. 7, 1988; and David E. Sanger, "A High-Tech Lead in Danger," *New York Times*, Dec. 18, 1988.
36. Kennedy, *Rise and Fall of the Great Powers*, 467.
37. Nathaniel C. Nash, "Japan's Banks: Top 10 in Deposits," *New York Times*, July 20, 1988.
38. Kent E. Calder, "Japanese Foreign Economic Policy Formation: Explaining the Reactive State." *World Politics*, July 1988, 520.
39. Theodore H. White, "The Danger of Japan," *New York Times Magazine*, July 28, 1985.
40. Broad, "Novel Technique"; and see the editorial "The Art and the Grasshopper," *New York Times*, Jan. 9, 1989, subtitled, "Why Is U.S. Prosperity Eroding? Japan's Lessons."
41. Calvin Sims, "U.S. Warned to be Strong in Sharp TV," *New York Times*, Nov. 23, 1988.
42. Armacost, "The United States in the Changing Asia," 1. Also see Peter T. Kilborn, "Bush Aides Study Ideas to Refocus Goals of Business," *New York Times*, Jan. 9, 1989.
43. Department of State, Bureau of Public Affairs, "US Economic Relations with East Asia and the Pacific," *gist*, January 1989.
44. Brzezinski, "America's New Geostrategy," 694. Also see Robert Gilpin, *The Political Economy of International Relations* (Princeton, N.J.: Princeton University Press, 1987), 328-336.
45. On Japan's increasing assertiveness in foreign policy, see Clyde Haberman, "The Presumed Uniqueness of Japan," *New York Times Magazine*, August 28, 1988, 39ff.
46. Brzezinski, "America's New Geostrategy," 693.
47. Ibid., 695.

Part Three

THE SECOND
AND
THIRD LEVELS

CHAPTER 8

National and Elite Styles in Foreign Policy: American and Soviet Perceptions and Behavior

CONCEPT OF STYLE: INSULAR AND CONTINENTAL STATES

In the previous chapters the game of international politics was analyzed in terms of the interactions among the states. It was assumed up to this point that states have similar interests, motivations, and internal structures and that their behavior is the product of the state system. Thus, at the first level of analysis, there was no reason to look inward—except in those instances in which states have not behaved as expected. Although the assumption that states are identical in nature is useful conceptually, it clearly does not suffice. To analyze and more fully understand the actual behavior of states, one must look not only at their interactions but also at individual states and their foreign policies—that is, their perception of themselves, their role in the world, and their behavior.

Nations develop distinct personalities or "styles" that affect the manner in which they conduct themselves in the international arena, whether they take the initiative or react to what other states are doing. This style reflects a country's historical experience, geographical position, political values and organization, and economic resources. Nations have unique histories; each reads its own past and draws certain lessons from it—or misreads it and learns the wrong lessons. Each state develops a certain picture of the system and possesses a repertoire of acts and responses derived from its domestic and foreign experiences. Each, to put it another way, perceives "reality" selectively from its particular perspective of *Weltanschauung* (worldview) or a "cognitive map"; in practice, each has a corresponding "operational code" or national style.

In no two states is this more obvious than the United States and the Soviet Union; their styles could not be more different. The United States is a

177

product of its long isolationism. Surrounded by fish to the east and west and weak neighbors to the north and south, the United States has had no security problem for most of its history. It has taken security for granted. In its early days, the country possessed only a small army and, until the turn of the twentieth century, a small navy; the military and its values were generally despised and felt to be the antithesis of the nation's democratic values. Indeed, when needed, the army was drawn primarily from citizen-soldiers or militia. The nation's main task was internal; domestic concerns held an absolute priority. It is no wonder that in an *insular* or island nation like the United States (and to a lesser extent in Britain, protected so long by the English Channel) foreign and domestic policies were thought to be entirely distinct. Events overseas appeared to have little to do with the development of democracy at home. European *continental* powers, bordering one another, could never afford to think of the domestic and foreign arenas as separate or independent. Unable to take security for granted, they gave priority to the conduct of foreign policy.[1]

For the United States, the stark contrast between the intense conflicts, violence, and often perceived immorality (sometimes disapprovingly referred to as Machiavellianism) of international politics, and the law and order, consensus, and generally peaceful change of democracy reinforced this tendency to separate international anarchy from domestic affairs. This contrast may not exist in the minds of people who have experienced internal tyranny from dictatorial regimes, revolution, or other forms of domestic violence; these peoples' experiences are closer to those of states living in an anarchical environment. Unfortunately, such domestic terror by governments against their own people, revolutionary violence, and the breakdown of law and order are widespread in the contemporary world.

This insular, democratic distinction between international and domestic systems, the result of the country's foreign and domestic experiences, led Americans to draw a further distinction between policies of "choice" and "necessity." The American approach to international politics was based on two beliefs: (1) that the United States had a choice about whether it would participate in international politics; and (2) that if it did, it could apply the same moral principles that governed domestic affairs. Americans, once they had gained independence from Europe, told themselves that they were different from the Europeans (Continental Europeans, anyway), who were addicted to power politics. Americans tended not only to associate the behavior of the European states with the character of their class societies but also to see a causal relationship between them. Conflict and war were associated with Europe's aristocratic or undemocratic governments; the United States, an overwhelmingly middle-class society whose outlook was liberal and democratic, was peaceful in its behavior. Almost a century of experience seemed to support the belief that democracies were peaceful in their foreign policies.[2]

Rejecting the power politics approach (an unsocialized attitude according to the state system's rules of the game), American political leaders were concerned primarily with realizing proven democratic principles in foreign policy as the United States became involved internationally. This contrasted to the Continental tradition. Influenced mainly by geography, European leaders spoke of the "necessities of state" and learned to cope with the conflict between morality and "reasons of state." They were in no position to accept the American assumption that nations' leaders did not have to act out of necessity. Living far from Europe, Americans, as democrats, believed that they had freedom of choice and that, in fact, they could choose the moral path in their foreign policies as they did in their internal ones. The resulting American approach has often smacked of excessive moralizing, if not self-righteousness, in the conduct of external affairs. Indeed, not to pursue policies believed to be consistent with democratic and moral principles arouses a sense of guilt and subjects these policies to moral condemnation.

The Soviet approach to international politics is quite different. Perhaps it is more appropriate to say *Russian* approach here because Russia was an old country before the Soviet regime came to power. Unlike the United States, Russia has a long history of invasions. It was attacked by, among others, the Mongols, Turks, Poles, Swedes, French (1812), Japanese (1904-1905), and Germans (1914-1917 and 1941-1945), and was defeated by many of them. Russia's leaders, like most leaders of the Continental states have, always felt vulnerable. Not protected by any natural barriers—oceans, channels, rivers, or mountain ranges—Russia has been invaded and beaten, or almost, so many times that its leaders have been rendered virtually paranoid about security. They did not assume the good neighborliness of surrounding states but their natural enmity. Peace was only a period that started after the last war and served as a time of preparation for the next one. The Russian state historically has dealt with its security problem by centralizing power in an authoritarian state, possessing large armies and, by pushing outward and keeping foreign threats as far away as possible.

Not all of Russia's expansion over the centuries, however, can be considered defensive. The same lack of natural barriers that did not stop invasions also could not prevent Russia's outward thrust of power for offensive purposes. Russia is the world's largest territorial state, covering one-sixth of the earth's surface. It no more became that large merely by repelling invasions than a man becomes rich by being constantly robbed. Indeed, Russia's history has been one of sustained territorial expansion, leading its neighbors such as Japan, which attacked Russia at the turn of the century, to regard it as a threat. Russia's advantage is that it lies in what is usually referred to as Eurasia's heartland at the crossroads of Europe, Asia, and the Middle East. This strategic location allows it to probe all along its borders for weak spots and expand where these exist. Zbigniew Brzezinski, President Jimmy Carter's national security assistant, said that Russia historically has been a "persistent aggressor" against its neighbors rather than their victim. That expansion, of course, alarmed Russia's neighbors and, instead of increasing Russian security, *decreased* it because those neighbors reacted by strengthening themselves.

Thus, even if Russian foreign policy is interpreted as mainly defensive, a cycle was established: "Insecurity generated expansion; expansion bred insecurity; insecurity, in turn, would fuel further expansion." [3]

Russia's leaders understood only too well the meaning of the phrase "reasons of state" and recognized that foreign policy frequently had to be given priority over domestic policy. Democracy with its decentralization of power, as practiced in the United States, did not take root in Russia; an American-style neglect of military power would have been an open invitation to foreign threats and would have negated opportunities for expansion when they arose. Soviet leaders inherited this historical experience when they came to power. They merely carried on the traditional way, with its emphasis on conflict and struggle, the potential enmity of other states, the importance of military power, and self-reliance. Communism was to accentuate these attitudes multifold.

These examples of the contrasting styles of an insular democratic state and a continental undemocratic state suggest that the concept of style can be very useful in clarifying the ways in which a nation and its policy makers are likely to view a specific situation, alternative courses of action, and the course selected. If, for example, a certain nation has acted repeatedly in a particular fashion in similar situations, one could then suggest that it has demonstrated certain distinctive characteristics in its foreign policy outlook and behavior patterns. [4]

AMERICAN NATIONAL STYLE

The U.S. national style is distinguished by seven characteristics in its external behavior that are uniquely "American." [5]

Isolationism Versus Interventionism

Fundamental to American experience is the nation's lengthy isolation from the quarrels of the great European powers. For almost a century the United States was able to devote itself to domestic tasks: strengthening the bonds of national unity, expanding westward, absorbing the millions of immigrants attracted by the opportunities of the country, and industrializing and urbanizing an entire continent. This freedom to concentrate on internal affairs cannot be explained entirely by the presence of the Atlantic Ocean and weaker neighbors to the north and south. As a democratic nation, the United States and its internal orientation must also be explained by the preferences of the electorate. Citizens in a democracy are concerned primarily with their individual and family well-being. All Western democracies, responding to public demands, have become welfare states to some degree. [6] Thus, government demands for service in the armed forces or for higher taxes to finance international obligations are bound to be viewed as burdens. And foreign policy will, on the whole, be considered a distraction from primary domestic tasks. The American citizen's intense concern with private and material welfare and almost compulsive striving for economic success—the measure of individual self-esteem—have long been noted. If, in an egalitarian society, a citizen is judged primarily by his or her material achievements, which indicate ability and bring varying degrees of respect, he or she will concentrate on "getting ahead." Money becomes the symbol of status and prestige; it is a sign of success, just as lack of success at earning money is considered a token of personal failure.

Given such a profound inward orientation, it is not surprising that the United States has turned its attention to the outside world only when provoked. First there had to be a danger so clear that it could no longer be ignored. This point cannot be overemphasized: the United States has rarely initiated policy; the stimuli responsible for its foreign policy have usually come from beyond its frontiers. The result historically was that U.S. foreign policy was essentially both reactive and discontinuous, a series of impatient responses to external pressures whenever there was "clear and present danger" and of returns to more important domestic affairs as soon as danger had passed.

Long-range commitments and foreign policy planning tended to be rare. The pattern, instead, was that of a pendulum: when it believed itself to be provoked, the United States swung from isolation to intervention; once the provocation was over, the United States withdrew again. The unrestricted German submarine campaign in 1917 led the United States into World War I. After Germany's defeat, the United States returned to its traditional isolationist stance. Then the Japanese attack on Pearl Harbor in 1941 brought the United States out of this posture again. After the victory over Germany and Japan, the country attempted to withdraw once more. Britain took the first moves in containing the Soviet Union; the United States, considering itself a friend of both, attempted to mediate impartially between the two! Only after Britain, exhausted by the second world war in this century, collapsed in the winter of 1946-1947 did the United States engage in the cold war. Only U.S. power could contain Soviet power.

Moralism and Missionary Zeal

The American attitude is further characterized by a high degree of moralism and missionary zeal arising from the nation's perception of itself as a unique and morally superior society. The United States was the world's first democracy, committed to improvement of the lot of ordinary people. Americans regarded themselves as the "chosen people." The New World stood for opportunity, democracy, and peace; the Old World for poverty, exploitation, and war. Abraham Lincoln phrased the point aptly when he said that the United States was "the last best hope on earth." Woodrow Wilson during World War I and Franklin Roosevelt during World War II expressed much the same view. Just as in 1861 the United States had not been able to remain half free and half slave, so in 1917 and again in 1941 Americans thought that the world could not continue half free and half slave. Each war was considered an apocalyptic struggle between the forces of darkness and the forces of light.[7] Moralism in foreign policy reflected the awareness and pride of a society that believed it had carved out a better domestic order, free of oppression and injustice.

Isolation from European power politics, therefore, was basically a means of safeguarding American morality and purity. Quarantining itself was the best way to prevent the nation from being soiled and tainted by the undemocratic domestic institutions and foreign policy behavior of European states. The American experiment had to be safeguarded against the corruption of power politics, and withdrawing from the state system and providing the world with an example were the only correct course. Once it became impossible to remain aloof in the twentieth century, however, the country went to the other extreme and launched crusades to destroy the nation—Germany—that had made it necessary to emerge from its isolationism. As a self-proclaimed superior country—morally and politically—the United States could remain uncontaminated only by eliminating those that might infect it. Once provoked, the nation acted as a missionary power and sought to make the world safe for American democracy by democratizing or Americanizing it. American crusading and American isolationism sprang from a single source.

America's wars fitted the pattern. Kaiser Wilhelm II's Germany in World War I (1914-1918) was a semiabsolutist monarchy; Adolf Hitler's Germany in World War II (1939-1945) was a fascist totalitarian regime; and Joseph Stalin's Soviet Union in the cold war (after World War II) was a Communist totalitarian state. They were all antidemocratic, evil systems led by evil men, and they had to be destroyed (or, at least, contained). American power was "righteous power." Either it was not to be used at all, or it was to be used totally in a moral cause—in defense of democracy. The German submarine campaign in 1917 was regarded as more than a series of attacks on American ships. President Wilson called it "warfare against mankind. This is a war against all nations.... The challenge is to mankind." Also, according to Wilson,

> The right is more precious than peace, and we shall fight for the things which we have always carried nearest our hearts—for democracy ... [and] for a universal dominion of right by such a concert of free peoples as shall bring peace and safety to all nations and make the world itself at last free.[8]

Similar words, although perhaps not quite so eloquent, were used during World War II and the cold war. For example, these thoughts were contained in President Harry Truman's 1947 speech, which became known as the Truman Doctrine:

> At the present moment in world history nearly every nation must choose between alternative ways of life.... One way of life is based upon the will of

the majority. . . . The second way of life is based upon the will of a minority forcibly imposed upon the majority . . . [and] it must be the policy of the United States to support free peoples who are resisting attempted subjugations by armed minorities or by outside pressure.[9]

Almost every succeeding president spoke similar words at some point during his term.

Depreciation of Power Politics

A third characteristic of the American national style follows from the liberal democratic values upon which the nation was founded and the resulting high moralism: a depreciation of power politics, with its connotations of conflict, destruction, and death. Strife is considered abnormal and only transitory; harmony is viewed as the normal condition among states. The use of power within the national political system is legitimate only in the service of democratic purposes; its employment in the state system can be justified only in the service of a moral cause. Specifically, in the state system power cannot be employed, at least without arousing guilt feelings, unless the nation confronts a morally unambiguous instance of foreign aggression. And when that happens, the United States must completely eradicate the immoral enemy that threatens the nation and its democratic principles. The presumption is that democracies are peaceful states because the people, who elect their rulers, do not like to go to war and suffer the resulting hardships and losses in lives and property. Therefore, the eruption of hostilities is attributed to authoritarian and totalitarian states whose rulers, unrestrained by democratic public opinion, wield power for their own personal aggrandizement. Their removal becomes a precondition of peace and the end of power politics itself. If the struggle for power cannot be avoided, it is to be abolished.

The American experience appears to support this belief in the normality of peace. Because the United States was a democracy and had enjoyed a long peace during the nineteenth century, lasting until 1917, the association was logical. Americans never asked themselves whether democracy had been the cause of peace or whether that peace had been the product of other forces. The frequent wars of Europe seemed to provide the answer, and European societies were viewed as undemocratic. It was because of this contrast that the United States had cut itself off from the Old World; the nation had to guard its democratic purity and virtue.

Distinction Between Peace and War

Arising from both this moralism and the depreciation of power is a fourth characteristic of the U.S. national style: the tendency to draw a clear-cut distinction between peace and war. Peace is characterized by harmony among nations, and war and power politics in general are considered atypical. In peacetime, little or no attention need be paid to foreign problems. Indeed, such problems would divert people from their individual, materialistic concerns and upset the whole scale of social values.

Once Americans are angry and the United States has to resort to force, however, the use of force can be justified only in terms of the universal moral principles with which the nation, as a democratic country, identifies. Resort to the evil instrument of war can be justified only by noble purposes and by the goal of the complete destruction of the immoral enemy that threatens the integrity, if not the existence, of these principles. Since American power has to be "righteous" power, only its full exercise can ensure salvation or absolution from sin. The national aversion to violence thus becomes transformed into national glorification of violence, and wars become ideological crusades to make the world safe for democracy—by converting authoritarian adversaries into peaceful, democratic states and banishing power politics for all time.[10] Once that aim has been achieved, the United States can again withdraw into itself. Although foreign affairs are annoying diversions from more important domestic matters, such diversions are only temporary; maximum force is applied to aggressors or warmongers to punish them for provocation and to teach them that aggression is immoral and will not be rewarded. As a result, American wars are total wars, fought to achieve total victory and the enemy's unconditional surrender. "There is no substitute for victory," said General Douglas MacArthur in Korea. To stop short of victory is to fight "a half-war." There can be no compromise with the enemy. Only its total defeat is acceptable.[11]

Divorce of Diplomacy from Force

The United States not only considers peace and war two mutually exclusive conditions, but it also divorces diplomacy from force, so that in wartime political considerations are subordinated to military considerations. Once the diplomats have failed to keep the peace through appeals to morality and reason, military considerations become primary. During wartime, the soldier is in charge. Just as medical doctors are responsible for curing their patients, so the military "doctors" must order the treatment of international society when it is infected with the disease of power politics. The United States then traditionally has rejected the concept of war as a political instrument; war has not been viewed as the continuation of politics by other means. Instead, it has been regarded as a politically neutral operation that should be conducted according to its own professional rules and imperatives. The military officer is a nonpolitical technician who conducts the campaign in a strictly military, efficient manner. And war is a purely military instrument whose sole aim is the destruction of the enemy's forces and its despotic regime, so that after its defeat the people can be democratized.

The same moralistic attitude that is responsible for the American all-or-nothing approach to war also militates against the use of diplomacy in its classic sense: to compromise interests, to conciliate differences, and to moderate and isolate conflicts. Although Americans regard diplomacy as a rational process for straightening out misunderstandings among nations, they also have been extremely suspicious of diplomacy. If the United States is by definition moral, it obviously cannot compromise, for a nation endowed with a moral mission can hardly violate its own principles. If it did, national interests would be undermined and the national honor stained. Moreover, to compromise with the immoral enemy is to be contaminated by evil. To reach a settlement with the enemy instead of wiping it out is to acknowledge American weakness. This attitude toward diplomacy, viewed as an instrument of compromise, reinforces the American predilection for violence as a means of settling international problems. War allows the nation to destroy its evil opponent, while permitting it to pursue its moral mission uncompromised.

Belief in U.S. Omnipotence

Twice in the twentieth century the United States has successfully dealt its enemies total defeat, thereby highlighting yet a sixth characteristic of the American national style: the belief that the United States is omnipotent and, once engaged in a conflict, can "lick anyone in the system." [12] Indeed, even earlier in the history of the country, American actions had met with quick success whenever the United States had been drawn into the international arena. At one time or another, Americans have beaten the British, Mexicans, Spaniards, Germans, and Japanese. Furthermore, the United States had never been invaded, defeated, or occupied (as most other nations had been). It had made mistakes, to be sure, but with its great power, it usually had been able to rectify them. For a nation that had the confidence to promise "the difficult today, the impossible tomorrow" failure would be a new experience.

Thus, prior to the cold war, American history had included only victories; the unbroken string of successes seemed evidence of national omnipotence. This belief in American invincibility tended to be reinforced by domestic successes. Historically, the United States was unique in that, with the single exception of the Civil War, it had never experienced national tragedy. Few other states have managed to avoid defeat and conquest. American policy makers usually have not been deterred by thoughts of failure, but, had failure in fact occurred, they could have expected a major political reaction because in a country that is believed to be all-powerful, the public will understand failure or defeat only as the result of national incompetence or treason. The nation cannot admit that its situation may not be resolvable through the proper application of force.

Pragmatism

A seventh and final characteristic of the U.S. national style is generally known as pragmatism. Again, it has been part of the nation's experience that when problems have arisen, they have been solved using whatever means were at hand. Americans have always been a "can-do" people and have prided themselves on their problem-solving abilities. Europeans invented radar and the jet engine, but Americans refined and developed these inventions, produced them on a large scale, and marketed them more effectively than the countries of origin. All problems have seemed solvable; they are only matters of "know-how." The question is not *whether* but *how*—and how quickly at that. This approach to foreign policy may be called the engineering approach:

> A pragmatic or instrumental approach to world problems typifies the Western policymaker. Not theoretical conceptions enabling him to relate policy to the general trends of events, but know-how in the face of concrete problem-situations is what he typically emphasizes. He wants to "solve" the immediate, given concrete problem that is causing "trouble," and be done with it. Accordingly, diplomatic experience—always of great importance, of course—is exalted as the supreme qualification for leadership in foreign policy. For experience is the royal road to know-how. It teaches the statesman how to negotiate with the Russians, how to coordinate policy with the allies, how to respond to emergencies, and so on.
>
> In facing foreign-policy problems it is not the Western habit to attempt first of all to form a valid general picture of the world-setting events in which the problems have arisen. The tendency is rather to isolate the given problem-situation from the larger movement of history and ask: what can and should we do about it? [13]

More specifically, the United States tends to tackle each problem as it arises. In the abstract, this approach may make sense. After all, until a situation has occurred and the "facts" are in, how can one react? The trouble is that by the time sufficient facts are in the situation may well be so far developed that it is too late to do much about it, or, if one tries, difficulties abound. The American quest for certainty is usually carried too far. Policy making involves tackling problems early enough that influence can still be brought usefully to bear. Often, however, it can only be brought to bear when there is still insufficient information. By the time the situation is clear, it may be too late for any effective action short of applying military power; it may even be too late for that. Pragmatism thus reinforces the reactive and discontinuous nature of the American conduct of foreign policy, along with the emphasis on the immediate and short run to the detriment of longer-term policy consideration. [14]

AMERICAN POLICY AFTER WORLD WAR II

The American approach to international politics reflects a series of simple dichotomies: domestic policy versus foreign policy, good peace-loving nations versus bad aggressor nations, isolationism versus crusading, war versus peace, force versus diplomacy. But fundamental to all of them is the self-image of the United States as the epitome of democracy and the defender of the democratic faith. The United States, the shining "beacon lighting for all the world the paths of human destiny" in peacetime (in the words of Ralph

Waldo Emerson), has been like a democratic St. George battling against evil aggressors.

During World War II this moral attitude led the United States to divide nations into those that were "peace-loving" (the United States, Soviet Union, and Great Britain) and those that were "aggressors" (Germany, Italy, and Japan). The former had to destroy the latter and thus sought unconditional surrender. The Western democracies crusaded for total victory. Once that objective had been achieved, the aggressors were to be entirely disarmed and peace preserved through the cooperation of peace-loving nations within the new United Nations. Power politics would be ended. Alliances, spheres of influence, and balances of power, President Roosevelt said shortly before his death, were to be replaced by an international organization, which would furnish an alternative and better means for preserving peace. As the evil nations had been defeated, no new aggressors were expected. The Soviet Union, an ally, was certainly not expected to become an adversary.

Although Soviet behavior had already changed by the time hostilities ceased, a period of eighteen months was to elapse before U.S. policy toward the Soviets was reassessed. The American public attitude toward the Soviet Union was still generally friendly and hopeful for peaceful postwar cooperation. The United States wished to be left alone to occupy itself once more with domestic affairs and the fulfillment of American social values. The end of the war presumably signaled the end of power politics and the restoration of harmony among nations. The emphasis was therefore on rapid demobilization. Only when Britain pulled out of the eastern Mediterranean and there was no longer any countervailing power on the European continent—and only after continued Soviet denunciations and vilifications of the United States and Britain—did America's leaders again commit themselves. For this commitment to be made, a major external stimulus was needed.

Cold War Crusade and Intervention in Vietnam

American identification of the Soviet Union as an enemy and aggressor resulted from Soviet actions in Eastern Europe, Iran, and Turkey. The Soviet Union then became the new enemy. Because international conflict was viewed as a contest between good and evil states, instead of a competition among states who all had legitimate interests, the American-Soviet struggle became transformed into another moral crusade. The Korean War, and especially the Chinese Communist intervention in it, turned a conflict that previously had been limited to Europe and aimed against the Soviet Union into a "global" conflict against communism. The contrast between American democratic values and the Soviet Communist values of what Washington saw as a united Sino-Soviet bloc, was striking. It was a clear instance of good against bad, and it fitted the traditional dichotomy between New World democracy and Old World autocracy.

The impact on policy was readily visible. For example, during the cold war years from 1946 to 1969 American policy makers put off any attempt to achieve a major political settlement with the Soviet Union until after communism had "mellowed"—that is, changed its character. Until then, negotiations were thought to be useless not only because of the expansionist aims of the Soviet leadership but also because such diplomatic dealings with the devil in the Kremlin would be immoral. Recognition of Communist China after Nationalist China's collapse became impossible, and mainland China's intervention in Korea only confirmed the American appraisal of Communist regimes as evil, even though the United States itself had precipitated this intervention with its march up to the Chinese frontier with North Korea.

If communism per se were the enemy, then the United States had to oppose it everywhere or, at least, wherever it seemed that counterbalancing American power could be applied effectively. Thus, the United States built up alliances in Europe (NATO), the Middle East (METO), and Asia (SEATO) around the Sino-Soviet bloc and fought two limited wars on the Asian continent. It also supported numerous anti-Communist regimes, mostly outside of Europe, whether they were democratic or not. Most of them were right wing; Chiang Kai-shek (Nationalist China) on Taiwan and Ngo Dinh Diem and Nguyen Van Thieu (and several in between them) in South Vietnam were typical of the dictators receiving U.S. support. Viewing communism as truly wicked, Americans counted all Communist states as uniformly evil. The recognition of differences among Communist states—and the exploitation of these divisions—was therefore difficult. Nationalism as a divisive factor within the Communist world was played down because of the belief that all such states were equally immoral. Above all, every issue of foreign policy tended to be framed as part of a universal struggle between democracy and totalitarianism, freedom and slavery. The expansion of any Communist country's power was viewed in Washington as an expansion of Soviet power, and, since a gain of power and security for the Soviet Union was equated with a loss of power and security for the United States, it is not surprising that the possible loss of Vietnam was viewed in terms of a domino image. If Vietnam fell, the rest of the dominoes in Southeast Asia were expected to fall, thereby profoundly altering the regional balance of power. That had to be prevented.

This international logic was reinforced by domestic politics as the anti-Communist justification for American foreign policy came back to haunt the policy makers. In Europe, communism was contained, but when Nationalist China collapsed, the Truman administration was attacked as "soft on communism." Indeed, the unquestioned assumption that the United States was omnipotent suggested that the American failure in China had been caused by treason within the U.S. government. If the nation was supposed to be omnipotent, then it could not be lack of strength that accounted for its "defeat." It could not be that there was a limit to the nation's ability to influence events far away from its shores. Such setbacks appeared to have resulted from American policies.

It was argued that China had fallen because the "pro-Communist" administrations of Roosevelt and Truman had either deliberately or unwittingly "sold

China down the river." This charge, which came primarily from the strong conservative wing of the Republican party (including Joseph McCarthy and Richard Nixon), was simplicity itself. American policy had ended in Communist control of the mainland. Administration leaders and the State Department were responsible for this policy. The government must, therefore, be harboring Communists and Communist sympathizers who were "tailoring" American policy to advance the global aims of the Soviet Union.[15] The "loss" of China was the fault of disloyal American leaders. Low morale among the Nationalist Chinese, their administrative and military ineptitude, and repressive policies that had alienated mass support were ignored, as were superior Communist organization, direction, morale, and ability to identify with popular aspirations. When supposed omnipotence failed, conspiratorial interpretations were the result.[16]

The effects on American foreign policy makers were several. Above all, they wanted to avoid being accused of "having lost" country A or B, or of "appeasing communism." The Democrats, accused by the Republicans during the 1952 presidential election (in which the Democrats were defeated) of having lost China, were supersensitive to such charges. The principal result was to make American policy more inflexible and interventionist than it might otherwise have been. This was especially true of policy in Asia where one result was the inability of any administration to recognize Communist China and exploit Sino-Soviet differences before Nixon's visit to mainland China in 1972. That visit took place after the Vietnam War had weakened America's anti-Communist consensus, and Nixon, a conservative Republican, who could hardly be accused of being "soft on communism," had been elected.*

The ultimate cost of this crusading policy was not the failure to recognize Communist China or exploit the Sino-Soviet split but the intervention in Vietnam. As the situation in Vietnam worsened in late 1961, it is not surprising that President John Kennedy introduced American military "advisers," particularly after the Bay of Pigs fiasco in Cuba and American inaction at the time of the erection of the Berlin Wall. Kennedy did not want the Democrats accused of being the party that had "lost Indochina," as it had "lost" China.

---

* The irony is that until 1988 it was conservative Republicans, claiming to be strongly anti-Communist, who could be more accommodating in policy toward China and the Soviet Union than liberal Democrats. In 1979 Jimmy Carter could not get the Strategic Arms Limitation Talks (SALT) II agreement through the Senate; in 1988, however, Reagan, was able to mobilize support for the Intermediate Nuclear Forces (INF) treaty and had he completed the Strategic Arms Reduction Talks (START) agreement, he could have gained support for it as well. In fact, the Soviets let it be known that Gorbachev wanted to sign an agreement on strategic weapons before the end of Reagan's term precisely because Reagan could attract the support needed whereas his successor, especially if he were a liberal Democrat, might fail.

The military advisers temporarily kept the situation in Vietnam from deteriorating. Kennedy's successor, however, had to deal with forestalling a defeat of the South Vietnamese. He intervened with American forces, the logical culmination of his predecessor's actions. From Truman on, each president had done just enough to prevent the loss of South Vietnam.

For each post-World War II president, increasing involvement in Indochina led to a major military intervention calculated as *less costly* than doing nothing and disengaging from Vietnam. In the context of American domestic politics, acquiescence in defeat was unacceptable.[17] The basic rule was "Don't lose Indochina." Each time the American administration came face to face with the possibility of disaster, it escalated the involvement and commitment not to lose Vietnam. Note the negative nature of the goal: to prevent a disaster. It was hoped that if the North Vietnamese found they could not win, they would finally just give up.

Post-Vietnam Withdrawal

The United States, seduced by the "illusion of omnipotence," was reasonably optimistic that it could win in Vietnam. After all, where had American power ever failed? Such optimism was expressed most strongly by the civilian policy makers. When a leading civilian government official was told that eliminating the guerrillas in Vietnam might take as long as it had in Malaya, he curtly responded, "We are *not* the British."[18] As hostilities in Vietnam dragged on and as American casualties and impatience grew,[19] American domestic politics became divided between those who advocated further escalation in the hope of attaining a clear-cut military victory and those who proposed withdrawal because victory seemed elusive. Indeed, these alternative responses sometimes were put forth by the same people, and President Lyndon Johnson found himself increasingly subject to opposing political pressures. To appease those calling for escalation, mainly conservative and hawkish elements in Congress, he did in fact escalate U.S. involvement. This decision was temporarily popular, but backfired when it failed to achieve victory. The other pressure was to withdraw, but to do this was to risk the charge of "appeasement." If he chose the middle course of neither expansion nor retreat, domestic opinion would split further, leaving the center weaker than ever. Whatever he did, the president was trapped, and he could count on little aid from his deeply divided party.

Not only did this all-or-nothing attitude erode Johnson's support, leading him to forgo seeking a second term and producing a Republican victory in the 1968 presidential election, but it also led to widespread American disillusionment with foreign policy and the use of power, especially the use of force. Power politics, it has been suggested, historically has been considered wicked, to be engaged in only by the states of the Old World. American power was supposed to be righteous power. The Vietnam War, which could be watched nightly on television in "living color," seemed to prove only that, in the exercise of power, the nation had forsaken its moral tradition. Driven by anticommunism, which exaggerated the cohesiveness and threat of the Sino-Soviet bloc, tempted to intervene in many places and to make widespread commitments in the name of anticommunism, and aligning itself with many a disreputable reactionary regime in the name of freedom, the United States appeared to have violated its own democratic and liberal principles. This use of power in Vietnam created guilt feelings. Power was viewed as a corrupting factor. It seemed better to concentrate on domestic affairs and to return to a historic duty: to complete the unfinished tasks of American society—that is, create a truly democratic nation in which the gap between profession and performance would be minimal and serve as an example for people everywhere.

Whereas power is viewed as evil and its exercise as tantamount to abuse, providing an example of a just and democratic society to the world is considered the moral thing to do. According to such liberal critics as former senator William Fulbright, chairman of the Senate Foreign Relations Committee until 1974, power had made the United States "arrogant." He counseled that the United States should focus its attention and resources "to serve as an example of democracy to the world" and to "overcome the dangers of the arrogance of power." More specifically, "the nation performs its essential function not in its capacity as a *power* but in its capacity as a *society*." [20] Similarly, Ronald Steel, in appraising the *pax americana*, has said the same thing more eloquently:

> It is now time for us to turn away from global fantasies and begin our perfection of the human race within our own frontiers.... America's worth to the world will be measured not by the solutions she seeks to impose on others, but by the degree to which she achieves her own ideals at home. That is a fitting measure, and an arduous test, of America's greatness.[21]

The optimistic faith that the United States, with its power and missionary zeal, could improve the world was thus replaced by a mood of disillusionment because, in the wake of the Vietnam War, it appeared that the wicked world outside could not be quickly or totally reformed and that the attempt would corrupt the nation. The characteristic swing pattern, which began with an attempt to reform the world, ended with the fear that the nation would forfeit its soul in the effort. It also renewed the determination to concentrate on the United States, and to improve national life so that the presumed American superiority and greater morality could once more spread to the world and be worthy of imitation. Setting an example for the rest of the world, instead of adulterating its own purity with power politics, was said to be the American task.

In this context, foreign policy is replaced by domestic policy, and power by virtue. America's influence, the critics suggested, should be derived solely from the United States' moral standing as a good and just society. Arms, alliances, and spheres of influence are not the answer. A redistribution of income, racial justice, environmental concerns—worthy ends in themselves—are favored as *substitutes* for a foreign policy that demands an extensive role in the world. The shift from military services to social services should bring happiness to the United States and protect the peace of the world. Whatever their prescription for U.S. foreign policy, the critics were characteristically American in their assessment of foreign policy. They too viewed policy in terms of dichotomies: between peace and war, abstention and total commitment, no force and maximum force, and passionate crusading and disillusioned withdrawal.

Détente I and Its Collapse

The détente of the 1970s was, because of this mood of isolationism, largely a tactic. President Richard Nixon and his national security adviser, Henry Kissinger, recognized two opposing forces.[22] One force was the popular desire to limit American involvement in the world because the country was weary of its cold war role, a weariness reinforced by the shock of OPEC's actions and oil price increases. The country had been shown that it was not militarily invincible; now it was also clear that it was economically vulnerable. The other force was the Soviet Union's achievement of strategic parity with the United States. Moreover, the Soviet Union had considerably upgraded its conventional capabilities, developing a sizable surface fleet plus airlift capability. Czarist and Soviet Russia had always been essentially an Eurasian, or Continental, power. Now, for the first time in its history, it had become a global power. As the Soviet Union's ability to neutralize U.S. nuclear power grew, its capacity to project its conventional power beyond Eurasia grew as well. Would the Soviet Union, in these new circumstances, continue to expand its influence only on land and in territory contiguous to its own? Or would it feel a new confidence and take greater risks, challenging the United States in new areas farther away from the Soviet Union? At the very moment when the United States was experiencing its greatest doubt about its own international role and when its strategic superiority that had helped it to "contain" the Soviet Union had eroded, the Soviet Union was more powerful and self-assured than ever before. The question was how could the United States contain the Soviet Union now? How could it be induced to follow a path of self-restraint? Were there nonmilitary levers to supplement, or even to replace, the military one?[23]

The Republican administration found the levers in exploiting the Sino-Soviet schism and enticing Moscow with trade and technology. Détente then was not so much a rejection of the cold war but a continuation of it by other means until the pendulum would swing back and the United States could once more assert its power internationally. The Soviets too had their tactical reasons for pursuing détente. Perhaps the chief one was economic. The Soviet Union's agricultural and industrial problems predated Gorbachev, but General Secretary Leonid Brezhnev was unwilling to risk *glasnost* and *perestroika* to reinvigorate the economy. The possible consequences in terms of domestic upheaval and the security of the Communist party's monopoly of power were too frightful. Brezhnev therefore wanted to import Western food, industrial plants, and modern technology rather than risk the structure of Soviet power.

To gain time and credit, he needed a period of relaxation internationally. The Soviet desire to slow down the Sino-American reconciliation and realignment, to legitimate the postwar European status quo, and to obtain arms control agreements reinforced the need for détente.

Détente I was undermined when the Soviets also sought to exploit the resulting relaxation of tensions. Not that the United States did not seek to make some unilateral gains itself, but Moscow, which replaced virtually all of its strategic missiles *after* SALT I in 1972 as it continued its massive nuclear and conventional military buildup, undertook expansionist efforts that were more sustained and deliberate. Moscow believed the 1970s to be a period of shift in the global balance of power from the United States to the Soviet Union; therefore, it was disposed to exploit this situation. It also saw a new radicalism rising in the Third World, and it hoped to attract new and reliable Marxist allies for the Soviet Union as former colonial states were detached from the imperialist camp. American reaction would be deterred by the Soviet attainment of nuclear parity. The United States, it believed, would have no choice but to face this "new reality" and accept these changes in alignment, whether it liked them or not.

> The international order was now viewed as being conductive to a pro-Soviet bandwagon, in which Soviet gains could cumulate rapidly. . . . [T]he Soviet leaders went through a period of high expectations about their ability to gain the advantages from detente, including the avoidance of confrontation, without sacrificing their commitments to exploit the rapidly growing opportunities for competitive gains in the Third World.[24]

By 1979—the year of the Soviet invasion of Afghanistan, the collapse of General Anastasio Somoza Debayle in Nicaragua and his replacement by the pro-Soviet Marxist Sandinistas, and the fall of the shah in Iran and the emergence of a militant Islamic anti-American regime—détente had collapsed.

The failure of détente I also spelled the end for Democratic president Jimmy Carter, who in 1976 defeated incumbent president Gerald Ford (successor to Richard Nixon, after he had resigned his office in the wake of the Watergate scandal). The Carter administration had reflected the nation's mood of withdrawal and guilt about the misuses of American power. Until the Soviet invasion of Afghanistan, it had rejected power politics. Had not this approach been responsible for America's involvement in Vietnam? The Carter administration therefore de-emphasized the East-West struggle, while focusing its attention on the Third World and the problems of nationalism, self-determination, racial equality, human rights, and poverty. Balance-of-power politics was being transformed into "world order" politics. In the dawning new age of interdependence among states, security as the primary issue was being replaced by a concern with welfare, the hierarchy of nations by greater equality, and the use of force by more peaceful cooperation among states to advance the greater good of all nations, with special emphasis on human welfare and individual dignity. Presumably, the wicked days of power politics were over. A more peaceful and just world was within grasp.

Humiliation and the Reassertion of U.S. Power

In late 1979 the Iranian seizure of American diplomatic personnel in Tehran as hostages sharply shifted the nation's mood again. The 444 days that the hostages were held were considered a national humiliation. One month after the attack on the embassy, the Soviets invaded Afghanistan, and again the United States felt helpless. It was not just that the other superpower felt it could act without considering U.S. reactions; even a middle-range power such as Iran, in the midst of revolutionary turmoil, thought it could act against American interests with impunity. All nations could see that in the wake of Vietnam the United States was determined to play a lesser role in the world. Congressional restraints on the president's ability to use the armed forces and Central Intelligence Agency for overt and covert intervention raised questions about America's will and capability to act.

As a further demonstration, defense budgets plummeted from 8.2 percent of the gross national product in fiscal 1970 to 5.2 percent in fiscal 1977, the lowest figures since before the Korean War. With the Soviets spending, according to the U.S. Central Intelligence Agency, an estimated 16 percent, if not more, on defense, this meant that the 1970s witnessed the largest reduction in American military strength relative to the Soviet Union in the entire postwar period.[25] Large defense requests citing the continuous and enormous growth of Soviet military strength were dismissed by Congress as a "Pentagon scare tactic" in the annual budget fight. When the sharp increases in Soviet missiles were noted, the response was that the Soviets were just "catching up." When they caught up, the reaction was that now they would stop. When they did not stop, the excuse was that the Soviets, after all, confronted not only the United States and NATO, but China as well. And as Soviet military power continued to grow steadily year after year, it was pointed out that the Soviets suffered from paranoia because of past invasions. Finally, as Soviet strength in strategic and conventional weapons grew beyond any conceivable defense needs—as Washington saw it—the ultimate excuse was that force no longer played a role in the post-Vietnam War world. The Soviets were wasting their money, and apparently they were too stupid to realize that the forces they were buying were no longer useful. In this political atmosphere, is it really surprising that the multiple indications of American impotence led to the humiliation at Tehran? Or that this slap in the face would once more arouse the nation to reassert itself?

President Carter's reaction to Afghanistan was twofold: the Carter Doctrine, committing the United States to the defense of the Persian Gulf oil kingdoms, and the imposition of economic sanctions on the Soviet Union. But despite Carter's belated recognition of the Soviet threat and the fact that power politics was not quite dead, Ronald Reagan, the former governor of California, was the beneficiary of this change of public mood. Why reelect Carter, the belated convert to the "hard line," when Reagan had been the genuine hard-liner all along? The pendulum had swung at least part of the way back to involvement and the reassertion of American interests and power in the world.

In 1980 President Reagan refocused the nation's attention on the Soviet Union, the East-West struggle, and the central issue of American security. He sought support for his reapplication of the classical containment policy in characteristic American style by depicting the East-West struggle as a moral conflict. According to Reagan, the Soviet Union was "the focus of evil in the modern world." And he told a Baptist convention, "There is sin and evil in the world and we are enjoined by the scripture and the Lord Jesus to oppose it with all our might." Reagan also stimulated and exploited a renewed pride in the nation and frequently praised the military and its service to the country.

Three characteristics of Reagan's foreign policy stand out.[26] First, he emphasized rebuilding American military strength, especially modernization of the nuclear arsenal. The results were the new B-1 bomber, the MX missile with ten warheads, and the new Trident submarine and Trident I and II missiles. He also proposed supplementing these offensive weapons with a defense against the incoming enemy missiles, called the Strategic Defense Initiative (SDI). Second, in its first term the administration strongly opposed arms control, which it blamed for America's weakened military position. The arms control positions it advanced were strictly intended to ward off public pressures to negotiate by making it appear that it was interested in arms control agreements. Third, the administration implemented what became dubbed the Reagan Doctrine; more accurately, it could be called a "rollback" policy.

This policy aimed to undo the results of Soviet expansion during the 1970s in Afghanistan (where Carter had begun helping the resistance), Angola, and Nicaragua. All three had become Marxist states, but all faced resistance movements. Assuming that the Soviets had overextended themselves, that the balance of power was shifting back to the United States, that the Soviet Union's critical problems were domestic (even before Gorbachev acknowledged this fact), and that except in Afghanistan only peripheral Soviet interests were involved, the Reagan administration believed that Moscow would not risk a confrontation with the United States. In Afghanistan, American military supplies allowed the resistance to the Soviet armed forces to survive until Moscow, tiring after eight and a half years of war, decided to withdraw. In Angola, fighting and negotiations continued until 1988 when a settlement was reached. In Nicaragua, the administration failed because the American-supported contras failed to win a popular base in the country and the Congress and public opinion, fearing another Vietnam, opposed the "covert" war the United States was waging to overthrow the Sandinista government.

It is ironic that by the end of his second term President Reagan had forged a new détente with the Soviet Union, retracted his statements about the "evil empire," and embraced Gorbachev's efforts to reform the Soviet Union. The president had also negotiated an intermediate nuclear forces treaty which abolished this entire class of missiles, and the two powers had made significant progress on a strategic arms agreement that would cut these offensive weapons by 50 percent. As opposed to earlier arms control agreements which had set ceilings on the numbers of weapons each country could possess, the Reagan administration set as its goal the radical reduction, if not the elimination, of nuclear arms. Its achievements in arms control were substantial, in part because of its negotiating tactics (Chapter 18), in part because of the need of the Soviet Union to slow down the arms race, and in part because SDI proved to be a potent bargaining chip at a time when Moscow wanted to avoid a costly arms race—and especially a high-technology one in an area in which it was already rapidly falling behind the Western powers. Although Reagan had been accused of stirring up a new cold war in his first years in power, he and Gorbachev had in fact inaugurated détente II, if not a more profound transformation of the superpower relationship. A new era of Soviet-American relations had begun. Détente I in the 1970s was the product of Vietnam and America's weaknesses and loss of will to continue its containment policy. Détente II was the result of Soviet weaknesses, especially internally, at a time of a revival of American pride and military strength.

SOVIET ELITE STYLE

The Communist 'Ruling Class'

Because foreign policy decisions are made not by nations but by a few decision makers, some analysts have suggested that perhaps the styles or operational codes of the political elite, the small group that makes policy, may be more useful analytically. The United States frequently has been called a one-class society; the basic values of American society have been essentially those of the liberal middle class. For this country, it can be argued, the policy elite and the masses share a fundamental set of beliefs, values, and attitudes: democratic liberalism. In other countries, where class differences are more obvious and the political elites are clearly separated from the mass of the population, the beliefs and values of the elites are usually easily identifiable. Even in countries such as the Soviet Union, which reject class distinctions and claim to be classless societies, the political elites are much more visible and far smaller in size than in Western societies, even those with clear-cut class structures. In the Soviet Union, the Communist party has until now monopolized all power, controlling both the government and the economy. It is this control that makes it the privileged "Soviet ruling class" or *nomenklatura* (this name derives from the secret system by which the party controls all appointments to political, administrative, military, police, and other jobs that it thinks are politically sensitive). The party admits and promotes within its ruling class, which theoretically does not exist. The *nomenklatura* has been estimated at about 750,000 or, with families, approximately 3 million or just over 1 percent of the population. But those who are its highest members and who run the party and state in Moscow and the provinces number about 100,000. Powerful and privileged, they live in exclusive apartments, shop at special stores, go to vacation resorts reserved for them, and have their own medical clinics and doctors. Their wealth comes from the possession of power, the reverse of the frequent Western pattern in which power stems from the accumulation of wealth. This top elite of the Communist class has also been called "partocrats." [27]

Ideology Versus Interest

Almost all debates over Soviet foreign policy revolve around the fundamental issue of the Soviet leaders' self-proclaimed adherence to the official ideology. Are they really motivated by Communist ideology, or do they use it merely to justify and expand their power? Are they seriously bent on fomenting world revolution, or are they trying to strengthen the Soviet Union as a nation—that is, are the Kremlin leaders fundamentally revolutionaries or nationalists? The first-level analysis revealed that ideologies are viewed merely as justifications for what leaders believe they must do to preserve and enhance their security interests in the state system. Ideologies are instruments for rationalizing what would have been done anyway. Ideology, therefore, is not a motivating force. All leaders, including Soviet leaders, think in terms of "national interest"; it is this interest that motivates the behavior of nation-states.[28] Ideology, it would follow, has not led the Soviets to adopt any policy that Soviet national interest has not demanded. It has been merely a means of promoting that interest. The manipulation of ideology to justify any and every change of foreign and domestic policy only "proves" that it is too flexible to be a guide to action.

From the moment the Soviet state was born, the Soviet Union still shared Eurasia with the same states (Germany, France, Britain, China, and Japan) as before the 1917 revolution. Therefore it had to deal with them as the czarist state would have done—that is, according to the balance-of-power logic. In the 1930s, for example, the Soviet state aligned itself first with France against the rising power of Germany and, as the British-French appeasement policy failed, then with Germany—its professed enemy, whose enmity it reciprocated—to delay its threat as long as possible. It hoped that Germany and the Western allies would stalemate each other on the western front if the allies did not win. After World War II, it frequently aligned itself with nationalistic and anti-Western regimes in developing countries, even when they banned the Communist party and arrested and sometimes executed Communist leaders. Ideology and proletarian internationalism were quickly sacrificed to whatever advanced the security and needs of the Soviet Union.

Now, seventy years after the Bolshevik Revolution, not only have the passions that animated the early leaders long been spent, but a new generation is taking over power. The earlier generation of leaders, born early in this century, rose to prominence in the thirties, and preserved their stranglehold on the top offices until the 1970s. They participated in the massive industrialization after 1928 and the victory of World War II. After Stalin's death, they hung on to power, resisting Khrushchev's efforts to change and revitalize the system while the economy stagnated and old patterns of behavior ossified. The new generation, born in the late 1920s, and early 1930s, raised in the system, loyal to it, and obviously its beneficiaries, are now seeking to make it work better, not to transform it.[29] Failure spells not only a decline in the standards of living when expectations are of improving standards, but also the decline of the Soviet Union as a superpower. Thus, the new leaders confront many problems. They will have to find answers to these as practical politicians, and, if anything, they will have to throw out much past dogma.

Ideology, Perception, and 'Operational Code'

Is the question asked earlier—in what ways, if any, does Soviet ideology affect Soviet leaders, especially the current generation, who are certainly not the "true believer" types of Lenin's generation—then still relevant? The answer is yes, ideology does matter, but this does not mean that in a specific situation the men in the Kremlin go to the library and search for guidance in the works of Marx and Lenin. There is no one-to-one relationship between ideology and policy. Indeed, from a practical point of view, the ideology appears largely irrelevant. Policy makers act in terms of threats to their security, opportunities for enhancing their influence, domestic politics, and other conditions. But the ideology is not irrelevant in the sense that it provides the Soviet leadership with a way of perceiving and interpreting "reality"—with *their* model of the world. Ideology in this context is what earlier was called an analytical framework that "organized reality" for its devotees. It is through ideological lenses that policy makers selectively perceive the world and understand it, define the 'national interest' and decide how to act.[30] Alexander George, a political scientist, has referred to this general Marxist-Leninist orientation to the world as an "operational code."[31] At its core are certain questions about political life: What is the "essential" nature of politics? Is it basically one of harmony or conflict? What is the fundamental character of one's opponents? What are the prospects for victory and should one be optimistic or pessimistic? How much control does one have over historical development, and how can one move it in the desired direction? What is the role of "chance"? And what are the best tactics to most effectively achieve one's goals? It is the answers to these questions that constitute the operational code and it is the resulting set of attitudes towards international politics that all Soviet leaders have shared up till now.

Very briefly, the basic tenets of Marxism-Leninism are:[32]

- Economic forces are fundamental. The organization of the production and the distribution of wealth is the foundation, or substructure, upon which society is built.
- The capitalist superstructure consists of (1) the owners of the means of production and wealth, and (2) those who work for them and are exploited by them. Class relations are essentially based on opposing interests and conflict. According to Marx, all history is the history of class struggle between the rich and the poor—between the slave owners and the slaves, the feudal, land-owning nobility and the peasantry, the capitalist owners of industry (the bourgeoisie) and the working class (the proletariat).
- The capitalist political system, like the class structure, reflects the nature of the economic system. The owners of wealth control the state and use its instruments—the army, the police, and other levers of governmental power—to keep control. They can also manipulate other means of control, such as the legal and educational systems and religion, to maintain their power.
- This type of system cannot be reformed. Superficial, or cosmetic, changes may be attempted in order to "buy off" the underprivileged and the exploited, but they cannot save the system. Contemporary capitalism is based upon private property and the profit motive. Their abolition is the prerequisite for the productive use of industry for the benefit of the many instead of the luxury of the few. But the nature of capitalism cannot be changed; attempts to create a socialist society will be resisted.
- The injustices of capitalism will come to an end, however, with the proletarian revolution. This revolution will occur when the proletariat has become the majority and is politically conscious of its own exploitation. This day of reckoning is historically inevitable.
- Lenin explained the failure of this "inevitable" revolution to occur in the Western industrial countries by imperialism and the massive capitalist exploitation of non-Western, or colonial, peoples. This global exploitation was so profitable that some of the profits trickled down to the industrial proletariat, so that its standard of living was improved, its revolutionary consciousness eroded, and its vested interest in capitalism strengthened. Domestic revolution was thus avoided by means of a policy of imperialism.
- The Marxist class struggle within the capitalist states was projected onto the global plane. The rich are now defined as the Western industrial states, the poor and exploited as the developing countries. This worldwide class struggle has become the critical conflict in the world.
- Only when the industrial states lose the cheap raw materials previously provided by the developing countries and the economic growth rate slows, so that unemployment increases and the standard of living declines, will the domestic proletariat again recognize that its interests

clash with those of the bourgeoisie. Then the class conflict will resume and will end in the proletarian revolution.

What is striking, and what shall be emphasized below, is that this ideology is fully compatible with—indeed, reinforces—the realist perspective of leaders of states socialized by the state system. The Communist emphasis is on conflict and change; all political relationships are viewed in terms of struggle, including war. Specifically, the general ideological outlook of leaders, with its total critique of capitalist society and way of analyzing the world, defines the foe for them, the ultimate aim, and a commitment to help history along to its predestined end. By positing the Soviet relationship with capitalist states as one of enmity and continuous struggle and by attributing to the latter hostile intentions, Moscow's sense of insecurity has been heightened even beyond traditional concerns; the external world has always been viewed as unremittingly threatening. The resulting determination to rely mainly on oneself, not allies, to be strong, especially militarily, not relaxing one's guard, and distrusting the enemy's professions of peaceful intent, are attitudes hardly unknown in the realist's world.

Definition of the Enemy and Revolutionary Aims

However weakened the hold of Marxist-Leninist ideology on Soviet leaders seventy years after the revolution, it does provide them with a set of core beliefs and attitudes that have profoundly influenced their view of the state system; the nature of politics, including international politics; and who their enemies are. Most of all, it defines their principal enemy and the historically appointed task of helping to bring about the new, postcapitalist order. This ideology does not merely embody a critique of contemporary capitalist society; it also projects communism as the desired state of existence for humanity.

Domestic justice and international peace can be realized only if the old capitalist order is swept away throughout the entire state system; all people are to be liberated from the social tyranny of capitalism and the scourge of war. Since 1917 this purpose has transformed Russia, a traditional great power, into *Soviet* Russia, a revolutionary state, committed to the secular mission of eliminating world capitalism. Soviet leaders historically have denied the legitimacy of what they have regarded as the prevailing international capitalistic order. Their ideology is thus contrary to the basic assumption of the balance of power: that each state has the right to exist, regardless of its domestic structure. The balance is supposed to protect all members of the state system. But the revolutionary state is revolutionary just because it *claims universal applicability for its values and ways of organizing domestic society and makes the domestic structures of all other states the central issue of international politics.*

No state in a pluralistic system can feel absolutely secure; yet each, though greatly concerned with its security, normally does not feel *so* insecure that it seeks universal domination to eliminate threats from all other states. It seeks security within a balance-of-power system that provides for its survival, as well as for the survival of other states. Conflicts are therefore *limited* and *pragmatic*; no state seeks another's elimination. Each recognizes the right of the others to exist. Communist ideology, by repudiating the legitimacy of capitalist states, however, transforms the international struggle between the revolutionary power and its adversaries into a *total* and *ideological* conflict. If one state feels compelled to destroy the domestic structures of other states and to transform them according to its own ideological values, that state must seek dominance or hegemony so that it can impose its will on them.

In a brilliant and eloquent passage, George Kennan described how this revolutionary approach to foreign policy has made a "mockery of the entire Western theory of international relationships, as it evolved in the period from the seventeenth to the nineteenth centuries." [33] He went on to say:

> The national state of modern Europe, bitterly as it might feud with its neighbors over the questions of *relative* advantage, was distinguished from the older forms of state power by its abandonment of universalistic and messianic pretensions, by its general readiness to recognize the equality of existence of other sovereign authorities, to accept their legitimacy and independence, and to concede the principle of live and let live as a basic rule in the determination of international relationships. . . .
>
> It was this theory that the Bolsheviki challenged on their assumption of power in Russia. They challenged it by the universality of their own ideological pretensions—by the claim, that is, to an unlimited universal validity of their own ideas as to how society ought to be socially and politically organized. They challenged it by their insistence that the laws governing the operation of human society demanded the violent overthrow everywhere of governments which did not accept the ideological tenets of Russian Communism, and the replacement of these governments by one that did. . . .
>
> The significance of this situation has been somewhat obscured by those Western historians and commentators who have been unable to perceive any difference in principle between the attitude of the Soviet Union toward the Western countries and that of the Western countries toward the Soviet Union. After all, they have said, were not the Western governments equally hostile to Russia? Did they not attempt to overthrow the Soviet regime by their intervention in 1918-1919? Could the challenge to existing concepts of international relations properly be laid only at the Soviet door? Was not the Western rejection of socialism as a conceivable governmental system just as important in the breakdown of the established theory of international life as the Soviet rejection of capitalism?
>
> It is my belief that the answer to the question is "No." Any unclarity on this point can lead to a grievous misunderstanding of some of the basic elements of Soviet-Western relations. There were, in those initial years of Soviet power, some very significant differences between anti-Sovietism in the West and the hostility which the Soviet leaders entertained for the Western powers. This hostility from the Communist side is preconceived, ideological, deductive. In the minds of the Soviet leaders, it long predated the Communist seizure of power in Russia. Anti-Sovietism in the West, on the other hand, was largely a confused, astonished, and indignant reaction to the first acts of the Soviet regime. Many people in the Western governments came to hate the Soviet leaders for what they *did*. The

Communists, on the other hand, hated the Western governments for what they *were*, regardless of what they did. They entertained this feeling long before there was even any socialistic state for the capitalists to do anything to. Their hatred did not vary according to the complexion or policies or actions of the individual noncommunist governments. It never has. . . .

Had the Soviet leaders contented themselves from the outset with saying that they felt that they knew what was good for Russia, and refrained from taking positions on what was good for other countries, Western hostility to the Soviet Union would never have been what it has been. The issue has never been, and is not today, the right of the Russian people to have a socialistic ordering of society if they so wish; the issue is how a government which happens to be socialistic is going to behave in relation to its world environment.[34]

The upshot of this new long-range mission that Soviet rulers assumed after 1917 was to reinforce historic Russian expansionism. Russian leaders had a right to feel insecure, given the frequency of invasions; the Soviet leaders' insecurity was even greater, given their ideological perception of the outside world as hostile. Indeed, this perception was so strong that they maintained a "garrison state" at home. No doubt, Soviet leaders also found the enmity of the capitalist world a convenient rationalization for preserving a totalitarian state and legitimizing their monopoly of political power. But their perception of states beyond their borders, especially in Europe, as bourgeois and dangerous, on top of a sense of historic vulnerability, appeared to them to demand constant vigilance and central control to deal with their enemies, whom they saw everywhere, abroad and at home. Even if offensive reasons for expansion are forgotten—for example, adding new members to the world of socialism— the unique combination of its great, almost paranoid, insecurity and its great power, the result of its sizable population, rich resources, and large industrial base, led to a policy of constantly seeking to enhance Soviet influence in order to maximize Soviet security.[35] But this search for virtually absolute security came, as Brzezinski suggested earlier, at the price of the insecurity of other nations, and as the latter took measures to increase their security, the cycle began again.

Marxism-Leninism as a Method of Analysis

Marxism-Leninism provides the Soviet leaders with more than a broad *Weltanschauung* and a definition of ultimate purpose as a guide to policy; it also provides a method of analysis that makes it possible to identify, explain, and comprehend the particular historical era that the world is passing through on the way to postcapitalism. In contrast to the more pragmatic American approach, in which leaders tend to react to each problem as it arises and to deal with each on its "merits," the Soviet approach is based on a type of broad conceptual approach that is rare in the United States. Kremlin leaders start with a broad picture of the world, the principal forces at work in it, and the direction of contemporary history.

Lenin asserted that capitalism had used imperialism to avoid domestic revolution, that the basic struggle between capitalism and communism had become worldwide, and that revolution would begin in what is now called the Third World. From the beginning, the Soviet leaders have seen their own revolution as not simply a single event in one country but part of a larger, continuing historical process.[36] Until 1917 the international system had been controlled by the West. European colonial rule had spread to all parts of the globe, and by the beginning of the century the United States, already dominant over Latin America, had begun to play a role in the Pacific area. The Russian revolution signaled the first defection from this Western-dominated international capitalist system. Furthermore, the revolution was the beginning of the end of this basically European-centered world order; the defection of Russia was only the first one.

According to the Marxist-Leninist interpretation of contemporary history, the projected decline of Europe was to be paralleled by the emergence of a new world order, the nucleus of which would be postcapitalist Soviet Russia. As the West's "raw materials appendages" in the Third World became increasingly conscious of their subordinate status, their exploitation, and their poverty, they would become more and more resentful. In their proletarian revolution against the West, they would be drawn to the Soviet Union. In stage one—World War I—the defection of Russia had occurred; in stage two— beginning after World War II—the "peoples' democracies" of Eastern Europe and China defected from the weakening world capitalist order. Initially Soviet Russia had been alone, confronted by "capitalist encirclement." After 1945 it was no longer alone, and the conflict became one between the capitalist and Communist worlds. As a greater number of Arab, Asian, and African nations became independent from colonial rule, Moscow leaders saw "the breakdown of the structure of Western dominion in the non-European parts of the world, the disappearance of most of what remained in the interwar periods (1919-39) of the great European colonial empires."[37]

It is hardly surprising then, given this interpretation of contemporary history, that the Soviet Union is committed to what is now called *national liberation.* It sees its support for national liberation movements, on the one hand, as helping to administer the final blow to the old international order, propped up by the United States since 1945, and, on the other hand, as promoting the creation of a new postcapitalist system centered on the Soviet Union. Even during the period of détente, Moscow always openly declared that détente did not mean the end of the ideological struggle and the abandonment of support for national liberation. The Soviet-Cuban-East German interventions in Afghanistan, Angola, Ethiopia, and South Yemen during the 1970s were consistent with this perspective. An ideology that provides its leaders with a general worldview, an understanding of the principal social and political forces at work in the world, and sufficient insight into history to grasp the "essence" of contemporary international politics is obviously not meaningless, a mere rationalization of policies that would have been pursued even if the ideology had never existed.

Commitment to Struggle and Caution

Indeed, once Marxism-Leninism had committed the Soviet leadership to elimination of the old order, the conflict between the Soviet Union and the Western industrial states, all of which were regarded as capitalist, became total and irreconcilable. For Marx, the basic "fact" of history was the condition of unending conflict between classes; for Lenin, it was the struggle between states controlled by antagonistic classes. For the Soviets then, politics is not a means of ultimate reconciliation. It is instead a bitter and unending series of campaigns to defeat the capitalist enemy. The only question is *kto, kovo?* (Who, whom?, meaning "Who will destroy whom?"), though history has already predicted the outcome.[38] But this formula is symptomatic of a basic outlook. Between adversaries, agreements can be only temporary, each only a tactical move in the struggle.

This struggle must be prosecuted with persistence; to end this historically ordained struggle would be tantamount to betrayal of the revolutionary mission. Victory over capitalism is the *raison d'être* of the movement. But while the goal is constant, tactics are flexible. Opportunities for the advancement of Soviet power are not to be forgone, but they are to be pursued only after the most careful calculation of the possible benefits versus the likely risks and costs. Soviet doctrine rejects adventurism and it counsels knowing when to stop pushing to expand and even to retreat before superior power. There is no special emphasis in Communist doctrine on the use of force, as there was in Nazi doctrine.

> The Kremlin is under no ideological compulsion to accomplish its purpose in a hurry. Like the Church, it is dealing in ideological concepts which are of long term validity, and it can afford to be patient. It has no right to risk the existing achievements of the revolution for the sake of vain baubles of the future.[39]

Soviet doctrine also accepts the tactical need for periods of relaxation of tensions or détentes when time is needed, as at present, to recoup the nation's economy to assure its future economic and military strength. It also accepts negotiations and agreements such as arms control accords to prevent a suicidal nuclear war (see Chapter 18), as well as measures to advance the purposes of the Soviet state in some other ways such as, attracting Western trade, technology, and credits to help modernize the economy. This does not necessarily mean, however, that the struggle against capitalism has been abandoned. Indeed, rather than postponing it, agreements may serve to further it if, for example, by defusing the enemy image, they drive a wedge between members of the opposing coalition (such as between Europeans and Americans) or relax the enemy's guard by feeding its hopes that the conflict is over.

Soviet doctrine is therefore very cautious.[40] Force has been used only where vital interests were at issue, Soviet intervention promised a quick solution at moderate costs, and the United States was unlikely to intervene. Even in Hungary in 1956 and Czechoslovakia in 1968, Soviet intervention was hesitant despite the obviously critical importance of preventing defections from the Warsaw Treaty Organization. They intervened neither in Yugoslavia when Stalin threw it out of the Soviet bloc in 1948, nor later in Romania when it showed independence in foreign policy, nor in China when relations tensed in the late 1960s, nor in Poland, where the regime's authority was being undermined in 1980-1981. All these states are close to or border the Soviet Union. Only in Afghanistan did Moscow make a miscalculation. Soviet behavior clearly reflected the memory of World War II's awful losses and destruction and a keen awareness of the catastrophic impact a nuclear war would have. If the Soviet Union used force only against its allies and friends, it was nevertheless repeatedly willing to challenge and test American commitments and resolve. But while willing to raise tensions, it always very carefully and unfailingly left itself a route for escape if the United States and the West reacted firmly; if not, it took another step forward.

According to the Soviet viewpoint, at least before Mikhail Gorbachev in 1985, good will is a quality absent from such an adversary relationship. Capitalist states do not possess decent intentions; by nature, their motives are hostile. Western conciliatory gestures and peaceful professions are dismissed as either hypocritical or propagandistic. When Western states sign arms control agreements, it is not because they seek genuine mutual accommodation but because they recognize the superiority of Soviet power and have no choice but to be compromising. Thus, Western acts of moderation and expressions for a better relationship have in the past provided Moscow with a rationale for further arms build-ups and continued pressure; the more arms, the more accommodating the West would be. In over thirty years, Kennan once wrote, he had never known a single instance of a non-Communist government being credited with a "single generous or worthy impulse."[41] All actions responsive to Soviet interests are attributed to "bowing to necessity," yielding to "outraged opinion" or some ulterior motive.

The Soviet Style, World War II, and the Beginning of the Cold War

Not surprisingly then, the ideological perceptions of Soviet leaders have enhanced the regime's insecurity and reinforced the traditional Russian approach to international politics of relying on oneself, not allies or professions of peaceful intent from potential adversaries; of regarding the outside world with deep suspicion, if not hostility; and of always being strong militarily to defend oneself and not relaxing one's vigilance. International politics has been a constant struggle. One result of these attitudes has been deepening suspicion and fear among the states coexisting with the Soviet Union. Perhaps the most significant characteristic of Soviet leaders' thinking has been their insistence on their superior insight into history. They claim that Marxism-Leninism has given them a greater ability to understand political events as a manifestation of an objective underlying reality which is defined by basic economic and social structures. Soviet leaders therefore, convinced that they have unsurpassed theoretical comprehension of the past, present, and future are bound to see the international environment as extremely hostile and to regard with deep distrust any Western state, however benevolent its expressed intentions or conciliatory its approach. Indeed, since the Soviet Union has assumed that the Western states are out to destroy it—as it has been bent on destroying the Western states—the Soviets' attitude toward what they have regarded as a capitalist-dominated system has bordered on paranoia.

Consequently, it was immaterial during World War II whether Stalin personally liked Roosevelt. Roosevelt's expressions of hope for peace and cooperation after the defeat of Germany were dismissed as "sentimental gestures," not reflecting "reality." On the eve of a 1985 summit conference with President Reagan, Soviet leader Mikhail Gorbachev was reported to believe that the United States was "a land controlled by wealthy capitalists and conservative business interests."[42] This image of the United States as a foe corresponded closely to the Marxist-Leninist view of a nation in which ordinary citizens are exploited by the ruling class and the purpose of government policy is to ensure the vested interests of the rich. Stalin *knew* that the deeper objective forces of the economic substructure, upon which the prevailing social and political superstructure rested, would determine Roosevelt's actions. In his view, the American president was merely a puppet—though perhaps a likable puppet—of Wall Street interests. Governmental decisions simply reflected the law of capitalism. How could anyone have persuaded Stalin otherwise, when he, like all other Soviet leaders, was absolutely convinced of his deeper insight into history, arising from his Marxist-Leninist training?

This suspicion of capitalist states has been constant since 1917.[43] When any state defines another as an enemy long enough and acts upon that assumption, it will come to see confirmation for its suspicions in the reaction of the other state, whether that reaction is firm or conciliatory. Toughness will be viewed as confirmation of the other state's enmity; conciliation will be seen as an attempt to soften, in order to strike when vigilance has been relaxed. All actions by capitalist states, as already noted, are regarded as reflecting only their hostility toward Soviet Russia; their behavior is never attributed to friendly motives or mistaken but correctable policies.

The intervention by Russia's former World War I allies after the Bolshevik capture of power in 1917 was seen as an attempt to restore the czar and the old order. The French attempt to contain Germany between the two world wars by means of an alliance with Poland and several other eastern European countries was viewed as an effort to keep the Soviets out of Europe. The appeasement of Hitler was perceived as a move to turn Nazi Germany away from attacking the Western states to an attack on the Soviet Union. Appeasement "opened the gates to the East." During World War II, from 1941 to 1945, Moscow viewed the United States only as a temporary ally. Once Germany had been defeated, the United States, the strongest Western capitalist power, would become the Soviet Union's principal enemy in the continuing struggle against capitalism. Leaders in the United States, thinking in terms of the country's historic approach to international politics, saw World War II as a temporary interruption of the normal, peaceful condition among nations. After the conclusion of hostilities, U.S. policy makers expected to live in harmony and friendship with the Soviet Union. The chief American objective in Europe from 1941-1945 was strictly military: the unconditional surrender of Germany in the quickest possible time, total victory, and the elimination of Hitler. A postwar balance of power against the Soviet Union played no role in the formulation of American wartime planning and strategy. Soviet policy makers, however, foresaw the postwar conflict and remained highly suspicious of the capitalist West.

To cite only one of many examples, the Soviets not unnaturally wanted the Western allies to invade Western Europe to relieve the pressure on the eastern front. They did not believe any of the Western explanations of why that could not be done in 1942 or 1943, especially the claim that the West lacked sufficient landing craft for an operation of such magnitude or that the United States and Britain were unwilling to risk cross channel invasion of France unless there were assurances that the invading forces would not be driven back into the water with enormous loss of life. The Soviets dismissed these as mere excuses. Why should the Western allies delay? Because, in the Soviet view, they were waiting to invade the Continent until Germany and the Soviet Union had bled each other white. Then they could administer the final blow to Germany and dictate postwar terms to the Soviet Union as well. In the wake of the retreating German armies, the Soviet Union consolidated its hold on Eastern Europe as a buffer zone to give it greater protection in the postwar conflict.

Ironically, given Stalin's expectations, the war years had created a great reservoir of good will toward the Soviet Union both in the United States and in Western Europe. The Soviet Union had borne the brunt of the German armies, and the heroism of the Red Army and the Soviet people was acclaimed everywhere. Stalin, the dictator who had collaborated with Hitler in 1939-1941, became "Uncle Joe," as American leaders spoke of a new era of good relations with the Soviets. In the United States and Britain, hopes for the postwar period were high. By and large, the Soviet Union was described in glowing terms—virtually as a democracy—just as it was later depicted in almost satanic terms. Concerned as the Soviet Union was about its security in Eastern Europe, in this atmosphere it should have been easily reassured.

Had the Soviet Union left Bulgaria, Hungary, Poland, and Romania to govern themselves domestically while securing control of their foreign policies, as it did in postwar Czechoslovakia, it could have avoided arousing and alienating the United States and Britain. The Western states accepted the Soviet contention that Eastern Europe was the Soviet Union's security belt, but they argued that freely elected coalition governments that included Communists could be friendly to both the Soviets *and* the West. President Eduard Benes in Czechoslovakia seemed a symbol of this model for Eastern

Europe, for the Czech Communists had, in a free election, won a plurality of the vote and were therefore the dominant partner in the coalition government. But even that kind of coexistence was unacceptable to the Soviet Union. Non-Communist parties by nature were regarded as anti-Communist because they allegedly represented class enemies. They were therefore to be eliminated from the Czech government, as they already had been in the rest of Eastern Europe. The Soviets overthrew the coalition government in Prague.

It may be that Soviet expansionist policy in the wake of the retreating German allies can be explained in terms of state-system behavior. Russian leaders long ago had been socialized by this system. It can hardly be doubted that their traditional power politics outlook has been intensified greatly by the ideological perceptions of Soviet leaders. For the latter, that outlook has raised their sense of insecurity; strengthened their view of capitalist states as extremely hostile; committed them to accept the idea of a long-run struggle; intensified their suspicion of capitalist states' professions of peace and friendship as tricks to deceive them and lower their guard; and deepened their reliance on themselves, especially their nation's military power. During World War II, Stalin, knowing that Roosevelt was the political leader of a capitalist state—in effect, a tool of Wall Street—could not believe that the president's statements of good intentions and good will were genuine, and that they reflected the hopes of the American people who had come to respect and admire the Soviet Union because of its war effort, endurance, and courage. Stalin's perception of Soviet Russia's role in the world also made it impossible for him to abstain from exploiting weaknesses to the south and west of the Soviet Union in an effort to extend socialism to a larger area. The relative security that the Soviet leader could have gained for his country by acting more cautiously was squandered because of his ideological thinking and behavior. This aroused British and then American opposition.

Effects of Ideology on Communist State Relationships

Communist ideology not only intensified the suspicions that already existed in the state system and hindered the establishment of alliances with Western states, but also impeded the formation of smoothly working alliances with other Communist states. The Soviet Union's suspicions of other Communist states was revealed when, right after the war, Stalin expelled Yugoslavia's Marshal Tito—a loyal Stalinist until then—from the Soviet bloc. Soviet suspicion was revealed even more dramatically in the Soviet Union's relationship with Communist China; it simply proved impossible for these two giants of the Communist world to maintain a long-term, mutually beneficial alliance. Conflicts among Communist nations were supposed to be nonexistent, for antagonism among states was ostensibly the result of the competing interests of their dominant classes. Communist states professed to be classless societies, and no strife between them should have occurred. The problem was that the Soviet Union was no longer the only powerful Communist state and its monopoly of "truth"—that is, its total control of decision making—was being challenged.

In part the Kremlin leaders had only themselves to blame for this under-mining of their authority. One of the functions of Communist ideology is to legitimate those who hold authority. Communist ideology, therefore, is de-signed to legitimate Soviet leaders both as rulers of the Soviet Union and—when the Soviet Union was the only socialist state—as directors of the international Communist movement. Just as there can be only one pope, there can be only one source of ideological pronouncements in a secular movement like communism. Moscow was this infallible source. But Beijing's leaders challenged this authority and the Soviet monopoly of political wisdom. In the resulting interparty conflict, each contender claimed the correct interpreta-tion of history and the true interpretation of party theology. Within years of Stalin's death, each country was denouncing the other for heresy. Claiming to be fundamentalists, the Chinese saw themselves as remaining true to Marx-ism-Leninism, which they believed the Soviets had betrayed. Moscow, the Communist Rome, and Nikita Khrushchev, the new Communist pope (and later Leonid Brezhnev), were thus challenged by Mao Ze-dong's Eastern orthodox church.

Compromise on common policies between the *Communist* Soviet Union and *Communist* China was to pose an insuperable obstacle. In matters of doctrine, when the purity of ideology is at stake, does not a policy of give-and-take represent contamination? How can mutual adjustments be made between two members of a movement in which differences of emphasis become issues of loyalty to the faith? How could the primacy, infallibility, and doctrinal purity of the Kremlin leaders be reconciled with Chinese claims to an equal voice, Maoist infallibility, and ideological fundamentalism? The Western allies, themselves pluralistic societies, can cope with pluralism and diversity. Com-munist states cannot, for their parties impose uniform domestic patterns in accordance with their ideological interpretations. Each is a totalitarian society precisely because the Communist party claims to be the bearer of revealed "truth," which must be imposed upon society because "the truth will make men free." Heresy must be ruthlessly eliminated. How can two such states, each convinced that its interpretation of the truth is the only correct one, coexist?

Nonrevolutionary great powers at least share a degree of toleration. If they are allies, as are France and the United States, they can resolve differences as mere conflicts of interest without the additional burden of a superimposed conflict between good and evil. When differences of interest continue to exist, they do not necessarily lead to complete rupture. The self-righteous—for the righteous always tend to become self-righteous—exhibit no such tolerance, however. When ideology is so intimately linked with power, as it is in Communist policy and decision making, then there can be only one "correct" answer. Divergent policies cannot be compromised, and these differences affect the entire range of relations. The resulting bitterness between Soviet and Chinese leaders over who was orthodox and who was heretical led to decades of extreme and vitriolic denunciations, worse than those each had ever aimed toward the United States.

Compromise was blocked by the insistence on doctrinal purity. A "correct" answer demands a single center of political authority and ideological orthodoxy. *Any relationship between Communist states, therefore, must be hierarchical in nature; it cannot be one of equality.* Either Moscow or Beijing must be the center of Communist theological interpretation *and* the source of policy for most, if not all, issues. Thus, it was not wholly surprising that the Sino-Soviet break occurred after the border clashes in 1969; nor was it surprising that Chinese fears of Soviet intervention led Beijing to look to Washington for protection.

It is also not surprising that the countries of Eastern Europe, instead of giving the Soviet Union the greater sense of security it sought when it transformed them into satellites, have only contributed to its insecurity, compelling it to intervene repeatedly militarily and politically, to station Soviet forces in most of them, and to subsidize their shaky economies at great expense to its own. Yet as events in Poland demonstrated in the 1980s, that country, and perhaps all of Eastern Europe have been emerging as a "region of potentially explosive instability, with five countries already in a classic prerevolutionary situation" of economic failures and political instability.[44] Should this, combined with Gorbachev's efforts to let the former satellites be responsible for their own domestic affairs, spark an explosion and Soviet intervention, endangering even Gorbachev's restructuring policies at home, it would again expose Soviet insecurity in the area and reinforce once again the strong anti-Soviet feelings existing in Czechoslovakia, Hungary, and Romania. Thus, there is surely an irony about the results of Soviet foreign policy. After forty-five years, the Soviet Union is the only Communist state surrounded by hostile Communist states. It has driven China into the arms of the West, and the East European countries, except perhaps for historically pro-Russian Bulgaria, greatly desire that they should be so lucky. In fact, Poland and Hungary are at present trying to "de-Communize" without provoking Soviet military intervention.

DO STYLES CHANGE? DETENTES I AND II

Continuity

One conclusion to be drawn from the above analyses of American and Soviet styles is their degree of continuity, how little their fundamental outlooks have changed. Nowhere is this more visible than in the collapse of détente in the 1970s.[45] Given current hopes for détente II—that it will blossom into an end of the cold war—the erosion of its predecessor deserves further examination. Basically, the cause of this erosion was less a question of personalities or individual policies than the sharply different and contrasting styles and perceptions of the two superpowers.

American Search for an End to Conflict

In their perception of the nature of politics—especially their image of conflict—Americans historically have emphasized an international harmony of interests, which has stood in stark contrast to the emphasis in the state system on the inevitability of conflict and differences of interest among states. Moreover, Americans have viewed conflict as an abnormal condition, whereas the Soviets have viewed harmony as an illusion. Prior to World War I, the United States, long isolated from Europe and therefore not socialized in the state system, did not accept the reality and permanence of conflicts among members of that system. Differences between states were not considered natural and certainly not deep or long lasting. Instead, they were attributed to wicked leaders (who could be eliminated), authoritarian political systems (which could be reformed), and misunderstandings (which could be straightened out if the adversaries approached each other with sincerity and empathy). Once these obstacles had been removed, peace, harmony, and good will would reign supreme.

Thus, every change of Soviet leadership during the post-World War II years aroused hopes in the United States for an end to the cold war. Perhaps, it was said, a more moderate leader would succeed, a more peaceful man. Terms such as *liberal* and *dove* were used frequently, in contrast to *conservative* and *hard-liner*. These hopes and terms were heard after Brezhnev's death in 1982 and his eventual succession by Gorbachev, just as they had been heard after Khrushchev was ousted as Soviet leader almost two decades earlier, as well as after Stalin's death in 1953. Or, it was believed, the Soviet system would be transformed from within. Again and again, the Soviet Union was expected to behave with restraint either because it needed Western economic assistance (right after World War II and again during the détente of the 1970s); or because its own industrialization would make the totalitarian regime superfluous; or because the need Soviet leaders had to satisfy their people's hunger for a higher standard of living would require them to shift resources from the military sector to investment in consumer goods.

If evil men were not replaced or evil systems not fundamentally changed, there was always the hope that if "misunderstandings" had given rise to the superpower struggle, they could be corrected, especially at summit conferences. Here American leaders could prove to their Soviet counterparts that they were sincere when they talked of peace and demonstrated their good will. The goal was to reduce the Soviet leaders' suspicions of American intentions and, if possible, win their friendship. If the leaders could just talk to each other face to face, realize that neither was a devil with horns but just an ordinary mortal, they could more easily see each other's point of view and, given good will, resolve their differences. The problem, then, appeared merely to be Soviet misperception of American leaders' desires for peace.

Conflict could be resolved by correcting this misperception. In this way the search for a cooperative, stable relationship with the Soviet Union could go on, regardless of past disappointments. An adversary relationship remains unacceptable to Americans; conflict and war are signs of failure.

Thus, it is hardly surprising that the United States becomes disenchanted so frequently, as it did with détente shortly after it was launched in the early 1970s. If the cold war was over, peace and a moderation of conflict should be the consequence. "Negotiations rather than confrontations" were to be the rule. But Soviet activities in Vietnam, Cambodia, Angola, Somalia, Ethiopia, South Yemen, and Afghanistan were seen as incompatible with the "spirit of détente." Americans expected Soviet leaders to restrain themselves—that is, to behave quite unlike Soviet leaders. Soviet ideological perception, however, makes acceptance of the status quo impossible. Changes in Soviet leadership may bring changes of emphasis in policy or tactics, but it does not change the *fundamental* perception of the United States as the enemy and of a commitment to a long-term struggle. The United States is the enemy because of what it is (a capitalist-imperialist state) and not because of what it does—that is, whether American policies are at the moment conciliatory.

Soviet Focus on Conflict

The Soviet emphasis during détente I, then, totally unlike that of the United States, was on the inevitable and irreconcilable struggle with capitalist states. Conflict was viewed not as the result of wicked capitalist political leaders—they might be very decent and likable—but as the inevitable result of the system they represented. There was nothing accidental about conflict. Genuine peace and harmony could come only after capitalism, the real cause of rivalry between states, had been eliminated and replaced by world communism. Until then, it was only natural, indeed imperative, to exploit existing opportunities in the Third World to advance Soviet influence. Attempts to explain or demonstrate to Soviet leaders the peacefulness or accommodating nature of American policies ran head-on into the fundamental conviction of Soviet leaders that history is inevitably going in their direction, that they have a superior—indeed, exclusive—insight into this historical process, and that they are obligated to help history along.

In contrast to the United States, which expected détente would result in the modification of Soviet behavior, Soviet leaders never believed or said that détente was incompatible with continued struggle. While Americans became disillusioned with détente, and cynicism about Soviet intentions replaced the initial confidence, the Soviets claimed not to understand why Americans should be so disappointed in détente. They were not doing anything very different from what they had been doing all along. The United States seemed to be overreacting. There had been no understanding between the two powers on freezing the status quo, and there had therefore been no violations. The United States and the Soviet Union clearly perceived détente differently and had quite divergent expectations. The former assumed détente would result in mutual restraint. The latter perceived that détente was the result of the new strategic parity; the loss of U.S. strategic superiority because of the massive Soviet missile build-up "compelled" the United States to behave with greater restraint. The logic was clear: continued Soviet strategic growth would require the United States to behave very cautiously while allowing the Soviet Union to act more boldly and exploit opportunities to extend its influence, as during the 1970s.

One point must be very clear: détente was seen as a symptom of America's growing weakness vis-à-vis the Soviet Union. It was the growth of Soviet strategic power that was "forcing" the United States to behave with "moderation." Military power—not the Soviet economy—has been the reason the Soviet Union regarded itself, and was regarded by the world, as a superpower. And because the Soviets also believed that their newfound strength was the cause for a less confrontational posture by the United States, the logical step was to add more. Military power "paid off." In the 1970s, while U.S. defense budgets declined significantly, the Soviets continued to invest heavily in the military, despite their having overtaken the United States in numbers of missiles, and despite the fact that this investment came at the cost of improving the Soviet people's standard of living and the continuing stagnation of the Soviet economy. This cost was willingly paid by the regime because military might was a measure of Soviet standing and political achievement in the world.

Above all, the contrast in the attitudes of the two countries toward power could not be more striking. The United States has always considered itself a morally and politically superior society because of its democratic culture. Its attitude toward the use of international power has therefore been dominated by the belief that the struggle for power need not exist, can be avoided through isolation, or can be eliminated. Moralism in foreign policy has proscribed the use of power in peacetime; power is to be employed only in confrontation with unambiguous aggressors, at which point the United States would be obliged to fight in behalf of a righteous cause. Power internationally, just as domestically, can be legitimated only by democratic purposes; otherwise, its exercise is evil and necessarily arouses guilt.

The Soviet belief in unceasing and irreconcilable conflict means acceptance of power as an instrument of policy, dedicated to the pursuit of Communist ends. But this power is used with care and restraint:

> [The Kremlin] has no compunction about retreating in the face of superior force. And being under the compulsion of no timetable, it does not get panicky under the necessity for such retreat. Its political action is a fluid stream which moves constantly, wherever it is permitted to move, toward a given goal. . . . But if it finds unassailable barriers in its path, it accepts these philosophically and accommodates itself to them. The main thing is that there should always be pressure, increasing constant pressure, toward the desired goal. There is no trace of any feeling in Soviet psychology that the goal must be reached at any given time.[46]

The Soviet use of power is not subject to cyclical swings from isolationism to crusading and back again, as the American pattern has been. To the Soviets, power is the raw material of international politics, to be applied discriminatingly and cautiously in the effort to achieve specific objectives and to probe for soft spots in the adversary's positions. Its use arouses no guilt; the only requirement is that it successfully advance Soviet goals. In the past, "adventurism" and "romanticism," which might have provoked the enemy and endangered the base of the world revolution, were avoided. The question is whether this attitude will prevail in the future as the Soviet regime, unable to provide its people with a higher standard of living and balanced diet, seeks to substitute foreign policy successes for domestic failures, and whether, in this quest for mass support and to demonstrate its own legitimacy, Soviet leaders will be tempted to resort to military power, the one asset they have in abundance.

Americans, believing that peace is a natural condition and that differences between states usually can be resolved through demonstrations of sincerity and good will, cannot comprehend an attitude so dedicated to struggle. Soviet leaders, because of their commitment, never hesitate to sacrifice opportunities to win good will in exchange for strategic gains. The expansion and consolidation of Soviet power in Eastern Europe, which helped to undermine the wartime alliance, was not the only time that the Soviets torpedoed good relations with the West. In 1955 the summit conference and the "spirit of Geneva" quickly fell before the Soviet arms deal with Egypt, which helped to precipitate the Suez War a year later. The ink was hardly dry on the first strategic arms limitation treaty when the Soviets supplied Egypt with the offensive arms that led to the Yom Kippur War in 1973 and nearly resulted in a military confrontation with the United States. During all the years of negotiations on SALT II, the Soviets never hesitated to extend their influence in Africa. Even while the Senate was debating SALT II and the survival of the treaty was in doubt, the Soviets expanded their influence to the Indian Ocean and Persian Gulf areas, intervening with their own troops in Afghanistan. Believing in economic determinism and irreconcilable class struggle, they rejected the idea that opportunities for advancing their cause should be passed up; good will among enemies locked in a deadly struggle seemed to them an illusion anyway.

Revisionist Explanation of U.S. Foreign Policy

Perhaps the most telling symptom of the American style in conducting foreign policy is the appearance after every major war of works reinterpreting the country's participation. The *revisionist* histories have certain common themes: the conflicts in which the nation had been entangled had not in fact threatened its security interests; the politicians had seen a menace where none existed, and this mistaken perception had been promoted by propagandists, who had aroused and manipulated public opinion—by soldiers with bureaucratic motives and, above all, by bankers and industrialists—the "merchants of death" of the 1930s, the "military-industrial complex" of the 1960s—who expected to benefit from the struggle. The United States' engagement in two world wars in this century (and in the cold war) had been a mistake; these wars had really been unnecessary, immoral, or both. Yesterday's apparent aggressor thus had not represented a threat to American security after all; on the contrary, the threat really came from within. Except for certain domestic forces, the United States could have continued to isolate itself from international politics.

Such revisionism is perhaps the deepest symptom of the American aversion to power politics. The distinguished American diplomatic historian Dexter Perkins wrote that revisionists always seek to convince the public that "every war in which this country has been engaged was really quite unnecessary or immoral or both; and that it behooves us in the future to pursue policies very different from those pursued in the past." [47] What is most striking about the revisionists' claims that the cold war was avoidable (based on second-level analysis) is that they really believe that, but for the United States' purported anticommunism and lack of sensitivity to Soviet interests, the conflict between the superpowers would not have erupted. It was American policy that aroused Stalin's fears and suspicions and led him to react aggressively and angrily. Stalin's ambitions were limited to Eastern Europe, where the Soviet Union had legitimate security interests. Thus, the cold war could have been avoided had the United States, animated by anticommunism, acted less provocatively.[48]

A change in *American* behavior has therefore been seen as the remedy. If the United States abandoned its anticommunism, revisionists have argued, there would be no need for cold wars, interventions, or large military budgets. Instead, Americans could build a truly just society at home, a wiser and more moral goal. Such a revisionist attitude, which seeks to deny the reality of international struggle and suggests that it can be avoided, has not in the past been found among the characteristics of Soviet style.

A Change? Gorbachev's 'New Thinking'

Yet clearly significant changes in mutual perceptions of the two superpowers have occurred since Reagan and Gorbachev assumed their respective offices. When he came into office in 1981, Ronald Reagan denounced the Soviet Union as an "evil empire." Sounding like an old-fashioned evangelist, he lambasted Soviet communism as "the focus of all evil in the world." [49] Furthermore, making the point that democracy and freedom were the waves of the future, he questioned the legitimacy and longevity of communism as a social and political system in both Eastern Europe and the Soviet Union. Simultaneously, he presided over a $2 trillion rearmament program, the largest of any administration in postwar history, and rejected any serious arms control efforts. By the end of his second administration, however, he had forged a new détente. Having denounced the first one, he met with his Soviet counterpart more times than Nixon had, signed an arms control agreement that for the first time eliminated an entire class of nuclear weapons, and was negotiating a 50 percent reduction in strategic arms when he left office. Just over forty years after an English prime minister in the United States spoke of an iron curtain coming down over Europe, the American president in London expressed his hope that it was being lifted and that a "new era" in U.S.-Soviet relations was about to begin. "What about your 'evil empire' talk?" Reagan was asked while walking around in Moscow's Red Square at the 1988 summit conference? He retracted the statement, saying it belonged to a different time—pre-Gorbachev.[50]

The implications of Gorbachev's domestic changes for Soviet foreign policy and U.S.-Soviet relations have aroused the hope that the cold war may be ending. Although Western observers for decades have argued that the Soviet economy needed more investment, requiring less investment in the military and a reduction in cold war tensions—only to be repeatedly disappointed—this time there appears to be more basis that it might happen. After first insisting that the Soviet Union could deploy intermediate nuclear forces (INF) in Europe while the United States could not deploy any, and walking out of all arms control negotiations unless the United States and its European allies accepted Moscow's one-sided position, Gorbachev not only resumed negotiations but also accepted the American double zero position that all intermediate nuclear forces, as well as short-range missiles, should be eliminated globally, not just in Europe. He also accepted a mutual inspection system of nuclear facilities in both countries to verify the INF treaty. In addition, the Soviet leader was anxious to pursue a strategic arms control agreement, involving radical reductions, and conventional arms control in Europe. Slowing the momentum of the arms race and improving superpower relations was clearly a high-priority item, a prerequisite for focusing more attention and resources on the economy and the political-social changes required to raise Soviet living standards and maintain its status as one of the two superpowers. The withdrawal from Afghanistan after eight years also suggests the new priority of domestic over foreign policy. Another indicator is the resolution of regional disputes between the superpowers in Angola involving the withdrawal of the fifty thousand Cuban troops, and Cambodia, involving the pullout of Vietnamese forces. Domestic reform is critical for Soviet society; it is also the basis for a new policy of détente.

In the meantime, Gorbachev also has made a number of important pronouncements on foreign policy. Whereas the historic Russian/Soviet pattern had been concerned only with Soviet security, without either sensitivity or concern for the security of its neighbors or other states, Gorbachev has talked of "mutual security," suggesting that he understands that Soviet restraint is a necessary prerequisite to producing and sustaining more friendly U.S. policies, which, after all, profoundly affect Soviet security—in contrast to the 1970s détente, which was torpedoed largely by Soviet expansionist efforts in the Third World.[51] Less security for the United States is not in the Soviet Union's interest, he said. Unlike his predecessors, Gorbachev recognized the implications of the security dilemma. The unilateral Soviet pursuit of security would lead only to greater distrust and instability as it compelled the United States to arm itself further. This is a significant shift from the prior Soviet view that security required the Soviet Union to be stronger than the United States. He also has talked of an increasingly interdependent world, a radical departure from the past focus on maximum Soviet self-reliance and a division between the capitalist and socialist worlds. Thus, the expectation is improved Soviet relations with other countries from whom Moscow could benefit economically. Militarily, the Soviet leadership, while continuing to claim that Soviet strategy is defensive, has recognized the concern of other states that this strategy has a strong offensive orientation, which may take the form of seizing the initiative and launching a preemptive attack on the United States if a nuclear war appeared imminent to launching a blitzkrieg against Western Europe. There has been a great deal of talk therefore of a shift in Soviet military doctrine toward a "nonoffensive defense," which will preclude a surprise attack by the Warsaw Treaty Organization armies, followed by a massive offensive thrust Westward. To ensure this and to reassure NATO, the Soviet Union has proposed reductions in the forces most needed for such operations: tanks, strike helicopters, and long-range aircraft. Acknowledging their numerical superiority in some of these categories, Gorbachev has asserted that the side that is ahead must accept asymmetrical cuts. To underline this position, he has offered to unilaterally demobilize 500,000 troops (10 percent of Soviet forces) and scrap 10,000 tanks over a two-year period; 50,000 troops and 5,000 tanks would be withdrawn from Eastern Europe. He has talked repeatedly as well of "our common European house" to Western Europe and has emphasized that security must be achieved by political means. Finally, he has called for an enlarged role for the United Nations in resolving international disputes.[52]

All this would suggest profound changes in the Soviet approach to the world. Future events will demonstrate whether in fact such changes are mainly declaratory or tactical to win time and to erode the Western image of the Soviet Union as an enemy so that the West, while relaxing its vigilance, will supply it with the technology and credits it needs. Much will depend on Soviet *domestic* events and the evolution of Soviet politics and society. The fact is, however, that every previous détente in the cold war has been followed by disillusionment in the United States and the West because Soviet actions unilaterally exploited that relaxation of tensions.[53] The "spirit of Geneva" in 1955 was followed by an arms deal with Egypt, producing a Middle Eastern war in 1956; Glassboro in 1967 was followed by military intervention in Czechoslovakia in 1968; SALT I in 1972 was followed by Soviet military assistance to Egypt and another Arab-Israeli war in 1973; and within a few months of SALT II in 1979 the Soviets intervened in Afghanistan. Nor had Moscow been deterred from its intervention in Angola and Ethiopia by the prospects of SALT II. In brief, Soviet actions torpedoed every "thaw" in the cold war. Therefore, Gorbachev's reforms are critical for the future of Soviet-

American relations. The Soviet Union may not become a Western democracy, but if Gorbachev's reforms do take hold, the change from a totalitarian system to a more pluralistic and open one may mean a less expansionist foreign policy and a greater willingness to live and let live with neighbors not sharing the Soviet social and economic system.

It is notable in this respect that Gorbachev's new chief ideologist in 1988 not only called for more experiments with market economies but also rejected the idea of a global struggle against the West. Avoiding war and ecological catastrophe, he said, "must outweigh the idea of a struggle between classes." [54] Gorbachev has made similar statements. Lenin, the father of the class struggle against the West and cited by every one of his successors for seventy years, was suddenly transformed into a man who had in fact placed the priority of human values and survival above class conflict! If this viewpoint indeed prevails in practice and Moscow abandons its historic Marxist-Leninist analytical framework and efforts to help history along its allegedly predestined path from capitalism to socialism—or, at least, subordinates the expansion of Soviet influence and search for unilateral advantage to greater cooperation with the West—Gorbachev's "New Thinking" will alter the principal reason for the Soviet conflict with the United States and the West.

Indeed, by late 1989 it looked as if the cold war might be ending more quickly than anyone had expected—and doing so in the area where it started—Eastern Europe. The forty-year conflict, as noted earlier, had begun with the imposition of Communist regimes upon the states of Eastern Europe and the division of Germany. This occurred because the Soviet Union was unwilling to accept a traditional sphere of influence in Eastern Europe in which its allies would be allowed to enjoy domestic autonomy as long as they were sensitive to the security interests of their great-power neighbor. Equating non-Communist governments with anti-Communist governments, Moscow insisted that Soviet security could be ensured only by Communist regimes that held a monopoly of power; power was not to be shared with parties representing class enemies. All subsequent efforts by the peoples of Eastern Europe to rid themselves of the unpopular and to them, illegitimate, regimes that governed them were quashed.

But the economic burden of supporting the failing economies of Eastern Europe (with the exception of East Germany), and the danger that suppressing further revolts (stemming from mass dissatisfaction with lack of food and other basic necessities of life) posed for his *perestroika* program, led Gorbachev to accept a more traditional sphere of influence. It started in Poland, where in 1989 the first free elections since World War II repudiated the Communist party and endorsed Solidarity, the trade union that had expressed the general state of unhappiness of the workers and Polish people at the beginning of the decade and had been outlawed as a result. Solidarity has now formed the first non-Communist government in postwar Eastern Europe. It continued in Hungary, where the parliament removed the word *People* from People's Republic and renamed the country the Republic of Hungary. At the same time, the Communist party, readying itself for a free election in 1990 in which other parties would be allowed to run, relabeled itself a social democratic party in the hope of surviving the elections. And it boiled over into East Germany. Initially, tens of thousands of refugees, mainly younger people, left through Hungary for West Germany. This was followed by spontaneous mass demonstrations in several East German cities demanding change. In what was truly a people's revolution, the old party and government leaders were replaced, and the new Communist party leader promised radical reforms, including free elections. As a token of the changes to come, he declared the end of restrictions on emigration and travel to the West. Hundreds of thousands of East Berliners then swarmed across the Berlin Wall in a mass celebration of their new freedom. The thaw resulting from Gorbachev's reforms in the Soviet Union had become a flood in Eastern Europe.

If any act could spell the transformation of the cold war, it was the symbolic destruction of the Berlin Wall on November 9, 1989.[55] It had become a symbol of what the cold war was all about: tyranny versus freedom. It had been built in 1961 to keep a people in, to prevent their escape to a better and freer life in West Germany. The opening of the wall, in which large holes were knocked to allow more and easier transit between East and West Berlin, was therefore also very symbolic (although, ironically like building the wall, opening it up again was to serve the same purpose: to keep East Germany's population in East Germany). Gorbachev, facing serious ethnic tensions and gross economic failure at home, wanted to unburden the Soviet Union of Eastern Europe. Unlike his predecessors, he was therefore willing to tolerate non-Communist governments on the condition that the states of Eastern Europe would remain members of the Warsaw Treaty Organization. Thus, the Polish government, for example, not only committed itself to remaining a member of the security treaty but, to reassure Moscow, also appointed Communists to the ministries in charge of the police and the armed forces. As the other Communist states in Eastern Europe were subjected to increasing domestic pressure for *perestroika*, it became clear that Eastern Europe was in the process of "de-Communizing."[56] Soviet troops would no longer keep Communist regimes in power.

For East Germany, that posed a special problem. If it reforms, becomes more politically pluralistic, and adopts a market economy, what is the rationale for its continued existence as an independent state? If it transforms itself into a replica of West Germany, why should the two Germanies not be unified once again? Given Germany's history, that causes much concern among its neighbors, both East and West. Whether such a Germany, if and when it comes about, will be neutralized or integrated into a democratic unified Europe remains to be seen. Obviously, a solution for the German problem must be found within the broader context of what Gorbachev calls the "common European house." But what is already clear is that from the Soviet Union to the intra-German border, communism as a social, economic, and political system has failed because it has been unable to provide its citizens with either a decent standard of living or freedom; it has produced only a plentiful supply of weapons. Less clear, but quite likely, is that eventually Poland and Hungary will prefer an Austrian-type neutrality, and that both superpowers will pull back their troops, allowing the two alliances that have confronted each other for forty years to dissolve.

Admittedly a number of assumptions underlie the optimism about the transformation of the superpower relationship: that both the domestic and foreign policy changes are irreversible; that Gorbachev will survive or, if he does not, that his successor, faced with the same internal and external situations, will continue on essentially the same course; that the ethnic tensions within the Soviet Union, especially in the Baltic states, will not explode; that the changes under way in Eastern Europe will remain nonviolent; and that, if *perestroika* succeeds, the economically more dynamic and politically more self-confident Soviet Union that will emerge will not once again resume an expansionist course in foreign policy. To ensure against this, it becomes critical that the Soviet Union gravitate toward a more open society. Only more popular participation in government can prevent a future sudden shift toward a more aggressive policy and a corresponding transfer of resources back to the military. In the meantime, as Soviet-American tensions subside, it should be remembered that whether the cold war ends or goes into a long remission, the Soviet Union—like the United States—remains a formidable nuclear power.

The principal difference between détentes I and II (détente II is likely to be a more genuine détente than the earlier one) then is twofold. First, in the 1990s domestic economic concerns are primary for both countries. Second, and more important, the two powers appear in phase with one another. In détente I, the United States, after Vietnam and the OPEC oil crisis, was dealing from weakness. Moscow, confident that the balance of power was shifting in its direction, decided to exploit this weakness. In détente II, the Soviet Union is dealing from a position of weakness, as demonstrated by its string of concessions in the negotiations on intermediate nuclear forces, its eagerness for arms control agreements and regional settlements, and its willingness to risk the dismantling of Communist regimes in Eastern Europe. The United States, by contrast, had under Reagan rebuilt its military power, regained much of its self-assurance in foreign policy, and contributed in large measure to Gorbachev's desire to relax international tensions because the military buildup and Reagan Doctrine made the cost of continuing the Soviet Union's imperial policy prohibitively costly. But the United States too is eager for agreements and, in President Bush's phrase, to proceed "beyond containment." It too has serious domestic problems: millions homeless, a drug epidemic, widespread crime, and a growing public health problem related to AIDS. Above all, the United States must focus more attention and energy on its own economic revival and competition with Japan.

For Review

1. What is meant by "styles" in foreign policy?
2. How have American isolationism and democracy shaped American perceptions and foreign policy behavior?
3. How have Russia's history and Communist ideology affected Soviet views of international politics, their enemies, and their objectives?
4. How do American and Soviet styles contrast?
5. Will Soviet domestic reforms change Soviet foreign policy behavior?
6. Did President Reagan and Soviet leader Gorbachev change American and Soviet perceptions of each other?

Notes

1. Arnold Wolters and Laurence W. Martin, eds., *The Anglo-American Tradition in Foreign Affairs* (New Haven, Conn.: Yale University Press, 1956), ix-xxvii.
2. Louis Hartz, *The Liberal Tradition in America* (New York: Harvest Books, 1955).
3. Zbigniew Brzezinski, "The Soviet Union: Her Aims, Problems and Challenges to the West," in *The Conduct of East-West Relations in the 1980s,* Part I (London: Institute of Strategic Studies, 1984), 4; and Richard Pipes, *Survival Is Not Enough* (New York: Simon & Schuster, 1984), 37-44.
4. Alexander L. George, "The 'Operational Code': A Neglected Approach to the Study of Political Leaders and Decision-Making," *International Studies Quarterly* (June 1969): 190ff.
5. An exhaustive analysis of the American "style" can be found in *Gulliver's Troubles, or The Setting of American Foreign Policy,* by Stanley Hoffmann (New York: McGraw-Hill, 1968), 87-213. See also Hans J. Morgenthau, *In Defense of the National Interest* (New York: Knopf, 1951); Robert E. Osgood, *Ideals and Self-Interest in America's Foreign Relations* (Chicago: University of Chicago Press, 1953); George F. Kennan, *American Diplomacy 1900-1950* (Chicago: University of Chicago Press, 1951); and John Spanier, *American Foreign Policy Since World War II,* 11th ed. (Washington, D.C.: CQ Press, 1988). For an application of this style—and Soviet style—to nuclear strategy, see for example, Colin S. Gray, *Nuclear Strategy and National Style* (Lanham, Md.: Hamilton Press, 1986). For a quite different interpretation of U.S. foreign policy, see Michael Parenti, *The Sword and the Dollar* (New York: St. Martin's Press, 1988), subtitled "Imperialism, Revolution, and the Arms Race," or Gabriel Kolko, *Confronting the Third World* (New York: Pantheon Books, 1988).
6. The hypothesis about democratic behavior offered by Klaus Knorr and others and discussed in Chapter 2 is generally supported by Gabriel A. Almond, who, in *The American People and Foreign Policy* (New York: Holt, Rinehart & Winston, 1960), strongly emphasizes the "extraordinary pull of domestic and private affairs even in periods of international crises." See particularly Chapter 3, with Almond's summation of the American value orientation.
7. Paul Seabury, *The Rise and Decline of Cold War* (New York: Basic Books, 1967), 39-45, offers some fitting quotations, especially a poem by Archibald MacLeish celebrat-

ing the *pax americana* as a preamble to the *pax humana* during World War II. The moralism of Secretary of State John Foster Dulles is discussed by William L. Miller, "The 'Moral Force' Behind Dulles' Diplomacy," *Reporter*, Aug. 9, 1956.

8. Quoted by Arthur S. Link, *Wilson the Diplomatist* (Baltimore: Johns Hopkins University Press, 1957), 89.

9. Quoted in Joseph M. Jones, *The Fifteen Weeks* (New York: Viking, 1955), 272.

10. Robert E. Osgood, *Limited War* (Chicago: University of Chicago Press, 1957), 28-45, focuses on this point in explaining the difficulties that the nation experiences in conducting limited wars.

11. John Spanier, *The Truman-MacArthur Controversy and the Korean War* (Cambridge, Mass.: Harvard University Press, 1959), 221-238.

12. Denis W. Brogan, "The Illusion of Omnipotence," *Harper's*, December 1952, 21-28.

13. Robert Tucker, *The Soviet Political Mind* (New York: Holt, Rinehart & Winston, 1963), 181-182.

14. There is in fact a very important eighth characteristic: the belief that political problems can be solved through economic means. For an elaboration of this characteristic, see Chapter 18.

15. Tang Tsou, *America's Failure in China* (Chicago: University of Chicago Press, 1963), 538-541. For a study of the accusation of a leading State Department figure by Senator Joseph McCarthy, see McGeorge Bundy, *The Pattern of Responsibility* (Boston: Houghton Mifflin, 1952), 201-220.

16. The repetitious pattern of conspiracy charges in American political life has been explored by Richard Hofstadter, *The Paranoid Style in American Politics* (New York: Vintage, 1967).

17. Leslie H. Gelb, *The Irony of Vietnam* (Washington, D.C.: Brookings, 1979), 220-226.

18. Bill Moyers, President Johnson's special assistant from 1963 to 1966, reports this comment in an interview with the *Atlantic Monthly* reprinted in *Who We Are*, ed. Robert Manning and Michael Janeway (Boston: Little, Brown, 1969), 262.

19. Larry Elowitz and John W. Spanier, "Korea and Vietnam: Limited War and the American Political System," *Orbis*, Summer 1974, 510-534; and John E. Mueller, *War, Presidents and Public Opinion* (New York: Wiley, 1973). Mueller comes to the startling conclusion that the war had no *independent* impact on President Lyndon Johnson's declining popularity, though the rate of the decline was the same as that for Truman during the Korean War. See also Milton J. Rosenberg et al., *Vietnam and the Silent Majority* (New York: Harper & Row, 1970).

20. J. William Fulbright, *Arrogance of Power* (New York: Vintage, 1967), 256-258.

21. Ronald Steel, *Pax Americana* (New York: Viking, 1967), 353-354.

22. Henry Kissinger, *White House Years* (Boston: Little, Brown, 1979), 115-130.

23. For analyses of the feasibility of economic leverage in the 1970s, see Samuel P. Huntington et al., "Trade, Technology and Leverage," *Foreign Policy*, Fall 1978, 63-106; and Herbert S. Levin, Francis W. Rushing, and Charles Movit, "The Potential for U.S. Economic Leverage on the USSR," *Comparative Strategy*, I (1979), 371-404.

24. Also see George W. Breslauer, "Ideology and Learning in Soviet Third World Policy," *World Politics*, April 1987, 436. Stephen D. Hosmer and Thomas W. Wolfe, eds., *Soviet Policy and Practice Toward Third World Conflicts* (Lexington, Mass.: Lexington Books, 1983); and Andrzej Korbonski and Francis Fukuyama, eds., *The Soviet Union and the Third World* (Ithaca, N.Y.: Cornell University Press, 1988).

25. John Lewis Gaddis, *Strategies of Containment* (New York: Oxford University Press,

1982), 320.

26. Spanier, *American Foreign Policy Since World War II*, 268-346.

27. Michael Volensky, *Nomenklature*, trans. by Eric Misbacher (New York: Doubleday, 1985); and Ilya Zemstov, *The Private Life of the Soviet Elite* (New York: Crane, Russak, 1985).

28. Samuel L. Sharp, "National Interest: Key to Soviet Politics," in Erik P. Hoffmann and Frederic J. Fleron, Jr., eds., *The Conduct of Soviet Foreign Policy* (Chicago: Aldine-Atherton, 1971), 108-117.

29. See Timothy J. Colton, *The Dilemma of Reform in the Soviet Union*, rev. ed. (New York: Council on Foreign Relations, 1986), 106-116; and Seweryn Bialer and Michael Mandelbaum, eds., *Gorbachev's Russia and American Foreign Policy* (Boulder, Colo.: Westview Press, 1988) for background and future domestic and foreign prospects.

30. Joseph L. Nogee and Robert H. Donaldson, *Soviet Foreign Policy Since World War II*, 3d ed. (Elmsford, N.Y.: Pergamon Press, 1988), 13-39.

31. Alexander L. George, "The 'Operational Code': A Neglected Approach to the Study of Political Leaders and Decision-Making," in Hoffmann and Fleron, *Conduct of Soviet Foreign Policy*, 165-190. Also see Nathan Leites, *A Study of Bolshevism* (New York: Free Press, 1953).

32. Arthur P. Mendel, *The Essential Works of Marxism* (New York: Bantam, 1961); Alfred G. Meyer, *Communism*, rev. ed. (New York: Random House, 1967); V. I. Lenin, *Imperialism, the Highest Stage of Capitalism*, rev. ed. (New York: International Publishers, 1939); and Joseph Stalin, *The Foundations of Leninism* (San Francisco: China Books, 1965).

33. George F. Kennan, *Russia and the West Under Lenin and Stalin* (Boston: Little, Brown, 1961), 179.

34. Ibid., 180-183 (emphasis in original). Used by permission of the publisher.

35. John Lewis Gaddis, "The First Fifty Years," in Mark Garrison and Abbot Gleason, eds., *Shared Destiny* (Boston: Beacon Press, 1985), 19-39.

36. Tucker, *Soviet Political Mind*, 185-189.

37. Ibid., 190.

38. Leites, *Study of Bolshevism*, 27-63.

39. Kennan, *American Diplomacy 1900-1950*, 118.

40. Hanes Adomeit, *Soviet Risk-Taking and Crisis Behavior* (London: George Allen and Unwin, 1982); Jan F. Triska and David D. Finley, *Soviet Foreign Policy* (New York: Macmillan, 1968), 310-349; and Stephens S. Kaplan, *Diplomacy of Power* (Washington, D.C.: Brookings, 1981) for a thorough analysis of the 190 incidents in which Soviet armed forces were used to achieve foreign policy aims.

41. Kennan, *American Diplomacy 1900-1950*, 182.

42. *New York Times*, Nov. 15, 1985.

43. For World War II and the beginning of the cold war, see Adam B. Ulam, *Expansion and Coexistence*, 2d ed. (New York: Holt, Rinehart and Winston, 1974), 314-455; Ulam, *The Rivals* (New York: Viking Compass, 1971), 3-151; Voitech Mastny, *Russia's Road to the Cold War* (New York: Columbia University Press, 1979); William Taubman, *Stalin's American Policy* (New York: Norton, 1982); and Hugh Thomas, *Armed Truce* (New York: Ahteneum, 1987).

44. Zbigniew Brzezinski, "America's New Geostrategy," *Foreign Affairs* (Spring 1988): 686; and Brzezinski, *The Grand Failure* (New York: Scribner's, 1989), 103-144.

45. Mike Bowker and Phil Williams, *Superpower Détente* (Newbury Park, Calif.: Sage

Publications, 1988).

46. Kennan, *American Diplomacy 1900-1950*, 118.

47. Dexter Perkins, "American Wars and Critical History," *Yale Review* (Summer 1951): 682-695.

48. For some of the revisionist histories that place the responsibility for beginning the cold war upon the United States, see D. F. Fleming, *The Cold War and Its Origins*, 2 vols. (Garden City, N.Y.: Doubleday, 1961); Gar Alperovitz, *Atomic Diplomacy: Hiroshima and Potsdam* (New York: Vintage, 1967); William A. Williams, *The Tragedy of American Diplomacy* (Cleveland: World, 1959); Gabriel Kolko, *The Politics of War: The World and United States Foreign Policy, 1943-1945* (New York: Random House, 1968); and Thomas G. Paterson, *Soviet-American Confrontation* (Baltimore: Johns Hopkins University Press, 1973).

    Evaluations of the Fleming-Alperovitz thesis, in which American anticommunism is blamed directly, may be found in Arthur Schlesinger, Jr., "The Origins of the Cold War," *Foreign Affairs* (October 1967): 22-52; J. L. Richardson, "Cold War Revisionism: A Critique," *World Politics*, July 1972, 579ff.; and John Spanier, "The Choices We Did Not Have: In Defense of Containment," in *Caging the Bear*, ed. Charles Gati (New York: Bobbs-Merrill, 1974), 128ff. The Gati book provides a discussion of Kennan's analysis and the policy of containment twenty-five years after the latter's anonymous article "The Sources of Soviet Conduct" in *Foreign Affairs* (July 1947): 566-582, later republished in *American Diplomacy 1900-1950*, 107-128. In that article Kennan had provided the Truman administration with a rationale for its containment policy. Finally, for an assessment of economic interpretations of American policy, see Robert W. Tucker, *The Radical Left and American Foreign Policy* (Baltimore: Johns Hopkins University Press, 1971). For an analysis that suggests either poor scholarship or deliberate distortion of the documents, see Robert J. Maddox, *The New Left and the Origins of the Cold War* (Princeton, N.J.: Princeton University Press, 1973).

49. Strobe Talbott, *The Russians and Reagan* (New York: Vintage Books, 1984).

50. Steven V. Roberts, "U.S.-Soviet Tension Is Now Receding—Reagan Declares," *New York Times*, June 4, 1988.

51. Seweryn Bialer, " 'New Thinking' and Soviet Foreign Policy," *Survival*, July/August 1988, 291-309; and Colton, *Dilemma of Reform in the Soviet Union*, 185-186.

52. David Holloway, "Gorbachev's New Thinking," *Foreign Affairs* (America and the World, 1988/89 issue): 69-71. For a very optimistic view, see Robert Levgold, "The Revolution in Soviet Policy," *Foreign Affairs* (America and the World, 1988/89 issue): 83-98.

53. Kissinger, *White House Years*, 119; and Richard C. Holbrooke, "For Whom the Kremlin Bell Tolls," *New York Times* (Op. Ed.), June 27, 1988, 21.

54. Bill Keller, "New Soviet Ideologist Rejects Idea of World Struggle Against the West," *New York Times*, Oct. 6, 1988.

55. For a recent proposal on how to end the cold war, see Robert S. McNamara, *Out of the Cold* (New York: Simon and Schuster, 1989).

56. Zbigniew Brzezinski, *Grand Failure*, whose subtitle, "The Birth and Death of Communism in the Twentieth Century," is both intellectually provocative and visionary as he focuses on what he calls the "terminal crisis of Communism." On the Soviet economy and how the West should and should *not* respond to Gorbachev, see Judy Shelton, *Coming Soviet Crash* (New York: Free Press, 1988).

CHAPTER 9

The Developing Countries: The Primacy of Domestic Concerns

FOREIGN POLICY AS A CONTINUATION OF DOMESTIC POLITICS

During the cold war years, the term *Third World* was used to describe the formerly colonial, mostly non-Western, largely nonwhite, poor or developing countries. But these nations did not constitute the unitary bloc implied by the label. There was considerable diversity among them: in history and experience, in religion and culture, in population and resources, and in ideology and political and economic systems. Some nations were more developed than others. Some had very large populations; many had small populations. Some possessed sizable resources; others were not well endowed. Some were governed by religious tradition (especially in the Islamic world), but most were secular. What united the majority of them was their past colonial history, their poverty, a determination to modernize, and a desire to fulfill the "revolution of rising expectations." In these respects, they were distinct from the First World (Western industrial nations) and the Second World (Soviet-led Communist nations). In their foreign policies, the Third World states generally preferred nonalignment—that is, independence from the two rival global power blocs—in the initial period of "newcomers" in the international system, and they were very much aware of their lack of influence and status in that system.

The status of the developing countries becomes even clearer by taking a look at the economic gap between the First and Third Worlds or between the rich North and poor South. The term *South*, like *Third World*, claims more than it should. Tanzania and Uganda are *South*, but Australia and New Zealand are *North*; South Korea and Taiwan are in between as newly industrialized coun-

225

tries (NICs). Geographically erroneous as it may sometimes be, the term *North-South* does have the advantage of emphasizing the frustration of most developing countries over the continued division of the world between rich and poor nations (see Figure 9-1). This division between rich and poor nations is, to be sure, somewhat oversimplified; a continuum between very rich and very poor is probably a more accurate image. While the distance between the extremes is growing, that between the developed countries and the top rank of the developing countries—the OPEC countries and NICs—is narrowing. Nevertheless, these countries constitute a minority of the developing nations. As the 1980s began, the North, including Eastern Europe, had a quarter of the world's

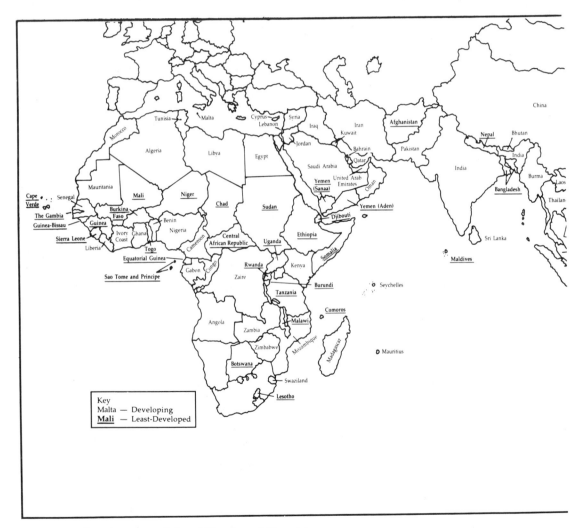

Figure 9-1 Developing and Least-Developed Countries

population and four-fifths of its income; the South, including China, had three-quarters of its population and one-fifth of its income.

The poorer nations have been united by a set of common attitudes: anger against their former colonial masters, the Western industrial nations, whom they blame for their backwardness and deprivation; a sense that they do not yet control their own political and economic destinies; and a determination to change the status quo as they seek a more equitable distribution of the world's wealth. The 1973 embargo of the Organization of Petroleum Exporting Countries (OPEC) against the United States and the quadrupling of oil prices first united the developing countries, even though the higher oil prices hurt most

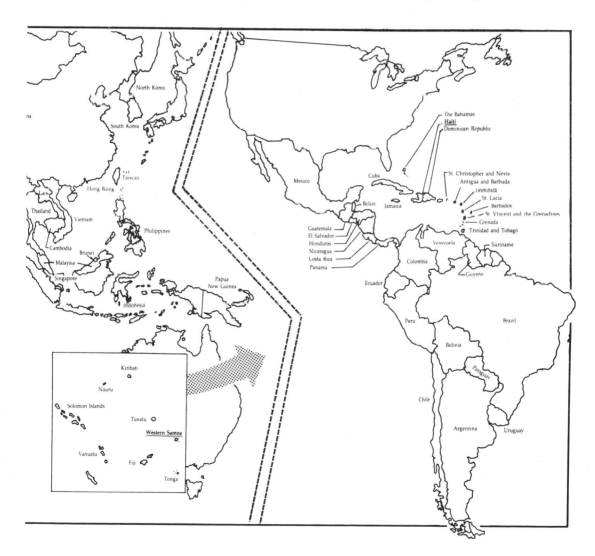

Table 9-1 Economies Classified According to Income Group (based on GNP per capita in 1983 U.S. dollars)

Low-income (less than $400)

East Africa
 Burundi
 Comoros
 Ethiopia
 Kenya
 Madagascar
 Malawi
 Mozambique
 Rwanda
 Somalia
 Tanzania
 Uganda
 Zaire

West Africa
 Benin
 Burkina Faso
 Cape Verde
 Central African Rep.
 Gambia, The
 Ghana
 Guinea
 Guinea-Bissau
 Mali
 Niger
 São Tomé and Principe
 Sierra Leone
 Togo

North Africa
 Sudan

Latin America and the
Caribbean
 Haiti

East and Southeast Asia
 Burma
 Cambodia
 China (excluding Taiwan)
 Lao People's Dem. Rep.
 Viet Nam

South Asia
 Afghanistan
 Bangladesh
 Bhutan
 India
 Maldives
 Nepal
 Pakistan
 Sri Lanka

Oceania
 Vanuatu

Lower-middle income ($400-$1,635)

East Africa
 Botswana
 Djibouti
 Lesotho
 Mauritius
 Swaziland
 Zambia
 Zimbabwe

West Africa
 Angola
 Cameroon
 Congo, People's Rep. of the
 Ivory Coast
 Liberia
 Mauritania
 Nigeria
 Senegal

North Africa
 Egypt, Arab Rep. of
 Morocco
 Tunisia

Latin America and the
Caribbean
 Belize
 Bolivia
 Colombia
 Costa Rica
 Cuba
 Dominica
 Dominican Rep.
 Ecuador
 El Salvador
 Grenada
 Guatemala
 Guyana
 Honduras
 Jamaica
 Nicaragua
 Paraguay
 Peru
 St. Christopher and Nevis
 St. Lucia
 St. Vincent and the
  Grenadines

East and Southeast Asia
 Indonesia
 Korea, Dem. People's
  Rep. of
 Mongolia
 Philippines
 Thailand

Southwest Asia
 Gaza Strip
 Lebanon
 North Yemen
 South Yemen
 Turkey

Oceania
 Kiribati
 Pacific Islands, Trust
  Terr. of the
 Papua New Guinea
 Solomon Islands
 Tonga
 Western Samoa

Upper-middle income (more than $1,635)

East Africa
 Namibia
 Réunion
 Seychelles
 South Africa

West Africa
 Gabon

North Africa
 Algeria

Latin America and the
Caribbean
 Antigua and Barbuda
 Argentina
 Bahamas
 Barbados
 Brazil

Table 9-1—Continued

Chile
Guadeloupe
Martinique
Mexico
Montserrat
Netherlands Antilles
Panama
Suriname
Trinidad and Tobago
Uruguay
Venezuela
Virgin Islands (U.S.)

East, Southeast, and
South Asia
Brunei
Hong Kong
Korea, Rep. of
Macao
Malaysia
Singapore
Taiwan, China

Southwest Asia
Cyprus
Iran, Islamic Rep. of
Iraq
Israel
Jordan
Syria

Europe
Greece
Malta
Portugal
Yugoslavia

Oceania
Fiji
French Polynesia
Guam
New Caledonia

**High-income
(oil exporters)**
Bahrain
Kuwait
Libya
Oman
Qatar
Saudi Arabia
United Arab Emirates

**Industrial market
economies**

North America
Canada
United States
(and Puerto Rico)

Asia
Japan
Europe
Austria

Belgium
Channel Islands
Denmark
Finland
France
Germany, Fed. Rep. of
Iceland
Ireland
Italy
Luxembourg
Netherlands
Norway
Spain
Sweden
Switzerland
United Kingdom

Oceania
Australia
New Zealand

**East European
nonmarket economies**
Albania
Bulgaria
Czechoslovakia
German Dem. Rep.
Hungary
Poland
Romania
USSR

SOURCE: My T. Vu, *World Populations Projections, 1985* (Baltimore: Johns Hopkins University Press, 1985) 436.

of them more than the West. Still, they supported OPEC because, for the first time, they sensed that the industrial nations were vulnerable and could be pressured by producer-cartels. Their firm belief that they were still the victims of the Western-dominated international economic system and that they must stand together to regain control of their fates led the Third World nations to move from nonalignment closer to confrontation with the West.

The desire to modernize, in short, molds the developing nations' perceptions of the world. Their foreign policies reflect this preoccupation with nation building. It has been said that, for a "new state, foreign policy is domestic policy pursued by other means; it is domestic policy carried on beyond the boundaries of the state."[1] This remained true in the 1980s as confrontation proved counterproductive and more developing countries turned for help to multinational corporations for capital and technology, and experimented increasingly with Western market ideas to lift themselves out of poverty (see Chapter 15).

NATIONAL SELF-DETERMINATION AND POVERTY

The right to national self-determination, a notion conceived in the West but denied by the Western industrial powers to their overseas territories, became a key issue after World War II. Throughout Asia and Africa, former colonies sought national independence and most gained it. The common denominator of this global nationalist revolution has been a fundamental urge to be free from the control of former colonial powers. From the beginning, colonialism contained the seeds of its own destruction. Humiliation and resentment of foreign domination stirred a "reactive nationalism" that asserted itself in terms of the very values by which the Westerners justified their rule—national self-determination, dignity, and equality. A nation must be master of its own destiny; no one must ever dominate it again or treat it condescendingly.

Accompanying this drive for national independence has been the determination to achieve a higher standard of living and to abolish the abject poverty and misery of past centuries. In the economically developing countries, people have continued to live on subsistence agriculture because they have not possessed the modern tools—factories, machinery, computers, and so forth—with which to increase productivity. A vast increase in productivity was the essence of the industrial revolution and the means for the "great ascent" out of poverty. Equally important, the developing countries have lacked the cultural values, social structures, and political order necessary for industrialization. Developing nations do not necessarily lack natural resources, however. They can in fact be divided between those that possess plentiful resources (for example, the oil states) and those that control either less desirable raw materials or very little of nature's wealth. But the hallmark of a developing country is its inability to attain self-sustaining economic growth and higher per capita income. Table 9-1 reveals the large number of developing countries with per capita incomes of less than $400 or within the $400-$1,635 range. For a contrast, note in Table 9-2 the by comparison astronomical per capita incomes of the ten wealthiest developed countries. Note further that these Western incomes have continued to rise, while those in the non-OPEC and non-NIC developing nations have been at a virtual standstill.

But the dividing line between developed and developing countries is not purely economic; it is also reflected in differences in infant mortality, life expectancy, general health, availability of consumer goods and housing (especially, bathing facilities and living space), calorie intake per person, education, and sources of energy.

Table 9-2 Per Capita Income of the Ten Wealthiest
Nations (U.S. dollars)

Country	Per Capita Income
1. Japan	$21,820
2. Switzerland	19,250
3. United States	18,400
4. Denmark	15,370
5. West Germany	14,890
6. Norway	14,650
7. France	13,000
8. Italy	12,955
9. Sweden	12,590
10. Britain	9,800

SOURCE: Central Intelligence Agency, *The World Factbook 1988* (Washington,
D.C.: Central Intelligence Agency, 1988).

For the affluent middle-class American who has never known what it is to
be poor, malnourished, and vulnerable to disease and the ravages of nature,
it is impossible to conceive of the life led by a typical family in a developing
nation. In the early 1960s Robert Heilbroner graphically conveyed what
such an existence would mean to an American suburban family then living
on $9,000-$10,000 a year:

> We begin by invading the house of our imaginary American family to strip it of
> its furniture. Everything goes: beds, chairs, tables, television set, lamps. We
> leave the family with a few old blankets, a kitchen table, a wooden chair. Along
> with the bureaus go the clothes. Each member of the family may keep in his
> "wardrobe" his oldest suit or dress, a shirt or blouse. We will permit a pair of
> shoes to the head of the family, but none for the wife or the children.
>   We move into the kitchen. The appliances have already been taken out, as we
> turn to the cupboards and larder. The box of matches may stay, a small bag of
> flour, some sugar and salt. A few moldy potatoes, already in the garbage can,
> must be hastily rescued, for they will provide much of tonight's meal. We will
> leave a handful of onions, and a dish of dried beans. All the rest we take away:
> the meat, the fresh vegetables, the canned goods, the crackers, the candy.
>   Now we have stripped the house: the bathroom has been dismantled, the
> running water shut off, the electric wires taken out. Next we take away the
> house. The family can move to the toolshed. It is crowded, but much better than
> the situation in Hong Kong, where (a United Nations report tells us) "it is not
> uncommon for a family of four or more to live in a bedspace, that is, on a bunk
> bed and the space it occupies—sometimes in two or three tiers—their only
> privacy provided by curtains."
>   But we have only begun. All the other houses in the neighborhood have also
> been removed; our suburb has become a shantytown. Still, our family is fortu-
> nate to have a shelter; 250,000 people in Calcutta have none at all and simply

live in the streets. Our family is now about on a par with the city of Cali, Colombia, where, an official of the World Bank writes: "on one hillside alone, the slum population is estimated at 40,000—without water, sanitation, or electric lights. And not all the poor of Cali are as fortunate as that. Others have built their shacks near the city on land which lies beneath the flood mark. To these people, the immediate environment is the open sewer of the city, a sewer which flows through their huts when the river rises."

And still we have not reduced our American family to the level at which life is lived in the greatest part of the globe. Communication must go next. No more newspapers, magazines, books—not that they are missed, since we must take away our family's literacy as well. Instead, in our shantytown we will allow one radio. In India the national average of radio ownership is one per 250 people, but since the majority of radios is owned by city dwellers, our allowance is fairly generous.

Now government services must go. No more postman, no more fireman. There is a school, but it is three miles away and consists of two classrooms. They are not too overcrowded since only half the children in the neighborhood go to school. There are, of course, no hospitals or doctors nearby. The nearest clinic is ten miles away and is tended by a midwife. It can be reached by bicycle, provided that the family has a bicycle, which is unlikely. Or one can go by bus—not always inside, but there is usually room on top.

Finally, money. We will allow our family a cash hoard of five dollars. This will prevent our breadwinner from experiencing the tragedy of an Iranian peasant who went blind because he could not raise the $3.94 which he mistakenly thought he needed to secure admission to a hospital where he could have been cured.

Then the head of our family must earn his keep. As a peasant cultivator with three acres to tend, he may raise the equivalent of $100 to $300 worth of crops a year. If he is a tenant farmer, which is more than likely, a third or so of his crop will go to his landlord, and probably another 10 percent to the local money lender. But there will be enough to eat. Or almost enough. The human body requires an input of at least 2,000 calories to replenish the energy consumed by its living cells. If our displaced American fares no better than an Indian peasant, he will average a replenishment of no more than 1,700-1,900 calories. His body, like any insufficiently fueled machine, will run down. That is one reason why life expectancy at birth in India today averages less than forty years.

But the children may help. If they are fortunate, they may find work and thus earn some cash to supplement the family's income. For example, they may be employed as are children in Hyderbad, Pakistan, sealing the ends of bangles over a small kerosene flame, a simple task which can be done at home. To be sure the pay is small; eight annas—about ten cents—for sealing bangles. That is, eight annas per gross of bangles. And if they cannot find work? Well, they can scavenge, as do the children of Iran who in times of hunger search for the undigested oats in the droppings of horses.[2]

Thirty years later, things are not much better for the average person in the Third World, and certainly not in Africa where in 1985-1986 and again in 1988 millions faced outright starvation. Home to twenty of the thirty least-developed states in the world was in Africa. Africa supports 400 million people on an economy about as productive as that of Illinois. Moreover, Africa has the highest birthrate of all the continental regions in the world.[3] It is thus not surprising that, as a former Pakistani finance minister once said, for the children who survive to the age of five years in the developing countries, life is a matter of "deprivation, desperation, and degradation. It is an intense, but mercifully a short struggle, as their life expectancy is no more than thirty years." Although life expectancy has risen in the developing countries, as has the standard of living in some, there remains a huge disparity in wealth between a minority of people who live in the North and the vast majority of those who live in the Third World. But it is not just that the North is so much wealthier than the South. It is that the former contains the bulk of the world's manufacturing capacity and, because of its economic power, dominates the international economic system—its rules and regulations and its international institutions of commerce and finance.[4]

'WESTERNIZATION' OF THE DEVELOPING COUNTRIES

Although the developing countries generally tend to blame Western capitalism for the conditions just described, the role of the Western industrial nations in forging the nationhood of these countries cannot be ignored.

Territorialization

Territorialization by the colonial powers usually defined the present frontiers of the developing countries. The Western powers drew arbitrary lines on the map, often straight through tribal or ethnic boundaries, and then imposed administrative and legal structures upon the resulting territories. All who lived within a particular structure were treated as if they belonged to a single nation. Thus India, in its quarrel with China over precisely where the Sino-India boundary lies in the Himalayas, has defined its claim by the line drawn by British colonizers.

Infrastructure

Another byproduct of colonialism has been the construction of harbors, roads, railroads, airports, telephone and telegraph lines, and factories, as well as the development of natural resources. These facilities have provided what economists call the infrastructure or capital overhead, the prerequisite for any major industrialization.[5] To be sure, Europeans did not undertake such projects for the benefit of the natives. The roads and railroads were used to carry resources and crops from the interior to the harbors; they were also used to move troops to quell uprisings and riots. Furthermore, the impact of these projects upon the traditional native economy and society was disruptive. The traditional patterns of life and expectations of the vast majority of peasants who had migrated from the land were altered in the cities. European-built centers of government, business, and communications offered the peasants who came there to work a new way of life and values. Urban life provided the "demonstration effect." [6] Europeans lived better and longer. Why, the natives wondered, could they not live as well and as long? They could hardly avoid awareness of the technical and scientific knowledge, tools, and skills that had given the Europeans their higher material standards, as well as their power. Why, the natives asked themselves, could they not learn these secrets? One point was especially noteworthy: Europeans believed that life could be improved here on earth and that poverty need not be accepted as one's fate.

Education

The urge to transform backward societies into modern societies thus began with the European introduction of urbanization, industry, wage-labor forces, and exchange economies. But the most significant contribution of Western colonialism was education of the social groups determined to lead their shackled nations into freedom and modernity. A relatively small and youthful group, this secular nationalist intelligentsia produced the leadership of revolutionary movements in the developing countries. Its members were doctors, journalists, civil servants, and lawyers; they had in common their "Westernization." Educated in Europe or the United States—or in Western schools in their own countries—they had learned Western ways. Even more significant, in the course of their professional training they had learned to think in characteristically Western rational and secular terms. This had revolutionary implications: for the Third World intelligentsia, it provided an escape from the traditions, customs, and privileges that had held their societies in the tight grip of economic, social, and political backwardness. Its simple but powerful message that human beings can be the masters of their own destinies was exhilarating, a promise of intellectual liberation from religious superstition, substituting rationalism for obsolete traditions and institutions.

Education then was the chief means by which Western political and social thought was diffused to non-Western peoples. As one political analyst has observed, "The future will look back upon the overseas imperialism of recent centuries, less in terms of its sins of oppression, exploitation, and discrimination, than as the instrument by which the spiritual, scientific, and material revolution which began in Western Europe with the Renaissance was spread to the rest of the world." [7] It was this Westernization that transformed members of the intelligentsia into leaders of the nationalist and modernist movements of their own countries. [8]

But, as intensely aware as the first generation of leaders and their successors were of the underdeveloped condition of their countries and as determined as they were to initiate development, they faced almost insuperable obstacles to the necessary economic "takeoff" and self-sustaining economic growth. Lack of national cohesion, rapidly growing populations, insurmountable hunger and malnutrition, a dearth of capital, and traditional social structures and values all have impeded the modernization of most of their societies, with grave foreign policy implications.

OBSTACLES TO DEVELOPMENT

Absence of National Unity

The first obstacle encountered in creating cohesive societies in developing countries is a lack of national unity. Leaders of the new nations have had to construct the very nations in whose names they once revolted against colonial domination. They have had to be "nation builders." The lives of the citizens of the new nation have been rooted in smaller communities, and their first loyalties are to tribes, regions, or religious, racial, or linguistic groups.[9] Loyalties are parochial, and attitudes are particularistic. These stand as formidable barriers to the formation of a national consciousness and devotion to national symbols and may, in fact, reach such intensity that civil war breaks out. Disunity, not unity, is the spirit of most new nations. The communities created by the colonial powers may have become "national" in the sense that the people living in them have rid themselves of foreign rulers. But their common resentment and aspiration to be free have often not developed into a shared allegiance to nations with artificial frontiers previously drawn by Europeans.

Indeed, once the colonial rulers that united them have gone, the new nations have tended to fall apart. When the British maintained order and public security in India, the Muslims, Hindus, and Sikhs could coexist; once Britain withdrew, their mutual fear and hatred of one another led to disintegration and bloodshed. The groups composing a new nation realize how little they have in common—indeed, how many things divide them. The issue facing new nations then is not whether they will develop economically, but whether they will survive as national entities. When people obey racial, religious, or tribal authority instead of legitimate national authority, secession and civil war may result. Ironically, the new nations face the task of nation building at a time when some Western states such as Belgium, Ireland, and Spain, are confronting similar demands for independence and greater self-government. But no advanced nation has yet fallen apart, unlike such new states as India, Pakistan, Nigeria, and Zaire. Of those new nations that have managed to remain united, many have had to cope with demands for greater autonomy, if not independence. Civil wars continue presently in the Sudan, Ethiopia, and Sri Lanka.

Race.   Integrating diverse masses into a new nation, forming a national consensus, is therefore crucial. Race is one element impeding this "integrative revolution." For example, many of the countries of Southeast Asia, such as Malaysia, contain many large minority groups, chief among them the ethnic (overseas) Chinese. In Singapore, they constitute the majority. Almost everywhere in Southeast Asia the Chinese act as distributors of consumer goods, bankers, investors, and shopkeepers. But while dominating Southeast Asian economic life, they have retained their language and customs, tending to isolate themselves; they remain foreigners in the nations where they live. Centuries of Chinese invasion and conquest have left a residue of suspicion that is only intensified by this cultural separatism. The result is fear, jealousy, discrimination, accusations of "alien exploitation," and occasionally, as after the abortive Indonesian Communist party coup in 1965, the slaughter of the Chinese population. Another example is the cruel expulsion of the Chinese from Vietnam in the late 1970s. The majority were forced out on unsafe boats after most of their money had been taken from them, and many drowned on the high seas. Most of these "boat people" found refuge in other Southeast Asian countries. Vietnam's anti-Chinese sentiment was one of the factors contributing to the brief Vietnamese-Chinese war in 1979.

It is not just the inhumanity of such behavior that is notable but also its counterproductiveness. In non-Communist states, such minorities play a critical role in the process of development. And, as noted, some traditional societies, such as in Southeast Asia, the Chinese minority are the entrepreneurs. In Africa, this role is often played by the Indian-Pakistani community. Hostile or discriminatory actions, such as expelling this minority, which happened in Uganda, or rioting and attacking their shops, which occurred in Kenya, are likely to hurt economic growth.

Religion.   A second element is religious animosity. When this sparks wars and leads to massive dislocation of millions and slaughter of hundreds of thousands, it seems incomprehensible—at least to Westerners, unless they have studied the Thirty Years' War of the early seventeenth century. When India gained its independence in 1949, it was partitioned into Hindu India and Muslim Pakistan because the Muslim minority wanted its own nation. The division was accompanied by a great blood bath in which more than half a million people died.[10] In the middle of all this were the Sikhs. Their prosperity as a result of India's agricultural revolution had led them to forget their religious background. This, in turn, resulted in a counterrevolution as young radicals, often from well-to-do families, were attracted to religious fundamentalism and the idea of establishing a Sikh nation in the Punjab, India's breadbasket. During the 1980s, this spilled over into violence as the Sikhs' convictions grew that they were being discriminated against by the Hindu-dominated national government. One victim was Indira Gandi, India's prime minister, who was assassinated by her Sikh bodyguards after she ordered Indian troops to attack the Sikhs' sacred Golden Temple, where militants had fortified themselves.

Religious divisions have tended to be disastrous. Internal religious differences have hampered nation building in Lebanon, where religious and political hostilities among Maronite Christians and other Christian sects, as well as Druse, Shiite, and Sunni Muslims, have all but destroyed the country. While their impacts have not been as devastating as in Lebanon, religious conflicts have occurred in other countries as well. In Nigeria, for example, the religious differences between the Muslim Hausas and the Christian Ibos fueled modern Africa's bloodiest civil war, which lasted three years and reflected tribal, regional, and economic divisions; over a million lives were lost. In the Sudan, conflict erupted between the black Christian South and the Arab Muslim North when the government tried to enforce the Islamic laws on the Christians. This conflict, combined with millions of refugees from Ethiopia and rioting in response to the government's removal of food subsidies, led to the overthrow of the government. But the fighting continued.

Regionalism.   Regional differences are a third divisive element, particularly when they are accompanied by the uneven distribution of resources and wealth. "Regionalism is understandable because ethnic loyalties can usually find expression in geographical terms. Inevitably, some regions will be richer than others, and if the ethnic claim to power combines with relative wealth, the case for secession is strong."[11] In India, this is the basis for the Sikhs' demands for greater autonomy, if not independence. When Pakistan was born and split between East and West Pakistan, separated by over a thousand miles, it was West Pakistan that became more prosperous, even though many of the resources were located in East Pakistan. This fueled the latter's resentment and revolt, which led to the establishment of Bangladesh and the further division of Pakistan.

Ethnicity.   Ethnic, nationality, or tribal divisions also contribute to disunity. Indeed, African tribal chieftains may invoke the same claim of national self-determination that the intelligentsia originally invoked on behalf of their nations. Moreover, because Europeans often split up tribal groups when drawing their artificial boundary lines in the conference rooms of Berlin, London, and Paris, the new nations' frontiers have tended to be unstable. Tribes freely cross frontiers in search of water and grazing lands; one part of a tribe may even try to break away from its "nation" to join the rest of the tribe in the neighboring nation. The result may be a frontier war such as that between Ethiopia and Somalia in 1977, when Somalia tried to unite with its ethnics in Ethiopia who sought to secede and join Somalia. One consequence was that the Soviets were forced to choose between two friends, Ethiopia and Somalia; together with the Cubans, the Soviets intervened on the side of Ethiopia, the larger nation. Tribalism also affects domestic politics. In some countries, such as Burundi, tribal warfare breaks out from time to time between the minority Watusis, who rule the nation, and the majority Hutus. In 1988 one of these eruptions resulted in the death of an estimated 20,000 people in one week; in 1972, 100,000 Hutus had been massacred. One major reason for the civil war in Angola during the 1970s was the exclusion of the largest tribal group, the Ovimbundu, from the Soviet and Cuban-supported government.

Sometimes problems related to race, ethnicity, religion, and regionalism occur simultaneously. Sri Lanka, for example, is presently disintegrating as a nation because of the conflict between the Buddhist Sinhalese and the Hindu Tamils.[12] On the island of Sri Lanka, which lies just south of India, the Sinhalese majority regards the Tamil minority with fear because the latter is backed by 50 million Tamils living in the southern Indian state of Tamil Nadu. Some of the more militant Tamils, who like India's Sikhs are demanding greater autonomy, if not their own state, organized a guerrilla movement known as the Liberation Tigers. Because the Sri Lankan army was unable to suppress them, Sri Lanka asked India, which had in the past provided sanctuary and training for the Tamil insurgents in southern India, to mediate the conflict. But the Tigers continued to resist even when Indian forces were sent in to disarm them. An Indian peace-keeping force of 80,000 thus became involved in the fighting. The fighting continued, and in 1989 Sri Lanka finally asked the Indians to withdraw.

Language.   New nations' lack of political and cultural cohesiveness is symbolized by the language problem, the fifth element in their disunity. Language is one of the most important factors in forming and preserving a sense of nationality. Uniformity of language not only helps people to communicate with one another but also promotes common attitudes and values. Group consciousness and common interests are stimulated in turn; people learn to think in terms of "we" as opposed to "they." Yet in many developing countries several languages are spoken, and any attempt to impose a single language is resisted. The prospects for national cohesion in these circumstances are not promising.

In India, the government has tried to make Hindi the official language in a nation with fifty major regional languages, fourteen of which are recognized officially. The fact is that English, the colonizer's language, has become the preferred language of many urban Indians, especially India's educated, rapidly expanding middle class. English is also the language of commerce, computers, finance, science, and social sciences, as well as of the leading newspapers, advertising, and growing television network. Even though it is emerging as the nation's first language, English is spoken only by about 150 million Indians, reflecting what may well be a schism between modern India and traditional India. Since the key decisions that affect most Indians' lives and the important discussions that are carried on in the news media are in English, most Indians may be increasingly cut off from public life. Yet efforts to make Hindi the national language have led to repeated rioting and violence. In neighboring Pakistan, the national language, Urdu, is spoken only by a minority.

Overpopulation

The second problem encountered in modernizing developing countries is overpopulation. Not all such countries have this problem, but where it exists, overpopulation casts doubt on whether a country can make any economic progress at all. In 1987 the world population passed the 5 billion mark and is increasing at an annual rate of just over 2 percent. For 1980-1985 the annual rate of population growth in the developed world was 0.64 percent, while that of the developing countries was 2.02 percent. Africa had the highest rate (3.01 percent), followed by Latin America (2.30); South Asia, including India (2.20); and East Asia, excluding Japan (1.20). All these rates, except Africa's, were down from earlier periods, suggesting a slowing of population growth. Even so, the figures for the population growth of specific countries remain startling. For example, in 1950 Mexico's population was 27 million; in 1987 it hit 83 million. China's population of 547 million in 1950 has since passed the billion mark. India will reach that figure by the turn of the century. Kenya has the highest population growth in the world: its 6 million people in 1950 had almost quadrupled by 1988; at a growth rate of 4 percent its 23 million population will reach 79 million in thirty years. Nigeria's population of 112 million, growing at a rate of 3 percent, will total 274 million in three decades.[13] In 1900 there was one European for every two Asians; in 2000, the ratio will probably be one to four. It is also estimated that by 2000 there will be two Latin Americans for each North American—and this is based on a 300 million population figure for the United States.

There is then a population explosion. World population first reached 1 billion in 1830, and by 1930 it had doubled. In 1960 the total was 3 billion people, nearly half of which was under twenty years old. The fourth billion took only another fifteen years. By the year 2000 the current population of 5 billion is expected to exceed 6 billion. Moreover, the inhabitants of Third World countries (including China) will constitute more than 80 percent of the world's population. Fewer than 20 percent—perhaps only 15 percent—of the rest of the world's citizens will live in North America, Europe, the Soviet Union, and Japan. Can this crowded earth continue to sustain such enormous increases in population, of over 1 million people every five days, despite the recent decrease in population growth in the Third World (see Table 9-3)?

Disturbance of Malthusian Checks. The developing countries have come face to face with the realities of the Malthusian problem: the constant hunger and grinding poverty that result when the population grows faster than the means of subsistence. More than 150 years ago the Reverend Thomas Malthus, a British cleric who was also an economist, predicted this fate for the Western world—unless population growth was limited by "positive checks" (such as wars and epidemics) or "preventive checks" (such as sterilization and contraception). The great economic progress of the West—despite the huge population increase since 1800—had seemed to refute the Malthusian prediction. Agricultural production increased to provide a plentiful supply of food, and

Table 9-3 Population Estimations, 1950 and 1980, and Projections, 2000-2100 (in millions)

	1950	1980	2000	2025	2050	2100	Total Fertility Rate 1980[a]	Year in which NRR = 1[b]
Selected Countries								
China	547	980	1,198	1,397	1,414	1,426	2.3	2005
India	350	675	1,001	1,361	1,605	1,778	4.7	2020
Indonesia	80	146	216	297	351	388	4.4	2020
Brazil	53	118	177	239	274	297	3.9	2015
Bangladesh	42	89	156	259	342	412	6.3	2035
Nigeria	32	85	169	329	472	600	6.9	2040
Pakistan	40	82	148	249	329	394	6.4	2035
Mexico	27	69	115	166	197	214	4.8	2015
Egypt	20	42	64	88	104	115	4.6	2020
Kenya	6	17	40	84	122	153	8.0	2030
Regions								
Developing countries								
Africa	223	479	903	1,646	2,297	2,873	6.4	2050
East Asia	587	1,061	1,312	1,542	1,573	1,596	2.3	2020
South Asia	695	1,387	2,164	3,125	3,810	4,328	4.9	2045
Latin America	165	357	543	748	868	944	4.1	2035
Subtotal	1,670	3,284	4,922	7,061	8,548	9,741	4.2	2050
Developed countries	834	1,140	1,284	1,393	1,425	1,454	1.9	2005
Total world	2,504	4,424	6,206	8,454	9,973	11,195	3.6	

SOURCE: Robert S. McNamara, "The Population Problem," *Foreign Affairs,* Summer 1984, 1113. Reprinted with permission.

[a] Total fertility rate is the number of children an average woman would have during her lifetime.

[b] NRR (net reproduction rate) refers to a level of childbearing in which each couple on average replaces itself in the next generation. This column thus projects a decline of the level of fertility to just a replacement level.

industrial production raised the standard of living to new heights. For years, therefore, Malthus's dire warning was ignored by all save diehard pessimists.

Unfortunately, the conditions that confront the developing nations are quite dissimilar to those experienced in the West. First, the Western industrial countries had far smaller populations when they began industrializing, and their subsequent population increases did not outdistance their economic gains. Ironically, the pattern in the developing countries to a significant degree has been brought about by the colonial powers. In the precolonial period the Malthusian "positive checks" had, in their own cruel way, contributed to some sort of balance between population and resources. But the

Western colonial states, by introducing modern medicine, upset the balance: more of the newborn survived, people lived longer, and populations began to increase at much greater rates.

Hindrances to Birth Control. Children in many of these countries are a religious, social, and even economic necessity. In India, for example, Muslims believe that children are a "gift of Allah," and the childless couple is pitied or despised; a woman does not even establish herself with her husband or his family until she has borne a son. A Hindu man needs a son to perform certain rituals after his death, and during life he needs sons to fight in village feuds or in tribal warfare. Furthermore, there is a fear of having *too few* children, for they may be needed to work in the fields and support their parents as the latter grow older. Children are in this sense a substitute for the social security payments or endowment policies common in the West. People, in short, are not poor because they have large families; they have large families because they are poor. Birth controls can be economically disastrous in these circumstances. The family is also the hub of life for Indian villagers. Weddings and births are festive social occasions, important village events. A woman's prestige may even be measured by the number of children, especially sons, that she bears. A voluntary reduction in the size of her family would in these circumstances strike at the very basis of her life.

For the developing countries, the following maxim may yet be painfully true: *industrial revolutions may be defeated by Malthusian counterrevolutions.*[14] In developing countries that have achieved economic growth, population increases may cancel most, if not all, of the hoped-for increase in living standards or savings for capital investment. How can these developing countries possibly provide adequate food, housing, education, health care, and jobs for all their people? The Aswan Dam, planned in 1955 and completed in 1970, added 25 percent to Egypt's arable land, but in those fifteen years, Egypt's population increased by 50 percent to more than 30 million. By the year 2000 the Egyptian population will double to more than 64 million if the present rate of growth continues. Mexico, with a population in 1980 of 69 million people and projected to add 50 million by the year 2000, must create 700,000 new jobs per year if its already high unemployment rate is not to increase even more, but the prediction is for only 350,000 jobs a year. In 1988 the UN Population Fund warned that within ten years the developing countries would have to increase their capacity to provide social services by 65 percent just to maintain their present living conditions. As it is, many Third World governments cannot cope with the current demands for jobs, education, housing, health services, sanitary systems, and other social services brought on by the shift of this ever larger population from the land to the city.

By the year 2000, more than half the world's people will live in overcrowded cities; and four of the six largest cities will be in the Third World.[15] Mexico City may be the world's largest city, growing from the present 15 million to 26 million; São Paolo, Brazil, will be 24 million; and Calcutta and

Bombay, both in India, will be 17 and 16 million, respectively (Tokyo will be also the third largest city with 17 million, and New York City will be just over 15 million). The masses of people will strain, if not collapse, the already inadequate social services and facilities such as transportation, sanitation, education, and housing. Of the top thirty-five cities in the year 2000, twenty-five will be in the developing countries. They may come to resemble huge slums surrounding small inner-city enclaves of middle-class dwellers and may, in turn, become the breeding ground of political radicalism and social turmoil.

In any event, the continued Third World "population bomb" with its critical growth rate in the age group of twenty to forty years (between 1980 and 2000 this age group will increase by 630 million, compared to 20 million in the developed countries, nine out of every ten children born today being born in the Third World) has dire consequences for the political and social stability of Third World countries. In the words of Robert McNamara, former president of the World Bank:

> Rapid population growth, in sum, translates into rising numbers of labor force entrants, faster-expanding urban populations, pressure on food supplies, ecological degradation, and increasing numbers of "absolute poor." All are rightly viewed by governments as threats to social stability and orderly change. Even under vigorous economic growth, managing the demographic expansion is difficult; with a faltering economy it is all but impossible.[16]

Unless these population trends are altered, the future may see mass misery, migrations, and violence result from widespread despair.

During the nineteenth century, Europe's population rose by approximately 0.5 percent per year; today, the poorer countries are growing at more than 2 percent per year, or by about 200,000 people a day. Yet, from the mid-seventeenth century to 1940, more than 60 million Europeans emigrated; from 1820 to 1940, 33 million went to the United States. During the 1970s, 7.5 million foreign workers as well as their 5.5 million dependents emigrated from southeastern Europe (Greece, Turkey) and North Africa (Algeria, Morocco, and Tunisia) to Western Europe. Before West Germany's economic downturn in the late 1970s, there were more than 1 million Turks in Germany; in Britain, the majority of immigrants were "colored" people from British Commonwealth countries. By the late 1970s, immigration to the United States stood near or at an all-time high; the country was the world's largest receiver of refugees and immigrants, the latter largely Spanish-speaking people from the Caribbean and Mexico. In the first decade of this century, legal immigration to the United States averaged 880,000 annually; by the early 1980s, the estimated legal plus illegal immigration averaged over 1 million annually (of whom more than 50 percent were Spanish-speaking). Can this influx continue?

Fertility, once the key to survival, seems to have become the curse of humankind (see Table 9-4). Despite a slight decline in its growth rate since

Table 9-4 Population and Economic Growth Rates of Selected Developing Countries, 1988

Country	Population Growth Rate	Economic Growth Rate
Angola	3.55	0.0
Brazil	2.37	8.2
Egypt	2.65	3.0
Honduras	3.11	3.5
India	2.01	4.8
Ivory Coast	3.81	-3.0
Kenya	4.21	5.0
Malawi	3.24	-0.3
Malaysia	1.98	1.8
Mexico	1.99	-3.8
Morocco	2.49	5.7
Nigeria	3.00	-3.4
Zaire	2.92	1.4

SOURCE: Central Intelligence Agency, *The World Factbook 1988* (Washington, D.C.: Central Intelligence Agency, 1988).

1970, the world population continues to rise by 90 million a year. Yet at the 1984 UN International Conference on Population, despite a World Bank study that predicted that even with the declining birthrate the world's population will double by 2050, the United States took a strong stand against abortion and family planning. Since 1974, U.S. law has prohibited the use of foreign aid for abortion, reflecting the domestic controversy over family planning. President Ronald Reagan's administration, strongly influenced by pro-life groups, strictly administered the law, withdrew its contribution to the UN Fund for Population Activities in 1986, and cut off all funds for nongovernmental organizations working in family planning if they supported abortions. Planned Parenthood, for example, had to cancel programs in eighteen African countries, despite the fact that only an estimated 30 percent of couples in developing countries outside of China use contraceptives. Remarkably, Secretary of State George Shultz could still say, "Rampant population growth underlies the third world's poverty, and poses a major long-term threat to political stability and our planet's resource base." [17] This was an accurate assessment, but U.S. policy during the Reagan years guaranteed a more crowded planet; and the Bush administration has shown no sign of changing this policy.

Malnutrition and Hunger

The third problem impeding modernization in the Third World is inadequate food supplies and growing malnutrition. The paradox of the developing countries is that, although the overwhelming majority of their populations live on the land, the peasants do not produce enough food. The emphasis instead has been on industrialization and such visible projects as steel factories and automobile plants with the hope that replication of at least the outward symbols of industrial society will raise living standards. This has usually led to the neglect of agriculture, which requires costly long-term investment in land reclamation and irrigation projects, fertilizer plants, and extension services. Furthermore, to the leaders of these countries, agriculture has meant poverty; it has been a constant reminder of colonial subjugation and of their continued status as suppliers of raw materials. But industry has symbolized freedom and national dignity. Given the continued swings in the prices of agricultural commodities, investing more money in food has been viewed, not surprisingly, without enthusiasm.

Yet food production must be raised to feed the rapidly growing populations. *An industrial revolution requires a prior or simultaneous agrarian revolution.*[18] Instead of being separate and distinct processes, agricultural development and industrial development are intertwined. An industrial revolution cannot occur without the provision of extra food to feed the urban population, and raising food production above the subsistence level requires the application of science and technology to farming. Britain, the first nation to industrialize, also had the highest agricultural productivity at the time. By contrast, most developing countries have to spend their hard-earned currency to *import* food.

Food imports stem from the dilemma facing developing countries: cheap food for urban workers means keeping prices down, but low prices provide little incentive for farmers to raise production. Higher prices for farmers, however, may lead to trouble, even rioting or a *coup d'état*. Most Third World governments, therefore, have failed to provide farmers with the necessary economic incentives to provide more food; few governments have had the courage to stake their own survival on this issue. Cheap food is used to curb economic and political unrest because high food prices are dangerous when wages are low and many people are unemployed or underemployed. Government policy, in short, has been a principal stumbling block to food production, leading several former "breadbaskets" to become empty baskets, no longer able to feed themselves and forced to import food.

Yet the Green Revolution, so-called because of its use of high-yield strains of grain and rice to increase production per acre, has been remarkably successful in several countries. Between 1954 and 1973 the food supply in the Third World increased sufficiently to feed an extra 1.3 billion mouths. India, once the recipient of American food aid, became self-sufficient in food and has even begun to export wheat. Thus, more and more developing countries have begun to realize that the rush to industrialize and the neglect of agriculture were wrong, and agricultural development finally is receiving the emphasis reserved in the late 1950s, 1960s, and 1970s for industrialization. China's impressive 50 percent increase of food production in just eight years from 1976 to 1984, like India's, is evidence of a change that points to the farmer, instead of the industrialist, as the key figure in pulling the developing countries up out of poverty and hunger. Together with large surpluses of food in North America and Western Europe, this suggests that Malthus's contention that population increases will outgrow the world's ability to feed its inhabitants was wrong.

Despite these improvements, during the 1980s an estimated 700 million people, according to the World Bank, still confronted the prospect of malnutrition despite the increases in food production since 1950. Africa and South Asia fall within the area of fastest population growth, suggesting that even India's claim to self-sufficiency may only mean the maintenance of a substantial diet and that tens of millions of India's population remain undernourished. Thus, one-third of the population of the Third World does not consume sufficient calories to sustain an active, working life, and one-fourth of the populations of Africa and South Asia do not receive enough calories to prevent stunted growth and health problems. Sizable increases in food production are therefore needed just to sustain the current population, let alone future growth. Indeed, the number facing malnutrition could rise if continued poor harvests in the North shrink food reserves and raise food prices. For low-income and food-deficit countries already having difficulties making ends meet, this would create serious problems requiring emergency assistance. In the longer run, the problem of whether food production can be accelerated to keep up with future population growth remains questionable, unless there is significant progress toward limiting such growth. On occasions, however, as in Ethiopia, two other factors account for malnutrition: civil war and governmental callousness.

Ethiopia's Soviet-style collectivization of land by its Marxist rulers had already created hunger and malnutrition prior to 1985, the year an extended drought brought death to millions. Incredibly, despite its people's starvation, Ethiopia spent $100 million the same year on the tenth anniversary celebration of its 1975 revolution which had abolished the monarchy. Had it not been for a foreign photographer, who sold his film to Western television, the widespread starvation accompanying the drought might not have become known outside of Ethiopia. The government had suppressed the news in favor of glorifying "Ethiopian socialism." Even after trucks and food had been shipped to Ethiopia, the regime gave priority to unloading Soviet arms over Western food and used the trucks for military purposes rather than for the transport of food to the starving. The government, moreover, would not allow food distribution in rebel areas. In any event, it was only the outcry in the West that compelled the Ethiopian regime to pay some attention to its starving people, and it was largely private Western relief agencies that transported the food, often in the face of government obstruction and incompetence. In 1987-1988, drought and civil wars (in Ethiopia, Sudan, and Mozambique) again produced famine in central and southern Africa. But in Ethiopia, hard hit once more, the government refused to allow foreign relief agencies to distribute food in certain areas because of the continuing internal strife.

Thus, the donated food piled up and millions were threatened with starvation. Despite the government, however, resourceful agencies got food through to the needy and avoided a repetition of the starvation of 1985.

Ethiopian indifferences to the suffering of its people unfortunately are not unique.[19] Today, developing country governments aware of food crises can call upon the reserve food supplies that Western governments put aside each year if their harvests are plentiful. If developing-country governments do not possess the administrative skills and organization for emergency relief, international relief organizations are available to help. The fact, however, is that governments for various reasons, including the desire not to publicize failures that reflect poorly on them, may not care about the feeding of their peoples—for example, in China from 1959 to 1962 in the wake of the "Great Leap Forward," a disastrous economic experiment in which several millions are believed to have starved; in Nigeria, where from 1967 to early 1970 the government encouraged starvation to bring the rebel province of Biafra back into the national fold, at the cost of perhaps 1 million ethnic Ibos who lived there; in East Pakistan in 1970, when the government, located in West Pakistan, responded slowly in the aftermath of a typhoon, resulting in not only about 100,000 deaths but also secession and the creation of the new state of Bangladesh; in Ethiopia, where the emperor, before 1974 when he was overthrown, tried to conceal news of a famine; and in Afghanistan, where after 1979 Soviet forces deliberately destroyed crops to force hungry peasants either into the Soviet-controlled towns and cities or out of the country.

Even if sufficient food were available because farmers are provided with the incentive of higher prices, many people in developing countries cannot afford to buy food, especially if prices rise.[20] During the 1974 world food crisis, for example, there was enough food to go around. The cause of hunger was simple: poverty and poor income distribution in the affected areas. The higher the price of food, the more widespread hunger will be because the poor already spend 60-80 percent of their income on food. Even in those countries where the Green Revolution increased food production—India, Pakistan, Bangladesh, and Mexico—malnutrition remains. The sub-Saharan region will continue to be a chronic food-deficit area, with a limited food supply and too many people. The key to reducing malnutrition and eliminating starvation is therefore an agricultural *and* industrial revolution.

Accumulating Capital for Modernization

A fourth overwhelming problem of backward, even stagnant, economies is how to accumulate the requisite capital needed to escape a past as "raw-material appendages" to the industrial powers. New nations recognize the need to build industrial economies to banish poverty, end economic dependence on the former colonial powers, and achieve international standing.

Developing countries are exporters of raw materials. Fifty nations rely on single commodities for export; others rely on two or three resources. Altogether, ninety-three developing countries rely on the export of crops or natural resources other than oil for more than 50 percent of their export earnings (see Table 9-5 for examples of developing-country exports). Theoretically, these countries should be able to earn sufficient capital from their exports to carry out large-scale industrialization because, ideally, as Western industrial nations continue to consume more, their demand for raw materials should rise. In practice, however, it usually has not worked out that way. The developing countries' dependence on exports of raw materials has limited their earning capacities. One reason is that their exports reflect every fluctuation in the Western business cycle. For example, as Western industrial economies approach full employment, the demand for and prices of materials rise. When these economies turn downward, as they did in the 1970s and economic growth remains low as in the 1980s, demand and prices decline. A drop of just one cent in coffee or copper prices can result in the loss of millions of dollars, sometimes tens of millions of dollars, for developing countries. As the Mexicans used to say, "A sneeze in the American economy can lead to pneumonia in Mexico."* Commodity prices during the last decade were the lowest in fifty years! A second reason for the limited earning capacities from exports is that advanced Western industrial technology has, in many instances, made it both possible and profitable to develop synthetics and other substitutes for western-imported raw materials. The demand for resources by industries no longer dependent on certain natural raw materials then decreases and prices drop. A final reason for developing countries' difficulties in earning money through their exports is their practice of producing more to compensate for low prices. The result is a glut on the international market, which drives prices even lower. For example, for Chile or Zambia, dependent solely on copper exports, the drop in price from $1.34 per pound in 1980 to 65 cents in 1985 was a disaster; the same has been true for Ghana and cocoa, Uganda and coffee, Cuba and sugar, and Chad and cotton.

The dilemma of many developing countries is agonizing. They desperately need capital, and they rely on their raw-material exports to earn it. But the harder they work to enlarge the volume of these exports to enhance their earnings, the less they may earn. At the same time, because of their frequent difficulties in producing enough food for their rapidly growing populations, they must buy food. They also must import the Western machinery required to boost their industrialization, the price of which is usually rising. The "terms of trade"—the developing countries' earnings from their exports versus the cost of their imports—are thus against them. Exports of raw materials then do not seem a likely route of escape from poverty for the non-OPEC developing countries dependent on commodity exports. Faced with higher oil

* In Colombia, dependent on coffee exports for legal income, a 40 percent drop in coffee prices, stemming from U.S. suspension of an international coffee agreement drives more farmers to produce and process coca. Yet Washington is simultaneously urging Colombia to eliminate its cocaine industry. An international price support program for coffee is clearly needed if farmers are to make a living.

Table 9-5 One-Commodity Countries

Latin America	Iraq	Burundi	Rwanda
Bahamas	*Crude petroleum*	*coffee*	*Coffee*
Petroleum products	Kuwait	Comoros	Seychelles
Bolivia	*Crude petroleum*	*Cloves*	*Copra*
Natural gas (1983)	Oman	Congo	Somalia
Colombia	*Crude petroleum*	*Crude petroleum*	*Live animals*
Coffee	Qatar	Gabon	Uganda
El Salvador	*Crude petroleum*	*Crude petroleum*	*Coffee*
Coffee	Saudi Arabia	The Gambia	Zaire
Jamaica	*Crude petroleum*	*Groundnut products*	*Copper*
Alumina	South Yemen	Guinea	Zambia
Mexico	*Petroleum products*	*Bauxite*	*Copper*
Crude petroleum	Syria	Lesotho	
Netherlands Antilles	*Crude petroleum*	*Diamonds*	**Asia/Pacific**
Petroleum products	United Arab	Liberia	Brunei
Suriname	Emirates	*Iron ore*	*Petroleum and*
Alumina	*Crude petroleum*	Libya	*products*
Trinidad and Tobago		*Crude petroleum*	Fiji
Petroleum and	**Africa**	Mauritania	*Sugar*
products	Algeria	*Iron ore*	Indonesia
Venezuela	*Crude petroleum*	Mauritius	*Crude petroleum*
Crude petroleum	Angola	*Sugar*	Papua New Guinea
	Crude petroleum	Niger	*Copper concentrate*
Middle East	Botswana	*Uranium*	Vanuatu
Iran	*Diamonds*	Nigeria	*Copra*
Crude petroleum		*Crude petroleum*	

SOURCE: United States Department of State, *Atlas of United States Foreign Relations*, 2d ed. (Washington, D.C.: Department of State, 1985), 54.

NOTE: Based on 1980-1983 export average; market economies only. One-commodity countries are those for which one commodity provides more than 50 percent of export earnings.

prices, a sharp drop in commodity prices, and shrinking Western markets because of the increase in oil prices, many developing countries began to borrow heavily in the 1970s, only to accumulate huge debts (see Chapter 14). The declining foreign aid from Western countries, especially the United States, did not fill this gap, and banks, given the debts, were not eager to loan more money. As a result, in the 1980s developing countries eagerly sought relationships with multinational corporations (MNCs), as aid and trade failed to bring in sufficient capital. But the MNCs often repatriated their profits rather than reinvesting in the countries in which they were earning their money; indeed, even the initial capital outlays may have come partly or wholly from local sources, diverting it from native investments. Certainly, with the debt repayments, more capital was by the mid-1980s going from South to North rather than the other way around.

Newly Industrialized Countries

The international economy is, however, in the process of major change (see

Chapter 7). While in the past the developed states imported raw materials and agricultural products from the developing countries, they are now increasingly importing finished goods. This change stems in part from a vast increase in the activities of multinational corporations (see Chapter 15). During the 1960s, the international economy began to be turned on its head as the MNCs invested in the poor nations to produce manufactures for export. As of 1985 more than half of these nations' exports were manufactured goods. The industrial nations now export agricultural goods to the poor states, a startling change from the previous pattern. Two political observers, Richard Barnet and Ronald Müller, have called this phenomenon the "Latinamericanization of the United States":

> Production of the traditional industrial goods that have been the mainstay of the U.S. economy is being transferred from $4-an-hour factories in New England to 30 cents-an-hour factories in the "export platforms" of Hong Kong and Taiwan. Increasingly, as the cars, televisions, computers, cameras, clothes, and furniture are being produced abroad, the United States is becoming a service economy and a producer of plans, programs, and ideas for others to execute. . . .
>
> The United States trading pattern is beginning to resemble that of underdeveloped countries as the number one nation becomes increasingly dependent on the export of agricultural products and timber to maintain its balance of payments and increasingly dependent on imports of finished goods to maintain its standard of living. . . . (Unlike poor countries, however, the U.S. also exports "software"— i.e. technical knowledge.) [21]

This turnaround situation presently involves only a handful of nations: the NICs in East Asia, Singapore's ASEAN colleagues (mainly Malaysia, Thailand, the Philippines, and Indonesia), and a few nations in other regions, such as Brazil in Latin America. Table 9-6 reveals the higher per capita incomes, higher life expectancy and literacy rates, and lower infant mortality rates of these nations in contrast to those of the more typical developing countries shown in Table 9-7. Indeed a look at these figures raises the question of whether the NICs can still be classified as developing countries, even if they are more rapidly developing ones.

But should the NICs, whatever their classification, be the model for the other developing countries? If they can take off economically, should not the other developing nations able to produce textiles, clothing, simple consumer electronics, and such products as shoes and toys take their place on the lower rungs of the development ladder? Probably not. [22] Potential NICs, like the commodity-exporting nations, confront a shrinking international economy. The 5 percent growth in the 1950s and 1960s fell back to 3 percent in the 1970s and fell further to just over 2 percent in the 1980s. In short, the rapid growth of the international economy through the 1960s permitted room for newcomers, but this may now be at an end. Indeed, the very presence of South Korea and Taiwan may be obstacles to the entry of new Koreas and Taiwans. Moreover, as Western industries decline and unemployment grows, protectionist pressures grow. In fact the more successful developing countries

Table 9-6 Profile of Eight Newly Industrialized Countries, 1988

Country	Population (millions)	Infant Mortality Rate (per thousand)	Life Expectancy	Literacy Rate (%)	Per Capita Income
Hong Kong	5.6	8	75 [a]	75	$7,550
Indonesia [b]	184.0	95	54 [a]	62	330
Malaysia [b]	16.3	25	68 men 73 women	65	1,600
Philippines [b]	63.0	48	61 men 65 women	88	540
Singapore	2.6	9	70 men 75 women	86	6,700
South Korea	42.7	29	64 men 71 women	over 90	2,800
Taiwan	20.0	11	70 men 75 women	94	3,640
Thailand [b]	54.6	43	62 men 66 women	82	790

SOURCE: Central Intelligence Agency, *The World Factbook 1988* (Washington, D.C.: Central Intelligence Agency, 1988).

[a] Men and women.

[b] Members of the Association of Southeast Asian Nations (ASEAN).

are at exporting, for example, textiles, clothing, and shoes, the more likely they are to face rising trade barriers such as the congressional legislation passed against these three items in 1988 and vetoed by President Reagan. Not surprisingly, the Third World has stopped growing since the early 1980s; many developing nations have even slipped backward. It is therefore doubtful that, for their development, they can rely on the export strategies adopted earlier by the NICs. Yet whether a strategy oriented toward production for the domestic market will be more successful for most developing countries also remains to be seen. Ironically, Communist China—which has been shifting to capitalist market methods—may become the new model for many of the nonexporting developing countries, if the squashing by its leaders of the pro-democracy movement in 1989 does not set the country back.

Cultural Transformation

The term *economic development* suggests a one-dimensional picture of the transition process from a traditional rural society to an advanced modern nation. Economic development implies that the only requirement for this

Table 9-7 Profile of Nine Typical Developing Countries, 1988

Country	Population							Economics		Type of Government
	Total (millions)	Growth Rate (%)	Infant Mortality Rate (per thousand)	Life Expectancy	Literacy Rate (%)	Ethnic Groups	Religious Groups	GNP (billion dollars)	Per Capita Income	
Brazil	151	8.2	70	62 men 67 women	76	Portuguese Italian German Japanese Amerindian Black	Roman Catholic	200.0	1,880	Federal republic
El Salvador	5	—	41	63 men	65	Mestizo	Roman Catholic	4.3	870	Republic
Ethiopia	48	3.0	145	38 [a]	35	Oromo Amhara Tigrean	Muslim Ethiopian Orthodox Aminist	5.4	110	Communist state
India	817	4.8	116	55 [a]	36	Indo-Aryan Dravidian	Hindu Muslim Sikh	200.0	250	Republic
Kenya	23	5.0	59	53 [a]	47	Kikuyu Luhya	Protestant Catholic	5.0	230	Republic
Nigeria	112	3.0	113	48 men 52 women	25-30	Hausa Fulani Yoruba Ibo	Muslim Christian	53.4	520	Federal republic
Pakistan	107	2.7	119	52 men	26	Punjabi Sindhi Pashtun Baluch Mahajir	Muslim	33.0	330	Islamic republic
Saudi Arabia	15	4.2	61	60 men 64 women	52	Arab	Muslim	85.0	6,030	Monarchy
Somalia	8	3.2	152	44 men 48 women	50	Somali	Sunni Muslim	1.4	200	Republic

SOURCE: Central Intelligence Agency, *The World Factbook 1988* (Washington, D.C.: Central Intelligence Agency, 1988).
[a] Men and women.

process is industry, that industrialization follows automatically from the formation of capital, and that mobilizing capital is therefore the crucial problem. Even when agricultural growth is included, as it must be, the term *economic development* is an oversimplification—indeed, a distortion—of the complex realities of modernizing a traditional society. Modernization is more than simply building steel mills and constructing dams. It means, above all else, changes in values, aspirations, and expectations. The necessary changes are not simply economic, but political, social, and cultural as well. Modernization is multidimensional; it aims at the complete transformation of society.

Traditional societies have not usually regarded economic activity as a prime concern of life. Even in Western history, money making was not always the chief pursuit. In the Middle Ages, for example, religion was the principal concern. The church condemned the charging of interest—a necessity in a monetary economy—as usury. The desire for profit was equated with greed, and economic competition was simply not part of the accepted way of life. This attitude toward interest and profits was, of course, inimical to business. A major break with this medieval attitude came with the introduction of the Protestantism of John Calvin in the sixteenth century. In contrast to Catholicism, it gave priority to earthly works. Industriousness, profits, savings, and investments were in this way legitimated by religion. Thrift, character, and hard work represented the earthly trinity.

It is hardly surprising that this "Protestant ethic" and capitalism became closely identified.[23] It was but a short way from Calvin to the eighteenth-century British economist Adam Smith, whose theory of capitalism was based upon recognition of the acquisitive passion that the Roman Catholic church had earlier condemned. Smith accepted the desire for gain as a fact of life, calling it "enlightened self-interest." *Laissez-faire* capitalism was merely to harness this acquisitive instinct to the public welfare.

In the contemporary world such a process of secularization is also critical. Today, the NICs embody this Protestant ethic with their "this world" attitude, their energetic and active orientation as opposed to contemplative life, and their positive view toward accumulating wealth which is combined with a willingness to postpone gratification, thereby gaining savings for further investment and capital accumulation.[24] This secularization has not gone unchallenged, however. Islamic fundamentalism, which has spread throughout much of the Middle East and West Asia since the late 1970s, is essentially an "other world" religion, a reaction against Westernization, and an attempt to uphold traditional society and values—and the status of the mullahs or religious leaders.[25] The process of modernization uproots the traditional society and historic social relationship, causing great personal insecurity while eroding customary and religious norms. It brings with it a "foreign" way of life, whose external manifestations such as rock music, dancing, public displays of affection between couples, and pornography are often as shocking for old societies as ostentatious displays of wealth by the newly rich (which are in striking contrast to the lifestyles of the ordinary people) and the omnipresence of foreigners doing business. Critics of modernization have called it "Westoxication."

Psychologically, modernization means recognition of the inferiority of both the old ways and old society and the superiority of the foreigner's—the Westerner's—way. The colonialists were the first to erode traditional society. Westerners may have been able to colonize the non-Western world because they had the guns, but to the natives guns were a symbol of a more advanced society. It was the inferiority of the traditional society and its way of life that made it possible for Western states to conquer these "backward" areas.

Not unnaturally, the West considered itself to be the model of what an advanced, modern society should be; where it led, others would follow. It was not a matter of coercion but of preference. Islamic fundamentalism is the most profound, most widespread, and angriest reaction to this phenomenon. It is also violently anti-American because the United States represents the most advanced secular Western society and is the most powerful Western state. Islamic fundamentalism asserts the dignity and worth of the ways of Islam, and it provides the mass of people untouched by the prosperity of Westernization—indeed, often displaced by it as, for example, when people are driven off the land into urban shantytowns—a sense of belonging and spiritual and emotional comfort. In Iran, this movement was led by the mullahs, the traditional religious leaders whose property had been confiscated by the shah and whose role in a modern secular society would be much less important than that of other groups. Islam not only has gained a firm grip in Iran, but rulers in other states from Pakistan to the Sudan and Egypt have either adopted Islamic laws or become sensitive to them. Its potential to spread among Muslims in other Arab countries, the Israeli-occupied West Bank, and potentially even the Soviet Union north of Afghanistan is a matter of concern to many.

But the reaction to the cultural transformation inherent in modernization occurs even in those societies that have achieved economic development and cultural changes. It is less severe, obviously, than in Iran, but Westernization spurs ambivalence about the price of success even in such a city-state as Singapore. Because traditional society with its emphasis on community values and hierarchy gives away in a modern society to individualism, achievement, reward, and social mobility, loss of "core Asian values" and preoccupation with self at the cost of the larger group has become a concern of Singapore's prime minister, Lee Kuan Yew. In Singapore, English is the primary language being taught in the schools, and business has brought in its wake Western television, books, magazines, and other cultural influences. What then is a Singaporean? [26]

NATION BUILDING AND CIVILIAN
AND MILITARY AUTHORITARIANISM

Building a nation that is in the initial stages of modernization is thus enormously difficult and complex, requiring a number of tasks. First, the new state must achieve national cohesion. Second, a set of legitimate governmental institutions must be created through which conflict can be channeled peacefully and compromise achieved. Otherwise, *coups d'etat*, rioting, revolutions, assassinations, and civil wars will remain the methods of resolving differences.[27] The third task is economic development. For new nations, the response to the "revolution of rising expectations" is important for humanitarian and political reasons and for the cause of nation building itself. The degree to which expectations are satisfied will be proof of the effectiveness of the new national government. Economic development produces a better life for each citizen; its significance is its *political* payoff. The leaders of new nations not yet solidly knitted together must prove to the people that what they, the leaders, are seeking to establish will be beneficial to the people. Otherwise, why should the people transfer their loyalty to the new nations? Economic development can in this way strengthen the fragile bonds of national unity and give new nations legitimacy.

But how does the leader of a new nation deal with these tasks? One way is to "nationalize" the people—that is, to inculcate in them national consciousness and loyalty and recognition of the national government as *their* government, its laws reflecting *their* adherence. The majority must acknowledge that they are citizens of one nation and that the national government has the legitimate authority to make decisions on behalf of the entire population. Such popular consciousness cannot be developed overnight. An entire people must, in a sense, go to school—to learn their nation's language and history (much of it mythical, devised for the purpose of fostering national identification) and to be brought into the mainstream of national life. Only then will national symbols stimulate deep emotion and a national community emerge.

After independence, many new developing countries were held together by their leaders who more than anyone else symbolized the new nation.[28] If they had led the nationalist movement before independence, they had agitated for freedom for years, propagated national mythology, and served time in jail as a result. They and their nations were thus in a very real sense identical. As the founders of these nations, they provided a kind of symbolic presence. Loyalty can usually be felt more keenly toward individuals who incorporate an idea such as the "nation" than toward the idea itself. The heroes in the new nations were transitional figures in transitional societies. They served the indispensable function of encouraging a shift from the traditional, parochial loyalties to tribe or region to broader loyalties to the impersonal nation-state. Moreover, these heroes usually had charisma—"a quality of extraordinary spiritual power attributed to a person . . . capable of eliciting popular support in the direction of human affairs." [29] They were, in fact, *substitutes* for their nations and for the national institutions that had yet to be built; they also conferred legitimacy upon the new nations and their governments.

They were usually supported by a single party as the principal instrument of national integration. Unlike Western political parties, which primarily represent the various interests within a nation, the single party in a developing country has a double rationale. First, the party is a means of socializing the traditionally "tribalized" people on a national basis, instilling in the people a sense of identification as citizens of a distinct national community. Just as the charismatic leader replaces the traditional chieftain, the nation is supposed to replace the tribe. The party claims to represent the nation. The second rationale of one-party rule is its alleged efficiency in mobilizing the economic and human resources of a nation for the purpose of modernization.[30] By American standards, such a one-party system is, of course, undemocratic. In the United States the opposition is a loyal opposition whose allegiance is to the same nation and values as the governing party. But in a new African nation the opposition's allegiance is often regional and tribal, and it thus represents the centrifugal forces in society. In these circumstances, a change in the form of government favoring greater democracy could result in disintegration of the state. The choice is *not* between democracy and dictatorship but between nationhood and disintegration. The problem is not one of restraining power to ensure individual freedoms, but one of accumulating sufficient power to ensure that the government will be obeyed.[31]

Because of the tenuous nature of the bonds holding a new nation together and the immense difficulties inherent in modernization, civilian one-party governments often give way to military governments. In the developing countries, the trend toward military control of government is widely established. In Africa more than half the nations were governed by the military in the mid-1970s; by late 1988 thirty-eight out of the forty-five sub-Saharan governments were one-party or military governments. More than two-thirds of the countries of Asia, Africa, the Middle East, and Latin America have experienced varying levels of military intervention since 1945.[32] The trends away from or toward military governments vary by region and circumstance. In the late 1970s, thirteen of Latin America's twenty republics were governed by generals, Haiti by a family dictatorship, and Cuba by a Communist dictator. That changed again in the 1980s. Eleven of the thirteen states elected civilian governments; only Chile and Paraguay remained right-wing regimes, and Chile was moving toward civilian democratic rule by the late 1980s. Several of the new civilian governments remain fragile, however, in large part due to the debt problem. The army remains visible in the background.

One reason for the past visible role of the military is that in Latin America, as in other Third World areas, the low level of political culture in and the fragile legitimacy of new states favors military-intervention in politics. In a modern nation with developed and accepted political institutions that contain and mediate conflict in society, the military would find it difficult to justify seizing power and demanding public obedience (or proving it possessed legitimate authority). In a new country, however, in which political obligation still follows largely along ethnic, religious, and racial lines and there is little agreement about the rules of the game, the military can seize power. Rather than a usurpation, such a seizure is claimed to be legitimate if embryonic political institutions and politicians appear to the public to have failed. Military rule may even be welcomed in situations where civilian leaders, overwhelmed by the massive problems confronting them, have proved themselves inept and indecisive, as well as lax, self-indulgent, and corrupt.

Yet the performance of military governments falls far short of expectations as well.[33] Not unnaturally, given the armed forces' organizational interests, the share of the national budget going to the military goes up dramatically in most instances of takeover (usually 50-75 percent of the previous budget), thus eating up whatever small increases in productivity may have been gained. Although economic growth is viewed as desirable, the military's interests come first—even at the cost of modernization. Furthermore, military leaders do not necessarily have the skills of economists and businesspeople in assessing alternative economic growth strategies, understanding fiscal policies, and directing large sectors of the economy. The economic record of military governments is hardly an enviable one, certainly no better than that of civilian governments.

Thus, the reputation of military regimes as reformers is, on the whole, undeserved. Although nationalistic military governments frequently claim to be progressive, determined to bring about redistribution of land and wealth and to enhance the people's welfare, their often militant rhetoric is in direct conflict with their corporate aggrandizement. In economies of scarcity, in which a gain for one group means a loss for other groups, increased military spending leaves less to redistribute. Moreover, armies more often than not represent one or two tribal or ethnic groups rather than a mixture of all the groups in the nation. Attempts to favor the communities from which much of the military leadership comes serve only to deepen the already existing social divisions.

Yet the image of many military regimes as progressive persists, largely because in areas where the traditional landed elite was still governing, as in much of the Third World, the military did, upon coming to power, redistribute land and wealth. The breakup of landed oligarchies, which provides greater social mobility and economic opportunities, clearly favors the rural and urban middle classes with which the officers identify. But where, as in Latin America, a relatively high level of modernization already exists and the lower class, especially the workers, is more politically self-conscious and mobilizable, military regimes will crack down if challenged. As a contender for sharing the power and wealth in society, a mobilized lower class is viewed as a threat to the military's corporate interests and to middle class interests in general. The result is the transformation of the military government into a defender of the social and economic status quo.

The military thus plays different roles in different societies. In traditional society, the middle class military becomes radical, and its coups are "break-through" coups; in middle class society, the military becomes a participant and arbiter; in mass society, the military becomes the conservative guardian of the prevailing order, and its coups are "veto" coups. In other words, the less developed the society, the more progressive is the military's role; the more developed that society, the more conservative and reactionary is that role.[34]

However poorly or well the "armed modernizers" govern and advance their nation's economic growth and welfare, military regimes are likely to remain common throughout the developing world.[35] Nevertheless, the trend away from authoritarianism among the NICs, especially in South Korea and Taiwan, and toward democracy in Latin America, is a hopeful sign. But admittedly, this trend is fragile and reversible. The debt problems of some of the new democracies such as Argentina and Brazil are so enormous that simply paying off the debt will eat up funds that should be used for economic development. Even worse, they are paying off these debts by austerity measures which could destabilize these societies and topple governments, leaving perhaps military or Communist dictatorships in their place.

FOREIGN POLICY IN THE BIPOLAR ERA

Because the leaders of the new states confront problems that are so vast and seemingly insoluble, they are tempted to play dramatic and popular roles on the international stage rather than concentrate on their nations' domestic needs. Indeed, foreign policy may help them accomplish their various internal aims.

Nationalization of Their People

First, leaders may use foreign policy to help them "nationalize" their people. Often the only force that initially united the people was hatred of the former colonial power, but this "reactive nationalism" tends to lose its force as a socially cohesive factor soon after independence. Thus, the only way to arouse people and keep them united is to continue the struggle against European colonialism or "imperialism" in general. The more tenuous the bonds uniting the members of a society, the more ardent will be the campaign against the "vestiges of imperialism." By asserting that the nation is once more the victim of the West, leaders seek to arouse the people and unite them against a common external danger. Anticolonialism thus does not end with the achievement of national independence. The struggle against "neocolonialism" must be continued until a measure of national unity and economic progress has occurred. "Anti-colonialism is a cement that holds together otherwise incompatible domestic factions. The cohesive function of the 'common enemy' must be perpetuated even when the foreign 'enemy' is no longer a real threat. . . . This, perhaps, is the reason why opposition to colonialism frequently grows more intense *after* independence." [36] Foreign policy thus serves as *a continuation of the revolution against colonial rule to preserve the unity of the new nation.*

Search for Identity, Status, and Dignity

Second, and closely related, the foreign policy of developing countries involves a search for identity, status, and dignity. Many of these countries are new nations, former colonies, with no national history, no commonly accepted political institutions, no domestic unity, and almost no strong national commitment among their populations. Even if they had a glorious past and are at present independent, the feeling that they are still subject to Western influence may lead to an assertive foreign policy:

> In short, the state's legitimacy is more easily asserted through its foreign policy than through its domestic policies and it is more apparent when performing on the international than on the national stage. Domestic issues divide the nation and disclose how little developed is its consciousness of itself; foreign issues unite the nation and mark it as a going concern.[37]

Foreign policy, therefore, is also *an effort* to *discover and establish the new state's personality and to affirm its identity as a nation separate from the former colonial power.*

Assertion of Equality

The new states are very conscious that the history of the international system is the history of inequality. By and large as developing states they are aware of their lower places in the hierarchy of states dominated by the superpowers and the Western industrial states (including Japan). While the leaders of the developing countries have vigorously asserted their equality as legally equal sovereign states in the United Nations, they bristle at being excluded from conferences and institutions that deal with issues that affect their countries, particularly economic and financial issues. The developing countries tend to see themselves as the West's "dependencies" who do not control their own destiny. Thus, a third aim of foreign policy is *to secure greater participation in decisions that have an impact upon their societies, and, more generally, to play a more influential role in the state system.*

Maximization of Foreign Aid

A fourth aim of the foreign policy of developing countries has been *to attract the external funds necessary for their domestic transformation from rural, economi-*

cally backward societies to urban-industrial societies with high standards of living. Bipolarity favored this quest. According to political scientist Robert Good,

> The possibility of "blackmail" is built into the very structure of Cold War competition. But from the point of view of the excessively dependent, relatively impotent new state, this is not blackmail. It is the equally ancient but more honorable art of maintaining political equilibrium through the diversification of dependence, the balancing of weakness—in short, the creation of an "alternative" lest the influence of one side or the other become too imposing. The attraction of Communist aid is enhanced for radical governments whose wariness of the intentions of the former metropole extends to the "capitalist-imperialist West" in general. Yet [even] conservative governments are receptive to Communist aid. They want it partly to placate their radical oppositions and to hasten development, but also, one suspects, to pursue the first requirement of operational independence—the creation of a rough equilibrium among foreign influences in the life of the country. Conversely, radical governments that have developed extensive relations with the Communist bloc may seek the re-establishment of compensatory links with the West.[38]

Preservation of Power

Fifth, nationalist leaders want to stay in power and, therefore, frequently seek to divert popular attention from domestic problems. At home only painfully slow progress can be made—the task of development is bound to be long and arduous—and the masses will tend to become increasingly restless and dissatisfied. The gap between their rising material expectations and satisfaction seems unbridgeable as increasing numbers of people become politically conscious and demand that their needs be met. In addition, increased movement from rural areas to the impersonal and unfamiliar cities disrupts the traditional loyalties and ties of the people; unable to find substitutes, they live isolated in a mass society. And the tendency to political fragmentation remains ever present. The pressure on national leaders to improve living conditions and build the new nation then is unrelenting. If these demands remain unsatisfied, the revolution of rising expectations may turn into a revolution of rising frustration, and the leaders and their governments may suffer declining prestige and support.

To preserve or recapture the people's support, stay in power, and stabilize the government, leaders are tempted irresistibly to assert themselves in foreign policy. In circumstances of economic stagnation, cultural alienation, and governmental insecurity, political leaders may try to preserve their power by externalizing domestic dissatisfaction; foreign scapegoats will be required to relieve internal stresses and strains. It is easier for leaders to play prominent and highly visible international roles—at the United Nations, at meetings of the nonaligned states, during visits to Moscow or Western capitals, for example—than to undertake the difficult work of modernizing their nation. Foreign policy, therefore, may serve the *purpose of exporting domestic dissatisfaction and mobilizing popular support for the government.*

CHARACTERISTICS OF NONALIGNMENT

A foreign policy of nonalignment favors the implementation of all these aims. Bipolarity made nonalignment feasible. By taking an in-between position, a new state could maximize its appeal to both the Soviet Union and the United States, as well as to their respective allies. The two superpowers would act as if they were suitors seeking to win the same woman. By occasionally hinting at a commitment, the new nation could gain leverage, despite its lack of power. Each suitor would then be compelled to demonstrate its serious intentions, usually with large amounts of foreign aid. The further a new state moved away from the West, the more eagerly the Communists would offer it assistance; the closer it moved to the West, the greater the number of Western loans or grants offered.

Although bipolarity favors nonalignment, not all non-Marxist, nonaligned countries implement this policy in the same way. The Yugoslavs consider themselves nonaligned, as do the Egyptians, Indians, Ethiopians, Malaysians, and Tunisians. Yet the dispositions of these countries range from pro-Soviet to pro-American. In a way, the problem of classifying the varieties of nonalignment is one of *time*. A regime may be looking eastward one moment and yet normalize its relations with the West the next. Ethiopia is pro-American one year; then the new Marxist regime shifts toward the East. But in Somalia, the Marxist government, once close to Moscow, shifted toward the United States when the Soviet Union switched its support from Somalia to Ethiopia, with which Somalia was in conflict. Egypt for many years seemed to be a Soviet pawn—indeed, in 1971 it formalized its association with a treaty of friendship and cooperation—but a year later it threw out its Soviet advisers and within two more years its president had reestablished diplomatic relations with the United States, called Secretary of State Henry Kissinger (who is Jewish) his "good friend and miracle worker," and denounced the treaty of friendship with the Soviet Union. Similarly, in the early 1970s India under Indira Gandhi signed a friendship treaty with the Soviet Union. But a few years later, after she had been defeated in a general election, her successor declared that his government would adopt a foreign policy of "proper nonalignment" and that the Indian-Soviet friendship treaty would not be allowed to interfere with India's relations with other countries—presumably the Western states. Upon reelection, Gandhi shifted again somewhat toward the Soviet Union, and, after she died, her son continued to stress the Indian-Soviet link.

Nonalignment is even more a matter of *issue areas*.[39] One such area is military. Egypt and India received vast amounts of military equipment from the Soviet Union, but Singapore was willing to make its naval base available to the West in the event of hostilities, and Tanzania once relied upon the military forces of its former mother country (Britain) to restore domestic order. Yet all these countries consider themselves nonaligned. Some even seek and gain military aid from both sides. The same is true for other issue areas such as economic assistance and trade, diplomacy, and ideology. For example, country A may appear to lean toward the West because it places a high priority on democratic values, receives most of its military hardware from the West, receives about equal amounts of economic aid from both sides, and gravitates more toward Western than Soviet diplomatic positions. (An exception is India, which, democratic tradition notwithstanding, has often gravitated toward the Soviets.) Country B, in contrast, is politically sympathetic to the East, a source of its military hardware; obtains much of its economic aid and trade from the West; and leans notably toward the East on diplomatic issues. (In this category Egypt is an exception. A one-party state, Egypt, with its "Arab socialism," has switched from a pro-Soviet stance toward rapprochement with the United States. It has also dismantled much of its brand of socialism to stimulate private initiative and attract foreign investments while retaining some public ownership over certain sectors of the economy.)

Even when a nonaligned country seems to lean more toward the Soviet Union or the United States, however, one must be careful about classifying it one way or another. The term *pro-Soviet* may reflect the general attitude and preference of national leaders (for example, the Sandinistas in Nicaragua), but it may also indicate positions that those leaders would have taken even in the absence of a cold war—if they are opposed to colonialism or apartheid, for example, which the Soviets also oppose. The same is true of a country that seems pro-American. For example, Anwar Sadat was first an Egyptian nationalist. When he made overtures to the West, it was because he knew U.S. leaders could better help him achieve his goal of recovering Egyptian lands lost in 1967 because they had influence in Israel and the Soviets did not. On balance, however, nonalignment more often than not has seemed—especially during the 1970s—to be pro-Soviet because of strong anti-Western attitudes.

The developing countries have attributed all sorts of ills—from their continued role as raw-material suppliers for Western industries to conditions in South Africa—to the West's "neocolonial" control. The conviction that the distribution of power between the First and Third Worlds has been stacked against them and that the West thereby keeps them poor and dependent has led the nonaligned countries to take increasingly anti-Western stands. If the many countries of Asia, Africa, and Latin America could be considered a cohesive bloc, it is because they share this set of attitudes.[40]

FAILURE OF DEVELOPMENT: INTERNAL OR EXTERNAL CAUSES?

Initial Western Development Models

Forty-five years after World War II, much of the Third World remains poor, illiterate, hungry, and unhealthy, despite an economic growth rate higher than that of the First World. The difficulty is that, because these countries started so far behind in per capita income, it has been virtually impossible for them to catch up. For example, a person earning $300 receives $330 when that income rises by 10 percent; another earning $3,000 receives $3,150 after a 5 percent increase. Indeed, from 1955 to 1980 per capita income in the United States, in constant dollars, grew from $7,000 to $11,500. In India, during the same time, it grew from $170 to $260. Thus, a gap of $6,830 in 1955 had almost doubled to $11,240 in 1980! In short, the income gap between rich and poor states widens, even if the poorer nation has a faster rate of economic growth. Some of the developing countries, to be sure, have managed surprisingly well, especially the resource-rich (particularly oil-rich) countries and the export platforms.

Nevertheless, many of the developing countries have remained just that, developing. This result has been contrary to the early models of development drawn up by Western social scientists as more and more colonial countries achieved independence. Essentially, it was said, nations went through certain stages of development. In this process, as in the development of individuals as they progress from childhood to old age, nations passed, according to the economists, through several "stages of economic growth," and, according to the political scientists, through a number of "stages of political growth." [41] At the end of their growth, the new nations would look like Western states: politically pluralistic, democratic, stable, and industrialized, with a high standard of living and a relatively equitable distribution of income. Peaceful was another characteristic often added, although sometimes it was left implicit. Development, thought of mainly to be the economic transformation of a traditional rural society into a modern urban-industrial one, was therefore also called *Westernization*. Having no models of global development to work with, Western social scientists, not surprisingly, looked back at their own societies and generalized about their evolution into modern societies. The paths the European states had trodden, therefore, seemed likely to be the ones the new states of Asia and Africa would walk along. The West, then, held itself up as the model for the rest of the world.[42] This was an ethnocentric view, but it was also an optimistic one. In effect, it promised that the developing countries, no matter how backward, will *inevitably* develop; they will make it, just as the countries of Europe and North America.

It was in this context that the United States and other Western states began to provide the developing countries with economic aid. Nations living at the poverty level, it was pointed out, could not squeeze the required capital out of their low-paid work force; foreign funds were therefore necessary to fan the fires of development. But aid did not help the vast majority of developing countries realize self-sustaining growth. Finding their status as recipients of Western "charity" rather humiliating, their slogan became "Trade, Not Aid." In an industrial world, they expected orders for their natural resources to earn the funds they needed for capital investment. This would enable them to diversify their economies and become less dependent upon single commodities for exports. This too failed as Western states protected their industries against developing country imports.

Increasingly, therefore, the First and Third Worlds took opposite views of why the developing countries have not been able to modernize. The Western industrial countries argued that the Third World's problems are primarily internal. They arise from overpopulation; ethnic, religious, and racial divisions; lack of natural resources; lack of professional training; government corruption and mismanagement; the low priority given agriculture; a hostile attitude toward private capital investment; and expulsion or mistreatment of productive minorities. The developing countries argued that they cannot modernize because they are the victims of an international economy dominated by the industrial West. The causes and cures of their underdevelopment, they claimed, are not internal but external. Specifically, they asserted that the reason for their economic backwardness is international capitalism.[43]

Developing-Country Dependency and World Capitalism

The difficulties that most developing countries face in earning money in the international market have already been noted. They are too dependent on single resources, and the prices of these resources fluctuate with the Western industrial economies. Competition among resource producers tends to lead to an oversupply, forcing prices downward. When Western industries substitute other resources or synthetics, prices are further depressed. In the meantime, the manufactured goods bought in the West tend to rise in price. The terms of trade do not favor the developing countries.

It is in this context that the developing countries have generally claimed that their relations with the industrial West have not changed much since colonial days. Formerly the colonies were governed directly from London, Paris, or other Western capitals. Since independence, the former colonies have achieved self-government but, they insist, their independence is only formal, not meaningful. Indeed, this formal independence masks the fact that *real* self-government does not exist. The developing countries remain tied to their former masters by the same economic chains that characterized the colonial era. These chains keep them dependent on the capitalist West. Politically independent in name only, the majority remain in *neocolonial* bondage as raw-material suppliers for Western industry.

As a result, they claim, their economies are not oriented toward their national needs, toward improving the lives of their own people. Their resources were, originally developed by the West and then used by Western industry for the production of goods that have raised the *Western* standard of living to the highest in the world. Decisions over their economies were, in brief, decided by foreigners for the benefit of foreigners. That is why the West grew rich while the developing countries remained poor. The relationship of the mother country to the colony was one of exploitation. The developing countries then are poor because they have been robbed; the Western states are rich because they have been the exploiters. Even today, the former colonies still provide Western industry with cheap raw materials—except for oil. The United States, Western Europe, and Japan are said to benefit enormously from this Western-dominated international economy. They are the *core countries* of world capitalism. (The Soviet-bloc economies are by and large, not part of the world trading system.) The developing countries constitute the *peripheries.* Thus the free market, which in theory benefits all nations, actually favors the strong and keeps the developing countries in a subordinate position.

Dependency is a relationship characterized by asymmetry, in which the economic growth of the developing countries is conditioned by events in the industrialized nations' economies. (Interdependence, in contrast, is characterized by greater symmetry.) The developing countries' dependency takes several forms. One is trade dependency; the developing countries depend on the industrial states for markets in which to sell their commodities and are obviously both sensitive and vulnerable to levels of demand. Another form is investment dependency. Western investors control key sectors of Third World economies: production of natural resources and any manufacturing that may have been developed. Foreign aid creates yet a third form of dependence.

A more radical viewpoint asserts that these economic chains are supplemented by Western political alliances and by military and police links to the developing countries' ruling elites, which have a vested interest in preserving this dependency relationship. These governing elites owe their social status, political power, and wealth to this exploitive arrangement. They are the Western capitalists' "front men"; their survival depends on the preservation of the status quo. By the same token, these elites have no strong ties to their own people. Ruling on behalf of foreigners, they are domestically unpopular and, as a result, resort to authoritarian regimes. If their power is threatened, covert or overt foreign intervention—usually by the United States since it is the world's most powerful capitalist state—may occur. U.S. foreign policy is therefore counterrevolutionary according to this viewpoint. Despite its verbal commitment to democracy, the United States in fact suppresses democracy abroad. In this way, the developing countries are "managed" by the United States and its Western partners, who are the real beneficiaries of the free market. Note that in this dependency argument underdevelopment is not a stage preceding the "stages of economic growth" but is the outcome of the international economy.

To sum up the overall developing country case: (1) the current old international economic order favors the states who organized it, the Western capitalist states; (2) the ex-colonial, now neocolonial states, occupy a subordinate and underdeveloped status because of international capitalism, not internal problems; and (3) a new international economic order is needed to right past injustices and bring about a more equitable distribution of wealth, status, and power among the nations of the First and Third Worlds.

CHANGING THE INTERNATIONAL ECONOMY: REVOLUTION OR REFORM?

Those who believe that the old international economic order is not only unfair but also permanent and that the global inequality of wealth is directly attributable to an inherently exploitive capitalism, prescribe a strategy of revolution as a solution. Because the United States and its Western allies are the preeminent capitalist states, and their domination of the international economy is viewed as the prerequisite for the continued exploitation of the peripheral states, a strategy of liberation must be used to destroy this link and America's role in the world economy. In theory, the best solution would be a revolution within the United States itself in which capitalism would be replaced with a socialist economy. By definition, a socialist United States would not exploit the developing countries and would allow them to live in political *and* economic freedom (under socialism, people no longer exploit each other, domestically or internationally, for profit). In practice, however, this is an unlikely solution. A more feasible course, it is suggested, would deprive the United States and its capitalist associates of Third World markets and resources. Cutting the economic links that bind the developing countries with the core states is an alternative strategy that can be achieved by revolutions that overthrow the capitalist puppet regimes in the Third World. Such revolutions may well involve guerrilla war, as in China and Vietnam. However the revolution is brought about, violence is the only way of gaining true national liberation.

The reformist approach agrees that an exploitive relationship exists between the Western industrial states and the raw-material producing developing countries but explains it differently. Instead of attributing the cause to capitalism and advocating a revolutionary solution because imperialism is a necessary expression of capitalism, the reformers blame the structure of the state system. In other words, the inequality of power between states with advanced economies and less-developed economies is the cause of the division between rich and poor nations, not the inherent nature of capitalism. The solution thus is to reduce this inequality of wealth and power. Initially, the prescription was "import substitution." The developing countries had to develop their own industries. They should not import the industrial and consumer goods they need but produce them themselves. This would require the temporary protection of their "baby industries" until they are able to compete internationally. Unfortunately, this solution, which tended to make industries uncompetitive behind their protective barriers, did not prove to be the correct one. It was in this context that in 1974 the new international economic order was offered as a solution.

The political objective of the developing countries was to change the international economy so that wealth would be more equitably distributed. Thus, they sought seven concrete goals:

1. Higher and more stable commodity prices (to provide steady income "decoupled" from Western economic fluctuations) so that they can plan for several years ahead, diversify their economies, and become less dependent on the sale of single resources.
2. Protection of their purchasing power through "indexing," linking the sale of resources to Western inflation rates and rising prices for Western machinery, weapons, and food.
3. Doubling or tripling of foreign aid and capital contributions from such institutions as the International Monetary Fund, and the World Bank, and more influence in these organizations.
4. Preferential Western tariffs for developing country exports, which would give them a competitive edge and enhance their earning capacity.
5. A voice in controlling the levels of production and prices of alternative sources of minerals, such as those found in the seabeds.
6. Deference of their debt, which had stood at $142 billion in 1974, but was to shoot up in succeeding years.
7. Greater control over the multinational corporations.

Although satisfaction of these demands would not constitute a revolutionary transformation of the international economy, it would constitute a new international economic order in which the Western states' perceived control of the economic rules of the game would be reduced.[44] The developing countries' demands reflected their struggle to end past humiliations and their determination to participate actively in shaping their futures.

Developing countries are deeply resentful of their past treatment and present lot in the system. It may be said that the poor and plentiful people of the southern half of this planet are no longer willing to be the "hewers of wood and drawers of water" for the rich states of the northern half. This attitude was the main reason why the poorer developing countries, though the hardest hit by OPEC policies, continued to support OPEC during the 1970s. The louder the rich Western countries squealed, the greater the delight of the Third World countries. As William Wordsworth wrote of the French Revolution, "Bliss was it in that dawn to be alive/But to be young was very heaven." A Third World poet might have written those lines in the winter of 1973-1974. If OPEC were successful, other developing countries could organize cartels for their raw materials and control production and prices—that is, lower production and raise prices.

Throwing off the alleged chains of economic dependence was the critical task for the developing countries. Clearly, though economics can be discussed rationally, the issues being negotiated in the 1970s and early 1980s were only partly economic. The discussion of the terms of trade was deeply symptomatic of a general assertion of non-Western nationalism against the West. The economic bargaining took place, therefore, between parties who were all too frequently and too deeply separated by wide psychological and cultural barriers.

Insisting that their poverty was the result of Western exploitation, the developing countries were really claiming that the West owed them a moral debt for past colonial sins, which it must pay off in more earthly coin. Charging that the West had plundered them in the past and continues to do so today, they repeated over and over that such "imperialistic exploitation" is wrong. Presumably, in their view, Western political organization, economic ideas, scientific inventiveness, and technological skills have had little to do with creating Western prosperity.[45] The attempt to induce a sense of Western guilt for past behavior was a shrewd tactic, however, because many Westerners feel ashamed and morally culpable for what their forebears did, even though the political standards and moral codes were quite different in the colonial age. Preparation for past errors seemed the right thing to do; helping the poor by narrowing the gap between them and the rich constituted, for those Westerners, a morally worthy cause, a way of gaining national redemption and of living up to the promise of a democratic way of life. The developing countries have little leverage, but by charging Western exploitation they hoped to place the West on the defensive. Morality, no less than arms, can be an effective weapon.

Latest Prescription: Western Free Market

Indeed, public discussions of a new international economic order often became diatribes. But the era of confrontation in the 1970s gave way to a more reflective attitude in the Third World in the 1980s. OPEC's influence had declined and resource cartels as a strategy for development no longer seemed appropriate (see Chapter 14). Confrontation with the West and demands for a new international economic order had gained little. The first half of the 1980s saw the economic growth rates of the developing countries decline sharply and the average incomes in most Latin American and sub-Saharan states drop while their debts accumulated. Commodity prices remained low. The South's lot, despite some significant exceptions, had not improved. In a more chastened mood, it was willing to look at other prescriptions.

The key to development is still capital accumulation. Economists, including those in the Third World, have found that considerable capital resources exist in the developing countries, especially in the more developed states in Latin America. But that capital is wasted by governments whose leaders indulge themselves with Rolls Royces and Mercedes or villas on the French Riviera or in Miami, whose bureaucracies are so oversized that they are a drain on the economy, and whose military forces spend too much on weapons for wars that they will never fight. The solution then returns to a standard capitalist prescription: an emphasis on internal savings, austerity, and investment in economic growth. Government, while taxing consumption heavily, should encourage industrial and agricultural development.

Critical to this 1980s shift in position was an increasing endorsement of the private marketplace. President Reagan's view of the "magic of the marketplace," which initially met with skepticism, seems to have gained support and placed on the defensive the more traditional view that free-market economies were inappropriate and that state-directed economies were the answer. Even more surprising, the developing countries were not alone in recognizing the importance of the market; even Communist China began experimenting with the profit motive and greater political decentralization.

In fact, more governments in all areas were showing a new interest in private enterprise—in large part because their state-controlled economies were going broke—and Asia was their model. Japan, of course, as well as South Korea, Taiwan, Hong Kong, and Singapore, Malaysia, and Thailand, were all growing rapidly and providing their people with better health and nutrition, lower infant mortality and longer life expectancy, and less illiteracy and more income. Certainly, the grinding poverty so visible in so much of the Third World is no longer seen in these societies. The average per capita income in Taiwan was $6,000 by the late 1980s (up from $500 in 1949), twice that of the average Korean ($2,826) and approaching that of Singapore ($7,000). Moreover, and very important, if any societies can be called "dependencies," they are South Korea and Taiwan (which were very dependent on the United States), Hong Kong (which was dependent on Britain), and Singapore (which was a small cog in the international capitalist economy). Even Japan's development was initiated during the American occupation after World War II. Yet, this dependency status has not prevented them from achieving successful economic growth and development far beyond the dreams of most developing countries.

Japan and its East Asian neighbors are, interestingly, "neo-Confucian" societies; they are relatively homogeneous in population, with a strong belief in the work ethic and a commitment to education. The governments of these nations have also played a strong role in their development, guiding their economies by setting economic priorities, working closely with corporate leaders to encourage their countries' export strategies, carrying out land reforms and rural development (while avoiding the "urban bias" of most developing countries), and investing heavily in education and human capital.[46] Above all, the governments have worked with and not against the market; government intervention has been based on market forces, thereby spurring private enterprise and economic efficiency and productivity. Whether, of course, the NICs are likely to be the model for other developing countries seeking to improve their lots, remains—as noted—more problematical because of their dependence on a growing world economy.[47]

Vanishing Soviet Model

While the early Western development models appeared increasingly irrelevant, the American system of a mixed economy, with its emphasis on private enterprise and competition, drew more attention. Simultaneously, fewer and fewer developing countries were attracted to the Soviet model. The Soviet Union's continuous problems in providing its citizens with a balanced diet, its failure to produce a sufficient number and variety of quality consumer goods, and its inability to keep up with Japan and the United States in the new industrial revolution made the Soviet economy more and more inappropriate as a model. Those nations outside the Soviet bloc that followed this model—such as Ethiopia, Cuba, and Nicaragua—themselves became examples of mismanaged economies. Soviet-style communism's main attraction for Marxist leaders and groups remained its ability to seize power by using its ideology to attract supporters and to organize them for revolutionary warfare (China, Vietnam, Nicaragua), as well as to provide its friends engaged in civil wars with Soviet and Soviet-bloc advisers, weapons, and troops (largely Cuban). But as an economic model for tilling the land or industrially producing nonmilitary goods, it was increasingly useless. In short, the Soviet Union can help its friends in the seizure and consolidation of power, but not in the modernization and management of their economies. Gorbachev too has recognized that the Soviet Union can no longer be a model for modernization of the developing countries. He now speaks of "market socialism" and future closure of inefficiently run factories. He is even trying to use the profit motive to stimulate farm production. In fact, Poland and Hungary are increasingly moving to shed their Soviet-imposed "command economies" in favor of Western capitalism!

Communist China too has turned away from what a Chinese leader called the "radical leftist nonsense" of Mao Zedong and has turned toward a more flexible economic system that has encouraged some private enterprise and property ownership.[48] Largely abandoning the collective farm, China has experienced a "great leap forward" in food production, and the Chinese are now introducing capitalist ideas to urban industries and services to stimulate development—with Western assistance. The widespread slogan, "To get rich is glorious," appeals to the Chinese. "Marx died 100 years ago," says Beijing's *People's Daily*. "There have been tremendous changes since his ideas were formed. . . . So we cannot use Marxist and Leninist works to solve our present-day problems" (see Chapter 7).[49] And China's leader, Deng Xiaoping, has said that it did not matter whether a cat was black or white (Communist or not), as long as it could catch the mouse. Until the 1989 crushing of the pro-democracy Soviet Union, where *glasnost* (political openness) was not accompanied by *perestroika* (economic restructuring), in China *perestroika* was not accompanied by *glasnost*. And whether the suppression of demands for it will set China back economically remains to be seen.

Domestic Instability, Civil Wars, and International Wars

In the original Western rationale for economic aid to the countries of the Third World, it is clear that, aside from simple humanitarian sentiments, security considerations were uppermost. Perhaps the basic reason for such concern sprang from a logic frequently articulated by government spokespersons, academicians, and journalists and thus often implicit in policy: that a world divided between rich and poor nations is an explosive world, endangering the stability of the international system. The vast majority of wars since 1945 have occurred in the Third World. Besides disputes over frontiers, these have been attributed primarily to the greater domestic instability of the developing countries. The result has been frequent civil wars. Indeed, most wars in the contemporary world are civil, not interstate. Thus, it becomes important to bring about greater domestic stability in the developing countries, by building more cohesive and viable political systems, reducing internal divisions between rich and poor, promoting economic growth, and taking the other measures discussed above. Evan Luard, an English political scientist, has argued that avoidance of civil wars will require, above all, alternative and legitimate means for change in society. Civil conflicts have occurred most frequently in countries with unrepresentative governments. In democratic countries, where there is likely to be less major discontent, civil conflict is less justifiable. Thus, a reduction in the incidence of war may be related most to the creation of more representative governments and open societies.[50] However correct these observations, the current internal conditions and problems of most developing countries do not suggest that one ought to be too optimistic about doing away with war among them. Quarrels over border territories, clashes promoted ·by groups seeking secession and their own states, and conflicts about who will control a nation (as in Afghanistan, Angola, El Salvador, Ethiopia, Lebanon, Nicaragua, the Philippines, and South Africa) currently continue. Violence is often thought to be the answer to resolution of these issues. The conditions for internal instability, in short, remain rife in all too many Third World states.

Many of these civil wars have become "internationalized"—that is, they result in foreign intervention (not just American or Soviet, but Chinese, Syrian, Vietnamese, Cuban, and South African as well). A partial list would be: the Greek civil war (1944-1949); the Chinese civil war (1946-1949); wars in the Philippines, Burma and Malaysia after World War II; and wars in Guatemala (1954), Cuba (1957-1959), Lebanon (1958), Laos (1960-1963, 1970-1975), Vietnam (1959-1975), the Dominican Republic (1965), Indonesia (1965-1966), South Yemen (1967), Cambodia (1970-1975, 1980-), Angola (1975-), El Salvador (1979-), Mozambique (1980-), and Nicaragua (1983-). These civil conflicts are therefore a matter of grave international concern lest they lead to an escalation of violence. In the past, the greatest danger was that they attracted the superpowers; luckily, this likelihood is diminishing currently (see Chapter 18).

For Review

1. How did the colonial experience shape the new states?
2. Why is the possibility of national disintegration perhaps the basic problem for many developing countries?
3. How are rapidly growing populations threatening the future of the

developing world?

4. What has prevented most developing countries from following the successful example of the newly industrialized nations?

5. How can one account for the Third World's dominant pattern of civilian and military authoritarianism?

6. How have bipolarity and nation building affected the developing countries' foreign policies?

7. In the developing countries' continued search for development, which countries are serving as their models—Western market economies, Soviet Union, or China?

Notes

1. Robert C. Good, "Changing Patterns of African International Relations," *American Political Science Review* (September 1964): 638.
2. Robert L. Heilbroner, *The Great Ascent* (New York: Harper & Row, 1963), 23-26. Used by permission of the publisher and A. D. Peters & Co.
3. Lawrence S. Eagleburger and Donald F. McHenry, "How the U.S. Can Help," *New York Times*, Nov. 29, 1985, and Albert Bressard, "The Time for Painful Thinking," in Jagdish N. Bhagwati and John G. Ruggie, eds., *Power, Passions and Purpose* (Cambridge, Mass.: M.I.T. Press, 1984), 59-60.
4. Brandt Commission, *North-South* (Cambridge, Mass.: M.I.T. Press, 1980), 32.
5. The disruption of traditional colonial society by the economic behavior of the Western industrial nations is analyzed in *The Emerging Nations*, ed. Max F. Millikan and Donald L. M. Blackmer (Boston: Little, Brown, 1961), 3-17; and Immanuel Wallerstein, *Africa: The Politics of Independence* (New York: Vintage, 1961), 29-43.
6. Barbara Ward, *The Rich Nations and the Poor Nations* (New York: Norton, 1962), 54.
7. Rupert Emerson, *From Empire to Nation* (Cambridge, Mass.: Harvard University Press, 1960), 6.
8. According to Klaus Mehnert,

   The term "intelligentsia" used to denote specifically those intellectuals who are experiencing internal conflict between allegiance to traditional cultures and the influence of the modern West. Within these terms of reference it is not the amount of knowledge or education that determines membership in the intelligentsia.... No man, no matter how learned, is classified as a member of the intelligentsia if he has retained his identity with his national background. As long as he remains integrated in his society and accepts the values of that society as his own, he is likely to remain essentially a conservative without that revolutionary spark which ... would class him as a member of the intelligentsia. If, on the other hand, he is an intellectual who has felt the impact of Western civilization and has been drawn into the vortex of conflicting ideas, he enters the ranks of the intelligentsia.... Within the intelligentsia, however, rebelliousness is a common characteristic. Beset with doubts about traditional cultural values, its members have felt a driving need to search for something new.

   Klaus Mehnert, "The Social and Political Role of the Intelligentsia in the New

Countries," in *New Nations in a Divided World*, ed. Kurt London (New York: Holt, Rinehart & Winston, 1964), 121-122.

9. See particularly Emerson, *From Empire to Nation*, 89-187, 295-359; Clifford Geertz, "The Integrative Revolution," in *Old Societies and New States*, ed. Clifford Geertz (New York: Free Press, 1963), 105-157; and Walter Connor, "Nation-Building or Nation-Destroying?" *World Politics*, April 1972, 219ff.

10. Michael Brecher, *Nehru: A Political Biography* (New York: Oxford University Press, 1959), 362-363.

11. Wallerstein, *Africa*, 88.

12. Steven R. Weisman, "Sri Lanka: A Nation Disintegrates," *New York Times Magazine*, Dec. 13, 1988, 34ff.

13. Anastasia Toufexis, "Too Many Mouths," *Time*, January 2, 1989, 48.

14. Alexander Gerschenkron, *Economic Backwardness in Historical Perspective* (New York: Holt, Rinehart & Winston, 1965), 28.

15. John T. McGowan, "Third World to Lead Surge in Growth," *USA Today*, May 9, 1986.

16. McNamara, "The Population Problem," *Foreign Affairs* (Summer 1984): 1119. Also Lester R. Brown, *In the Human Interest* (New York: Norton, 1974).

17. *New York Times*, July 25, 1985.

18. W. Arthur Lewis, *The Evolution of the International Economic Order* (Princeton, N.J.: Princeton University Press., 1978).

19. Nick Eberstadt, "Famine, Development & Foreign Aid," *Commentary*, March 1985, 25-31; and Arch Paddington, "Ethiopia: The Communist Use of Famine," *Commentary*, April 1986, 30-39.

20. Francis Moore Lappé and Joseph Collins, *Food First* (Boston: Houghton Mifflin, 1977); and John Warnock, *The Politics of Hunger* (New York: Methuen, 1987).

21. Richard J. Barnet and Ronald E. Müller, *Global Reach* (New York: Simon & Schuster, 1975), 216-217; Lewis, *Evolution of the International Economic Order*, 34-37.

22. Robin Broad and John Cavanaugh, "No More NICs," *Foreign Policy*, Fall 1988, 81-104.

23. See R. H. Tawney, *Religion and the Rise of Capitalism* (Baltimore: Penguin, 1947).

24. Peter L. Berger, *The Capitalist Revolution* (New York: Basic Books, 1986), 161-70.

25. Robin Wright, *Sacred Rage* (New York: Lindon Press, 1985).

26. Steven Erlanger, "In the Global Village, Seeking an Exit," *New York Times*, Nov. 5, 1988.

27. Samuel P. Huntington, *Political Order in Changing Societies* (New Haven, Conn.: Yale University Press, 1968), 1.

28. Wallerstein, *Africa*, 98.

29. Ibid., 99.

30. See, for example, Julius Nyerere, quoted in *The Ideologies of the Developing Nations*, by Paul E. Sigmund, Jr. (New York: Holt, Rinehart & Winston, 1963), 199 (emphasis in original).

31. Wallerstein, *Africa*, 96.

32. General analyses of the role of the military in new nations are found in: Morris Janowitz, *The Military in the Political Development of New Nations* (Chicago: University of Chicago Press, 1964); S. E. Finer, *The Man on Horseback*, rev. ed. (Baltimore: Penguin, 1976); John J. Johnson, ed., *The Role of the Military in Underdeveloped Countries* (Princeton, N.J.: Princeton University Press, 1962); Huntington, *Political Order*, 192-263; Edward Feit, "Pen, Sword and People:

Military Regimes in the Formation of Political Institutions," *World Politics*, January 1973, 251ff.; and Feit, *The Armed Bureaucrat* (Boston: Houghton Mifflin, 1973). For the dominant role the military played in Latin America from 1962 to 1973, see Alain Rouguié, trans. Paul Sigmund, *The Military and the State in Latin America* (Berkeley, Calif.: University of California Press, 1988).

33. See Eric A. Nordlinger, "Soldiers in Mufti," *American Political Science Review* (December 1970): 1131ff.; and Nordlinger, *Soldiers in Politics* (Englewood Cliffs, N.J.: Prentice-Hall, 1977) for the best overall evaluation of the military in power. This analysis has been heavily influenced by Nordlinger's judgments.

34. Huntington, *Political Order*, 192-263. The Huntington-Nordlinger view of the different roles the military plays in different societies is questioned by Robert W. Jackman, "Politicians in Uniform," *American Political Science Review* (December 1976): 1078-1097.

35. Finer, *Man on Horseback*, 21.

36. Robert C. Good, "State-Building as a Determinant of Foreign Policy in the New States," in *Neutralism and Nonalignment*, ed. Laurence W. Martin (New York: Holt, Rinehart & Winston, 1962).

37. Ibid., 8-9

38. Ibid., 11.

39. Cecil V. Crabb, Jr., *The Elephants and the Grass* (New York: Holt, Rinehart & Winston, 1965), 20-38.

40. For the evolution of nonalignment from 1955 to 1983, see Robert A. Mortimer, *The Third World Coalition in International Politics* 2d ed. (Boulder, Colo.: Westview Press, 1984).

41. W. W. Rostow, *Stages of Economic Growth* (New York: Cambridge University Press, 1960); and A. F. K. Organski, *The Stages of Political Development* (New York: Knopf, 1965).

42. Tony Smith, "Requiem or New Agenda for Third World Studies?" *World Politics*, July 1985, 533-544.

43. Ibid., 544-558; Brandt Commission, *North-South*; Barbara Ward, Lenore D'Anjou, and J. D. Runnalls, eds., *The Widening Gap* (New York: Columbia University Press, 1971); Mitchell A. Seligson, ed., *The Gap Between Rich and Poor* (Boulder, Colo.: Westview Press, 1984); and Gabriel Kolki, *Confronting the Third World* (New York: Pantheon Books, 1988).

44. Stephen D. Krasner, *Structural Conflict* (Berkeley, Calif.: University of California Press, 1985).

45. For a critique of dependency, see Robert Gilpin, *The Political Economy of International Relations* (Princeton, N.J.: Princeton University Press, 1987), 263ff. For a rebuttal of this view, see Nathan Rosenberg and L.E. Birdzell, Jr., *How the West Grew Rich* (New York: Basic Books, 1985).

46. Gilpin, *Political Economy of International Relations*, 301-302.

47. Ibid., 303-304.

48. *New York Times*, Feb. 21, 1985.

49. Orville Schell, *To Get Rich Is Glorious* (New York: Pantheon Books, 1985).

50. Evan Luard, *War in International Society* (New Haven, Conn.: Yale University Press, 1987), 406-407.

CHAPTER 10

The Games
Policy Makers Play

A FOCUS ON DECISION MAKERS

Whereas the first level of analysis (the state system) focuses on "outside-in" explanations, the second and third levels of analysis emphasize "inside-out" explanations for nations' foreign policies. The difference between the latter two levels is that the second level does so by identifying the sources of state behavior in the character of the state and its political/ideological style, while the third level zeroes in on the individuals who make specific decisions. It is one thing to learn from the second level of analysis what one nation's "operational code" may be and use it to analyze and understand the general thrust of its policy, and it is another to know that insular and continental states, for example, show different patterns of behavior. But within each category states do act differently, and one can use the decision-making approach to account for these differences in state behavior.

The decision-making approach to understanding the foreign policy of a country is based on a close look at the specific personnel officially responsible for making foreign policy.[1] When one speaks of a state doing this or that, one is really speaking of those officials, the policy decisions they make, and how they implement them. The state, in short, equals the official policy makers whose decisions and actions constitute its policies. Decisions are the "output" of the domestic political system. By focusing on decision makers, this approach emphasizes, first, how they *see* the world. What is important is not what the international system is like objectively, but how policy makers perceive it. It is on their perceptions that these officials act or, for that matter, do not act; reality does not exist outside of policy makers' definitions of it.

As noted earlier, a balance-of-power analysis can explain what British prime minister Neville Chamberlain should have done to counter Adolf

Hitler in the 1930s, but not what he did. Without studying the prime minister and his advisers and without analyzing their perceptions of Hitler, the goals of Nazi Germany, and the Versailles peace treaty, first-level analysts could not tell why the British did not choose another course of action, or why they bungled and brought on the war they had hoped to avoid. Such an analysis was thus not very helpful. A useful analysis would have included Chamberlain's misperception of Hitler as simply a German nationalist who, while seeking some territorial adjustments, had otherwise only limited ambitions. Such an analysis would also have focused on the pacifist nature of British public opinion, still guided by memories of horrible losses during World War I. The strength of this opinion acted as a constraint upon British political leaders, even had they wished to contain Germany.

Rational Actor Model

One model of decision making—the *rational actor model*—is central to the first-level analysis. Each state is viewed as a unitary actor, and each calculates by what means it can best achieve its ends or objectives. It does this in four clearly separate steps: (1) selecting objectives and values, (2) considering alternative means of achieving them, (3) calculating the likely consequences of each alternative, and (4) selecting the one that is most promising. Henry Kissinger wrote in 1957 that if American policy is to seek security and peace, it cannot be based on a strategy of massive retaliation against the Soviet Union when confronted with limited challenges. To respond in this manner would only ensure American suicide; not to respond at all would be tantamount to surrender. Both courses are therefore irrational. The only rational option in these circumstances is "limited war." [2] This rational model underlies not only analyses of international politics and specific foreign policies but also other spheres of decision making. In the competitive games nations play, with their informal rules, each player creates a strategy designed to lead to "victory." There are usually several options, and players must decide at points during the game which play is the best in terms of the ultimate goals.

Governmental Politics Model

The other model is the *governmental politics model.* It focuses on the executive branch of government and especially on the bureaucracies whose official responsibility is to formulate and execute foreign policy. Indeed, this model is usually referred to as the *bureaucratic politics model.* The term *governmental politics* is used here because it must also include the legislature, at least in free countries, as well as interest groups, the mass media, and the various publics that together constitute public opinion. The bureaucracy, in short, is viewed in its broader governmental and societal setting. The emphasis is on the *pluralistic nature of decision making* in which, in general, the actors' views reflect their organizational positions and interests. For example, a foreign service officer in the State Department sees the world quite differently than a military officer. And in the Defense Department, an army officer is likely to define what U.S. defense policy should be quite differently than a navy or air force officer. Policy makers' perceptions of the national interest depends on the position in government they occupy. This emphasis on the roles individuals play as officials has been aptly summed up by the phrase, "*Where you stand depends on where you sit.*" Policy in these circumstances is formulated through conflicts among many actors with different perceptions, perspectives, and interests, but also through reconciling these differences. These two elements of the policy struggle will determine who receives what and when.

Political scientist Graham Allison has illustrated the difference between rational and bureaucratic policy making.[3] When in the late 1950s the Soviet Union tested its first intercontinental ballistic missile (ICBM), American leaders became very concerned about a possible "missile gap" favoring the Soviets. Following the rational model, they concluded that the Soviet Union would exploit this technological breakthrough, mass-produce ICBMs, and use them to pressure the United States to concede territorial changes in central Europe, specifically in the symbolically significant western half of Berlin. In terms of the balance of power, the Soviets had achieved a major technological breakthrough, which, if fully exploited before the United States could test and deploy an ICBM, could give them superior power. Rationally, in terms of the rules of the game of the international system, that is what the Kremlin leaders should have done—at least, that is what American policy makers expected them to do. Had the United States been the nation to test the first ICBM, it would have gone into large-scale production, which would have strengthened the American hand in relation to the Soviet Union. It would have seemed the logical thing to do.

If the same American policy makers had used the governmental politics model, however, they would have been more cautious in drawing this conclusion. The Red Army controlled the missiles, and it was unlikely to abandon suddenly the traditional definition of its role on the ground in favor of intercontinental strategic deterrence with ICBMs. The very thought would be alien to an organization preoccupied with land defense and a role limited to Eurasia. A dramatic shift of deterrence from the army to another service certainly would have been accompanied by an observable policy struggle. The development of a large ICBM force would have required a vast transfer of funds to that other service, creating interservice rivalries and quarrels. The different models, then, offered grounds for quite different assessments of what the Soviets would do and implied quite different American defense and foreign policies. The incoming administration of John Kennedy, acting upon the rational model, initiated a more numerous intercontinental missile deployment than it would otherwise have done. It was not until after the Cuban missile crisis in 1962, that the Soviets began the extensive buildup that resulted in the achievement of strategic parity. And the dangerous confrontation in Cuba occurred because the Soviets sought to reduce the imbalance in strategic weapons by placing intermediate-range missiles (of which they had plenty) in Cuba.

Before these two decision-making models are examined in more detail, it must be noted that, although these models can be used in explaining other countries' foreign policies, American examples and the American policy process are used here because of readily available materials, the many decisions that have been made in Washington since World War II, and the greater familiarity of American readers with latter-day U.S. history.

CRISIS DECISIONS

The rational actor model is probably the most relevant to explaining and understanding crisis decisions. A crisis is characterized by a number of features: decision makers are taken by surprise; they feel that they must make decisions rapidly; and they perceive that vital interests are at stake.[4] In these circumstances, decisions cannot be made in the routine manner characteristic of bureaucracies. The element of surprise is likely to forestall use of standard operating procedures in management of the crisis. The need for quick decisions will limit the number of officials involved. Above all, the perception that vital interests are at stake will quickly centralize the decision making and take it to the top: to the president and the chief presidential advisers in the United States, and equivalent officials in other governments.

These characteristics of crises, then, tend to be highly functional. The usual drawn-out haggling over differences in policies between different bureaucracies, the separation of powers between the executive and Congress, and all the efforts of interest groups to influence policy, if not to undermine it, are, so to speak, short-circuited. The different ways in which crises are managed by the government means that the policy process works speedily and efficiently, free of the traditional domestic pressures, for the short duration of crises. And the fact that crisis decisions flow upward to the top officials has another important consequence: the careful and cautious management of superpower crises. A crisis obviously results in stress and anxiety, and there is always the possibility of rash or impetuous actions. Another possibility is that policy makers may not examine all the alternative options and may choose the wrong one because some officials are reluctant to express doubts about the policy being adopted.

Psychologist Irving Janis has argued that conformity is especially common within a relatively small circle of leading officials because there is a great deal of pressure to conform to "groupthink." [5] "Dovish" views tend to be suppressed within a group whose members are trying to impress one another with their toughness. The more cohesive the group, the greater is the inclination of its members to reject a nonconformist; the greater the desire to remain in the group, the more likely an individual with doubts about a proposed policy will suppress them and go along with the majority. If others too suppress their reservations, the so-called consensus on policy will clearly be a superficial one. More serious, however, is the possibility that, because searching questions about the policy are not asked, the nation will misman-age a crisis. Nevertheless, although policy mistakes have been made when U.S. policy makers were confronting what they believed to be a second- or third-rate opponent, they have been very cautious and keenly aware of the dangers of a miscalculation when facing the Soviet Union. The risks and costs of not examining all alternatives, and not scrutinizing the assumptions upon which they were acting, were all too clear—and a clear antidote to groupthink.

Rise of Decision Making to the Top

One characteristic of the decision-making process then is that decision making rises to the top of the governmental hierarchy—specifically, to the president and the president's closest advisers. Some will be statutory advis-ers, such as the secretaries of the chief foreign policy agencies; others will be people both in and out of government whose judgments the president particularly trusts. During the potentially explosive Cuban missile crisis of 1962, the executive committee that managed the crisis included President John Kennedy and Vice President Lyndon Johnson; the secretaries of state and defense; their seconds in command; the director of the Central Intelli-gence Agency; the chairman of the Joint Chiefs of Staff; the president's special assistant for national security affairs; and other individuals such as the secretary of the Treasury, the attorney general (the president's brother), the president's special counsel (perhaps his closest friend after his brother), an ambassador just returned from Moscow, and President Harry Truman's former secretary of state.[6]

Central Role of the President

A second characteristic of making crisis decisions is the central role of the president, who interprets events and evaluates the stakes in the crisis. Kennedy's "reading" of the situation he confronted during the Cuban Missile Crisis, the consequences this situation might have for American security, and his political future and ability to lead the nation were responsi-ble for his actions. (The latter two factors can hardly be separated, for the external challenges, as the president sees them, do not really leave a choice of accepting a loss of personal prestige without a loss of national prestige. For the president of the United States, personal and national cost calcula-tions tend to be identical.)

Kennedy saw the installation of Soviet missiles in Cuba as a personal challenge, with potentially damaging national effects. In response to earlier congressional and public clamor about possible Soviet offensive missiles in Cuba—as distinct from ground-to-air or ground-to-ship defensive missiles—Kennedy had publicly declared that the United States would not tolerate offensive missiles on an island ninety miles off the Florida coast. Intended primarily as a declaration to cool domestic criticism that had come largely from Republicans, Kennedy's statement had also led Soviet leaders to respond that they had no intention of placing missiles in Cuba. Kennedy thus was pledged to act if the Soviets lied—as it turned out they had—unless he wished to be publicly humiliated. If he did not act, the Soviet leaders would not believe other pledges and commitments the president had made or inherited from his predecessors. At least, that is how Kennedy perceived the situation.

He saw the consequences as very dangerous because he feared that Soviet premier Nikita Khrushchev had interpreted previous acts—the abortive 1961 Bay of Pigs invasion of Cuba and the inaction of U.S. troops when the Berlin Wall went up the same year—as signaling a lack of will, an absence of sufficient determination to defend American vital interests. Khrushchev spoke openly of an American failure of nerve. It was not so much the effect of the Soviet missiles upon the military equation between the two powers that mattered, although that was important; it was the political consequences of the *appearance* of a change in the balance of power that were deemed critical by Kennedy. The Soviet Union was supposed to be on the short end of the missile gap, but Kennedy feared that American inaction would persuade the world that Soviet claims of missile superiority were accurate. This would lead allied governments to fear that, in the new situation in which the United States would be vulnerable to nuclear devastation, they could no longer count on this country to defend them. Above all, it might tempt the Soviets to exploit the situation and to seek to disrupt American alliances—especially the North Atlantic Treaty Organization. Khrushchev already had restated his determination to eject the Western allies from West Berlin. If Khrushchev succeeded in Cuba, why should he take Kennedy's pledge to defend West Berlin seriously? And if he did not, would not Soviet and American troops soon be clashing in an area where they would be hard to separate?

The real irony of the Cuban missile crisis is that Kennedy was also determined to seek a more stable and restrained basis for coexistence with the Soviet Union during his years in office. This long-range goal, which hardly had the massive support it would have later, could not be realized if Khrushchev did not take Kennedy seriously and tried to push him around. Then serious negotiations, in which each party would recognize the other's legitimate interests, would be impossible. A major change in the cold war atmosphere was at stake, in addition to the United States' reputation for power and willingness to keep commitments. Domestically, of course, another "defeat" in Cuba, discrediting Kennedy's foreign policy, was bound to affect his personal standing with his party, Congress, and the public. It also would lead to strong right-wing Republican pressures to be more forcible in foreign policy and would give less priority to the president's liberal domestic reform program. Thus, the foreign policy and domestic pressures for Kennedy to act were overwhelming.

But if he wanted to get the missiles out of Cuba, he was also determined to avoid a nuclear war. Kennedy had considered alternative responses to the Soviet missiles in Cuba, ranging from diplomatic pressures and a secret approach to Fidel Castro to precision air strikes at the missiles, invasion, and blockade. Feeling strongly that he had to act to impress Khrushchev, Kennedy chose the blockade as the option most likely to attain the removal of the Soviet missiles. Although the blockade could not by itself achieve this objective, it was a sign of American determination. It permitted the United States the option of increasing the pressure on the Soviet regime later if the missiles were not removed. It also provided a relatively safe middle course between inaction and invasion (or an air strike), which might provoke the Soviets. Finally, it placed on Khrushchev the responsibility for deciding whether to escalate or de-escalate the crisis. It is significant that, thanks to information provided by a U-2 "spy plane," the administration had a whole week to debate the meaning and significance of the Soviet move, its likely military and political effects on American security interests, the different courses of action open to the United States, and which course was most likely to achieve removal of the Soviet missiles without precipitating nuclear war. Many crises simply do not afford such time for preparation and the careful consideration of alternatives. Even during the missile crisis, the initial reaction of most of the president's advisers had been to bomb the missile sites. Slowing down the momentum of events is crucial if impulsive actions are to be avoided. So is White House management of crises.

Role of the Bureaucracy

The third characteristic of crises is the subordination of bureaucratic interests to the need to make a decision to safeguard the "national interest." The crisis is accompanied by a sense of urgency, as well as by the policy makers' perception that the nation's security is at stake and that war looms. Thus, although decision making has risen to the top levels of the government, and the men and women in those positions reflect their departmental points of view, they do not necessarily feel themselves limited to representing those points of view. Organizational affiliation is not a good predictor of those points of view. Senior participants in crises behave more as "players" than as "organizational participants." Secretary of Defense Robert McNamara did not reflect the Joint Chiefs' readiness to bomb and invade during the Cuban missile crisis (just as late in the Vietnam War he was to disagree increasingly with their views and recommendations); he became the leading proponent of the blockade. Other players in that crisis did not even represent foreign policy bureaucracies—the two men closest to the president, the attorney general and the president's special counsel, along with the secretary of the Treasury and a former secretary of state, for example, represented only themselves. The bureaucratic axiom that "you stand where you sit" is thus not necessarily correct, at least during a crisis.

The bureaucracy's principal role in a crisis is carrying out the policy. This especially applies to the military because use of the threat of force, if not some limited application of force, becomes quickly visible in such a confrontation. Military organizations, like all organizations, operate according to certain standard operating procedures. While these serve the purpose of the organization, they may not serve the policy-makers' goals of preventing a dangerous escalation and preserving the peace. Thus, the air force, when asked about the possibility of a "surgical strike" on the missiles, dusted off old plans drawn up for an invasion of Cuba and simply added the missiles to hundreds of other targets—that is, the air force produced a disproportionate response which might have led Moscow to respond differently if it suspected the U.S. goal was not only the withdrawal of Soviet missiles but—despite the president's words—the elimination of Castro as well. And the navy wanted the blockade to be imposed outside the range of Cuban-piloted Soviet MIG fighters, while Kennedy wanted the blockade pulled in to give Khrushchev extra time to think about his next move. Both goals were legitimate, but obviously they were incompatible. The president's goal, however, took precedence because of the crucial need to slow operations down. The risks of war by inadvertence are real. No one wants war, but a loss of control in the implementation phase of a crisis may provoke an unintentional escalation.

Role of Congress

Finally, decision making in a crisis is characterized by congressional non-involvement. Congressional leaders usually are called in and informed of the president's decision just before he announces it publicly. This form is followed as a matter of courtesy. But their advice is not requested. Presidents consider themselves more representative of the country than any senator or House member and as representative as Congress as a whole. Interestingly, Kennedy, after informing a congressional delegation of his decision to blockade Cuba, did ask for its opinions. When the response was to question the utility of the blockade and to propose an air strike instead, Kennedy reacted angrily. After the members left, he consoled himself by saying that had they had more time to think it over they also would have decided on the blockade. If presidents assure themselves like this, why indeed consult members of the legislative branch? In any event, in crises what choice do the latter have but to support the only president the country has at the moment?

DECISION MAKING AS A PLURALISTIC POWER STRUGGLE

Multiple Actors

The governmental politics model of decision making is characterized first by multiple institutional actors: the three branches of the federal government.

In foreign policy matters, the principal participants are the executive and legislative branches. Within these institutions there are a multitude of departments, organizations, staffs, committees, and individuals concerned with foreign policy. Within the executive branch, there are (1) the president, the national security adviser, and the adviser's staff; (2) the senior foreign policy departments—the State and Defense Departments and the Central Intelligence Agency (CIA); (3) the junior departments—Agency for International Development (AID), U.S. Information Agency (USIA), and Arms Control and Disarmament Agency (ACDA); and (4) departments with domestic jurisdictions that occasionally deal with foreign policy issues falling within their areas of expertise—Departments of the Treasury, Commerce, and Agriculture. On the legislative side, both the Senate and the House are divided into many different party groupings and committees—the latter being subdivided even further into subcommittees.[7]

This institutional pluralism is supplemented by organized groups representing many economic, ethnic, racial, religious, and public interests. But they are less involved in security policy than in domestic/intermestic affairs. The reason is easy to understand. Interest groups have abundant knowledge of and experience in internal affairs, but on foreign policy issues they rarely have comparable information and skill. In addition, interest groups are consulted regularly by the respective executive departments while domestic/intermestic legislation is being drawn up, but in foreign policy the departments tend to be their own constituencies and spokespersons. The responsible agencies have their own experts and are in contact with other experts, be they at the RAND Corporation or at Harvard University. Although there is a fairly stable structure of societal interest groups concerned with domestic/intermestic policies, the comparable structure in the traditional area of foreign policy concerned with security issues is weak and at times even ephemeral. Business groups and labor may be interested in particular tariff issues when certain industries and their employees are exposed to foreign competition, or an ethnic group may be stimulated by disputes involving a specific country, such as Israel or Greece. Yet continuing concern with foreign policy as a whole is usually lacking; it is largely intermittent and tied to special issues. This is generally true as well for public interest groups or nonethnic one-issue groups concerned with such specific issues as the Panama Canal or an arms control agreement, although from time to time these groups may exert considerable influence on such issues.

In short, the main differences between foreign and domestic policy making are that the latter involves more participants in both the executive and legislative branches and that interest groups and public opinion are more active. The larger the number of actors and, the more important the stakes that key legislators, committees, and lobbyists perceive at issue, the more difficult it will be to arrive at policy decisions (see Table 10-1). Negotiations will be long and very difficult, and compromises acceptable to so many involved parties will not be reached

Table 10-1 Policy Characteristics

Type of Policy	Chief Charac- teristics	Primary Actors	Principal Decision Maker	Role of Congress	Role of Interest Groups	Relations Among Actors
Crisis	Short run; bureaucracy & Congress short-circuited	President, responsible officials, individuals in & out of government	Executive (president-ial preemi-nence)	Postcrisis legitimation	None	Cooperation
Noncrisis (security)	Long run; bureaucratic-legislative participation	President, executive agencies, Congress, in-terest groups, public opinion	Executive bureaucracy	Congres-sional parti-cipation	Low to moderate	Competition and bar-gaining
Domestic (welfare)	Long run; bureaucratic-legislative participation	President, executive agencies, Congress, in-terest groups public opinion	Executive-congres-sional sharing	High	High	Competition and bar-gaining

SOURCE: This table is modeled on one in Randal B. Ripley and Grace A. Franklin, *Congress, the Bureaucracy, and Public Policy* (Homewood, Ill.: Dorsey, 1976), 17.

without immense effort, if they can be arranged at all. In these circumstances, the president's ability to initiate, lead, and maneuver will be seriously circumscribed. For the traditional security issues where no immediate tangible interests are perceived to be at stake, the president is generally—although not always—acknowledged to have greater expertise. In contrast, domestic issues involve many concerns, especially material ones, that arouse many actors who believe they are just as expert and experienced as the executive. Presidential involvement, therefore, does not guarantee successful domestic negotiations. On key issues, presidents, lacking votes, may be reluctant to enter the policy arena at all, lest failure and an impaired reputation for "getting things done" result. The contrast to most foreign policy issues is striking; there presidents can normally count on achieving their aims, building successful records, benefiting their political parties, and presumably helping the nation.

Conflict

A second characteristic of the governmental politics model of decision making is conflict among actors. Because the president is both the nation's chief diplomat and the commander in chief of its armed forces, this conflict occurs primarily within the executive branch, among executive departments that are responsible for formulation and implementation of foreign policy (although conflict between the executive and legislative branches of government also occurs—in fact, the two branches rarely speak with a single voice).[8] Conflict may arise, for example, between the State Department and the Defense Department. And within the State Department, the head of the bureau for European and Canadian affairs may express a view quite different from those of the heads of the Inter-American or African bureaus. In the Defense Department, the position of the air force may differ from those of the army and navy. Indeed, within each service there are differences, as between the Strategic Air Command and Tactical Air Command, or as among the surface navy, strategic submarine navy, and aircraft-carrier navy. In the Senate, the Foreign Relations Committee may clash on a specific issue with the Armed Services Committee, and subcommittees of each committee may disagree with one another. This situation must be multiplied by the other committees and subcommittees in both houses. Each of these institutions, bureaucracies, committees, and interest groups develops intense organizational identifications, and all are determined not only to survive but also to expand their influence in the policy-making process. Furthermore, each, viewing a problem from a special perspective, is likely to develop strong convictions about the content of policy, especially when "national interests" are involved and the organization or department thinks that it has a vital contribution to make. Institutional struggles between the executive and legislative branches, as well as within each branch and within executive departments, are consequently the norm.

This kind of policy-making process is often condemned as "parochial," on the assumption that more comprehensive—more "correct"—solutions to all policy problems could be found were it not for the selfish and narrow points of view of the various participants in the policy process. Adherents to this view ignore the fact that in any pluralistic institution, diverse convictions compete. Different policy recommendations are offered as solutions to the problems being considered, and these recommendations represent a fairly broad spectrum of choice. Just as in a democracy different groups and individuals have the right to articulate their values and interests, so the various parts of the executive and legislative branches have the right to articulate their own policy views and seek to protect their own interests. The issue is not which policy positions and recommendations are correct; clearly, there is not a single correct policy. *The issue is how to reconcile conflicting interpretations of what the correct policy ought to be.* This reconciliation of the policy preferences of the various "players" is complicated by the many players outside the executive branch.

Consensus Building

The third characteristic of the governmental politics model of decision making, stemming from the first two, is reconciliation of these different points of view to build a consensus or majority coalition so that decisions can be made. Negotiating thus occurs throughout the executive branch as officials and agencies in one department seek support in another or attempt to enlist the aid of the president or the White House advisers to achieve their goals. The process is one of widening the base of support within the executive branch and then seeking further support in the two houses of Congress, gaining allies through continual modification of the proposed policy. The official policy "output" that emerges represents the victory of one coalition formed across institutional lines over an opposing coalition of the same kind.

More specifically, a coalition across institutional lines can be, for example, an alliance among the personnel of a particular desk in the State Department, of a specific service in the Defense Department, of various bureaus in the Departments of the Treasury and Commerce, or of several committees in Congress. It may be opposed by personnel of other desks, services, bureaus, and committees in the same or other departments or the legislative branch. Such a coalition usually holds together only for the specific issue being considered. A different issue requires mobilization of a different coalition. The reason is that in the United States political parties are undisciplined, and party loyalty cannot be counted upon automatically for any given presidential policy. Great energy must be expended on this task. *Policy is therefore not only a matter of which point of view seems to have the most merit and pertinence; it is also a matter of who has power and exercises it the most effectively.* The resulting intragovernmental policy struggle is every bit as intense and persistent as intergovernmental conflicts.

Incrementalism and Crisis

A fourth characteristic of the governmental politics model of decision making is the effect of conflict and coalition building on policy output. One of the most important results of continuous bargaining within the "policy machine" is that policy in any area moves forward one step at a time and tends to focus on fleeting concerns and short-range aims.[9] This is usually called *incrementalism*. Another word is "satisficing." Policy makers, as this word suggests, do not sit down each time they have to make a decision and go through the rational procedure of decision making. They do not try to isolate which values and interests they wish to enhance, examine all the means that might achieve these goals, calculate the consequences of each, and then select the one most likely to be successful. Policy makers have neither the time nor resources to go through this process. Instead, they pick the policy that is likely to be the most satisfactory, and they judge it by whether the policy has been successful in the past. If so, why not take another step forward on the same path?

The presumption is that what has worked in the past will work now, as well as in the future. In addition, once a majority has been forged, the "winning" coalition, after a hard struggle and probably much bloodletting, will normally prefer modification of the existing policy to another major fight. The presumption is, of course, that a policy will result, which is not necessarily true. Negotiations among different groups with conflicting perspectives and vested interests can produce a stalemate and policy paralysis.

As a result, policy tends to vacillate between incrementalism and crisis, either because incrementalism is not adequate to a developing situation or because stalemate produces no policy at all. It may be said with reasonable certitude during "normal" periods, low external pressure on the policy machine favors continuation of existing policies; during crises, high pressure tends to produce innovative reactions, perhaps because a stalemated policy machine must have an *external trigger* to undermine the coalition supporting the status quo. A crisis may break up coalitions, may awaken a sufficiently great sense of danger to dampen the pluralistic struggle, even if only for a short time, and may create a feeling of urgency—and therefore a common purpose—among the various participants in policy making. In addition, suggested earlier, crisis policy is decided in an inner circle, composed of the president and a few top officials and trusted advisers; at a time of perceived danger these officials function relatively free of departmental points of view and interests. The usual process of consensus or coalition building is thus short-circuited.[10] There are, then, two policy processes: the pluralistic advocacy system and the crisis management system, the latter involving top officials (assistant secretaries and up), the former a broader mix of interests.

Because the U.S. political system, with its multiple actors, often tends to produce a stalemate, it is during crises that policy makers can most easily shift policy. For example, it took the bombing of Pearl Harbor in 1941 to harness the strength of the United States and direct it toward warding off German and Japanese threats to the nation's security. Before December 7, 1941, President Franklin Roosevelt had taken only intermittent measures to help England survive after the defeat of France, but he had faced constant opposition at home. After Japan's attack, however, the president, who had called himself "Dr. New Deal"—the physician called in to cure a sick economy—became "Dr. Win the War"—the physician who could mobilize the nation's full resources to defeat its enemies. Similarly, after World War II, it was the overwhelming Soviet threat that allowed Truman to mobilize the country for containment; before the threat became so obvious that it could no longer be ignored, Truman had been unable to take the necessary countermeasures. Again, it was Castro and his attempts to stir anti-American revolutions in Latin American countries that allowed President Kennedy to mobilize support for the Alliance for Progress, which was intended to help relieve some of the potentially revolutionary problems in the Southern Hemisphere.

Need for Time

A fifth characteristic of the policy-making process, implicit in the analysis thus far, is its time-consuming nature. Incrementalism suggests a policy machine in low gear, moving along a well-defined road rather slowly in response to specific short-run stimuli. Normally, a proposed policy is normally discussed first within the executive branch. It then passes through official channels, where it receives clearances and modifications as it gathers a broader base of support on its way "up" the executive hierarchy to the president. Constant conferences and negotiations among departments clearly slow the pace. The process takes even longer when the policy requires extensive congressional participation and approval. On domestic/intermestic policy particularly, potential opponents can occupy many "veto points" to block legislation within Congress. Such veto points are the numerous House and Senate committees and subcommittees that hold hearings on legislation and the floor debate and votes in both chambers. Should both houses of Congress pass the legislation, the differences between the two versions must be compromised and resubmitted to both for final approval. Only then does the legislation go to the president for a signature. Should the president veto it, it will go back to Congress, which can override the presidential veto, but only by a two-thirds vote. The advantage of this slow process lies with those who oppose specific pieces of legislation, for it is difficult for legislation to jump all the hurdles along the route to final approval and enactment. This process, admittedly, is more common in domestic than in foreign policy because of the president's greater responsibility and freedom to make policy in the latter area.

Given this slow negotiating process, the formidable obstacles, and the great effort needed to pass a major new policy, old policies and the assumptions upon which they are based tend to survive longer than they should. For example, policy based on the assumption that the Communist world is cohesive continued even after the Sino-Soviet conflict had surfaced in the late 1950s, and preoccupation with strategic deterrence persisted long after the need for a limited war capacity had been painfully demonstrated in the Korean War.

Appealing Packaging and Shared Images

A sixth characteristic of the governmental politics model is the premium placed on attractive and appealing policy packaging and advertising arising from the competition among groups involved in the policy-making process. This means that rather than presenting complex and sophisticated reasons for a particular policy position, proponents will try to make it more acceptable by oversimplifying the issues, tying their "product" up with a pretty moral ribbon, and overselling it by insisting that it will definitely solve the buyer's problems. The sellers may indeed exaggerate these problems to enhance the buyer's feeling that he or she absolutely needs the policy "product" being offered.[11] In foreign policy, the presentation of issues in terms of anticommunism versus communism, good against evil, hardly promoted understanding of the real issues involved and made it difficult to adjust policies to a changing international environment and a changing Communist world. The threat of Russia, simply as a great power, was real enough; that it was Soviet Russia constituted an even greater threat. Nevertheless, the menace of "international communism" was exaggerated, partly because it was an effective device for persuading various governmental agencies to accept certain policies, and partly because it helped mobilize majority support in Congress and the country for those policies.

More specifically, the commonly shared assumptions upon which decision makers operate—their shared biases or images—help to determine which decisions are made. If anticommunism is the bias, those who try to "sell" their preferences in terms of these "shared images" have a good chance of putting together a majority coalition. Those whose preferences are not in line with these assumptions, however, lose out.

Public Debate

The seventh characteristic of this model is the usually public nature of American foreign policy decision making. In a democracy, public involvement is inevitable. Although policy may be made primarily by the executive, its limits are established by public opinion. No British government before 1939 could have pursued a deterrent policy toward Hitler, and no American government before the fall of France in 1940 could have intervened in Europe to preserve the balance of power. In general, however, public opinion tends to be permissive and supportive as far as presidential conduct of foreign policy is concerned.[12] The public is aware that it lacks information and competence in this area, which is remote from its everyday involvement, and it looks to the president for leadership, information, and interpretation of that information. Only when setbacks arise or painful experiences pinch the voters will public opinion on foreign policy be expressed, the limits of public tolerance broadly clarified, and perhaps the party in power punished. Even though most of the time public opinion does not function as a restraining factor, policy makers are always aware of its existence, however amorphous it may be. Because mass opinion does not tend to take shape until *after* some foreign event has occurred, it can hardly serve as a guide for those who must make policy; nonetheless, the latter will take into account what they think "the traffic will bear," because they know that if a decision is significant enough, there is likely to be some crystallization of opinion and possibly retribution at the polls.

Reflecting public opinion, Congress was, until the Vietnam War, usually *supportive* of the president's foreign policy. Throughout most of the post-World War II period, Congress had followed the president's lead, and its role had been essentially reactive and peripheral. The executive initiated and devised foreign policies, which Congress rarely rejected. Primarily, its role was to legitimate those policies in either the original or amended form.[13] The record of American foreign policy from 1945 to the mid-1960s shows clearly that all major presidential initiatives were accepted and supported by Congress.[14]

This situation has changed since the Vietnam War, however, as Congress, reflecting the erosion of the previous cold war consensus, has become both more skeptical of presidential wisdom in foreign policy and more assertive on the many international issues facing the United States. This assertiveness was evidenced in the congressional passage of legislation to restrict the president's use of force and subversion. But more than anything else, the Vietnam war itself raised the congressional sense of confidence and competence in foreign policy. It surely could do no worse than the executive branch. Issues were more thoroughly debated, executive judgments were accepted less readily and evaluated more critically, and restraints were imposed on the president's ability to use the armed forces and overt intervention, as well as the Central Intelligence Agency and covert intervention, without legislative knowledge and consent (thus President Reagan, restrained by Congress from lending military assistance to the contras fighting to overthrow the Marxist government of Nicaragua, sought to bypass Congress and the Constitution by seeking private funding of such assistance, thereby initiating the so-called Iran-contra scandal). Particularly important since Vietnam has been the shift in the role of the media from one of communicating and explaining official policy to one of questioning and criticizing policy. In this more adversarial role, the press, and especially the television news, have unquestionably affected and influenced public debate and opinion on foreign policy issues. In summary, amid an absence of consensus on what the role of the United States should be in the world, partisan conflict and institutional rivalry, as well as a disbelieving press, it has become increasingly difficult for the president to provide the leadership the country needs.

POLITICS OF STRATEGIC DEFENSE

The seven characteristics discussed in the preceding section by no means exhaust the characteristics of the foreign policy process in the federal government, but they are the most obvious and are reflected in the following case study of the politics of strategic defense. In 1983 President Reagan proposed his Strategic Defense Initiative, or "Star Wars" as his critics dubbed SDI because it relied largely on space-based defenses. A look back at the original antiballistic missile (ABM) decision made by President Johnson during the 1960s will place SDI in some perspective. That decision provides a keen insight into governmental decision making and is especially important because the ABM treaty, incorporated into SALT I, became part of the controversy over SDI. In the 1960s the United States' deterrent policy was based upon a retaliatory capability (see Chapter 12). It was generally assumed that a defense of either the missiles or the U.S. population was unnecessary. The deterrent forces were supposed to be invulnerable to a first strike, and, if they were, it was assumed that the people in the cities were also protected; no enemy would be foolish enough to attack America's cities if the United States could retaliate in kind. A first strike made sense only if U.S. retaliatory capability could be destroyed; therefore, as long as this force was invulnerable, the enemy would be deterred.

From time to time, however, the defense of either the population and/or America's land-based deterrent forces has been proposed and debated publicly. The first time was in 1967 when Secretary of Defense Robert McNamara made a speech that seemed to make no sense because it included contradictory themes. On the one hand, he denounced the ABM—designed to knock down incoming missiles or warheads before designated targets were hit—as an expensive venture that would stimulate another round of the arms race and leave the United States less secure in the end; on the other hand, he proposed building a "small" ABM system against the Chinese (who were verbally more radical and militant than the Soviets but had few ICBMs)! To say the least, it was a strange speech, but it reflected the opposing views on defense within the government.[15]

Antiballistic Missile: Contestants and Arguments

On the anti-ABM side were McNamara and Secretary of State Dean Rusk, as well as the Arms Control and Disarmament Agency. All believed that the decision to deploy ABMs would mean a spiraling and costly arms race and would destroy all chances for a stabilization of the American-Soviet deterrent balance. McNamara believed that such deployment would virtually preclude any possibility of initiating arms limitations talks with the Soviets. He was also skeptical of the technical feasibility of the proposed ABM. The secretary, however, was in the minority within his own department on this question. The Pentagon's Office of Defense Research and Engineering, concerned with development of modern weapons, and its Office of Systems Analysis both supported deployment of ABMs. Within the Defense Department only the Office of International Security Affairs agreed with McNamara.

The principal bureaucratic supporters of the ABM were the armed services, which, in contrast to their situation on most defense issues, were united in their support. Although the army, navy, and air force each "saw a different face of ABM and reached different conclusions,"[16] the very fact of this interservice agreement is worth noting. Earlier, McNamara had exploited divisions among the services to prevail on issues of defense spending. Their united front, however, compelled him to go above the services and to appeal directly to the president. Different departments and, indeed, different bureaus within the various departments thus all saw different "faces" of the same ABM problems and had different stakes in the issue.

Congress too had interests and stakes in the ABM debate. Supporting the services were several senior members of the Senate Armed Services Committee, including Chairman Richard Russell, John Stennis, and Henry Jackson. These Democratic senators were supporters of Johnson's Vietnam policy and had been friends of the president when he served as the Democratic majority leader in the Senate during the administration of Dwight Eisenhower. Indeed, Johnson had served with them on the Armed Services Committee and trusted their judgment. He was particularly close to Russell.

In arguing their case, proponents and adversaries often emphasized different factors. Supporters stressed that the Soviets had already developed such a system, that it threatened the U.S. deterrent capacity, and that the ABM would save American lives. They argued that an ABM would provide Americans with an extra bargaining chip in any negotiations on a mutual defensive-weapons limitation. Opponents, however, were less concerned about the Soviet deployment of ABMs than about the potential for a new arms race. Another factor that concerned them was the price tag. Estimates of the cost of an ABM system ranged from $30 billion to $40 billion.

View from the Presidency

In the presence of these opposing pressures, no decision below the presidential level was possible. But a president's stake in any given issue is always greater than that of anyone else, and the White House perspective is different from that of any other player. For one thing, unity in the administration is a primary goal. Thus, Johnson sought to avoid, if at all possible, a direct break with McNamara. They were already at odds over the war in Vietnam, but the president still valued his secretary of defense too highly to reject his advice out of hand. McNamara viewed the ABM choice as a direct confrontation between himself and the Joint Chiefs of Staff, and he would have seen a decision to deploy the system as a rejection. In addition, a president also needs congressional support for foreign and domestic policies. A negative decision on the ABM would have alienated key senators who were also longtime friends and colleagues whose opinions and convictions Johnson respected. But presidents are more than the chief officers of their administrations and chief architects of legislation to be submitted to Congress. They are also the heads of their parties and concerned with reelection and their parties' fortunes at the polls. The Republicans were already talking of an ABM gap, threatening to do to the Democrats what Kennedy and Johnson had done to Nixon in 1960—use the potentially powerful charge of neglecting the nation's defenses. Johnson, who had not yet decided to forgo a reelection bid, had to be worried about the possible impact of such an accusation.

But presidents must take other considerations and pressures into account as well. They know that in the final analysis they are responsible for the country's security and protection. Others can advise them, but only presidents can make the required decisions, and it is they who will be judged not only by the people but also by history.[17] And that judgment is their ultimate stake. They will be compared to others: George Washington, Thomas Jefferson, Abraham Lincoln, Theodore Roosevelt, Franklin Roosevelt, Harry Truman. No one who occupies the White House (or its equivalent in other countries) can possibly ignore his or her future historical reputation. Johnson, whose involvement in Vietnam was already arousing popular and congressional criticism and casting doubt upon his place in history, was keenly interested in a major arms limitation agreement with the Soviet Union to help his standing at that time and in the future; he needed a major breakthrough in the area of international reconciliation.

Minimal Decision Making

In this situation, given the "pitfalls" he saw in the ABM issue and the stakes he had in it, yet buffeted by conflicting pressures, the president would have preferred to make no decision at all and to allow the proponents and opponents of ABM to reach some kind of compromise among themselves. The problem of gaining presidential support for one side or another thus is not limited to reaching presidents, but also includes persuading them to make decisions. Their tendency is to procrastinate or to make only a "minimal decision." "How to decide without actually choosing" is the way political observer Warner Schilling aptly put it, in connection with another important presidential decision:

> The President did make choices, but a comparison of the choices that he made with those that he did not make reveals clearly the minimal character of his decision. It bears all the aspects of a conscious search for the course of action which would close off the least number of future alternatives, one which would avoid the most choice. . . .
> . . . One of the major necessities of the American political process [is] the need to avert conflict by avoiding choice. The distribution of power and responsibility among government elites is normally so dispersed that a rather widespread agreement among them is necessary if any given policy is to be adopted and later implemented. Among the quasi-sovereign bodies that make up the Executive the opportunities to compel this agreement are limited.[18]

Truman put this need to gain support to decide policy in fewer and more picturesque words: "They talk about the power of the president, how I can push a button and get things done. Why, I spent most of my time kissing somebody's ass." [19]

The critical question thus became: What will be the nature of the ABM compromise? At least part of the answer became clear in a meeting between Johnson and McNamara and Soviet premier A. N. Kosygin in Glassboro, New Jersey, in June 1967. Johnson pressed the Soviets for a date for the opening of arms limitation talks. This declaration would allow him to postpone the decision on the ABM. But Johnson did not receive an answer. Kosygin described the Soviet ABM system as defensive and therefore unobjectionable. As a weapon that would save lives, it was, in the Soviet premier's judgment, a good weapon that would not destabilize the arms balance and was not a proper subject for strategic arms limitation talks. McNamara's principal objection to the ABM had been refuted by the Soviets. Consequently, Johnson no longer saw the ABM as a possible stumbling block to beginning arms limitations talks.

Johnson then made his minimal decision: to adopt a small anti-Chinese ABM system. McNamara announced the decision in his contradictory speech. He said, on the one hand, that the most effective way to overcome a Soviet ABM was to saturate the defense with offensive missiles, suggesting that the Soviets could do that to the United States as well. On the other hand, should the Chinese be as irrational as their militant revolutionary rhetoric suggested, a "thin" or small ABM system might help to deter a strike. In one sense, McNamara had won a victory against the Joint Chiefs of Staff and ABM supporters in Congress, who favored a "thick" or nationwide anti-Soviet (and more expensive) ABM system. The very fact that he made the speech showed that he had by no means suffered a major defeat on this issue. He could view the president's decision as leaving open the possibility that the system would never be deployed at all if the Soviets would later agree to limitation of mutual defensive weapons. The administration had come out *not* in support of deployment but only in support of increased funding for the procurement of certain ABM parts that would require a long lead time. But the administration had publicly changed its position, and that represented a victory for ABM supporters in Congress and the Joint Chiefs. Proponents of the more extensive system viewed the change in the administration's position as a hopeful sign and expected that they could accomplish their goal later. There were as yet no "winners" or "losers." Compromises had prevented that.

The fight over ABM continued into the Nixon administration. At the time, the large Soviet missile buildup, which overtook the United States in the number of ICBMs and to which there seemed no end in sight, was perceived as an increasing threat to U.S. ICBMs. The fear was that the number of missiles plus the number of warheads the Soviets would place on them over the coming years, would give the Soviet Union a first-strike capability. President Nixon, therefore, switched the ABM from defending cities to defending ICBMs. This would counter the possibility of a successful Soviet strike and help keep the mutual deterrent balance stable.

Nixon also wanted a bargaining chip for the Strategic Arms Limitation Talks (SALT). There had been no U.S. missile buildup, so he could not trade some of them against the larger number of Soviet missiles. The ABM might be the only thing the United States could trade. As it turned out, the strategic arms limitation treaty placed a low limit on ABMs (the Soviets had already deployed about sixty around Moscow), so low that the United States abandoned it. At the same time, as the two powers agreed to freeze all offensive systems for a five-year period during which they would negotiate mutually acceptable ceilings on all strategic systems.

Neither Johnson nor Nixon were strongly committed to a strategic defense. Johnson was concerned that the Republicans would make the lack of an ABM defense a key issue in the next presidential election, and he was also worried about his relations with his own secretary of defense and several senators whose friendship and support he needed for his Great

Society domestic reform program. Nixon, in his turn, wanted a trade-off between defensive and offensive systems at a time when the public and Congress were in an antimilitary mood and the defense budget had reached its lowest percentage of the gross national product since 1950, *before* Korea.

Star Wars

President Reagan, by contrast, was committed to a strategic defense and did not think of SDI as a bargaining chip.[20] Moreover, Reagan's advice on some sort of defensive system had come from outside the government, primarily from Edward Teller, the "father" of the hydrogen bomb. There was no pressure within the executive branch or Congress for SDI. Indeed, at the time of the president's speech proposing it, the Defense Department's assessment of a strategic defense was that it was not feasible. Many in the administration were surprised by the president's speech. Unlike McNamara's speech, which reflected the various bureaucratic pulls, the SDI conclusion to Reagan's speech apparently had been added by the president at the last moment. The idea had not been submitted to the relevant departments for their examination, analysis, and recommendations. The president surprised most members of his administration.

This is not to say that SDI reflected a momentary whim. Reagan had expressed concern both before and immediately after he became president that the U.S. population was not being defended. The strategic balance when he assumed the office of presidency was, in his judgment (although not that of most experts), shifting in the Soviet Union's favor. Whether or not it was, the president worried about the long-term consequences of a deterrent balance that depended upon the threat of wiping out millions of Russians. Would it not be better to build deterrence upon a defense that would shoot down incoming missiles and protect, rather than incinerate, the civilian population of *both* countries? And, if the Soviets were behind the United States technologically, he offered to share SDI technology with them.

The security of the United States was not Reagan's only reason for advancing SDI, domestic politics was another. The president was seen by many as a militant anti-Communist crusader. He and other members of his administration had made a number of careless comments about nuclear war. Moreover, members of the administration had talked of *nuclear war fighting,* of *limited nuclear war,* and of *prevailing* in a nuclear exchange, not of deterrence. Partly because of all this talk, partly because détente had ended and the United States was embarking on a major modernization of its strategic forces, and partly because the administration was clearly opposed to arms control, many people feared a possible nuclear war. The media, physicians, Catholic and Methodist bishops, and other groups made constant reference to a "nuclear winter" and "the day after"; the nuclear freeze movement gained a large public following. In these circumstances, the president was on the defensive, especially against the bishops who denounced the immorality of using, if not possessing, nuclear weapons—which, in effect, was tantamount to saying that nuclear deterrence was immoral. SDI placed the president back in charge and gave him the initiative in the nuclear debate. If nuclear war was bad for the nation's health and bad for Americans' souls, why not propose a nuclear shield that would protect the population? Why not seek mutual assured survival instead of mutual assured destruction? "War-monger" Reagan thus stole his critics' antinuclear thunder. There was something profoundly ironic about the most conservative president in postwar history adopting the nuclear abolitionist stance of the most left-wing nuclear disarmers.

Strategic Defense Initiatives 1-3

In his speech the president proposed that SDI be able to render missiles "impotent and obsolete." A three-phase system, SDI would try to shoot down missiles while they were in their initial boost phase, lasting about five minutes; it would then try to destroy the multiple warheads after they had separated from the missiles in mid-phase flight (an infinitely more difficult task because of the far larger number of targets); and last, a terminal defense would try to destroy the warheads that had escaped. Nevertheless, SDI was controversial from the beginning. However shrewd a move in the context of American politics, it also suddenly undermined the deterrent basis on which U.S. and Western security had rested for four decades. Deterrence assumed that the threat of retaliation and extinction was sufficient to prevent an attack; SDI assumed that deterrence would fail. Moreover, it turned out that there was not one but three SDIs. SDI 1—the president's proposed nonnuclear population defense shield based in space—was quickly dismissed by most technologists and arms controllers. Such a futuristic system was deemed so complex and technically demanding that it was doubtful that it could offer the 100 percent protection the president had promised. Even if it were 80-90 percent effective—which was dubious—enough Soviet missiles would be able to penetrate the "space shield" to still destroy the United States. The point was that no matter how good U.S. technology might be eventually—and no one was likely to know that for a decade or two—it was questionable whether SDI would work perfectly the first time it was needed. Indeed, because no full-scale test of all the components could be carried out beforehand, the Congressional Office of Technology Assessment thought SDI would be a "catastrophic failure." [21]

Moreover, because the Soviets were hardly likely to accept the president's assurance that the United States would share this new technology with them so that both powers could substitute SDI for their offensive missiles simultaneously—as Gorbachev sarcastically remarked, the Americans would not even share their oil-drilling technology with the Russians—SDI was likely to stimulate not one but two arms races. One way the Soviets could seek to overcome SDI was by flooding it with more warheads than it could possibly handle. This meant a further Soviet offensive buildup, just as the United

States had responded to the Soviet ABMs in the 1970s by MIRVing or multiplying the warheads on its missiles to inundate and thereby overwhelm any Soviet defenses. Simultaneously, the Soviets would accelerate their own SDI research. Thus, the critics said, SDI would result in offensive and defensive arms races, which would be enormously expensive and in the end leave both powers less secure than before.

SDI 2 did not create such intense controversy. Relying largely on then-or-soon-to-be-available technology (fundamentally ground-based), SDI 2 was limited to missile protection. Given the large numbers of Soviet missiles and increasingly accurate warheads with their potential for a first strike, SDI 2 had some appeal. It would reduce the potential vulnerability of land-based missiles, thereby stabilizing the deterrent balance. Because such a defense was not based mainly on exotic space-based technologies, it also would be more affordable and feasible. And, unlike a population defense, a defensive capability of 50 percent would suffice. If the potential attacker knows that even half of the enemy's adversary's missiles will survive to retaliate against it, it will remain deterred. Not surprisingly, many military officers, including the Joint Chiefs of Staff (who hoped for an only 30 percent shoot-down rate) and members of Congress, skeptical about SDI 1, were attracted to SDI 2, and the Senate Armed Services Committee specifically went on record favoring this more attainable goal.

One critical difference distinguished SDI 1 from SDI 2. It was assumed that with the deployment of SDI 1 offensive missiles would be eliminated. They would become "impotent and obsolete" and therefore could be scrapped. With SDI 2, however, it was assumed that offensive missiles would remain; deterrence, rather than being abolished, would be made safer by sending the message to the other side that it cannot prevent a devastating second strike—even if it struck first. SDI 2 was also compatible with further arms control efforts.

SDI 3 was the *Soviet* perception of the president's proposal as an offensive, not defensive, system. If SDI 1 could not be made "leak-proof" against an attack by thousands of warheads, a certain number of which would still be able to penetrate it to create enormous destruction, it could be effective against a retaliatory blow already weakened by the opponent's first-strike capability. This, the Soviets claimed, was what the Reagan administration was really seeking. Interestingly, the Soviet objection to SDI was the same as the U.S. objection to Soviet ABM deployment in the early 1970s. Washington had viewed the Soviet ABM as part of a first-strike strategy, since Soviet military doctrine had emphasized a preemptive strike if nuclear war appeared likely and destruction of as much of the U.S. retaliatory capacity as possible to limit damage to itself. The ABMs might then further weaken the retaliatory blow by the remnants of the crippled U.S. forces, reducing the damage to the Soviet Union even further. In fact, SDI's aims remained defensive, although the military sought to promote the use of lasers offensively against satellites.[22]

Incentive or Obstacle to Arms Control?

The Reagan administration, worried that U.S. ICBMs were becoming more vulnerable to a Soviet attack, had from the outset sought a radical reduction of Soviet ICBMs and warheads to reduce this danger. But it had little to offer the Soviets in return. SDI thus proved, no doubt to Reagan's surprise, a powerful counter. In part, this stemmed from the Soviet fear of SDI as part of an offensive strategy. It stemmed as well from the fear of Soviet leadership—beset with a stagnating economy at home and already unable to keep up with Western technological advances—that SDI research would result in a quantum leap forward in the very area in which the United States had a successful past and the Soviet Union did not: technological innovation. The consequences of such a leap forward would be even further setbacks for the Soviet Union technologically. Moreover, the expense of a Star Wars race would have profound consequences for the Soviet standard of living, already low.

Thus, the Soviet interest in preventing SDI deployment, or at least slowing it down and allowing Soviet science to catch up, was intense. The research could continue in the laboratories; that could hardly be prevented. But there was to be no testing or deployment of any SDI technology in space, as the two powers had agreed in the 1972 ABM treaty. SDI had thus given the Reagan administration the lever with which to gain a radical reduction in the Soviet first-strike capability. SDI, like the U.S. ABM, was potentially a very powerful bargaining chip. But while Nixon had been willing to use the ABM that way, Reagan was unwilling to do so. The president clung to his vision, talking of SDI as if it were already a reality instead of a research program that could only in ten to twenty years reveal whether SDI was even technologically feasible. Unwilling to accept any limitations on U.S. research and *testing*, Reagan rejected Gorbachev's "grand compromise" of a 50 percent cut in offensive weapons, even as his secretary of state and others were seeking to negotiate such an agreement and make it so attractive that neither the president nor other SDI supporters could turn it down.[23]

Thus, instead of being a bargaining chip, SDI became an obstacle to an arms control agreement on strategic weapons. The Soviets repeated over and over that they should not be expected to greatly reduce the numbers of their strategic missiles when they did not know whether they had enough to cope with SDI. Again, they were merely repeating President Nixon's argument that he could not accept limits on U.S. offensive missiles until he knew whether the Soviets intended to deploy a nationwide ABM system. If the Soviets were going to deploy such a system, Nixon had said, the United States would need large numbers of missiles to penetrate this defense; if not, the United States was willing to accept an upper ceiling on missile deployment. Now Gorbachev presented Reagan with the same argument, but the president would not accept the linkage between the offensive and defensive arms races that had made SALT I possible in 1972.

It was hard to understand why the president was not more compromising on SDI because he was not being asked to abandon his vision, and the Soviets were willing to make him a good offer while SDI research could continue in the laboratories. But what the Soviets were unable to achieve, Congress did. SDI stimulated governmental politics in the form of an executive-legislative confrontation. The Congress, especially the Democrats, who controlled the House and, after the 1986 midterm election, the Senate as well, had never been enthusiastic about SDI, about whose purposes, feasibility, and costs even the administration appeared to be divided. The enormous cost of SDI at the time of a huge budget deficit, was an additional factor inciting Congressional resistance. Finally, there was the arms control impact; the likelihood that SDI would accelerate the defensive and offensive arms competition was very critically regarded by members of Congress who favored arms agreements. Indeed, there was a good deal of skepticism about the shift from deterrence to defense. The Senate specifically insisted that SDI concentrate on protecting missiles, contending that protection of the population was impossible. The result was that Congress cut funding for SDI every year after 1985.

The biggest skirmish in this battle, however, came over the 1972 ABM treaty.[24] The Reagan administration, determined to go ahead with SDI, wanted to test elements of SDI in space rather than just confine its research to the laboratories. Thus, it asserted a "broad" interpretation of the treaty that would allow such testing. This led to a confrontation with Congress, especially the Senate and Senator Sam Nunn, who had become chairman of the Senate Armed Services Committee after the Democrats regained control of the Senate in 1986. Nunn, the Senate's leading expert on military affairs, reviewed the record of the ABM treaty negotiations and found that the Senate had consented to the "narrow" treaty submitted by the Nixon administration. Thus, for the administration to unilaterally change the treaty that had been signed with Moscow and ratified by the United States would lead to a "constitutional crisis" with the Senate. Just to make sure, the Senate Armed Services Committee voted an amendment to the 1988 defense authorization bill which blocked any testing activities that violated the traditional reading of the ABM treaty.

Faced with congressional reductions in funding and a confrontation with the Senate over the ABM treaty, Reagan tried to commit his successor and the Congress to SDI by pushing for early deployment with currently available technology by the mid-1990s, even though it would not be the SDI the president had proposed and early deployment required a lowering of the system's performance requirements. A Senate study showed that it would stop only 16 percent of the warheads fired in a full-scale attack. Even a report by a 1987 panel of the American Physical Society, composed of leading physicists on exotic weapons technologies—all of whom had access to the research and development being done on SDI—stating that it would be ten or more years, perhaps the next century, before it would be known if these technologies were even feasible, did not deter the administration.[25] Reagan was clearly concerned that if deployment had not started before the end of his administration, SDI would be downgraded after he left office, becoming a bargaining chip and a long-term research program.

Even before the 1988 election results were known, General James Abrahamson, the air force general in charge of the SDI research program, resigned, declaring that a new administration would want to take a fresh look at SDI. The resignation probably symbolized the end of the idea of a comprehensive space-based missile shield deployment. This was not stated, but what was offered almost simultaneously was a vastly scaled version of the 1987 plan for early deployment. Within the executive branch, the opposition of the Joint Chiefs remained strong. They were very worried lest the enormous expense of even the original space-based deployment plan, estimated at $115 billion (even without the research and development cost on the more exotic future technologies), would eat up the resources needed for virtually all other military programs in a period of budgetary restraints. In fact, there were cheaper alternatives: shifting more land-based missiles to sea; making greater use of the mobile missiles on land; and most of all, concluding a strategic arms control agreement that cut the number of missiles by as much as half.

Back at the White House, one of the biggest remaining unknowns about SDI was domestic politics, which had been largely responsible for its origin and which continued to haunt it. Precisely because SDI had been a vision rather than a strategic program, and because it had been so bitterly criticized (especially by Democrats) for accelerating the nuclear arms race rather than abolishing the likelihood of nuclear war, the Reagan administration had made support for SDI a loyalty test. SDI thus became a "Republican weapon." Michael Dukakis, the 1988 Democratic presidential candidate, had denounced the entire program and, although he backtracked on SDI research, he declared SDI largely a waste of money badly needed for many more pressing domestic programs. The election of George Bush to succeed Reagan in the White House therefore gave SDI at least a partial new lease on life. Conservative Republicans remained loyal to SDI, and they were a strong faction with the Republican Party. Bush, however, remained subject to the same constraints as his predecessor: the technical-scientific limits; the opposition from the still Democratic-controlled Senate, especially Senator Nunn who favored only a limited system against accidental launches; and the huge Reagan-inherited budget deficit. Thus Bush was in a good position to achieve the "grand compromise" deal on missiles if he downgraded SDI from a vision to a long-term research program on the feasibility of the exotic technologies involved and perhaps limited any development to ground-based interceptors to protect missiles and bombers (although even that was questionable if Bush were to shift to mobile ICBMs).[26] According to initial indications, that indeed is the way the new administration will likely proceed. Bush, like Nixon, may use SDI as a bargaining chip to achieve radical reductions in offensive weapons. In fact, that was the deal the Soviets offered the administration soon after it came into office: a 50 percent cut in strategic forces; a prior agreement on SDI would not be necessary as long as the United States did not violate the

1972 ABM agreement. This would allow START to be completed, permit Gorbachev to avoid a high-tech arms competition that would interfere with his transfer of military resources to his failing civilian economy, and allow Bush to claim that he had not sacrificed SDI (while Gorbachev knows that Congress, already lukewarm in its support of SDI, would be even less likely to fund it after a START agreement that reduces U.S. concerns about the Soviet missile threat to American deterrent forces).

AMERICAN POLITICAL PROCESS AND FOREIGN POLICY DECISION MAKING

'Where You Stand Depends on Where You Sit'

This slogan sums up the decision-making approach. In contrast to the first-level analysis in which each state is considered a unitary actor, at the decision-making level each government is viewed as a composite of multiple actors. Instead of regarding foreign policy as a product of a rational choice among several options that maximize a chosen value such as security, analysts focus on the many conflicting values, perspectives, and interests that result in a specific policy.[27] The "games nations play" are the result of the "games bureaucrats play" to enhance their personal influence, as well as that of their own agencies. The same can be said of nonbureaucratic players, although the center of decision making remains in the executive branch.

President Johnson's decision to go ahead with the anti-Chinese ABM system is not easily explainable in terms of the rational actor model. The decision might not have been made had it not been for congressional and bureaucratic pressures, for the president really was primarily interested in starting the SALT talks and avoiding an expensive and possibly destabilizing arms race. But even for a president, there are constraints. Specifically, Johnson wanted to avoid a break with influential senators, as well as with his own secretary of defense, over ABM. The political costs of such breaks were greater than he was willing to pay. He also had to consider the probable electoral costs if he decided to avoid any ABM decision. So he compromised—he made a minimal decision, satisfactory to all the chief actors, who thought that they had "won" the president over to their position. In fact, he had kept his options open for a more definitive decision in the future.

The president was merely one of many players. To be sure, he may have been "first among equals," but his ability to impose his decisions was limited by the other players. Johnson did not want an ABM but was pushed into taking the first minimal step toward acceptance of it. He could not ignore the Joint Chiefs' coalition with powerful leaders in the Senate. The president, according to the organizational charts of the executive branch, may be the "boss" and presumably can order the Joint Chiefs, for example, to do or not to do what he or she chooses, but in reality, the relationship is more equal, and the participants bargain with one another. A close relationship between military leaders and a powerful congressional committee and ranking legislative leaders or a threat of resignation by military leaders (which reportedly occurred during the Vietnam War) forces the president and the secretary of defense to persuade their subordinates.

As the ABM case illustrates, the "foreign policy" decision that emerges from this bureaucratic system, which in turn is set in the broader governmental system,

> is not necessarily "policy" in the rational sense of embodying the decisions made and actions ordered by a controlling intelligence focusing primarily on our foreign policy problems. Instead it is the "outcome" of the political process, the government actions resulting from all the arguments, the building of coalitions and countercoalitions, and the decisions by high officials and compromises among them. Often it may be a "policy" that no participant fully favors [or the system is] more responsive to the internal dynamics of our decision-making process than to the external problems.[28]

Presidential Initiative and Leadership

The case of the ABM reveals the constraints, especially within the executive branch, on presidential leadership and initiative in foreign policy.[29] The SDI scenario, however, usually illustrates why the presidential perspective is usually preeminent in what political scientist Robert Art has called "innovative policy." First, presidents can seize for themselves certain specific policy areas, such as Nixon and SALT I, détente with the Soviet Union, and reconciliation with China; Carter and SALT II and the Israeli-Egyptian peace negotiations; and Reagan and the "space shield." "The ability of bureaucracies to independently establish policies is a function of Presidential attention. Presidential attention is a function of Presidential values. The Chief Executive involves himself in those areas which he determines to be important."[30] Whereas the bureaucratic politics model emphasized policy as the product of intrabureaucratic bargaining, it is probably more correct to say that, to a large degree, bureaucratic influence is a function of presidential—and, it ought to be added, congressional and public—inattention. The bureaucracy plays its largest role in routine daily affairs, its smallest during crises.

A president can also structure the organization for making foreign policy decisions. Nixon did so by making Kissinger his national security adviser, a kind of supersecretary of foreign affairs, giving him a fairly sizable staff and clearly ignoring the established bureaucracy or subordinating it to the White House. Kissinger's staff asked the established bureaucracy for policy papers on certain areas or policies, gathered them together, evaluated the alternatives, and, once the president had selected the best policy, sent the decision back to the bureaucracy for implementation.[31] Foreign policy decisions resulting from primarily bureaucratic infighting and compromise, rather than of rational responses to perceived external challenges and problems, were to be avoided as much as possible. Bureaucratic interests were to be subject to presidential perspectives and interests.

Reagan's problems in foreign policy during his two terms, especially the Iran-contra affair, were often due to disorganization. In contrast to Nixon who had one national security adviser, Ford who had two, and Carter who had one, Reagan had six! Moreover, the first four had little competence or experience in foreign policy. Worse, the president set broad directions but showed little interest in the details of policy or in close involvement on a daily basis (except for monitoring the U.S. hostage situation in Lebanon and the contra war in Nicaragua). Thus, there was no one to resolve key conflicts, especially between the secretaries of state and defense until the latter resigned in 1987.

A president also chooses cabinet officials. And, although they do represent the various bureaucracies and agencies in government, they also normally reflect the president's general views and values, for they owe their places in the history books to the person who appointed them and they are likely to feel some gratitude. They know too that the president, if displeased, can fire them and that most of them are expendable. Moreover, the president can ignore them; the president decides whom to listen to and whom to exile from the policy-making circle. Kennedy chose to heed McNamara rather than Rusk. During the Vietnam War, Johnson eliminated powerful and respected men such as McNamara from his administration when they increasingly opposed his bombing policy, and he simply did not listen to others. Nixon, during his first term, listened to his national security adviser and paid little attention to his secretary of state. Reagan for most of his eight years listened to Secretary of Defense Caspar Weinberger; only in his last years did Secretary of State George Shultz gain the president's ear.

Executive-Legislative Conflict

The bureaucratic politics model, by focusing also on the executive branch, tends to downplay the important role of Congress in the policy process. Prior to the Vietnam War, Congress generally supported the president's policy, largely because they shared a set of common anti-Communist images. Nevertheless, electoral politics and executive-legislative conflict permeated the conduct of foreign policy—as the nation's Asian policy after Nationalist China's collapse and Communist China's birth amply demonstrated. The Republican attacks on the Democrats paralyzed even Eisenhower, the moderate Republican, but particularly Democratic presidents remained fearful of improving relations with Communist China and, more broadly, of any "appeasement of communism." Knowing the great difficulties that they would have with Congress if they defied it, these presidents were afraid to assume anything less than strong positions against Communist China. When President Johnson was informed that South Vietnam was collapsing, he responded that he was not going to be the president who saw Southeast Asia go the way of China.

The price of all this was very high. Had China been recognized in early 1950, the Truman administration might have more accurately assessed how the Chinese would react to U.S. intervention in Korea. Had American observers been stationed in Peking (now Beijing), the Kennedy and Johnson administrations would have known that the war in South Vietnam was not part of Chinese Communist expansion and U.S. involvement might have been avoided. Better relations with China might have been established earlier and the increasing Sino-Soviet conflict exploited to bring about a parallel reduction in American-Soviet tensions.

With the erosion of the cold war's anticommunism, executive-legislative conflict has affected virtually the whole range of American foreign policy. Congressional questioning and criticism of presidential policy grew during the 1970s and 1980s.[32] The Vietnam War discredited the leadership of the executive branch and its expertise in foreign policy; the Watergate scandal and revelations about the CIA and Federal Bureau of Investigation (FBI) added to congressional determination to be more assertive in foreign policy in a period in which there was no new consensus on which to base policy. In the early days of détente, when Kissinger wanted to supplement the military stick with economic carrots to induce more restrained Soviet behavior, the Senate added the Jackson-Vanik amendment on Jewish emigration from the Soviet Union to a commercial treaty. Because of this attempt at interference with its domestic affairs, Moscow rejected the treaty, thus reducing the economic leverage the United States might have gained. The Senate also almost undermined the Panama Canal treaties and failed to vote on SALT II, which effectively killed it. Congress as a whole imposed an arms embargo against Turkey to punish it for its 1974 invasion of Cyprus, which was launched to protect the Turkish minority there from a Greek attempt to unite Cyprus with Greece. But Congress as an institution is more splintered than ever before: party loyalty has further declined; the authority of committee chairs has been reduced; and subcommittees have become more numerous and influential. Given this high degree of decentralization, pressure groups have gained increased access to congressional policy makers. Especially active are ethnic groups, such as Greek-Americans, who favor the Turkish embargo, and American Jews, who have made it difficult for American administrations to take an even-handed position on Middle East affairs. Whenever the executive has pressed Israel to be more conciliatory in peace negotiations, Congress has undermined the effort. Simply put, it has become much more difficult for a president to mobilize Congress on foreign policy issues; obstructing, delaying, changing, and even emasculating policy have become considerably easier.

Congress has become especially sensitive to any presidential use of force, and in 1973 it passed the War Powers Act over President Nixon's veto to avoid more Koreas and Vietnams. This resolution required the president to consult with Congress before using American forces and required Congress to approve presidential use of force after sixty days (or the troops would have to be withdrawn). While Congress generally has gone along when presidents have used force in a quick, effective, and successful manner as in the invasion of Grenada or attacks on Libya as reprisals for terrorism, it has been far more reluctant to support the president if the actions appeared to involve the United States in "another Vietnam." Thus, President Reagan's support for the government of El Salvador and, even more so, his support for the contras in their war with the Sandinista government in Nicaragua, did not always receive the backing he wanted. Congress was far more willing to question presidential wisdom than in the pre-Vietnam days, particularly when it feared that if military assistance did not work, U.S. troops might have to be sent in to do the job.

By and large, all presidents since Nixon have refused to invoke the War Powers Act. They have considered it an encroachment on their commander-in-chief powers and, politically, they have feared—as Reagan did in the Persian Gulf—that if they invoked it, Congress would seize the opportunity to end American involvement at the first sight of heavy American casualties. Eisenhower resorted to covert means to overthrow Guatemala's government in 1954, and Kennedy used Cuban refugees to invade Cuba in 1961. But Reagan's attempt to use proxies in Nicaragua was unsuccessful. Congress opposed the intervention and the constant headlines in the press and leadoff stories on the television news made a charade of the term *covert*. Congress, fearful of another Vietnam, thus had placed restraints on the presidential conduct of foreign policy. Not that Congress was opposed to all interventions; it had, however, become far more selective and discriminatory in those it would support. It expected the president to make a strong case that such interventions would promote national security.

OTHER SYSTEMS, DIFFERENT DECISION MAKING

Although the U.S. government is used here as an example of pluralistic decision making, the same type of analysis can be applied to other governments such as the Soviet or British. In the Soviet Union too there are multiple bureaucratic interests behind the authoritarian facade: party, army, policy, industrial, and agricultural interests, all of which have representatives to voice their needs and grievances. Conflict among these actors occurs within the Soviet government, but, in contrast to that of the U.S. government, its bureaucracy historically has not mobilized interest group or legislative and popular support for its policy preferences. Until Gorbachev, the Communist party had commanded the legislature; the Supreme Soviet has had no independent role. Outside the government, groups such as the trade unions historically have not existed autonomously. The Communist party has controlled all appointments, promotions, and demotions. And there has not, until recently been a tradition of freely expressed public opinion in the Soviet Union. Bargaining and coalition building in the making of domestic and foreign policy occurred within the party framework.[33]

Gorbachev, who is currently trying to mobilize popular support against the bureaucracy—like Jimmy Carter and Ronald Reagan, he seems to be running against the government!—presumably will benefit from the experience of Nikita Khrushchev, who succeeded Stalin and was too innovative for his colleagues. His attempts to stir up the Soviet economy led to a number of different proposals which, quite apart from their merit, met strong opposition. Among other things, Khrushchev wanted to cut the bureaucracy in Moscow and send officials out to the provinces. The bureaucrats, however, preferred life in the Soviet capital. Other programs aroused opposition because they were seen to weaken the bureaucracy's central control and preeminence. Khrushchev's humiliation in the Cuban missile crisis as well as what were called his "harebrained" domestic schemes led to Brezhnev's *coup d'état* in 1964. Whether Gorbachev's even more daring and extensive reforms will avoid such a fate remains to be seen.

Still, a comparison of the American and Soviet political systems suggests that making a decision in the Soviet Union has in the past been considerably easier than in the United States, and, once a decision is made, it has been easier to execute. One need but note how, despite illness and old age, the doddering Brezhnev hung onto power for five years until his death, even though critical decisions, especially with regard to the economy, needed to be made. Once solidly in power—in the pre-Gorbachev era they did not arouse too much opposition from colleagues and the many bureaucracies— Soviet leaders were hard to dislodge. Khrushchev may have been the exception rather than the rule, serving as a warning to his successors not to be too innovative or upset vested interests. The problem, as the Brezhnev era was to demonstrate, was that this type of governing could not reverse the nation's economic stagnation and its lag behind the West technologically and scientifically. Thus, Gorbachev has no choice but to be innovative and upset vested interests.

The British system of government resembles that of the United States in that many of the same types of players participate in the policy process. A prime minister's cabinet colleagues represent different institutional and socioeconomic interests, and he or she cannot neglect the members of the party in the House of Commons because the party cannot be led where it does not want to go (in fact, in recent years the Labor party in Commons has been greatly influenced by militant constituencies outside of Parliament). Kenneth Waltz has argued that a prime minister tends to avoid innovations in policy unless he or she has gained support from cabinet colleagues and the rank and file:

> Seldom will a prime minister try to force a decision widely and genuinely unpopular in his party. The prime minister must preserve the unity of the party, for it is not possible for him to perpetuate his rule by constructing a series of

majorities whose composition varies from issue to issue [as in the United States]. He is, therefore, constrained to crawl along cautiously, to let situations develop until the necessity of decision blunts inclinations to quarrel about just what the decision should be.[34]

Incrementalism thus seems to be as much a feature of British government as of American government. Continuity of policy, slow adjustment to changing circumstances, policy deadlocks, and evasion of issues until they become crises are features in common. Innovations in policies are few and far between.

Nevertheless, unlike the U.S. government, the British government is not characterized by a separation of powers or, more accurately, separate institutions sharing powers; rather, the executive and legislative branches are unified. And because, unlike American political parties, British parties are disciplined, the prime minister has much greater control over his or her members in the House of Commons than a president has over party members in Congress. It would be inconceivable for a British prime minister to sign a SALT II treaty and then not see it gain parliamentary approval. When a prime minister and the cabinet decide to adopt a policy, they can mobilize the necessary party support and carry out that policy. A president can never be sure.

DECISION MAKING AND INTERNATIONAL NEGOTIATIONS

Finally, the governmental politics model holds several important implications for international negotiations. One implication is how difficult the negotiations are likely to be, quite apart from the substantive complexity of the problems being negotiated. Misunderstandings, failures of communication, disappointed expectations, and even failure of the negotiations between two countries may easily result when each set of national policy makers for foreign affairs is so deeply engaged in its own bureaucratic and governmental "games" that it does not pay sufficiently close attention to the other side. Even between countries as close as Britain and the United States, negotiations can break down because the Londoners are negotiating with other Londoners and Washingtonians with other Washingtonians in trying to formulate policy. "Their self-absorption is a day-and-night affair; it never flags. They calculate accordingly and act to suit. So do their counterparts inside the other government.... Comprehension of the other's actual behavior is a function of their own concerns."[35]

Another implication is that in negotiations between two highly bureaucratized governments, the international negotiations are only one of *three* simultaneous sets of negotiations; the other negotiations are those between the governments and those among the various participants within each government. Kissinger used to complain that it was easier to negotiate with the Soviet leaders than to negotiate an agreed-upon policy in Washington; this complaint may be common in many capitals.[36]

For Review

1. What is the governmental politics decision-making model?
2. How does this decision-making model explain different types of policies?
3. What are the chief characteristics of both crisis and noncrisis policy decisions?
4. What does a case study of the Strategic Defense Initiative reveal about the American political process, especially the roles of the presidency and the Congress?
5. How can this American model of decision making be applied to other countries and international negotiations between states?

Notes

1. See Roger Hilsman, *To Move a Nation* (Garden City, N.Y.: Doubleday, 1967); Graham T. Allison, *The Essence of Decision* (Boston: Little, Brown, 1971); Morton H. Halperin, *Bureaucratic Politics and Foreign Policy* (Washington, D.C.: Brookings, 1974); Morton H. Halperin and Arnold Kanter, eds., *Readings in American Foreign Policy* (Boston: Little, Brown, 1973); and David C. Kozak and James M. Keagle, eds., *Bureaucratic Politics and National Security* (Boulder, Colo.: Lynne Rienner, 1988).
2. Henry A. Kissinger, *Nuclear Weapons and Foreign Policy* (New York: Harper & Row, 1957).
3. Graham Allison, "Conceptual Models and the Cuban Missile Crisis," *American Political Science Review* (September 1969): 716.
4. Oran Young, *The Politics of Force* (Princeton, N.J.: Princeton University Press, 1968), 6-15; Charles F. Hermann, ed., *International Crises* (New York: Free Press, 1972); and Phil Williams, *Crisis Management* (New York: John Wiley, 1976).
5. Irving Janis, *Victims of Groupthink* (Boston: Houghton Mifflin, 1972).
6. For the Cuban missile crisis, see Elie Abel, *The Missile Crisis* (New York: Bantam Books, 1966); Alexander L. George et al., eds., *The Limits of Coercive Diplomacy* (Boston: Little, Brown, 1971); and Robert F. Kennedy, *Thirteen Days* (New York: Norton, 1967).
7. For elaboration, see John Spanier and Eric M. Uslaner, *American Foreign Policy Making and The Democratic Dilemmas*, 5th ed. (Pacific Grove, Calif.: Brooks/Cole, 1989).
8. See Samuel P. Huntington, *The Common Defense* (New York: Columbia University Press, 1961), 123ff., for formulation of defense policy.
9. Charles E. Lindblom, "The Science of Muddling Through," *Public Administration Review*, Winter 1959, 79-88.
10. Theodore J. Lowi, *The End of Liberalism* (New York: Norton, 1969), 160-161.

11. Ibid.

12. Francis E. Rourke, "The Domestic Scene," in *America and the World: From the Truman Doctrine to Vietnam*, Robert E. Osgood, ed. (Baltimore: Johns Hopkins University Press, 1970), 147-188; William R. Caspary, "The 'Mood Theory': A Study of Public Opinion and Foreign Policy," *American Political Science Review* (June 1970): 536-547; and James N. Rosenau, "Foreign Policy as an Issue Area," in Conference on Public Opinion and Foreign Policy, *Domestic Sources of Foreign Policy* (New York: Free Press, 1965).

13. Former secretary of state Dean Acheson offers some amusing and somewhat sarcastic comments on the way Senator Arthur Vandenberg helped to legitimate presidential policy during the crucial days after 1945. See *Present at the Creation* (New York: Norton, 1969), 223.

14. James A. Robinson, *Congress and Foreign Policy-Making*, rev. ed. (Homewood, Ill.: Dorsey Press, 1967). For the early postwar period, see Daniel S. Cheever and H. Field Haviland, Jr., *American Foreign Policy and the Separation of Powers* (Cambridge, Mass.: Harvard University Press, 1952), 106ff. For the post-Vietnam days, see John Spanier and Joseph L. Nogee, eds., *Congress, the Presidency and American Foreign Policy* (Elmsford, N.Y.: Pergamon Press, 1981).

15. This section relies heavily on the account by Morton H. Halperin, "The Decision to Deploy the ABM: Bureaucratic and Domestic Politics in the Johnson Administration," *World Politics*, October 1972, 62ff. For the development of the ICBM, see Edmund Beard, *Developing the ICBM* (New York: Columbia University Press, 1976).

16. Halperin, "Decision to Deploy the ABM," 67-69.

17. Halperin, *Bureaucratic Politics and Foreign Policy*, 81-82.

18. Warner R. Schilling, "The H-Bomb: How to Decide Without Actually Choosing," in Halperin and Kanter, *Readings*, 253, 255.

19. Quoted in *Time*, January 25, 1968.

20. For the background of SDI, see Ashton B. Carter and David N. Schwartz, eds., *Ballistic Missile Defense* (Washington, D.C.: Brookings, 1984); and Philip M. Boffey et al., *Claiming the Heavens*, subtitled "The New York Times Complete Guide to the Star Wars Debate" (New York: Times Books, 1988). Two anti-SDI books are Sidney Drell, Phillip Farley, and David Holloway, *The Reagan Strategic Defense Initiative* (Cambridge, Mass.: Ballinger, 1985); and Robert McNamara, *Blundering into Disaster* (New York: Pantheon, 1986). Two pro-SDI books are Zbigniew Brzezinski et al., *Promise or Peril* (Lanham, Md.: University Press of America, 1986); and Keith B. Payne, *Strategic Defense* (Lanham, Md.: Hamilton Press, 1986). Also see Harry Waldman, *The Dictionary of SDI* (Wilmington, Del.: Scholarly Resources, 1988) for the terminology of SDI. For historical and Soviet perspectives, among other issues, see Samuel F. Wells, Jr. and Robert S. Litwak, *Strategic Defenses and Soviet-American Relations* (Cambridge, Mass.: Ballinger, 1987). The Congressional Office of Technology Assessment reports, the second one of which is very critical, may be found in *Strategic Defense Initiative* (Princeton, N.J.: Princeton University Press, 1988). The economic aspects are examined in Rosy Nimroody (for the Council on Economic Priorities), *Star Wars* (Cambridge, Mass.: Ballinger, 1987).

21. Warren E. Leary, "Report Depicts 'Star Wars' as an Unworkable System," *New York Times*, Apr. 25, 1988.

22. William J. Broad, "U.S. Promoting Offensive Role for 'Star Wars' " and "Military to Ready Laser for Testing as Space Weapon," *New York Times*, Nov. 27, 1988, and Jan. 1, 1989, respectively.

23. See Strobe Talbott's *The Master of the Game* (New York: Knopf, 1988) for details of the "grand compromise" negotiations and the progress made during the Reagan administration.

24. William J. Durch, *The ABM Treaty and Western Security* (Cambridge, Mass.: Ballinger, 1987); and Gerald M. Steinberg, *Lost in Space* (Lexington, Mass.: Lexington Books, 1989).

25. William J. Broad, "The Star Wars Program Prepares for a Year of Reckoning," *New York Times*, Nov. 29, 1988.

26. Talbott, *Master of the Game*.

27. Halperin and Kanter, *Readings*, 3.

28. I. M. Destler, *Presidents, Bureaucrats, and Foreign Policy* (Princeton, N.J.: Princeton University Press, 1972), 64, 74.

29. For the critique that follows I am indebted to Robert J. Art, "Bureaucratic Politics and American Foreign Policy: A Critique," *Policy Sciences* 4 (1973): 467-490; and Stephen D. Krasner, "Are Bureaucracies Important?" *Foreign Policy*, Summer 1972, 159-179.

30. Krasner, "Are Bureaucracies Important?" 168. Krasner's emphasis on the state as a unified actor pursuing its "national interest" is elaborated in his *Defending the National Interest* (Princeton, N.J.: Princeton University Press, 1978).

31. Destler, *Presidents, Bureaucrats, and Foreign Policy*, 118-152. For a more recent and favorable assessment, see Robert J. Strong, *Bureaucracy and Statesmanship* (New York: University Press of America, 1986); Alexander L. George, "The Case for Multiple Advocacy in Making Foreign Policy," *American Political Science Review* (September 1972): 751ff.; and Janis, *Victims of Groupthink*.

32. Spanier and Nogee, *Congress, the Presidency and American Foreign Policy*; John Rourke, *Congress and the Presidency in U.S. Foreign Policymaking* (Boulder, Colo.: Westview Press, 1983); and William P. Quandt, *Camp David* (Wash., D.C.: Brookings, 1986).

33. Zbigniew K. Brzezinski and Samuel P. Huntington, *Political Power: USA/USSR* (New York: Viking, 1964), 196-197; and Darrel P. Hammer, *The Politics of Oligarchy*, 2d ed. (Boulder, Colo.: Westview Press, 1986). Also see Arnold L. Horelick, A. Ross Johnson, and John D. Steinbruner, *The Study of Soviet Foreign Policy* (Beverly Hills, Calif.: Sage, 1975), for an evaluation of decision-making models as they have been used in studying Soviet politics.

34. Kenneth N. Waltz, *Foreign Policy and Democratic Politics* (Boston: Little, Brown, 1967), 59-62.

35. Richard E. Neustadt, *Alliance Politics* (New York: Columbia University Press, 1970), 66.

36. For the Reagan administration's internal fights on arms control, see Strobe Talbott, *Deadly Gambits* (New York: Knopf, 1984), and *Master of the Game*.

CHAPTER 11

Foreign Policy: A Conclusion

FOCUS ON PERCEPTION

The single thread that runs through the preceding chapters is *perception:* the way nations, political elites, specific bureaucracies, and individual leaders see the world, the way they define vital issues and the international role their countries should play. It quickly becomes clear that although states see the same "reality," they view it differently. The United States and the Soviet Union see their conflict with each other as the primary one; the threat each poses to the other is the key to their foreign policies. National security is their critical concern. The developing countries view the struggle for modernization and a more equitable distribution of status and wealth in the state system as the chief issue. Their focus is on North-South tensions; the East-West competition is of secondary interest to them, although they are not reluctant to use it to advance their goals. The resulting emphasis in international politics on conflicts of interests should not therefore be surprising. Individual policy makers often view the world through the lenses of their own organizations, and their policy recommendations tend to reflect their organizations' interests. The result is a conflict of interest within government as well and competition among multiple versions of what is truly in the national interest. Even presidents are subject to constraints in pursuing their policies.

Policy makers, whether their views are filtered through national, elite, or bureaucratic lenses, are persuaded that the way *they* see the world is correct. It is the *other* policy makers in the other states who see the world incorrectly. Each nation can justify its perceptions and policies and marshal an impressive array of facts and historical analyses. How can that be? Do the facts not speak for themselves? We can, after all, neither ignore them nor mistake them. Facts are facts. Or are they? The truth is that a fact as such does not possess any meaning. What gives it meaning is an observer's perceptual framework, influenced by personal experiences, beliefs, and interpretations of history. This image of the world leads the observer to select a specific fact from the thousands available. But why was that particular fact chosen? The answer is our selective vision. It not only allows us to pick out some facts and ignore others—those picked tend to be consistent with our way of viewing the world—but also gives meaning to those we select, thereby allowing us to understand the world better. This is as true for nations as it is for individual policy makers (or outside observers) and bureaucracies.

Misperception and Conflict

The cold war has illustrated certain objective geopolitical realities. The U.S. objective before World War II, as afterward, was to prevent the domination of Eurasia by any hostile power. The Soviet Union, which after the collapse of all the prewar great powers was the only great power remaining, already spanned all of Eurasia. American power was the only power able to balance Moscow's. The Soviet Union, with its fresh memories of Germany's invasion—the second in this century—and its enormous losses, was determined that this pattern not be repeated. It therefore pushed outward into Eastern Europe to keep the enemy, whoever it might be, as far away from Russian soil as possible. Thus, as so often before, two great powers, allied to defeat a common enemy, fell out with one another and became adversaries. The momentum of great-power rivalry, as old as history itself, then became an additional factor. Sparta versus Athens, Rome versus Carthage, France versus England (plus the rest of Europe at various times), England versus Germany, all preceded the post-1945 conflict. Influence, status, and power were the stakes; each considered the other a security threat. These "structural" causes of the cold war—causes inherent in the decentralized nature of the state system—were intensified by the ideological and cultural differences between the two societies, such as the individualist versus collective philosophy, democracy versus authoritarianism, private enterprise versus state ownership of property. Thus, the roots of the U.S.-Soviet conflict, in terms of both interests and values, were real and were not easily resolvable. Even though the superpowers in the Gorbachev era are moving away from viewing each other as "mortal enemies," they may, by virtue of their power and geographical location, remain "global rivals."[1]

The *subjective* reality of Soviet leaders after World War I—their perception of reality—made it virtually impossible to work out a postwar modus vivendi or mutually acceptable working arrangements, as in 1815 when czarist Russia, also trying to protect itself from another invasion, pushed outward and seized control of the then Duchy of Warsaw, much to the consternation of Russia's fellow victors. George Kennan has argued that this post-1917 subjective reality stemmed from Soviet ideology, which tended to see the United

States as only a temporary ally during World War II. As a capitalist state, the United States was viewed as an enemy, what were intended to be American declarations of good intent and hopes for postwar peace were interpreted as mere rhetoric which, if anything, was intended to deceive and relax the Soviet Union's guard. Thus, the Soviet Union's "own aggressive intransigence with respect to the outside world began to find its own reaction. . . . It is an undeniable privilege of every man to prove himself right in the thesis that the world is his enemy; for if he reiterates it frequently enough and makes it the background of his conduct he is bound eventually to be right." [2]

The American reaction to the Soviet perception of the United States as the enemy, as in World Wars I and II, took on the character of a crusade. With its tendency to see the world in terms of friend and foe, moral and immoral, U.S. foreign policy, initially limited to reacting to specific Soviet moves, soon spilled over into a global anticommunism. These differing perceptions and behavior patterns accounted for much of the intensity and bitterness of the superpower competition, the failure of a détente to emerge before the 1970s, and the collapse of détente I. They accounted as well for the refusal of the United States to recognize the new mainland Chinese government for thirty years after it proclaimed its existence, to exploit the growing Sino-Soviet schism after 1956, and to not intervene in Vietnam in 1965.

John Stoessinger, a longtime student of the effects of perceptions on nations, has noted the frequent gap between image and reality. Therefore, nations "live in darkness," he has argued: "Great nations struggle not only with each other, but also with their perceptions of each other." [3] In saying that perception may be almost as critical a factor in accounting for a state's behavior as objective reality, he and other analysts are implicitly, if not explicitly, drawing a line between correct perceptions and misperceptions. These misperceptions can aggravate or prolong, if they do not cause, con-flict, as well as make peaceful resolution difficult, if not at times impossible.

Thus, even though both the United States and Soviet Union had good reasons for wanting détente in the 1970s, it did not last long because each one understood its meaning differently and therefore held different expectations. The Soviets assumed that the United States was interested in a relaxation of tensions and agreements with Moscow because of the Soviet Union's new military strength. Therefore, Brezhnev and the Kremlin felt that they could exploit opportunities for expanding Soviet influence with impunity. The United States would have to accept the resulting changes in the status quo. The men in the Kremlin at no point saw such behavior as incompatible with détente or believed that their own behavior would once more aggravate tensions and bring on a new cold war. In exaggerating the constraints on the United States, the Soviets badly miscalculated, for with the Soviet invasion of Afghanistan, the United States did an about-face in policy.

American disillusionment with détente had grown over the years. Détente was supposed to restrain the Soviets and reinforce the status quo. Thus, Soviet behavior resulted once more in a strong anti-Soviet policy, which, even had Carter been reelected, would in most respects (except for the possible support of the contras in Nicaragua) have been similar to Reagan's. While America saw the Soviet moves in the 1970s as incompatible with détente, it did not see some of its own moves, such as promoting an Arab-Israeli peace while displacing Soviet influence in the region, as a unilateral search for advantage. The cooperation required therefore to maintain détente was risked by both Moscow and, to a lesser extent, Washington. It is precisely on this point of being aware the Soviet behavior might affect America's just as the latter's behavior affected the Soviet Union that Gorbachev has broken with his predecessors.

Causes of Misperceptions

Why do national leaders so often misperceive the true nature of the world they face? The reasons are multiple. Both the British prewar and American wartime experiences showed, as already noted, how reluctant democracies are to recognize threats—in both cases from revolutionary states. Traditional states assume one another's right to exist; they are therefore at a disadvantage when a revolutionary state appears. Wishing to preserve peace and maintain their own tranquillity rather than face serious threats to their national security which entail costly rearmament programs and risks of war, democracies prefer to believe that the revolutionary state is really like themselves—that is, it has only limited, legitimate objectives which can be satisfied by patience, good will, and compromise.[4] In other words, democracies are tempted to interpret their challengers' demands and behavior in familiar, favorable, and recognizable terms as if revolutionary states were in fact traditional states like themselves. Thus, the British thought Hitler was just another German nationalist, while the Nazi dictator justified every move he made in terms of the principle of national self-determination, the basis of the Western-imposed peace treaty at the end of World War I. Claiming that the Western powers had violated their own principles, he undermined the legitimacy of the territorial settlement and disguised his ultimate intentions of making Germany the dominant world power while paralyzing the will of Britain and France to oppose him. They recognized Hitler's claims as just and could not be sure that he was merely exploiting the principle of self-determination until he violated it. In the hope of preserving peace, they wanted to believe him when he said that his claims were limited and that he too wanted to preserve peace.

American history and experience reinforced this democratic unwillingness to admit the existence of international conflict and the U.S. stake in the outcome. In both world wars, the United States stayed out until its enemies attacked. The United States would not have declared war had not the Germans in 1917 launched their unrestricted submarine campaign to starve Britain into submission and, in the process, sunk American ships. Had Hitler not stupidly declared war on the United States after the Japanese attack on

Pearl Harbor, the American war effort would have been directed only at Japan, and Germany, the greater threat, might have defeated Russia and Britain. In fact, it is questionable whether the United States, with a divided public, would have declared war on either Germany or Japan had it not been for the Japanese attack on Pearl Harbor. The ultimate decisions to go to war were made by Germany and Japan. The United States did not take the initiative even though the balance of power in Europe and Asia was at stake.[5] Unable to act wisely, the United States was saved by its enemies from the consequences of its behavior. Thus, it is not surprising that during World War II American leaders were generally optimistic about postwar relations with the Soviet Union. Just as the British had thought of Hitler as another Bismarck, who after unifying Germany in 1870 had declared that Germany would support the status quo, American policy makers thought of Stalin as another czar concerned only with securing historic *Russian* goals.

More specific explanations of misperceptions can vary from policy makers' misreading of history to their personalities. In a biography of Dean Acheson, President Truman's secretary of state during the early days of the cold war, Gaddis Smith, a historian, argued that underlying Acheson's thought and policy advice was "an extraordinarily articulate expression of thoughts which guided American foreign policy for a third of a century after the outbreak of the Second World War. An appraisal of Acheson must therefore be an appraisal of the nation's behavior in world affairs for an entire generation."[6] In Smith's interpretation, Acheson's general image of the world and what ought to be the American role in it was shared by his successor, Eisenhower appointee John Foster Dulles, as well as by Presidents Truman, Eisenhower, Kennedy, Johnson, and Nixon. All were heavily influenced by their generation's experiences and perceptions. Postwar U.S. leaders had been tempered in the crucible of the 1930s; the career of Hitler and the appeasement at Munich, as well as the Nazi-Soviet pact, had made deep impressions on them.

Even more specifically, this generation had learned from the interwar period that the American isolationist stance had helped to bring on World War II and that American participation in the defense of Western Europe after World War I would have helped to deter Hitler. Isolationism no longer seemed a feasible policy; expansionistic totalitarian movements, whether Nazi or Soviet, had to be contained. A second lesson was that appeasement only whets a dictator's appetite—it seemed better to stand firm against demands and "present arms." Soviet policy was expansionist and aggressive and had to be resisted, by force if necessary. "Driven by the ghost of Hitler,"[7] of concessions made from a position of weakness, and of failure to match the adversary's military strength, this generation had learned that peace cannot be preserved solely by good intentions. Military power and, if necessary, force were required.

Acheson and a host of postwar American policy makers therefore approached American-Soviet relations as a deadly contest. Soviet totalitarianism had to be contained and its expansionist attempts dammed, until some day that nation mellowed. Inflexible American policies, distrust of all Soviet and other Communist states, and an inability to recognize the diversity within the Communist world were the results, as was the unnecessary prolongation of the cold war.[8]

Whereas Smith and other analysts have attributed misperceptions to drawing the wrong lessons from history, political scientist Ole Holsti has attributed them to other factors. For example, Holsti pointed to the rigid personality and equally inflexible anti-Communist view of Secretary of State John Foster Dulles.[9] Holsti argued that Dulles drew a distinction between the Soviet state and the governing Communist party, between Soviet national interests and Marxist-Leninist ideology with its universal revolutionary goals, and between the Soviet people and Soviet leaders. The consequence of these distinctions, Holsti claimed, was that in Dulles's mind the American quarrel was with the Soviet leaders, whose aims reached beyond legitimate and limited Soviet interests. The United States was not in conflict with the Soviet people, who, had they been represented by a democratic rather than a totalitarian government, would have pursued only limited national interests and not global expansionism. Soviet expansionism, in Dulles's view, was the cause of the cold war. The United States had to prevent the spread of "atheistic communism" and be constantly on guard against Communist attempts to lull the West.

Given Dulles's black and white image of the world—which is of central importance to the misperception approach—all incoming information had to be filtered through his particular perceptions: what fitted his preconceived image was accepted, and what did not fit was filtered out. The image thus remained intact. *Psychologic* is the term sometimes used to describe this tendency to see what we want to see and to reject contrary evidence; psychologists call it a "reduction of cognitive dissonance." On the basis of Dulles's public statements, Holsti argued that various Soviet pronouncements and moves, including a major reduction in the size of the Soviet army during Dulles's tenure as secretary of state, were not recognized as possible concessions and attempts to relax tensions. They served only to reinforce his preexisting views of the Soviet Union and were interpreted as signs of Soviet weakness and attempts to win a respite to recoup strength for a more effective and successful struggle with capitalism. A more flexible, less suspicious personality, Holsti has suggested, might have been more receptive to new and conflicting information; presumably, this kind of person might also have made a more serious and sustained effort to test Soviet intentions and perhaps to bring about what is now popularly known as détente.

Correct Perceptions: World War II and the Cold War

If misperceptions may cause, magnify, or prolong conflict, then it follows that correct perceptions will either prevent or restrain conflict; at least, they will not blow it out of proportion to the interests at stake. But this is not necessarily true either. States that perceive each other all too correctly also go to war. For example, it was while Neville Chamberlain misperceived the nature of Hitler's aims that Britain tried to appease him. Once the prime minister's perceptions had been proved erroneous by events, however, and he saw Hitler for what he really was, Britain declared war on Germany. The British prime minister's incorrect perception of Hitler and his attempts to come to an understanding thus avoided conflict for several years, giving Nazi Germany time to build up its armed forces and expand its strategic position.[10] Had Chamberlain understood Hitler's aims earlier and risked war before Germany strengthened its military and expanded its territory, the world might have been spared a war—or, at least, a long war.

During World War II, President Franklin Roosevelt, in characteristic American wartime fashion, focused U.S. policy on Germany's defeat and a total victory. Once the war would be over, "normalcy" would be restored. Roosevelt was confident he could win the Russian leader's trust and cooperation. Typical of the American approach that to win a friend one had to be a friend, the president simply projected his domestic experience. At home he dealt constantly with other politicians; as a democratic politician, socialized in the arts of negotiation and compromise, he believed that all problems were solvable. Stalin was just another politician, and, as reasonable men, he and Stalin could compromise differences and avoid conflict. But Stalin was a product of a different political culture. While Roosevelt was optimistic about the future, as were the majority of Americans, Stalin's policy was based upon the assumption of the inherent antagonism between capitalism and Soviet socialism.

The irony was terrific. While Roosevelt basically viewed Stalin as a Russian Roosevelt, Stalin saw Roosevelt as a capitalist Stalin! To Stalin, the president was the leader of an imperialist state, a tool of Wall Street. To Stalin, there was no fundamental difference between Roosevelt and Hitler, also a leader of a capitalist state. No real distinctions between Nazi fascism and American democracy existed. All capitalist states were believed to be hostile; Nazi Germany was simply the most extreme capitalist state. After Germany's defeat, the United States would take its place, and the conflict of the two social systems would continue. Thus, Stalin dismissed all of the president's professions of peace and good will. Capitalist leaders, he *knew*, possessed no such feelings for the Soviet Union. They were merely using words of good intentions to lull the Soviets into relaxing their guard. Roosevelt—and Churchill—were "adversaries who would do unto him approximately what he would do unto them, assuming they got the opportunity." [11]

Had Roosevelt understood that he and Stalin held opposite conceptions of what the postwar world would be like, he might have advocated different policies opposing Stalin, and Truman might have resisted demobilizing U.S. military strength once the war was over. The enormous conventional power of the United States—it did not need to use the threat of the atom bomb—

could have provided political leverage that Stalin would have understood. Protests over Stalin's brutal "satellization" of Eastern Europe were disregarded as the Soviets, after Germany's defeat, established themselves in the center of Europe and then attempted to expand into Iran, Greece, and Turkey. It was President Truman's accurate perception of Soviet behavior, as exhibited in these events, that led to the Truman Doctrine and the containment policy.

Misperceptions thus ensured the occurrence of World War II and the cold war; probably neither was avoidable. *Correct perceptions by the two democracies finally led each to recognize the stakes at issue and take a firm stand.* Had they done so earlier, they would have been in a stronger position for their respective conflicts. But democracies appear reluctant to acknowledge that there are states that wish them ill. Rather than face the unpleasant fact that they confront enemies, it is more comforting to explain away enemies as unfortunate victims of past history (invasions, mistreatments), or to believe that no vital interests are threatened. In this connection, former president Nixon has observed the following about contemporary superpower summitry:

> Summit meetings between leaders of the United States and the Soviet Union have become essential if peace is to be preserved. Such meetings will contribute to the cause of peace, however, only if both leaders recognize that tensions between the two nations are due not to the fact that we do *not* understand each other but to the fact that we *do* understand that we have diametrically opposed ideological and geopolitical interests.... [T]he United States and the Soviet Union have one major goal in common: survival.... The purpose of summit meetings is to develop rules of engagement that could prevent our profound differences from bringing us into armed conflict that could destroy us both.[12]

That is why such meetings continue as the cold war fades.

Correcting Misperceptions

Thus, misperceptions can cause conflicts and possibly wars; they also can prevent states from recognizing emerging threats and acting to forestall them. How can such misperceptions be corrected? Of all the ways, disaster appears to be a chief one. Policy (as Chapter 10 revealed) tends to be incremental; what worked yesterday will work today and tomorrow. As long as a particular policy appears to be successful, it will not be questioned, even if circumstances change. Policy makers and bureaucracies, as already noted, see what they want to see and reject contrary evidence. It is only when policy fails disastrously that it tends to be reexamined. For example, Britain's appeasement policy appeared to be successful in avoiding another war until 1938; when events then demonstrated Germany would continue its expansion, British policy began to shift and oppose German moves. But by then it was too late to contain German expansion peacefully. As another example, the American-Soviet alliance during World War II began to come apart over Soviet control of Eastern Europe; postwar Soviet pressure on Iran, Greece, and Turkey shifted the relationship from recent allies to adversaries. President Roosevelt's efforts to establish an era of Soviet-American cooperation after Germany's defeat lay shattered. It was the collapse of the wartime expectations that led to the containment policy. Soon spilling over into an anticommunism crusade, it lasted for two decades—until the Vietnam disaster.

Yet despite this anticommunism, the possibility of committing mutual suicide had already led the United States and Soviet Union to initiate arms control negotiations and agreements even before Vietnam. In the early 1970s, these were extended to the central strategic systems of the two superpowers as President Nixon pursued a policy of détente toward the Soviet Union and rapprochement with China. Perhaps no better proof exists that even before the occurrence of disaster, perceptions can and often do change as circumstances change. Nuclear weapons, precisely because of their awesome nature and the certainty that their use would be catastrophic, have been a greater teacher of reality.

During the 1950s, Nixon had been a militant anti-Communist. In the 1970s, he pursued a flexible, nonideological, pragmatic balance-of-power foreign policy. Moreover, China's revolutionary and anticapitalist posture and rhetoric did not stand in the way of improving relations with the United States when the Soviet Union seemed a growing threat. The philosophies of Marx and Mao were simply subordinated to the balance of power. In 1989, the most anti-Communist American president of four decades ended his years in office having endorsed his Soviet counterpart and his reform efforts, signed the INF treaty, and made major advances toward a 50 percent reduction in strategic arms.

And, *if* rhetoric turns into action, it is Gorbachev who has made perhaps the most startling declarations, once he decided that the Soviet Union's future as a superpower was in danger unless he could shake up the stagnant Soviet economy. His references to "mutual security" are a significant departure from past Soviet thinking about Soviet defense policies. The Soviet leader virtually admitted that in the past the Soviet search for military security had produced American feelings of insecurity and reactions which, in turn, jeopardized Soviet security. Thus, the original Soviet policy was counterproductive. Each power, the Soviet Union and the United States, he has said, needs to be more sensitive of the impact of its defense policy on the other. That would be novel for Moscow, whose constant, almost paranoid scramble for more security has in the past subscribed to the maxim that the more power gained, the greater Soviet security. Conversely, the less power and security the adversary had and felt, the better. Gorbachev's declaration thus represented "a major discontinuity in the Soviet way of thinking. . . . If the conceptual modification is implemented in practical Soviet defense policies its importance will be immense." [13] What was surprising was not only the emphasis on defense policy, but also the underlying willingness to admit that Soviet policies might be responsible for the conduct of other nations. This was simply unheard of. The collapse of détente I, according to Gorbachev's predecessors, was not attributable to the continued Soviet military buildup in the 1970s or to Soviet interventions in Angola, Ethiopia, and elsewhere; these activities were merely cited as pretexts by anti-Soviet U.S. cold warriors who wanted to torpedo détente. This Soviet admission of an action-reaction pattern may in fact be a prelude to a stabler détente II and an end to the cold war as Gorbachev's words are translated into basic policy changes.

BACK TO THE LEVELS OF ANALYSIS

All this being said, the perceptions of leaders cannot be divorced from the larger context. Before World War II British public opinion was pacifist, and the prime minister accurately reflected this feeling. Further indicating Britain's desire for peace, Churchill's warnings were ignored, and he did not become a member of the government until the war broke out; indeed, he did not become prime minister until after the initial disasters of the war. During that war, President Roosevelt's hopes and attitudes represented U.S. opinion. Most Americans wanted to believe that there were no basic conflicts between the United States and Russia. According to General Eisenhower: "The ordinary Russian seems to me to bear a marked similarity to what we call an 'average American.' " [14] How, given such views, could the United States have initiated an anti-Soviet policy against an ally who had borne the brunt of the fighting and whose wartime courage and endurance were much admired? The democratic nature of England in the late 1930s and the United States in 1945-1946 thus prevented these nations from formulating policies that would have contained their enemies more effectively. In short, the misperceptions of Chamberlain and Roosevelt have to be explained in terms of the larger social setting.

They also have to be explained in terms of their adversary's deceptive tactics, of taking only limited steps, each one of which appeared reasonable and legitimate in terms of security or Western principles of national self-determination, thereby catering to the democratic state's belief that no basic threat existed and that all problems were negotiable and resolvable. British and American policy makers may have preferred to believe that good relations were possible with Germany and the Soviet Union—in fact, the latter nations made it a point to continually assure the democratic states that they shared the desire for peaceful and harmonious relations.

Because the issue of perception cannot really be separated from the broader state system context, what are some of the key issues that policy makers' perceptions, bureaucratic and governmental politics, and public opinion must heed if they are to deal intelligently with the threats and opportunities all governments face in advancing their nation's interests?

Defining the National Interest

It should be fairly obvious by now that the notion of "national interest" is of little help analytically. No political leader, bureaucrat, legislator, or interest group spokesperson is likely to advocate a policy that is *against* the national interest; these individuals, to maximize the appeal of the policy solution they are advancing, wrap up their advocacy with the suggestion that their particular preferences are in the nation's best interests. There is no objectively defined national interest. While geography may instill in succeeding generations of policy makers similar ideas about how they should define their country's security interests in geographical terms—for example, czars and commissars have both shown an interest in Eastern Europe because of its importance for Russia's security—even these ideas tend to change as technology and other conditions, including especially domestic politics, change. By and large, even if the term "national interest" took into account any state's multiple interests, it would remain largely meaningless. The best that can be said for it is that this interest is whatever the government says it is. For example, Jimmy Carter supported SALT II; Ronald Reagan opposed it (although for most of his two terms he observed its terms).

American leaders in the nineteenth century consistently defined U.S. security in terms of hegemony over Latin America, or at least over Central America. Since the Sandinistas took control of the government in Nicaragua, a country of only 3 million people, does it constitute a threat to American security? Should it be overthrown because it considers itself an implacable foe of "U.S. imperialism" and has ties to Havana and Moscow? Or will it suffice to make sure that the Sandinistas do not export their revolution to their neighbors and that they commit themselves to not allowing a Soviet base to be built in their country from which the Soviet Union could threaten the United States (as in Cuba in 1962)? Clearly, there is considerable disagreement over whether Nicaragua constitutes a threat to the United States and if so, how much of a threat. On economic issues, is it a vital security interest to preserve the U.S. steel industry—at the cost of huge government subsidies—because steel is a key ingredient in war materiel? Or can the United States become dependent on cheaper steel imports, which in peacetime keep inflation down and provide consumers with less expensive goods than technologically lagging U.S. mills with highly paid workers could? Does U.S. prosperity require that the United States protect its markets and industries from "unfair" foreign competition or are free trade and competition in fact the best remedy for reviving American industries? Again, here there are many differences of opinion. And if the U.S. economic troubles are not turned around, which political commitments does it eliminate—in Latin America, Western Europe, the Persian Gulf, Middle East, or Asia? Such a debate would arouse great controversy.

While there are answers to all these questions, they are anything but clear in most cases. This would be so even if policy makers' parochial interests did not influence their perceptions and policy preferences. Normally, only in a crisis does the government appear united in its stance. But everyday policy decisions, security or economic, have to be forged from a set of diverse views and conflicting opinions.

Who Threatens These Interests?

It is not enough to define what a nation's interests are; it is also important to clarify who threatens them and how, or who may do so in the foreseeable future and under what conditions. Indeed, the two issues are inseparable, for the specific interests to be defended or advanced can be selected only in the context of specific relationships with other countries. In part, the answer stems from a potential or actual adversary's power. This power, as already noted, is hard to calculate because of the number of its components, the mixture of tangible and intangible elements, the fact that these components are rarely static, and the difficulties incurred in "adding" them up (see Chapter 7). Moreover, depending on the specific situation, only some elements of power are even relevant and applicable, while others are totally useless. But even more difficult than calculating another nation's power is calculating another state's intentions.

At the heart of the Reagan administration's initially hard anti-Soviet line and emphasis on large-scale rearmament was a judgment about Soviet intentions and the meaning of the Soviet military buildup. Thus, despite the quantifiable nature of weapons, such calculations may not by themselves tell us much more than that they exist. We must understand what their existence means. For example, what was the purpose of the enormous strategic and conventional military buildup begun by the Soviets in 1964 to catch up with the United States, behind which they had lagged so long? Was it to achieve parity militarily, as well as psychologically, and attain recognition equal to that of the United States? Was it undertaken because the Soviet Union needed larger forces to confront NATO to the west and China to the east? Was defense the primary motive for a country that had been invaded repeatedly throughout history? Or was the correct impression, widespread in the West, one of a new Soviet arsenal—including airlift and sealift capabilities developed over a decade and at huge cost—that was offensive and far larger than anything required for defense? Counting weapons, therefore, is not enough; more important is what people believe the weapons mean.

The question of intentions becomes even more difficult in the economic realm because it is America's allies who are the threat. Are America's economic problems largely the result of its own doing or the result of the unfair tactics of its allies in dumping goods on the international market and protecting their home markets? Are the Japanese, as some Americans charge, pursuing economic domination of world markets and doing so with the same energy, determination, and ruthlessness that they once sought by military victory over the United States? Or are the Japanese correct when they say that the United States' Japan-bashing is part of an effort to blame others for America's economic problems rather than accepting responsibility for them? Whatever the judgment, given the interdependent relations among the Western countries and their fierce competition economically, what should and can be done when they need one another politically and militarily?

What Is Domestically Feasible?

Whatever the rational and intelligent response to a particular foreign policy situation, domestic politics and opinion will determine how much maneuverability a government will have. A pacifist British public opinion and an isolationist mood in the United States during the 1930s meant that both governments were constrained in what they could do. It is not accidental that Churchill, who warned of the folly of appeasing Hitler, was out of power and out of favor during the "gathering storm." Nor is it accidental that President Roosevelt retreated back into passivity after his 1937 speech advising the democracies to quarantine dictators was met with a storm of criticism.

Similarly, during the cold war years the anti-Communist consensus limited the flexibility of U.S. foreign policy, such as recognizing Communist China. Vietnam dispersed this consensus into three belief systems: cold war internationalism, essentially the continuation of the old cold war consensus, which focused on the bipolar East-West struggle and saw security as the main issue of international politics; post-cold war internationalism, which focused on North-South issues and saw social and economic issues as primary; and semi-isolationism, which focused on domestic issues and viewed the Soviet Union as a minor threat (the first two belief systems are detailed in Table 11-1).[15]

The cold war internationalist position has been generally identified with the Republican party in the post-Vietnam era, the post-cold war internationalist position with the Democrats. These positions do not, of course, correspond perfectly, given differences within and between each party, and the related rivalry between the presidency, occupied by the Republicans from 1969 to 1989 (with the exception of the single term of Jimmy Carter), and the Congress, mainly controlled by the Democrats. Thus, conflict and controversy between the executive and legislative branches, influenced by the effects a policy may have on a party's fortunes in the next election (the next election being never more than two years away), has become the norm. Presidential leadership, once assumed, can no longer be taken for granted; legislative support, almost automatic for over two decades (except on Asian policy), is no longer assured. The use of force by presidents has come to be regarded especially critically by the Congress. "No more Vietnams" haunts this generation of Americans, much like "Munich" and "appeasement" haunted their predecessors. As the party that involved the United States militarily in Vietnam, the Democrats have been especially opposed to military interventions since that time.

By What Methods?

Even if policy makers agree on the aims they wish to pursue and mobilize legislative and public support, the question of how best to achieve these objectives remains and itself can become a matter of intense debate. For example, to avoid a threat to its security in its own backyard, should the United States overthrow the Nicaraguan government or contain it? Does opposing it only drive the Sandinistas into the arms of the Cubans and

Table 11-1 Two Foreign Policy Belief Systems

	Cold War Internationalism	*Post-Cold War Internationalism*
Nature of the international system		
Structure	Bipolar (and likely to remain so) Tight links between issues and conflicts	Complex and interdependent (and becoming more so) Moderate links between issues and conflicts
World order priorities	A world safe from aggression and terrorism is necessary precondition for dealing with other issues	International regimes for coping with a broad range of issues, with high priority on North-South ones
Conception of interdependence	Encompasses security issues ("domino theory")	Encompasses economic/social issues
Primary threats to the United States	Soviet and Soviet-sponsored aggression and terrorism Military imbalance (favoring Soviet Union) Soviet ability to engage in political coercion based on nuclear blackmail	North-South issues (for example, rich-poor gap) which threaten any prospects for world order International environmental problems Danger of nuclear war
Soviet Union		
Nature of the system	Model totalitarian state	Great power
Driving force of foreign policy	Aggressive expansionism	Seeks parity with United States Defensiveness (exaggerated view of defense needs may create further tensions)
Appraisal of recent foreign policies	Highly successful	Moderately unsuccessful
Soviet-American relations		
Nature of the conflict	Genuine conflicts of interest Largely zero-sum	Some real conflicts of interest but exaggerated by hard-liners on both sides Largely non-zero-sum
Appraisal of détente	A dangerous delusion	Some useful first steps
Appraisal of SALT process	Skeptical; dangerous as conducted in the past	Some useful first steps

Table 11-1—Continued

	Cold War Internationalism	Post-Cold War Internationalism
Primary dangers of war	Military imbalance will lead Soviets to threaten vital U.S. and Western interests Recent successes will make Soviets more aggressive, perhaps recklessly so	Uncontrolled arms race Both sides equally likely to misperceive other's actions, leading to unwanted war
Linkages	Vital to link issues	Decouple issues
Third World		
Role in present international system	Primary target of Soviet and Soviet-inspired subversion and aggression	Primary source of unresolved social/economic problems that must be resolved to create a viable world order
Primary source of Third World problems	Subversion and aggression by Soviet Union and its proxies (Cuba, Libya, etc.) Left-wing authoritarian governments	Legacies of western colonialism and imperialism Right-wing authoritarian governments Structural flaws in the international system
Primary U.S. obligations	Help provide security from aggression and terrorism, but on a selective basis (to strategically important ones: oil producers, etc.)	Economic and other forms of nonmilitary assistance Play a leading role in structural systemic changes (new international economic order, etc.)
Prescription for American foreign policy	Rebuild military strength to regain a position of parity with the Soviet Union Rebuild collective security system Active U.S. role in the world is a necessary but not sufficient condition to create a stable and just world order	Stabilize relations with the Soviet Union in order to free energy and resources for dealing with North-South and other high-priority issues Active U.S. role in the world is a necessary but not sufficient condition to create a stable and just world order

SOURCE: Ole R. Holsti and James N. Rosenau, "Consensus Lost: Consensus Regained? Foreign Policy Beliefs of American Leaders, 1976-1980," *International Studies Quarterly* (December 1986): 380-381.

Russians? Will more friendly relations attract the Sandinistas away from Havana and Moscow and move it in to a more nonaligned position? Will American security vis-à-vis the Soviet Union be enhanced by a unilateral nuclear arms buildup or arms control? Should an arms control effort place ceilings on certain weapons, greatly reduce each side's arsenal across the board, or even seek the elimination of all strategic nuclear weapons? Should arms control be pursued by diplomatic negotiations and formal agreements, or by each side taking unilateral steps on the expectation that the other will reciprocate?

A look at how the "game is played" follows.

For Review

1. Why is the perception of nations, political elites, specific bureaucracies, and individual leaders so important in the conduct of foreign policy?
2. What are some of the causes of their misperceptions?
3. How do the correct perceptions of policy makers affect the likelihood of conflict and war?
4. How can misperceptions be corrected?
5. How do perceptions relate to the key issues all policy makers face?

Notes

1. Seweryn Bialer, " 'New Thinking' and Soviet Foreign Policy," *Survival*, July/August 1988, 303.
2. George F. Kennan, *American Diplomacy 1900-1950* (Chicago: University of Chicago Press, 1951), 111-112.
3. John G. Stoessinger, *Nations in Darkness* (New York: Random House, 1971), 5; and Stoessinger, *Why Nations Go to War* (New York: St. Martin's Press, 1974).
4. Henry A. Kissinger, *Nuclear Weapons and Foreign Policy* (New York: Harper & Row, 1957), 317-320.
5. Robert A. Divine, *The Illusion of Neutrality* (Chicago: University of Chicago Press, 1962), 280-281.
6. Gaddis Smith, *Dean Acheson* (New York: Cooper Square, 1972), 414.
7. Ibid., 423.
8. Gaddis Smith, "The Shadow of John Foster Dulles," *Foreign Affairs* (January 1974): 403-408. Also see Townsend Hoopes, *The Devil and John Foster Dulles* (Boston: Little, Brown, 1973).
9. David J. Finlay, Ole R. Holsti, and Richard R. Fagen, *Enemies in Politics* (New York: Rand McNally, 1967), 25-96.
10. Williamson Murray, *The Change in the European Balance of Power, 1938-1939* (Princeton, N.J.: Princeton University Press, 1984).

11. William Taubman, *Stalin's American Policy* (New York: Norton, 1982), 39.

12. Richard Nixon, "Superpower Summitry," *Foreign Affairs* (Fall 1985): 1.

13. Bialer, " 'New Thinking,' " 298.

14. Dwight D. Eisenhower, *Crusade in Europe* (New York: Doubleday, 1952), 457, 473-474.

15. Ole R. Holsti and James N. Rosenau, "Consensus Lost: Consensus Regained?: Foreign Policy Beliefs of American Leaders, 1976-1980," *International Studies Quarterly* (December 1986): 380-381.

Part Four

HOW TO PLAY—
POLITICALLY,
MILITARILY,
ECONOMICALLY

CHAPTER 12

The Balance
of Terror

BARGAINING AND CONFLICT RESOLUTION

How states live together and on what terms is the product of diplomacy or bargaining, which decides "who gets what, when and how." Bargaining encompasses three tasks: (1) defining a state's interests; (2) communicating them to the party or parties with whom conflicting interests are to be negotiated; and (3) conducting the actual process of negotiation.[1] Such negotiations may be conducted by chiefs of governments at summit meetings, professional diplomats, or, on certain occasions, military officers or special emissaries. They may be bilateral, between two states, or multilateral, among three or more states. They may be carried on publicly in an open forum and in the glare of constant publicity and media exposure, or secretly and privately (although in democracies the results will be made public and will usually need public approval). Finally, such negotiations may be formal, and include the officials who are trying to negotiate a compromise between conflicting positions using face-to-face meetings or messages transmitted between governments by ambassadors. Or they may be tacit—that is, when governments talk to one another indirectly, sending each other signals about how vital an issue is to them and frequently informing an adversary not to interfere (such as by calling up the reserves or placing troops on alert or moving them to another country or even fighting). Thus, bargaining is going on between states not only when diplomats gather and talk to one another but also when no formal meetings take place.

An example of formal negotiations was the Reagan administration's bargaining over intermediate nuclear forces (INF) in the early 1980s. A few years earlier the Soviets had deployed SS-20 missiles within the Soviet Union to cover targets in Western Europe. Then during the Carter years the countries in Western Europe asked the United States for a similar deployment of U.S. missiles to neutralize the SS-20s, which they perceived to be a means of political intimidation. One of the proposed American missiles, the Pershing II, was capable of reaching Soviet territory. Moscow vehemently opposed such a counterdeployment, arguing that an overall military, including nuclear, balance already existed in Europe when British and French nuclear forces were counted, and that the American missiles would upset this balance. Subsequent negotiations failed, however, because the Soviets insisted that only they could deploy modern INFs; they would not accept even a single American missile as they, despite their claim of an existing European balance, continued to emplace more SS-20s. Moreover, they threatened a series of reprisals if the United States deployed any missiles, most notably to break off all arms control negotiations.

Many Europeans, already nervous about talk out of Washington about "nuclear war fighting" instead of deterrence and some of the harshest denunciations of the Soviet Union and communism since the cold war began, took to the streets in mass demonstrations against the plans of the U.S. and West European governments to balance the Soviet missiles. The fear of a new cold war, even nuclear war, was high and the Soviets sought to exploit these fears. In the United States, the Reagan administration was faced with the antinuclear freeze movement. When the first U.S. missiles were deployed nevertheless, the Soviets walked out of the arms control negotiations, saying they would not return until all U.S. missiles were withdrawn. Thus, the Soviets raised the pressure on the United States and its allies, testing NATO's will and waiting to see whether the Western allies would change their position and accept the Soviet one, as European governments continued to face huge mass demonstrations opposing the NATO position.

But the United States and its allies persisted. The position of the Reagan administration, initially rather hostile to arms control negotiations and bent on launching a huge unilateral rearmament program, was that if Moscow wished to avoid the deployment of U.S. intermediate nuclear forces, neither superpower should deploy INF. It did not expect Moscow to accept its "0-0" proposal, however, because it meant the elimination of Soviet missiles that the United States had not yet matched. But 0-0 sounded good and, it was hoped, it would calm the protests and place the blame for the U.S. deployment on the Soviets. If they had accepted 0-0, the U.S. reaction would not have been necessary. Two developments led the Soviets to eventually change their minds, however, and accept not only 0-0 but also the elimination of all intermediate *and* short-range missiles on a global basis. One was Gorbachev's succession to power and his priority of reforming the Soviet economy. The other was Gorbachev's desire to relax heightened tensions with the United States, and to avoid a new potentially expensive arms race in space stemming from the additional Reagan plan for a Strategic Defense Initiative (SDI). Not only did the Soviets return to all arms control negotiations, but they accepted virtually the entire range of U.S. proposals on INF.

The administration had "hung tough." Initially, probably not even caring about making a deal, it had avoided any appearance of eagerness. Then it had insisted on the U.S. deployment in Europe and had strengthened the U.S. bargaining position in two ways: first, by deploying, among other missiles, Pershing IIs, and second, by announcing SDI. That really worried the Soviets because not only would a new arms race divert enormous resources needed domestically, but they lagged behind in the very technology at issue. Thus, the Reagan style of bargaining demonstrated elements of classic hard bargaining—more traditionally a Soviet characteristic—and, created assets that the Soviets considered threatening, thereby giving them the incentive to be more compromising and to settle on terms favorable to the United States. SDI was particularly instrumental in bringing Moscow back to the bargaining table. Moscow was eager to conclude an INF agreement as a first step toward a strategic arms reduction in which it would offer a radical reduction in the Soviet forces that worried Washington in return for a deal on SDI. Thus, hard bargaining, patience, a refusal to bow to public pressures to be more conciliatory, deployment of weapons (just as Moscow) for political bargaining—not military use—and use of SDI as a potentially powerful bargaining chip for a future trade-off in strategic arms negotiations (except that Reagan liked SDI and refused to trade) paid handsome dividends.

An example of tacit diplomacy[2] occurred in 1965 when the United States intervened in Vietnam to prevent the loss of South Vietnam to the North. By destroying enemy forces, or at least by inflicting heavy and sustained casualties on the enemy, the United States hoped to weaken the Communist side and to strengthen South Vietnam. Then either the North Vietnamese would finally call off the war or, if negotiations took place, the United States and South Vietnam would have more leverage. Thus, the fighting itself was the bargaining. And although there was no visible or explicit negotiating—U.S. diplomats did not meet with North Vietnamese diplomats at some neutral spot in Switzerland—negotiations were going on constantly. North Vietnam had already stated its expectation of unifying Vietnam. Any solution short of taking over the South was unacceptable. The United States rejected that solution; it intervened massively to prevent unification as the South Vietnamese army failed. It expected an improved position on the battlefield to be reflected in the terms of any final settlement. Formal talks are only a minor part of such tacit negotiations, if they occur at all. Note that the issue for Washington was not that of peace; it could have had peace at anytime—on North Vietnam's terms. The critical issue was peace on what terms. Determined to protect South Vietnam, it decided to fight. The fighting was not an alternative to peacetime diplomacy; it was a violent continuation of the bargaining process.

Whether diplomacy is explicit or tacit, resolution of a conflict does not necessarily always take the form of compromise. In fact, there are at least four kinds of conflict resolution: (1) that in which both states lose, (2) that in which neither state wins, (3) that in which one state wins everything, and (4) that in which both states are partial winners and partial losers in a compromise agreement.

Loss by Both States

The best example of the first kind of conflict resolution is the concept of deterrence. The deterring side seeks to prevent an adversary from initiating the use of force by making such action much more costly in the calculations of the would-be aggressor than any possible benefits. In the context of the U.S.-Soviet conflict and their possession of nuclear weapons, the deterrer seeks to prevent the opponent from attacking by announcing, in effect, "You may kill me if you attack me, but I will kill you before I die." Thus, deterrence is based on the ability to retaliate even after the enemy's first strike. Mutual deterrence is said to be equivalent to mutual suicide. The United States even calls its capacity to destroy the Soviet Union an "assured destruction" capability. The reciprocal capacity is called "mutual assured destruction," or MAD—probably not a bad name for a strategy in which everyone loses.

Victory for Neither State

When neither party can win, the conflict resolution is called a *stalemate*. It can occur under a variety of conditions: when both parties have exhausted themselves in the struggle, when both are unwilling to invest greater resources in a struggle that is not critical, when both are unwilling to escalate because the risks are too great, when a third party (perhaps one or both of the superpowers or the United Nations) intervenes and calls a halt to the conflict, or when new problems and priorities arise.

In the Korean War the United States, unwilling to escalate the war by attacking China, sought instead to exhaust the Chinese through a war of attrition. In Vietnam the American strategy of physical attrition was designed to exact so heavy a price in bombing damage of North Vietnam and battlefield deaths that at some point the North Vietnamese would stop trying to take over the South. In Korea a stalemate resulted when the battle lines were drawn along the thirty-eighth parallel, approximately where the war had started. In Vietnam, however, U.S. strategy failed.

Victory for One State

Probably the most obvious form of conflict resolution is a clear-cut victory for one side. It occurs when one side is much stronger than the other, or the issue no longer seems important enough to cause the other side to take great risks to defend its position. Diplomatically, a complete victory for one side is relatively rare. The Munich settlement of 1938 is one of the most infamous examples. Germany won a total victory over Britain and France by threatening war. The American victory over the Soviet Union in the Cuban missile crisis of 1962 is another example. President Kennedy did not overtly threaten war; the possibility was inherent in the confrontation. A wartime illustration is the allied victory over Germany, Italy, and Japan in World War II. Other examples include the Soviet interventions to crush the Hungarian rebellion in 1956 and the Czechoslovakian uprisings in 1968, and the Vietnamese Communists' defeat of France in 1954 and of the United States two decades later.

Compromise

Compromise is probably the most common form of conflict resolution. Both states win part of what they want and give up part of what they want. The two sides may "split the difference," or one side may gain more than the other. The settlement is likely to reflect the perceived power relationship of the two states, their respective willingness to run risks and make sacrifices, or the importance each attaches to the issue in dispute. A compromise may be easier to achieve among states friendly to one another than among adversaries; a higher degree of mutual trust may be the critical ingredient.

The search for compromise, especially among adversaries, may be promoted by the use of force (as in the Egyptian-Syrian attack on Israel in 1973), the threat of force (as in the conflict between the United States and the Soviet Union over Berlin in 1948-1949), the offer of rewards (as when the United States offered North Vietnam in 1973 the withdrawal of American forces, continued Communist control of captured areas in South Vietnam, and U.S. economic aid), or a mixture of the proverbial sticks and carrots (most agreements).

NUCLEAR REVOLUTION AND BALANCE OF POWER

Expansion of Violence

A nation's military strength is an important component of its power, for, as the English political observer, E. H. Carr wrote, "War lurks in the background of international politics just as a revolution lurks in the background of domestic policies." [3] Ironically, democracy, which was expected to abolish war, multiplied the importance of this component many times over. One democratic assumption used to be that only irresponsible rulers were belligerent; for them wars were merely an enjoyable and profitable "blood sport." In this view, it was the people who paid the price of wars with their lives and their taxes. If peace-loving people could hold their rulers accountable, wars would be eliminated and peace secured. Democracy would then bring an era of good will—of individual freedom and social justice at home, of peace and harmony abroad. The world would be safe for democracy because it would be democratic. Government by the people, of the people, and for the people would ensure perpetual peace. [4]

Instead, democracy became tied to nationalism, and the two gave birth to the "nation in arms." Once people were freed from feudal bondage and granted the right to some form of self-government, they came to equate their own well-being with that of their nation, and it seemed only reasonable that the nation should be able to call on them—the citizens—for defense. Not surprisingly, it was the 1789 French Revolution that brought people into contact with the nation-state. One result was the first system of universal military service. When supreme loyalty of the citizens' was to the nation, the nation in arms followed logically. Democracy and nationalism thus enabled France to mobilize fully for total war and destroy its opponents completely.

This change was one reason why the Congress of Vienna in 1815 reacted with such horror to the revolution, which had unleashed mass passions and all-out war. Previous wars had been restrained because men had identified not with nations but with smaller units, such as like towns or manors, or with universal entities, such as embodied in the Roman Catholic church. The armies of the *ancien régime* were composed largely of mercenaries and lowly elements of society such as debtors, vagrants, and criminals—men who were animated neither by love of country nor by hatred of the enemy, but who fought because they were paid or compelled to do so. States lacked sufficient economic resources to maintain sizable armies. Indeed, their tactics were determined by the need to limit expenses. And to keep casualties low the emphasis was on maneuver rather than on pitched battle. The revolution enlisted popular support, however, and mass armies aroused by nationalism began to fight in defense of their countries. Frenchman Bertrand de Jouvenel described this "new era in military history" as "the era of cannon fodder." [5]

It remained only for the Industrial Revolution to produce the instruments that enabled men to kill one another in greater numbers. Modern military technology brought total war to its fullest realization.[6] Mass armies were equipped with mass-produced weapons that were ever more destructive, making it possible for nations to inflict progressively greater damage on one another in shorter and shorter periods. In the seventeenth century, it took thirty years for the states of central western Europe to slaughter half the population of central Europe. In the second decade of the twentieth century, it took only four years for them to bleed one another into a state of exhaustion and, for some, collapse. But the atomic bomb, and especially the hydrogen bomb, made it possible to inflict catastrophic damage in minutes, or at most hours, that previously had taken years, and this catastropic damage was tantamount to near destruction.

Destructive Nature of Nuclear Weapons

With the ascendancy of strategic air power and nuclear weapons, human beings had then the means with which to accomplish their own extermination. Cities—indeed, whole nations—could be laid waste in a matter of hours, if not minutes. The effectiveness of that kind of strategic air power against a highly urbanized and industrialized society is no longer a matter of dispute. Nuclear bombs are so destructive that they make World War II bombing attacks appear trivial by comparison. Atomic bombs, such as those dropped on Hiroshima and Nagasaki, were surpassed in destructive power within a few years by the new hydrogen bombs. Kilotons were replaced by megatons (1 megaton equals 1 million tons of TNT). A single U.S. Strategic Air Command B-52 bomber can carry 25 megatons of explosive power—or 12.5 times the explosive power of all bombs dropped during World War II, including the two atomic bombs! [7]

Physical Effects and 'Nuclear Winter.' A nuclear explosion has four phyphysical effects: blast, fire, immediate radiation, and long-term radiation.

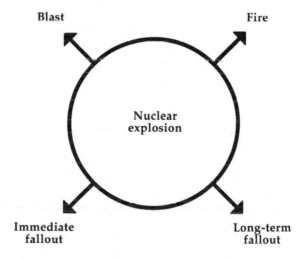

The blast, or shock wave, is the almost solid wall of air pressure produced by an explosion, creating a hurricane-type wind. The blast from a low-altitude bomb exploding in a city will collapse all wooden buildings within six miles of ground zero for a 1-megaton bomb, within fourteen miles for a 10-megaton bomb, and within thirty miles for a 100-megaton bomb. For brick buildings, the figures for the same bombs are four, nine, and eighteen miles, respectively, and for sturdier buildings, the distance ranges from three to twelve miles.

The thermal impact of a bomb can be heightened by a higher-altitude explosion or airburst. The heat generated by a 1-megaton bomb is tremendous, producing second-degree burns of the skin up to nine miles from ground zero; a 10-megaton bomb has the same effect up to twenty-four miles; a 100-megaton bomb up to seventy miles.[8] Furthermore, the heat in most instances would ignite wooden houses and other combustible objects (from plastics and furniture in homes to gas lines and furnaces) over the same range. World War II demonstrated that the real danger from fire, even when started with ordinary incendiary bombs, is the fire storm.[9] In a fire storm the intense heat from the fire rises, heating the air in turn. As the difference in pressure between the hot and colder air sucks in fresh oxygen to feed the hungry flames, the process builds in intensity. Air rushes in at ever greater speeds until wind velocity surpasses gale force. The flames, whipped by the wind and fed further by the gas, oil, and other incendiary materials of the homes and streets of the burning city, leap upward, stabbing high into the air, enveloping the stricken area. Everything burns in this tomb of heat and flame. There is no escape. Those who have not yet been crushed in their shelters are asphyxiated by lack of oxygen or by carbon monoxide poisoning; if they seek to escape into the burning streets, their lungs are seared, and their bodies, exposed to the intense heat, burst into flame. During the 1943 attack on Hamburg, the fire storm caused a ground temperature of 1,400 degrees Fahrenheit. Indeed, near the center of the fire storm the temperature exceeded 2,200 degrees Fahrenheit.

The third and fourth effects of a nuclear explosion, the radiation impact, can be maximized by a surface burst or a low-altitude explosion. The resulting fireball—a large, rapidly expanding sphere of hot gases that produces intense heat—scoops up debris and converts it into radioactive material. The fireball of a 10-megaton bomb has a diameter of six miles. The heavier particles of debris fall back to earth within the first few hours. Besides the immediate radiation in the area of explosion, longer-term, lighter particles "fall out" during the following days and weeks over an area the size of which depends on the magnitude of the explosion, the surface over which the explosion occurs, and meteorological conditions. The American 15-megaton thermonuclear explosion of 1954 in the Pacific Ocean caused substantial contamination over an area of 7,000 square miles (equivalent to the size of New Jersey). Under more "favorable" conditions, the fallout could have covered an area of 100,000 square miles (equivalent to the areas of New Jersey, New York, and Pennsylvania).

Fallout can emit radiation for days, months, and even years. The power of this radiation depends on the amount absorbed by humans and animals.[10] A dose of 100-200 roentgens causes radiation sickness, a combination of weakness, nausea, and vomiting that is not fatal, although it can result in disability. At 200 roentgens, radiation becomes very dangerous: disability is certain, and death can come within a month. The possibility of death increases until, at 500 roentgens, it is certain for 50 percent of those exposed to the radiation. Above 600 roentgens, the number of deaths continues to mount, and deaths occur more rapidly.[11] Radiation also has two other effects: cancer and genetic transmutations that may affect subsequent generations.

Considering the overwhelmingly destructive character of a single nuclear weapon and the large number of them that the United States and the Soviet Union possess, a coordinated nuclear attack on either power's major urban and industrial centers would be catastrophic, reducing everything to rubble and leaving the population dead or injured, with little hope of help. Most hospitals, doctors, nurses, drugs, and blood plasma would be destroyed, as would the machinery for the processing and refrigeration of food and the purification of water. Medical "disaster planning" for a nuclear war is meaningless. Not surprisingly, nuclear war has been called "the last epidemic." In addition, there would be no transportation left to take survivors out of the smoldering ruins and into the countryside; most, if not all, of the fuel would have burned up. Estimates of casualties in such a coordinated urban strike range from 30 percent to 90 percent of the population, depending upon the yield of the bombs, the heights at which they were exploded, the weather, civilian protection, and preparations for coping with the aftermath of such an attack.[12]

If cities are the main targets in a nuclear war, Soviet premier Nikita Khrushchev's remark that the survivors will envy the dead appears all too true. A 1977 Department of Defense study estimated that 155 million to 165 million Americans would be killed if all explosions were detonated at ground level and no civil defense measures existed. If half the explosions were airbursts, the casualties would be reduced to 122 million.[13] Other studies show equally high figures, although some differ by 20 million fatalities or so. Even "low" figures such as 55 million dead are staggering and unprecedented in the history of human existence, particularly when it is recalled that these are only the casualties that will occur immediately and within thirty days of the attack (see Figure 12-1). Deaths occurring afterward from injury, radiation, starvation, and general economic chaos are not included. Total fatality figures would be much higher.

Today, we are more aware of some of the side effects of nuclear explosions. In 1983 some scientists issued a warning that nuclear war may destroy the ozone layer in the stratosphere.[14] This layer protects all living things from ultraviolet solar radiation, which destroys protein molecules. In addition to death, destruction, and radiation, therefore, extensive ozone depletion could destroy the food chain of plants and animals upon which humans and animal life depend for survival. As if this were not sufficient, these scientists also concluded that fires from large-scale attacks on Soviet and American cities in a nuclear war would create so much smoke that it would filter out sunlight, thereby creating a "nuclear winter." The Northern hemisphere would be plunged into darkness by plumes of dust and soot suspended in the stratosphere; this would cause extensive freezing of the earth's surface, including lakes and rivers, even during the summer, leading to the extinction of a major portion of plant and animal life. Such a freeze might last weeks, months, possibly even years. The implications of a nuclear winter are twofold: (1) even if the initiator of a nuclear war could launch a surprise attack and destroy most of the opponent's retaliatory capability, the first-strike state would be the victor only briefly because the nuclear winter would soon cripple it as well; and (2) because the nuclear winter would spread from the Northern to the South-

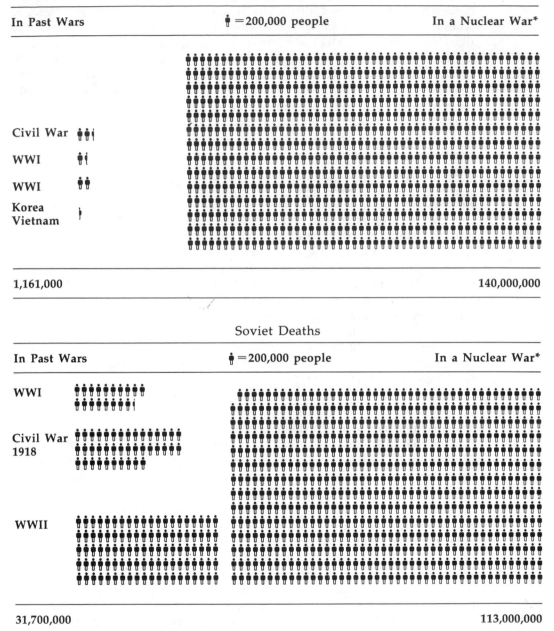

Figure 12-1 American and Soviet Deaths in Past Wars and in a Projected Nuclear War

ern hemisphere, the human race could become extinct. Scientists continue to debate whether in fact nuclear war would unleash such a deep freeze and how long it would last. But clearly the environmental effects of a nuclear war can no longer be considered secondary to the results of blast, fire, and radiation.

Psychological Effects. The psychological impact upon the survivors will be as devastating as the physical destruction. The elimination of a nation's largest cities, the deaths of more than 100 million of its citizens, and the wrecking of industries, communications, and transportation all would undermine the confidence of those who survived. A nation in ruins is not likely to retain its *élan vital* or entertain optimistic expectations for the future. It took Europe, especially France, more than forty years to recover from the psychological wounds of World War I and the loss of a generation on the battlefields. A quicker recovery after World War II was brought about primarily by extensive infusions of American economic aid. European losses then are minor compared with those incurred in a nuclear attack. Not only cities but the very fabric of social life would be destroyed. Henry Kissinger noted in the late 1950s:

> Any society operates through confidence in an orderly succession of events, either natural or social. A catastrophe is an interruption in what has come to be considered natural. The panic it often produces is the reflection of an inability to react to an unexpected situation and attempt to flee as rapidly as possible into a familiar and, therefore, predictable environment. If a familiar environment remains, some confidence can be restored. Most natural catastrophes can be dealt with, because they affect only a very small geographic area or a very small proportion of the population. The remainder of the society can utilize its machinery or cooperative effort to come to the assistance of the stricken area. Indeed, such action tends to reinforce the cohesiveness of a society, because it becomes a symbol of its value and efficiency. The essence of the catastrophe produced by an all-out thermonuclear war, however, is the depth of the dislocation it produces and the consequent impossibility of escaping into familiar relationships. When all relationships, or even most relationships, have to be reconstituted, society as we know it today will have been fundamentally transformed.[15]

Nuclear Impact on the Balance of Power

The impact of this awesome power on the conduct of international politics has been revolutionary.[16] Before 1945 war was still considered a rational instrument of policy, despite the rapidly increasing costs of modern warfare. States usually preferred to accept these costs rather than submit. Nuclear weapons, however, endanger the very substance of national life. Rather than helping to preserve civilization, the new instruments of violence promise to destroy it through the "assured destruction" of society. What possible goal could be "worth" the cost of self-immolation? How could a nation defend its political independence and territorial integrity if, in the very act of defense, it could be sacrificing itself? Nuclear war can know no victors; all the contestants will be losers. *Total wars may have been compatible with weapons of limited destructive capacity, but they are incompatible with "absolute weapons."*

The conclusion to be drawn from this general principle is that the main function of strategic military strength in the nuclear age is *deterrence* of an all-out attack. Deterrence protects a nation's security by preventing an attack rather than by defending the nation after an attack. The opponent is threatened with such massive retaliation that it dare not attack. The assumption is that, faced with the risk of virtual suicide, the enemy will desist. Mutual deterrence between two states, each seeking to protect its own security interests, thus becomes a matter of conflict resolution. "I won't destroy you, if you don't destroy me" is the offer of each side to the other. "We shall both lose if you attack me because I shall retaliate" is the answer.

In this extraordinary situation the role of nuclear power is that it is *not* to be used. Its primary value is in peacetime; if war erupts, it will have failed. The decisive test of arms is no longer vanquishing the enemy in battle; it is not having to fight at all. Furthermore, deterrence must be perpetual. There can be no margin for error. The frequency of war throughout history suggests how often deterrence failed. But because no weapon was so destructive that failure spelled extinction, such mistakes were not irreparable. The critical issue for the military was not whether it could prevent the outbreak of hostilities but whether it could win on the battlefield. This is no longer true. The superpowers today possess overwhelming power yet are completely vulnerable to attack and destruction. Thus, modern nuclear warfare would be irrational. Nuclear technology has so vastly augmented the scope of violence and destruction that total war can destroy the very nation that wages it and can do so in a matter of hours, not years.

In sum, the balancing of power historically has had two purposes: (1) protection of individual states and (2) protection of the state system as a whole. Peace has not been the chief aim. When states have been secure, peace has followed; when states have not been secure, they have gone to war. The philosophy of "peace at any price" has been rejected by states. But nuclear weapons have changed all that; security can no longer be given priority over peace. Security and peace have become virtually identical. The deterrent function of the balance has therefore become supreme. To fight a war—a total war—is no longer feasible.

U.S. ARMS CONTROL DOCTRINE

Rationale

For a state to deter its opponent, it must have the forces to launch a massive retaliation. Before World War II, states normally had military forces with which they hoped to prevent enemy attack, but these forces were never nearly as strong as the forces that could be mobilized if war actually broke out. Since war was not fatal, there was no reason to keep large and expensive forces continuously ready. Plowshares were to be converted into swords after the attack. This attitude was particularly prevalent in the United States. Protected by two oceans and thus not subject to invasion or even air attack, it had time to mobilize its vast power after it entered a war. But nuclear deterrence requires peacetime readiness of all the forces required for retaliation if an enemy attack occurs. If deterrence is to be permanent, the enemy must never doubt that it would be committing suicide should it strike first.

The need for a wartime offensive capability is thus constant and requires unfailing concern with effective delivery systems. This is a difficult problem because of the rapid technological changes that have occurred every few years since 1945. These changes have become critical in determining the stability of the nuclear balance of power. Even the early nuclear delivery systems tended to destabilize the postwar equilibrium because of the ability of fast bombers to execute surprise attacks. It is true, of course, that even before the development of high-speed bombers surprise attack had been possible. The Germans had achieved it against the Soviets in 1941, despite the large-scale movement of troops to Poland that it had necessitated, and the Japanese had been highly successful at Pearl Harbor a few months later. The speed of postwar bombers, however, made surprise attack even more feasible, particularly since it would no longer have to be preceded by massive troop or ship movements.

Although during the first two decades of the cold war the United States sought to deter a Soviet attack by threatening to drop enough bombs to virtually wipe the Soviet Union off the map, this threat would have been meaningless if most American bombers could have been destroyed in a surprise attack. The surviving bombers would then not have been able to retaliate with sufficient destructiveness. Moreover, not all of them would have had enough fuel to reach their targets. Soviet fighters and ground-to-air missiles, alerted for the arrival of those bombers that did reach Soviet territory, would have been able to shoot down many, if not most. The few that did manage to penetrate Soviet defenses might no longer have been able to wreak catastrophic damage. Indeed, the level of damage might have been acceptable to Soviet leaders if it meant the elimination of their deadliest enemy.

The vulnerability of bombers to a nuclear Pearl Harbor thus rendered the balance of power very unstable because of the enormous advantages gained by the side that struck the initial blow. Possessing only bombs was insufficient to ensure that war would not result. The possibility of eliminating the opponent's retaliatory bombers—bombers above ground being considered "soft" targets—constituted a powerful incentive to attack. The consequent balance was therefore a delicate one.

What conditions might instigate an opponent's first strike against one's own retaliatory force? And what could be done to prevent such an attack and "stabilize" mutual deterrence? [17] These questions preoccupied students of arms control in the late 1950s and 1960s. Proponents of arms control rejected the feasibility of general disarmament and assumed that neither conflicts among states nor nuclear weapons would be abolished. Instead, the best hope for earthly salvation seemed to lie in the "control" of armaments. In a competitive state system, deterrence was recognized as the only feasible policy. It had to be improved, however, to be made "safe."

Preemptive and Preventive Strikes.   Arms control thus supplemented the more traditional defense policies, as its aim was identical: to protect the national security by deterring war. Whereas disarmament stressed the reduction of a nation's military capability, either completely or partially, arms control emphasized the elimination of American and Soviet incentives to strike first. Two presuppositions underlay arms control: (1) despite the continuation of their political conflict, both nuclear powers shared a *common interest in avoiding nuclear war,* and (2) both possessed delivery systems that raised tensions by providing a strong and *independent incentive* for a first strike.[18] Of paramount importance is hitting first because, in the nuclear age, to come in second is to lose. Policy makers thus might be tempted to launch a first strike.

It is useful here to recall the first law of preservation in the state system: Be suspicious. One side's gain—and any proposal by a potential adversary is assumed to have advantages for itself—is usually considered the other side's loss. The fear of loss is particularly acute in the military sphere, where each party is hypersensitive to the possibility of being inferior. Few arms agreements have existed in history precisely because states, driven by their sense of insecurity, prefer to add arms to their already existing arsenals to ensure that they will not find themselves lacking. *Arms control thinking, however, is based on the assumption that one side's gain is not necessarily the other's loss; both sides can gain simultaneously.*

If the only defense is indeed an offense, then a *preemptive strike* is a particular danger during crisis periods. It differs from a *preventive strike,* in which the aggressor coolly plans the strike beforehand with confidence that it can obliterate the opponent; that is, the attacker picks a specific date and then sends its forces on their way, regardless of possible provocation. In a preemptive strike, however, the attack is launched to forestall a strike by the enemy. In this instance the aggressor believes that the opponent is about to strike; it therefore strikes first to destroy the enemy's forces before they take off. The attack results from moves on the other side that are interpreted as menacing.[19]

The role of a possible miscalculation in precipitating a preemptive strike is clear. The signs that an opponent is about to launch an attack are likely to be ambiguous. The opponent may simply be taking measures to make its own strategic force less vulnerable and thereby to enhance its deterrent stance. For instance, during the years the United States and Soviet Union possessed mainly bombers, the opponent might have sent many of them into the air to avoid having them caught on the ground; by making them less vulnerable to sudden destruction, the opponent might have tried to prevent the other side from launching an attack. But the action itself could easily have been misinterpreted as the prelude to an attack. In a situation of mutual vulnerability, in which the "nice guy" finishes last, delay can prove fatal.

Offensive action may therefore be the only wise course. Thomas Schelling, one of the "founding fathers" of arms control thinking, has described the odd logic of preemption: " 'Self-defense' becomes peculiarly compounded if we have to worry about his striking us to keep us from striking him to keep him from striking us." [20] What is important, in short, is not what state A intends to do but state B's perception of state A's intentions. In this type of hair-trigger situation, the interpretation cannot be conservative. Because the survival of the nation is at stake, it is necessary to assume the worst. To return to the example used earlier, the strategic bombers of both sides were, of course, ready at all times to take off on their missions. When one side places a large number of them in the air, the possibility of a sudden attack increases. Even defensive actions, intended merely to enhance one's deterrent power, may intensify international tensions or touch off nuclear conflagration. Paradoxically then, the very weapons intended to deter nuclear war may well precipitate it.

Stabilizing Mutual Deterrence.   How then can a preventive war and especially a preemptive strike be forestalled? The answer is to make each side's retaliatory or second-strike forces invulnerable. *A second-strike force is one that can absorb an initial blow and still effectively perform its retaliatory mission.* The deterrent force that matters is that part likely to be left after an initial enemy attack; the size of the force before the attack is less relevant. In the bomber era, an invulnerable deterrent force was impossible. The solution was twofold. First, instead of relying on one weapons system for deterrence, several systems were to be developed so that if one became vulnerable as technology changed, the others would still be safe and deterrence would be assured. It was best to err on the side of safety. Thus, the United States and the Soviet Union developed a triad consisting of bombers, intercontinental ballistic missiles (ICBMs), and submarine-launched ballistic missiles (SLBMs) (see Table 12-1 and Figure 12-2). Second, solid-fuel missiles that can be fired instantly became the backbone of the deterrent forces. They can be dispersed more easily than bombers, which are generally concentrated at a relatively small number of bases, the location of which is easily discoverable. Missiles, unlike bombers on the ground, can also be hardened, or placed in underground concrete silos that can withstand the enormous pressure from the blast of a nuclear explosion. Most important, sea-launched missiles—in contrast to stationary ICBMs—can be concealed and made mobile by placing them in nuclear submarines whose exact locations are not known to the enemy.

Table 12-1 U.S. and Soviet Strategic Launchers (and Warheads), Summer 1988

Type of Launcher	United States	Soviet Union
ICBM	1,000 (2,366)	1,386 (6,412)
SLBM	640 (5,472)	942 (3,378)
Intercontinental bomber	423 (4,845)	160 (680)

SOURCE: Center for Defense Information, "U.S.-Soviet Military Facts," *The Defense Monitor*, vol. 17, no. 5 (1988): 1-4.

NOTE: International Institute for Strategic Studies, *The Military Balance, 1988-1989* (Reading, England: Eastern Press, 1988) has identical figures except that it lists 17 Soviet long-range bombers.

This dispersal, hardening, mobility, and concealment of missiles deprive a surprise attack of its rationale. The entire justification for a first strike had been to surprise the opponent with its bombers on the ground and to destroy them. But when the opponent's retaliatory power is basically invulnerable, obliterating the enemy's cities will benefit the aggressor very little. Surprise no longer confers any significant advantage to the side that hits first. The enemy's first strike cannot destroy the ability to strike back. The fact that a second-strike force will remain is the best guarantee against war. *Invulnerable deterrents stabilize mutual deterrence.*[21] Once the advantage of an initial attack has been greatly reduced, if not eliminated, the incentive to strike at all and the possibility of war also disappear.

Characteristics of Arms Control

U.S. arms control thinking is composed of three critical elements. First the number of nuclear weapons needed to achieve the "assured destruction" of the other society determines how many weapons each side needs, not the number of weapons possessed by the opponent. Second, deterrence requires urban areas to be left vulnerable to attack as "hostages." And third, second-strike forces must be invulnerable, so that the enemy can never believe that it can destroy enough forces to survive a retaliatory strike.

Parity in Numbers of Weapons. *The balance of capability does not necessarily require equal numbers of bombers and missiles.* A balance is achieved when each side, after absorbing an initial blow, has a second-strike force able to destroy the opponent's homeland. The best size for such a second-strike force may vary quite a bit in the views of U.S. and Soviet leaders. For example, SALT I, the 1972 agreement on offensive arms, froze the strategic missiles of the United States at 1,054 ICBMs and 656 SLBMs. The Soviet Union was permitted to have 1,618 ICBMs and 740 SLBMs. The treaty seems to have given the Soviets a hefty advantage of 2,358 missiles to 1,710, although it seems less

**Nuclear Weapons
on Land-based Missiles (ICBMs)
Soviet Union 6,412, United States 2,366**

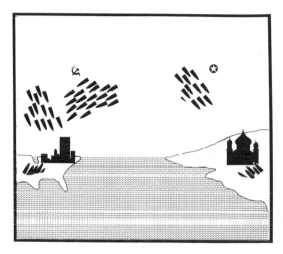

Each ◣ = 200 weapons.

**Nuclear Weapons
on Strategic Submarines
Soviet Union 3,378, United States 5,472**

Each ◣ = 200 weapons.

**Nuclear Weapons
on Strategic Bombers
Soviet Union 680, United States 4,845**

Each ◣ = 200 weapons.

**Total Strategic
Nuclear Weapons
Soviet Union 10,470, United States 12,683**

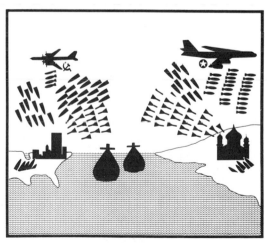

Each ◣ ◣ ◣ = 200 weapons.

Figure 12-2   Breakdown of Strategic Nuclear Weapons, Soviet Union and United States, 1988

unequal when it is noted that approximately 450 U.S. bombers, as opposed to 150 Soviet bombers, were allowed.

According to U.S. leaders' arms control thinking, even if most U.S. land-based missiles were destroyed in their silos by Soviet ICBMs, the sizable bomber fleet plus nuclear submarines, each one armed with sixteen to twenty four multi-warheaded missiles, would remain. Could Moscow therefore really risk launching a strike on the assumption that it might be able to destroy enough of the U.S. second-strike force to prevent the latter from inflicting overwhelming retaliatory damage on the Soviet Union? Would not such a move represent a reckless gamble—a "cosmic roll of the dice," as Harold Brown, Carter's secretary of defense, called it—even if the total Soviet strike force was larger than that of the United States by several hundred missiles? [22]

Thus, although superpowers are capable of destroying each other, they long ago reached a plateau—variously called *parity, sufficiency, mutual deterrence, nuclear stalemate,* and *balance of terror*—in this capability. The nuclear balance, or mutual deterrence, is not sensitive to numerical variations if each side retains an invulnerable deterrent force capable of the assured destruction of the enemy's society. Parity then may be defined as a relationship in which each superpower can destroy the other, regardless of who strikes first—in short, what has usually been described as mutual assured destruction. [23]

Vulnerable Populations and Economies.   *Urban industrial areas are deliberately left unprotected as hostages.* In 1964 the Soviets began to deploy an antiballistic missile (ABM) system around Moscow. By itself, the Soviet ABM constituted no problem. The problem lay in the possibility of an extensive ABM deployment to protect the Soviet urban population. If such ABMs were capable of shooting down a large percentage of missiles in a retaliatory strike—or if the Soviets believed they could—it might weaken the U.S. capability to deter.

Deterrence depends upon the ability to hold the adversary's population hostage: a Soviet ability to greatly reduce America's capacity to inflict unacceptable losses upon Soviet cities might, by eliminating the possibility of suicide, tempt the Soviets to risk launching a preventive or preemptive strike. Anything that detracts from the superiority of the offense to inflict assured destruction on the opponent tends to destabilize mutual deterrence, which is based on a *vulnerable population and invulnerable offensive forces.* An ABM protecting cities is a "bad" weapon in the sense that it can endanger nuclear deterrence. [24] In SALT I, for all practical purposes, the United States and Soviet Union abandoned the ABM and left their cities vulnerable to each other.

Invulnerable Retaliatory Forces.   Because invulnerable second-strike forces are the key to the stability of mutual deterrence, *the weapons produced and deployed must be the "right" kind.* Whether a weapon is right or wrong, good or bad, depends on whether it will help to stabilize the balance or to destabilize it; these terms have no moral connotations in this context.

Bombers, when they constituted the backbone of deterrence, were bad because they were vulnerable to attack. Missiles, because they can be dispersed, protected in silos, or moved around and concealed underwater, are good; it is not so easy then for a surprise attack to destroy one's retaliatory capacity. Indeed, in the early 1960s it was believed that once both powers possessed invulnerable missiles, peace would be guaranteed because there would be no point in attacking. Moreover, it was expected that once each power had reached the level it needed to retaliate, the arms race would end.

MAD and Technological Innovation

It was these ideas that led the United States and Soviet Union during the 1970s to stop pursuing strategic defenses and to first freeze their offensive forces for a five-year period in SALT I, before negotiating equal ceilings in SALT II and proceeding to significant reductions in SALT III (see Table 12-2). In short, SALT was viewed as a process, as a series of agreements which would be negotiated over time. But by the time SALT II was agreed upon in 1979, arms control concepts were being undermined by technological innovations[25] and changes in military doctrines.[26]

Just as technology had stabilized mutual deterrence with single-warhead missiles that were not especially accurate (they were accurate enough to hit cities, but not accurate enough to hit missiles in their silos), so technology in the 1970s appeared to be undermining this stability, first with multiple warheads (or MIRV multiple independent reentry vehicles), and then with increasingly accurate guidance systems. MIRVs once more made it possible for both superpowers to strike first. If both the United States and the Soviet Union had, for example, 1,000 ICBMs with single warheads, a surprise attack on the other would not be feasible. On the assumption that it takes two warheads to destroy one missile, it would take 2,000 ICBMs to eliminate the opponent's 1,000 ICBMs. If, however, one side had three warheads per missile and the other eight, then the latter gained the capability to destroy the former's missile sites with a fraction of its ICBM force. It would have ICBMs to spare. Missiles that had that capability were called counterforce weapons.

In actuality, the United States has over 2,300 ICBM warheads, 1,500 of them on 500 Minuteman III missiles plus 500 on an additional 50 MX missiles when all are soon in place. The Soviet Union has 1,400 ICBMs; 308 of these are the gigantic SS-18s, most with 10 warheads on each missile, and 350 are SS-19s with 6 warheads apiece, for a total of more than 6,000 warheads.

Either the SS-18s or the SS-19s could destroy most of the 1,000 U.S. ICBMs by launching five warheads against each silo.[27] Soviet military doctrine in the nuclear age has heavily stressed striking first if war is about to erupt in order to destroy as much of the U.S. retaliatory force as possible before it can be launched; it has not stressed absorbing the first blow and then retaliating. Such a preemptive blow is also referred to as a "disarming" or "damage-limitation" strike.

Table 12-2 Provisions of Salt I and II

	SALT I (1972)		SALT II [a]
	US	*USSR*	*US and USSR*
Total of all strategic delivery systems	1,710	2,358	2,250 (including bombers)
Intercontinental ballistic missiles (ICBMs)	1,054 (550 with MIRVs)	1,618 (minus 210 older ICBMs which could be scrapped and replaced by SLBMs)	820 (all with MIRVs: Soviets could keep 308 heavy missiles such as the SS-18 allowed by SALT I)
Submarine launched ballistic missiles (SLBMs)	656 (496 with MIRVs)	740 (plus 210 SLBMs)	1,200 (SLBMs *and* ICBMs with MIRVs)
Bombers	(450, excluded under SALT I)	(150, excluded under SALT I)	1,320 (SLBMs, ICBMs with MIRVs, plus bombers with ALCMs)
			930 (single warhead ICBMs, SLBMs, and bombers without ALCMs)

NOTE: MIRVs = multiple independent warheads or reentry vehicles; ALCMs = air-launched cruise missiles.
[a] Unratified by the United States. The Reagan administration, however, observed its limits until 1986.

This trend toward counterforce, as distinct from countercity or counter-value, attacks was worrisome for two reasons. First, for each side it placed a premium on striking first, "to use 'em [the ICBMs] or lose 'em," especially in a time of crisis when the superpowers confront one another toe-to-toe.*

---

* An illustrative situation occurred in 1988 in the Persian Gulf when the captain of the cruiser *Vincennes*, believing that an Iranian jet fighter armed with missiles was flying toward his ship, and recalling an earlier incident in which the U.S.S. *Stark* had allowed an Iraqi jet to get too close—resulting in the death of thirty-seven of its crew and a near sinking when the jet mistakenly attacked that ship—decided to fire his missiles. He destroyed instead an Iranian civilian airliner with 290 people on board. Trying to protect his ship, acting on available information, and having only three or four minutes to make a decision, the captain made the only rational decision he could in that compressed amount of time and in circumstances in which he had just been engaged in a fight with three Iranian attack boats and sunk two of them.

Second, because if both powers really believe that they can limit their strikes to the opponent's military forces and prevent an escalation to all-out nuclear war, they might risk a nuclear attack in the belief that they can avoid mutual annihilation. Bismarck, the Prussian Chancellor who united Germany in 1870, defined the so-called security dilemma well when he said that no "government, if it regards war as inevitable even if it does not want it, would be so foolish as to leave to the enemy the choice of time and occasion and to wait for the moment which is most convenient for the enemy"—even if a preventive war was, as he also called it, "committing suicide from the fear of death." [28]

Strategic Arms Control Record

If counterforce was not really compatible with stable mutual deterrence, what did this mean for arms control? There can be no question that arms control has been generally popular with the public because of its association with better Soviet-American relations. But the record of arms control regimes has been mixed (see Table 12-3).[29] Liberals were disillusioned with the high ceilings that they found incompatible with arms limitation. They charged that SALT I and II allowed the arms race to go on; the agreements merely codified the existing forces each possessed and modernization plans. It was not uncommon to point out that after more than a decade of arms control negotiations following SALT I, the superpowers' arsenals were much larger than they had been in 1972. Conservatives were upset because the SALT negotiations had not prevented the Soviet achievement of parity in the early 1970s or the modernization that after 1972 increasingly threatened U.S. deterrent forces. They also accused Moscow of systemmatically violating the agreements it had signed in its continuous quest for strategic superiority and a warfighting and war-winning capability. But in fact, liberals and conservatives alike have exaggerated both the promise and danger of arms control.

By establishing ceilings, arms control reduces the uncertainty each superpower has in estimating the other side's military buildup. Not sure of what the opponent's plans are, each tends to make "worst case" assumptions. The likely overestimation of what the opponent may acquire—based on the principle of "it's better to be safe than sorry"—will then result in overbuilding. This in turn will cause the opponent to react, if not overreact, in an ever-upward cycle. Arms agreements therefore have contributed to a more predictable atmosphere. This may in fact have been SALT's principal contribution to arms control regimes. For the United States, this is especially important because its knowledge of Soviet plans is bound to be less than Soviet knowledge of U.S. plans. In fact, Washington, using worst-case assumptions thought it was facing "gaps" in bombers in the 1950s and missiles in the 1960s. Thus, the SALT process was a recognition by both superpowers of the dangers of an unconstrained arms race and of the need to moderate the security dilemma.

SALT also sought to preclude the defensive-offensive arms linkage. The development and deployment of defensive weapons would only escalate the

Table 12-3 Objectives of Arms Control and Relevant Agreements

Objective	Agreement	Year
Quantitative and qualitative limits	SALT I ABM agreement	1972
Strategic delivery systems	SALT I interim agreement on offensive arms	1972
	Vladivostok guidelines	1974
	SALT II[a]	1979
Eliminating all intermediate nuclear forces (INF)	INF agreement	1988
Direct communication between U.S. and Soviet leaders during crises	Hot-line agreement	1963
	Hot-line modernization agreement	1971
Barring nuclear weapons from specific regions	Antarctica treaty[b]	1959
	Outer-space treaty[b]	1967
	Seabed treaty[b]	1971
Discouragement of nuclear proliferation	International Atomic Energy Authority[b]	1954[b]
	Nonproliferation treaty[b]	1968
	Nuclear Suppliers' Club	1975
Limiting of nuclear tests	Limited test-ban treaty[b]	1963
	Threshold test-ban treaty[a]	1974[a]
	Peaceful nuclear explosion treaty[a]	1976[a]
Banning nonnuclear weapons of mass destruction	Biological weapons convention	1972

[a] Signed but not in force because of Senate refusal to ratify.

[b] Multilateral agreements.

offensive arms race in order to overwhelm any defensive shield. An assured destruction strategy, thus required further acquisition of offensive weapons. The ABM treaty specifically recognized this defensive-offensive linkage by stating that without an ABM limitation curbing the offensive arms competition would be difficult. In one sense then the ABM agreement was the prerequisite for the SALT process—that is, the process of first establishing equal offensive ceilings (after freezing these forces first) and then reducing them. Likewise, SALT I was the prerequisite for SALT II.

Unfortunately, by the time SALT I had been negotiated, the United States had already begun to deploy multiple warheads. Thus, the defensive-offensive linkage helped *destabilize* a process whose central concern was to stabilize mutual deterrence. MIRV was the U.S. response to the Soviet deployment of an ABM system around Moscow which, Washington believed, might be the prelude to a nationwide deployment. By multiplying warheads on its missiles, the United States could overwhelm any Soviet defensive system and still destroy Soviet society. Had the SALT negotiations started in 1968, as they were supposed to, and not been delayed first by the Soviet invasion of Czechoslovakia and then by a change in American administrations, MIRV might have been stopped.[30] But by 1972 it was too late, the long-term impact of MIRV was destabilizing. Ironically, the effect of START (Strategic Arms Reduction Talks, the Reagan administration's name for SALT) has been to cut the numbers of strategic launchers and warheads by 50 percent in order to reduce each side's counterforce capability, a capability neither would possess but for MIRV. But even more ironically, President Reagan had by this time introduced the Strategic Defense Initiative to counter the threat of Soviet missiles to America's population and its ICBMs. Unlike SALT, however, START lacked a framework; there was no agreement on the role defensive systems should play in the deterrent equation. Thus, a START treaty could not be negotiated during the Reagan years.

The question remaining here is: Why did the United States not give up MIRV after 1972 when the SALT I treaty had ensured that America's single warheaded ICBMs could get through to deliver their assured destruction punch? The principal reason is the same one that makes arms control negotiations so difficult: In a bipolar competitive game, the side that has gained what it believes to be a major technological breakthrough will seek to exploit its perceived advantage.

Perhaps the best evaluation of the SALT process is the following:

> What is most striking about the arms control experience surveyed here is what it did not do. Those who hoped arms control would bring about major reductions in existing or planned inventories or slow the introduction of new and more capable technologies have little grounds for satisfaction. Nor do those who looked to arms control as a means for constraining the emergence of a large, modern Soviet arsenal capable of destroying a significant proportion of U.S. strategic retaliatory forces. Even the contributions of the ABM Treaty, arms control's chief accomplishment, are of uncertain durability. The treaty may merely have codified the postponement of a race in defensive systems until advancing technologies made effective defenses possible.
>
> What emerges above all is the modesty of what arms control has wrought. [It] has proved neither as promising as some had hoped nor as dangerous as others had feared.[31]

This conclusion should hardly be surprising. The fact that the two superpowers have managed to negotiate arms control agreements at all is surprising. Historically, states have enhanced their security by unilateral measures, largely arms buildups. The idea that a nation that has become vulnerable should seek to supplement traditional military measures by cooperating with the adversary who threatens its security to *decrease* that security threat is a novel one. Cooperation among enemies is *not* the norm.[32] When it does happen, it is subjected to all the competitive pressures that make them rivals in the first place.

One of the ironic results of arms control regimes is that they rechannel the arms competition from the weapons controlled to newer technologies. SALT I froze missile launchers because silos and submarines were easy to count; this constraint shifted the new race to multiple warheads. Like the Darwinian theory of natural selection, limitations on weapons simply stimulate the evolution of species not restrained.[33] Some of the most successful arms control agreements, taken to stabilize mutual deterrence, have not in fact been formal bilateral agreements producing treaties but unilateral moves, such as the U.S. shift from bombers to the triad. Arms control has become unavoidable in the nuclear age, but obviously it is not a magic cure for the arms race and the political rivalry that feeds it. Yet it can ease that rivalry, while also serving as an indication of improved superpower relations.[34]

ARMS RACE AND NUCLEAR PEACE

Rationale for Arms Competition

Would it in these circumstances be correct to say that the continuing nuclear arms race in offensive and defensive weapons is very dangerous and is likely to end up in a nuclear war? It is widely viewed that arms races are in fact the cause of war and that basically armaments and peace are incompatible—more specifically, the more armaments, the greater the danger of war. The logical conclusion is to reduce arms to ensure peace. Sir Edward Grey, Britain's foreign minister on the eve of World War I, made this classic statement on arms races:

> The moral is obvious: it is that great armaments lead inevitably to war. If there are armaments on one side there must be armaments on other sides. While one nation arms, other nations cannot tempt it to aggression by remaining defenceless. . . . The enormous growth of armaments in Europe, the sense of insecurity and fear caused by them—it was these that made war inevitable.[35]

This sweeping generalization may sum up the conventional wisdom on the relationship of arms to war, but it is too simple. For one thing, arms races may result in war, but not all wars are the result of arms races. There is no evidence that arms races preceded the Russo-Japanese War (1904-1905), the Korean War (1950-1953), the Vietnam War (1965-1973), or the British-Argentinian War over the Falkland Islands (1983), to cite but a few of the many wars in this century. Among the causes of World War II, in fact, was Britain's refusal to match Germany's growing military strength, thus upsetting the European balance. Arms races have also sometimes been called off when they reached a certain point, as in the Anglo-German naval race, which ended in 1911 and was not the reason for Britain's declaration of war in 1914. After World War I, the Washington Naval Conference restricted the battleship fleets of the United States, Britain, Japan, Italy, and France according to a fixed ratio and declared a ten-year "naval holiday" for new battle-ship construction (it was extended five more years in 1930).

Arms races, which, like wars, cannot be isolated from the political circumstances that produced them, take different forms. For example, the race may be part of a process of competitive modernization among states seeking to preserve the status quo. Each fears falling behind the others in keeping weapons technologically up-to-date. Or it may be part of a political struggle between a status quo state and a revisionist state. In this context, the former's decision to match the latter's increase in capability sends a *political* message: it refuses to acquiesce in a major shift of the power balance. The resulting arms race is a measure of their political rivalry. The arms race did not produce this rivalry, nor will the race end until there is some political settlement of these powers' differences. The arms race, in brief, is a test of national will, especially on the part of the status quo power (a test that Britain failed in the 1930s).[36]

To the extent that the balance will dissuade a revisionist state from attacking a status quo one, entry into an arms race by the latter can be considered a "necessary surrogate for war."[37] And one observer, agreeing that the arms race is a substitute for war, has said that while it may be an expensive substitute, it is cheaper than fighting a war.[38] In short, an arms race is a bloodless way to demonstrate to the adversary that it would lose if war should occur. Whether the race ends in war will depend, as noted earlier, on the accuracy of the power calculations and intentions of the adversaries.

The term *arms race* implies an action-reaction process; one side builds up and the other responds in an ever-upward spiral. This implies that at some point war will erupt in a "spontaneous combustion." It is inevitable as each side piles up more arms. (Those who assert this thesis assume that the time at which the war erupts, or the specific events and crises that are the immediate cause of the war, are of no importance![39]) This action-reaction thesis, however, pays little attention to the fact that in the superpower arms race neither the Soviet Union nor the United States, by far the wealthier and more productive society, has ever built all the weapons it could. The United States built many bombers; the Soviet Union built relatively few. Moscow deployed an ABM system around the capital city; Washington did not deploy any ABMs.

This action-reaction process also suggests that if one state stops racing and begins to reduce its arms, the other side will reciprocate. Actually, quite the reverse may happen. The adversary may see a slowdown as an opportunity to strengthen itself and gain an advantage, not necessarily to attack but to enhance its political leverage. During the Nixon-Ford years, when U.S. defense expenditures dropped to the lowest percentage of the gross national product since before the Korean War in 1950, Soviet military spending is estimated to have increased to between 12 percent and 17 percent of the Soviet GNP.

Rather than action-reaction, *anticipated* action-reaction would be a more accurate description. One side sees the other test a weapon or begin the production or deployment of a new weapon, and it assumes the worse—a full-scale deployment or an attempt to seek strategic superiority or a first-strike capability. For example, when the Soviets test an ICBM and then repeatedly claim that it is being mass produced, the fear of a "missile gap" leads the United States to undertake a large-scale ICBM buildup which proves to have been an overreaction when several years later it becomes clear that the Soviets have relatively few missiles. Or when the Soviets deploy ABMs around Moscow, the United States, anticipating eventual full-scale national deployment to protect the Soviet population, the U.S. multiplies the number of warheads on its missiles so that it can still penetrate Soviet defenses and destroy the Soviet Union. In the first instance, the Soviets, fearful of the missile gap that they confronted, planted missiles in Cuba; this technological shortcut to narrowing the gap created a dangerous crisis. In the second case, the ultimate result, once the Soviets also acquired MIRVs and both had improved guidance systems, was to destabilize the balance of power.

Yet, as these examples suggest, one reason for the arms race within the broader superpower rivalry is a hedge against the uncertainties of technological advances, or the opponent's intentions. American sensitivity to Soviet arms developments was compounded by two additional factors: (1) the need for nuclear arms to compensate for the lack of NATO conventional forces and to deter superior Warsaw Pact conventional forces; and (2) the electoral process in which possible charges of neglecting the nation's security has tended to lead the party in power to build enough weapons to ward off such domestic attacks (see Chapter 6 and the ABM-SDI case study). Even "bargaining chips," weapons to be traded for Soviet concessions, were no longer always tradeable once these weapons mobilized congressional-industrial-labor constituencies and public opinion.

How Much Is Enough?

Within this process, it may well be therefore that both the United States and the Soviet Union have acquired too many arms. But the key question is how many missiles does it take to deter the other side? No one really knows. For the United States, is it the 1,000 ICBMs already built? After all, no war has started. Or would deterrence be implemented by 500 or even 200 missiles? In the absence of a war, how can one prove that an event did not occur because of a certain level of armaments? Thus, the numbers of weapons will always be a debatable and controversial topic.

This topic is complicated even more by the way one answers these questions: How many of the deterrent forces will be operational at the time of the attack? How many of these forces are likely to be destroyed in an enemy attack (assuming the United States will retaliate only after it has absorbed a first strike)? How many surviving missiles will malfunction on takeoff or during flight? How many missiles will miss their targets? Because the number of forces operational at the time of a first strike and the number destroyed are unknown, the caution against relying on forces that are too small is obvious. There is another reason for caution: small forces would presumably be easier to destroy in a first strike and therefore would have less credibility as a deterrent because the surviving forces might not be able to retaliate. In the nuclear balance, there is safety in numbers. With sizable forces on both sides, the attacker cannot be certain of a successful first strike. Political scientist Michael May has described it thus: "Numbers of nuclear weapons systems must remain high if the futility of a first strike is to remain obvious; if undetectable cheating is to remain unimportant; and if the U.S. and the U.S.S.R. are to remain secure in their deterrence regardless of what other nuclear powers may do."[40] Large forces, in other words, reduce each power's sense of vulnerability and therefore help reduce compulsions to preempt. May has omitted one other advantage of large forces: to guard against the opponent's achievements of technological breakthroughs. With small forces, there is a much greater need to seek assurance that one's forces are invulnerable.[41] In short, the issue is not so much the capability for "overkill" as the capability to "mutually kill" one another.

Thus, while numbers are not unimportant, the composition of the deterrent forces remains key to the stability of the deterrent equation.[42] Because deterrence is the chief aim, should one rely only on one system—for example, bombers—even if one possesses plenty of them? Is there not greater safety in diversity? Can one not legitimately argue that the three systems each superpower possesses—bombers, ICBMs, and SLBMs—make deterrence that much more certain? Possession of several systems greatly complicates an attacker's ability to destroy all of the opponent's retaliatory forces and makes it far more difficult to defend against a second strike.

To be sure, counterforce weapons are destabilizing. Thus, in a counterforce environment, a limited SDI deployment to protect ICBMs might some day make sense, because it might restabilize the deterrent balance. But other means might be equally helpful at less expense and more speedily. Because the current instability related to land-based missiles stems principally from the disproportion between the numbers of accurate warheads and launchers, a shift from multiple warheads back to a single warhead per missile, as on the projected Midgetman, would be the most desirable solution. Such a missile will be less threatening and consequently less likely to provoke a first strike, an accompanying move by both superpowers away from a counterforce strategy would also be important. Another solution might be mobile missiles because even accurate warheads cannot hit moving targets; a greater shift of missiles to the sea is yet another option. Arms negotiations will play a critical role as well. A START agreement that will cut the most destabilizing forces by 50 percent can contribute greatly to the stabilization of mutual deterrence, even if the overall reduction in strategic weapons is more likely to be in the 30-35 percent range (see Table 12-4).[43]

Table 12-4 Outline of a Probable START Agreement

Total (U.S. and Soviet) strategic delivery systems (ICBMs, SLBMs, bombers)	1,600
Total (U.S. and Soviet) strategic weapons (carried on delivery systems)	6,000
Total (U.S. and Soviet) ballistic missile warheads	4,900
Reduction in Soviet heavy ICBMs	50%
Reduction in Soviet ballistic missile throw-weight (size of warhead)	50%

SOURCES: Max M. Kampelman, "START: Completing the Task," *Washington Quarterly*, Summer 1969, 5-16; and Robert Einhorn, "Strategic Arms Reduction Talks: The Emerging START Agreement," *Survival*, September/October 1988, 387-401.

Mutual Vulnerability and Nonbelligerency

But even if these reductions do not occur, the nuclear peace should hold for three reasons.[44] First, the enormous destructive power of each nuclear weapon which, when multiplied by the huge stockpiles (even after a 50 percent reduction of both superpowers), means that nuclear war risks national survival. Should a nuclear exchange begin with attacks primarily restricted to bomber bases and missile fields, it is doubtful that such a "limited nuclear war" would not in the heat of war escalate to attacks on cities.[45] Second, if either side were ever tempted to undertake a preemptive strike, the chances are that operationally many things will go wrong and therefore such a first strike will not succeed in destroying most of the opponent's ICBM/bomber retaliatory capability. The likelihood that a small percentage will survive and be used in a retaliatory blow means that a first strike becomes too great a risk to take. Third, this risk becomes even greater because of the large size and multiplication of strategic forces. Submarines, especially American submarines, remain invulnerable; as the range of their missiles increases, they can roam over larger portions of the ocean, making themselves even harder to find. In fact, they could, if necessary, fire from their home ports and reach their targets. So can the latest Soviet submarines. Altogether, then, the likelihood of committing suicide remains much too high for either side to risk launching a first strike.

The fear of a nuclear Armageddon, a fear shared by both the United States and the Soviet Union, thus remains the best guarantee of peace. For better or worse, regardless of specific weapons systems or military doctrines, we live in a MAD world. In the words of Thomas Schelling: "I like the notion that East and West have exchanged hostages on a massive scale and that as long as they are unprotected, civilization depends on the avoidance of military aggression that could escalate to nuclear war." [46]

In these circumstances the avoidance of nuclear war is the only sensible course. But neither power can by taking only unilateral measures make itself more secure. U.S.-Soviet security has become interdependent; each one's security is dependent upon what the other does. While each power can and must continue to take unilateral steps to improve its security, they must be supplemented by bilateral cooperation. Realist theory may focus on the conflict of interests between states, but as arms control negotiations suggest, cooperation among adversaries is required as well. The U.S.-Soviet relationship has increasingly become an adversary partnership. Despite their long rivalry, their desire to survive also compels them to cooperate on arms control. Their rivalry accounts for the difficulties encountered in both arriving at and maintaining agreements. Suspicion that one or the other might be cheating to gain an advantage is inherent in their adversarial relationship. That they have continued to negotiate on arms control despite their conflicts, often angry feelings, and bitter words of denunciation testifies to the powerful impact of nuclear weapons. Cooperation among adversaries, it is worth repeating, is not normal in international politics; the security dilemma is more often the norm.

That the period since 1945 has not witnessed another world war is even more powerful testimony to the awesome character of nuclear weapons.[47] Despite the horrors of World War I, the great powers of Europe stumbled into World War II only twenty-one years after the first one had ended. The almost five decades that have passed since the conclusion of the second war have served as Europe's longest period of peace in the twentieth century. Even the states that precipitated two of the bloodiest wars in history have been at peace with one another (with the exception of Greece and Turkey on the periphery of Europe). This absence of *total* war between the superpowers and their allies testifies to the discipline and restraint the "bomb" has imposed upon the exercise of power by the United States and the Soviet Union. Rather than eliminating the human race, nuclear weapons appear to be eliminating large-scale war among the world's most powerful states, both nuclear and nonnuclear. According to Schelling:

> ... 40 years of living with nuclear weapons without warfare are not only evidence that war can be avoided but are themselves part of the reason why it can be; namely, increasing experience in living with the weapons without precipitating war, increasing confidence on both sides that neither wishes to risk nuclear war, diminishing necessity to react to every untoward event as though it were a mortal challenge.[48]

Since 1945 in fact there has been only one war between two great powers, the United States and Communist China, although China claims it was not officially at war because the Chinese troops in Korea were all "volunteers" and the United States defined that conflict as a "limited war." This forty-five-year record is unprecedented. Indeed, John Kennedy's national security assistant, McGeorge Bundy, has asserted that the nonuse of nuclear weapons has become so firmly established that each ten-year period has turned out to be less dangerous than the one before.[49]

Nuclear arms not only have prevented a total war between the United States and the Soviet Union, despite the scope and intensity of their rivalry, but also have led them to manage their crises very carefully when they have erupted: in Berlin (1948-1949 and again repeatedly from 1958-1961), in Quemoy and Matsu in the Taiwan Straits (1954-1955 and 1958), and especially in Cuba during the missile crisis (1962). A crisis is defined in terms of a high expectation of violence. Vital interests are at stake, and one power has challenged the status quo which the opponent resists. If the possible use of violence underlies behind much of international politics, this possibility rises close to the surface during crises. In this sense crises stand at the crossover point from peace to war, even if their occurrence suggests that the balance is being kept. As dangerous as crises are, none has escalated into war, as probably would have occurred in the prenuclear period when the penalty for going to war did not include the ultimate price of extinction. In both deterrence and crises the powers have resorted only to threats of force, not the use of force. That significant shift is the result of nuclear weapons and is the reason why the period since 1945 has been called the age of deterrence and crisis management. Deterrence has given rise to arms control and a sustained effort to stabilize the balance to ensure that nuclear war will never be fought. The fact that the last direct U.S.-Soviet confrontation occurred in 1962 testifies to the increasing focus of the two powers on crisis avoidance.[50]

Despite the Reagan administration's efforts to abolish the specter of nuclear war by means of a technical solution—Star Wars—it is ironic and probably closer to the truth to say that *if nuclear weapons were eliminated, relieving fears of a nuclear holocaust, wars between the major powers might become more likely because such hostilities would be considerably less damaging.* There is clearly a trade-off between the destructiveness of war and the likelihood of war. Total wars are incompatible with "absolute weapons," but they are not incompatible with weapons of more limited destruction. Thus, the abolition of nuclear arms, if it were possible, would present a cruel dilemma: it would remove the fear of national, if not global, suicide, but it also would make it feasible once more to use war as an instrument of state policy whose gains might exceed its losses. Fear of nuclear punishment inhibits the use of force; without that fear a major war might have broken out. It is not that the great powers would resort to conventional warfare lightly. The destruction and loss of life in the two world wars were immense, and none of the European states would wish to repeat the experience.[51] Indeed, a large-scale conventional war with today's weapons would be considerably more destructive. Perhaps even in the absence of nuclear weapons war might not break out. But can it be doubted that it is the fear of *extinction* that is the ultimate incentive to be cautious and guard against misperceptions and miscalculations? The possibility that even the slightest chance of a war will spark a nuclear conflagration has kept the peace in Europe since the end of World War II.

For all of the horror of that conflict in which casualties far exceeded that of World War I, there were victors and losers—and even the latter recovered. If there were only conventional weapons, one side might risk initiating a war because the ultimate penalty would *not* be suicide but perhaps victory. Nor need the cost of such a conventional conflict necessarily be high if a state can quickly achieve its goal—not necessarily total victory—with a new version of the German *Blitzkrieg*. But the scale of destruction of a nuclear war is incomparably greater; the difference between vast losses, from which eventual recovery is possible, and the certainty of a nearly complete annihilation from which recovery is unlikely, cannot be ignored. Thus, eliminating nuclear weapons would reduce the risks and costs of a possible war, weakening deterrence; what was unthinkable now becomes thinkable. Then, it may be that we could no longer say: "Perhaps the most striking characteristic of the postwar world is just that—that it can be called 'postwar' because the major powers have not fought each other since 1945." [52]

For Review

1. How can power, especially military power, be used to resolve conflicts among states?
2. What impact have nuclear weapons had on warfare, traditionally the ultimate instrument of persuasion?
3. What are the requirements of deterrence?
4. How does arms control help "stabilize" mutual deterrence?
5. What is the record of U.S.-Soviet arms control negotiations?
6. Which is the more likely result—peace or war—in the arms race?

Notes

1. Fred C. Ikle, *How Nations Negotiate* (New York: Harper & Row, 1964); Arthur S. Lall, *Modern International Negotiation* (New York: Columbia University Press, 1966); and William Zartman and Maureen Berman, *The Practical Negotiator* (New Haven, Conn.: Yale University Press, 1983). For the history of diplomacy, see Harold Nicolson, *The Evolution of the Diplomatic Method* (New York: Macmillan, 1955).
2. The emphasis on tacit bargaining, as distinct from traditional diplomatic negotiations, was introduced by Thomas C. Schelling, *Strategy of Conflict* (New York:

Oxford University Press, 1963). Also see Schelling, *Arms and Influence* (New Haven, Conn.: Yale University Press, 1966).

3. Edward H. Carr, *The Twenty Years Crisis, 1919-1939* (New York: Macmillan, 1951), 109.

4. See, for example, Immanuel Kant, *Perpetual Peace*, trans. Carl J. Friedrich in *Inevitable Peace* (Cambridge, Mass.: Harvard University Press, 1948), 251-252.

5. Bertrand de Jouvenel, *On Power*, trans. J. F. Huntington (Boston: Beacon Press, 1962), 148.

6. The interrelations between war and industrial power are well treated in *War and Human Progress* by John U. Nef (Cambridge, Mass.: Harvard University Press, 1950); and in *Men in Arms*, rev. ed., by Richard A. Preston and Sidney F. Wise (New York: Praeger, 1970), 176ff. For the impact of democratization and industrialization on U.S. military performance, see Walter Millis, *Arms and Men* (New York: New American Library, 1956).

7. Arthur T. Hadley, *The Nation's Safety and Arms Control* (New York: Viking, 1961), 4.

8. Ralph E. Lapp, *Kill and Overkill* (New York: Basic Books, 1962), 37; and Scientists' Committee for Radiation Information, "Effects of Nuclear Explosives," in *No Place to Hide*, ed. Seymour Melman (New York: Grove Press, 1962), 98-107. Also see Richard Rhodes, *The Making of the Atomic Bomb* (New York: Simon & Schuster, 1988).

9. A vivid account of a fire storm is given in *The Night Hamburg Died* by Martin Caidin (New York: Ballantine, 1960), 80-105, 129-141. The German estimate of those killed by British bombers in Hamburg was 60,000. The U.S. B-29 attack on Tokyo, March 9-10, 1945, burned up sixteen square miles and killed 84,000 people, most of whom were burned to death or died from wounds caused by fire. In contrast, the Hiroshima atom bomb killed 72,000 people. The most destructive attack ever, however, was the two-day Anglo-American bombing of Dresden in February 1945: 135,000 people were killed. On this attack, see David Irving, *The Destruction of Dresden* (New York: Holt, Rinehart & Winston, 1964). For the origins of the city bombing undertaken by the United States and what the author critically calls "the creation of Armageddon" in the subtitle, see Michael S. Sherry, *The Rise of American Air Power* (New Haven, Conn.: Yale University Press, 1987).

10. Lapp, *Kill and Overkill*, 53-54.

11. Ibid., 77.

12. Office of Technology Assessment, *Effects of Nuclear War* (Washington, D.C.: Government Printing Office, 1980), 159.

13. Ibid., 159.

14. Paul R. Ehrlich, Carl Sagan et al., *The Cold and the Dark* (New York: Norton, 1984). In the same genre, though hardly "scientific," see Jonathan Schell, *The Fate of the Earth* (New York: Avon Books, 1982). For a critical appraisal of the "nuclear winter" and its impact on nuclear strategy, see Albert Wohlstetter, "Between Unfree World and None," *Foreign Affairs* (Summer 1985): 962-994; and for an appraisal of its scientific basis, see Stanley L. Thompson and Stephen H. Schneider, "Nuclear Winter Reappraised," *Foreign Affairs* (Summer 1986): 981-1005.

15. Henry A. Kissinger, *Nuclear Weapons and Foreign Policy* (New York: Harper & Row, 1957), 79. See also Office of Technology Assessment, *Effects of Nuclear War*; and Arthur M. Katz, *Life After Nuclear War* (Cambridge, Mass.: Ballinger, 1981).

16. Glenn H. Snyder, "Balance of Power in the Missile Age," *Journal of International Affairs* 14 (1960): 21-34.

17. This continuing concern with different strategies and changing weapons systems is discussed by William W. Kaufmann, *The McNamara Strategy* (New York: Harper & Row, 1964). For overall views of U.S. strategy and arms control, respectively, see Lawrence Freedman, *The Evolution of Nuclear Strategy* (New York: St. Martin's Press, 1981); and Gregg Herken, *Counsels of War*, rev. ed. (New York: Oxford University Press, 1987).

18. Fine introductions to the field of arms control can be found in: Hedley Bull, *The Control of the Arms Race*, 2d ed. (New York: Holt, Rinehart & Winston, 1965); and Thomas C. Schelling and Morton H. Halperin, *Strategy and Arms Control*, 2d ed. (Elmsford, N.Y.: Pergamon-Brassey, 1985).

19. In Schelling's words:

> The 'equalizer' of the Old West [the pistol] made it possible for *either* man to kill the other; it did not assure that *both* would be killed. . . . The advantage of shooting first aggravates any incentive to shoot. As the survivor might put it, "He was about to kill me in self-defense, so I had to kill him in self-defense." Or, "He, thinking I was about to kill him in self-defense, was about to kill me in self defense, so I had to kill him in self-defense." But if both were assured of living long enough to shoot back with unimpaired aim, there would be no advantage in jumping the gun and little reason to fear that the other would try it.

Schelling, *Strategy of Conflict*, 232-233 (emphasis in original).

20. Ibid., 231.

21. Ibid., 232.

22. For an early discussion of the lack of any payoff from a position of strategic superiority that the Soviet Union might achieve, see Benjamin S. Lambeth, "Deterrence in the MIRV Era," *World Politics*, January 1972, 221ff.

23. David Holloway, *The Soviet Union and the Arms Race*, 2d ed. (New Haven, Conn.: Yale University Press, 1984), 49.

24. Jerome B. Wiesner et al., *ABM: An Evaluation of the Decision to Employ an Antiballistic Missile System* (New York: Signet, 1969); and Johan J. Holst and William Schneider, Jr., eds., *Why ABM? Policy Issues in the Missile Defense Controversy* (New York: Pergamon Press, 1969).

25. Matthew Evangelista, *Innovation and the Arms Race* (Ithaca, N.Y.: Cornell University Press, 1988).

26. Derek Leebaert, ed., *Soviet Military Thinking* (Boston: Allen & Unwin, 1981); and Joseph D. Douglas, Jr. and Amoretta M. Hoeber, *Soviet Strategy for Nuclear War* (Stanford, Calif.: Hoover Institution Press, 1979). For the United States, see Desmond Ball and Jeffrey Richelson, *Strategic Nuclear Targeting* (Ithaca, N.Y.: Cornell University Press, 1988).

27. Robbin F. Laird and Dale R. Herspring, *The Soviet Union and Strategic Arms* (Boulder, Colo.: Westview Press, 1984), 53-54.

28. Quoted by Fritz Fischer, *The War of Illusions* (New York: Norton, 1975), 377, 461.

29. Albert Carnesdale and Richard N. Haass, eds., *Superpower Arms Control* (Cambridge, Mass.: Ballinger, 1987).

30. Raymond L. Garthoff, "SALT: An Evaluation," *World Politics*, October 1978, 20-21.

31. Carnesdale and Haass, *Superpower Arms Control*; and Condoleezza Rice, "SALT and the Search for a Security Regime," in Alexander L. George, Philip J.

Farley, and Alexander Dallin, eds., *U.S.-Soviet Security Cooperation* (New York: Oxford University Press, 1988), 293-306.

32. Rice, "SALT and the Search for a Security Regime," 302.

33. Bruce D. Berkowitz, *Calculated Risks* (New York: Simon & Schuster, 1987).

34. Alan B. Sheer, *The Other Side of Arms Control* (Winchester, Mass.: Allen & Unwin, 1988).

35. Quoted by Paul Kennedy, *Strategy and Diplomacy 1870-1945* (London: Fontana Paperbacks, 1984), 165. Also see the annual studies by the Stockholm International Peace Research Institute, *SIPRI Yearbook,* for a similar contemporary viewpoint.

36. Michael Howard, *The Causes of War,* 2d ed. (Cambridge, Mass.: Harvard University Press, 1984), 18-20.

37. Ibid., 21.

38. Geoffrey Blainey, *The Causes of War* (New York: Free Press, 1973), 141. For a critical view of the U.S.-Soviet arms race, see "But No 'Race,' " *Foreign Policy* (Summer, Fall 1974): 3-20, 48-81.

39. Blainey, *Causes of War,* 137. Also see Richard N. Lebow, *Between Peace and War* (Baltimore: Johns Hopkins University Press, 1981).

40. Michael M. May, "The U.S.-Soviet Approach to Nuclear Weapons," *International Security,* Spring 1985, 487; and Joseph S. Nye, Jr., "Farewell to Arms Control?" *Foreign Affairs* (Fall 1986): 1-20, for a balanced analysis of the effects of reductions on contemporary arms control negotiations.

41. Joseph S. Nye, Jr., "The Role of Strategic Nuclear Systems in Deterrence," *Washington Quarterly,* Spring 1988, 50.

42. On SALT I, see John Newhouse, *Cold Dawn* (New York: Holt, Rinehart & Winston, 1973); on SALT II, see Thomas W. Wolfe, *The SALT Experience* (Cambridge, Mass.: Ballinger, 1979); and Strobe Talbott, *Endgame* (New York: Harper & Row, 1979). More broadly, on the do's and don't's of arms control to avoid nuclear war, see Graham T. Allison, Albert Carnesdale, and Joseph S. Nye, Jr., *Hawks, Doves, and Owls* (New York: Norton, 1985).

43. Robert Einhorn, "Strategic Arms Reduction Talks: The Emerging START Agreement," *Survival,* September/October 1988, 390; and Max M. Kampelman (the Reagan administration's START negotiator), "START: Completing the Task," *Washington Quarterly,* Summer 1989, 5-7.

44. Robert Jervis, *The Illogic of American Nuclear Strategy* (Ithaca, N.Y.: Cornell University Press, 1984); and Spurgeon M. Keeny and Wolfgang K. H. Panofsky, "MAD vs. NUTS: The Mutual Hostage Relationship of the Super-powers," *Foreign Affairs* (Winter 1981/82): 287-304.

45. Desmond Ball, "Can Nuclear War Be Controlled?" (London: International Institute for Strategic Studies, 1981). Also see Paul Bracken, *The Command and Control of Nuclear Forces* (New Haven, Conn.: Yale University Press, 1983); and Bruce G. Blair, *Strategic Command and Control* (Washington, D.C.: Brookings, 1985). But for the devastating consequences of even a limited nuclear war, see William Daugherty, Barbara Levi, and Frank von Hippel, "The Consequences of 'Limited' Nuclear Attacks on the United States," *International Security,* Spring 1986, 3-45.

46. Thomas C. Schelling, "What Went Wrong with Arms Control?" *Foreign Affairs* (Winter 1985/86): 233.

47. For other views, see Robert Jervis, Richard Ned Lebow, and Janice Gross Stein,

Psychology & Deterrence (Baltimore: Johns Hopkins University Press, 1985); Evan Luard, *War in International Society* (New Haven, Conn.: Yale University Press, 1987), 396-398; and John E. Mueller, *Retreat from Doomsday* (New York: Basic Books, 1989), appropriately subtitled "The Obsolescence of War." On the lengthy postwar arms race, see Charles R. Morris, *Iron Destinies, Lost Opportunities* (New York: Harper & Row, 1988).

48. Schelling, "What Went Wrong with Arms Control?" 233.

49. McGeorge Bundy, *Danger and Survival* (New York: Random House, 1988), 616. Also see Werner Levi, *The Coming End of War* (Beverly Hills, Calif.: Sage Publications, 1981); and a critique of Mueller's, *Retreat from Doomsday* by Robert Jervis, "The Political Effects of Nuclear Weapons: A Commentary," *International Security*, Fall 1988, 80-90.

50. George et al., *U.S.-Soviet Security Cooperation*.

51. Mueller, *Retreat from Doomsday*, 93-116.

52. Jervis, "Political Effects of Nuclear Weapons," 80. Also see his *The Meaning of the Nuclear Revolution* (Ithaca, N.Y.: Cornell University Press, 1989).

CHAPTER 13

The Use
of Force

LIMITED WARFARE IN THE NUCLEAR AGE

Nuclear weapons made an all-out war suicidal for the superpowers. Thus, the only kind of war they could use safely to advance their purposes was a "limited war." [1] Although the use of total force was considered irrational, it did not follow that *any* use of violence was irrational. The two superpowers could directly, or indirectly through allies and friends, pursue their goals through a limited war, especially if either superpower presented its opponent with a limited challenge to which the latter could respond *only* with all-out war. The latter could then confront an agonizing dilemma: if it responded, it would risk suicide; if it wanted to avoid that disaster, it could simply not respond and retreat from what it had previously defined as a vital interest.

Following World War II the United States enjoyed virtual immunity from attack until the mid-1950s, for the Soviets did not explode their first atomic bomb until late 1949, and the Soviet long-range air force did not undergo major development until 1954. The Soviet Union, however, was vulnerable to Strategic Air Command (SAC) bombers, whose American bases were supplemented by a global string of bases around the periphery of what was then the Sino-Soviet bloc. Yet, even under such favorable conditions, it was not rational for the United States to fight a total war in response to a limited provocation. The credibility of commitments is related to the importance of the interests at stake. A power may risk a major war in defense of itself and its principal allies but not of lesser states in areas of secondary concern. The ineffectiveness of threats of all-out war in deterring limited Soviet probes was clearly demonstrated when North Korea attacked South Korea in June 1950. The Soviets were apparently quite willing to acquiesce in, if not initiate, this use of force by an ally, despite the United States' overwhelming strategic superiority. Obviously, they did not expect direct U.S. retaliation in response to North Korea's invasion of South Korea. The subsequent war in Korea, however, became a model for the only kind of warfare possible between nuclear powers.

Definition of Limits

A limited war is a war fought for limited political purposes.[2] In contrast to the aims of total war, which generally include the complete destruction of the enemy's military forces and its government, the aims of limited war fall far short of total victory and unconditional surrender. Perhaps the most obvious goal is the capture or recapture of strategically located or economically important territory. In the Korean War the North sought to take over the South and to establish Communist control over the entire Korean peninsula; the North then would have, in the metaphor used by the Japanese, "pointed the Korean dagger straight at Japan's heart." It helps to recall that the precipitating cause of the Russo-Japanese War of 1904-1905 was Russia's penetration of Korea from Manchuria. Japan at that time offered to divide Korea at the thirty-eighth parallel, but the czarist government refused. As a result, Japan attacked Siberia. Japanese security demanded that the southern half of Korea remain free of Russian control. In June 1950, when Japan served as a base for American forces, the U.S. reaction was similar. After Nationalist China's collapse, the United States needed Japan as an ally. It thus had to defend South Korea; otherwise Japan would have been neutralized.

Another reason for the U.S. intervention was to preserve the recently formed North Atlantic Treaty Organization. Europeans remembered America's retreat into isolationism after World War I. Was the United States' just-proclaimed commitment to Western Europe's defense then a credible commitment? South Korea was not, admittedly, an ally of the United States, but it was a friend. Through the United Nations the United States had sponsored an election that had brought the South Korean government into power and then had assisted the new government with military and economic aid. Would the United States now defend its protégé or abandon it? The United States had little choice but to defend South Korea to keep the confidence of the NATO allies.

Moreover, the United States was concerned with a broader goal. President Harry Truman recalled that during the 1930s the democracies had not moved to halt the aggressions by Germany, Italy, or Japan. This failure to do so eventually led to World War II. The United States wanted a postwar world free from aggression. A failure to act in South Korea might encourage further Communist inroads.[3]

All of these objectives could be ensured by defending South Korea; they did not require, as in past American wars, the complete defeat of the enemy. In short, U.S. goals were limited and compatible with restoring the status quo. They did not require the enemy's unconditional surrender or the removal of its government. To forget the goal was to risk escalating the war.

The Victor's Restraint and the Opponent's Survival. In limited war—an alternative to fighting all-out nuclear war while preserving the balance of power—the existence of the opponent's state cannot become the issue. This is the first constraint of limited war. Halting the opponent's violations of one's interests is the issue. Unconditional surrender or total victory cannot be the goal. The "winner" on the battlefield must therefore forego winning a total victory; the "loser" will then not be compelled to escalate the conflict by, for example, calling on friends to intervene. The Korean War again provides a good example of this situation. The United States at first sought only the restoration of the status quo. But once the North Korean forces had been driven back to the thirty-eighth parallel, the United States, seeing an opportunity to unify all Korea and to destroy a Soviet satellite regime, changed its objective. But by turning around the dagger once aimed at Japan and thus endangering the political survival of the North Korean regime, the United States provoked Chinese intervention.[4] China's entry into the conflict intensified the fighting and risked escalating the war even more. Leaders in Washington, afraid that striking back against China *in* China would trap the United States into a full-scale war on the Asian mainland or precipitate World War III, reverted therefore to their original aim. They had learned the consequences of what could occur in the nuclear age if the United States followed its historic policy of seeking a total victory on the battlefield.

Noninvolvement of Major Powers. The forces of the superpowers also must not engage each other directly if a war is to be limited, not that total war would be inevitable if U.S. and Soviet forces (and during the early days of the Chinese-Soviet alliance in the 1950s, Chinese forces as well) were to clash. But their participation in combat would increase the difficulty of controlling the conflict. The great powers seem to be well aware of this second constraint. The United States and the Soviet Union have been extremely careful about where they have confronted each other, as in Western Europe—like porcupines making love! Incidents involving direct clashes between American and Soviet forces have been scrupulously avoided.

It is significant that a limited war, such as the Korean War, occurred outside of Europe and in an area from which U.S. forces had been withdrawn. After the U.S. intervention, the fighting was between the troops of North Korea, the Soviet Union's ally, and the troops fighting under the flag of the United Nations. The Communist Chinese troops that later intervened were not sent officially by the Chinese government. The government in Peking (now Beijing) never declared war and never accepted responsibility for the Chinese troops in Korea, which were declared to be "volunteers." Nor did the United States declare war on North Korea or on Communist

China; U.S. troops were regarded as part of the UN force fighting a "police action." The absence of a declaration of war and the use of volunteers may seem rather obvious fictions, yet such fictions help to keep wars limited.

Geographical Constraints. A third constraint is geographical: limited wars generally have been confined to the territory of a single nation. The Yalu River served as the frontier between North Korea and China during the Korean War, and even after the Chinese intervention the war was not extended beyond it. Bombers were not sent to hit targets in Manchuria. The Korean War was thus fought only in Korea (see Figure 13-1). Moreover, each side allowed the other some clearly demarcated "privileged sanctuaries"—inviolable areas for reserve troops, supplies, and air and naval bases. In a limited war, to attack these areas is to risk removing one of the constraints on the scope of the conflict. Manchuria was such a sanctuary for the Communists during the Korean War, although many in the United States demanded that it be bombed. The United States also possessed privileged sanctuaries within the actual area of the fighting. For example, no air attacks were launched against either Pusan or Inchon, the two largest ports through which most of the supplies for the UN forces were channeled. If either port had been bombed frequently, UN operations might have been seriously hampered. Similarly, Communist Chinese jet fighters did not attack UN troops in the field, American air bases in South Korea, or aircraft carriers off the coast; instead, they were limited to the Yalu River area, defending the bridges.

Nonuse of Nuclear Weapons. A final constraint on limited wars is the refusal to use tactical or battlefield nuclear weapons. If these weapons were employed, the critical dividing line between conventional and nuclear weapons would have been crossed and a dangerous precedent set. Once a small "tactical" nuclear weapon is used, escalation is unavoidable, for by what logic can larger "strategic" weapons be refused if they can be used more efficiently against larger targets? Nuclear weapons of any kind are also a political liability. The stigma attached to their use is such that whatever military advantage they might offer would be offset by the storm of criticism their use would arouse worldwide, even from allies, making them politically counterproductive. This would especially be the case if nuclear weapons were used again against Asians, stirring accusations that the United States uses them only against nonwhite races.

Limitations and Escalation. If these principal constraints are present, wars can be limited. The belligerents agree to these limits by *tacit* bargaining on the battlefield. However ridiculous such restrictions may appear from the military point of view, the principal aim of observing them is to provide an incentive to the enemy to accept similar restraints. The limitations must be clearly drawn: precisely because they are *not* formally negotiated but tacitly agreed upon, the terms must be qualitatively distinguishable from possible alternatives. Frontiers and the distinction between conventional and nuclear weapons are so crystal clear that it is relatively easy to agree on them tacitly; once these limits have been violated, however, it is far more difficult to draw new lines. Nonuse of tactical nuclear arms is simple and unambiguous, easily understood and observed.[5]

Limitations attached to a limited war in fact tend to reinforce one another; conversely, the more they are violated, the more tenuous the limitation. Permitting air attacks on previously off-limit targets, for example, will not lead immediately and automatically to total war, but it will lead to an escalation of the conflict. Because the removal of each constraint tends to weaken the capacity to limit the conflict, when one side does escalate, this step should be taken only after the most careful consideration. After each step up the escalation ladder, cautious leaders should pause to see whether the opponent will desist and whether further escalation is necessary.[6] The result may be a paradox. On the one hand, limited goals are established to avoid escalation. On the other hand, if one belligerent refuses to accept limited goals, escalation could become necessary to compel a more conciliatory stance.

REVOLUTIONARY WARFARE

Revolutionary or guerrilla conflict, even more than conventional limited war, reflects the restraints imposed upon the use of force by nuclear weapons. The Soviets call this kind of conflict wars of "national liberation." In the developing countries, guerrillas aim to capture state power in an effort to use it to completely transform the social and political structures and economic organizations of their country.

One advantage of such wars over conventional limited wars is that they do not raise the issue of aggression and the response to that aggression (as in Korea) as clearly; the initiators remain free of the stigma *aggressor*. There is no single moment when a major attack commences across a well-defined frontier. David Galula, an expert on such conflicts, has compared conventional war and revolutionary war:

> In the conventional war, the aggressor who has prepared for it within the confines of his national territory, channeling his resources into the preparation, has much to gain by attacking suddenly with all his forces. The transition from peace to war is as abrupt as the state of the art allows; the first shock may be decisive. This is hardly possible in the revolutionary war because the aggressor—the insurgent—lacks sufficient strength at the outset. Indeed, years may sometimes pass before he has built up significant political, let alone military, power. So there is usually little or no first shock, little or no surprise, no possibility of an early decisive battle. In fact, the insurgent has no interest in producing a shock until he feels fully able to withstand the enemy's expected reaction.[7]

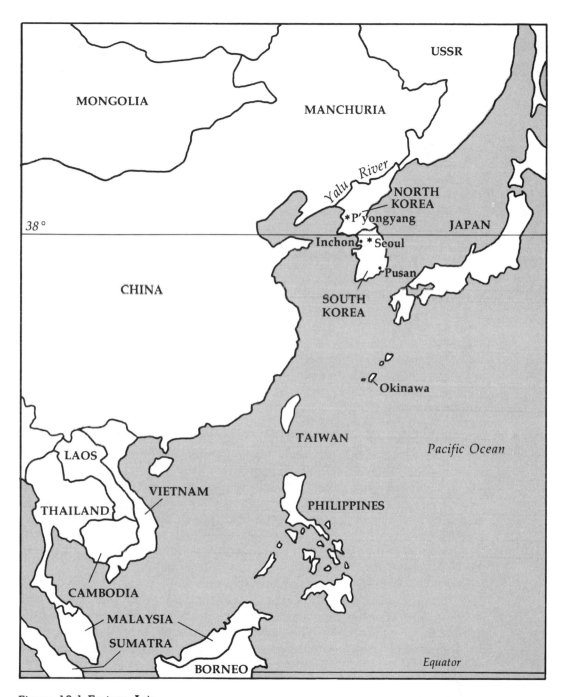

Figure 13-1 Eastern Asia

Guerrilla wars also tend to be lengthy. If the guerrillas were as strong as, or stronger than, their opponent, they would seek quick victory in conventional battle. But their very weakness compels them to whittle away at the enemy's strength bit by bit. This process of attrition can go almost unnoticed in the outside world until the last stage of the war, when the guerrillas are poised to defeat their weakened and demoralized opponent. By then it is usually too late for effective countermeasures, especially military intervention by a friendly external government seeking to help the local government. Waging guerrilla warfare is thus considerably safer than fighting a regular war in the nuclear age.

Guerrilla Strategy and Tactics

In the initial phase of a revolutionary war, the weaker guerrillas are strategically on the defensive; tactically, however, they are always on the offensive. To wear down the enemy they adopt *hit-and-run* tactics. Mobility, surprise, and rapid military decisions characterize their operations. They fight only when there is a good chance of victory; otherwise, they do not attack and, if engaged, quickly disengage. Their attacks are swift, sudden, and relentless. There is no front line in such a war. The front is everywhere, and the guerrillas can strike anywhere. Guerrilla tactical doctrine is perhaps most aptly summed up in Mao Zedong's well-known formula: "Enemy advances, we retreat; enemy halts, we harass; enemy tires, we attack; enemy retreats, we pursue." [8]

Rather than inflicting major defeats on the enemy, these tactics result in harassment, confusion, and frustration. The guerrillas do not engage in conventional battle until the last stage of the war because they are too weak throughout most of the hostilities. Physical violence is important, but it is the *psychological impact* of the war that is decisive. Although the enemy cannot be beaten physically, its *will to fight* can be eroded in two ways. First, the regular army can be demoralized. Suffering one minor defeat after another, rarely engaging the enemy directly in battle, and forced increasingly on the defensive by the guerrillas' tactics, the army loses its offensive spirit as it finds its conventional tactics useless. The determination to stay and fight declines, and stamina is sapped.

Second, and even more important in undermining the enemy's will to fight, are measures taken to isolate the government either by capturing the support of most of the population or by neutralizing popular support for the regime in power. Control of the population is essential if the guerrillas are to achieve their objective of internal conquest. The populace provides them with recruits, food, shelter, and, above all, intelligence. To surprise the enemy, guerrillas must know where to strike and when. To be able to choose favorable moments to fight and escape when government reinforcements suddenly arrive, they must know all of their opponent's moves.

Victory is one way of impressing the people. As government troops become demoralized and defensive and, as they increasingly appear unable to provide the population with elementary security in daily life, the government loses whatever allegiance it has had. It is the peasants—the majority—who are most concerned about their future. If they think the guerrillas will win the war, they are unlikely to antagonize them but will cooperate instead. Selective terrorism also helps to elicit cooperation. Its aim is to reaffirm the weakness of the government by attacking mainly local government officials. Obviously, wholesale and indiscriminate terrorism would alienate the very people whose support the guerrillas seek to win, although on occasion massive execution or the burning of an entire village is used to influence other villages and towns. The guerrillas have made their point vividly when they can show the peasants that the government is not able to protect even its own officials.[9] Furthermore, by eliminating these officials, often with all the villagers forced to watch, the guerrillas break the link between the government and the majority of the people, restricting the government's authority largely to the cities.

Guerrillas, however, achieve popular support mainly because of an effective *social strategy* in which they identify themselves with a popular cause or grievance.[10] Communist guerrillas do not usually present themselves as Communists, nor do the people support them because they are Communists or desire establishment of a Communist state. The guerrillas present themselves simply as representatives for existing social causes and aspirations. If the people are resentful of continued colonial rule or of a despotic native government, the guerrillas take up the cry. If certain classes seek social and economic justice, the guerrillas demand it on their behalf. The guerrillas identify themselves as liberators and reformers, promising that they can satisfy rising expectations. In South Vietnam the Viet Cong appealed to the peasants by pointing out that they were working in the landowners' rice fields for the landowners' benefits. When the landlords fled to the cities, the Viet Cong told the peasants that they no longer had to pay exorbitant and exploitative rents (or taxes); the peasants owned the land, and the Viet Cong would protect them if anyone sought to take it away. The result was a deep schism between the government in Saigon and the peasantry.

This social strategy is basic to the guerrillas' revolutionary warfare. Although the military component is important, it is neither the most significant nor the distinguishing characteristic of this particular kind of war, especially as it is waged by Communist parties whose entire social outlook is based on a class analysis and class struggle. Indeed, the struggle begins before the military phase of the war begins. In each village and hamlet the revolutionary party establishes its cells, seeks local control and support, and thus diminishes the base of popular support for the government. That a large proportion of the population tends to be neutral in the war, waiting to see who is likely to win, is partly the result of this *preemptive* social strategy. Whereas the revolutionaries' maximum goal is to mobilize the population to fight with them against the government, their minimum aim is to prevent the population from fighting on the government's side.

As the war goes on, the government becomes increasingly isolated socially and weakened militarily, so that only a final blow is needed to topple it. This last step involves conventional battle, unless, as in Cuba and South Vietnam before American intervention, the entire governmental structure and authority have already disintegrated. The defeat of the French forces at Dien Bien Phu in Indochina in 1954 broke France's determination to hold onto its old colony, yet the French garrison at Dien Bien Phu consisted of only one-fifteenth of the total number of French troops in Indochina. The French suffered 12,000 casualties, including prisoners, but the estimated Vietminh casualties were greater—15,000. Since its total force was not as large as that of the French, the Vietminh clearly had been badly hurt. Nonetheless, this single battle sapped France's will to resist.[11] The French decided to end the long and—for them—futile fighting.

Guerrilla warfare may at times seem militarily primitive, for guerrilla weapons do not begin to compare with the highly intricate weapons in Western arsenals. Guerrillas may receive sophisticated weapons, but their success does not depend upon them. Politically, however, guerrilla warfare is "more sophisticated than nuclear war or . . . war as it was waged by conventional armies, navies, and air forces."[12]

Primacy of Political over Military Factors

No counterrevolutionary war can be won by conventional military means alone: *a purely military solution is impossible.* Interestingly, the successful guerrilla and counterguerrilla leaders of the past two decades have not been military men.[13] In China, Mao—a student, a librarian, and subsequently a professionally trained revolutionary—defeated Chiang Kai-shek, a professionally trained soldier. In Indochina, Ho Chi Minh, a socialist agitator, and General Vo Nguyen Giap, a French-educated history teacher, defeated four of France's senior generals. Fidel Castro was a lawyer, and Ramón Magsaysay, who led the counterguerrilla war in the Philippines, was an automotive mechanic turned politician. In short, the orthodox military officer has generally been unable to cope with the unorthodox nature of guerrilla warfare.

In the final analysis, the government can win its war against the revolutionaries only if it alleviates the conditions that have led the peasantry to support the revolutionary party in the first place. For example, in Malaya (now Malaysia) the British promised independence during the war there from 1946 to 1960. Because they had already granted independence to India, Pakistan, and Burma, their word was credible, and the Malayans had a stake in the government's struggle. The Communists were thus stripped of their guise as liberators from colonialism. Many Malays fought alongside British troops. The contrast with the situation in Vietnam is striking. In the first Indochina War from 1946 to 1954 the people supported the Vietminh as national liberators because the French refused to grant them full independence. Ho Chi Minh became a symbol of Vietnamese nationalism. Anti-Communist Vietnamese who had fought with the French against the Vietminh (as anti-Communist Malays had fought with the British) were never able to compete with Ho for this nationalist identity. After 1954 they appeared to many—including many in the West—as puppets of France. This image was reinforced by their lack of social conscience and concern. Indeed, the government's suppression of political opponents, critics of the war, and advocates of settlement with the Viet Cong only fortified this image.[14]

Popular confidence, then, is the indispensable condition for successful antirevolutionary warfare. Military countermeasures alone are never adequate; troops trained in the tactics of unconventional warfare must be supported by political, social, and economic reforms. A British colonel summed up the essence of counterguerrilla warfare in this way: "There has never been a successful guerrilla war conducted in an area where the populace is hostile to the guerrillas. . . . The art of defeating the guerrillas is therefore the art of turning the populace against them." [15] The major task of antirevolutionary warfare is thus fundamentally *political*. Guerrillas are a barometer of discontent, which must be ameliorated, as it is the decisive element in victory or failure. Perhaps the French experience in Algeria offers the clearest evidence. By 1960 the French had actually won the military war against the Algerian guerrillas. The Algerian National Liberation Army no longer possessed even a battalion-sized unit. And by the end of the war in 1962, the Algerian guerrillas had, according to French army sources, fewer than 4,000 troops left (10,000, according to other, more sympathetic French sources) out of a total of almost 60,000 three years earlier.[16] French military tactics therefore had been as effective in Algeria as they had been ineffective in Indochina. Nevertheless, the French lost the war because it could not be won *politically*. The Algerian population was hostile; so were France's NATO allies and the nonaligned states. The suppression of a nationalist movement was politically unpalatable and infeasible in an age when the right of all former colonies to rule themselves was almost universally recognized and asserted. In such circumstances the use of conventional military force may be self-defeating.

UNITED STATES IN VIETNAM AND SOVIET UNION IN AFGHANISTAN

The preceding analysis should largely explain why in the second Indochina War from 1965 to 1973 it was difficult for the United States to cope with guerrilla warfare in Vietnam.[17] American military leaders had been trained traditionally. They saw this war, like other wars, as essentially a military, not political, undertaking.[18] All that was necessary, they believed, was to apply American technology and know-how to the problem. Could the world's mightiest nation, with its huge army led by well-trained officers and supported by the might and knowledge of American industry, not defeat a few thousand black-clad Asian guerrillas? It was easy to indulge in the illusion of omnipotence. The United States had, after all, beaten far greater powers. France's earlier failure was blamed on the alienation of the Vietnamese nationalists and on an army that was not well equipped or led and had poor air support. Presumably, none of these factors would hamper the United States.

Hubris (the Greek word for overweening pride) proved a great impediment, however. In effect, the United States was so powerful and so sure of success that it believed it could fight a guerrilla war simply by changing the rules and fighting according to the American concept of war.[19] This concept emphasized the achievement of victory through attrition of the enemy's forces. The soldier's concern was strictly military; politics was not the military's business. This division of labor suggests that the crucial political reforms would be postponed until after the guerrillas had been defeated. The additional advantage, according to the military, was that the United States would be fighting the war, thereby avoiding the difficulties and frustrations of cooperating with the ineffective South Vietnamese army, which was expected only to stay out of the way. But this policy and ordering of priorities guaranteed failure. Surely the war could not be won primarily by foreign troops; instead, an indigenous army with a will to fight and support from a sizable portion of its people was required. Indeed, how could the South Vietnamese government establish its own identity and claim the allegiance of its people if it was seen as essentially an American puppet, completely dependent on the United States politically, militarily, and economically?

U.S. Military Strategy and the Erosion of Public Support

To defeat the North Vietnamese forces sent into South Vietnam, the U.S. military adopted a conventional offensive strategy of "search and destroy." While the American military focused on the task of decimating the North Vietnamese forces, the Communist government in Hanoi matched the military buildup in South Vietnam. *America's aim was physical attrition; North Vietnam's was psychological exhaustion.*[20] The United States was irrevocably committed to a seemingly interminable war that eventually eroded the patience of the American public. Indeed, the search-and-destroy strategy that left the cities essentially undefended was an invitation to a Viet Cong attack. The dramatic Tet offensive of 1968 in which the Viet Cong infiltrated many South Vietnamese cities and towns not only revealed the folly of U.S. strategy but also forced Americans to ask whether the war could be brought to a successful political and military conclusion at all.[21] Psychologically, the Tet offensive was the beginning of the end for the United States in Vietnam, as the American public, increasingly beset by doubts about the wisdom and costs of a war that seemed to have no end, became more and more disillusioned. Tet sapped American will and determination. But it was not an American military defeat. Quite the contrary, the Viet Cong suffered such an enormous defeat that the North Vietnamese bore the burden of the fighting thereafter.

Americans like to win their wars quickly. Within one year Americans were fed up with "Truman's war" in Korea and the continuing, apparently futile loss of American lives. This mood contributed to the defeat of the Democrats in the 1952 presidential election, as it did again in 1968 following the Vietnam War. A long-drawn-out, indecisive engagement does not fit the traditional American all-or-nothing approach, and guerrillas can exploit this impatience by simply not losing.[22] In total war, when the public perceives a serious threat to the nation, it is willing to mobilize fully and make sacrifices; guns are automatically placed ahead of butter. In a limited war, where by definition the security threat is a limited one, the public does not automatically give priority to the prosecution of the war. When the national security is seen as directly and greatly threatened, people are willing to accept tax increases, a draft, rationing, and inflation; in a limited war situation, this is not so. Neither in Korea nor in Vietnam did the United States mobilize fully. Because the aim was not the total defeat of the enemy, most men were not drafted and industry was not generally converted to military production. For the vast majority of Americans, life went on pretty much as before, and guns, therefore, had to compete with the continuing demands for butter by the many interest groups in society.

The erosion of public support for these wars testifies to the fact that in a guerrilla war such as that waged in Vietnam there are two battlefields: "one bloody and indecisive in the forests and mountains of Indochina, the other essentially nonviolent—but ultimately more decisive—within the polity and social institutions of the United States." [23] The Viet Cong could not invade the United States, nor could they militarily defeat American forces in Vietnam. Their entire strategy was one of protracted conflict to wear down the adversary's *will*. General Giap, the victor over the French at Dien Bien Phu and the strategist of the war in the South against the United States, had a shrewd political estimate of the Western democracies' determination to continue fighting an inconclusive war for very long:

> The enemy will pass slowly from the offensive to the defensive. The blitzkrieg will transform itself into a war of long duration. Thus, the enemy will be caught in a dilemma: He has to drag out the war in order to win it and does not possess, on the other hand, the psychological and political means to fight a long-drawn-out war.[24]

Orthodox military doctrine thus led to the adoption of counterproductive strategy. American officers had not heard the axiom that a conventional army in a guerrilla war loses if it does not win, whereas guerrillas win if they do not lose. They could not grasp the fact that the United States could win all the battles, yet lose the war. Winning this kind of war demands a strategy that does not downgrade the political and psychological factors. The United States military, however, selected a strategy guaranteed to lose and then blamed its lack of success on the flow of men and weapons from North Vietnam. In this way, military leaders could avoid acknowledging their faulty strategy in the South, the main place where the war could be won, and could argue for more intensive bombing of the North. While this bombing had only a limited effect in Vietnam, it had a major impact in the United States.

The bombing, more than any other issue, deeply divided the American population and antagonized even friendly Western nations. It made the United States appear a bully and North Vietnam the underdog. It aroused international sympathy and support for the Hanoi government, and it stirred many an American conscience. The fact that the bombing brought many people out for anti-American demonstrations all over the world was as significant as the actual battles—and seemingly more decisive. It made it even more difficult to handle the war "politically at home and diplomatically abroad." [25] And it shifted the onus of the war from Hanoi to Washington as well as intensified the U.S. desire to get out of a war in which there was no light at the end of the tunnel. In 1973 the United States withdrew militarily from the war, although ground forces had already been replaced increasingly by the South Vietnamese army.

Who Won? Who Lost?

In the final analysis the North Vietnamese won the war in 1975 even though the 1973 settlement had left the South Vietnamese government with a reasonable chance of survival. The North won for three reasons. First, the American public had had it, and, when North Vietnamese forces invaded South Vietnam openly in 1975, the United States refused to intervene again. Second, the South Vietnamese regime fell, not only because of its military errors and panic but, more fundamentally, because of its political weakness in mobilizing broad popular support throughout South Vietnam. And third, the North Vietnamese were absolutely determined to win, unify, and govern all of Vietnam, regardless of cost.

The Vietnam War showed the limitations, if not the outright uselessness, of employing force in unfavorable political circumstances. The fact that in 1963—two years before the U.S. intervention in Vietnam—President John Kennedy acquiesced in the South Vietnamese military's overthrow of Ngo Dinh Diem was evidence of the political bankruptcy and catastrophic failure of American policy. After the first Indochina War between the Vietminh and French, General Walter Bedell Smith, head of the American delegation to the 1954 Geneva conference, reportedly said that any second-rate general should be able to win in Indochina if there was a correct political atmosphere. Without such an atmosphere, not even a first-rate general could win. According to Smith, "Sound politics in Vietnam was the precondition of military victory, not that military victory was the precondition of sound politics." [26] Military intervention by an external power in unfavorable political circumstances can result only in political failure and the loss of that power's prestige.

It took eight years for the United States to learn that lesson, and almost nine years for the Soviet Union to do the same after it intervened in Afghanistan in support of its Communist government. Having seized power in 1978, the Communist party in Afghanistan had alienated much of the population with its Marxist and antireligious policies in a profoundly Muslim society. The Soviets intervened in 1979 to prop up the government whose forces were losing the resulting civil war.

Soviet policy also failed. The Soviet military thought it too could disregard the rules of guerrilla warfare with firepower and mobility, but it believed that it would succeed where the Americans had failed. Earlier, Mao, recognizing the guerrilla strategy of separating the government from the people and winning their support for the guerrillas' cause, had used the analogy of fish (guerrillas) in water (the people) to underline the guerrillas' need for the people's support. The Soviets, with 115,000 troops in Afghanistan, reassessed Mao's strategy. Because the Afghan resistance, also known as the *mujahedeen* or holy warriors in this Muslim society, was based on popular support, "the easiest way to separate the guerrillas from the population [was] to empty the fish bowl and capture its contents. In other words, an effective counterstrategy in the face of guerrilla action involves massive reprisals, sometimes including the extermination of a large part of the population." [27] Underlying this approach was the assumption that "the war would be won by the side that succeeded in making terror reign." [28] The indiscriminate use of Soviet airpower was especially effective, destroying most of the Afghan villages. More than 5 million refugees—almost a quarter of Afghanistan's population of 15 million before the invasion—fled to Pakistan (approximately 3 million) and to Iran (about 2 million) during the war. Two million people are "internal refugees." The size of the Afghan refugee flow is historically unprecedented.

For a while it appeared as though Soviet power would grind down the resistance, as heroic as it was. But beginning in 1986, American-supplied, hand-held Stinger antiaircraft missiles and similar British missiles made a difference because they neutralized Soviet air dominance. Losing more than one aircraft a day, the Soviets had to abandon their helicopter gunship raids, which had been effective against the guerrillas. Once this occurred, the war turned around, and the resistance gained control of about three-quarters of the countryside, confining the Soviets and their Afghan allies to the major cities and towns and the roads connecting them.

Although Moscow had limited its commitment of troops to one-fifth of the U.S. forces in Vietnam, and it had no protests in the street or a critical media reporting unfavorably on the war, the Soviet Union finally decided after over eight years of fighting, to pull out from what Gorbachev called a "bleeding wound." If after fighting the *mujahedeen* twice as long as the Nazis, the Soviet Union could not win the war, it was better to desist. Resources had to be conserved for solving the severe economic problems at home. Thus the Soviets, like the United States, appear to have lost a war against guerrillas at an officially admitted cost of 15,000 dead and 35,000 wounded (figures which are probably higher in fact). An estimated 1 million Afghans had also died. Interestingly, the Soviet Communist party has implied in a secret circular that the decision to send troops into Afghanistan was an error; other Soviet commentators have more bluntly stated that this decision reflected an excessive tendency in Soviet foreign policy to use force.[29] In short, both superpowers, highly industrialized and possessing large military forces and huge nuclear arsenals, were defeated by guerrillas in peasant societies, although there is one difference: the Communist government in Afghanistan has survived so far because the guerrillas have not been effective in conducting a conventional war against government forces and because in anticipation of victory, the various ethnic and religious guerrilla factions began quarrelling and killing one another in jockeying for power before they had disposed of their common enemy.

WAR BY PROXY

Because nuclear weapons have made nuclear war too costly to fight, the use of force, as distinct from the threat of using force, is safe only in limited wars. It is not accidental that it is the age of suicidal weapons that has witnessed this revival of a more limited form of conflict; nor that the superpowers, anxious to control the risk of escalation, have been inventive in coming up with a variety of ways of engaging each other without direct confrontation. One of these ways became especially prominent during the 1970s—war by proxy. The Soviets used it in both Angola and Ethiopia by supplying military advisers, arms, and large numbers of Cuban troops to fight on the side of the government. In addition, to ensure governmental control for these self-proclaimed Marxist regimes, the Soviets supplemented troops with East German policemen and other Soviet-bloc personnel.

The point of using proxies is to avoid direct superpower confrontation. Employing a "stand-in" makes the attempt to change the status quo less provocative to the other side. Thus, rather than confronting the United States directly, which might be perceived by Washington as a direct challenge to U.S. interests (thereby requiring some sort of American reaction), Moscow presented its challenge by means of a proxy, thought to be viewed by Washington as less provocative. The main benefit of proxies is that Moscow can keep a lower profile than if it intervened itself. There is another benefit as well: someone else does most of the dying. Proxies, then, substantially reduce the danger of a possible superpower confrontation to and represent another refinement of the techniques devised in the nuclear era.

Under the so-called Reagan Doctrine, the United States during the 1980s was active in supporting guerrilla movements against Marxist regimes, especially in Angola, Afghanistan, and Nicaragua to reverse what it saw as Soviet expansion in the 1970s. These proxy wars not only provided the same benefits but also furnished an alternative to the open use of American forces. The fact that both superpowers resort to war by proxy shows that, in the age of absolute weapons, the superpowers have increasingly shifted their conflict to the lower levels of the spectrum of violence, when they have used force at all. Such conflicts are therefore often referred to as "low-intensity conflicts."

A DECLINE IN THE USE OF FORCE?

Growing Third World Capacity to Resist

It is widely asserted that force is of declining utility because, first, weapons of mass destruction are useless, and, second, limited wars, such as the U.S. effort in Vietnam, tend to be expensive failures. The first reason confuses a lack of use with a lack of *political* usefulness. The correlation between nuclear arms, the absence of any great-power war, and the careful management of crises testifies to the utility of military power in maintaining the status quo and general peace. The second reason has more substance, for the use of force by Western democratic states against Third World countries has declined. Several factors have contributed to this decline.

One significant factor has been the rise of nationalism. Ever since the French Revolution, the growth of nationalism has made it increasingly difficult to conquer *and* pacify foreign territories and populations. The conquered peoples of Europe resisted their Nazi oppressors. Today, even a weak Third World country with a strong sense of national identity—and foreign attack can be a powerful stimulant to nationalism—can make the use of force against itself extremely costly. In Vietnam, by the time American forces disengaged in 1973 after eight years of fighting, the costs had far exceeded any conceivable gains. The loss of over 50,000 American lives, thousands of injuries, expenditures of approximately $150 billion, and the use of overwhelming firepower on behalf of an authoritarian government were too costly in terms of the nation's self-image. The American army, which suffered from discipline, drug, and racial problems, paid the price in low morale and was saved from collapse only by the end of the war. The political turmoil and social divisions within the United States were a heavy additional price. Pacification can thus be made so costly and difficult for a foreign power that it will give up its effort, if it is not deterred from intervening in the first place. This has been equally true for the Soviet Union. In eight and a half years and with over 100,000 troops it was unable to pacify Afghanistan. It too withdrew.

Increasing Northern Costs

In the nineteenth century, it was Western technology, in addition to the absence of nationalism and the will to resist, that helped the European colonial countries conquer much of the non-European world. In the words of the English couplet, "Whatever happens, we have got / The Maxim gun, and they have not." That huge technological advantage in combat is un-likely in the future. Nationalism added to the lethal character of modern conventional weapons may well deter future great-power interventions in developing countries because of the cost in lives and materiel that the latter countries may exact. Arms themselves are becoming lighter, more portable, and more accurate. And precision-guided munitions (PGMs) are becoming inexpensive enough for even smaller countries, or guerrilla movements, if they do not receive them free from one of the superpowers (as the Afghan rebels did from the United States). When a relatively inexpensive missile presents a genuine threat to a multibillion-dollar aircraft carrier off its coast or to a multimillion-dollar aircraft in its sky, a great power will think twice about intervening. Even in brief uses of force, such as the air attacks the United States employed in Libya in 1986, the aircraft carriers have been kept well out to sea and the attacks carried out in the evening or at night to minimize losses. States such as Syria, Iran, Cuba, and Nicaragua, although small, are well armed, and the United States would have to use substantial forces and expect sizable losses in actions against them. It is not accidental that in the 1980s the United States used force against Libya, a third-rate power whose ruler was politically unpopular even the Arab world, and Grenada, "protected" only by 700 Cubans, almost of all them construction workers.

Northern Moral Constraints

National self-determination is a fundamental democratic principle. In fact, it was in the name of national self-determination that the colonies demanded their freedom after World War II. Thus, when a Western nation with a predominantly white population and a colonial past attempts to coerce one of the non-Western, largely nonwhite former colonies, guilt and moral repugnance are aroused in democratic societies. Examples are the opposition within Britain and the Commonwealth countries to the Suez War in 1956, President Kennedy's apprehension that the use of U.S. forces in Cuba in 1961 would alienate the very progressive elements in Latin America whose support was necessary to the success of the Alliance for Progress, and America's domestic resistance to the Vietnam War (as well as criticism in allied countries) from 1965 to 1973.

Moreover, where guerrillas appear to be fighting against what is per-ceived as political oppression and social injustice, U.S. intervention on the other side, the side of apparent repression, arouses opposition. Unlike the two world wars, which were straightforward fights between dictatorships and democracies that aroused moral support rather than revulsion, an inter-vention on the side of those less than 100 percent democratically pure mobilizes political opposition. If interventions occur, the public is likely to be divided and world opinion critical.

Constraints are applied then not only to the actual use of force against a potential adversary but also to the scope of this force. Nothing stimulated domestic protest more than the air war against North Vietnam, and the protest influenced the conduct of the war. The Johnson administration felt so vulnerable on this issue that it limited its attacks to certain kinds of targets, such as bridges and railroad lines, that would not cause extensive civilian damage and loss of life. President Nixon, unable to use ground forces because of the uproar about American casualties, gradually withdrew them. When he blockaded and heavily bombed North Vietnam in 1972, however, he precipitated intense protests from members of Congress, influential journalists, and the public. The Christmas bombing, which Nixon claimed would compel the Hanoi government to accept a cease-fire (which it did shortly after, whether because of the bombing or not), was especially harshly criticized.

These constraints on the use of force because of domestic opposition to war tend to narrow the gap between the power of the Western Goliath and the developing country David. Goliath, beset by inner doubts about the merits of his cause and accused of ruthlessness, finally gives up because he calculates that the costs of continuing his attempts to coerce David are no longer acceptable. They are disproportionate to the end to be achieved. David, highly motivated by a strong sense of nationalism and determined to win (or, at least, not lose), is encouraged by his enemy's problems, which, he expects, will sooner or later force Goliath to quit. David therefore calculates that the cost of complying with Goliath's demands is far greater than that of not complying.

Resolve, in short, is a critical factor in the conduct of revolutionary warfare. If a country's will to keep on fighting can be eroded, its superior military capability can be neutralized; indeed, the capability may as well not exist. British scholar Andrew Mack has said that for this reason

> the [Chinese Communist] slogan "imperialism is a paper tiger" is by no means inaccurate. It is not that the material resources of the metropolitan power are in themselves underestimated by the revolutionaries; rather, there is an acute awareness that the political constraints on their maximum deployment are as real as if those resources did not exist, and that these constraints become more rather than less powerful as the war escalates.[30]

Thus, adding up the components of power—even the conventional ones—would not have resulted in an accurate prediction of the outcome of the Vietnam War. Nevertheless, big Western democratic nations have tended to lose long, small wars since 1945.

Public scrutiny of every aspect of war has made a tremendous difference. When the democracies use force, they cannot do so as they did a hundred years ago. The media report on every facet of the hostilities, no matter how embarrassing or politically damaging it may be to the government. After the Argentinians seized the Falkland Islands, the British launched a successful expedition to recover them. Among other things, they sank the Argentinian cruiser *General Belgrano*, with heavy loss of life. For this act, the British government was heavily criticized at home and abroad. One British observer noted:

> It was an important military victory for Britain, yet it turned into a political defeat because of the premium that the international community put on the appearance of avoiding escalation. Any military action which is not self-evidently for defensive purposes . . . becomes an outrage. *Measures such as economic sanctions or blockades are deemed more acceptable than any military action which tends to lead to direct casualties.*[31]

In short, the Western democracies can no longer act in accordance with the idea that "all's fair in love and war."

By contrast, before the recent Afghanistan war the absence of open societies was generally seen as beneficial to the Soviet Union, other Communist states such as Cuba, and most developing countries. It was widely believed that the costs of intervention could be more easily sustained in such countries, where public opinion does not play the strong independent role it does in the West and therefore does not exert a restraining or inhibiting influence on authoritarian government leaders. Not only has the Soviet Union repeatedly intervened in Eastern Europe, as well as in Afghanistan, but, together with Cuba, it has also intervened in Angola and Ethiopia in Africa. Yet the cost of fighting the war in Afghanistan and the cost of supporting Cuban forces fighting on behalf of the Marxist regimes in Angola and Ethiopia and Vietnamese forces fighting against local insurrections in Cambodia appear to have caused Moscow to think twice about future interventions.

Thus, the above conclusion might be revised to say that great powers—democratic *or otherwise*—tend to lose protracted, small wars more often than not. Historically, there has been a dramatic turning point. Although the weak cannot defeat the strong on the battlefield (the traditional objective of war), they can wear them out and win the war politically on the great power's home front. In short, it is not necessary to defeat a great power in battle; it is enough not to lose. In a protracted conflict, the key is preserving public support. Today, wars are lost because political leaders miscalculate their people's willingness to fight a long war.

Prerequisites for Future Interventions: Dominican Republic Model

It appears that the principal prerequisites for future Western interventions are: a worthy cause, the assurance of relatively few casualties, and good chances for successfully achieving one's objectives in a short period of time. The U.S. intervention in the Dominican Republic in 1965 to forestall "another Cuba" in the Caribbean was virtually without cost. U.S. Marines ended the domestic fighting and withdrew, and a free election established a stable government.[32] In Grenada in 1983 the operation again was quick and relatively painless, ending with a withdrawal of U.S. troops and an election. These operations were the opposite of those in Korea and Vietnam, which were lengthy, did not achieve their objectives quickly, and were expensive in lives and materiel, as well as in economic and political costs in the United States.

There were, of course, reasons for the U.S. successes in the Dominican Republic and Grenada. Both are islands and therefore could be isolated by air and naval power. In both cases, U.S. troops held overwhelming numerical and technological superiority; in Grenada, 8,000 troops faced only 700 Cubans, most of them not professional soldiers. But it still took the United States three days to conclude its military task.[33] British operations against the Falkland Islands were similarly successful because the site was isolated and the Argentinian troops, although larger in numbers, were not as well trained as the British.

There is only one problem with the Dominican Republic model, however. There are only so many small islands! What about other areas where the United States has "vital interests" at stake? In 1984 Secretary of Defense Caspar Weinberger, reflecting the U.S. military's post-Vietnam attitudes, defined such interventions in terms that would, if followed, virtually preclude any future intervention.[34] Weinberger not only demanded that any U.S. intervention be undertaken with "the clear intention of winning"—presumably achieving a complete military victory, unhampered by political constraints—but also called for any such action to have the support of Congress and the American people. Yet initially such support existed in both Korea and Vietnam; the problem was that it evaporated as the war continued. To require continued support as a precondition of intervention is in fact an excuse for nonintervention.

It is perhaps because the United States has run out of small islands and weak opponents and seeks to avoid future protracted land wars such as in Korea or Vietnam that covert operations and air strikes, such as those against Libya in 1986 in response to terrorism, have some appeal. But if such air strikes were to be carried out against more formidable opponents such as Iran and Syria, which are also engaged in supporting terrorism, and American losses in planes and crews rose, would the approval ratings for U.S. actions remain high or decline? One need but look at the U.S. intervention in Lebanon in 1983 for an answer. Shortly after 241 marines sent there as part of an international peacekeeping force were killed by a terrorist bomb, President Reagan withdrew all U.S. troops from that country before there were more casualties and before they could become an election issue in the presidential election. High casualty figures thus are seen as an electoral liability.

Similarly, covert operations, undertaken in that supposedly beneficial zone between diplomacy and war, suffer from exposure in America's open society. Long-term commitments, such as U.S. support of the contra war against the Marxist government of Nicaragua, cannot be carried on without news leaks. What then is the point of covert operations when they headline American newspapers and television news? Even covert wars are difficult to sustain if the public, Congress, and the administration are all at odds, especially because of fear that eventually the United States will become militarily involved in "another Vietnam," as the cry goes, even if the situation is totally different. Thus, covert operations, certainly large-scale ones, are not an alternative to the direct use of force.

One overt operation was a successful alternative to the direct use of force, however, in 1987 the United States committed itself overtly to the protection of oil tankers belonging to Kuwait, an ally of Iraq in its war with Iran. It "reflagged" the tankers as American and then provided them with naval escort. Several shooting incidents with Iran followed as Iran attacked oil tankers in retaliation against Iraqi air attacks on tankers to and from Iran. In effect, the United States, officially neutral in the war, tilted toward Iraq, the weaker party, because it did not want to see Iran win that war, become the dominant Persian Gulf power, and thereby threaten the oil kingdoms upon whom the West—especially the Europeans and Japanese—were very dependent. The United States preferred a stalemate as the solution. The Reagan administration was also successful in gaining the participation of several key NATO allies in the Gulf, all interested in protecting their own shipping, and its measured retaliations against the Iranians provoked no escalation as both the United States and Iran were careful to avoid war. The allied support and the absence of casualties after a mistaken Iraqi attack on a U.S. frigate with a loss of lives undoubtedly were major reasons for public support, even though this was a long-term operation.

Resorting to Force: A Global Shift in Attitude

Since World War I the rising costs of war have led the industrial democracies—Western Europe, Japan, and, increasingly, the United States—to question the legitimacy of war or, at least, offensive war. The issues that are likely to compel them to use force are becoming more and more narrowly defined in terms of self-defense, however difficult it is in reality to distinguish between the offensive use of force and self-defense. There is a growing perception by the public that war, and even the threat of force, for coercive purposes is illegitimate. Since the ill-fated Suez invasion of 1956, European military forces have declined in their capacity to project their power beyond Western Europe. Britain had to stretch itself and remove much of its navy from NATO duties to recapture the Falkland Islands. Even then the United States had to help with intelligence and certain supplies. Moreover, Europe's defense of itself seems a growing and unwelcome burden for the Europeans. The states of Europe, with their large combined pool of military personnel, great industrial strength, and potential military power have too long relied on the United States for their defense to a far greater degree than their resources suggested they should.

In the era since the Vietnam War, American vital interests also have been defined more and more selectively. The memory of the war has haunted U.S. policy makers; when they have considered intervention with ground forces in the Third World, with the exception of Grenada and a half-hearted effort in

Lebanon, force has not been used. In both El Salvador and Nicaragua, Congress and U.S. public opinion were strongly opposed to intervention— hence the increasing reliance on covert intervention and support of proxies with military aid and advisers.

Communist states were not similarly constrained by the principle of national self-determination. Self-determination until 1989 was regarded as illegitimate by the Soviet Union in Eastern Europe, where it has used force several times. Opposition to Soviet domination is defined as "counterrevolutionary" and "reactionary," rather than as legitimate attempts by Hungary, Czechoslovakia, and Poland to gain control of their own destiny. In the non-Western world, however, the Soviet Union has used self-determination as a means of reducing or eliminating Western influence. The governments or movements that the Soviet Union supported were defined as those of national liberation, and the factions that opposed them were condemned as "reactionary" and "imperialist."

But the Soviet attitudes too appear to be changing as a result of experiences in Afghanistan and the cost of supporting pro-Soviet governments in Africa and elsewhere. Vietnam has withdrawn its troops from Cambodia; Cuba is withdrawing its troops from Angola. In Eastern Europe, the transition from Communist to non-Communist governments continues. And in the Third World, even if there were opportunities as in the 1979s, Soviet proxy intervention is unlikely. The trend is toward the opposite: disengagement from Third World rivalry and confrontation.

The developing countries themselves strongly support national self-determination, the legitimizing principle on which rest their claims to independence from colonial masters. But they interpret it in two ways: against the West and against one another, for many of the former colonies lay claim to people and territory of neighboring states on the basis of ethnic identification. For the developing countries the principle of self-determination can thus justify intervention. For example, Vietnam invaded Cambodia in 1978. China, in turn, temporarily invaded Vietnam. Egypt intervened in Yemen in the 1960s, and Yemen and South Yemen clashed in the late 1970s. Syria sent its forces into Lebanon during the latter's civil war in 1975-1976, and their presence seems permanent. And since the early 1950s, India has seized the Portuguese colony of Goa on the Indian subcontinent, intervened in East Pakistan during the Pakistani civil war, and been instrumental in depriving Pakistan of its eastern territory and destroying it as a rival. In addition, Tanzania invaded Uganda in 1979 to overthrow its dictator, and the 1980s saw Iraq attack Iran, Somalia invade Ethiopia, Argentina seize the Falkland Islands, and Libya invade Chad. Rather than a decline in the use of conventional force, there has been a global shift in attitudes toward the utility of force.[35] Can it be doubted that it was the Argentinians' belief that Britain would do nothing that led them to seize the Falklands by force? One suspects that but for the presence of Britain's prime minister Margaret Thatcher—the "iron lady"—that country would have acquiesced in Argentina's seizure of the Falklands. In any event, increasingly many newer states are behaving just as states have behaved for centuries.

This shift in the use of force since World War II constitutes in fact a dramatic reversal. Europe is peaceful now but heavily armed. Over the last 150 years, the trend in Europe has been one of a decline in warfare, although this has been balanced by increased casualties per war, especially the two world wars in this century. During roughly the same 150-year period, Western colonialism restrained the frequency of war in Asia, Africa and Latin America. But since 1945, 89 percent of all wars have occurred in the Third World, with the fewest in Latin America and the most in Asia.

For Review

1. What is a "limited war"?
2. What are the constraints that keep a limited war from escalating?
3. How does guerrilla warfare differ from conventional warfare?
4. Why did the United States lose in Vietnam and the Soviet Union lose in Afghanistan?
5. Why are Third World states more likely to fight future wars than the Western industrial states, formerly the most active warfare states?

Notes

1. The two best introductory books on limited war are by Henry A. Kissinger, *Nuclear Weapons and Foreign Policy* (New York: Harper & Row, 1957); and Robert E. Osgood, *Limited War* (Chicago: University of Chicago Press, 1957).
2. Kissinger, *Nuclear Weapons*, 140.
3. See Harry S. Truman, *Years of Trial and Hope*, vol. 1 of *Memoirs* (Garden City, N.Y.: Doubleday, 1958), 332-333.
4. See John Spanier, *The Truman-MacArthur Controversy and the Korean War* (Cambridge, Mass.: Harvard University Press, 1959), 84-134; and Allen S. Whiting, *China Crosses the Yalu* (New York: Macmillan, 1960).
5. Thomas C. Schelling, *Strategy of Conflict* (Cambridge, Mass.: Harvard University Press, 1960), 75; and Schelling, *Arms and Influence* (New Haven, Conn.: Yale University Press, 1966), 137-141.
6. Herman Kahn, *On Escalation* (New York: Holt, Rinehart & Winston, 1965), 38-41. On controlling escalation, also see Richard Smoke, *War* (Cambridge, Mass.: Harvard University Press, 1978).
7. David Galula, *Counterinsurgency Warfare* (New York: Holt, Rinehart & Winston, 1964), 9-10.
8. *Mao Tse-tung on Guerrilla Warfare*, trans. Samuel B. Griffith (New York: Holt, Rinehart & Winston, 1961), 103-104. For the Vietminh's seven rules for the conduct

of guerrilla warfare, see Otto Heilbrunn, *Partisan Warfare* (New York: Holt, Rinehart & Winston, 1962), 78-79.

9. In South Vietnam, for example, more than 15,000 village officials were murdered between 1957 and 1965. See Bernard B. Fall, *Viet-Nam Witness: 1953-56* (New York: Holt, Rinehart & Winston, 1966), 293.

10. Jeffrey Race, *War Comes to Long An* (Berkeley: University of California Press, 1972), 141ff.; Heilbrunn, *Partisan Warfare*, 145-146; and George K. Tanham, *Communist Revolutionary Warfare* (New York: Holt, Rinehart & Winston, 1961), 143. On the different components of strategy, see Michael Howard, "The Forgotten Dimensions of Strategy," *Foreign Affairs* (Summer 1979): 975-986.

11. Tanham, *Communist Revolutionary Warfare*, 32, 97.

12. Griffith, Introduction to *Mao Tse-tung on Guerrilla Warfare*, 7.

13. Charles W. Thayer, *Guerrilla* (New York: Harper & Row, 1963), 42-60.

14. Bernard B. Fall, *The Two Viet-Nams*, 2d ed. (New York: Holt, Rinehart & Winston, 1964); Denis Warner, *The Last Confucian* (New York: Macmillan, 1963); and Stanley Karnow, *Vietnam* (New York: Viking, 1983), 128-239.

15. Quoted in Heilbrunn, *Partisan Warfare*, 34. On the decisiveness of civilian loyalties, see Chalmers A. Johnson, "Civilian Loyalties and Guerrilla Conflict," *World Politics*, July 1962, 646-661. Also see Johnson, *Autopsy on People's War* (Berkeley: University of California Press, 1973).

16. Fall, *Two Viet-Nams*, 346-347. The Algerian example also clearly demonstrates that counterterror is not effective in ending guerrilla warfare.

17. This section is not concerned with judgments on whether the United States should have intervened in Vietnam, only with the manner in which force was used. Judgment is, of course, implicit in such an analysis. Ultimately, it reflects on the issue of the original intervention, for, if the conclusion is that force was exercised ineffectively—indeed, counterproductively—it may also be deduced that the intervention should have been avoided in the first place. This judgment, to be sure, is pragmatic, not moral. For moral and legal judgments on the war, see, among others, Telford Taylor, *Nuremberg and Vietnam* (New York: Bantam Books, 1971); and Richard A. Falk, Gabriel Kolko, and Robert J. Lifton, eds. *Crimes of War* (New York: Vintage, 1971). For a contrary point of view defending the war's legality, see Guenter Lewy, *America in Vietnam* (New York: Oxford University Press, 1978), 223-270, 343-373. My own pragmatic judgment on Vietnam is much the same as Donald Zagoria's in *Vietnam Triangle: Moscow, Peking, Hanoi* (New York: Pegasus, 1967), xiii—namely, that American strategy and tactics raise "serious doubts in my mind whether we as a nation have the wisdom, the skills and the manpower to cope with civil wars."

18. General Lewis W. Walt, assistant commandant of the U.S. Marine Corps, confessed in 1970 that when he visited Vietnam in 1965 he thought of it as a conventional war like the Korean War (*New York Times*, Nov. 18, 1970). General Earle Wheeler, chairman of the Joint Chiefs of Staff, held the same opinion, as reported by Roger Hilsman, *To Move a Nation* (Garden City, N.Y.: Doubleday, 1967), 426.

19. Robert Thompson, *No Exit from Vietnam* (New York: McKay, 1969), 13-17; and Lewy, *America in Vietnam*. Both authors stress that the United States, by waging a conventional conflict, was guilty of misconduct of the war.

20. Henry A. Kissinger, *American Foreign Policy* (New York: Norton, 1969), 104.

21. Thompson, *No Exit from Vietnam*, 40-74.

22. Andrew J. R. Mack, "Why Big Nations Lose Small Wars: The Politics of Asymmet-

ric Conflict," *World Politics*, January 1975, 175-288. Also see John E. Mueller, *War, Presidents, and Public Opinion* (New York: Wiley, 1973); and Larry Elowitz and John Spanier, "Korea and Vietnam: Limited War and the American Political System," *Orbis*, Summer 1974, 510-534.

23. Mack, "Why Big Nations Lose Small Wars," 177.

24. Quoted in Fall, *Two Viet-Nams*, 113.

25. Townsend Hoopes, *The Limits of Intervention* (New York: McKay, 1969), 82. For an assessment of "coercive violence" in Vietnam, see Wallace J. Thies, *When Governments Collide* (Berkeley: University of California Press, 1980), 349-374.

26. Theodore Draper, *Abuse of Power* (New York: Viking, 1967), 29, 30. For balanced interpretations of why the war was lost, see Timothy J. Lomperis, *The War Everyone Lost—and Won* (Washington, D.C.: CQ Press, 1987), 176. Also see Lawrence E. Grinter and Peter M. Dunn, eds., *The American War in Vietnam* (Westport, Conn.: Greenwood Press, 1988).

27. Claude Malhuret, "Report from Afghanistan," *Foreign Affairs* (Winter 1983/84): 427. On Soviet intervention, see Thomas T. Hammond, *Red Flag Over Afghanistan* (Boulder, Colo.: Westview Press, 1984); and Rosanne Klass, ed., *Afghanistan, The Great Game Revisited* (New York: Freedom House, 1988).

28. Malhuret, "Report from Afghanistan," 428.

29. Bill Keller, "Secret Soviet Party Document Said to Admit Afghan Errors," *New York Times*, June 17, 1988.

30. Mack, "Why Big Nations Lose Small Wars," 139-140.

31. Lawrence Freedman, "The War of the Falkland Islands, 1982," *Foreign Affairs* (Fall 1982): 209 (emphasis added).

32. Bruce Palmer, Jr., *The Dominican Intervention* (Lexington: University Press of Kentucky, 1988).

33. For three books very critical of the armed forces' preparations for fighting in the future, see Edward N. Luttwak, *The Pentagon and the Art of War* (New York: Simon & Schuster, 1984); Arthur T. Hadley, *The Straw Giant* (New York: Random House, 1986); and Richard A. Gabriel, *Military Incompetence* (New York: Hill and Wang, 1985).

34. For Weinberger's speech, see *New York Times*, Nov. 29, 1984. Also see Harry Summers, *On Strategy* (New York: Dell, 1984); and General Palmer Bruce, Jr., *The 25-Year War* (Lexington: University of Kentucky Press, 1984). Eliot A. Cohen's "Constraints on America's Conduct of Small Wars," *International Security*, Fall 1984, 151-181, provides a good analysis of why the U.S. military resists fighting what he prefers to call small wars. Also see Stephen T. Hosmer, *Constraints on U.S. Strategy in Third World Conflicts* (New York: Crane & Russak, 1987).

35. A similar thesis has been suggested in "Is International Coercion Waning or Rising?" by Klaus Knorr, *International Security*, Spring 1977, 92-110; and Knorr, "On the International Uses of Military Force in the Contemporary World," *Orbis*, Spring 1977, 5-27.

CHAPTER 14

The International Political Economy and Statecraft

PAST SEPARATION OF POLITICS AND ECONOMICS

Until 1973, the year of the oil embargo against the United States and the quadrupling of oil prices by the Organization of Petroleum Exporting Countries (OPEC), analysts of international politics had largely ignored the economic dimensions of relations among states. Security considerations—*high politics*—were primary, and, not unnaturally, the shadow of "the bomb" had led to an emphasis on deterrence, crisis management, and limited warfare. The behavior of states was explained primarily in terms of the state system. Economics or welfare concerns were relegated to a subordinate, indeed peripheral, position; the term *low politics* is in that sense appropriate.

In part, this separation of politics and economics sprang from the nineteenth-century *laissez-faire* or free-market economic theories. Classical capitalist economists painted a natural economic order that was independent of politics and worked best when governments interfered as little as possible with the laws of supply and demand. The economic sphere, which was based on private property and the profit motive, would provide for citizens' material wants. Private enterprise, through the laws of the marketplace, would maximize manufacturers' profits by providing what consumers wanted. The political sphere, that of government, was concerned with safeguarding the nation from foreign threats and preserving law and order domestically. But it was not to intervene and upset the market. Economics and politics were thus viewed as two separate orders, divorced from one another. Because they enhanced the standard of living, economic activities were regarded as good. Politics, however, was tolerated only as a necessary evil because the government had to tax citizens to raise the revenues to support the army and police. Concerned with such things as fighting wars and keeping order at home, government activities were thought to have little or no role in improving the lives of ordinary people. Politics, therefore, was thought to be "bad." Since 1973, this separation of economics and politics has disappeared: indeed, the term *political economy*, to emphasize their inseparability, has come back into vogue.[1]

NATIONAL INDEPENDENCE AND SELF-SUFFICIENCY

... In Wartime

Sovereign nation-states guard their independence jealously, even when they believe the world is becoming more interdependent. In pre-World War I Europe most professional soldiers thought that no war could last very long precisely because of the high degree of economic interdependence.[2] Countries would not be able to mobilize large armies and pay for such a war without risking mutual bankruptcy and social revolution. War plans aimed at quick victories, but the opposite happened. Once it was realized that the war was not going to end quickly, the industrial economies demonstrated their enormous potential power when they were mobilized for the long haul. The war lasted four years before Germany's exhaustion led to the end of hostilities.

The fate of Britain during the war underlines how important it is that the great powers be as self-sufficient as possible. Even though it was the first nation to industrialize, the world's most powerful country for most of the nineteenth century, and the country that demonstrated that a prerequisite for the Industrial Revolution was an agricultural revolution, Britain neglected its production of food, as industry demonstrated its capacity to increase the country's wealth and power. By World War I Britain had become a food importer. Moreover, as a resource-poor state, Britain had to import the raw materials needed for the manufactured products it exported to earn a living. A new weapon, the submarine, thus became a threat to Britain's lifelines. The Germans, who had built only a small fleet of submarines (like the British, they had spent most of the money allocated for the navy on battleships), almost managed to starve Britain into submission. But by declaring an unlimited submarine campaign against all shipping to England, including neutral American ships, the Germans provoked the United States to enter the war.

During World War II the German threat to British lifelines was even greater. After France's defeat in 1940, when Britain was left alone to carry on the fight against Germany, the Battle for the Atlantic became critical for Britain's survival as well as the prerequisite for an ultimate victory over Germany. Especially after the United States declared war against Germany in December 1941, this battle was waged fiercely until the Allies won it in May 1943. Once the sea lanes to Britain were secured, U.S. troops, landing craft, and other supplies needed for the invasion of France could be shipped to the British Isles.

Just as the Germans used submarines, the British tried to use the naval blockade during World War II to defeat Germany by slow strangulation.[3] But it was a strategy doomed to failure. German industry produced synthetic oil, rubber, and wool; the neutral states—such as Russia (until Germany attacked it), Sweden, and Spain—supplied materials Germany needed; and, of course, Germany conquered most of Europe and looted it for whatever it wanted. Without these supplies Germany would have been vulnerable to a blockade. Germany instead built up its military forces quickly and then rapidly conquered the raw material and financial base needed for a long war.[4]

. . . In Peacetime

Because states are not generally self-sufficient and must obtain what they need through trade in the absence of conquest, one of the economic tools they frequently use in conflict is an embargo. An embargo prevents the shipment of certain products or even all products to the targeted country. During the cold war, in what might be called economic warfare or a strategy of denial, the United States regulated exports to the Soviet Union. All products that might have had some sort of military application or could have contributed to the economic strength of the Communist state were placed on the embargo list. Although America's allies in the North Atlantic Treaty Organization (NATO) were somewhat less restrictive in the goods they embargoed, the overall consequence was that the economies of the West and the East remained separate and independent. There is no evidence, however, that these Western attempts at coercion resulted in Soviet political compliance, and the cold war years until 1962 were among the most tense and conflict-filled of the postwar era.

As the cold war gave way to détente, it was part of U.S. diplomatic strategy to bridge this gap and make the Soviet economy more dependent upon that of the United States. One tactic was use of the productivity of American industry and agriculture to offer the Soviets "carrots." The Soviet economy was already stagnating in both the industrial and the agricultural sectors. Economic growth had declined seriously, leading to especially serious stagnation in the electronic, computer, and petrochemical industries. The implications for Soviet military power and for the attraction of Soviet communism as a model for the developing countries were serious as well. Moreover, the regime was unable to deliver more consumer goods or fulfill its promise of more meat and a balanced diet for the Soviet people. Because the Brezhnev regime judged fundamental structural reforms of their centrally controlled and directed economy as too risky politically, it was logical for Soviet leaders to turn to the West for technology, food, and credits with which to buy what they needed. Secretary of State Henry Kissinger and, after him, President Jimmy Carter were quite willing to offer the Soviet leaders economic "rewards" if they acted with greater restraint in foreign policy.

Thus, the U.S. government used trade with the Soviet Union as a political lever. Kissinger attempted to create a *tactical linkage* that would use trade to change Soviet international behavior. The Soviets were asked to pay not only an economic price for what they wanted but also a political price. When the Soviets acted with self-restraint in ways acceptable to the United States, they were to be rewarded; when they did not, they were to be punished. The economic spigot was to be turned on and off. The sanctioning state's assumption was that if the adversary's needs were sufficiently great, it would behave in the desired manner to avoid a cutoff of trade. In other words, the Soviet Union would contain itself!

Limitations of Using Trade as a Political Lever

Practice, as distinct from theory, quickly revealed the limitations of using the Soviets' need for computers, oil drilling equipment, and wheat as a political lever to reward their restraint and punish their expansionism.

U.S. Domestic Objections. One limitation soon became clear; the United States could turn the economic spigot on but could not so easily turn it off.[5] American farmers let President Gerald Ford know in 1975 that if he expected their votes he had better not try another grain embargo against the Soviet Union. He did not. But in 1979, after the Soviet invasion of Afghanistan, President Carter embargoed 17 million tons of grain, most of it earmarked for Soviet livestock feed. Presidential candidate Ronald Reagan promised farmers that he would end the embargo if elected (despite his tough anti-Soviet rhetoric).

Clearly, the eagerness of U.S. banks, corporations, and farmers to trade with the Soviet Union and the pressures that they can exert on Washington mean that this kind of leverage cannot be used frequently. Indeed, the Soviets may manipulate U.S. economic interests more skillfully than American leaders can because American interest groups will seek to avoid confrontation and "unpleasantness" to protect their profits. (So much for capitalist enmity toward communism!) Thus, if the cost of sanctions to domestic interests is too high, public support for sanctions will erode. The lesson is clear: shooting oneself in the foot is not painful for the targeted nation.

Availability of Alternative Supplies. A second limitation was that the Soviets could buy technology and wheat from Western Europe, Japan, and other countries. Trade and credits are satisfactory bargaining tools only when the items that an adversary needs cannot be obtained elsewhere. Even if the U.S. government were to stand firm, foreign businesses and farmers overseas would be all too happy to receive the contracts. The Soviet Union could, in fact, play one Western country off against another and gain economic benefits despite its political behavior. Embargoes, in short, tend to be leaky when Western countries need markets for products.

SUPERPOWERS AND THEIR ALLIES: AID AND TRADE

In the difficult years that followed World War II, the United States, the Soviet Union, and their respective allies took economic measures to strengthen their positions. The United States created the Marshall Plan, several West European states formed an economic union, and the Soviet Union created economic ties with Eastern Europe and other allies.

Marshall Plan

The United States resorted to economic means to advance its foreign policy goals from the very beginning of the cold war. It was, in fact, Western Europe's economic collapse that finally made it impossible for the United States to return to isolationism, as it had done after World War I. Just as Britain's weakening position had brought the United States into World War I in 1917 and close to World War II in 1941 even before Pearl Harbor, so Britain's postwar collapse left the United States no alternative but to commit itself in Western Europe.

On the surface Britain's crisis was an economic one. As an island nation, it depended for survival on international trade. It had to trade or die because it had become almost completely urbanized and had neglected its agriculture. Except for coal, it had to import most of the raw materials for its industries: cotton, rubber, wool, iron ore, timber, and oil. In December 1946, despite an American loan and a severe austerity program that included rationing bread, Britain received what was almost a knockout blow: one of the severest cold spells in European history. In Britain the transportation system came to a virtual standstill; trucks and trains could not move, barges were frozen in rivers, and ships could not leave their moorings. Industry could not be supplied with fuel, and factories were closed. By February 1947 more than half of Britain's factories lay idle. When the thaw finally arrived, Britain was beset by floods. It took months to recover.

In the meantime, the export drive had collapsed. Britain had come to the end of its economic rope. The financial editor of Reuter's news service saw the true dimensions of the winter disaster: "The biggest crash since the fall of Constantinople—the collapse of the heart of an Empire—impends. This is not the story of a couple of snowstorms. It is the story of the awful debility in which a couple of snowstorms could have such effects." [6]

The European collapse thus posed a fundamental question to the United States: Is Europe vital to American security? The answer was never in doubt. Two world wars had demonstrated it, and the collapse simply reaffirmed it. The U.S. commitment was demonstrated by the grant of billions of dollars in

Marshall Plan funds to stimulate economic recovery and by the establishment of the NATO military alliance. The American role in Europe was akin to that of a doctor treating a patient—the prescribed cure was a massive injection of dollars. Only such an aid program could restore Europe's prewar agricultural and industrial production, close the dollar gap, and stimulate a revival of European *élan vital*, political stability, economic prosperity, and military strength.

European Economic Community

The infusion of Marshall Plan dollars was imaginative, but the French use of economics was even more so. France, after the experiences of 1870, 1914, and 1939, suffered a natural fear of Germany. The French were alarmed at American plans for the revival of the German economy, even though these plans were intended to benefit the economies of all the countries of Western Europe. For the French, the question was how to contain Germany's great power. Since the unification of Germany in 1870, France had attempted to deal with the greater inherent strength of this aggressive and militaristic neighbor by forming alliances to balance German power. Before World War I, France had found an ally in czarist Russia; in the interwar years, Poland, Czechoslovakia, Romania, and Yugoslavia had all been allied with France. Yet none of these alliances had saved France from attack. British, and especially American, power had been more important. As World War II was coming to a close, the French responded in its traditional fashion. Because Germany was still regarded as its number-one enemy, France entered into the French-Soviet Treaty of Mutual Assistance of 1944, which was quickly rendered obsolete by the cold war.

The failure of the traditional balance-of-power technique, by which an inferior power seeks to balance a stronger one, led France to adopt a revolutionary means of exerting some control over German power: European integration. Through the creation of a supranational community, to which Germany would transfer certain sovereign rights, German power would be controlled. Only in this manner would German strength be prevented from harming the rest of Europe. Instead, it would be channeled into support for European welfare and security.

France made its first move in the direction of a united Europe in May 1950, when it proposed formation of the European Coal and Steel Community (ECSC), to be composed of "Little Europe" (France, Germany, Italy, Belgium, the Netherlands, and Luxembourg). The aim was to entwine German and French heavy industry to such an extent that it would become impossible to ever separate them. Germany would never again be able to use its coal and steel for nationalistic and militaristic purposes. German use of political and military power derived from the industrial Ruhr area was to be eliminated for all time. War between Germany and France would become not only unthinkable but impossible.

The French showed great political astuteness in their selection of heavy industry as the first to be integrated. Coal and steel are the basis of the entire industrial sector, a sector that cannot possibly be separated from the overall economy. Success of the ECSC would exert pressure on the unintegrated sectors of the economy, and, as the benefits of pooling heavy industry became clear, other sectors would follow suit. The ECSC was regarded as the first stage in an attempt to create a wider market in one particular area of the economy, and it was expected that this approach would be extended gradually to such other areas as agriculture, transportation, and electricity. Eventually, it would lead to the creation of a single European market and efficient mass-producing industries. Industry, labor, and agriculture would all benefit. The ECSC was thus the forerunner of the European Common Market (later known as the European Economic Community, or EEC), formed in 1958. The EEC was designed to integrate the entire economies of its members and eventually to transform the separate nations into a United States of Europe, in which countries such as France and West Germany would become states in a federal union.

COMECON

The Soviets had a different way of organizing the economies of Eastern Europe following World War II. After initially forming "mixed" companies (the Soviet Union held a 50 percent interest but wielded total control), the Soviets founded the Council for Mutual Economic Assistance, known in the West as COMECON. When Stalin died, his successors decided to treat all of Eastern Europe as a single economic region, in which each country would produce certain items for the whole region. Poland would mine bituminous coal, East Germany would produce lignite and chemicals, and Czechoslovakia would manufacture automobiles. If each country were specialized, all countries would have to cooperate. The aim was to link the political and economic interests of the Communist countries and to create a high degree of interdependence among them. Economic specialization was to be the means of making Eastern Europe dependent on the Soviet Union and of isolating the Soviet bloc economy from the West. (After 1962 Mongolia, Cuba, and Vietnam joined COMECON and were integrated into the Soviet bloc.)

But such specialization was increasingly resisted as states sought to be self-sustaining in areas they thought important. Despite the underlying political purposes, neither COMECON nor the national planning of the individual East European countries could quite meet national aims, especially that of providing a higher standard of living. Although the regimes in Eastern Europe before 1989 were for forty years kept in power by the Soviet army, the increasingly nationalistic outlooks of most of them gave them a degree of legitimacy. Economic improvements, such as those in Hungary in the 1970s, helped strengthen this legitimacy, just as economic failure, as in Poland in the 1980s, weakened the authority of the regime.

Ironically, the inability of Moscow to provide substantial assistance during the 1970s and 1980s compelled the six countries of Eastern Europe to trade with the West, including the United States.[7] By the end of 1987, Eastern Europe's debt had grown to $81 billion. By 1989, all of Eastern Europe was potentially explosive.[8] Economic failure or political unrest, on top of a historic hatred of Russia, was the dominant pattern in Poland, Hungary, East Germany, Czechoslovakia, and non-Soviet-dominated Yugoslavia. Thus, the choice Eastern Europe faced was either embracing Communist central planning and orthodoxies and coping with further economic stagnation, or encouraging private initiative, and loosening ideological constraints.

Faced with staggering economic and ethnic problems at home, Gorbachev decided to unburden himself of the political and economic costs of supporting Communist regimes that despite efforts to enhance their legitimacy remained hated by the peoples they had for so long oppressed. Instead of intervening militarily to deal with any explosions and trying to maintain the Soviet-imposed Communist governments in power, as his predecessors had done, Gorbachev decided not to use force and accept the results of what can only be called genuine people's revolutions first in Poland, then in Hungary, East Germany, Czechoslovakia, and Bulgaria. He was willing to permit his Warsaw Treaty Organization allies to "de-Communize" and move toward democracy and economic market reforms as long as they remained within the alliance—although one result eventually of allowing free elections may be the demand by successor governments to withdraw Soviet troops and for Moscow's acceptance of their neutral status, like that of Finland or Austria. Additionally, COMECON is likely to disintegrate as potentially flowering Eastern European market countries find it harder to coexist with older, planned economies and the more market-oriented countries seek closer relationships with the EEC and individual Western nations.[9]

Aid to Cuba

Outside of Eastern Europe, the Soviet Union had economic problems with its allies and friends. Given its own difficulties in providing its population with sufficient food, its lack of experience with tropical agriculture, and its industrial economy oriented toward heavy industry and arms rather than consumer goods, the Soviet Union was unable to assist its new-found friends in Angola, Ethiopia, and other countries. With an economy that could not produce prosperity for its own people, it could do even less for its allies and friends, whether Communist or not.

Cuba was the most visible example. In the years since 1959 when Fidel Castro came to power Cuba has been unable to diversify its economy and become less dependent on sugar exports for its living. Indeed, Castro, having broken what he condemned as the "imperialist" economic relationship with the capitalist United States—in which Cuba was largely dependent on the U.S. market for the sale of its principal commodity—found himself in the same type of imperialist relationship with the Soviet Union! He still supplied mainly sugar; only his client had changed. Because Cuba was the Soviet Union's foothold in the Western Hemisphere, Moscow subsidized Cuba's economy. During the 1970s, Cuba's attraction grew as Castro represented Soviet interests as a leader of the Third World's supposedly nonaligned states. Cuban troops also helped Moscow's friends achieve power in Angola and consolidate power in Ethiopia. By the late 1980s, the estimated yearly Soviet subsidy for Cuba was said to be $7 billion. It is not surprising that the Soviet Union was unwilling to repeat this costly experience in Chile, Ethiopia, and Nicaragua.

In one thing the Soviet economy did excel—weapons production. The Soviets, often with Cuban assistance, could help friendly, self-professed Marxist-Leninist groups come to power, but could do little for them afterward economically. The possibility of Western economic aid and technology was in these circumstances a tool of potentially great influence and a limit on how far some of these states could turn toward the Soviet Union.

SUPERPOWERS AND SECONDARY ADVERSARIES: QUOTAS, BOYCOTTS, AND EMBARGOES

Economic pressures are used by the superpowers not only in dealing with one another and their chief allies, but also frequently in other conflict situations. Three examples have involved the United States and countries in Latin America.

Cuba, Chile, and Panama

After Castro assumed power in Havana in 1959, Cuba's relationship with the United States grew more contentious. Evidence of Cuban alignment with the United States' principal enemy led the administration of Dwight Eisenhower to try to both punish and warn Castro by suspending imports of 700,000 tons of sugar that remained unshipped out of Cuba's total 1960 U.S. quota of approximately 3 million tons. A quota is an import level for a particular product established by the importing government for a specific time period. This amount can be sold at a price higher than the international market one. For Cuba, whose entire economy was based on sugar production, this suspension was a form of pressure. The United States was trying to punish Castro, if not to eliminate him. Despite the loss of a sure American market, Cuba was not deterred from turning toward the Soviet bloc, even after the United States embargoed all exports to the island (except food and medicine).

A decade later in Chile, Salvadore Allende came to power, despite U.S. attempts to prevent his doing so because of his radical left-wing views. The Nixon administration then cut off all American short-term bank credits for

Chile. To make up for this loss, Allende obtained even more credits from the Soviet Union, China, a number of East European countries, Argentina, Brazil, Mexico, Finland, France, West Germany, the Netherlands, Spain, Sweden, and Japan. Most of these credits, however, were tied to purchases in the creditor countries to boost their own exports. Chile, therefore, could find no substitutes or spare parts for its American-made machinery and no comparable industrial technology. The copper industry, the source of Chile's international earnings, and the transportation system (cars, buses, and diesel trucks) were seriously affected. Only massive Soviet financial support could have saved Allende's regime. But the Soviet Union was not prepared to underwrite the runaway inflation and socially divisive domestic policies that resulted from Allende's own policies rather than from American pressure.[10]

In 1988 the United States tried to use its economic power against a nearby target: Panama.[11] If great-power primacy in the international system, or for that matter American hegemony in this hemisphere, meant anything, it should have been a simple matter to eliminate General Manuel Noriega, the head of Panama's armed forces who had been indicted by two Florida grand juries for drug-running. The Panamanian economy was very vulnerable to American pressure. The U.S. dollar was Panama's currency. By freezing all Panamanian government assets in American banks, withholding payments of canal revenues and taxes by American companies doing business in Panama, and depositing these monies instead into an escrow account to be used by a post-Noriega government acceptable to the United States, Washington caused a severe cash shortage. Banks could not meet payrolls, and the financial system, already badly managed and debt ridden, was brought close to collapse. Together with mass demonstrations against Noriega, which had already been going on for some time, the severely damaged Panamanian economy was expected to force him out of office within a few weeks. How could Noriega govern if he had no cash?

But Noriega could not have cared less about the hardships of the Panamanian people. He consolidated his power by replacing officers not completely loyal to him and strengthening his links to Cuba, Nicaragua, and the Medellin drug cartel in Colombia. After three months Noriega was still in power, and the United States retreated from its goal by reportedly offering to drop the drug charges and not requiring him to leave Panama if he stepped down (but in effect he could then run Panama through his loyal lieutenants). In the meantime, the United States had so severely damaged Panama's economy that it will probably take years to recover, even with American aid. And worse, it had most hurt the formerly pro-American professional and middle classes. Above all, Noriega has made the United States look—to paraphrase Richard Nixon's comments on Vietnam—like a pitiful, helpless giant, an impotent superpower. Reagan had declared that this "tin horn" dictator had to go, and Noriega successfully stood up to him as all of Latin America and the rest of the world watched.

In 1989 the failure of the United States to aid in a coup attempt by some of Noriega's fellow officers after President Bush had encouraged such a coup, appeared to underline U.S. impotence and Noriega's defiance. Why did the United States not use force? It had troops in the Panama Canal Zone, and it had reinforced them (the United States is scheduled to turn the canal over to the Panamanians by the end of the century). Even before this coup, the United States might have used force with a very good pretext. Earlier that year, Noriega had nullified the results of an election the opposition had won at the polls. Thus, American intervention might have placed the elected opposition leaders in power. But because of the precedent of using U.S. armed forces stationed in a foreign country to overthrow its government and even more because of Latin American fears of "Yanqui intervention" and opposition to such intervention, force was not an option, and the United States continued to look weak and ineffective. Ironically, given the popularity of the antidrug cause at the time and U.S. support of the Colombian government trying to suppress the Medellin drug barons, there was strong congressional support for the use of force.

What conclusions can be drawn from these three examples? In Cuba, U.S. economic pressure was unsuccessful. In fact, the eventual elimination of the sugar quota strengthened Castro's popularity at home, diverted Cuban attention from the regime's failures, and allowed Castro to use the United States as his scapegoat while simultaneously urging his people to work harder and rally to his cause. Attempted economic coercion also brought him admiration throughout Latin America precisely because of his successful defiance of the United States. Probably no amount of U.S. economic aid could have dissuaded Castro from enacting his role as a revolutionary leader. Thus the lesson to be learned: economic sanctions may serve only to arouse nationalism and to rally public support for the targeted regime. In short, they can have opposite effects from the ones sought.[12]

Another lesson to be drawn from the Cuban experience is that sanctions will inflict only temporary pain if alternative sources of supplies and export markets are available. A nation is vulnerable only if it is largely dependent on one product and trades mainly with one country. Castro was able to simply switch markets. Cuban sugar was sold to the Soviet bloc, which also became the source of products that Cuba had previously imported from the United States. Given the diversity of available markets, any targeted regime can survive with very little discomfort.

The Chilean example confirms these lessons, although at first the collapse of Allende's regime suggested the opposite—that is, that American economic pressures abetted by CIA activities can subvert a regime. Allende's government could have survived if Allende, like Castro, had presented himself as the leader of all his people. Instead, he declared, "I am not president of all Chileans." He saw himself as representing only some Chileans—the poorest segments of society—and not the others. The latter included not only the rich but also the middle classes, even the *petit bourgeoisie*.

Allende deliberately relinquished the possibility of arousing nationalist sentiment in support of his policies. Instead, he divided the Chileans and pursued a highly inflationary policy to satisfy "his" Chileans. Political scientist Paul Sigmund has thus described Allende's mistakes and the lesson that can be learned from them:

> Defiance of international corporations and foreign governments need not lead to economic or political collapse. The Allende policy, however, which combined inflation with deliberate class polarization, was a formula for disaster.
>
> The lesson, if there is one, in the relations between the United States and the Allende government is that a government which is determined to nationalize U.S. companies without compensation and to carry out an internal program which effectively destroys its ability to earn foreign exchange cannot expect to receive a subsidy to do so from either the U.S. government or from U.S. private banks. It may, however, receive some assistance from other countries either for political (aid to a fellow "socialist" country) or economic (encouragement of exports) reasons—at least for a time. What it cannot do is blame all its problems on foreign imperialists and their domestic allies, and ignore principles of economic rationality and effective political legitimacy in its internal policies. No amount of foreign assistance can be a substitute for these, and *no amount of foreign subversion or economic pressure can destroy them if they exist.*[13]

A government that enjoys domestic support can successfully resist attempts at economic coercion and subversion.

The economic pressure against Panama also failed because Noriega controlled the armed forces and the opposition could not prevail in these circumstances. The Reagan administration may have been misled, however, by its experience in the Philippines where a 1986 popular uprising led to the ouster of President Ferdinand Marcos. But the Philippines had been different; the Church and business community had turned against Marcos and the armed forces had splintered. After a clearly fraudulent election leading to Marcos's reelection, former military loyalists had turned against him, neutralizing those troops still supporting him and throwing their support behind Corazon Aquino, Marcos's opponent in the election.

Economic Coercion and High Politics

Economic sanctions, like force, are political instruments.[14] Like war, they seek to achieve specific political aims: to compel the targeted state to comply with the preferred policies of the sanctioning state (Kissinger's economic linkage policy toward the Soviet Union); to deter or, if not to deter, to punish an adversary (Carter's grain embargo against Moscow); to eliminate a perceived hostile regime (Castro and the Eisenhower sugar quota or the Reagan-Bush squeeze of Panama); or to communicate disapproval toward an adversary (all of the preceding examples).

But almost all of these examples of publicly imposed sanctions failed to achieve their political objectives. The main reason for failure was not only that the targeted nations were usually able to avoid economic pain, but also that their leaders and populations recognized that their stake in maintaining their policies was high. Compliance was considered to be the surrender of each nation's dignity and independence to decide its own future. The Soviets learned this lesson in the late 1940s, when Stalin cut off all trade and aid to Yugoslavia after his quarrel with Marshal Tito. Stalin failed in the effort to eliminate Tito, who simply shifted to American and West European markets, while the people rallied to his support. Indeed, as a leader of the Yugoslav guerrilla movement against the occupying Nazi armies during World War II, Tito had come to symbolize Yugoslav nationalism.

It is also a lesson that the Soviets taught the United States in 1975, when the former rejected a commercial agreement because of American demands that they change their policy on emigration, especially for Jews. No power, and certainly not a great power, will admit publicly that it has mistreated its own citizens; none will promise to improve its behavior under pressure. Domestic affairs are considered the business of the national government and of no one else. To insist on domestic changes is an affront. The Soviets therefore turned down the agreement. (By contrast, quiet, behind-the-scenes diplomacy had gained the release of 35,000 Soviet Jews in 1973.)

In a clash between a nation's vital interests and economic benefits, high politics takes priority over low politics. *Attempts at economic coercion are generally self-defeating when the target state believes high-politics issues are at stake;* instead such attempts strengthen the morale of the targeted nation and stiffen its resistance to negotiations. Indeed, what is usually overlooked when sanctions are applied is that even if the leaders of the targeted state wished to comply, they cannot. They would be accused of capitulating to foreigners' demands and jeopardizing their nations' security and independence. In short, they would lose domestic support if they complied. Even in Panama, where many *Panamanians* hoped the United States would succeed, pressure did not work.

One has to ask why, given this failure rate, states indulge in applying sanctions at all. One reason is that sanctions—for example, against South Africa—are a way of expressing displeasure with another nation's policy and defusing domestic critics. Banning South African gold coins from sale in the United States and barring bank loans to South Africa (which the banks were already doing) were symbolic sanctions; they were not intended to impose any real pain. But mass media attention and other factors led to growing popular anger and demands for more severe sanctions. The administration, resisting, was dragged behind the strong public and congressional sentiment that, as the leading democratic nation, the United States had to impose more than symbolic sanctions. Otherwise, the critics asserted, the United States would appear as if it approved of the South African regime and apartheid (a policy of strict racial segregation and discrimination against nonwhites). Moreover, the United States would be criticized bitterly by the black African nations, and it would alienate those blacks who would some day govern South Africa. Given these reasons, it was not surprising that Congress overrode President Reagan's veto of its sanctions measure; the president, it was stated, was out of step with public opinion on this issue. Although South African exports to the United States, its largest trading partner, then declined (more so than to the other industrial countries), they flourished with the mainly newly industrialized Asian countries. Many of these countries do not have diplomatic relations with the white minority government; nevertheless, clandestine trade relations exist. South Africa also trades with a number of black African nations. Overall in 1987, South Africa *increased* its trade.

In this case, as well as Panama, an embargo was applied because there was little else that could be done. For domestic and international reasons, Reagan could not send in U.S. forces. With military action ruled out, sanctions were seen as better than nothing; at least they avoided—or were supposed to avoid—the appearance of the United States as helpless. Carter had done the same thing in 1979 when Iran seized the U.S. embassy in Tehran. Unable to gain the hostages' release, the president halted the purchase of Iranian oil. But because the United States purchased only a small amount of Iranian oil, this cutoff was basically symbolic. To a frustrated American public, the president's move gave the impression of action just short of the use of force, which, it was widely believed, would result in the hostages' death. The real hope of the president was that the action would limit the political damage from the incident. For a while it did, but Carter's failure to secure the hostages' freedom month after month finally hurt him in the next presidential election, contributing to his defeat by Reagan. Why then do governments—especially democratic ones—continue to use sanctions? In large part, they do so to minimize domestic damage and to avoid the image of impotency at home and abroad.

SUPERPOWERS AND THE THIRD WORLD

Economic Aid

The unequal distribution of wealth between the First and Third Worlds was the original reason for the distribution of Western economic aid to the developing countries. It was feared that if the gap between the rich and poor nations widened, the resulting social instability and political turmoil would give rise to revolutionary conditions. In the postwar bipolar system, it was believed, that situation would benefit the Soviet Union and its allies.

For the developing countries, the distribution of power in the immediate postwar world enhanced their ability to attract the funds needed for their development. Because the superpowers were unwilling to risk total war, and each hoped to win friends and influence people in the developing areas, foreign aid became an instrument of policy. In the nuclear age, aid was a substitute for arms. According to political scientist George Liska, "In our times, economic activities are not an alternative [to war]; they are a substitute.

They are no longer a preferable alternative to clearly feasible war and to equally despicable but apparently dispensable power politics. They are instead a substitute for practically self-defeating major war, and they are more than ever an instrument of the again respectable politics of power." [15] Foreign aid thus became an instrument of economic warfare in the political competition for influence. The Soviet aid program, begun in the mid-1950s, was generally confined to states that were either politically vital (such as India) or strategically located (such as Egypt).[16] In particular, aid was given to those states that were perceived by the West as "troublemakers"—Egypt, Iraq, Algeria, and Cuba, for example. Furthermore, the Soviets did not necessarily demand economic justification of a project as a condition for aid. They furnished aid to build the Aswan High Dam in Egypt and a steel mill in India, in each instance responding to a request by the host country for such support. In brief, they often spent their money on highly visible projects.

Yet the Soviet Union's aid program was not as successful as one might have expected. One reason was Soviet performance. The Soviets at times failed to deliver the quantities of goods promised. They engaged in questionable practices (such as reselling Egyptian cotton at prices lower than those in the world market and thus underselling Egypt's own cotton).[17] They delivered poor-quality crude oil, wormy wheat, and unsatisfactory machinery, and they permitted shoddy construction. Yet the defects of the Soviet aid program should not be overstressed. The American program suffered similar failures and was inferior to the Soviet program in certain respects.[18] For example, not needing legislative approval of annual foreign-aid appropriations, the Soviets were able to commit themselves for years in advance, allowing the recipient nation to plan a long-range economic program. They also had the flexibility to exploit favorable new situations as they arose and mobilize their best engineers and technicians if they so desired. Finally, no citizen, official, ethnic group, or farm lobby in the Soviet Union embarrassed the government by denouncing the recipient country.

During the cold war years, Soviet aid did not fundamentally achieve more because Soviet long-range political aims did not coincide with the aspirations of the developing countries. Short-range Soviet goals, however, were often compatible with national independence and nonalignment in foreign policy. Indeed, one of the attractions of Soviet aid was that it strengthened the newly independent nation by reducing its otherwise exclusive dependence on its former colonial country or on the United States. But ultimate Soviet aims diverged sharply from the objectives of the new states.

The people of most of these nations keenly remembered their long colonial subjugation; they were not about to substitute Soviet colonialism for the Western variety. Their nationalism was directed against *any* foreign control, and this posed a real dilemma for the Soviets. When the Soviets did not interfere in domestic politics, they enjoyed good relations with the recipient nations (such as India). But when they sought to pressure a government to support Soviet positions, attempted to overthrow governments, or refused to support governmental goals, they alienated friendly states (such as the Sudan, Egypt, and Somalia).

The principal purpose of the American aid program, after it had shifted from Europe to the developing countries, was to help stop communism. Indeed, the term *economic aid* is actually something of a misnomer.[19] The giant portion of American aid in the 1950s and 1960s was *military aid* to support mainly the armies of allied nations around the Sino-Soviet periphery: Nationalist China, South Korea, South Vietnam, Pakistan, and Turkey. Such military assistance was viewed as a form of economic aid, for the recipient nation spent less of its own resources on military forces and instead invested more heavily in economic development, assuming it would invest in a military force without aid. In 1981, Reagan's first year in office, security-related assistance represented 50 percent of total U.S. aid; in 1987 that figure stood at 62 percent, and it would have been higher had the administration's aid request been fully granted.[20]

Economic aid has usually been identified with *development loans*.[21] In the past, American policy makers were eager to promote economic growth. They feared that some of the more important new nations, should they fail to transform themselves into unified, urban, industrialized societies, might adopt communism as a more efficient way of modernizing. Implicit in the American promotion of economic growth was the assumption that poverty would benefit the Communist cause; aid was intended to prevent Communist expansion. Conversely, it was assumed that economic development would nurture more open societies and democratic institutions, which would in turn ensure peaceful international behavior.[22]

Since the 1970s, however, there have been significant changes in aid policies. For example, both of the superpowers became aware that "instant development" was an unrealistic expectation. The enormous efforts they had made and the disappointing results they had obtained tired and disenchanted the two principal competitors. Both also recognized that aid did not necessarily buy allies or votes. Moreover, the Soviet Union had become increasingly disillusioned with the more radical nationalist leaders it had once sought as partners against the West. By 1965 several of them had been deposed; in addition, in each instance the successor regime had claimed that a principal reason for the *coup d'état* had been economic stagnation and domestic chaos. Similarly, the United States had become disenchanted with those who had bitten the hand that fed them. Competition for the Third World also seemed less urgent as other external and domestic commitments became more pressing, especially in the early to mid-1970s when Western economies were hit by high oil prices, inflation, and unemployment all at the same time. Once the rivalry resumed after 1975, the principal instrument of competition was military aid (see Chapter 18).

As a result, American aid has declined in relation to the rising gross national product. In the late 1940s, Marshall Plan aid totaled 2.75 percent of GNP. By the beginning of the 1970s, nonmilitary aid had fallen to 0.29

percent of GNP, the lowest of all major donor countries. In 1986 American aid constituted 0.0018 percent of GNP! That being the first year of a congressional effort to substantially reduce government expenditures under the Gramm-Rudman-Hollings act, foreign aid was cut, and the amount has been cut every year since. Defense, by contrast, received 6 percent of the national income (but even that figure is below the 10 percent of the 1950s). Today, of the leading seventeen economic powers, the United States remained last in foreign aid given. Small countries such as the Netherlands, the three Scandinavian countries, and Belgium have been among the leading donors—until 1989 when Japan became the world's largest donor. American aid was extended to 102 countries by the late 1970s, although eight of them received 75 percent of the total.

Most developing countries receive "so little aid that it is too small to make the difference between war and peace, friendship and enmity, or development and underdevelopment." [23] Currently, 40 percent of all aid goes to Israel and Egypt. This leaves little for human needs programs or emergencies, such as helping the new democratic government in the Philippines' recover after the gutting of its economy by the previous dictatorial regime. In any event, during the Reagan years, the emphasis in development programs was on the larger role for private enterprise: less government intervention in the economy, more private enterprise, and attractive conditions for foreign capital investment were the prescription. And given the failures of so many countries' economic planning and state-controlled industries, and the successful examples of the newly industrialized countries, the Reagan prescription had wide appeal.

The Soviet Union too changed its foreign aid program substantially.[24] In the early 1960s, Soviet advice to the new states was drawn straight from Marxist-Leninist theory: expand the public sector of the economy to gain control over the economy, expropriate and nationalize private foreign and domestic firms to keep profits for reinvestment, and orient economic relations toward the Soviet Union and its friends to break the Western imperialist economic chains that allegedly keep the developing countries underdeveloped. This approach has changed, however. Soviet leaders since the mid-1960s have de-emphasized—in very un-Marxist fashion—state control and nationalization of industry and have suggested that private capital, even *Western* capital, can play an important role in the modernization of new nations. They have also pointed out the need for more balance between industrial and agrarian development.

Since the Brezhnev years, Soviet economic assistance also has reached a low point.[25] The inability of the Soviet Union to provide economic development assistance on the scale expected by its Third World friends is a serious handicap in its efforts to influence the less-developed states. The Soviets simply have too many economic problems at home to afford the endless demands for economic aid. One Cuba to support at an estimated $12 million to $14 million per day in the late 1980s and a Vietnam costing approximately

$2 million a day are enough! Angola, Ethiopia, Nicaragua, and other pro-Soviet Marxist states, which even among the developing countries are the least successful economically, have been told to rely basically on their own efforts; the Soviets will only help to the extent of their ability. This attempt to discourage the expectations of its client states reflects Moscow's rising costs.[26]

With the decline in both American and Soviet aid and the high cost of oil in the 1970s, the developing countries began to borrow billions of dollars and to go deeply in debt. The result was the "debt bomb." Such private capital is available from two important sources: one source, which is examined below, is money loaned by banks to either business or government; and the other is multinational corporate investments in enterprises ranging from traditional raw material extraction to manufacturing plants (see Chapter 15).

International 'Debt Bomb'

By 1988 about thirty developing countries had collectively run up an astronomical $1 trillion debt, much of it loaned by some of the West's largest multinational banks and the rest by governments and the international lending agencies such as the International Monetary Fund (IMF). Approximately $440 billion was owed by Latin American countries, and three-quarters of this amount was owed by Argentina ($54 billion), Brazil ($117 billion), Mexico ($105 billion), and Venezuela ($32 billion).[27] In the early 1980s, the expectation was that should a significant amount of this debt be repudiated, it would bankrupt many banks and create a financial crisis in Western countries. Since that time, the latter have seemingly learned to live with this debt and to manage it.

The root of the debt crisis is the rise in oil prices from $3 a barrel to $34 a barrel that occurred from 1973 to 1982. The oil-producing countries earned huge amounts of "petrodollars," much of it then invested in the West or deposited in Western banks. But the developing country oil consumers were hard hit by the steep increase in their oil bills. Simultaneously, Western economic aid also dropped off as the Western economies slumped. The developing countries therefore had to choose between greater belt tightening or going into debt to buy oil, to continue their economic development, and to pay for imported food. Eager banks, holding surplus petrodollars, were only too eager to lend them money. This was, of course, very profitable for the banks, which competed with one another to extend loans and did not worry very much about being repaid. The developing countries used their commodities as collateral; a few borrowers, such as Mexico and Venezuela, were oil producers and wanted the money to develop their oil resources further.

The developing countries, however, could not repay their loans because commodity prices fell sharply. This stemmed mainly from the recession affecting the economies of the industrial countries, whose demands for raw materials declined. If an oil producer such as Mexico could not pay off its debt in these circumstances, how could other countries pay as well, especially those such as Kenya, Bangladesh, and Zaire that depend on the export of one item such as coffee, jute, and copper? Chile, also dependent on copper exports, suffered a painful setback as a debtor when copper prices fell by more than 50 percent from $1.50 a pound in 1980 to 62 cents a pound by 1985. It lost $29 million for each penny drop in the copper price. For the agricultural economies of Central America, this was a disaster. They suffered several years of no growth or negative growth and increased unemployment in a region already suffering considerable domestic upheaval and international strife.

Another reason the debts of the developing countries became such an unbearable burden was the stronger U.S. dollar. When they had borrowed the money, the developing countries thought that the dollars could be repaid easily. The United States was suffering from a major inflation in the late 1970s, and the developing countries expected to repay their loans with cheaper dollars. But in the early 1980s the dollar's value rose sharply relative to other currencies because of the huge Reagan budget deficits, and interest rates remained high. Inflation was gradually brought down, however.

Even to pay off the annual interest on their loans, the developing countries had to borrow more money. To prevent these countries from defaulting on the loans they could not pay back, the banks, ironically, loaned them more! The debtors had their bankers over a barrel; the bankers feared that the debtors might organize a debtor cartel and repudiate their loans. Increasingly, in fact, the debtors did rebel. To obtain more funds, the banks or the IMF asked the recipient governments to cut government spending, balance their budgets, bring down inflation with wage controls, and get their economies in order. The resulting austerity, as subsidies for social programs were cut and food prices rose, led to riots in the Dominican Republic, the invasion of supermarkets in Rio de Janeiro, and strikes throughout Latin America. Over the preceding forty years, Latin America's economy had grown, permitting limited benefits for the people in housing, health, and education. All that was wiped out as exports fell.[28] Paying the annual interest left little capital for investing in economic development, let alone in social programs. In fact, to the degree that they are now paying back their loans, the developing countries are exporting capital they need. In 1987 Latin America paid 30 percent of its export receipts to international banks and institutions; Argentina and Venezuela paid 50 percent. The total the Latin American nations paid out over what they received from the developed countries was just over $30 billion, triple the amount in 1983. Altogether they have paid out $160 billion on the over $400 billion debt.[29] It is not surprising, therefore, that economic growth has stopped, inflation has destroyed the savings of the middle class, and everyone's living standards have declined. Foreign aid in these circumstances can do little to help.

The dilemma is obvious: if the debtor nations default on their loans, they will endanger their credit ratings. Or they can tighten their belts and receive new loans but risk domestic political explosions as living standards fall and the division between the rich and poor grows. The implications for American security interests are obvious. Most of the Latin American debtors are democracies, but several of these democracies are new and fragile. Their political futures may be endangered and dictatorships of the left or right may return in an area where authoritarianism has a long tradition. It was debt or democracy for such new democracies as Argentina and Brazil.[30]

Peru in these circumstances decided to repay only 10 percent of its export earnings (and lost its credit worthiness when it defaulted on a $180 million repayment). Brazil declared it would not pay its debt with recession, unemployment, and hunger, but it finally reversed itself because the banks retaliated by reducing trade credit lines and delaying other loans. Castro advised the Latin American states not to pay their debt at all. Indeed, it is surprising that a debtor cartel has not been organized by Argentina, Brazil, and Mexico. But this may have more appeal as living standards continue to decline and unemployment grows.[31]

The Latin American countries were not totally without a case. The U.S. deficit, which initially had raised the value of the dollar, was a major reason for their difficulties in repaying their loans. Each percentage increase in American interest rates added tens of millions, if not hundreds of millions, of dollars to what they owed. In 1984 a 1 percent increase added $600 million to Argentina's debt, and, in the words of its president, "jeopardized his country's social peace." [32] Even though the value of the dollar declined after 1985, the dollar has remain expensive because the Latin American currencies have also declined in value. Unlike the United States, whose debt exceeds that of Argentina, Brazil, and Mexico, the Latin American countries have not been able to follow the U.S. recipe for cutting *its* debt to its Western allies and trading partners: driving the value of the dollar down by half and in effect telling its Japanese and German creditors that the United States will repay only half of its debts.[33] Take it or leave it! The short-term solution for rescheduling the Third World debt—that is, simply stretching out the time for repayment—thus continues but it does not suffice because what the developing countries have paid back has amounted to a huge transfer of funds from those countries to the rich developed ones, exceeding by far the inflow of capital from the latter. Thus, while avoiding crises in the short run, such a solution only postpones the critical issue of eventual repayment.

In recognition of this fact, the United States in 1985 accepted the Latin American position that growth-oriented policies, not austerity programs, were more likely to enable the Latin American countries to meet their financial obligations. According to a plan proposed by then Treasury secretary James Baker, economic growth would be encouraged by rewarding countries that adopted market-oriented policies with increasing support from the commercial banks as well as the World Bank. But the banks, understandably, refused to extend further credit, and the Baker Plan was therefore inadequately funded. The fact that in the 1980s the growth rates of the industrialized democracies were lower than during the troubled 1970s did not help either. Because the banks began to recognize that they were unlikely to collect much of what they are owed anyway, large-scale debt cancellation seemed a more appropriate strategy. Moreover, the outflow of capital from developing to developed states could not continue. The latter theoretically were to invest in the poorer nations to help develop them. Instead, in 1988 the Latin debtors transferred $50 billion to Western states, $12 billion more than in 1987. This capital was needed at home if development was to be resumed. In 1988 France took the initiative and announced that it would cancel one-third of the debt of sub-Saharan African countries and urged its allies to do the same.[34] While the latter did not cancel debts, they did agree to much more time for repayment, partial forgiveness of debts, and reduced interest rates on loans, thus alleviating the immediate burdens of countries too poor to cope with their debts. Such major international lending agencies as the World Bank have suggested an outright cancellation of the debts of the poorer developing countries. In *Time's* appropriate comment, "never in history have so many nations owed so much with so little promise of repayment." [35] In 1989, in fact, the United States proposed, and the 151 members of the World Bank accepted, a debt strategy to reduce the $1.3 trillion Third World debt by $70 billion. A debt cancellation of Latin American countries need not, as once expected, destroy the private banks or seriously damage the American financial system. It might instead gain new customers for U.S. goods and slash the trade deficit, since it was the onset of the debt crisis and the loss of previously growing Latin American markets that was one main cause of the trade imbalance. America's southern neighbors accounted for up to one-third of U.S. exports. Moreover, it might help stabilize the new Latin American democracies, if it is not already too late. One thing is certain: if the debt crisis is not resolved and sets off further rioting, as in democratic Venezuela in 1989, with more than 300 dead and thousands wounded, Latin America's young democracies may be endangered, giving rise to leftist radicals or military rightists. Whether a 20 percent reduction in the debt, as the banks have negotiated with Mexico under the U.S. Brady Plan, named after Bush's Secretary of the Treasury, Nicholas Brady, would have a sufficient impact on resolution of the debt problem even if it is extended to other states remains a question. Most observers tend to be pessimistic.

U.S. Trade with the Developing Countries

The American interest in preventing the debt bomb from exploding is a matter of national interest. American exports to the Third World have become larger than those to Canada and Western Europe. The EEC used to be America's premier export market, but U.S. prosperity has now become increasingly intertwined with the developing countries. The United States, in brief, has a growing interest in the development of Third World countries. The following figures from the State Department in the mid-1980s underscore the importance of the less developed countries (LDCs) to the U.S. economy:

> *U.S. benefits from LDC prosperity:* Partly as a result of post-1973 income growth in the oil-producing countries, LDCs have become an increasingly important market for U.S. manufacturers.

Over the last decade, the proportion of our manufactured exports purchased by LDCs has increased by one-third. In 1983, LDCs purchased more than $75 billion worth (about 38%) of U.S. merchandise exports, exceeding U.S. exports to Western Europe and Japan combined. . . .

LDCs are an important market for U.S. agricultural goods. Of the $36 billion of agricultural products we exported in 1983, $15 billion worth (about 43%) went to LDCs; more than 70% of our wheat exports and more than two-thirds of our rice exports went to LDCs.

At the end of 1983, U.S. private direct investment in the LDCs totaled $51 billion, about 22% of our total private direct investment abroad. As the LDCs become more stable and prosperous, they become more attractive candidates for investment, which should stimulate further economic growth. . . .

LDCs produce materials critical to the functioning of the U.S. economy. They supply more than half of our imports of such important metals as tungsten, bauxite, tin, and cobalt and provide 100% of the natural rubber, cocoa, and hard fibers we consume.

It has been estimated that about 70% of bilateral U.S. assistance disbursements and 50% of our contributions to multilateral development banks are spent on U.S. goods and services. In 1983, our total economic assistance to LDCs was $8 billion, $4.9 billion of which was bilateral. Hence our bilateral economic assistance expenditures last year can be expected to generate about $3.5 billion worth of U.S. exports of goods and services.[36]

By the 1980s, the developing countries were not only sources of key minerals and other commodities besides oil but also a growing market for American products. Thus, American stakes in this trading relationship with the developing countries had grown in ten years to the point where their growth or nongrowth affected U.S. well-being and economic performance. The United States therefore needs to help the debt-ridden Latin American states. Debtor countries cannot buy American goods. In fact, the debt had deeply cut exports to these countries, raising the U.S. unemployment level in the mid-1980s, by some estimates, to one million workers! The Treasury Department has estimated that for every $1 billion lost in exports, 25,000 Americans lose their jobs. It also has been estimated that if the debt problem could be resolved and the developing countries could resume their growth, they could by the year 2000 consume as much as 50 percent of all U.S. exports.[37] Even before then, ending the policy of telling the Latin American countries that they must pay interest on their debts rather than purchase U.S. goods could be very beneficial. Indeed, "Brazil has 140 million potential consumers of U.S. products, more than Japan and over twice the population of Germany. On our border, Mexico has 80 million potential customers, a market more accessible to American manufacturers than Korea or Taiwan."[38] In any event, the developed states, to maintain high employment and economic growth, are increasingly seeking markets for their products in other industrial mass consumption societies but are competing for markets in the Third World.

OPEC

Energy Crisis. The year 1973 was marked by the Yom Kippur War in the Middle East. That same year OPEC's Arab members, who held the world's largest oil reserves, instituted an embargo against the United States and the Netherlands to protest those countries' political support of Israel. The Arab states also planned monthly production cutbacks for the other non-Communist industrial states. In addition, OPEC raised oil prices from $3 to $12 a barrel. It was this ability to control supplies and prices that made OPEC a powerful producer-cartel and at the time a model for the developing countries of how to use their control over certain resources to enhance their bargaining strength and income. OPEC's impact upon the Western industrial countries was devastating. Its actions caused not only minor inconveniences to consumers, who had to pay more for gasoline and other oil-based products, but also a profound upheaval in entire economies, ways of life, and standards of living. OPEC also upset the plans for economic growth of many states, developed and developing alike. Economic issues rose to the top of the international agenda and became intensely politicized. The "energy crisis"— high oil prices and a lack of secure supplies—was born.

In the Western industrial nations and Japan, the quadrupling of oil prices immediately affected living standards. Families could no longer buy as much because gasoline and heating oil, as well as plastics, synthetics, and other oil-based materials, became much more expensive. Food prices also rose, because cultivation and distribution depended upon energy. The rising price stoked Western inflation, already high, and simultaneously precipitated the worst recession since the Great Depression of the 1930s, with very high unemployment rates. This "stagflation" in turn made recovery more difficult. The economic growth rates of all industrial countries were set back. Western Europe and Japan, the United States' principal allies, were hit much harder than the United States, for they were far more dependent upon OPEC oil. The large consuming nations no longer appeared to be in control of their own economies. Anti-inflationary policies could not be effective as oil prices continued to rise. By the spring of 1980 the Western countries had 18 million unemployed, and the figure was still going up. An estimated $240 billion to $250 billion worth of industrial capacity lay idle. The reported 1982 unemployment figure for the twenty-four major industrial democracies was more than 30 million people!

The energy crisis starkly demonstrated the fragility of all Western economies. Relatively inexpensive oil had led to the neglect of vast coal deposits in Europe and the United States. From 1955 to 1972 Western Europe's use of coal had shrunk from three-quarters of total energy sources to about one-fifth, while the share of its energy from oil rose from one-fifth to three-fifths. The American experience was similar. In 1964 the United States was still the world's leading oil producer; in 1965 the Middle East overtook that position. In 1970 U.S. production peaked and then started declining. By 1976 the industrial West—Western Europe, the United States, and Japan—consumed 65 percent of the world's oil production. This meant that they increasingly used oil from other nations. The Middle East and Africa, who have two-thirds of the world's oil reserves, consumed only 4 percent.

It was this oil-hungry world that OPEC faced when it broke the monopoly of Western oil companies. OPEC's power is clear from the American example. The United States became an importer in the 1970s. By 1976 it was importing 42 percent of its oil at a cost of $35 billion a year. Of its total consumption of 17.4 million barrels per day (mbd), it was importing 7.3 mbd (with 42 gallons per barrel). Almost 40 percent of this imported oil came from the Arab members of OPEC (AOPEC), four of which—Saudi Arabia, Kuwait, Iraq, and the United Arab Emirates—along with Iran, possess more than 50 percent of the world's known reserves and produce 40 percent of its supplies (see Figure 14-1).

By the summer of 1979, the United States was importing 45 percent or 9 million barrels *each day* out of a total of 21 million barrels used *each day*. From 1973 to 1979, American oil imports had increased more than 40 percent. Despite the clear warnings of 1973-1974, these imports increased, rather than decreased, its dependence. In 1973, 70 percent of the oil the United States imported was from OPEC; by 1977 this figure had risen to 86 percent. The percentage of these imports from AOPEC rose from 22 to 43 percent. Then in late 1978 and early 1979, disaster struck. The Iranian cutback in oil production after the collapse of the shah stretched supplies so tightly that prices increased almost 100 percent in less than one year.[39] By December 1979, the price of oil stood at $24 a barrel, up from about $13 a barrel in January 1979. (Some countries, however, were already selling their oil for up to $40 a barrel in the tight market.) American oil costs for that one year alone rose $28 billion. By the spring of 1981, the average price had risen to $36 a barrel, an increase in just over a year of more than 100 percent. In 1982 the price stabilized at $34 a barrel, $21 higher than the price in 1973. Forecasters were unanimous that the future would be one of scarcity and persistent price increases.

Minipowers Versus Great Powers.   There was an irony in this situation. None of the oil-producing states could be considered a major power, not even Iran with its substantial population. Most of these states had small populations, little industry, and virtually no military muscle. All they had was oil! But with that oil they were able to influence not only the domestic affairs but also the Middle Eastern policies of the non-Communist industrial states. Japan first and then Western Europe acceded to Arab demands to show more sympathy for the Palestinian cause. Even the United States, long a major supporter of Israel, decided to play a more even-handed role, and shortly after the 1973 war Kissinger began trying to bring about a more lasting peace in the region. The weak had come to seem omnipotent, the strong impotent. It appeared that the world had turned upside down as one by one the Western

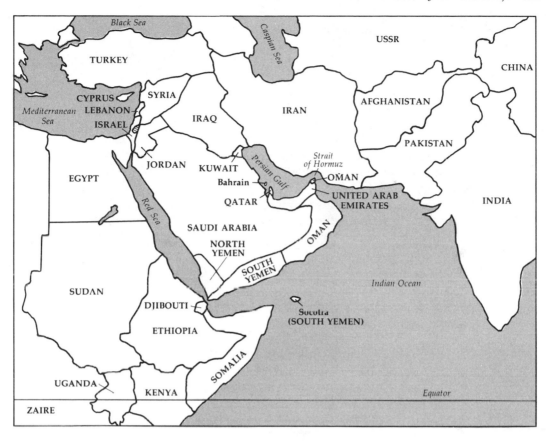

Figure 14-1   The Middle East and Northeastern Africa

states, former rulers of these small countries and still military giants relative to OPEC's members, complied with some Arab wishes. Clearly, power relations do not always follow the rule that the nation that can produce "more bang for a buck" can achieve its demands and successfully resist the demands of others.

Some OPEC members' highly public and dramatic use of their economic power seems to contradict the earlier conclusion that the exercise of economic sanctions is counterproductive. The most powerful military states in the world passively accepted high rates of inflation, recession, the declining value of the dollar, and continual oil price increases. Could there be much doubt that OPEC's price increases were far more damaging to the West than the loss of West Berlin, the placement of Soviet missiles in Cuba, or the loss of South Vietnam could ever have been? Can we disagree with political scientist Robert Tucker's conclusion that "it is the oil cartel, and not the rising military power of the Soviet Union, that has formed the greatest threat in the 1970s and early 1980s to the structure of American interests and commitments in the world"? [40]

The key question, however, remains: How could modern countries, with larger populations and sizable armed forces, repeatedly acquiesce in the raising of oil prices, which devastated their economies? One need but look at the obvious disparities in population and size of armed forces between some of the leading Arab oil producers and Western consuming nations at the time oil prices were at their peak. Were the oil barrels of the Arab and non-Arab OPEC members more powerful than the West's gun barrels? The very question suggests part of the answer: the West refused to use force in a situation in which a half century earlier would have resulted in a swift recourse to force. [41] OPEC claimed it had the right to determine prices for its oil and to deny that oil to Western nations through an embargo or reduced production. The West, by its acceptance of such measures, legitimated OPEC's claim. It interpreted the principle of national self-determination to mean that if another country owns resources, it can do with them what it pleases, regardless of the difficulties inflicted on itself and the rest of the world. In these circumstances, the use of force could only be considered illegitimate.

Indeed, this interpretation of the principle of national self-determination by the West led it to acquiesce in the virtual disregard by some OPEC members of their contracts. As Walter Levy, a noted oil expert, said in 1980 at the end of a decade of rising oil prices:

> The producing countries . . . in fact do not recognize as binding supply or price arrangements even if freely concluded by them. Recently they have gone so far as to change agreed-upon prices retroactively. This, they argue, they are entitled to do under the doctrine of sovereign control by producing countries over their natural resources. . . .
>
> Because of the fear of being arbitrarily cut off from supplies, Western nations and their [oil] companies now accept within a wide range practically any economic or political terms that a producing country may impose upon them. [42]

Leverage, Cartels, and Oil Gluts.   OPEC's strong bargaining position for the decade after 1973 reflected five conditions. First, the West was so dependent on imported oil that even sharp increases in price did not reduce demand by very much. Second, there were limited possibilities for substituting other energy sources for oil in the short run. Third, a small number of producer nations controlled most international trade in this commodity. Fourth, the exporting nations had common political or economic goals. And fifth, the oil producers were invulnerable to embargo by consumer nations.

But cartels tend to sow the seeds of their own destruction by driving prices up to levels that (1) cause consumers to do with less or (2) cause new producers to enter the field. Thus by the early 1980s, the conditions that had given OPEC its leverage during the 1970s began to change. First, the steepness of the price increases resulted in genuine conservation measures, such as designing more fuel-efficient cars, commercial jets, housing, and appliances.

Second, the number of non-OPEC oil sources increased: for example, Alaska, Mexico, and the North Sea (Norway and Britain). Third, the production of alternatives such as coal and natural gas began to increase. The high price of oil made coal and natural gas more profitable, resulting in expanded production. In addition, it stimulated research into such areas as oil shale, solar energy, and synthetic fuel, although the subsequent oil glut led to cutbacks in this research. Only nuclear energy did not expand much because of popular opposition in many Western countries. Fourth, OPEC members were often at odds with one another. As the 1980s began, Iran and Iraq were at war, and Libya sought the overthrow of the Saudi monarchy for allegedly allying itself with the United States and Israel and betraying the Arab cause. Fifth, the global recession led to a sharp reduction in the demand for oil.

The consequence of the decreased demand for oil was an oil glut and a downward pressure on prices. OPEC's eightfold increase in prices from 1973 to 1980 had by 1982 resulted in a drop in its share of the world oil market from almost 60 percent to less than 40 percent. Production was down 22 percent from 1981 and 45 percent from 1979. The official price of $34 per barrel of oil fell to $28. The decline of oil consumption continued, and non-OPEC oil production increased. OPEC's future as a producer-cartel was in jeopardy. No longer able to firmly control the price of oil, its production by 1985 was down to 16 mbd from the 1979 high of 32 mbd. OPEC's members competed with one another for the largest share of the remaining oil market (while non-OPEC oil increased from 17 mbd to more than 27 mbd). The unofficial price at which members were willing to undersell one another fell further to below $20 by early 1986, dropping to the $10-$12 range. Since 1973-1974, the West had paid more than a trillion dollars to OPEC, the largest forced transfer of wealth since the Spanish conquistadors plundered gold from ancient Peru. But this economic "bleeding" ended. The United States had by 1985 cut its dependence on oil imports to less than 30 percent from the 1977 peak of 46 percent; and, more important, it had shifted the source of most of its oil imports to Western Hemisphere countries (Canada, Mexico, and Venezuela).

OPEC, trying to survive, urged its members to eliminate the oil glut by sticking to the production cuts it set for each member. But that only gave rise to internal tensions. The oil-producing states with large populations needed all the money they could earn to support their development plans (Nigeria) or pay for their wars (Iran and Iraq); cutbacks in production and revenues tended to be resisted. OPEC's problems were also worsened by a price war with non-OPEC oil producers, especially Britain, which had become a large producer (1 mbd). OPEC's goal was to retain its share of the world oil market, which had dropped from 66 percent in 1976 to less than 30 percent in 1987. In these circumstances, Nigeria, for example, desperate for income, now matched a British or Norwegian price reduction to not lose sales. In effect, OPEC was no longer even pretending to be a cartel. Oil prices were expected to fall further unless the non-OPEC oil producers, also fearful of rapidly falling prices, would agree to stabilize prices.[43] In 1988 OPEC met with seven non-OPEC members—Angola, China, Colombia, Egypt, Malaysia, Mexico, and Oman—who were collectively producing about half the output of OPEC's thirteen members. But no agreement was reached on how much the non-OPEC states and OPEC should cut oil production. Indeed, a few months later, even OPEC, although producing 2 million barrels a day more than the established collective limit of 16.6 barrels, could not agree on further cuts. But once the fighting between Iran and Iraq ceased and the cheap oil prices had once more raised demand, prices climbed back to $18 a barrel, and the Saudis let it be known that they expected further price increases.

Can OPEC be pronounced dead? Not yet. Consider these facts: oil remains an essential fuel; oil consumption still exceeds new discoveries by a ratio of two to one; OPEC controls three-quarters of the world's known oil reserves; an upswing of the Western economies, stimulated by cheaper oil, will raise the demand for OPEC oil, strengthen its bargaining position, and render the Western industrial states vulnerable again to pricing pressures and possible supply disruptions; and political upheavals and political uses of oil remain a possibility. By 1987, U.S. imports had once more risen sharply from their lowest level of 1984 and become almost as important a component of the trade deficit as imported manufactured goods. In 1988 oil imports exceeded 50 percent, surpassing the record of 48 percent set in 1977. If oil prices remain stable and moderate, this figure may rise to 60 percent or higher, and the United States will again be very dependent on imported oil. Europe imports more than 60 percent of its oil and Japan almost all of its energy requirements.

Six other possibilities, however, also remain for the future: (1) producer manipulation of oil supplies for economic or political purposes (the Yom Kippur War, 1973); (2) shortages of oil stemming from domestic unrest and revolution (Iran, 1979); (3) conflict among oil-producing states, reducing oil production (Iran-Iraq War, 1980-1988); (4) OPEC once more pulling together, cutting production, and raising prices because of the large common losses (indeed, it has attempted to overcome past differences since 1988); (5) OPEC and non-OPEC states reaching agreement on production quotas to raise prices; or (6) to keep the world dependent on oil and to make alternative fuels less competitive, the oil producers make oil available to consuming nations at affordable prices and avoid both the sharply rising prices for consumers of the 1970s and the price competition among oil producers of the 1980s.

For the developing countries, OPEC appeared in the 1970s to be the example of how to use their control of resources to raise prices. The UN Conference on Trade and Development (UNCTAD), which mainly represents the developing nations who possess many of the resources that other states (especially the developed ones) import, encouraged the formation of resource cartels during the 1970s because higher prices obviously were the way to raise Third World incomes and thereby redistribute the global wealth. But efforts to fix prices for tin, bauxite, potash, lead, zinc, copper, nickel, sugar, cotton, timber, and jute all failed. The principal reasons were the availability of substitutes and adequate supplies of these commodities. Indeed, higher prices encourage the appearance of output from new sources in the international market. One current exception to these developing country failures is rubber; natural rubber is more heat- and tear-resistant than the synthetic rubber used for the condoms and gloves popularized by the AIDS epidemic.

ECONOMICS AND POWER

Instrument of the Wealthy

As already noted in Chapter 7, there is historically a clear correlation between economic power, military power, and the rise and fall of the great powers. Since the Industrial Revolution, it has been the economically most advanced powers—first Britain, then Germany, Japan, and the United States—who have been the most active players and exercise the principal influence. The powers who fell behind economically even when they had large populations—such as Austria, Hungary, France, and czarist Russia—saw their status and influence diminish as each in turn was defeated in battle.

Wealthy nations have been able to afford not only all types of guns but also a whole range of nonmilitary instruments. As a result, they have not had to resort to force in the pursuit of their objectives as often as the weaker states. The more economically advanced states have been able to use their "economic weapons" by offering or withholding foreign aid, making food available in a time of need, providing their businesses with the incentives to invest private capital in other countries (trade follows the flag), exporting the advanced technology other countries seek, and opening or closing their markets to foreign products (see Chapter 15). These and other weapons are means of exercising leverage. Withholding aid may help force another nation to comply with one's demands; offering access to one's markets may achieve the same purpose. Indeed, the wealthy states do not need to resort to force as frequently as the less wealthy states.

Kenneth Waltz has reminded us that the " 'non-recourse to force' is the doctrine of the strong," or what Karl Marx called the replacement of the cannon by capital. E. H. Carr illustrated the point long ago: "Great Britain's unchallenged naval and economic supremacy throughout the nineteenth century enabled her to establish a commanding position in China with a minimum of military force and of economic discrimination. A relatively weak power like Russia could only hope to achieve a comparable result by naked aggression and annexation." [44]

This issue of the superior economic power of the West is at the heart of Third World countries' current complaints that the international political and economic order is grossly unfair, and dominated by the First World, which makes the economic rules and receives the giant share of economic and political benefits. They see the international laws of supply and demand as "stacking the deck" against them. These complaints would not have surprised Friedrich List, a nineteenth-century German political economist, who, after studying the economy of Britain, the world's first industrial state to champion free trade, advised Germany against free trade:

> I saw clearly that free competition between two nations which are highly civilized can only be mutually beneficial in case both of them are in a nearly equal position of industrial development, and that any nation which owing to misfortune is behind others in industry, commerce, and navigation ... must first of all strengthen her own individual powers, in order to fit herself to enter into free competition with more advanced nations.[45]

The free market may well be a superior mechanism for allocating goods, when those competing and exchanging goods are of approximately equal strength. But when one nation is clearly more advanced economically, free trade benefits that nation more because it is able to penetrate the markets of weaker countries. If the latter do not protect themselves with tariffs to keep cheaper foreign imports out, home industries can never develop. During the initial stages of development, new industries are bound to be more expensive. Free trade is thus the weapon of the strong; tariffs to protect "infant industries" while they grow to efficiency are the weapon of the weak.

The laws of the free market are *not* neutral. Power is the "invisible hand" determining the distribution of wealth. Among nations that are equal in economic power, economic relations may well breed interdependence, as in the EEC and among the EEC, the United States, and Japan. Between the economically strong and the economically weak, however, the inevitable result is the dependence of the latter. Economic weapons, then, remain "preeminently the weapons of strong Powers."[46]

Increasingly, it appears that this is also true among the economically strong states. Some are simply more advanced than others. Their relationship may be one of interdependence, but this relationship may be an asymmetrical or unequal one. The United States was the champion of free trade when it was the world's strongest economic power. Today, in an increasingly interdependent economy, it seeks protection of various industries from foreign competition (see Chapter 15). The strong do not need protection; the weak do.

Conditions for Economic Coercion

If wealth gives states positions of general influence, the actual exercise of economic coercion by any state depends upon three conditions: (1) a high degree of control over the supply of goods or services the targeted state needs; (2) the intense need of the targeted state for the economic goods or services; and (3) a calculation by the targeted state that compliance with the demands made on it is less costly than doing without these goods or services.[47] These conditions gave OPEC leverage during the 1970s and early 1980s, even though its members possessed few of the normal components of power. The industrial countries' lives were so dependent upon imported oil that any major disruption would have played havoc with their economies. Paying higher prices was preferable to doing without. But these three conditions are frequently not present, as the examples of sanctions against Cuba and Yugoslavia, among others, show.

Sanctions are most effective if applied collectively; individual national sanctions are rarely effective. The critical condition is the cost calculation. Compliance is least likely if the cost to the targeted or coerced nation is perceived to be its national independence or what is sometimes called its national honor or prestige. States prefer to suffer economic or low politics deprivation before yielding to high-politics demands. Political scientist Richard Olson has suggested, therefore, that since the many instances of failure are all examples of publicly visible coercion, economic coercion must be exerted invisibly:

> In most cases of economic coercion, the sanctions are more subtle, they are applied in areas in which the target is the solicitor: aid, investment, finance, and technology. Trade sanctions are usually highly visible.... Furthermore, trade, however unequal the terms, is a partnership in which groups in both the sender- and target-countries stand to lose when sanctions are applied. This is much less the case in the more subtle and complex areas of international technology transfers, finance, investment, and aid. Ours is a capital- and technique-scarce world, with keen competition among LDCs for what is available....
>
> First World governments, their aid agencies, international financial institutions such as the World Bank or the regional development banks, private bank consortia, and multinational corporations are, for many LDCs, integral and influential parts of the domestic economy and policy-making apparatus. Dependency is indeed vulnerability; as George Ball has asked in apparent commiseration: "How can a national government make an economic plan with any confidence if a board of directors meeting 5,000 miles away can by altering its pattern of purchasing and production affect in a major way the country's economic life?" [48]

Also according to Olson, "Relatively covert, subtle economic sanctions will ultimately be *politically* effective with only moderate, purely *economic* effects." [49] The dependency of the target permits the exercise of economic coercion without publicity and patriotic rallying around the flag in that state. Delays in delivery of spare parts, drying up of credit, decline in value of investments, reduction of multilateral and bilateral loans, and refusal to refinance debts—not publicly announced cuts in quotas or embargoes—are more effective, though less visible, means of coercion.

Visible or invisible, it is well to remember that sanctions are not cost-free, as farmers, businesspeople, and bankers in the United States and Western Europe have learned. Indeed, sanctions may involve substantial costs to the nation or nations seeking to punish or coerce another nation. A key question, therefore, is always whether imposing sanctions is worth the trouble.

Coercion Versus Rewards

States have been more successful in attaining their aims by offering economic rewards than by depriving target nations of economic products and services. Rewards provide economic improvement and higher standards of living. Such rewards led to Western Europe's economic recovery after World War II and to the strengthening of NATO. They laid the foundation upon which European nations have been integrating their economies and establishing the basis for possible political union and status as a third superpower. They have twice helped attract the Soviet Union to détente. And, although economic aid in its various forms may not have given either superpower the degree of influence it would have liked to develop (although many economic projects and technical-assistance programs were successful), it has helped stabilize regimes (at least in the short run) and enhance the independence of some new nations, allowing them to resist seduction or pressure from the other superpower. Economic rewards at least provide incentives for improved political relations, as Gorbachev's behavior has demonstrated.

Economics and Morality

Finally, appearances of morality are not unimportant in the relations among nations and in the shaping of national reputations. The exercise of the economic weapon appears more moral than the military one, or perhaps we should say less immoral. In reality, it may be no more or less immoral. A wartime blockade, for example, may cause just as many—or more—people to starve to death as would be killed by high explosives in a series of air raids. Similarly, granting a nation political independence, even though economically it is dependent on foreign markets and not fully in control of its own destiny, generally seems less immoral than direct political control by a foreign occupying power. Carr called the popular distinction between dollars and bullets an illusion. Power is "one and indivisible," he argued.

> It uses military and economic weapons for the same ends. The strong will tend to prefer the minor and more "civilised" weapon because it will generally suffice to achieve his purposes; and as long as it will suffice, he is under no temptation to resort to the more hazardous military weapons. But economic power cannot be isolated from military power, nor military from economic. They are both integral parts of political power; and in the long run one is helpless without the other. . . . But generally speaking, there is a sense in which dollars are humaner than bullets even if the end pursued be the same.[50]

For Review

1. What are the main economic tools used by states in conflict?
2. What conditions are necessary for one state to actually undertake economic coercion of another?
3. Why is it easier to compel a state to comply on low-politics issues than on high-politics issues?
4. What roles has foreign aid played in the relationship between the superpowers and their allies, as well as between the superpowers and the developing countries?
5. What is the developing country "debt problem," and what are its domestic and international effects?
6. Are such developing country resource cartels as OPEC likely to be able to use their control over certain resources to enhance their bargaining strength and income?

Notes

1. The impact of economics on international politics and the uses of economic means for political ends were first explored in: David H. Blake and Robert S. Walters, *The Politics of Global Economic Relations*, 3d ed. (Englewood Cliffs, N.J.: Prentice-Hall, 1987); Joan E. Spero, *The Politics of International Economic Relations*, 2d ed. (New York: St. Martin's Press, 1981); and C. Fred Bergsten, *The Future of the International Economic Order* (Lexington, Mass.: D. C. Heath, 1973). See also various articles by Bergsten: "The Threat from the Third World," *Foreign Policy*, Summer 1973, 102-134; "The Responses to the Third World," *Foreign Policy*, Winter 1974-1975, 3-34; and "Coming Investment Wars?" *Foreign Affairs* (October 1974): 153-175. Finally, see C. Fred Bergsten and Lawrence B. Krause, eds., *World Politics and International Economics* (Washington, D.C.: Brookings, 1975).
2. Theodore Ropp, *War in the Modern World*, 2d ed. (New York: Collier, 1962), 203-204.
3. Paul M. Kennedy, *The Rise and Fall of British Naval Mastery* (Malabar, Fla.: Robert E. Krieger, 1982), 306-309.
4. Williamson Murray, *The Change in the European Balance of Power* (Princeton, N.J.: Princeton University Press, 1984), 4-27.
5. See Walter C. Clemens, Jr., *The U.S.S.R. and Global Interdependence* (Washington, D.C.: American Enterprise Institute, 1978) for a skeptical interpretation of the likely impact of interdependence on the Soviet Union. Also see Elliot Hurwitz, "The Politics of Soviet Trade," *New York Times*, Aug. 25, 1980.
6. Quoted in *The Fifteen Weeks* by Joseph M. Jones (New York: Viking, 1955), 80. An excellent book that conveys the feelings of this period in both Europe and the United States is Theodore H. White, *Fire in the Ashes* (New York: Sloane, 1953). See also White, *In Search of History* (New York: Warner Books, 1979), 263-306.
7. John Tadiabue, "Soviet Letting Trade Partners Shop Around in Hard Times," *New York Times*, Jan. 4, 1988.
8. Zbigniew Brzezinski, "America's New Geostrategy," *Foreign Affairs* (Spring 1988):

686.

9. Bill Keller, "Gorbachev's Hope for Future: 'A Common European Home,'" *New York Times*, Nov. 30, 1989.

10. Joseph L. Nogee and John W. Sloan, "Allende's Chile and the Soviet Union," *Journal of Interamerican Studies and World Affairs* (August 1979): 339-365.

11. Richard Millett, "Looking Beyond Noriega," *Foreign Policy*, Summer 1988, 46-64; and Steven Erlanger, "U.S. Economic Warfare Brings Disaster to Panama," *New York Times*, June 9, 1988.

12. Andrés Suarez, *Cuba* (Cambridge, Mass.: M.I.T. Press, 1967), 86.

13. Paul E. Sigmund, "The 'Invisible Blockade' and the Overthrow of Allende," *Foreign Affairs* (January 1974): 339-340 (emphasis added).

14. Richard S. Olson, "Economic Coercion in World Politics: With a Focus on North-South Relations," *World Politics*, July 1979, 472-479; and Anna P. Schreiber, "Economic Coercion as an Instrument of Foreign Policy: U.S. Economic Measures Against Cuba and the Dominican Republic," *World Politics*, April 1973, 387-413. Also see Otto Wolff von Ameringen, "Commentary: Economic Sanctions as a Foreign Policy Tool?" *International Security*, Fall 1980, 159-167; James M. Lindsay, "Trade Sanctions as Political Instruments: A Re-Examination," *International Studies Quarterly* (June 1986): 153-173; and Roy Licklider, "The Power of Oil: The Arab Oil Weapon and the Netherlands, the United Kingdom, Canada, Japan and the United States," *International Studies Quarterly* (June 1988): 205-226.

15. George Liska, *The New Statecraft* (Chicago: University of Chicago Press, 1960), 3.

16. See Joseph S. Berliner, *Soviet Economic Aid* (New York: Holt, Rinehart & Winston, 1958), 179-180; and Hans Heymann, Jr., "Soviet Foreign Aid as a Problem for U.S. Policy," *World Politics*, July 1960, 525-540. Also see Wynfred Joshua and Stephen P. Gibert, *Arms for the Third World* (Baltimore: Johns Hopkins University Press, 1969).

17. Berliner, *Soviet Economic Aid*, 171-177.

18. Heymann, "Soviet Foreign Aid," 538-539. For 1986 Soviet aid, see Department of State, *Warsaw Pact Economic Aid Programs in Non-Communist LDCs* (Washington, D.C.: Government Printing Office, 1988).

19. For the classification of aid generally followed here, see the excellent article by Hans J. Morgenthau, "A Political Theory of Foreign Aid," *American Political Science Review* (June 1962): 301-309.

20. David R. Obey and Carol Lancaster, "Funding Foreign Aid," *Foreign Policy*, Summer 1988, 141-155.

21. For a good study of cold war American aid programs, see Joan M. Nelson, *Aid, Influence and Foreign Policy* (New York: Macmillan, 1968).

22. This assumption was never made explicit in the doctrine of foreign aid for reasons analyzed by Robert A. Packenham, "Developmental Doctrines in Foreign Aid," *World Politics*, January 1966, 194-225; and Packenham, *Liberal America and the Third World* (Princeton, N.J.: Princeton University Press, 1973).

Also see Eugene R. Black, *The Diplomacy of Economic Development* (New York: Harper & Row, 1966), 19, 23. For a general analysis of the conditions necessary for democracy to flourish, see Seymour M. Lipset, *Political Man* (Garden City, N.Y.: Doubleday, 1959), 45-67.

23. Obey and Lancaster, "Funding Foreign Aid." On Japan's rise to number one donor, see David E. Sanger, "Japan to Be No. 1 Giver of Foreign Aid," *New York Times*, Jan. 20, 1989.

24. Elizabeth Kridl Valkenier, "New Trends in Soviet Economic Relations with the

Third World," *World Politics*, April 1970, 415-432; and Valkenier, *The Soviet Union and the Third World* (New York: Praeger, 1985). Also see Jerry F. Hough, *The Struggle for the Third World* (Washington, D.C.: Brookings, 1986).

25. Carol R. Saivetz and Sylvia Woodby, *Soviet-Third World Relations* (Boulder, Colo.: Westview Press, 1985), 134-135, 142-147.

26. Francis Fukuyamu, "Gorbachev and the Third World," *Foreign Affairs* (Spring 1986): 715-731.

27. Diana Tussie, *Latin America in the World Economy* (New York: St. Martin's Press, 1983).

28. Carlos Fuentes, "The Real Latin Threat," *New York Times*, Sept. 15, 1985.

29. Alan Riding, "Latins Want Bush to Help on Debts," and Clyde H. Farnsworth, "Money Loss Grows for Poorer Lands, World Bank Finds," *New York Times*, Nov. 29, 1988, and Dec. 19, 1988, respectively.

30. Abraham F. Lowenthal, "Threat and Opportunity in the Americas," in annual issue entitled "America and the World 1985," *Foreign Affairs* (1985): 558-561.

31. *New York Times*, Sept. 26, 1985. Also see Harold Lever and Christopher Huhre, *Debt and Danger* (Boston: Atlantic Monthly Press, 1986).

32. *New York Times*, May 11, 1984.

33. Richard Rothstein, "Give Them a Break," *New Republic*, February 1, 1988, 22.

34. Peter T. Kilborn, "U.S. to Give Poor Lands More Time to Repay Debts," *New York Times*, June 21, 1988; and Steven Greenhouse, "Fund Plans to Forgive African Debt," *New York Times*, June 9, 1988.

35. Quoted by Robert Gilpin, *The Political Economy of International Relations* (Princeton, N.J.: Princeton University Press, 1987), 317.

36. Department of State, Bureau of Public Affairs, *U.S. Prosperity and the Developing Countries* (Washington, D.C.: Government Printing Office, January 1985).

37. Charles William Maynes, "America's Third World Hand-ups," *Foreign Policy*, Summer 1988, 134.

38. Rothstein, "Give Them a Break," 24.

39. On the collapse of the shah, see George Lenczowski, "The Arc of Crisis," *Foreign Affairs* (Spring 1979): 796-820; Richard Cottam et al., "The United States and Iran's Revolution," *Foreign Policy*, Spring 1979, 3-34; and especially Gary Sick, *All Fall Down* (New York: Random House, 1985).

40. Robert W. Tucker, "Oil and American Power," *Commentary*, September 1979, 39.

41. See Louis J. Halle, "Does War Have a Future?" *Foreign Affairs* (October 1973): 20-34; Klaus Knorr, *On the Uses of Military Power in the Nuclear Age* (Princeton, N.J.: Princeton University Press, 1966); and Knorr, "The Limits of Power," in *The Oil Crisis*, ed. Raymond Vernon (New York: Norton, 1976), 229-243.

42. Walter J. Levy, "Oil and the Decline of the West," *Foreign Affairs* (Summer 1980): 1003-1004.

43. Youssef M. Ibrahim, "Gulf War's Fallout," *New York Times*, Dec. 17, 1987.

44. E. H. Carr, *Twenty Years' Crisis, 1919-1939* (London: Macmillan, 1951), 130.

45. Quoted in Edward Mead Earle, "Adam Smith, Alexander Hamilton, Friedrich List: The Economic Foundations of Military Power," in *Makers of Modern Strategy* (Princeton, N.J.: Princeton University Press, 1943), 140.

46. Carr, *Twenty Years' Crisis*, 131.

47. Klaus Knorr, "International Economic Leverage and Its Uses," in *Economic Issues and National Security*, ed. Knorr and Frank Trager (Lawrence, Kan.: Allen Press, 1977), 99-125; and James A. Nathan and James K. Oliver, "The Growing Impor-

tance of Economics: Can the United States Manage this Phenomenon?" in *Evolving Strategic Issues*, ed. Franklin D. Margiotta (Washington, D.C.: National Defense University Press), 73-99.

48. Olson, "Economic Coercion," 477, 481.
49. *Ibid.*, 485.
50. Carr, *Twenty Years' Crisis*, 131, 132.

CHAPTER 15

The Multinational Corporate Revolution and Interdependence

GOING GLOBAL

It has been said that the rise of the multinational corporation represents the "central macroeconomic event of the postwar world" because it has globalized technology, production, investment, and marketing.[1] In the 1960s, American multinational corporations (MNCs) set the pattern for this globalization by spreading to Europe as they sought to exploit the business opportunities represented by the Common Market (more formally known as the European Economic Community), avoid the tariffs the latter would have imposed on their products had they been exported from American factories to Europe, and save on transportation costs. American corporations, given their size and ability to mass-produce goods, were in an advantageous situation to compete with European corporations, many of whom still produced mainly for the home market despite the (not always successful) efforts of European states to eliminate internal barriers to trade and the free movement of capital and labor.

But the growth of American MNCs and their extension to Europe, important as it was, was less fundamental than the spread of American mass-production techniques to Japan, as well as to the newly industrialized countries (NICs)—Hong Kong, Singapore, Taiwan, and South Korea—and a few other developing countries. Prior to the 1960s, American workers had been paid high wages because their productivity was high. The technology, training, and management that backed up the worker had not yet been transferred or duplicated overseas. In the 1960s they were. Japan was the first to combine the high labor productivity of America with the low labor costs of Asia. Earlier, rising industrial states such as Britain, Germany, and the United States had become major economic powers by being innovators and focusing first on the home market. Japan chose the path of imitation and an export strategy.[2] The target markets were those of the industrial West, especially the United States, which was the world's biggest market because of its combination of a large population, high affluence, and considerable consumer spending, much of it on credit (unlike in Japan or, until recently, in Europe). The Japanese deliberately concentrated on such industries as steel, shipbuilding, automobile, and consumer electronics, which in the United States were unionized, high-wage sectors, thereby giving the low-wage producer the competitive advantage. Others then followed Japan's example. As the value of the Japanese yen rose against that of the dollar in the latter 1980s, thereby increasing prices for Japanese goods, countries such as South Korea and Taiwan exploited this advantage. In 1987, the year Japan produced more cars than the United States, South Korea operated the world's most modern steel mills, and Taiwan's central bank had reserves of nearly $70 billion, second only to Japan's.*

To protect itself, Japan too has gone multinational, moving production to low-wage countries or to the countries where its most lucrative markets are. The Hyundai Excel, one of the best-selling cars and thought by many to be purely Korean, was designed by Japan's Mitsubishi, which also supplies the transmission and electronics and has a sizable investment in Hyundai.[3] Fearing U.S. protection and attracted by the size of the market, Japanese corporations such as Honda have been building plants in the United States. Collectively, the Japanese car producers in this country were one of the four major automobile producers. Honda manufactures more cars in the United States than in Japan and will soon export more than 50,000 cars back to Japan!

Going "multinational" is not confined to American and Japanese firms. Europe too has its giants such as Nestlé (Switzerland), Philips (the Netherlands), Michelin (France), and British Petroleum. After 1992, European firms are likely to become more competitive, both in Europe and in the international marketplace. In fact, there are now three major industrial areas in the world: North America, Western Europe, and the Pacific Rim countries. The latter confront the more mature industrial economies with a new reality. America's former protégés are now full-fledged competitors increasingly producing goods they had previously imported—and at far lower prices.

Two things are striking about the new economic globalism. First, very visible to travellers are the familiar names and products encountered abroad. McDonald's restaurants are found in Tokyo, Paris, and now even in Moscow. Michelin radial tires are fitted on American cars, and Nikon cameras and Toyota cars and vans are used widely on all continents. Second, and less visible and well known, is the increasing multinational manufacturing of prod-

---

* Most popular brands of athletic shoes are made in Korea, where workers' wages have risen to $450 a month. Thai and Chinese workers, by contrast, make $30 a month. The Koreans are moving increasingly into electronics and automobiles.

ucts most consumers identify solely with their own countries. Thus, AT&T sells telephones produced in Singapore, and IBM sells computers whose parts come from Japan and other Asian countries. The globalization of the American car is well along. Since the early 1970s, Chrysler has imported small cars and trucks made by Mitsubishi and sells them under the Plymouth and Dodge labels; Mitsubishi V-6 engines power various Chrysler cars. The Ford Probe and Mazda MX-6 come off the same Japanese-managed assembly line near Detroit. While they look different, these cars are only dissimilar versions of the same car. Engines and transmissions for both cars are designed and manufactured by Mazda in Japan; seats, tires, and batteries are American-made. Probe's styling is Ford's. These two cars are only one example of the extensive ties developing between American automakers and their Japanese rivals. Ford is planning other future models with Mazda, in which it has a 25 percent interest, and exploring collaboration with Nissan. General Motors (GM) owns 42 percent of Isuzu. The Chevrolet Spectrum is an Isuzu-made import, and the Spring is a Suzuki import (GM owns a 5 percent interest in Suzuki). GM will be a major supplier for Isuzu vehicles to be produced at Isuzu's new plant in Indiana. In a joint venture with Toyota known as the United Motor Manufacturing Company, GM also produces the Chevrolet Nova and Toyota Corolla FX-14 in a plant in California managed by Toyota.

Increasingly, unless a company is willing to "go multinational" and arrange intercorporate alliances and cooperation, its future may be in trouble, be it in manufacturing, marketing, finance, or other services. Because cars, for example, are produced all over the world, manufacturers favor tire companies that can supply them wherever they are. Thus in 1988, Pirelli of Italy and Bridgestone of Japan fought a take-over battle over Firestone Rubber & Tire Company.[4] In the emerging global tire market, a company has to be a global player to compete effectively. The United States, being such a huge market, made the fight for control of Firestone critical for both companies. Bridgestone won, joining Goodyear and Michelin as a company to be reckoned with in both the United States, where it can serve the increasing number of Japanese car plants, and Europe where Firestone had extensive operations. A German tire company, Continental, which gained access to the American market by buying Uniroyal and Japan's Sumitomo Rubber, has an 85 percent interest in Britain's Dunlop. Goodyear produces tires in Brazil for sale on the West Coast to compete with Korean tires offered to West Coast distributors at 15 percent below Goodyear prices. Goodyear and Michelin are seeking entree to South Korea because of its growing importance as a car maker.

A global strategy, then, is becoming imperative for companies seeking to survive and prosper in an increasingly *interdependent* economy, in which each nation, to assure national prosperity, must participate. A strong market presence in the United States, Europe, and Japan has become essential. Transnational joint ventures, mergers, licensing, production, and marketing arrangements among manufacturers which result in market entry, technological exchange, and lower production costs in the competitive global economy obviously place companies that do not establish similar links in a potentially dangerous situation.

As companies shift much of their production to the developing countries, blue-collar employees in the developed countries are decreasing in number (foreign companies in the United States also insist on nonunion labor). Growth in employment comes in nonmanufacturing and non-blue-collar jobs as America "de-industrializes." [5] The multinationalization of production means that capital is mobile, moving to where production costs are low. An American company has no economic reason to pay American workers a wage of about $15 an hour if Korean or Taiwanese or Mexican workers will do the same tasks for $3 an hour—hence the term *outsourcing*. For example, Boeing now imports almost 30 percent of the parts for its planes: tail cones come from Canada, aluminum skin panels from Japan, Rolls-Royce engines from Britain, and various tail sections from Italy, Ireland, and China. Thus "sourcing" is competitively driven, even as it is applied to labor. With production moving offshore, even in the high-technology sectors such as computers and telecommunications, and companies increasingly using robots in the manufacturing process, industrial job security and downward pressure on wages are the new facts of life for American labor. The castoffs often find themselves in lower-paid service jobs ("flipping hamburgers"), and to make ends meet many families now have two wage earners. But, citing the postwar stagnation of British industry, one expert has said that "a country, an industry or a company that puts the preservation of blue-collar manufacturing jobs ahead of international competitiveness . . . will soon have neither production nor jobs. This attempt to preserve such blue-collar jobs is actually a prescription for unemployment." [6]

The result of all this is that while American MNCs remain competitive and profitable, America as a country is becoming less competitive. For a nation whose industries were once the envy of the world and whose products were widely desired abroad—"Made in the USA" was a label denoting high quality and a reasonable price—having to compete in the international marketplace has been a shock. Too long used to having the huge American market largely to itself and never having to export much to be profitable, U.S. industries have found the sudden exposure to global, and especially Japanese, competition to be a brutal experience. That Americans invented color television, the videocassette recorder, and the microwave oven, virtually all of which are now produced by the Japanese and South Koreans and are flooding the U.S. market, stands as an indictment of American industry and management. Between 1970 and 1987, for example, U.S. industry saw its proportion of the color television market shrink from 90 percent to 10 percent.[7] Today, the Japanese view their competitors in most areas of consumer electronics as the newly industrialized Asian countries, not the United States.[8] The Reagan administration's policy of cutting taxes while greatly raising defense expenditures, thereby creating a trillion-dollar debt and gigantic trade imbalances as the high value of the dollar in the early-to-mid-1980s hurt U.S. export industries and agriculture, did not help either (see Chapter 4). Of the top twenty nations with which the United States traded in the late 1980s, it had a surplus with only three. America imported more than it sold to West Germany, Italy, and Japan, whom it defeated in war, as well as Canada, Mexico, and such countries as Sri Lanka, Bangladesh, and the Ivory Coast. The upshot of all this for labor was a new sense of insecurity and vulnerability. Like the decreasingly competitive sectors of American industry, labor expressed its concerns in terms of complaints about unfair foreign competition and the search for protective legislation. Once an advocate of free trade, the United States now seeks "level playing fields" at a time when the nation has acquired a healthy stake in the international economy. About 10 percent of its gross national product is exported to the rest of the world, up from about 4 percent in the 1960s. Moreover, one-third of its cropland is committed to exports. Approximately one-quarter of the after-tax profits of U.S. corporations comes from overseas operations (this figure excludes their exports from the United States because these constitute domestic earnings).[9] Finally, as described earlier, banks have lent huge sums abroad.

Corporations Without Countries

What has brought on the "transnational organizational revolution in world politics"?[10] Modern means of rapid transportation and communication are one factor; another is the technical and organizational capabilities to operate across long distances. This revolution became very visible in business in particular because of the emergence of strong consumer-oriented economies in the industrialized First World and because of the evolution of high-technology industries such as electronics. Exporting had also become increasingly disadvantageous for many industrial concerns. Because of lower local labor costs and transportation costs in the importing country, corporations decided that they could remain competitive only if they established manufacturing facilities there. They thus are better able to sell their goods in the local market, as well as in the U.S. market when they ship their less expensively made overseas products back home. U.S. corporate investments in Europe after the formation of the European Economic Community (EEC) in 1958 were enormous, and the companies resulting from these investments were very successful.

American corporations, accustomed to coping with the different regulations of various states in the United States, adapted better than many of their European competitors to operating within the EEC. European firms, which historically have confined themselves to protected national markets, usually lagged behind U.S. corporations. The transnational business organization operating in multiple markets shifts its resources from one country to another as needed; its aim is to maximize profits, and the various national markets function as parts of a single larger one, in which capital, technology, and other resources can be shifted at will. American firms, thinking in continental terms, thus became more "European" than European firms. In fact, the largest corporations in Europe are presently American.[11] This overseas investment pattern suggests that the growth of the MNC is a rational response to new business opportunities, as well as a defensive move to protect overseas markets to which these firms had previously exported. Using the tools of modern business available in the 1960s—telexes, telephones, and jetliners—American MNCs were able to coordinate operations and pursue a virtually global business strategy. European and Japanese MNCs have repeated this pattern.

The early observers of the MNCs interpreted this expansion of MNCs optimistically. According to them, if there were no interference with the free international movement of capital, technology, and goods, the MNCs would create a new world of plenty for all and conflict for none. Each MNC was viewed as an independent actor. With its managerial skills and technology, it could stimulate economic development, eventually abolishing poverty throughout the less-developed areas. Thus, its corporate selfishness would lead to maximum global welfare. Furthermore, in a world divided by nationalism, the MNCs could provide the impetus for creation of a world community. George Ball, a former undersecretary of state, argued that the MNC, which he called "Cosmocorp," had outgrown the state; national boundaries were anachronistic, because they confined MNC activities.[12] Unlike traditional imperialism, which presumably encouraged the state to open up new lands for business to exploit, the new business corporation sought not territorial and political control but access to different markets. In this multinational context, the Cosmocorps' managers were the new "globalists"—the advance men and women of "economic one-worldism," who viewed the globe as a single market or, in management expert Peter Drucker's phrase, "a global shopping center."

Dependent upon foreign states for permission to produce and sell within their frontiers, these managers regarded states, national egotism, and assertive foreign policies as contrary to their interests. Their primary loyalty was to the corporation, rather than to the nation, and global corporate interests took precedence over national interests. MNCs needed peace; national rivalries were economically too costly from their perspective. MNCs would therefore act as a major restraint on foreign adventures as peace and profits became interdependent. For this reason, the MNCs were looked upon as likely to replace nation-states as the most visible and potent actors on the world scene. Welfare politics would replace power politics. The MNCs, having burst through the confining jurisdictions of national sovereignty, would bring a better life to all peoples. Unable to fulfill their citizens' expectations, nation-states would then become anachronisms. The managers of IBM, General Motors, Exxon, General Electric, Coca-Cola, Xerox, and other large MNCs make decisions daily that have a more immediate and visible impact on consumers' lives than governments. The chief executive officers of such companies, it has been asserted, have the organization, technology, money, and ideology to manage the world as an integrated unit. The MNC managers claim that they can succeed where conquerors and empires have failed.[13]

Will the Nation-State Survive?

Do MNCs threaten the viability of nation-states and the future of the state system? It is easy to understand why states are anxious and concerned about the MNCs in their territories. Even advanced industrial states are wary. Multinational corporations represent high technology. Will other industrial economies become their "technological colonies"—that is, dependencies of the country whose MNCs possess the most advanced technology and skills? A French observer wrote in the late 1960s:

> Electronics is not an ordinary industry; it is the base upon which the next stage of industrial—and cultural—development depends. In the nineteenth century the first industrial revolution replaced manual labor by machines. We are now living in the second industrial revolution, and every year we are replacing the labor of human brains by a new kind of machine—computers.
>
> A country which has to buy most of its electronic equipment abroad will be in a condition of inferiority similar to that of nations in the last century which were incapable of industrializing. Despite their brilliant past, these nations remained outside the mainstream of civilization. If Europe continues to lag behind in electronics, she could cease to be included among the advanced areas of civilization within a single generation.[14]

By the early 1970s, just after these words were written, American MNCs already controlled 80 percent of Europe's computer business, 90 percent of its microcircuit industry, 50 percent of its transistor industry, and 65 percent of its telecommunications. In addition, they controlled sizable portions of more traditional industries, such as the automobile (40 percent) and synthetic rubber (45 percent). Concern that the MNCs would come to control the technologically most advanced, most rapidly growing, and most profitable sectors of industrial economies was understandable, even though at the time American firms owned only 5 percent of overall European corporate assets. This European fear of falling behind the United States (and now Japan as well) has not changed. It is the reason that the EEC countries have decided to make another effort to unite in 1992, and that Britain, West Germany, and other U.S. allies stated in the 1980s that they wanted to participate in the Strategic Defense Initiative (SDI) research. These governments were profoundly skeptical about SDI but understood that the research, for example, in laser beams could have peacetime applications in such areas as basic science, industry, and health. Now, of course, the United States shares the fear of what will happen as foreign corporations buy up more and more American industries and America becomes more dependent on foreign technology (especially in the area of electronics). American observers now write books voicing concerns similar to those voiced by the Europeans not long ago.[15]

Another worry about MNCs is their huge size and assets compared with the gross national products of the host states.[16] This issue is particularly sensitive in the developing countries, which fear that MNCs will dominate their economies, "repatriating" profits and draining capital from states that need it. Additional complaints are that they fail to produce the goods needed for modernization. For example, Coca-Cola attracts money that could be spent on such necessities as milk, meat, vegetables, and educational materials. MNCs are also said to impose Western culture and consumer-oriented values upon their host countries (the term "cultural imperialism" is often used).[17] These fears about the MNCs, however, have changed significantly as the developing countries' needs for the MNCs have grown because of the decline of foreign aid and the drop in commodity prices. The generally poor economic performances of many developing countries, previously committed to publicly run economies, have led their governments to reassess the value of private enterprise and capital.

But whether an MNC operates a manufacturing plant in Europe or an extractive industry in the Third World—and it is the former that has attracted most American investment capital[18]—the common fear in the host country is that the MNC will exploit its power in a way that will hurt national interests. For example, if an MNC finds the investment climate no longer suitable in one country, it can pick up its chips and move to another country, leaving behind unemployment and ill-feeling. Or, because other states seek to attract the MNC, it can play one state off against the other. During the cold war the United States attempted on occasion to use MNCs as instruments of its foreign policy, forbidding shipment of certain products to designated countries. This restriction applied to all U.S. corporations, domestic as well as multinational. A foreign country, wishing to pursue a friendlier policy toward a U.S. adversary or simply to improve its balance of payments, could thus be prevented from trading these restricted products if they are manufactured by a subsidiary of an American MNC. The apprehensions of nations about the control over their own economies have been strengthened by MNC political interference, such as International Telephone and Telegraph's efforts at subversion in Chile and bribes offered and subsidies paid by Lockheed and other firms to governmental and political leaders in many countries for orders or the right to sell their products. Host governments are understandably sensitive to infringements of their right to maintain control over their economies and foreign policies. Many Americans share this fear nowadays as foreign money has poured into the United States in the 1980s, buying up everything from luxury homes in Hawaii to shopping malls, large merchandisers, industries, and now farmland. America appears up for sale—and cheaply too.

Yet states will probably survive the challenge of the new transnational business actor. The reason: some conflict between the two is unavoidable, they need each other. Their conflict is complementary. According to political scientist Samuel Huntington,

> It is conflict not between likes but between unlikes, each of which has its own primary set of sanctions to perform. It is, consequently, conflict which, like labor-management conflict, involves the structuring of relations and the distribution of

benefits to entities which need each other even as they conflict with each other. The balance of influence may shift back and forth from one to the other, but neither can displace the other.[19]

Indeed, the MNC appears to strengthen rather than weaken the state, because it needs the latter's permission for access to its territory. The multinational corporation may well be one of the leading reasons for the increasing role of the state in economic affairs and the extension of state power into the economic realm. In Europe, for example, governments intervened in the economic sphere to create domestic conditions to counterbalance the size and influence of American corporations. This will be even truer after 1992 when the European Economic Community's expected last steps toward economic integration will stimulate mergers and more efficient and competitive European and global MNCs. In the United States, too, the government is increasingly involving itself in the economy to ensure "fair play" in international trade and to assure that the country will be competitive in modern technologies.

Host countries are also setting the terms of access to their markets and establishing MNC-host relations in which they benefit in the form of employment, taxes, balance of payments, transfer of technology, and acquired managerial skills, while simultaneously permitting the MNCs to earn enough to want to stay. Some hosts establish employment quotas for nationals, require MNCs to locate in so-called depressed areas (for which they may, however, receive tax incentives), forbid layoffs, and demand the training of whatever local workers are required (which may, however, be subsidized). Almost all host countries set dates by which time they will own 51 percent of the company. They also may set export figures for the MNCs (with which some may be reluctant to comply to avoid competing with their own brands in other countries). In recent years, MNCs, in return for access to markets, have increasingly complied with these kinds of demands by the host countries. The result has been greater cooperation between host states and MNCs. One observer has noted:

> In short, sovereignty is no longer at bay in most countries. To be sure the degree of this shift in power differs from country to country, and from industry to industry. It is virtually complete in most industrial host countries and some developing countries as well, and is well underway in many other developing countries.[20]

In turn, corporations essentially want to be left alone to do their business, although the fear remains that the large MNCs will interfere in national politics. Their interest in politics stems from their desire to gain access to a nation's market and a hospitable environment in which to make money. MNCs are very flexible. They will work with a democratic government in a democratic society and with despotic and even racist governments in other countries (just as the Roman Catholic church historically has come to terms with all types of governments to have access to their people).[21] In the short run, the MNCs may well reinforce the status quo in the societies in which they operate. In the long run, however, they may help undermine the status quo—in non-Communist societies, at least—by making visible new technologies, ideas, social and cultural values, and ways of life that challenge, especially in the developing countries, the more traditional cultures. As relations with host nations have become closer, however, MNCs' relationships with their home nations have grown more and more distant. Labor, particularly, has become protectionist, opposing what the unions call the "export of jobs" to developing countries, especially Taiwan, South Korea, and Singapore. Political pressures have grown on the U.S. government to restrict the outflow of investment capital when the nation is suffering from high unemployment and balance-of-trade deficits (more money going out to pay for imports than coming in from exports). But the stakes are high, for they are "nothing less than the international division of production and the fruits thereof." [22]

Meaning of Interdependence

The growing interdependence of the Western industrial democracies has been amply illustrated. Interdependence means not only that their economies are becoming more intertwined, but also that they are becoming more vulnerable to one another because of their interconnectedness—that is, one nation can hurt another. An interesting example is the case of Toshiba, which during the Reagan years was found to be guilty of selling the Soviets the American machinery needed to make their nuclear submarine propellers quieter (before, the noisiness of Soviet submarines had allowed the U.S. Navy to keep track of them). This gross violation of U.S. security enraged Congress to the point of considering a ban on all Toshiba products for a number of years. But U.S. manufacturers, among whom AT&T, IBM, General Electric, Honeywell, Xerox, and Hewlett-Packard were the most prominent, lobbied against such legislation; they had all become too dependent on Toshiba electronic components for their products. This very dependence on foreign suppliers for critical components of arms is (as noted in Chapter 7) increasingly worrisome to U.S. officials. Thus, Congress, in seeking to punish just one foreign MNC, would be hurting U.S. industries and jobs as well.

In a broader sense, can the United States pressure the Japanese to import more American products? Within limits, yes, but those limits are quite narrow because the two countries need one another and neither can pressure the other too much without hurting itself. According to former Carter national security adviser Zbigniew Brzezinski,

> America needs Japanese capital to finance its industrial renovation and technological innovation; it needs Japanese cooperation in protecting its still significant global lead in creative R&D and in opening up new scientific frontiers for both peaceful and military uses; it needs Japanese participation in securing through enhanced economic development such geopolitically threatened yet vital areas as the Philippines, Pakistan, Egypt, Central America, and Mexico. Japan needs American security protection for its homeland; it needs open access to the

American market for its continued economic well-being and, through cooperation with America, secure access to a stable and expanding world market; it needs
to maintain and even expand its collaborative academic research facilities that are
so central to Japan's continued innovation.[23]

One American need is not mentioned above: Japan's willingness to buy U.S.
Treasury bonds during the Reagan budget deficit years to help cover America's military spending spree and maintain American commitments at a time
they exceeded the nation's economic capability.[24] Had the Japanese not
bought these bonds as the value of the dollar declined and, therefore, the
value of Japanese holdings, the U.S. economy could have quickly sunk into a
depression. As it was, in October 1987 concern over the continued huge U.S.
deficit led to a stock market crash. It may not be the last warning.

The intertwining of corporate and national economies is often described by
the term *interdependence*. Two characteristics of interdependence are sensitivity and, more important, vulnerability.[25] If events in one nation's economy
affect another nation's economy but the latter can take countermeasures to
minimize the consequences, the latter's economy is sensitive but not vulnerable. But if such remedial measures are unavailable, it may be hurt because it
is vulnerable to another nation's actions. Two or more countries are interdependent when none of them can withdraw from a relationship without each
being hurt by doing so. In the opposite situation, all benefit from their
interdependence. For example, because an inflation or recession tends to be
transnational, its consequences are not likely to be confined within the
originating nation's frontiers. Remedial actions will therefore require cooperative action; unilateral action will not suffice. Thus, all the Western industrial
states were sensitive and vulnerable to OPEC's sharp price increases during
the 1970s; simultaneous recession and inflation were among the results. But as
OPEC kept driving the prices up, non-OPEC oil production was stimulated.
The result was a surplus of oil and a drop in oil prices and OPEC income.
OPEC thus hurt itself. No national economy is autonomous any longer,
immune to events elsewhere.

Interdependence, while applied mainly to economic issues, is not confined
to them. Militarily, for example, the United States and the Soviet Union are
interdependent. If either tries to destroy the other, it will itself be destroyed
by the retaliation. Each is not only sensitive to what arms the other may
acquire but also potentially vulnerable. It is this interdependence that has led
the two powers, despite their enmity, to cooperate with one another on arms
control. Nevertheless, security regimes, as noted earlier, are rarer and more
limited in scope than economic ones.[26] The reasons are not hard to uncover.
For example, if an arms agreement breaks down because one side will no
longer abide by the agreed-upon arrangements, the price may be very high.
States are reluctant to enter security arrangements unless they can verify that
the terms are being kept and, if not, they can minimize their vulnerability. In
the postwar period, of course, the abilities of the superpowers to monitor each
other have grown enormously, especially since the launch of the first satel-

lites in the early 1960s.[27] Furthermore, because both have sufficient security, given their nuclear strengths, a violation of or withdrawal from a security arrangement will not have a fatal impact; there will be time to take remedial action. Nevertheless, strategic arms control agreements remain fragile in a competitive environment, especially when deterrent forces possess an increasing first-strike capability. If, by contrast, economic arrangements break down, the likelihood of immediate, critical damage is very small. "As a result, states know that they can readily verify compliance with economic agreements and will have time to discuss possible violations and, if need be, adjust to them. These favorable conditions facilitate trust and diminish the risks of cooperating." [28] The crucial differences, then, between security and economic arrangements "lie in the costs of betrayal, the difficulties of monitoring, and the tendency to comprehend security issues as strictly competitive struggles."[29]

While economically interdependent relationships are then more prevalent than military ones, such relationships are not necessarily symmetrical. The Europeans and Japanese were much more dependent on OPEC—and especially Arab—oil than the United States, an oil producer, and not long before an oil exporter itself. All Western nations therefore were sensitive to OPEC's actions but the United States was less vulnerable than its allies. Indeed, not all interstate relationships, even economic ones, are interdependent. Basically, it is the nations of North America (Canada and the United States), and America's European allies and Japan—all developed, pluralistic, democratic societies—that have become interdependent. Indeed, the degree of interdependence among them is so great that all Western governments have to worry about the "ricochet effect." [30] For example, when the United States persuades the Japanese to place a ceiling on car imports, the Europeans worry lest the consequences will be greater imports of cars to Europe, affecting European car manufacturers and jobs.

By contrast, the relationship between the First World and most of the Third World countries (excluding the newly industrialized and OPEC countries) remains one of inequality or dependency. And since 1945 the relationship between the First and Second Worlds has been largely one of independence because the United States has discouraged trade that might help the Soviet Union militarily. How much of that will change as U.S.-Soviet relations improve significantly remains to be seen. Interestingly, however, the structure and operation of the international economy reflects this threefold political division of the world.[31] Indeed, the existence of interdependence among states who are allied to one another suggests that trade follows the flag. American power created this alliance system, and the corporate extensions came later. But if political action created an interdependent economic relationship in its wake, the subsequent economic conflicts among allies were to have profound effects on the cohesion of these alliances as the international "free-trade" economy, initially dominated by the United States, became increasingly divided by competitive mercantilist policies.

FREE TRADE AND THE INTERNATIONAL ECONOMY

This state of affairs came about slowly. After World War II the American economy emerged healthy and preponderant. Those of Europe and Japan were shattered. The United States therefore took the lead in organizing alliances against the Soviet Union and in establishing an international economy in which trade would flourish, stimulating economic growth and prosperity among its allies. The General Agreement on Tariffs and Trade (GATT) was the principal organization created in 1947 to deal with the trade issue. Its basic philosophy and goal was one of free trade. Liberals had long believed that unhampered trade would result not only in maximum economic welfare for the participating states but also in more peaceful relations among states. Each state would benefit from such trade and therefore had a vested interest in continuing its trade relationship. Because war would disrupt trade and hurt a nation's prosperity, it was counterproductive. Thus, GATT was designed to create free trade among states by gradually lowering tariff barriers and stimulating trade. This emphasis on free trade was stirred not only by a belief in prosperity and peace but also by the memories of the depression years of the 1930s when each of the Western industrial states had cut imports while stimulating its exports by various means.[32] This economic nationalism had been unworkable, however. When country A had cut imports and exporting country B could not earn money by trading, how could B buy goods from A? The end result had been a decline in world trade and a deepening of the depression. Thus, it should not be surprising that after World War II, the United States would believe that free trade was good economically and politically. This belief was reinforced by self-interest. With the world's most powerful economy, the United States would obviously benefit from free trade—that is, access to other nation's markets. Similarly, in the nineteenth century when Britain had been the world's first nation to industrialize, it had advocated free trade.

The effects of free trade in the postwar period were everything everyone had expected. GATT grew from twenty-three member states in 1947, mainly Western, to ninety-six in 1989, including a number of Communist states (both China and the Soviet Union have expressed their desire to join). By cutting tariffs substantially in successive rounds of negotiations, GATT could claim much of the credit for the postwar growth of world trade and production. Consumer demand after World War II was explosive and sustained economic growth. According to political scientists David Blake and Robert Walters, it appeared "that the lessons of the 1930s had been learned; international oversight of national foreign economic policies has been successful in promoting production and in curtailing the excesses of economic nationalism with its negative economic and political consequences."[33]

But these "good times" ended during the 1970s because of three events. One was détente. The Western alliance had, on the whole, remained cohesive while all its member states perceived the Soviet Union as a threat. But this perception changed during the détente years. National interests, once more or less subordinated to the collective interests of the alliance, began to assert themselves more forcefully. The second event was the revival of the European and Japanese economies. American economic supremacy, which had been unnatural anyway because it resulted largely from the destruction of European and Japanese industry, began to decline. After 1945, the United States had 50 percent of the world's gross national product; by the late 1980s, that figure was 23 percent, still substantial but relatively a steep drop. This figure represented both a genuine U.S. decline and what was earlier referred to as the rise of "the others." National economic interests therefore tended to come to the fore and cause divisive conflicts. The third event was the shock of OPEC's actions, supplemented by the later fall of Iran's shah, which led to skyrocketing oil prices and simultaneous recession and inflation among Western oil-importing states. All these occurrences reinforced this trend of emphasizing economic issues.

If foreign policy has among its purposes the protection of a nation's economic welfare, then the preoccupation with employment, inflation, economic growth, and stable oil supplies was understandable. But it also intensified intra-alliance conflicts. The decline of the United States as the economically dominant power in the West meant that the rules of the (economic) game were harder to establish and enforce. States that once had little choice but to go along now had a choice. Thus today, economic cooperation has become much more difficult as Western governments respond primarily to domestic pressures, not that of their allies and friends.[34]

MERCANTILISM AND 'EVEN PLAYING FIELDS'

Whereas free trade is aimed at global prosperity, the new mercantilism of today is concerned primarily with maximum national welfare.[35] Originally, in fact, free-trade theory had been a reaction to the older mercantilism practiced by the states of Europe during the sixteenth, seventeenth, and eighteenth centuries. States in that era were interested in enhancing their power and wealth; increasing their power meant increasing their wealth and increasing their wealth meant increasing their power. States, therefore, encouraged exports and discouraged imports to maximize wealth. Exports earned the gold needed to support armies and growing civil governments. Mercantilism rejected the free-trade school's optimism that states' economic interests were basically harmonious; instead, it believed that economic interests were in conflict (see Table 15-1). Mercantilism also repudiated the belief of interdependence—the free-trade belief brought up-to-date—that nations must cooperate in finding solutions; instead, it placed its emphasis on unilateral action.

Table 15-1 Comparison of Free-Trade and Mercantilist Ideas About the International Economy

	Free Trade	*Mercantilist*
Actor	Multinational corporation	State
Nature of economic relations	Clashing interests and harmony	Clashing interests and conflict
Goal of economic activity	Maximization of global welfare	Maximization of national welfare
Economic-political assumption	That economics should determine politics	That politics determines economics

SOURCE: Adapted from Table 6, "Comparison of the Three Conceptions of Political Economy," in Robert Gilpin, *U.S. Power and the Multinational Corporation* (New York: Basic Books, 1975).

Now, the term *mercantilism* has been revived to describe policies adopted initially by the Europeans and the Japanese, but also increasingly—at least in agriculture—by the United States. Today's mercantilism is based on protection of employment and production, stimulation of exports, and reduction of imports to gain and maintain a favorable trade surplus. A trade surplus for one nation, however, is balanced by another's trade deficit; all states cannot achieve surpluses simultaneously. This means that economic growth and jobs for one state result in a decline of both in another. Mercantilism, therefore, compels states to compete for the largest possible share of the world market to ensure their national welfare and economic security.

Japan's aggressive export policy (the success of which it owes to the efficiency of its industries), the inventiveness of its engineers (thanks to its educational system), and the quality production and consumer appeal of its products have already been noted. While considered a private-enterprise economy, Japan's economy is in fact guided by the Ministry of International Trade and Industry (MITI) which, acting as an economic version of the famous old Prussian General Staff, selects the industries that are to grow and targets the countries whose markets are to be penetrated. It coordinates these plans with research and investment capital. Japan's state-guided trade policy not only has made Japan an economic giant but has made its policies suspect as well.[36] One of Reagan's secretaries of commerce, in condemning Japan's trading practices as "unfair," gave voice to the widespread fear that Japan's "export policy has as its object not participation in, but dominance of, world markets."[37]

The Western Europeans have subsidized the products of their less-competitive industries, such as steel, to undersell American-made products in the United States. But in no area has this been more irritating to the United

States than in agriculture. For years the efficiency of U.S. agricultural production has allowed the United States to serve as the breadbasket for the rest of the world. In 1981, a banner year, American farmers exported a record 162 million metric tons of food worth $44 billion.[38] Throughout the 1970s, when dollars were flowing out at a record level to pay for oil, large agricultural sales on the international market were the main reason the trade imbalances did not become even larger. But since 1981, the volume of these exports has declined, despite the continued export of U.S. grain to the Soviet Union. This has resulted in part from the high value of the dollar in the early 1980s, and in part from surplus production by other countries. Western Europe, once a large importer of American food, now overproduces because of the subsidies paid to its farmers. These surpluses are then "dumped" on the world market because, as inefficient producers, Europeans price their farm products too high to compete internationally. This will not be easily remedied, however, for at its core the EEC is a bargain between French agriculture and German industry, both looking for a wider European market (although West German farmers benefit from this deal as well). Agricultural competition then is becoming intense, and the United States is no longer the world's breadbasket.

But the problem is not limited to Europe: India is beginning to export grain; China's agricultural production has increased greatly in recent years; and other developing countries, such as South Korea and Thailand, will soon become greater agricultural producers and exporters. Many of these developing countries were also food importers until recently. Competition among old and new food producers for a share of the international market is thus the prospect for the future. Indeed, 1985 American grain exports were down by about 50 percent from the 1981 level of 48 million metric tons, and this surplus grain cost the United States approximately $20 billion per year to store. The U.S. government therefore decided in 1986 to do what other countries have been doing: subsidize farm products for export and sell them at competitive world prices. While 1988 was again a good year for U.S. farm exports because of poor weather in Europe and South Africa, the drought in the American Midwest raised grain and soybean prices. Droughts are temporary, however, while overproduction remains recurrent. America's competitors are undoubtedly determined to preserve their market shares.

The results of the growing economic conflicts among the interdependent Western states are several. First and most obvious, although politically and strategically the U.S. role remains that of a superpower—in fact, it is the only power capable of defending the non-Communist world by balancing Soviet power—economically the United States can no longer fulfill that superpower role. The U.S.-West European-Japanese alliance, the foundation of U.S. security and economic well-being, once cemented by a clearly visible Soviet threat, is now increasingly divided by commercial and financial rivalry as the Soviet menace has receded. Furthermore, the United States has not been holding its own in this competition, particularly with regard to Japan (see Chapter 7).

Second, this competition has, among other things, led—and will lead—to a series of trade wars or, what might be called more accurately, "subsidy wars," as each partner subsidizes its less-efficient manufacturers or agricultural sectors so that they can export their goods by undercutting their rivals' prices. Such subsidies are part of the broader protectionist strategy demanded by domestic pressures to prevent unemployment, the closing of increasingly uncompetitive plants, or inefficient farmers. The year 1989 started with a brief dispute between the United States and Europe, a trade war seen by some foreign trade experts as a harbinger of things to come when the EEC states make their final moves toward integration in 1992.[39] The Japanese have subsidized even efficient industries so that they can dump their products on the international market and drive their competitors out of business—for example, the production of 64K chips for computers. Such "trade wars" are thus properly named: they are the economic equivalent of military coercion.

Third, fair or unfair, this competition has led to widespread resentment and ill-feeling, charges of "uneven playing fields," and cries for "fair competition." As the world's largest and most affluent consumer market, the United States is the target of Japanese, EEC, and Third World exports.[40] While much of the competition was fair and U.S. consumers obviously liked imported goods, the United States nevertheless negotiated a series of "voluntary" restraints on steel, automobiles, television sets, shoes, and textiles, to cite but a few, in response to domestic pressures (but despite these ceilings on imports, the U.S. industries declined). While such pressures have to varying degrees protected industries and agricultural sectors, they also have been costly to the American taxpayer. Prohibiting or reducing imported goods reduces competition and the incentive to hold prices down. It does protect the industries that because of their inefficiency are the least equipped to survive, but it does so at a high cost to the entire economy. It also invites retaliation against American goods, leaving everyone worse off than if all markets had remained open. Every American family of four has already paid $1,000 a year to protect various industries and jobs from foreign competition.

While the American market, despite some restrictions, remains the magnet for other nations' imports, Japan is again an example of a country tenaciously guarding its industries against imports from the United States and Europe. Imports into Japan (as well as the newly industrialized countries) have been held to an extremely low level—the lowest of any industrialized country—not by imposing tariff barriers, which are lower than those of the United States, but by other means. The Japanese usually claim that their products are the best, while American goods are shoddily made and unreliable—claims that have all too often been true. But even where such charges are not true, there is strong cultural and political resistance by the Japanese to buying foreign products, ranging from spark plugs and telecommunications gear to agricultural staples and baseball bats. Thus in 1987, the U.S. trade deficit reached $60 billion, a record. This resistance is only slowly being overcome, after lengthy, item-by-item negotiations, amid mutual recriminations. The Japanese are forever inventive in rejecting imports—for example, pharmaceuticals that may have been tested extensively elsewhere but not in Japan. The Champion spark plug company, after being turned down in a bid to equip a particular brand of Japanese automobile, then offered its product for nothing and was still turned down!

But the Japanese, proud of their economic efficiency and accomplishments, have become resentful of what they call "Japan-bashing" and feel that the pressures on them to open up their markets to more American exports and efforts to impose ceilings on Japanese exports to the United States reflect a declining, increasingly uncompetitive American economy.[41] They have a case. Even if the Japanese complied with American demands and bought all the citrus fruit, beef, medical equipment, car telephones, and other products the United States feels they should buy, it would reduce the trade deficit with Japan only by a few billion dollars. If both countries wiped out all barriers to trade, the trade deficit might grow as voluntary restraints on imports were lifted.[42] Americans are drawn to Japanese products, even when higher priced than similar American ones, because of the quality of Japanese production. The fundamental problem is not unfair trade—as unfair as it often is or appears to be—but American productivity and quality, the nation's low savings rate (and, therefore, investment in new capital or machinery), and business, with its focus on mergers, buy-outs, and short-term returns for investors. America's trade problems do not stem principally from other nations' actions. Indeed, but for Japanese competition, America would not be recovering some of its competitiveness. Nevertheless, the mutual resentments and recriminations, translated into a rising anti-Americanism in Asia (not only in Japan and the "little Japans" but in other countries as well) and antialliance—especially anti-Japanese—feelings in the United States, are harmful to the alliances. American anger is especially strong because it is the very allies that the United States helped to recovery after the war that are alleged to be not only competing unfairly but also destroying the U.S. economy. Yet the fact that the U.S. budget deficit has been financed by the dollars earned by the Japanese from their trade surpluses with the United States suggests the critical importance of Japan to America financially and the danger to this country and the world of inflaming Japanese nationalism. The U.S. domestic economy is all too vulnerable to Japanese decision making.

Europe too has restricted imports; unemployment has been high and economic growth low since the 1970s. Europeans have favored détente even when the United States has not, because they are seeking markets in the East to replace markets lost to the Japanese and Americans. Europe's openness and fast economic growth after the war helped the development strategy and involvement in the world economy of the newly industrialized countries. But those European industries that played so large a role in Europe's rapid postwar growth have been hard hit by Japanese and NIC competition. As a result, various European nations have placed severe restraints on Japanese imports. The United States has already expressed its concern that Europe, with its over 300 million people (customers) will become a protectionist bloc—"Fortress Europe"—rather than a key player in a prosperous and growing international economy.[43]

Finally, but by no means the least important, is the impact of this mercantilism on the developing countries. The EEC has become one of the world's largest sugar exporters, impoverishing producers in the Philippines, the Caribbean, and Central America. The EEC's export policy is similar for other crops. Indeed, the developing countries were already hurt by the general slowdown of the world's economy, which has led the industrial countries to resort to mercantilism. The Third World's prospects for economic growth depend on the industrial countries' demands for their natural resources and markets for their manufactured products. But the decline of commodity prices, the Western tariff and nontariff barriers, and the Third World's debt problem dim the hopes of the developing countries for development, exacerbating an already grave situation as incomes decline and poverty worsens.

This mercantilist challenge to the more liberal international economic order of free trade will not be easy to deal with, although the security and prosperity of the U.S.-West European-Japanese alliance depends on the outcome. On the one hand, efforts to cooperate are being made. The Japanese, realizing that their economic strategy of maximizing exports and minimizing imports is generating adverse reactions in the United States and Western Europe, have become increasingly aware that Japan must expand its domestic market and become more of a consumer/importer society and less of a saver/exporter. Such a shift has already started, and European and Asian imports to Japan are up. Despite concessions won by U.S. negotiators, however, American companies have not taken much advantage of these opportunities. Nevertheless, despite economic forecasts, Japan's stimulation of domestic demand as well as the sharp drop of the dollar and the rise of the yen, Japan's high exports have continued![44] America's monetary strategy to make U.S. products cheaper and Japan's more expensive to correct the imbalance of trade worked only so far. Japanese companies made themselves even more efficient, while U.S. consumers remained devoted to their Japanese products, almost regardless of price. Driving the dollar down further, therefore, will only result in making "America for sale" even more cheaply than it already was.

All the industrial countries also recognize the growing burden of spending $100 billion a year on farm subsidies, which continue to increase while many governments are attempting to cut fiscal deficits. In the late 1980s, farm subsidies amounted to $26 billion for the United States, $23 billion for the EEC, and $15 billion for Japan. The United States, Europe, and Japan agree that farm supports must be cut. They are bad for budgets, bad for prices, and bad for the developing countries' economies. President Reagan proposed dealing with this problem by ending agricultural supports by the year 2000. The problem, however, is that farmers in all the developed countries are well organized and politically powerful. In Japan the farmers, who are among the world's most inefficient, have managed to pressure the government to pay them five to ten times world prices for the rice they produce to maintain Japanese self-sufficiency. The elimination of subsidies may put those in power out of power. Japan's governing party receives large contributions from beef and rice farmers. Europeans too have political clout, although the EEC has agreed to cut—but not eliminate—subsidies among member nations. Because each nation would worry that if it ended farm subsidies and the others did not (even if they said they would), it would lose markets to its rivals; such an accord is unlikely.

Governments are thus subject to contradictory pressures. The forces of interdependence compel them to cooperate to find collective solutions. Western leaders meet annually at an economic summit conference demonstrating their awareness that no unilateral solutions are possible. But none can forget their voters at home. Markets may be global but political constituencies still end at the border of their nation-states. Thus to increase its exports and cut back imports, the United States drove down the value of the dollar, lowering the price of American-made goods and raising those of foreign products. Basically, this was tantamount to a beggar-thy-neighbor policy, reducing U.S. trade deficits by slowing down the economies of America's allies. Germany, like Japan, could have contributed to reducing the U.S. trade deficit by stimulating the domestic economy, absorbing more of its own products, exporting less to the United States, and buying more American imports. But Germany, fearful of setting off inflation and upsetting voters, declined. Thus, these summits have become more social affairs and photo opportunities. The future of trade may therefore be "managed trade." Rather than supply and demand in an unregulated market, trade relations will be negotiated according to the principle of reciprocity.[45] The 1988 U.S. trade law emphasized the protection of American workers from foreign competition, not free trade. "Fair trade" is enshrined in the legislation, meaning that the United States will play tit-for-tat with such countries as Japan and the NICs that now have easy access to the U.S. market. The whole point of the legislation was to boost American exports by pressuring other countries to lower their trade barriers. The United States has entered the mercantilist age in full force. And European officials, pointing to the period after 1992, say the EEC will also demand "reciprocity."

The worst of all scenarios would be the emergence of three huge regional blocs. The first would be the EEC members in Europe. The second would be Japan and the newly industrialized Pacific Rim countries in East Asia. Japan's industries, in search of cheaper labor, are largely relocating in the Pacific Rim NICs, and the latter are increasingly exporting goods to Japan. This has already resulted in closer economic relations among these Asian countries, with Japan gaining a position of preeminent influence. The third superbloc would be the United States and Canada in North America. Already possessing the largest trading relationship between any two countries, the United States and Canada have signed a free-trade agreement, which could lead to an integration of the automobile, energy, banking, transportation, and other industries. This core market might eventually encompass the Caribbean and Central American countries, as well as Mexico (Australia and New Zealand, as well as Taiwan and Malaysia have expressed their interest in similar bilateral agreements). Such essentially protectionist blocs would certainly be incompatible with alliances, if these remain desirable, against the Soviet Union, which is likely to be the political and economic beneficiary as Europe, Japan, and perhaps even the United States all eagerly extend Moscow credit.

Thus, now the Western alliances are poised between economic nationalism and, potentially, economic warfare and interdependence. Which will be the stronger force in future years? Strong strands of interdependence exist among the Western states and between them and the NICs as well as the OPEC countries. The state system's principal characteristic may be its anarchical nature, but, as also noted, conflict and competition are not the only consequences of this decentralization. Coexisting states also need a degree of order and regularity. Thus, cooperation has also been a feature. States have never possessed total freedom to do whatever they wished. But the focus has been on state autonomy and conflict rather than on restraint and cooperation. It is this autonomy that now appears to be a constraint on economic matters; indeed, interdependence not just promises greater restraints on states but also requires a greater degree of cooperation if states are going to solve the economic and financial problems they face. Will interdependence, rather than economic nationalism and commercial competition, then increasingly characterize world politics and will the state system of the future be a more harmonious and peaceful one?

EROSION OF HIERARCHY

The developments examined in the last four chapters have profoundly affected the traditional power hierarchy and go a long way toward explaining why in contemporary international politics the powerful often appear weak and the weak powerful. First, in large part because of the new nations that emerged from the colonial era, the principle of national self-determination has been firmly established globally. The great powers may violate this principle from time to time, but usually such violations arouse cries of condemnation and extract a political price. Second, the nuclear revolution and the emergence of nuclear parity between the United States and the Soviet Union have led both powers to recognize that a nuclear war cannot be won and to declare that it must not be fought. Despite massive armaments and political-ideological hostility, the superpowers—indeed, all the war-prone major powers—have been at peace for forty-five years, an unprecedented achievement. The fear of nuclear war has restrained their use of force to limited wars and proxy interventions; and concern about escalation has led them increasingly to favor the latter. Third, great-power efforts to suppress lesser states have become more costly if not counterproductive. In the prenationalistic age, it had been easy to conquer basically passive populations, but in the postcolonial world nationalism has meant that native political leaders can mobilize their peoples to resist. In fact, easy access to modern weapons has given them the capability to resist for a long time and to extract a price greater than the large powers have been willing to pay. Economic coercion has not been much more successful. Fourth, the growing interdependence, particularly among the Western allies but also between them, the NICs, and leading OPEC countries, has further complicated the exercise of the traditional means of influence.

The great powers, to be sure, are hardly impotent; they have many means of exercising power. Their military power allows them to extend protection to other nations; their economic power means that they can offer all sorts of economic rewards; their economic vitality in this technological age, and the attractiveness of their cultural and social values make them models for others to follow; and there is always that ancient skill diplomacy, which permits those adept in its uses to convert assets such as these into genuine influence on the international scene. Nevertheless, the accumulated effect of the four changes in contemporary international politics listed above has been to erode the historical hierarchy or structure of dominance based on military power. An astute observer, noting these trends in the 1970s, commented:

> Clearly, if the inequalities that have traditionally marked state relations are to decline, the institution that has afforded the primary means for maintaining inequality must also decline. The effective challenge to inequality requires, at the outset, that the more extreme forms of self-help—especially military force— no longer perform their time-honored functions. Provided that physical coercion of the weak by the strong has largely lost its former utility, as many now believe, nothing would appear to be of comparable moment in altering the hierarchical structure of international society. It is in the assumption that the rising material and moral costs of employing force now effectively inhibit—or very nearly so—the strong from resorting to force against the weak that we must find one of the root sources, if not *the* root source, of the challenge to inequality.
>
> Nor is it reasonable to expect that a growing disutility of military power will have no effect on the economic power wielded by the strong. Although disparities in economic power remain in a world where military power is presumed to be increasingly at a discount, the effects of these disparities must surely be altered as well and in the same direction....
>
>   ...[R]ecent experience has shown that even against a very small state, and one with a vulnerable economy, the effectiveness of economic coercion alone may prove surprisingly limited. In part, this is so for the evident reason that economic coercion permits the weak alternatives that physical coercion does not. Then, too, the limited effectiveness of economic coercion may in some

measure be attributed to the same sources that limit the effectiveness of physical coercion. While the legitimacy of the former has not been subject to the same standards as has the latter, economic coercion has been called increasingly into question. . . . This argument draws added force once it is recognized that economic coercion can only have its full effects to the extent it leaves open the option of physical coercion.[46]

Does all this mean that there may be a growing disjunction between power and order in the contemporary international system—that is, greater disorder? Has the "natural order" been turned upside down? In either case, how can international conflict be restrained, if not overcome? A closer look at this question follows.

For Review

1. Why are Western corporations increasingly going multinational?
2. What conditions have made this "transnational revolution" possible?
3. What is interdependence and how has it affected relations among nations?
4. Why has the free-trade regime been increasingly supplanted by mercantilism?
5. Will trade wars or cooperation be the result, and why?

Notes

1. Michael Moffitt, "Shocks, Deadlocks, and Scorched Earth: Reaganomics and the Decline of U.S. Hegemony," *World Policy Journal* (Fall 1987): 557.
2. Peter F. Drucker, "Japan's Choices," *Foreign Affairs* (Summer 1987): 923-924.
3. Ibid., 931.
4. Jonathan P. Hicks, "A Global Fight in the Tire Industry," *New York Times,* Mar. 10, 1988.
5. Peter F. Drucker, "The Changed World Economy," *Foreign Affairs,* Spring 1986, 775. Also see Louis Uchitelle, "Trade Barriers and Dollar Swings Raise Appeal of Factories Abroad," *New York Times,* Mar. 25, 1989; and "U.S. Businesses Loosen Link to Mother country," *New York Times,* May 21, 1989.
6. Ibid., 777.
7. Martin Crutsinger, "U.S. Edge in Technology is Slipping," *Gainesville Sun,* Sept. 8, 1988.
8. David E. Sanger, "Japanese Electronics Thrive Despite Asian Competition," *New York Times,* Dec. 18, 1988.
9. Richard N. Cooper, "International Economic Cooperation: Is It Desirable? Is It Likely?" *Washington Quarterly,* Spring 1988, 91.
10. Samuel P. Huntington, "Transnational Organization in World Politics," *World*

Politics, April 1973, 333ff. Also see Abdul Said and Lutz R. Simons, eds., *The New Sovereigns* (Englewood Cliffs, N.J.: Prentice-Hall, 1975); and Charles P. Kindleberger, ed., *The International Corporation* (Cambridge, Mass.: M.I.T. Press, 1970).

11. Robert L. Pfaltzgraff, *The Atlantic Community* (New York: Van Nostrand Reinhold, 1969), 80, 108-110.

12. George W. Ball, "Cosmocorp: The Importance of Being Stateless," *Atlantic Community Quarterly*, Summer 1968, 168.

13. Richard J. Barnet and Ronald E. Müller, *Global Reach* (New York: Simon & Schuster, 1975), 13.

14. J. J. Servan-Schreiber, *The American Challenge* (New York: Avon, 1969), 42.

15. Martin Tolchin and Susan Tolchin, *Buying into America* (New York: Times Books, 1988). See David E. Sanger, "Key Technology Might Be Sold to the Japanese," *New York Times*, Nov. 27, 1989, detailing the possible sale of a semiconductor equipment plant, which would leave the United States almost completely dependent on Japan for the tools to make future generations of computer chips. As before, Americans pioneered this technology. Yet the Bush administration is considering cutting even the small amount of government financing of U.S. high-tech that now exists because it opposes an industrial policy (like Japan's) in the name of the free market. See John Markoff, "Cuts Are Expected for U.S. Financing in High-Tech Area," *New York Times*, Nov. 16, 1989.

16. Robert Gilpin, *The Political Economy of International Relations* (Princeton, N.J.: Princeton University Press, 1987), 242-252, assesses the pros and cons of the impacts of MNCs on host countries.

17. A strong indictment of the MNCs may be found in Barnet and Müller, *Global Reach*.

18. David H. Blake and Robert S. Walters, *The Politics of Global Economic Relations*, 3d ed. (Englewood Cliffs, N.J.: Prentice-Hall, 1987), 91-94; and Joseph S. Nye, Jr., "Multinational Corporations in World Politics," *Foreign Affairs* (October 1974): 162.

19. Huntington, "Transnational Organization," 366.

20. C. Fred Bergsten, "The Coming Investment Wars?" *Foreign Affairs* (October 1974): 125ff.; and C. Fred Bergsten, Thomas Holst, and Theodore H. Moran, *American Multinationals and American Interest* (Washington, D.C.: Brookings, 1978).

21. Ivan Vallier, "The Roman Catholic Church: A Transnational Actor," in Robert O. Keohane and Joseph S. Nye, Jr., eds., *Transnational Relations and World Politics* (Cambridge, Mass.: Harvard University Press, 1972), 135-140.

22. Bergsten, "The Coming Investment Wars?" 148.

23. Zbigniew Brzezinski, "America's New Geostrategy," *Foreign Affairs* (Spring 1988): 696.

24. Gilpin, *Political Economy of International Relations*, 328-336, in a section subtitled, "Japanese Subsidization of American Hegemony."

25. Robert O. Keohane and Joseph S. Nye, Jr., *Power and Interdependence*, 2d ed. (Boston: Little Brown, 1988), 12-16.

26. Charles Lipson, "International Cooperation in Economic and Security Affairs," *World Politics*, October 1984, 12.

27. John Lewis Gaddis, "The Long Peace: Elements of Stability in the Postwar International System," *International Security*, Spring 1986, 123-125.

28. Lipson, "*International Cooperation*," 17.

29. Ibid., 18.

30. Cooper, *"International Economic Cooperation,"* 92.
31. Joan E. Spero, *The Politics of International Economics Relations,* 2d ed. (New York: St. Martin's Press, 1981), 12-18.
32. Blake and Walters, *Politics of Global Economic Relations,* 11-14.
33. Ibid., 14.
34. For a more optimistic view of regime maintenance, see Robert O. Keohane, *After Hegemony* (Princeton, N.J.: Princeton University Press, 1984).
35. Kevin T. Philipps, *Staying on Top* (New York: Random House, 1985).
36. Paul Kennedy, *The Rise and Fall of the Great Powers* (New York: Random House, 1987), 463. For a detailed analysis, see Chalmers Johnson, *MITI and the Japanese Miracle* (Stanford, Calif.: Stanford University Press, 1982).
37. Quoted by Theodore H. White, "The Danger from Japan," *New York Times Magazine,* July 28, 1985, 42. Also see Clyde V. Prestowitz, Jr., *Trading Places* (New York: Basic Books, 1988), Ch. 1, especially 13, 21-14; and James Fallows, "Containing Japan," *Atlantic Monthly,* May 1989, 40-54.
38. *New York Times,* April 20, 1986.
39. Milton Freudenheim, "Beef Dispute: Stakes High in Trade War," *New York Times,* Jan. 1, 1989.
40. Moffitt, "Shocks Deadlocks," 569; and Bernard K. Gordon, *Politics and Protectionism in the Pacific* (London: International Institute of Strategic Studies, 1988), 14-17.
41. Susan Chira, "New Pride Changes Japan's View of U.S.," *New York Times,* June 28, 1988. See, for example, the article by the chairman of the Sony Corporation: Akio Morita, "Something Basic Is Wrong in America," *New York Times,* Oct. 1, 1989.
42. Martin E. Weinstein, "Trade Problems and U.S.-Japanese Security Cooperation," *Washington Quarterly,* Winter 1988, 22.
43. Steven Greenhouse, "The Growing Fear of Fortress Europe," *New York Times* (Business section), Oct. 24, 1988.
44. Susan Chira, "U.S. Currency Policy Speeds Japan in Vast Economic Role," *New York Times,* Nov. 27, 1988; and David E. Sanger, "Warning from Tokyo on Trade and Dollar," *New York Times,* Jan. 18, 1989.
45. Prestowitz, *Trading Places,* appropriately subtitled "How We Allowed Japan to Take the Lead." Also see Jagdish Bhagivati, *Protectionism* (Cambridge, Mass.: M.I.T. Press, 1988) for an analysis of the opposing forces of protectionsim and global corporate competition.
46. Robert W. Tucker, "A New International Order?" *Commentary,* February 1975, 43-44.

Part Five

FROM STATE SYSTEM TO GLOBAL SYSTEM

C H A P T E R 16

Preserving Peace
in the State System

Can the problem of how to preserve peace be resolved *within* the existing state system? Can the behavior of states be restrained, and can states be made more responsible? Can peace be achieved through cooperation among states in an international organization such as the United Nations, and through international legal and moral norms? For many of its advocates, the United Nations—the first approach to preserving the peace discussed in this chapter—symbolizes the expectation that war will be abolished because, ideally at least, it embodies the new spirit of internationalism that is supposed to replace national egotism. In the words of former senator and chairman of the Senate Foreign Relations Committee J. William Fulbright, the United Nations is an institution intended to protect "humanity from the destructiveness of unrestrained nationalism" and therefore to be strengthened by subordination of short-run national needs to long-run international needs.[1]

Two other approaches to preserving the peace stress the self-restraint that states would have to exercise if they obeyed international law (second approach) or behaved more morally (third approach). How realistic are these three approaches to making the state system safe for humanity? If they offer practical solutions, the abolition of the state system may not be necessary; if they do not, the case for the creation of a new world order may be stronger.

UNITED NATIONS

To understand the United Nations, it is necessary to understand what it is *not*. It is not the "great peacemaker" and solver of all problems. It is not a superstate, usurping members' sovereignty and imposing its will on them.

Nor is its behavior independent of states' national interests and political considerations. UN decisions are not made according to some impartial, nonpolitical, and therefore purportedly superior standard of justice. The organization is not above politics because it cannot exist or act independently of its members' politics. Rather, it reflects the political interests, attitudes, and problems of its member states. It is only the channel through which the power and purposes of its members are expressed. The United Nations is not a substitute for power politics; it only registers the power politics of the state system. It is a mirror, not a panacea; it has no magic wand by which it can resolve all international problems. It cannot transcend the cold war or anticolonial struggles; it must function in the world as it exists. And it cannot solve any problems that its members, because of conflicting interests, are not prepared to solve. Its failures demonstrate only its members' inabilities to reach agreement.

First Phase: Preservation of the Wartime Grand Alliance

Because the United Nations is not a superstate but a body registering its members' political interests, attitudes, and problems, its functions can best be understood in terms of the changing conditions of the state system. After its birth in 1945, the United Nations in its first phase reflected the hope that, once victory over Germany had been won, cooperation among great powers would continue and peace would be maintained. Primary authority for the preservation of peace and security in the United Nations was vested in the Security Council (originally composed of eleven members, six of them on two-year rotation; the total membership has since been raised to fifteen, with ten members on a two-year rotation). Real authority, however, was to be exercised by the five permanent members: the United States, Soviet Union, Britain, France, and China (at first Nationalist China and subsequently Communist China). With the approval of at least seven members of the Security Council, including all the permanent members, the council could take enforcement action against aggression. Each permanent member of the council could veto such action, however. Any decision made was then to be obeyed by all members of the United Nations. Through an oligarchical structure that reflected the global distribution of power, the great powers were thus able to become the masters of the United Nations. Indeed, the United States and the Soviet Union, the only two great powers remaining in 1945, were the real masters. As long as the two superpowers could maintain harmony, peace would be preserved.

The security system thus was directed only against the smaller nations; if they disturbed the peace, they could be squashed if the great powers could agree to take punitive action. The United Nations was, in the words of one delegate to its first conference, "engaged in establishing a world in which the mice could be stamped out but in which the lions would not be restrained." [2] The purpose of the veto was to prevent one of the great powers from mobilizing the United Nations against another great power.

Because a decision to punish a great power for aggression would precipitate global war, the

> insertion of the veto provision in the decision-making circuit of the Security Council reflected the clear conviction that in cases of sharp conflict among the great powers the Council ought, for safety's sake, to be incapacitated—to be rendered incapable of being used to precipitate a showdown, or to mobilize collective action against the recalcitrant power. The philosophy of the veto is that it is better to have the Security Council stalemated than to have that body used by a majority to take action so strongly opposed by a dissident great power that a world war is likely to ensue.[3]

Conflicts among great powers were to be handled *outside* the United Nations under collective self-defense arrangements, which did not require prior Security Council authorization for individual or joint military action in response to an attack.

Second Phase: American Instrument for Prosecuting the Cold War

As the two superpowers took opposite sides at the beginning of the cold war, the United States sought to mobilize the support of the United Nations for the containment of the Soviet Union and thus to associate its own policies with the humanitarian, peaceful, and democratic values underlying the organization. The transition from the first to the second phase was most dramatically illustrated in the Korean War. The United States felt it had no choice but to oppose the Soviet Union, but it acted under UN auspices. Soviet absence from the Security Council on the day of the vote to intervene in Korea enabled U.S. opposition, but such an absence was not likely to occur a second time. The United States therefore introduced the "Uniting for Peace" resolution in November 1950 to transfer primary responsibility for the preservation of peace and security to the General Assembly should the Security Council be paralyzed by a veto. Constitutionally, this transfer of authority should not have been possible. The General Assembly only had the authority to debate, investigate, and make recommendations on issues of international peace and security; it could offer no recommendations affecting matters on the Security Council's agenda. By placing an issue on its agenda then, the council supposedly could reduce the assembly to a debating society.

The Americans argued, however, that the United Nations' responsibility for the preservation of international peace and security should not be abandoned just because the Security Council was paralyzed. If the council could not fulfill its "primary responsibility" for this function, the assembly would have to assume the task. It need hardly be added that in the assembly, as it was then constituted, the United States could easily muster the two-thirds majorities needed for important resolutions from among members of the North Atlantic Treaty Organization (NATO) countries, the older British dominions, the Latin American republics, and one or two

Asian states. The Soviet Union was, of course, consistently outvoted, though it was still able to use the body as a forum for its own point of view. American policies were therefore legitimated by world public opinion.

American use of the assembly to support anti-Communist policies did not last long. Just as the configuration of power underlying the original Security Council—the wartime alliance—had changed shortly after the establishment of the United Nations, so the political alignment at the outbreak of the Korean War was not destined to survive even that war, despite the Uniting for Peace resolution. The United States had received UN support at first for two reasons. First, an overwhelming number of member nations, including the nonaligned states,[4] saw in the North Korean aggression a test of the United Nations itself. If the organization failed to respond, it would follow the League of Nations into the dustbin of history. Second, the smaller powers saw in the transfer of authority on security matters to the assembly an opportunity to play a larger role than assigned to them in the original UN charter. But Communist Chinese intervention in Korea in late 1950 made American-sponsored use of the United Nations as an instrument of collective enforcement against the Communist bloc more difficult. The involvement of a major Communist power and the possibility that the American government might accede to strong domestic pressures to extend the war to China by air bombardment, naval blockade, and the landing of Nationalist Chinese forces on the mainland, dramatized the wisdom of the UN architects' original effort to prevent the organization's involvement in military conflicts among great powers. The danger of a large war, which might even bring in the Soviet Union, was simply too great.

In addition, the twelve Arab-Asian members of the General Assembly were determined to remain nonaligned in the cold war. Their earlier support for American intervention in Korea had been motivated by their concern for the United Nations as an institution. It was essential that North Korean aggression be met, and, because the United States had the strength to take appropriate measures, the Arab-Asian members had approved of the original American reaction. But they had no desire to participate in collective measures against one side or the other, which in effect would have forced them to become allied to one of the cold war blocs through the mechanism of the UN voting procedure.

The question was how to prevent a military clash between the great powers and, simultaneously, to avoid becoming aligned in the cold war themselves. The answer was to shift the function of the United Nations from enforcement to conciliation.[5] The United Nations was to serve as an instrument of mediation in conflict between the great powers. The original assumption that peace could be preserved by having five lions, led by the two biggest lions, act as world guardians was replaced with recognition of the imperative to keep the lions from mauling one another to death—and trampling the mice while they were at it.

Third Phase: Preventive Diplomacy

A third phase of the United Nations thus began. In the first phase the members had been dedicated to preserving the wartime Grand Alliance; in the second, the United Nations had become an American instrument for prosecuting the cold war. This phase had begun to fade during the Korean War. By exerting great pressure, the United States could still, in the spring of 1951, obtain the two-thirds majority needed in the General Assembly for a condemnation of Communist China. Yet already it had to make concessions to muster these votes—the price being that it not follow the condemnation with additional military or economic measures. Instead, the United States was to give primary emphasis to conciliatory efforts of the Arab-Asian bloc—supported by most of the NATO allies, which were also concerned about possible escalation of the conflict—to end the war. By 1955 the United Nations had reached adolescence, and it matured quickly as the number of newly independent members, especially African, grew rapidly after 1955. In 1955 six new Asian and North African states were admitted to the organization; the next year four more were added. In 1960 the number of new states admitted was seventeen, mainly from sub-Saharan Africa. By 1974 Asian, African, and Latin American states made up three-quarters of the 138 members (see Table 16-1). Both the American and the Soviet blocs previously had used the United Nations for their own cold war purposes, but the neutral bloc soon learned how to use the organization to erase the vestiges of Western colonialism as quickly as possible. The General Assembly was a particularly good forum in which to voice anticolonial sentiments and state demands for the new international economic order (the global redistribution of wealth and power between rich and poor countries).

In this third phase, the United Nations could not help becoming involved in the cold war. The Soviet Union and the United States, to be sure, did not allow the organization to interfere in *their* respective clashes. The Soviets had no intention of permitting the United Nations to intervene in Hungary or Czechoslovakia. Nor would the United States permit it to become involved in negotiations over the post-1958 Berlin crises, Cuban problems,[6] and the war in Vietnam. East-West issues were debated only; no action was taken. The superpowers handled their own direct confrontations. But, on the periphery of the cold war, the United States and the Soviet Union were constantly tempted to interfere in the conflicts arising from the end of colonialism. Such interference, by threatening the peace and involving neutrals in the cold war, was bound to lead the nonaligned nations to take protective action. The United Nations was for them more than a political platform. It was also a shelter in which they sought refuge from great-power pressure. In this third phase, they thought of the United Nations as *theirs,* and they were determined to use it to remain nonaligned.

The chief function of the United Nations thus became "preventive diplomacy"[7]—that is, the stabilization of local conflicts *before* either of the superpowers could become involved and provoke its antagonist's intervention. To

Table 16-1 United Nations
Membership, 1946-1985

Year	Members
1946	55
1950	60
1955	76
1960	99
1965	107
1970	127
1975	144
1985	159

SOURCE: Successive issues of the *United Nations Yearbook*
(New York: United Nations, 1946-1985).

describe it differently, preventive diplomacy was intended to keep American-Soviet clashes from extending beyond the cold war zone. At the same time, by containing the cold war, the small nations could safeguard their independence and control their own future to some extent. The mice were to keep the lions apart so that they could not grapple with each other and trample them. The chief means of stabilization was establishment of a "United Nations presence" in these peripheral quarrels. The organization thus functioned as a fire brigade, devoted to minimizing potential hazards. It could not douse a fire, but its presence could signal that fire was imminent or had already broken out and should be controlled quickly.

In a real sense, the United Nations has performed a crucial function in a highly combustible world. But to perform this role, it has needed not only the support, or at least acquiescence, from the superpowers but also the active support and participation of the Third World countries. The contribution of the latter to the stability of the state system has stemmed from two tendencies. The first is the tendency of developing-country problems to spill over into the international arena. One example is a clash between states in a region when each party has friends in the superpower camps. This kind of clash occurred during the Israeli-Egyptian war in 1956, when France and Britain intervened militarily on Israel's side and the Soviet Union supported Egypt diplomatically—and even talked of firing missiles at Paris and London. Another example is the disintegration of a state, which happened in the Congo after it attained independence in 1960. In the resulting civil war, competing factions seeking to reunify the country sought outside help.

The second tendency is for these kinds of developing-country problems to attract the attention of the Soviet Union and the United States, leading to possible confrontations and military conflict. The two superpowers are attracted, of course, because these problems may bring to power groups favorable to one side and thus inimical to the other, or they may lead to regional expansion that would benefit one side and hurt the other. If one of the two superpowers is unwilling to tolerate what it sees to be a local or regional setback, it will intervene; if it fears that its opponent may intervene, it may make the first move. In either instance, it risks counterintervention. The conflicts that have arisen on the periphery of the American-Soviet rivalry thus have tended to feed the major confrontation between the two superpowers.

Interstate Conflict in the Middle East.   The United States and the Soviet Union have actively competed for influence in the Middle East since 1955, when the Soviets and the Egyptians concluded an arms agreement. The rivalry of the superpowers was superimposed on Arab-Israeli hostility and intra-Arab competition. Diplomatic support, economic aid, and military assistance from the two superpowers fueled the Arab-Israeli conflict through several wars. Without this competition for influence, the fundamental struggle could not have continued. Who else would have provided the Arab armies and the Israeli army with equipment?

With each war in the Middle East the possibility of superpower involvement became greater. In 1956, when the British, French, and Israelis captured the Suez Canal, the Soviets threatened to rain rockets on Paris, London, and Tel Aviv. The Soviets were putting on a show, and it was a good one. Hostilities had already ceased, thanks to American pressure on its allies to desist, but the Arabs, apparently believing that Soviet threats had led to the cease-fire, were grateful to the Soviets. The Soviets were primarily responsible for precipitating the 1967 Arab-Israeli war, for they had deliberately floated false rumors of an Israeli force poised to invade Syria. The Syrians, naturally, reacted immediately. What then could Egypt, the current acknowledged leader of the Arab world, do but mobilize its forces and send them into the desert? Moreover, the Soviet fleet made its first appearance in the Mediterranean, presumably as a symbol of Soviet commitment to the Arabs and as a warning to the United States not to interfere while the Arabs, with their enormous amounts of Soviet military equipment and training, defeated the Israelis. Israel won again, even more quickly than in 1956. This time, however, it kept the territories that it had captured. They were to be traded for genuine peace and recognition by the Arabs of Israel's right to exist. But no Arab leader would even sit down with Israeli representatives to talk.

In 1973 Egypt and Syria launched yet another attack to recapture the 1967 territories. Despite initial successes, their armies were finally thrown back. As Egypt's armies stood on the verge of defeat, the Soviets mobilized paratroopers and threatened unilateral intervention if American forces would not join Soviet troops to enforce the cease-fire that the two superpowers had agreed upon. The United States placed its forces throughout the world on alert as a warning to the Soviet government against such an intervention, and the crisis passed as the United States pressured Israel to obey the cease-fire. But the administration of Richard Nixon also sought to avoid an Egyptian defeat and complete Israeli victory; total humiliation for one side and total victory for the other were not judged conducive to persuading the two sides to sit down together and talk about troop disengagement and a possible peace settlement. Another reason the United States sought such a settlement was the fear that another Arab-Israeli war might precipitate a direct superpower clash.

How many more wars can the Middle East sustain without engulfing the world in nuclear flames? For both superpowers the stakes in the area are enormous. Each has its allies or friends which depend upon it for political, military, and economic support. Yet these states are not fully controllable; each one of them has its own interests and ambitions, in pursuit of which it may draw its great-power protector and benefactor into the conflict. Who manipulates whom? In 1972, when the Soviets apparently refused to supply Egypt with offensive arms to launch a war to recapture the territories lost in 1967, Egypt sent its Soviet advisers home. For the men in the Kremlin the possible defection of Egypt from the Soviet camp would have been a serious blow, jeopardizing the Soviet Union's political influence and gains in the area. Therefore, in 1973 the Soviets supplied Egypt with the arms it wanted, and the Yom Kippur War, with its near superpower confrontation, was the result. It appears that the tail wagged the dog. Great powers are not in complete control and cannot therefore fully restrain their small-power client states. Conflict among regional rivals may therefore balloon beyond control.

Civil War in Africa. The Republic of the Congo (now Zaire) became an independent state in 1960. But the Belgians, unlike the British and the French in most of their colonies, had not trained native leaders to take over. Thus, complete disorder soon prevailed, and the native army rioted. The Belgian settlers fled, and to protect them Belgium flew in troops. The Congolese premier, Patrice Lumumba, interpreted the Belgian action as an attempt to restore colonial rule and appealed to the United Nations to compel the Belgians to withdraw. The Soviets immediately supported his appeal and condemned Belgium, accusing it of acting as a front for "NATO imperialism." An even more serious situation developed when the province of Katanga (now Shaba) seceded. Katanga's rich copper mines were the Congo's main source of revenue, and secession threatened the survival of the entire nation. Lumumba demanded that the United Nations crush Katangan president Moïse Tshombe's mercenary army and help to restore Congolese unity.

When his demand went unheeded, Lumumba appealed to the Soviet Union for help against the "colonialists." He received both Soviet diplomatic support and military supplies, and it looked as if the Soviet government was about to establish an important base in Africa. Lumumba thereupon was dismissed from office by Congolese president Joseph Kasavubu, whom the United States supported to prevent the establishment of a Soviet foothold in central Africa. The Soviets, however, refused to recognize Lumumba's successor, insisting that only the parliament had the right to dismiss Lumumba and that, as it had not done so, he was still the legitimate Congolese prime minister and must be restored to his office. The subsequent murder of Lumumba exacerbated the situation.

The national coalition government of the Congo, formed in early 1961, faced a major crisis from the beginning, a crisis that could only benefit the Soviet Union unless a solution was found. The government, committed to a policy of nonalignment, had national reunification as its first objective. Failure to achieve this goal would undermine its authority and lead to collapse from political and financial weakness. The transfer of power to a more radical pro-Communist government would then be a real possibility. The central government, to head off its own collapse, might even turn toward the Soviet Union, just as Lumumba had done. In either instance there would be a Soviet-American confrontation in the Congo.

Role of the United Nations. It was in such situations—in which the two superpowers were drawn into confrontations that threatened the peace of the world—that the United Nations in its third phase played its most important role. Just as the Security Council was the intended focus of authority in the first phase and the General Assembly the focus in the second phase, the secretary-general was the principal actor in the third phase. No longer merely the principal administrative officer of the organization, the secretary-general, largely through partnership with the nonaligned nations, became its leading political officer. It was Secretary-General Dag Hammarskjöld who, by establishing the precedent of a UN presence in troubled areas, first assumed the role of "custodian of brushfire peace." The most dramatic expression of this custodianship was the establishment of a "nonfighting international force" for political, not military, purposes. The size of the force, drawn primarily from states not involved in the particular dispute, and its firepower are not as significant as its political presence, which forestalls the use of Soviet or American forces.

During the Suez crisis in 1956, a UN Emergency Force (UNEF I) supervised the withdrawal of British, French, and Israeli troops from Egypt. It did not seek to *compel* withdrawal through combat. The cease-fire agreement was the prerequisite for its use, yet the mere fact that it was available made it easier to obtain British, French, and Israeli agreement to withdraw. Once withdrawal had been completed, fewer than 5,000 UN soldiers were left to guard the Israeli-Egyptian frontier and to maintain peace in that area. Symbolically, it was Nasser's demand that these forces be withdrawn in 1967, leaving Egypt and Israel to confront each other directly, that led to the Six-Day War. Similarly, the interposition of UN forces between Israeli and Egyptian troops after the 1973 war helped keep the peace. These forces stood between hostile troops on both the Egyptian front (UNEF II) and the Syrian front (UN Disengagement Observer Force, or UNDOF) as American secretary of state Henry Kissinger patiently negotiated disengagements of the combatants as a prelude to more comprehensive peace negotiations.

Not all peace-keeping operations have been as successful (see Table 16-2). The force sent into southern Lebanon in 1978 to cope with the Palestine

Table 16-2 Selected UN Peace-Keeping Operations, 1948-Present

Date	Location	Purpose
1948-present	India and Pakistan	To monitor cease-fire between India and Pakistan
1956-1967	Egypt	To secure cease-fire between Egyptian, Israeli, British, and French troops in Sinai Peninsula
1960-1964	The Congo	To ensure Belgian troop withdrawal and prevent civil war
1964-present	Cyprus	To prevent fighting between Greek and Turkish Cypriots (UN troops have maintained buffer between the two communities since partition in 1974.)
1973-1979	Sinai Peninsula (Egypt)	To observe cease-fire between Israel and Egypt
1974-present	Golan Heights (Israel)	To observe cease-fire between Israel and Syria
1978-present	Lebanon (southern area north of Israeli border)	To confirm Israeli withdrawal from area and restore security

Liberation Organization attacks on northern Israel (and Israeli retaliation) was unable to deal with the PLO presence. In 1982 the Israelis invaded Lebanon to try and finish the PLO off, in the process sweeping the UN force aside. It was one thing to interpose UN soldiers between two opposing armies and prevent further violence when the superpowers had agreed that further fighting might escalate and involve them, but quite another to stop guerrillas infiltrating across a border. Even the Israelis, for all their punitive retaliatory strikes before 1982, did not succeed in this—hence their invasion.

Conditions for Peace-Keeping Forces.   At least three conditions are imposed on such an international force. First, it must be neutral and must therefore exclude permanent members of the Security Council. Second, the nation upon whose territory the force is to show its "presence" must grant permission for such entry. In this way, the host nation, as a sovereign state, exercises some control over the composition of the international force and can exclude troops from nations it considers unfriendly or undesirable. It can also demand the withdrawal of these troops, as Egypt did in 1967. Even had the secretary-general not agreed to their withdrawal, he would have had no option; UNEF I was a small force and not fit for fighting. (Israel had refused to accept UN forces on its side of the frontier with Egypt; had it done so, it would have been protected against an Egyptian strike by their very presence.) UNEF II, however, was placed under the jurisdiction of the Security Council and thus differed in this respect from UNEF I, which had been created by the General Assembly. Because the presence of UN forces had to be approved every six months, they could not be terminated during that period except with the unanimous consent of the five permanent Security Council members. A veto by any one of them at the semiannual meeting could end a mission.

The third condition is that the UN force not intervene in any purely internal conflict and become party to the dispute. In Egypt in 1956 and again in 1973, the force was not used to impose a specific settlement on Nasser and Sadat, respectively; it merely disentangled the combatants. The UN presence was not intended to deal with the causes of the two wars but with their effects. The same was true in the Congo, though with a special twist. It was precisely the United Nations' refusal to interfere in the domestic politics of the Congo that created most of the difficulties. After the Congo had disintegrated, the head of the "national" government insisted that the UN operation in the Congo crush the secession of Katanga. In the end, the international organization could not isolate itself from the Congolese civil war. The effect of UN *non*intervention was to freeze the schism and to ensure the collapse of the Congolese government because Katanga's rich copper mines were the major source of national revenue. Although UN forces eventually did fight to crush the secession of Katanga, the third condition of domestic nonintervention remains. One need look no further than the American-organized multinational force in Beirut in 1982-1983 for contrast; when the United States became partisan in the civil war, the mission turned into a disaster.

The nations of the Third World, it must be noted, can use this preventive diplomacy function *only* if the superpowers permit them to do so. The assumption underlying the pacifying role of the nonaligned states is that both the United States and the Soviet Union wish to avoid escalating conflict in their desire to avoid nuclear war. This gives them a vested interest in keeping peripheral conflicts under control. They will thus at least acquiesce in the establishment of a UN presence: "It cannot be done *against* the major parties; it cannot be done *by* them; it can only be done *for* them and by their leave." [8]

In conflicts not involving direct American-Soviet confrontations, especially to achieve preventive diplomacy, four alternative kinds of UN action are possible: a pro-Western action, an impartial action, no action at all, or a pro-Soviet action. Obviously, the American preference is that order; the Soviets prefer the exact reverse. Neither extreme is really feasible, but the difficulty is that between the remaining alternatives the United States prefers impartial, neutralizing action, whereas the Soviet Union prefers inactivity. The United States fears that inactivity will lead either to a Soviet advantage or to a collapse requiring American intervention—and Soviet counterintervention. It also hopes that impartial action will accomplish pro-American results. Conversely, the Soviets hope that inaction will produce pro-Soviet results and prevent American intervention. The Soviets fear that the course preferred by the United States may indeed yield results detrimental to Soviet interests.

Consequences of Preventive Diplomacy. By limiting the scope of marginal conflicts and seeking to stabilize tense situations, preventive diplomacy has on the whole served U.S. purposes better than Soviet ends. For example, in Egypt in 1956 and 1973, UN forces helped preempt possible Soviet intervention. In the Congo in 1961 UN intervention eliminated the bridgehead the Soviets had established. The Soviet Union was therefore frustrated; from its perspective, the moving force in both crises, but especially in the Congo, had been the secretary-general, and the results demonstrated the need for a Soviet veto over his actions. The Soviets proposed a "troika" plan, calling for the appointment of three secretaries-general, each representing one of the major blocs in the world. The Soviets sought to supplement their actual veto in the Security Council and their virtual veto in the General Assembly (where they usually found enough votes among the nonaligned states to prevent a two-thirds majority vote against them) with a hidden veto at the top of the Secretariat. This veto would ensure that the United Nations could not do anything that was in any way detrimental to Soviet interests.

The nonaligned states unanimously opposed the troika plan to hamstring the secretary-general. They valued the organization as the bastion of their independence and "neutralist" positions in the cold war. Because of Soviet refusal to pay for UN peace-keeping operations and American insistence that the Soviet Union must pay if it was not to lose its voting rights in the General Assembly, the international body became deadlocked and remained so until American leaders saw that they would receive little support for stripping the Soviet Union of its voting rights in the assembly. They were then willing to recognize instead the principle that no great power must pay for peace-keeping operations it regards as detrimental to its interests.

It is inconceivable that the United States would have been any more likely than the Soviet Union to financially support operations that were injurious to its national interests. Indeed, when the United States abandoned its position, it declared that it too reserved the right not to pay for future peace-keeping operations of which it disapproved. Although at the time this move may have been a face-saving way out of an awkward situation, the United States went further than the Soviets and reduced its overall contribution to the United Nations in 1971 from 40 to 25 percent of the annual budget. Later, it was to withhold its annual contribution to compel reforms enhancing American influence in the organization and withdraw from one of the United Nation's specialized agencies to voice its displeasure about the anti-Western—especially anti-American—attitudes and emotions that appeared to characterize the United Nations in general in the fourth phase of its development.

Can the United Nations Prevent Wars?   Although the United Nations has managed to prevent the continuation and escalation of fighting in which one or both of the superpowers have not been participants themselves, it should be emphasized that this success is not to be confused with the prevention of war. That is one lesson of the war in 1967, when Egypt exercised its sovereign right to expel UN forces. Sometimes wars do not even come under the jurisdiction of the United Nations. For example, in 1971 Pakistan brutally crushed an attempt by East Pakistan to secede and become independent. Claiming that the proposed secession was a domestic matter, the Pakistani government rejected UN intervention. India, burdened by 10 million refugees from East Pakistan and eager to eliminate its only rival on the subcontinent, went to war with Pakistan, helped establish the state of Bangladesh, and sent the refugees back there. India too rejected UN intervention. When the Vietnamese invaded Cambodia in 1978 to overthrow the pro-Chinese Pol Pot government and impose a pro-Vietnamese government—after which Chinese forces crossed the frontier with Vietnam to teach the Vietnamese a lesson—none of these Communist states wanted a debate on aggression in Indochina. It would have been too embarrassing. Nor have all conflicts in Africa received attention in the halls of the United Nations. In 1977 Somalia actively supported, perhaps even sponsored, an uprising in the Ogaden area of Ethiopia; later the Ethiopians, with Soviet-Cuban support, moved toward Somalia's border, but no debate occurred. Nor was there debate when Idi Amin of Uganda provoked Tanzania in 1978, and, in the subsequent war, Tanzanian troops deposed him. Similarly, the Iraqi attack upon Iran in 1980 was never placed on the Security Council's agenda; nor was Libya's invasion of Chad in the same year.

Civil wars, with their potential for spilling over into interstate conflict, and the barbarous treatment of people by their own governments usually are not placed on the international agenda either. While the Nigerian government was engaged in civil war against the Ibos in the secessionist state of Biafra from 1967 to 1970, approximately half a million people died, but the issue was not debated in the United Nations because many developing countries did not wish to legitimate Biafra and encourage secession in their own countries. After its victory in Cambodia, the Communist government of Pol Pot adopted a barbarous policy of genocide against its own people, yet this problem never appeared on the United Nations agenda. An estimated 3 million of Cambodia's 8 million people reportedly died as a result of these policies before the regime was forcibly replaced in 1979 by a Vietnamese puppet regime. These issues have not even been discussed by the United Nations because that body consists of sovereign states, which means that each has the right to exclude any intervention aimed at protecting the rights of individual citizens. But the increasing number of wars that are *not* brought before the Security Council raised a serious question about the continued relevance of the United Nations on peace and security issues.

Fourth Phase: First World–Third World Confrontation

The period following 1973 was a heady one for the developing countries. The success of the Organization of Petroleum Exporting Countries (OPEC) in its control of worldwide oil prices suggested that the former colonies need no longer take a back seat to their former masters, the Western industrial democracies. The developing countries' strategies of modernization had by and large failed. Western economic aid was declining and "import substitution" had not stoked the fires of development; producer-cartels were thought to be a better strategy. With its global forum and public attention, the United Nations was the obvious place to publicize Third World grievances. In fact, the developing countries controlled the General Assembly, where they had organized the United Nations Conference on Trade and Development (UNCTAD) in 1964. By the mid-1970s, UNCTAD was 120 members strong, and the "Group of 77" had emerged as an informal working coalition to push issues of interest to the developing countries. Thus, it was in the assembly that the developing countries focused the international spotlight on the relationship of the rich and poor nations, expressed their anger and resentment, blamed the West for their continued underdevelopment, and demanded a new international economic order in 1974.

Anti-Western Phase. The years of confrontation after 1973 were filled with strident rhetoric both within the United Nations and within the nonaligned movement outside. The Western countries were continually criticized for past and present exploitation of the developing countries even while they were being called upon for assistance. The Communist countries, which offered virtually no material help, suffered no rebuke and even enjoyed acclaim for their view that poor countries are poor because they have been exploited by the rich. The temper of the developing countries, most of which in the past had prided themselves on nonalignment, was symbolized by their 1979 meeting in Cuba. Vietnam and North Korea, which, like Cuba, were not nonaligned at all, attended this meeting and tried to influence the assembly to support Soviet policy. Although the subsequent Soviet invasion of Afghanistan aroused the overwhelming disapproval of the nonaligned countries, later nonaligned meetings did not hesitate to criticize American policies while abstaining from mentioning Soviet policies. Even in calling for the withdrawal of Soviet forces from Afghanistan, the reference was to "foreign forces"; the nonaligned refused to mention the Soviet Union by name. The 101-nation 1986 meeting in Zimbabwe condemned the United States by name fifty-four times—including for "state terrorism" against Libya—and the Soviet Union not once. (Only at the 1989 meeting were there signs for the first time of a shift from the anti-U.S. policy.)

Thus, not a double but a triple standard seemed to prevail. The Western democracies, particularly the United States, were frequently condemned by name, while the Soviet bloc, especially the Soviet Union, if criticized at all, was criticized in milder tones and often only by implication. The developing countries themselves rarely criticized one another. Because Israel was usually seen as a Western state, to attack it was to attack the West and the United States. Indeed, it was the Middle Eastern situation that first suggested the possibility that the United Nations was entering a fourth, anti-Western phase. In 1974 the General Assembly invited the head of the Palestine Liberation Organization, a nonstate actor whose acts of terrorism and hijacking it had debated only a few years earlier, to address it. It treated PLO leader Yasir

Arafat as a head of government and greeted him with sustained applause while limiting the time for an Israeli reply, which was delivered to a virtually empty auditorium. Simultaneously, the Arab-African-Asian majority, supported by the Communist states, barred Israeli participation in the previously nonpolitical United Nations Educational, Scientific, and Cultural Organization (UNESCO). In addition, the assembly ousted South Africa from its sessions because of that nation's racial practices after the Security Council, which exercises ultimate suspension power, had refused to do so. Finally, the PLO, as well as SWAPO (South West African People's Organization in Namibia), were given "permanent observer" status at the United Nations. Both even receive UN funds—all in the name of national liberation and their status as future states.

In 1979, however, the most dramatic confrontation in the General Assembly occurred. That was the year that Idi Amin, then president of Uganda and chairman of the Organization for African Unity (OAU)—a man who had voiced approval of the slaughter of Israeli athletes at the Munich Olympics and who had said that Adolf Hitler's only error had been not killing more Jews—claimed to speak on behalf of forty-six African members when he charged that the United States had been colonized by Zionists and that Israel had no right to exist. A coalition of African, Asian, Arab, and Communist nations also oversaw passage of a General Assembly resolution equating Zionism with racism. A similar resolution was passed almost unnoticed in the closing weeks of the 1979 session. The earlier resolution, sponsored by the Arab states, also proclaimed the Palestinians' right to independence and sovereignty but failed to recognize the same right for Israel. Thus by accepting this resolution, the majority in the General Assembly recognized the rights of Palestinians, as defined by leaders who refused to accept the rights of the nation of Israel, over whose birth the United Nations had presided.

Concern for human rights also became very selective, especially during the 1980s. There was a "Special Rapporteur" on human rights for El Salvador but not for Nicaragua. And Israel and South Africa remained the perennial targets. Most of those attacking the policies of U.S. allies were themselves authoritarian regimes whose human rights records were very poor. Thus, the result was sometimes bizarre, as when, for example, Iran and Vietnam condemned Israel as a "non-peaceloving state" (because peaceloving, according to the UN Charter, is a prerequisite of membership; to declare a state to be the opposite means that potentially it could be expelled). Symptomatic of the United States' diminished ability to mobilize the United Nations in behalf of Western interests were the thirty vetoes it cast from 1981 to 1986, and its departure from the International Labor Organization from 1977 to 1980 and UNESCO in 1983.

An Arena for Opposition or Conflict Resolution? In the early 1980s, former U.S. ambassador to the United Nations Jeanne Kirkpatrick voiced an additional charge.[9] Not only did the developing countries frequently vent their anti-American sentiments, she said, but the United Nations, by repeatedly debating the same issue and sometimes calling for sanctions (usually against Israel and South Africa), generated "a process of conflict extension, polarization, and exacerbation." Rather than facilitating the resolution of disputes, the United Nations was debating hardened positions, embittering the contending nations. American successes, she observed, increasingly amounted to little more than blocking anti-American resolutions. U.S. policy thus added up to not much more than "damage control," such as warding off attacks on Israel.

The reason for this outcome, Kirkpatrick pointed out, was the increase in bloc voting. There was the East European bloc, the twenty-member Arab bloc, the twelve-member European Economic Community plus Japan, the forty-two-nation Islamic Conference, and the more than 100-nation nonaligned bloc (of which approximately one-third are African states and which includes the above members of other developing-country groupings). The General Assembly had grown to 159 members in which every state had one vote, whether it was Communist China, with more than 1 billion people, or St. Christopher-Nevis, a microstate with a population of less than 100,000. Thus, the thirty-eight microstates with populations of fewer than 1 million had an influence in the United Nations totally disproportionate to their size, population, wealth, and financial contribution to the UN budget. (The ten major industrial nations contribute 80 percent of the UN budget, while the eighty smaller countries contribute less than 1 percent; yet the latter are part of the General Assembly's majority which decides the budget.) With this organization into blocs, the developing country-Soviet bloc coalition, for example, could easily muster anti-Western majorities in the General Assembly and most of the specialized agencies, such as UNESCO, while often ignoring other critical peace and human rights issues, especially those they did not want aired (see Table 16-3).

The upshot, Kirkpatrick said, has been twofold: (1) the United Nations has become increasingly less relevant to many of the world's problems, and (2) its capacity for conflict resolution has decreased as repeated condemnations have made it even more difficult to find a compromise solution. Moreover, reasoned debate has more and more fallen prey to ritualistic and repetitive slogans whose aims are, directly or implicitly, to condemn the United States, and which only serve to aggravate conflicts rather than resolve them. The "all-too-familiar scenario," said Kirkpatrick,

> features one victim, many attackers, a great deal of verbal violence and a large number of indifferent and/or intimidated onlookers.
>
> In these carefully staged productions, the Security Council serves as the stage, the presence of the world press ensures an audience, the solidarity of the "blocs" provides a long procession of speakers to echo, elaborate and expand on the original accusations. The goal is isolation and humiliation of the victim—creation of an impression that "world opinion" is united in condemnation of the targeted nation. The enterprise more closely resembles a mugging than either a political debate or an effort at problem solving.[10]

In these circumstances, and particularly because the United Nations was widely regarded as unfriendly to American values and interests (as during its second phase when it was unfriendly toward the Soviet Union), the United States played "hard ball" with funds for the upkeep of the United Nations. In 1985, the U.S. Senate passed a resolution reducing the American contribution to the UN annual budget from 25 percent to 20 percent by October 1986 unless the UN voting formula of one state, one vote was changed. That resolution called for the United Nations to shift to a system in which each member state's voting strength on budget matters was proportional to its financial contribution. The four largest contributors—the United States, Japan, West Germany, and France—would then have slightly more than 50 percent of the vote and control of the budget. The current formula, it was charged, represented "taxation without representation."

After carrying out a self-examination, the United Nations recommended in 1986 that the largest contributors have a proportional influence, to be ensured by requiring budget decisions by consensus. Thus, presumably, the larger donors could veto the budget. In 1988 the United States was $467 million in arrears and owed an additional $65 million for peace-keeping operations, reflecting its frustration with the United Nations' anti-Western bias and its wasteful, inefficient ways. But, just as the United Nations was facing the possibility of bankruptcy, President Reagan released $44 million outstanding for 1988, promised an additional $144 million for 1989, and committed the nation to paying all past debts over a number of years. But the Congress paid no heed. In 1989 it cut $123 million from the $715 million that President Bush had requested for the UN budget; the $96 million that Bush had wanted to pay as the first installment on the over $400 million that the United States was in arrears was eliminated as well. Congress even cut $30 million from the $111 million that the country contributed for UN peace-keeping operations. The timing could not have been worse, the United Nations was once more increasing its mediating and peace-keeping operations and serving both American and Soviet interests at a time the superpowers were moving away from the cold war.

Fifth Phase: Revival of Peace Keeping

In the late 1980s, several events occurred that allow the United Nations to once again play a prominent role in world affairs.[11] First, the Third World's confrontation with the West had come to naught. The demands for a new international economic order had failed. Given their own economic problems and the failure to solve them, as well as their need for Western assistance, including that of the multinational corporations, the developing countries moderated their tone; market solutions and private capital became more attractive. Second, the Soviet Union, which had for over a decade aligned itself with the Third World's complaints against the West, sought a respite from more conflict to focus on its domestic problems. It thus saw the United Nations as an institution that would both help resolve some of the entangle-

Table 16-3 UN Member Countries, 1945-1985

	Americas		*Europe*	

1945 (Original members)	Argentina
	Bolivia
	Brazil
	Canada
	Chile
	Colombia
	Costa Rica
	Cuba
	Dominican
	  Republic
	Ecuador
	El Salvador
		Guatemala
		Haiti
		Honduras
		Mexico
		Nicaragua
		Panama
		Paraguay
		Peru
		United States
		Uruguay
		Venezuela
			Belgium
			Belorussia
			Czechoslovakia
			Denmark
			France
			Greece
			Luxembourg
			Netherlands
			Norway
			Poland
			Turkey
				Ukraine
				United
				  Kingdom
				USSR
				Yugoslavia

1945-1965	Jamaica Trinidad and Tobago		Albania Austria Bulgaria Finland Hungary Iceland Ireland Italy Malta Portugal Romania Spain Sweden	

1965-1985	Antigua and
	  Barbuda
	Bahamas
	Barbados
	Belize
	Dominica
	Grenada
	Guyana
		St. Christopher
		  and Nevis
		St. Lucia
		St. Vincent
		  and the
		  Grenadines
		Suriname
			East Germany
			West Germany	

SOURCE: Department of State, *Atlas of United States Foreign Relations*, 2d ed. (Washington D.C.: Government Printing Office, 1985), 18.

NOTE: As of 1990, no new states had been added.

ments it had gotten itself into (and sought relief from) and handle future Third World crises in which it wished to avoid becoming involved. Gorbachev specifically called for a more active role for the Security Council

Table 16-3—Continued

Asia/Oceania		Africa	
Australia		Egypt	
China		Ethiopia	
India		Liberia	
Iran		South Africa	
Iraq			
Lebanon			
New Zealand			
Philippines			
Saudi Arabia			
Syria			
Afghanistan	Pakistan	Algeria	Mali
Burma	Singapore	Benin	Mauritania
Cambodia	Sri Lanka	Burkina Faso	Morocco
Cyprus	Thailand	Burundi	Niger
Indonesia		Cameroon	Nigeria
Israel		Central African	Rwanda
Japan		Republic	Senegal
Jordan		Chad	Sierra Leone
Kuwait		Congo	Somalia
Laos		Gabon	Sudan
Malaysia		Gambia	Tanzania
Maldives		Ghana	Togo
Mongolia		Guinea	Tunisia
Nepal		Ivory Coast	Uganda
North Yemen		Libya	Zaire
		Madagascar	Zambia
		Malawi	
Bahrain	Solomon Islands	Angola	Mauritius
Bangladesh	South Yemen	Botswana	Mozambique
Bhutan	United Arab	Cape Verde	São Tomé and
Brunei	Emirates	Comoros	Principe
Fiji	Vanuatu	Djibouti	Seychelles
Oman	Vietnam	Equatorial Guinea	Swaziland
Papua New Guinea	Western Samoa	Guinea-Bissau	Zimbabwe
Qatar		Lesotho	

and the use of peace-keeping forces in regional conflicts. He also proposed establishing a number of "war-risk reduction centers" around the world that would watch for and monitor military activities. To show Soviet confidence in the organization, he paid Soviet back-dues to the United Nations, including almost $200 million for peace-keeping operations the Soviet Union had long opposed.

Third, the United States, which had found that going it alone—when, for example, it invaded Grenada, bombed Libya, and ignored the International Court of Justice (World Court) on Nicaragua—was the preferred course during the time the United Nations and some of its agencies had become platforms for anti-Western propaganda, also saw renewed possibilities for strengthening the United Nations and furthering U.S.-Soviet cooperation. Finally, the late 1980s was a period in which no country or bloc was really in charge of the international organization. The West had dominated in the early stages of its development, only to be succeeded by the developing countries. But the new primacy of the Security Council had decreased their influence in the General Assembly. U.S. interest in the organization was revived by the success of the United Nations in ending the eight-year Afghan war, with the subsequent Soviet withdrawal. In fact, it was the UN undersecretary-general for special political affairs who had patiently mediated the 1988 agreement between Pakistan, which had supported the Afghan rebels and had not recognized the Communist regime as Afghanistan's legitimate government, and the latter, whose sole support was the Soviet Union. The United Nations also supervised the Soviet pull-out.

But even before this occurred, some prominent Americans had called for a larger role for the Security Council and the United Nations itself in world affairs. For example, George Ball, undersecretary of state during the Kennedy and Johnson administrations, had noted that the presence of a UN peace-keeping force in Lebanon after Israel's 1982 invasion might have spared the lives of the over 200 U.S. Marines assigned to a multinational peace-keeping force (composed of several NATO countries) who were killed after that force became involved in the civil war in that country. Former Carter secretary of state Cyrus Vance and Nixon secretary of defense Elliot Richardson had pointed out that in 1987, the United Nations, not the United States, should have reflagged nonmilitary vessels in the Persian Gulf. They argued that because UN peace-keeping operations in the past were "widely respected and rarely attacked, even in zones of bitter conflict," and U.S. reflagging only fueled tensions with Iran, such a move would have cooled tensions and assured commercial shipping peaceful passage.

While this advice went unheeded, the United Nation's success in Afghanistan (where forty observers oversaw the soviet withdrawal) was followed by a role for that organization in the Persian Gulf once Iran stated in 1988 that it wanted to end the war. The subsequent cease-fire was monitored by a 412-person UN military observer group, while Iran and Iraq, with the help of UN Secretary-General Javier Pérez de Cuéllar, sought to find mutually acceptable terms to conclude their almost eight-year-long hostilities. Peace-keeping was suddenly back in style. During the same period, the United Nations outlined plans for ending the sixteen-year war in the Western Sahara between Morocco and the Polisario guerrillas. Two thousand United Nation troops would be sent to the area, and the UN would administer the former Spanish colony of Western Sahara until a referendum could be held. Another country, Namibia, or Southwest Africa, became an independent state in 1989 after the U.S.-brokered agreement had provided for South African forces to pull out from that country in return for a Cuban troop withdrawal from Angola, its northern neighbor, where the South Africans had supported the guerrillas against Angola's Marxist government. When that war ended, an estimated 4,500 military personnel and 1,000 police officers were needed to ensure the truce and oversee free elections. Secretary-General de Cuéllar has also offered to become involved in talks on the withdrawal of Soviet-supported Vietnamese troops from Cambodia (see Table 16-4). In addition, he is participating in negotiations between the leaders of the Greek and Turkish communities on Cyprus on the reunification of that divided island state. And the five Central American presidents have asked the secretary-general to assist in carrying out a peace plan for that area. A force of 2,000 troops was scheduled to be sent to the Nicaraguan-Honduran border in late 1989 to guard the former against infiltration as contra troops were disbanded.

About 10,000 UN troops are already deployed in the Sinai Peninsula between Egypt and Israel, in the Golan Heights between Syria and Israel, in Cyprus, in Lebanon, and on the Indian-Pakistani frontier. If the United Nations becomes involved in all the peace-keeping operations in the Western Sahara, Namibia, Cambodia, and elsewhere, the cost may increase from $235 million to $1.5-$2 billion.

Improved U.S.-Soviet relations have enabled the Security Council to become a more effective means of resolving long-standing regional disputes. In the past, most UN peace-keeping operations were related to Third World conflicts, primarily the product of the decolonization process. Because, if allowed to go on, these conflicts threatened to pull in the superpowers, the peace-keeping forces provided a buffer. But in Afghanistan, Angola, and Cambodia the superpowers were directly involved. There, Soviet troops or Soviet proxies—the Cuban and Vietnamese armies—had placed friendly regimes in power in the 1970s, and during the Reagan years the United States had supported the rebels. Although in the past the superpowers had kept the United Nations out of the East-West rivalry, they now found it a useful means of resolving some regional disputes that had long soured their relationship. Specifically, the United Nations had shown once more how, by acting as a third party, it could allow the contestants to save face and extract themselves from situations that had become too burdensome.

In a combustible world the United Nation's role is a very important one. But this does not mean that it can prevent or halt wars; the latter can be achieved only if the participants want to stop and are looking for help to do so. Secretary-General de Cuéllar's efforts to mediate the 1982 Argentinian-British dispute over the Falkland Islands failed. Also in 1982, the Security Council was ignored, if not defied, when it called repeatedly and unani-

Table 16-4 Recent U.S.-Soviet Regional Settlements or Efforts at Resolution

War Site	War Initiated	Diplomatic Resolution Initiated
Afghanistan	1979: Soviets invade Afghanistan.	1988: Moscow announces withdrawal.
Iran-Iraq	1980: Iraq attacks Iran.	1988: Iran accepts UN cease-fire resolution.
Angola	1975: Portugal withdraws from Angola.	1988: Peace talks begin between Angola, Cuba, South Africa, and the United States.
Cambodia	1978: Vietnam invades and occupies Cambodia.	1988: Peace talks begin in Indonesia.
Nicaragua	1981: U.S.-supported contra war begins.	1988: Truce and cease-fire precede Sandinista-contra negotiations.

mously for a cease-fire in Lebanon and for Israel to withdraw its troops. Prior to 1988 as well, the United Nations had been unable to convince the Soviet Union to withdraw its troops from Afghanistan, to influence Vietnam to pull out of Cambodia, to end the Iran-Iraq war, or to resolve the conflicts in Nicaragua and El Salvador. An editorial in the *New York Times* summed up the situation:

> The problem is that an assembly of nations called "sovereign," or subject to no higher authority, can never be more than the sum of its members. Nations can behave inside the UN only as they behave outside, bartering interests, including their interest in peace. But the Charter notwithstanding, they insist on the right to redress grievance by force, which is what distinguishes a nation from province, county, town or individual.
>
> To yield that right, nations would need a common parliament to write laws, courts to interpret them and police to enforce them. They would have to disarm and pay taxes to a protecting authority instead. The United Nations cannot evolve into such a higher authority; it was designed to foreclose it, to let peoples relate only inter*nationally*, through the prism of their armies.
>
> That does not mean the UN is useless as mediator when any parties want to avoid war. But it does mean that anarchy—the absence of higher authority—is the desired, if undesirable condition.[12]

In short, the sovereignty of the member states will limit the contribution of the United Nations to resolving nations' security problems. But at the same time that organization helps to limit the impact of anarchy. Indeed, in a world of sovereign states it is necessary to underline certain limitations of the United Nations because expectations about its role are so often unrealistic— and the disillusionment about it therefore so deep—that the organization is then rejected as useless.

Limitations and Benefits of the United Nations

Not an Alternative to Power Politics. The United Nations is *not* a substitute for power politics. To idealize the organization—that is, to expect it to rise "above that sort of thing" and to be superior in morals and general demeanor to the nation-states that are its members—is not only unwarranted but also likely to breed disillusionment and cynicism. Unrealistically high expectations, when disappointed, result in declining support for its highly important preventive diplomacy. The United Nations is not simply a debating society. Speeches there articulate conflicting views and make the world more aware of key issues that are likely to be troublesome. UN representatives from various nations are also able to gather informally to try to reconcile differing interests and to arrange compromises out of the limelight.

No Authority over the Superpowers. Although the United Nations is neither a world government nor totally impotent, it is not very influential when it comes to dealing with the superpowers. In 1979 the General Assembly demanded that Vietnam withdraw its troops from Cambodia after two attempts to censure Vietnam in the Security Council had been vetoed by the Soviet Union. The assembly resolution, sponsored by Vietnam's non-Communist neighbors and supported by many developing countries, was ignored by Vietnam. And all this came after the Security Council had briefly discussed the Vietnamese invasion of Cambodia, only to drop it quickly. In 1979-1980 the Security Council agreed that Iran should release the American hostages held in the embassy in Tehran. Because seizure of diplomatic personnel threatened to make diplomacy itself impossible, such unanimity was to be expected. If the United Nations could not speak for the safety of diplomats, what could it speak for? But when Iran continued to hold the hostages, economic sanctions were vetoed by the Soviets in the Security Council. (The United States did not take the issue to the General Assembly, allegedly because a supportive vote there would have had no legal force, but actually because a majority could not be obtained. Domestic support for U.S. military action against Iran was also lacking.) When the Security Council called for Soviet military withdrawal from Afghanistan after its 1979 invasion, it was vetoed by the Soviets. The assembly, however, did vote 104-18 (with 30 states not voting) to condemn the Soviet move, a rare occurrence in the United Nations.

Influenced by National Interests. Because the United Nations reflects the real world and not the ideal world, it should not be surprising that all member nations continue to follow their national interests, regardless of how moralistic and altruistic their rhetoric. When the Soviet Union and the Communist bloc nations were a minority in the second phase of the United Nations, the Soviet Union could counter majority resolutions in the Security Council only through its veto power as one of the council's five permanent members. It did indeed cast many vetoes, partly because the United States, using diplomacy as a tool of propaganda, repeatedly introduced resolutions to which it knew the Soviet Union would object. Precisely because the United Nations is associated in the popular mind with idealism, the United States was able to place the Soviet Union in a position of seeming to obstruct the peaceful work of the organization and to align itself with the majority in the pursuit of all that is good and true. The United States, however, did not have to cast a single veto; it had majority support in the Security Council. In using majority votes to reject Soviet proposals, the United States was exercising what has been called a "hidden veto"—a negative vote hidden beneath a democratic cloak.

Not until 1966, when enough nonpermanent members had been added to the Security Council to jeopardize American control of that body, did the United States, faced with the fact that many developing countries were participating with the Soviet Union in an anti-Western coalition, begin to cast vetoes in the Security Council. Moreover, the United States refused to sign the 1982 Law of the Sea Treaty, withdrew from UNESCO in 1983 because of that organization's politicization of issues before it and its anti-Western orientation, and rejected the jurisdiction of the International Court of Justice when Nicaragua brought charges of U.S. aggression before the court in 1984.

Double Standards.   Because the United Nations represents its constituents and because these nations pursue their national interests through the organization, it follows that the United Nations reflects double standards of judgment. When Israel retaliates against one of its Arab neighbors for brutal guerrilla attacks and outright murder, it is likely to find itself condemned by a majority of members because the Arab states, both as developing nations and as Muslim nations, have lots of friends. The guerrillas and the Arab states harboring them will not be similarly condemned. The United States cast its second veto in the United Nations when Israel, having exacted reprisals for the murder by Palestinian terrorists of several members of the Israeli Olympic team in Munich in 1972, was about to be condemned in the Security Council. And, although South Africa is frequently condemned, the developing countries never censured Idi Amin for the as many as 300,000 murders carried out under his rule and the persecution and expulsion of 60,000 Asians from Uganda, or Burundi for the over 100,000 Hutus reportedly killed within its borders in 1972 and the estimated 20,000 people killed in 1988, or Cambodia for its genocide. "The countries of the Third World are not subject to criticism or attack, even by each other, while any part of the rest of the world which can be labelled racist or imperialist must be held accountable."[13] In the eight-year Iran-Iraq war, a war between Third World states, Iraq was not condemned for invading its neighbor in 1980; nor has either side been condemned for its brutal treatment of each other's prisoners of war. Yet there have been some signs of change in the reluctance of Third World countries to denounce one another, as in a 1988 UN human rights report which for the first time revealed that serious human rights violations were occurring in Iran.

Not Representative of World Opinion.   The United Nations does not represent "world public opinion," which allegedly restrains state behavior. Most states cannot be considered democratic, although many claim to be. Many are authoritarian, whether civilians or military officers are in charge, and public opinion on national issues has no means of expression in such countries. Nor do they allow competing political parties or a free press and other mass media. The masses hear only what their governments wish them to hear. In addition, a government's public statements may not reflect its private views.

In any event, the absence of a world public opinion in the United Nations reflects the existence of many nations with varied historical traditions, philosophies, ideologies, and political and moral standards. There is little consensus among countries on what is moral and what are acceptable standards of behavior. Certainly there is nothing equivalent to those that exist in modern Western political systems. What does exist, however, is a set of *governmental* views and opinions, which are often mistaken for "world public opinion." When a government solemnly declares in the United Nations that "our people wish to express their outrage" or whatever else, it is presenting its own opinion as the *vox populi.*

A state is admittedly sensitive to what other states think of its actions, and it may take prospective reactions into account in deciding on its aims, how they are to be achieved, and how to explain them publicly. Concern for other states' opinions is an everyday affair, evidenced by extensive public relations and propaganda efforts. And no state relishes a UN vote against it, for the popular image of the United Nations as a "good" organization, symbolic of humanity's desire for peace, is deeply rooted. Nevertheless, when governments feel strongly about an issue, they will pursue their aims, regardless of the *national* opinions expressed in the General Assembly and Security Council. The Soviet invasions of Hungary, Czechoslovakia, and Afghanistan are examples. Moreover, Iran continued to hold American hostages, despite a disapproving vote in the Security Council.

Adaptability.   Finally, as a benefit, the United Nations has demonstrated its adaptability in a world in flux. It was originally established on the assumption that the great powers would cooperate, with the added safeguard that, if they could not cooperate, a veto would preclude any attempt to ride roughshod over a great power. It seemed preferable to paralyze the Security Council and to prevent action, for that would reflect the genuine stalemate outside the United Nations. Abolishment of the veto might have cured the Security Council's impotence, but it would also probably have meant war. When one great power opposes another, it is the better part of wisdom to attempt to negotiate differences rather than to outvote one of the parties and then to try to enforce the majority decision. In any event, the United Nations was not permanently paralyzed in its area of primary responsibility, keeping the peace. This function was first shifted to the General Assembly, then to the secretary-general, and then back to the Security Council. Thanks to this flexibility, the United Nations has demonstrated a vitality that its predecessor, the League of Nations, never exhibited during the period between the two world wars. It has survived and performed some vital functions during four decades of changing American-Soviet relations, the appearance of many new states, and the subsequent division between rich and poor nations. None of these is more important than its mediating and peace-keeping functions.

INTERNATIONAL LAW

In a decentralized system, international law exercises little restraint on state behavior when vital interests are at stake. On the whole, however, states generally do obey legal norms which tend to reinforce the restraints imposed by calculations of power and prudence. But if the limited impact of international law can be attributed to the primitive nature of the state system rather than any inherent lack of merit, the fact that in routine matters—which is the stuff of everyday behavior—it does constrain states in their relationships with one another demonstrates once more that the international system is not one of pure anarchy but of qualified anarchy.

Sources of International Law

Not surprisingly, given the nature of the international system, the states themselves are the principal source of international law. Most international law is customary. Certain norms of conduct that have evolved over a long period of time have at some point become accepted as binding by the states that have followed them; new states tend to accept them automatically. Customary law, then, rests on a general consent. The other principal kind of international law is treaty law. Unlike customary law, which is applicable to all states, treaty law binds only the parties that sign and ratify the treaties. As two states alone can hardly establish a general rule of conduct, treaty law usually reflects agreement by a large number of states. In 1982, for example, 117 nations, mainly Third World, voted for a new treaty governing the use and exploitation of the seas. The United States voted against the new Law of the Sea, however, as did West Germany and Britain, and forty-six other nations abstained.

Despite widespread opinion to the contrary, states usually obey international law because they need it. The rise of states as independent political units made the development of law necessary. Each sovereign state enjoyed complete jurisdiction and authority over its own territory and people, but it enjoyed neither beyond its boundaries. As states are compelled to coexist, however, they have to regulate their relations. If they are to stay in official contact, they must exchange representatives, which means that the rights and immunities of diplomats have had to be defined so that they can be protected on foreign soil. Other matters that have had to be covered include how title to territory is acquired (a matter that retains some importance because of continuing frontier disputes), ceded, and recognized. Also to be dealt with are a state's jurisdiction over its territorial waters, its air space, and aliens on its soil; conditions under which treaties come into effect and are terminated; legal methods for resolving disputes; and conduct of warfare and determination of the rights of neutrals.

The 1982 Law of the Sea, for example, covers such issues as territorial waters (twelve nautical miles from the coastline); the right of "innocent passage" through territorial waters for all ships, including military; the right of ships to pass through international straits (for example, Gibralter or Hormuz) that do not become territorial waters; a 200-mile economic zone in which coastal states have the exclusive right to fish and other marine life; a 350-mile zone for the exploitation of oil, gas, and other resources; and arrangements for the mining of seabed nodules of copper, nickel, cobalt, and zinc. The United States, as well as West Germany and other European Economic Community countries, did not sign the treaty, largely out of fear that the organization in charge of the mining would be controlled by the developing countries. Still, coexistence requires rules.

Obedience and Disobedience of International Law

It should now be obvious why states do not normally violate international law—indeed, why it is virtually self-enforcing, except in the area of warfare. Legal norms provide a degree of order and predictability in an all too uncertain and chaotic environment. States expect to benefit from the reciprocal observance of obligations; if a particular state gains a reputation for not keeping its agreements, other states will be reluctant to sign further agreements with it, and reprisals may occur as well.

This rule is as true for Western states, among which customary international law originated, as for non-Western states. It has sometimes been held that Western-derived international law is unacceptable to the Third World and that the law must therefore be developed further to reflect the values and interests of the latter. But this view has led to confusion. On the one hand, the non-Western states are attempting to articulate their economic and political interests, shaped mainly by their desire for modernization, so that they can play a more influential role in the state system. On the other hand, they seek to express their resentment of a legal order that mirrors primarily the interests of the rich and powerful Western states. The new countries have thus accepted the prevailing law, invoking it in disputes with other states when it favors them, while seeking certain changes—for example, in the areas of foreign investments and property and the settlement of claims after expropriation and nationalization of such holdings. Yet even on the latter issue, it is suspected that as some of the newer states gain greater stakes in the international system and become exporters of capital, their views will move closer to those held by the more industrialized Western states.

Because of the anarchical nature of the state system, international law has its shortcomings, however. The international legal system, unlike a national or municipal one, exists in the absence of a supranational legislature. Customary law and treaty law are substitutes for legislated rules. The difficulties inherent in a decentralized system are clear: states may disagree about when a custom becomes a legal norm; they may differ in defining their obligations because even well-established customary law may be unclear on specific details; and there is no accepted authority to impose a uniform interpretation. Law that evolves over time is also slow to adapt to rapidly changing conditions; as a result, it may become obsolete. Treaty law may not be subject to such obsolescence, but it does not apply to nonsignatories. Few treaties are signed by even a majority of states, let alone all states. This may mean that while parties to a treaty are bound by its terms with regard to each other, their relationship to nonparties continues to be based on customary law. Treaty law, like customary law, may also suffer from a lack of specificity. Nor is there a supranational executive to impose sanctions when international law is violated as in domestic systems, although, as one noted British international legal expert, J. L. Brierly, has noted:

> The weakness of international law lies deeper than any mere question of sanctions. It is not the existence of a police force that makes a system of law strong and respected, but the strength of the law that makes it possible for a police force to be effectively organized. The imperative character of law is felt so strongly within a highly civilized state that national law has developed a machinery of enforcement which generally works smoothly, though never so smoothly as to make breaches impossible. If the imperative character of international law were equally strongly felt, the institution of definite international sanctions would easily follow.[14]

In a sense, the word *law* is a misnomer in this context. A proper designation would be *norm*, a prescribed rule of conduct to which one *ought* to adhere; to not adhere to it may bring a bad conscience, disgrace, or even social ostracism. A law is similar, except that violation also leads to legal sanctions (fines, jail sentences, or executions). But there is no international government with a superior force that can be applied to those states that break the law. The principal shortcoming of international law, in these circumstances, is that its subjects decide when it applies! No state is indicted, tried, and punished. States normally obey international law and accept their obligations under it because it applies to everyday relations. On the whole, the routine business of coexistence makes light demands on states and does not have major political significance. When the law is violated, it is because of issues that involve high political stakes, and the offended party usually applies its own sanctions.

International Law and the 'National Interest'

Such violations are relatively few in number but tend to be dramatic and sensational when they occur, thus giving rise to the impression that international law is weak. For example, during the 1950s the United States sent U-2 intelligence planes over the Soviet Union in the name of national security, even though the Soviet Union has legal jurisdiction over its own air space and had given no permission for such flights. Cuba, as a sovereign state, has a perfect right to welcome the strategic missiles of the Soviet Union on its soil, and the United States has no legal right to demand their withdrawal. Yet American security interests and the balance of power with the Soviet Union were perceived to require such withdrawal in 1962. The United States therefore blockaded Cuba, but, because a blockade is legally a *casus belli*, a reason for war, this action was called a quarantine. In these and similar instances, it would be more correct to say that international law is *restricted* in the range of its application, rather than that it is weak or ineffective. This limited range of application contrasts greatly with the broad freedom of independent action that states claim for themselves.[15]

States thus ignore international law when it would restrain them from doing what they believe they must do in their interest. When Italy invaded Ethiopia in 1935, international lawyers thought that Italy had violated the League of Nations Covenant and that sanctions ought to be invoked. Yet Britain, and especially France, wished Italy to remain a friend and potential ally against the new Germany of Hitler. To apply sanctions would be to alienate Italy and to make it more difficult to keep the European balance. International law is also a problem for smaller states concerned with their security. For example, Israel, surrounded in the 1950s and 1960s by states that were clearly hostile and refused to recognize its right to exist, struck preemptively in 1956 and 1967, when it believed that its enemies were about to attack. Yet such a war is generally considered illegal.[16]

In 1979 Iran seized the U.S. embassy in Tehran, even though, according to international law, embassies are regarded as parts of the nation they represent and diplomats are legally immune to seizure and captivity. The new militant Islamic regime insisted that the United States had violated international law since World War II by interfering in Iran's domestic affairs by supporting the shah. It demanded his return for trial (and presumably execution) for what it condemned as his cruel tyranny and alleged subservience to the United States. In short, Iran claimed that the United States had violated international law and that seizure of the embassy and its personnel—labeled spies rather than diplomats— was retribution for past injustices and therefore legitimate. The United States took the case to the International Court of Justice, which found that the hostage-taking was illegal and the hostages should be freed. Iran ignored the ruling. The United States then took the matter to the UN Security Council, where the Soviet Union cast a veto. In these circumstances, the United States fell back on self-help and attempted the ill-fated hostage rescue mission. In this instance, self-help was the only course left to protect America's legal rights.

Disputes fall into two categories: (1) those that are amenable to settlement on a legal basis or *justiciable*, and (2) those that are political or *nonjusticiable*.[17] Political disputes are usually nonjusticiable, not because there is no law that can be invoked but because they involve vital interests. If a state is dissatisfied with the status quo—for example, the settlement imposed upon it at the end of a war—it does not appeal to the law for a remedy because the law upholds the status quo. On the basis of existing law, an appeal for legal revision would be disallowed; agreements are binding. The question of revision is not judicial; it is political. Consequently, judicial methods are of no avail. In the 1930s, for example, Germany knew that it was violating the Versailles peace treaty and that international law would support the territorial status quo. Because it rejected the status quo, Germany would not submit its claims to an international court. This kind of dispute can be resolved peacefully by negotiations and compromise but not by appeal to the law. The distinction between a legal and political problem is therefore arbitrary, reflecting a state's attitude toward the status quo. Still, it is a critical distinction, as became clear in 1984 when Nicaragua took the United States to the International Court of Justice, accusing the United States of intervening in its internal affairs by supporting counterrevolutionary actions against its government and of mining and blockading its ports. The court ruled unanimously that the United States must halt such actions and by a 14-1 vote that, as a sovereign state, Nicaragua's political independence "should be fully respected and should not be jeopardized by any military or paramilitary activities." [18]

When Nicaragua took the case to court, however, the United States announced that it would not accept the court's judgments in matters relating to Central America for a period of two years. The United States accused Nicaragua of misusing the court for political and propaganda purposes and of hiding efforts to export revolution to its neighbors. The latter, the United States claimed, provoked the U.S. assistance to the contras.[19] Calling the court's findings "clearly erroneous," the U.S. State Department claimed that the issues "represented political questions that are not susceptible to resolution by any court" under the UN Charter. The implication of this statement was that if the court proceeded to hear Nicaragua's arguments and evidence and ordered the United States to stop supporting the contras, the United States would defy the court, which, of course, could not compel compliance. The United States also stated a broader rule: in the future it would refuse to participate in "cases of this nature." After October 1985, the United States announced, it would formally cease to recognize the authority of the World Court except in nonpolitical cases.

The U.S. decision to flout the court was widely criticized. The United States was supposed to stand for the law and be a law-abiding country, but it refused to participate in the court and accept its verdict. "It's like Al Capone saying he refuses to recognize the jurisdiction of the criminal court. It's the most compelling admission of guilt one can imagine," said one of the American lawyers arguing Nicaragua's case. The Reagan administration's defense was summed up by a quote from Winston Churchill, made in reference to the democracies' observance of international law during the 1930s: "It would not be right or rational," Churchill reportedly said, "that the aggressor powers should gain one set of advantages by tearing up all laws and another set by sheltering behind the innate respect for the law of their opponents." [20] Nicaragua was openly proclaiming its right—indeed, its revolutionary duty— to intervene in neighboring El Salvador to help the guerrillas there overthrow its government. Should respect for international law prevent the United States from defending its interests? The fact remains that two-thirds of the 159 UN member nations, including the Soviet Union, while technically subject to the court's jurisdiction, have placed limits on the court's authority.

States create the law, interpret it, and decide when to obey it. The International Court of Justice has no compulsory jurisdiction. Refusing to submit a dispute to it is the legitimate right of sovereign states. Because most states do not submit issues of vital interest to legal resolution, most international law enforces itself. And because international law would not have evolved had it not been useful to states, it is not surprising that the compliance record is high. Nevertheless, no state will submit a case on an important issue if it feels it may lose—and certainly not cases that involve vital interests. The United States, knowing it would probably lose the Nicaraguan case, did what might have been expected. By the same token, Nicaragua, a weak state, took the case to court to help strengthen its political and psychological position relative to the United States. The reverse was true with Iran. Iran knew the law and did not show up to argue its case; the United States, however, did, not so much because it expected Iran to obey the court's ruling but to strengthen its political and moral case.

Interestingly, and indicative of international law's utility, in 1988 the Reagan administration proposed to Moscow that the two countries allow the World Court to arbitrate a list of disputes arising from some sixty treaties and conventions they had signed and that they agree in advance to accept the court's verdicts. Thus the United States moved to once again accept the court's jurisdiction in areas that do not threaten national security interests. And Moscow agreed, in a radical shift from the past when it did not allow the court to settle such quarrels. But this does not change the fundamental fact that on issues vital to them, states will ignore international law. No more gruesome reminder of this fact exists than Iraq's violation of the prohibition of gas warfare by using poison gas against Iranian troops and, after the fighting ceased, against its own Kurdish minority. But, except for the United States, the world yawned. To be sure, an international conference was called in 1988 in which Iraq participated, but it was neither condemned or punished; Iran was not even mentioned. In turn, it raised the key question of what international law means in a system so conspicuously unable and unwilling to control such a gross violation.[21]

MORALITY OF NATIONS

The anarchical nature of the state system also limits the impact of moral norms on the competition and rivalry of states. Indeed, in probably no sphere of human endeavor is there a greater gap between actual behavior and professions of moral principles and declaration of noble intentions than in international politics. A frequent definition of a diplomat is "an honest man sent abroad to lie for his country." A man or woman who slays another human being is normally called a killer; if apprehended, tried, and, convicted, the killer is isolated from society in prison or, in many countries, put to death. But a person who kills other people called enemies on behalf of his or her country is hailed as a hero, presented with medals, and sometimes even immortalized in a statue or on a postage stamp. Ordinary soldiers receive veterans' benefits from a grateful country. A leader of the Italian unification movement once said, "If we did for ourselves what we are doing for Italy we should be real scoundrels."

The usual explanation for the alleged immorality of states is that their concern for their security requires them to do "whatever must be done." In a domestic system of law and order, the resulting sense of security allows individuals and groups to act with at least some degree of morality, but in the international system the absence of law and order means that all states, like the cowboys in a lawless western town, must go armed and must be prepared to shoot when their lives are endangered. According to the philosophy of Thomas Hobbes, the war of every man against every other man in a state of nature arose not from fear of death but from fear of *violent* death at the hands of another. In the resulting state of perpetual war nothing was unjust. The idea of right and wrong, justice and injustice, simply had no place. The present state system is essentially a Hobbesian jungle; in a jungle one must behave appropriately. The "nice guy" is devoured.

In such a system it is perhaps wise to adapt and to play the game of nations, however rough that game is at times. For a national leader, being a good person and possessing moral intentions are not enough. Prime Minister Neville Chamberlain of Great Britain was such a person. More than anything, he wanted to avoid another war with Germany and to spare his people another awful bloodletting. Surely, preserving the peace was a moral goal. Peace is precious, not to be sacrificed lightly, and to be forfeited only if absolutely unavoidable. Had Chamberlain been a less noble individual, had he been more willing to take up arms and risk surrendering peace, he might have saved the peace he so treasured.

This line of thinking suggests that power and morality are antithetical. If, on the one hand, a state is concerned with security and power, it must throw off morality as so much excess baggage. But if, on the other hand, it seeks to act morally, it will suffer badly in the international struggle. This position, however, is false. Acts by individuals and groups, subnational or national, all involve moral considerations: decisions involve choices, and the choice of one course over another is influenced by moral predispositions, which are inherent in larger social values. In an international context, it is more accurate to say that *the closer relations among states move toward enmity, the more likely the states are to adopt policies normally considered immoral; the closer relations move toward friendship and the more secure the states feel, the more moral will be the conduct of their foreign policies.*[22]

Whatever the degree of morality that influences states in different situations, the source of this morality lies within the states themselves, giving rise to the following points.

Nationalism and Morality.   States identify their interests with morality. Clearly, no state is going to admit publicly that its actions are unethical. President Julius Nyerere of Tanzania once said on behalf of his country and the "poor nations" of the world:

> I am saying it is not right that the vast majority of the world's people should be forced into the position of beggars, without dignity. In one world, as in one state, when I am rich because you are poor, and I am poor because you are rich, the transfer of wealth from the rich to the poor is a matter of right; it is not an appropriate matter for charity. . . . If the rich nations go on getting richer and richer at the expense of the poor, the poor of the world must demand a change, in the same way as the proletariat in the rich countries demanded change in the past.[23]

The developing countries believe they are poor because the Western industrial states are rich. They therefore have a legitimate grievance based on the West's plunder of their resources and continued "capitalist" exploitation. The Western countries owe them reparations and help as a moral obligation and historic duty. This formulation is the essence of the claim for a new international economic order. The definition of what is moral and what is immoral is egocentric—and obviously very practical if it induces guilt feelings among the former colonial powers so that they seek to relieve those feelings by means of "alms for the poor."

Different Definitions of Morality.   States define morality differently, as President Nyerere's words illustrate, according to whether they are satisfied with their position in the state system. A status quo state, which benefits from the current distribution of power, will espouse a morality identified with the interests of the larger state system and will emphasize peace. If its interests coincide with those of most other members of the system, there is no occasion for challenges from the latter: upholding peace will give the state a political and psychological advantage against challengers, which must threaten war or actually go to war to effect change and can therefore be denounced as aggressors and warmongers. The status quo state stresses the need for diplomacy, claiming that no problem is insuperable and that all can be settled by patient and sincere negotiations rather than by unjustified intimidation or force. The peace of a region—of the world—should be everyone's prime consideration; no injustice or wrong, however strongly felt, is worth the even greater injustice of war and the sacrifice of peace.

In contrast, a revisionist state that seeks to transform the status quo to its own advantage will attempt to avoid being morally discredited by claiming that it is underprivileged, that it is a "have-not" state, and that it seeks only equality or national self-determination. A good example occurred at the November 1976 UN General Assembly meeting when a resolution was passed linking South Africa's apartheid policy with Western governments and especially with the government of Israel. This resolution called the South African government "illegitimate," having "no right to represent the people of South Africa." It declared support for "the legitimacy of the struggle of the oppressed people of South Africa and their liberation movement, by all possible means, for the seizure of power by the people." [24] This resolution was an open call for the use of violence, justified in this instance by the morality of the goal—the end of discrimination and the equality of all people, black and white. The challenger must convince other states that the status quo demands alteration because it is no longer morally justifiable.

Here again morality can be a very practical instrument. The weak usually have few other weapons, and appeals to morality in states where public opinion is accessible to foreign persuasion can be effective. If the international system could be made to function according to moral principles, the inequality of power among states would not matter. It would even work to the advantage of the weak. It is also noteworthy that the moral issues raised publicly in international forums and those not raised reflect political circumstances and votes taken in international organizations. For example, the issue of the human rights of blacks in South Africa has been made an international issue by black African states in the United Nations, but the issue of the human rights of black Africans in some black African states whose rulers abuse the political and civil rights of their subjects has not been raised in the same forum. Black leaders do not want to raise the issue of human rights in their own states, and they have enough votes to prevent it.

Moral Restraints on National Behavior.   Although it is not surprising that states try to justify themselves, it would be a mistake to assume that "anything goes" just because officials who decide specific policies stamp them "morally approved." The domestic principles of a state can and do act as restraints on its behavior. For example, many Britons, as well as many people throughout the English-speaking world, disapproved of the British intervention at the Suez Canal in 1956 because they believed colonialism was no longer legitimate and the invasion of Egypt unjustifiable in an age of nationalism.

Similarly, many people in the United States—and in much of the rest of the world—found American support of the Saigon government in Vietnam illegitimate. In that "civil war" Hanoi's leaders were widely identified with the principle of national self-determination. How could the democratic United States support an autocratic regime that denied every democratic principle to which the United States professed commitment, in a war against those who were fighting for national unity and independence? In addition, the often massive use of force against a small unindustrialized country—on which the United States dropped more bombs than it had dropped on Germany and Japan combined during World War II—seemed outrageous. The means used to wage the war and the destruction wrought appeared excessive to many in light of the proclaimed moral purposes of the intervention. Both the ends and the means of U.S. policy in Vietnam were widely questioned.

These two examples are part of a growing normative restraint—anchored in the values of Western democratic societies—in military confrontations between the First and Third Worlds. The use of force in such conflicts, short of a clear threat to national security or prestige, is now widely regarded as illegitimate in the West. In 1974, after the Organization of Petroleum Exporting Countries quadrupled oil prices and caused a surge in Western inflation and unemployment, no Western power thought of using force. OPEC's right to set prices, even to withhold oil, was recognized.

Historian Arthur Schlesinger, Jr., once rather picturesquely remarked that a nation's foreign policy is the face that it wears to the world, and, if this policy embodies values that appear incompatible with the nation's ideals, either the policy will lose public support and have to be abandoned, or the nation will have to toss its ideals overboard. A nation, like an individual, must in the final analysis be true to itself, or the "consequent moral schizophrenia is bound to convulse the homeland."[25] During the Cuban missile crisis in 1962, to cite only one example, when President John Kennedy and his advisers were debating whether to attack or blockade the island, Robert Kennedy argued strongly against attack on the grounds of American tradition. A surprise attack, which would kill thousands of Cuban civilians, seemed inconsistent with that tradition. The United States was not like Japan, and his brother, the president, was not like Tojo Hideki, who had launched the surprise attack on Pearl Harbor. There were, of course, other reasons—"practical" reasons—that helped the government to decide in favor of the blockade, but morality unquestioningly contributed to the decision. The moral factor was also perceived by Robert Kennedy to be politically beneficial. A surprise attack, he declared, "could not [have been] undertaken by the United States if we were to maintain our moral position at home and around the globe. Our struggle against Communism throughout the world was far more than physical survival—it had as its essence our heritage and our ideals and these we must not destroy."[26]

One of the more interesting recent moral phenomena in the United States has been the rejection of nuclear arms by American Catholic and Methodist bishops.[27] Up to the 1980s it had been widely agreed that nuclear war was bad for one's health. This was hardly news; the threat to biological survival was the reason for the policy of deterrence. But groups such as the Physicians for Social Responsibility began to reemphasize this message as if it were new. Their stated intention was to counter widespread mass complacency about the dangers of the arms race and the use of nuclear weapons. It was the context within which this message was promulgated that was new.

The point was not to reinforce support for deterrence but to point to its failure; the message focused on "the day after." The only solution to this terrible nuclear problem was nuclear disarmament.

But if the physicians pointed to the danger that nuclear arms posed for people's bodies—a nuclear war would be "the last epidemic"—the bishops pointed to the consequences that their possession posed for people's souls. The use of nuclear weapons was condemned as immoral, even in retaliation against an enemy's first use. Nuclear war was contrary to the churches' teachings and could not, therefore, receive their blessings. The defense of a free society was not a sufficient cause for having such weapons. Because deterrence stems from the possession of nuclear weapons *plus* the will to use them if the enemy strikes—it is *not* just the product of the possession of these weapons—denunciation of the determination to use them, whether for moral or other reasons, means that deterrence no longer exists. At best, it becomes a sheer bluff. Besides, if the use of nuclear weapons is immoral, then deterrence must be immoral too. One cannot have a morally acceptable deterrent strategy without an operational doctrine governing its use. Basically, the moral position points to a unilateral nuclear disarmament. Here it is useful to remember that the only time a nuclear weapon has been used was at the end of a war against a fanatical enemy who did not possess the bomb and therefore could not retaliate in kind.

The bishops' position is an interesting offspring of the increasing Western reluctance to use any kind of force except in strictly defensive circumstances to ward off "aggression." Deterrence had not been questioned on moral grounds until the 1980s, and the bishops' stance raised a host of questions. Was not the purpose of deterrence to prevent war? Was not prevention of a nuclear attack moral, even if the way this goal was achieved was by producing nuclear weapons? Were not the latter the lesser evil and the prevention of nuclear war the greater moral good? (The French Catholic bishops thought so.) Can the threat of using nuclear weapons be equated morally to their actual use? In short, can one jump from the condemnation of nuclear war to the rejection of a deterrent strategy? Would not the two churches' positions also lead to policies that would, if adopted, result in the greatest of all evils, a nuclear attack or the submission to a foreign, antireligious, dictatorial power?[28] Is survival the highest moral good of both churches' teachings? Or is it justice? Should a moral nuclear strategy not only deter nuclear war but also help contain the expansion of a system of government that all Western states agree is tyrannical? And have not nuclear weapons achieved *both* objectives since World War II? In short, have not the moral attacks on deterrence ignored the forty-year history of deterrence?

Morality in an Insecure World

A nation, particularly a democratic nation, thus can find itself in a dilemma, caught between its values and its security interests, at least in terms of its immediate foreign policy. It is, after all, always easier to justify short-term deviations from the nation's values if it can be maintained that in the long run the deviations protect the values. Noted earlier were the tensions inherent in any U.S. policy that calls for alliance with undemocratic states to enhance U.S. security. Similar, but more shocking to many Americans, is the tension between the democratic ethos and security that has been revealed in a number of other ways: assassination plots by the Central Intelligence Agency (CIA) against foreign leaders, especially Fidel Castro; the overthrow of a legitimately elected government in Chile; the "secret" bombing of Cambodia; and the Reagan contra war. The dilemma of making foreign policy in the face of conflicting pressures and values is finding a way to *achieve some of the principal objectives with minimum sacrifice of other equally important objectives.* In giving priority to competing objectives, how does a state balance security and welfare; security, democracy, and individual liberty; and security and peace (see Chapter 4)? The problem is *not* simply how to choose between one element and another, but how to achieve the best combination of all the elements.

There is no more dramatic or tragic illustration of this dilemma than the events leading up to the seizure of the U.S. embassy in Tehran in 1979. The shah, admittedly both dictatorial and ruthless, was also strongly pro-American. He had supported President Anwar Sadat of Egypt in his search for peace after 1973, and he had long supplied oil to Israel, even during the 1973 war. The United States in turn firmly supported the shah over the years. In 1953, for example, the CIA had restored him to power after he had been forced to flee his country. But there is not much doubt that the shah's secret police used torture, and it was always clear that the shah was quite unpopular. American interests, however, were equally clear: control of the strategic Persian Gulf and plentiful supplies of oil. In 1979 Iranian oil constituted only 4 percent of American consumption, but U.S. allies in Europe and Japan were very dependent on it.

Could there have been a greater disaster for the United States and its allies than the shah's collapse? Oil prices shot up virtually 100 percent in one year because of reductions in Iranian oil supplies and the resulting tight world market. Egypt lost a staunch friend and had to buy its oil elsewhere, as did Israel, which felt even more insecure now that Iran was also militantly anti-Israel and supported terrorist groups in Lebanon. These groups, among other things, established a presence in southern Lebanon on Israel's northern frontier. Furthermore, the security of the Persian Gulf, which the United States had counted on the shah to guard, was now endangered by a zealous religious regime bent on fomenting an Islamic rebellion against the United States and overthrowing pro-Western Arab Muslim leaders in the oil kingdoms along the Persian Gulf. To prevent such an occurrence during the Iran-Iraq war, the United States sent a naval armada into the Persian Gulf when the war appeared to be going well for Iran.

It is also questionable whether the Iranians themselves were better off under this regime, which was bent upon restoring traditional customs. It banned Western music, dance, and drink; tried to crush all opposition; and killed its enemies in ways all too reminiscent of the shah's own dictatorial rule. Modernization fell by the wayside, and the economy declined, creating large-scale unemployment and inflation. Was American support for the shah "criminal"? [29] Indeed, given the subsequent actions of Iranian-supported terrorist groups against the United States in the Middle East, including twice blowing up the American embassy in Beirut and killing 241 U.S. Marines in a suicide attack, this question is all the more pertinent. Morally, a nation may not approve of some of its allies and friends, but should it therefore disassociate itself, even seek to replace its government, regardless of the character of the government that may follow? [30]

Morality as an Incentive to Crusades

While morality may serve generally as a constraint on state behavior, despite the frequent dilemmas involved in moral choices, it can also "unrestrain" or unleash foreign policy. For example, an attempt to impose moral values on another state may transform a conflict of interest, perhaps resolvable through hard bargaining, to a conflict of moral philosophies, between good and evil, which tends not to be resolvable peacefully. Viewing the international arena as one in which St. George must always be slaying dragons leads to a complete misunderstanding of the nature of international politics. Rather than being used to analyze the behavior of states in terms of their sense of insecurity, their legitimate interests and aspirations, the great difficulties involved in coexisting, and their common and conflicting interests, international politics becomes a matter of virtue and vice, in which purity is used to vanquish villainy. And, if the struggle among states is viewed as a struggle between right and wrong, those who *know* they are right all too often become zealots and crusaders. Like a religious fanatic, a state convinced that it represents morality easily and rapidly strikes poses of absolutism and self-righteousness.

Translated into foreign policy—as postwar American foreign policy has amply demonstrated—such moralism has several undesirable results, two of which are failure to recognize other governments because of moral disapproval and unwillingness to meet with adversaries to reconcile conflicting interests. In addition, states that view themselves as moral arbiters also exhibit a crusading spirit in peace and war, which makes it difficult for their governments to distinguish between vital and secondary interests and may even entice them into disputes that involve only peripheral interests (as in the American intervention in Vietnam). Finally, a nation imbued with the crusading spirit is likely to transform war into total war, to seek the unconditional surrender of the infidel. Crusaders remain oblivious to the fact that total military victory may make a postwar balance of power much more difficult to attain. Thus, moralism not only results in misunderstanding of international politics but, when applied to policy, also guides it on a course that in most instances will be detrimental to the state's own interests. Countries in which fanaticism has led to rigidity and self-righteousness are intolerant of other countries; thus coexistence with them becomes very difficult, if not impossible. Zeal and peace are mutually exclusive, for zeal gives rise to intervention in order to reshape and reform other states. Do democratic states have a moral mandate to remake other states in their own images? Indeed, can any state really expect—should it have the right to expect—to do more than influence the foreign policy behavior of another state when the latter impinges on its interests? Should foreign policy also concern itself with reforming another state domestically and make virtue a key criteria for its foreign policy?

In international politics the moral thing to do may be to avoid "the histrionics of moralism" and to restrain the tendency to self-righteousness and moralizing. It may be morally satisfying to appear noble and altruistic, but the impact of such aspirations on international politics has generally been to make national positions more rigid, render diplomacy less able to reconcile conflicting positions, and transform wars into total wars. In the words of George Kennan, "In a less than perfect world, where the idea so obviously lies beyond human reach, it is natural that the avoidance of the worst should often be a more practical undertaking than the achievement of the best, and that some of the strongest imperatives of moral conduct should be ones of a negative rather than a positive nature"—as in the strictures of the Ten Commandments.[30]

What is the bottom line? It is that moral questions and claims may be simple to state, but they are not simple to answer. Moral judgments that seem easy at first glance often turn out not to be so clear-cut. Furthermore, what one party calls moral is not necessarily moral to another. There are no universal standards of morality or of justice. This lack of agreement in turn reflects the decentralized nature of the state system. There do not, then, appear to be solutions to the security problem in the state system.

For Review

1. What is the United Nations, and how has it evolved over time?
2. How has the United Nations contributed to the preservation of peace?
3. What is international law?
4. Does international morality exist?
5. In what ways have international law and morality restrained the behavior of states?

Notes

1. J. William Fulbright, "In Thrall to Fear," *New Yorker*, January 8, 1972, 59.
2. Quoted in *Power and International Relations*, by Inis L. Claude, Jr. (New York: Random House, 1962), 59.
3. Ibid., 160; and Inis L. Claude, Jr., *Swords into Plowshares*, 4th ed. (New York: Random House, 1971), 80-86.
4. Egypt, because of its complaint that the United Nations had not supported it in the war against Israel in 1947-1948, was an exception.
5. Ernst Haas, "Types of Collective Security: An Examination of Operational Concepts," *American Political Science Review* (March 1955): 40-62, examines this transition from "permissive enforcement" to "balancing."
6. Only after the Cuban missile crisis of 1962 had already been resolved was the organization to be used in Cuba—and then it was to check that all Soviet missiles had been removed. But, because Fidel Castro refused to submit to international inspection and the United States was certain that all the missiles had been shipped back to the Soviet Union, the United Nations remained uninvolved.
7. Andrew Boyd, *United Nations* (Baltimore: Penguin, 1963), 85ff.; Inis L. Claude, Jr., *The Changing United Nations* (New York: Random House, 1967), 23ff.; Arthur L. Burns and Nina Heathcote, *Peace-keeping by U.N. Forces* (New York: Holt, Rinehart & Winston, 1963); and Linda B. Miller, *World Order and Local Disorder* (Princeton, N.J.: Princeton University Press, 1967). For one of the less successful ventures, see Bjorn Skogno, *UNIFIL* (Boulder, Colo.: Lynne Rienner, 1988), an analysis of international peace-keeping in Lebanon from 1978 to 1988. For an overall assessment of peace-keeping in the Middle East since 1974, see John Mackinlay, *The Peacekeepers* (Winchester, Mass.: Unwin Hyman, 1989).
8. Inis L. Claude, Jr., "Containment and Resolution of Disputes," in *The U.S. and the U.N.*, ed. Francis O. Wilcox and H. Field Haviland, Jr. (Baltimore: Johns Hopkins University Press, 1961), 101-128 (emphasis in original).
9. *New York Times*, Jan. 30, 1982.
10. *New York Times*, March 31, 1983.
11. Edward C. Luck and Toby Trister Gati, "Gorbachev, the United Nations, and U.S. Policy, *Washington Quarterly*, Summer 1987, 19-35.
12. *New York Times*, Sept. 11, 1982 (emphasis in original). Also see by former UN secretary-general Kurt Waldheim, "The United Nations: The Tarnished Image," *Foreign Affairs* (Fall 1984): 93-107.
13. Rupert Emerson, "The Fate of Human Rights in the Third World," *World Politics*, January 1975, 224.
14. J. L. Brierly, *The Law of Nations*, 6th ed. (New York: Oxford University Press, 1963), 73. Also see Werner Levi, *Law and Politics in the International Society* (Beverly Hills, Calif.: Sage, 1976).
15. Brierly, *Law of Nations*, 74.
16. Hedley Bull, *The Anarchical Society* (New York: Columbia University Press, 1977), 108-109, 143-144.
17. Percy E. Corbett, *Law and Society in the Relation of States* (New York: Harcourt, 1951), 77-79.
18. *New York Times*, Nov. 15, 1984.
19. *New York Times*, Jan. 19, 1985.
20. Quoted by Michael A. Ledeen, "When Security Preempts the Rule of Law," *New*

York Times, April 16, 1984.

21. Charles Krauthammer, "The Curse of Legalism," *New Republic,* November 6, 1989, 44.

22. Arnold Wolfers, *Discord and Collaboration* (Baltimore: Johns Hopkins University Press, 1962), 54.

23. Quoted by P. T. Bauer and B. S. Yamey, "Against the New Economic Order," *Commentary,* April 1977, 27.

24. *New York Times,* Nov. 10, 1976.

25. Arthur M. Schlesinger, Jr., "National Interests and Moral Absolutes," in *Ethics and World Politics,* ed. Ernest W. Lefever (Baltimore: Johns Hopkins University Press, 1972), 35.

26. Robert F. Kennedy, *Thirteen Days* (New York: New American Library, 1968).

27. National Conference of Catholic Bishops, *The Challenge of Peace* (Washington, D.C.: United States Catholic Conference, 1983); and *New York Times,* Dec. 26, 1985. For the final draft, see *New York Times,* April 27, 1986. For a critical evaluation, see James E. Dougherty, *The Bishops and Nuclear Weapons* (Hamden, Conn.: Archon Books, 1984).

28. Charles Krauthammer, "On Nuclear Morality," *Commentary,* October 1983, 48-52. Also see Robert W. Tucker, *The Nuclear Debate* (New York: Holmes & Meier, 1985), and Joseph S. Nye, Jr., *Nuclear Ethics* (New York: Free Press, 1986).

29. If so, most of the world's leaders can be called "criminal," for few have not supported regimes that have jailed domestic opponents and violated human rights. Indeed, many rule their own countries in this manner.

30. For two critical views of U.S. policy toward the shah, see Richard W. Cottam, *Iran and the United States* (Pittsburgh: University of Pittsburgh Press, 1988), and James A. Bill, *The Eagle and the Lion* (New Haven, Conn.: Yale University Press, 1988).

31. George F. Kennan, "Morality and Foreign Policy," *Foreign Affairs* (Winter 1985/86): 213.

CHAPTER 17

Peace Through Transformation of the State System

FROM MICRO- TO MACROPOLITICS:
FROM DOOM TO SALVATION

International organizations, international law, and morality may mitigate the basic anarchical character of the state system, but they do not fundamentally change state behavior. There being no ultimate protector, states generally have little choice but to assume the worst, and because they act on these worst assumptions, they stimulate their neighbors and other potential adversaries to do likewise. The latter's behavior then confirms the original assumptions and outlook of the former. According to the proponents of a world government, if the security dilemma is inescapably built into the state system, then perhaps the only way to elude it is to devise methods of overcoming the decentralized nature of the international system.

The bomb, they assert, is the reason for the urgent need to build a world state and reproduce internationally the law and order and peaceful change that exist within the more advanced domestic systems (see Chapter 5). The reason is all too obvious: deterrence cannot last forever. Sooner or later, if the cold war lasts, there will be a nuclear war. It will destroy not only the United States and Soviet Union but most of humanity. Deterrence and arms control may delay its eruption, but nuclear war cannot be avoided forever. Moreover, this is not just a matter for the United States and the Soviet Union to decide; the entire world has a stake in the prevention of nuclear war. It is therefore necessary to transcend the state system. Only by overcoming its decentralized nature can peace be ensured.

With the cold war fading, low-politics issues are cited for the urgency of changing the structure of the state system.[1] In a global economy national solutions for managing national economies no longer suffice; interdependence requires transnational management. The population growth rate, as noted (Chapter 9), clearly has worldwide implications. It destabilizes national societies when they are unable to fulfill popular expectations (leading to massive legal and illegal migration to the developed world, among other things); places greater pressure on global resources; leads to widespread deforestation to provide firewood and to make more room for people and farms; and even affects the world's atmosphere (the greenhouse effect). Birthrates are not therefore a solely national problem, to be solved at the national level; they are a global problem to be solved at the global level, requiring a global authority.

It is environmental problems, however, that have most dramatically pointed to the inadequacy of national solutions. For example, in the summer of 1988 medical wastes washed up on the Atlantic beaches of New England, New York and New Jersey. It was as if the earth were saying "enough is enough; no more pollution." Four environmental issues stand out. The first is the greenhouse effect or the warming up of the planet's atmosphere. This occurs when waste gases, chiefly carbon dioxide and flurocarbons (the industrial chemicals that carry chlorine up to the ozone layer), which otherwise would escape into space, trap heat from the earth's surface. The experts disagree only about how rapid and disastrous the effects of this phenomenon will be. The second issue is the depletion of the ozone layer over Antarctica (and potentially the Arctic). This layer screens out the sun's ultraviolet light, but when thinning or holes occur in it, higher rates of skin cancer and other damage to humans, crops, and forests result. The third environmental issue is the spreading acid rain and other atmospheric pollution that threaten the survival of forests and lakes. And the fourth issue is toxic and solid-waste disposal, symbolized in 1988 by the barge from New York City that after five months at sea was unable to dump its load. In fact, America and the industrial countries of Europe are trying to turn West Africa into a huge dumping ground. Thus, the earth's natural life-support systems all seem to be suffering catastrophic decline. Some environmentalists have even warned that the human use of water, air, land, forests and other systems is pushing these systems over the "thresholds" beyond which they cannot absorb use without permanent change and damage.

As if the tasks of preventing war or ecological disaster were not enough, some observers argue that the vast disparity of wealth between the rich and poor nations, as well as the large-scale poverty in the developing countries, also require a fundamental change in the attitude and structure of the contemporary state system. Every human being has the right to economic well-being. People also have a right to self-determination and self-government and to social and political justice within their societies (the "inalienable rights" of freedom, self-expression, and human dignity). To ensure peace and build a more harmonious "spaceship earth," it is therefore incumbent to build a more decent and humane world without poverty and social injustice.

Thus, high- and low-politics issues appear to demand a shift from the state system to a global one—from an emphasis on national interests to the common interests of humankind, from power politics to planetary politics. Nuclear bombs, overpopulation, ecology, and political and social needs impel national leaders to change habits and ways of thinking inherited from an earlier, prenuclear age. In a period when the problems facing the world are increasingly transnational, traditional ways of looking at the world can only result in disaster for all humankind. It is a matter of either doom or salvation.

It is claimed, in other words, that *our concepts of state behavior are outdated*. Reflecting the experiences of the historical state system, our thinking has not yet caught up with the "necessities" of a rapidly changing world. Thus, international politics can no longer afford to focus on the states in the system, their objectives, and their interactions. The focus must be enlarged from the individual nation-state—the "micropolitics" examined up to this point—to world politics or "macropolitics." According to political scientist Richard Sterling, this requires posing questions central to its global concerns: What is the *international* interest? Which policies and institutions appear to benefit all people, and which appear to benefit some but not others? Which are likely to disadvantage them all? One must also ask what any given nation-state contributes to the international interest and judge the value of any particular national interest in terms of the answer to that question.[2]

But hoping that national leaders will adjust to the era of world politics by asking themselves what is in the international interest and guiding themselves by it will not suffice. It is one thing to declare that states can no longer think in narrow, parochial, nationalistic terms and to demand that they think in more enlightened global terms. But how is that to be achieved in an essentially anarchical system? The logical answer is that the structural constraints must be overcome. The present system must be replaced by a world government. Governments preserve peace and maintain law and order on the domestic scene. If a government can be created that would supersede the governments of sovereign nations, it can, like national governments in their own spheres, ensure global peace and find solutions to the world's low-politics problems.

WORLD GOVERNMENT THROUGH FEDERALISM:
THE AMERICAN EXAMPLE

It is often argued, by analogy, that under the American Articles of Confederation, the states retained their sovereignty and continued their quarrels. But, under the Constitution, the states were reduced in status to nonsovereign members of a new federal system in which the government could apply national law directly to individuals and had the responsibility and the authority to ensure domestic tranquility. Can it not be argued then, as advocates of world government do, that the American Constitutional Convention was the "great rehearsal" [3] for a global convention that will transfer the sovereignty of all nations to a world government, the purpose of which will be to ensure global peace through establishment of the rule of law? Such partisans seem to believe that wherever a legal order is established— that is, wherever government applies law directly to its citizens—government functions as a peace-keeping institution. What leads them to this conclusion? Inis Claude has suggested that one factor is the attractiveness of certain terms and the images that they produce in people's minds—terms such as *government* and *law and order:*

> A clue may perhaps be found in the intimate association between the idea of world government and the fashionable theme of world rule of law. Law is a key word in the vocabulary of world government. One reacts against anarchy— disorder, insecurity, violence, injustice visited by the strong upon the weak. In contrast, one postulates law—the symbol of the happy opposites to those distasteful and dangerous evils. Law suggests properly constituted authority and effectively implemented control: it symbolizes the supreme will of the community, the will to maintain justice and public order. This abstract concept is all too readily transformed, by worshipful contemplation, from one of the devices by which societies seek to order internal relationships, into a symbolic key to the good society. As this transformation takes place, law becomes a magic word for those who advocate world government and those who share with them the ideological bond of dedication to the rule of law—not necessarily in the sense that they expect it to produce magical effects upon the world, but at least in the sense that it works its magic upon them. Most significantly, it leads them to forget about politics, to play down the role of the political process in the management of human affairs, and to imagine that somehow law, in all its purity, can displace the soiled devices of politics. Inexorably, the emphasis upon law which is characteristic of advocates of world government carries with it a tendency to focus upon the relationship of individuals to government: thinking in legal terms, one visualizes the individual apprehended by the police and brought before the judge.[4]

Apart from the seductive quality of certain terms and the favorable images they create, the key argument of proponents of world government is that peace depends primarily upon the creation of a government that, because of its superior power, will be able to enforce the law upon individuals. This argument, however, shows that these proponents misunderstand the function of government and exaggerate the coercion necessary to maintain law and order. Admittedly, government power does play a role in preserving peace. A peaceful society is—at least to a degree—a policeful society. At the same time, however, as evident in the earlier analysis (Chapter 5), this power is not the principal factor in achieving peace, particularly in democratic societies. There have simply been too many civil wars, *coups d'état,* revolutions, and secessions to justify as much trust as world federalists place in the establishment of government as a solution for the disorder inherent in the international system. If a national government fails to produce law and order and is unable to keep the nation united, then how confident can one be that world government is the answer to anarchy and war?

The fact is that domestic peace results from the political negotiations and compromises required by the constantly changing distribution of power among conflicting, but usually organized, interests with a common political culture. It is not the application of law to individual violators and their imprisonment for disobeying the law that are primarily responsible for domestic peace. Neither is it the policeman swinging a club or the judge hearing a case and sentencing citizens who broke the law. Most citizens obey laws not out of fear but out of habit, respect, and recognition of their legitimacy. Peace is essentially the result of constant political adjustment and accommodation, accomplished through the efforts of the much-maligned politicians. When groups and classes have what they consider genuine grievances and unfulfilled aspirations for which they seek—but are unable to find—redress, then disorder, rioting, and civil war are likely. Applying a law that sanctifies the status quo becomes an incitement to conflict, not a solution. The issue then is not what the law is but what it should be. The analogy of catching the individual lawbreaker and applying sanctions is hardly appropriate; indeed, it is irrelevant.

The example of American nation building—from confederation to federation—in fact offers evidence that the belief that the mere creation of government is an answer to conflict is mistaken. Those who argue for world government consistently underrate the difficulties encountered in forming the United States of America. They want to show that if the will to organize a world government is present, it can be done. This falsifies history. More than will is required; a common political culture or sense of community is necessary. Such a sense of community is apparent in the Preamble to the U.S. Constitution, which declares that the Founders' purpose was to establish a "more perfect union." There was already a union, formed during the long colonial period and tested in the war for independence; it had only to be made "more perfect." By 1787 Americans already shared a language, a common cultural tradition, and a democratic heritage:

> The thirteen colonies formed a moral and political community under the British Crown, they tested it and became fully aware of it in their common struggle against Britain and they retained that community after they had won their independence. . . . The community of the American people antedated the American state, as a world community must antedate a world state.[5]

The final test of this union came during the Civil War, in which the issues of slavery and the country's values had to be settled before the United States could become a durable political community. And it is precisely the absence of an equivalent sense of global community or political culture that makes it impossible to establish a world government—along with, it should be added, a historical amnesia in which the civil wars and political disorders of the West have been forgotten and the past romanticized, especially that of the United States and Britain.

SUPRANATIONAL COMMUNITY BUILDING THROUGH FUNCTIONALISM

If the establishment of a democratic world government by means of federation is hardly likely to occur in the near future, is there then another way to overcome the divisiveness of present-day nationalism and establish on an international basis the sense of community that is the basis of government? Several political scientists have studied this issue empirically. How have political units in the past been integrated into larger political organizations, the authority of which then superseded their own? How relevant are these historical examples to the contemporary problem of integrating nation-states into a supranational political community?

Eliminating the 'Security Dilemma'

Three of the terms just used—*integrating, supranational,* and *political community*—are noteworthy. Karl Deutsch and several associates who analyzed various instances of integration of political units in the preindustrial era have defined *integration* as "the attainment, within a territory, of a 'sense of community' and of institutions and practices strong enough and widespread enough to assure, for a 'long' time, dependable expectations of 'peaceful change' among its population."[6] Closely related is the term *supranational,* which refers to the formation of a community and institutions above those of the integrating states. This community would have the authority to make on behalf of the states political decisions that would require their obedience (as the American federal government has authority superior to that of the individual states). *Supranational,* then, is not to be confused with the term *international.* An international or intergovernmental organization is an organization composed of states. Its decisions are reached through negotiation and compromise among the states, not imposed from above. Finally, according to political scientist Amitai Etzioni, a *political community* is

> a community that possesses three kinds of integration: (a) it has an effective control over the use of the means of violence (though it may "delegate" some of this control to member-units); (b) it has a center of decision-making that is able to affect significantly the allocation of resources and rewards throughout the community; and (c) it is the dominant focus of political identification for the large majority of politically aware citizens.[7]

Among states the threat of violence remains a key element in the resolution of differences, but the chief characteristic of a supranational organization is the absence of intimidation and war. The anarchical model of the state system, with its frequent focus on threat and counterthreat, force and counterforce, is no longer applicable. Deutsch and his colleagues have called such an enlarged supranational organization a "security community."[8] Historically, they distinguish between two kinds of such communities: the *pluralistic* security community, composed of states that retain their national autonomy while forming specific and subordinate agencies of cooperation on particular matters (such as those formed by the United States and Canada or by Norway, Denmark, and Sweden), and the *amalgamated* security community, in which states surrender autonomy to a new set of central political institutions (as did the separate provinces of Italy and of Germany at the time these countries were unified and born in the nineteenth century). Deutsch found that pluralistic security communities are easier to achieve and more durable; amalgamated security communities are more difficult to establish and more likely to fail.

The main point of studying this building process was to discover how states have learned to redefine their national interest in terms of peacefully cooperating with one another and to overcome their historic patterns of regarding each other as potential adversaries.[9] More specifically, study has focused on the transformation of Franco-German hostility into Franco-German friendship; after three wars in seventy years, this was a fundamental change in attitude. This transformation occurred within the context of the post-World War II creation of the European Economic Community, none of whose members expects any longer to go to war against any other member.

The movement toward a united Europe that has followed World War II has been the principal experiment undertaken by industrialized states in supranation building. Interested in the conditions essential to produce a successful amalgamated security community, Deutsch and his colleagues, not surprisingly, found that some of the conditions present in preindustrial amalgamations were also present in the experiment that began in 1950 with the formation of the European Coal and Steel Community (ECSC) and produced eight years later the European Economic Community (EEC) (see Figure 17-1). The European experience provides the sole modern example of nation-states seeking to integrate themselves into a larger political unit by shedding sovereignty and nationalism. It also, if successful, would be the first of perhaps several regional building blocs upon which a globally integrated world order could be based.

Conditions for Supranation Building

One condition for building a United States of Europe was a compatibility of values and expectations among the amalgamating states. The six original EEC members, sometimes called the Inner Six, certainly had such a compatibility. All were pluralistic societies (although Germany and Italy recently had been fascist states), and each had representative political institutions. In the larger countries—West Germany, France, and Italy—as well as in smaller Belgium, the governing Christian Democrats shared a European outlook and held similar views on social welfare, the free market, and other issues.

A second condition was that the political elites of the integrating countries believe their way of life to be distinctive. To them, the iron curtain was more than an ordinary political division; it separated the "West" from the "East," thus forming two distinct geographical and cultural entities. Christian Democrats were particularly disposed to think of the East-West conflict

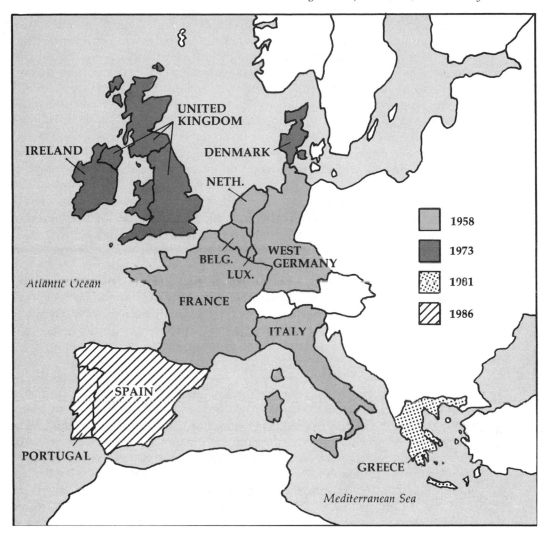

Figure 17-1 European Economic Community

in terms of the historic struggle between Christendom and the "barbarian" invaders from the East, such as the Mongols and the Turks. Russia, usually regarded as non-European, now fitted this role. For the Christian Democrats, the defense of "civilization" once again required Western countries to subordinate their own differences and unite in the struggle against the Communist Soviet Union.

A third condition of particular significance in amalgamation was the expectation of mutual economic benefit. For the Inner Six, this benefit was to be realized in two ways: (1) through the mutual elimination of trade barriers, import quotas, and other restrictions; and (2) through establishment of a common tariff to protect this market. European industry would then enjoy an enormous potential market, and efficient enterprises would presumably expand and modernize to take advantage of this enlarged market. By the same token, inefficient enterprises unable to compete—and unwilling to make the effort—would be closed. Business in general would profit from European integration. Labor would acquire a similar stake in the new Europe as production rose and the level of employment and real wages followed. To be sure, workers in less efficient industries would lose their jobs, and they might have to move to other areas in search of new employment. But in general the EEC would produce more jobs. Consumers also would benefit from the expanding economy. As they saw national economic barriers tumbling and industry converting to techniques of mass production—large-scale production at reasonable cost and with sufficient wages to enable consumers to buy in quantity—they too would recognize the advantages of the EEC.

These conditions, then, are among those necessary for the existence of a supranational community. Others include superior economic growth, high political and administrative capabilities in the participating units, unbroken links of social communication, broadening of the political elite, mobility of individuals, and multiple avenues of communication and transaction.[10]

Process of Supranation Building

But how about the *process* of integration? How does it occur? Functionalists think they know. David Mitrany, the father of this school of thinking, assumed that the *vertical* divisions between states, which produce conflict and war, can be overcome by tying the various functional areas of the economies of different countries together *horizontally* to resolve their common social, economic, and humanitarian needs.[11] He regarded these needs as essentially nonpolitical and noncontroversial, for they involve such values as welfare and social justice rather than national security and prestige. As each area of need is tackled, a transfer of state authority to supranational institutions will occur; as the satisfaction of more needs is undertaken, more and more authority will be transferred to supranational institutions. Thus, sovereignty will be whittled away until at some point nations find themselves brought very close together in this ever-expanding web of activity. They will then have a greater stake in maintaining peace and transferring national authority to new supranational organs. As political scientist Frederick Schuman aptly phrased it, integration of the various functional areas could bring "peace by pieces."[12] Mitrany called it a "working peace system," distinct from peace safeguarded by the balance of power. In Mitrany's words, "the problem of our time is not how to keep nations peacefully apart but how to bring them actively together."[13]

Ernst Haas was the first to study this process of integration in great detail after the start of the movement toward a more unified Europe. Like Mitrany and Jean Monnet, the French master planner of the New Europe, Haas found the driving force behind integration to be economic self-interest. There had to be something in it for everyone. Haas also emphasized, as did the French government when it launched ECSC, the importance of step-by-step economic integration. In 1950 Foreign Minister Robert Schuman of France proposed that the Inner Six pool their coal and steel industries in the ECSC. The choice of coal and steel, the backbone of industry, was deliberate, for it would tie together German and French heavy industry to such an extent that it would become impossible to separate them. Germany would never again be able to use its coal and steel industries for nationalistic and militaristic purposes.

Economic Spillover. Because the coal and steel sector forms the basis of the entire industrial structure, Haas has suggested that it was chosen for its economic "spillover." The ECSC would exert pressure on the unintegrated sectors of the economy, and, as the benefits of pooling heavy industry became obvious, these other sectors would follow suit. The ECSC was thus the first stage in an attempt to create a wider market. It was expected that this approach would be extended gradually to other functional areas of the economy such as agriculture, transportation, and electricity, with the eventual creation of a federal European state enjoying a huge market and a highly developed mass-production system. Once integration had been set in motion, it would pick up momentum on its own.

The first economic spillover occurred in 1958, when the Inner Six established the European Economic Community, then known as the Common Market. Their aim was the formation of an economic union. All tariffs, quotas, and other restrictions hampering trade among themselves would be completely eliminated; in turn, they would establish a common tariff to reduce imports and to keep as much of the market for themselves as possible. Furthermore, they would gradually abolish restrictions on the movement of labor, capital, and services within the community. Finally, the Inner Six established a third community, Euratom, for the generation of industrial energy. Together, the ECSC, EEC, and Euratom would constitute a European political community.

Political Spillover. Apart from economic spillover, the most important effect Haas stressed was political spillover. If the Common Market was to be and if it was to be more than just a customs union, there had to be a uniform set of rules to govern the economic and social policies of the member countries.[14] For example, if one nation should adopt a deflationary policy, its industries would be able to undersell those of its partners and capture their markets. Clearly, this kind of development had to be guarded against. Or, if a nation, after abolishing its tariffs for a specific industry, then subsidized that industry's production or imposed an internal tax on competitive foreign goods, it would gain an obvious advantage for its own industry. Such discrimination by a single government had to be forbidden. Uniform rules could not be established, however, for simply preventing deviant behavior; affirmative action was also required. Because prices reflect production costs, which in turn partly reflect national regulation of wages, hours, working conditions, and social welfare programs, the industries of a nation with lower standards have an advantage over competitors in neighboring states. A single set of standards in such areas as minimum wages, maximum hours, and welfare programs was therefore considered necessary. In addition, as workers would be able to move from one country to another in search of employment and better jobs, there had to be a single social security program for all six nations. This increasing need to harmonize the social and economic policies of the Inner Six would demand a single governmental center for policy formulation in Europe. Common policies would require common institutions with supranational authority.

In real terms, such supranational authority, one observer has noted, "starts to come into play when a state agrees . . . to carry out decisions to which it is itself opposed. Most obviously, such a situation arises when it has agreed to be outvoted if necessary by other states—either by a simple or by some weighted or qualified majority." [15] Common institutions with supranational authority extending beyond trade and tariff matters play a central role in furthering the larger political community:

> If economic integration merely implied the removal of barriers to trade and fails to be accompanied by new centrally made fiscal, labor, welfare, and investment measures, the relation to political integration is not established. If, however, the integration of a specific section (e.g., coal and steel), or of economics generally (e.g., the "General Common Market") goes hand in hand with the gradual extension of the scope of central decision-making to take in economic pursuits not initially "federated," the relation to the growth of political community is clear.[16]

The development of a political community is demonstrated most readily by interest group activity. In a developed supranational economy, those whose interests are affected by the decision-making institutions, adversely or otherwise, will organize to lobby at the supranational level to influence particular decisions. One is reminded of the United States, where various interest groups lobby at the state and federal levels. In an open, pluralistic society, interest groups and political parties (as aggregates of interest groups) normally act at whatever level of government important political policies are decided; this pattern has indeed been the aim of the EEC's founders. Interaction between decision-making institutions and the multitude of interest groups was considered of vital importance to the political integration of the Inner Six.[17]

Social Spillover. In the long run, however, the self-interests of various groups will not suffice. A truly federal Europe must have popular support as well. Eventually, the political spillover leads to social spillover: the transfer of national loyalty to the supranational community:

> As the process of integration proceeds, it is assumed that values will undergo changes, that interests will be redefined in terms of a regional rather than a purely national orientation and that the erstwhile set of separate national group values will gradually be superseded by a new and geographically larger set of beliefs. . . .
>
> As the beliefs and aspirations of groups undergo change due to the necessity of working in a transnational institutional framework, mergers in values and doctrines are expected to come about, uniting groups across former frontiers. The overlapping of these group aspirations is finally thought to result in an accepted body of "national" doctrine, in effect heralding the advent of a new nationalism. Implied in this development, of course, is a proportional diminution of loyalty to and expectations from the former separate national governments. Shifts in the focus of loyalty need not necessarily imply the immediate repudiation of the national state or government. Multiple loyalties have been empirically demonstrated to exist.[18]

Based upon the logic of the integration of economic, political, and social functions, the EEC was designed to develop into a United States of Europe through three stages: a *customs union*, an *economic union*, and a *political and social union*.

Limits of Functional Logic

Three fundamental assumptions underlay this logic: (1) that economic and social, or low-politics, problems could be separated from political and security, or high-politics, issues; (2) that the ever-widening vested interests and habits of cooperation formed in the low-politics area would spill over into high politics; and (3) that there would be a massive shift of loyalty from the nation to the new supranational community as citizens—producers, laborers, farmers, and consumers—came to recognize the economic benefits of the new and larger community.

Inseparability of Economics and Politics. The ups and downs of the European unification movement reflect on the validity of these assumptions. It should not have come as too great a surprise to discover that in practice, even if not in theory, social and economic affairs are not neatly separable from political considerations. The modern industrial welfare state testifies to this. Virtually no social or economic issue—whether it be farmers' subsidies, corporate survival, women's rights, or abortion—stands outside the realm of political controversy and action. This is just as true in international politics. Years ago, Inis Claude asked:

> Is it in fact possible to segregate a group of problems and subject them to treatment in an international workshop where the nations shed their conflicts at the door and busy themselves only with the cooperative tools of mutual interests? Does not this assumption fly in the face of the evidence that a trend toward the politicization of all issues is operative in the twentieth century?[19]

States have remained jealous guardians of their sovereignty, national identities, and military strength. France and the other five countries of the Inner Six may pool their coal- and steel-producing facilities to increase their standards of living, but it is quite another story when it comes to coordinating their foreign and defense policies. For example, France and Britain (which joined the EEC, together with Ireland and Denmark, in 1973) each possess small nuclear forces. But, despite the advantages that combining these forces might have for the two countries and the other EEC countries, they have been unable to do so because the EEC members could not agree on a common foreign policy that such a nuclear force would serve.

Indeed, the original impetus for the formation of a united Europe was political, not economic. The French sought to insure themselves against any future danger from German rearmament and aggressive policies, as well as to gain equality of status and influence with the "Anglo-Saxons" in the Western alliance. More broadly, France viewed the ECSC as the initial step toward a French-led United States of Europe. Europe was not to be merely a region of butchers and candlestick makers, as implied by the later term *Common Market*, but a world power ranking with the United States and the Soviet Union. Otherwise, how could Europe stand on its own feet and play a role again in world affairs? A divided and weak Europe would remain subordinate and subservient to the United States.

Success, an Obstacle to Political Unity. Nor did the economic spillover have quite the results it was supposed to have had. Economically, of course, there can be no doubt that the EEC has been successful. Its twelve members with 325 million consumers constitute the largest market in the world. As a single unit, the EEC possesses great bargaining strength on economic issues, and it has been responsible for tariff reductions among all the industrial countries and easier access to one another's markets. Trade among the six founding members has grown even faster, and this growth has probably been a major factor contributing to the industrialization of France and northern Italy.

Ironically, the very economic success of the EEC proved to be one of the greatest obstacles to further political spillover. As the national wealth of EEC members rose, the urgency for further integration declined. The functional analysts had emphasized that fulfillment of some needs would result in growing support for the integration of other sectors of the economy and further development of new supranational attitudes. But contrary to these expectations, economic gains through the customs union seem to have led to protection of the status quo and reduced support for further integration.[20] The citizens and interest groups who gained the most economically from the European unification movement attributed those benefits largely to their own governments. Thus once more, the confidence in nation-states, supposedly lost as a result of defeat in World War II and the postwar economic collapse, was enhanced.

Even more ironically, the post-1973 recession, which lasted into the 1980s, also strengthened the concern with national interests. Member states tried to protect industries and jobs by keeping out imports from other EEC states. This policy, in turn, made EEC decisions more difficult to reach as governments, facing voter wrath, were less able to make the necessary compromises. France and Italy, for example, waged a "wine war" when French growers tried to keep out cheaper Italian wine. In fact, because farmers possessed power disproportionate to their numbers, the EEC was swimming in lakes of wine and building mountains of butter, dumping surplus food on the international market, competing with U.S. farmers, and undermining the competition of the poorer nations of Asia and Latin America. The increasing national resistance to free trade was accompanied by growing government support for troubled industries.

At a time when cooperation was not always present in the low-politics arena, one could not be too optimistic about its transfer to the high-politics arena. Admittedly, in the 1980s there were indications of new life in the European unification movement. Greece joined the EEC in 1981, and Spain and Portugal joined in 1986. Like Greece, which had been admitted after it shed its right-wing regime, Spain and Portugal were rather fragile democracies. The rationale for their admission was obviously the extension and stabilization of democracy in these countries, making democracy more secure throughout Europe. The EEC admitted these countries even though all three were less developed industrially than the other EEC nations, and the larger number of members made efforts to integrate more difficult.

But, although the EEC countries were prosperous and at peace, the United States of Europe remained a distant objective. The automatic spillover from the economic to the political arena had not been automatic enough. More than thirty years after the launching of the ECSC and more than twenty years after the EEC began its life, nationalism and the nation-state were alive and well in Western Europe. National loyalties remained. Only in the long run may generational changes result in greater attraction to a new Europe for those born after World War II, whose values are said to be largely "post-bourgeois." [21] (Bourgeois values are based mostly on individual material and physical security, whereas postbourgeois values are based more on community values and intellectual and esthetic satisfaction. Adherents to the latter tend to be more cosmopolitan than parochial in their identifications.)

Future of the European Economic Community. The functionalists' belief in "the victory of economics over politics," in short, may have been exaggerated, as has the emphasis on the domestic conditions for integration. The neglect of external conditions as a motivation for integration is particularly ironic given the bipolar environment that stimulated the drive for a United States of Europe. Indeed, just as the Soviet threat had spurred the movement, so its momentum has slowed down as the perceived Soviet threat has diminished. As the defeated and discouraged Continental states recovered and the unique circumstances in which integration was launched changed, the larger vision seems to have dimmed.

In 1984 a special committee of the EEC, convened to address the problem of declining confidence in the EEC, stated that Europe is in a state of crisis and counseled that "Europe must recover faith in its own greatness and launch itself on new ventures—the setting up of a political entity." [22] But the committee was very cautious in offering recommendations. The fact was that the nations of Europe no longer thought of themselves as partners in the great enterprise of "building Europe." Each concentrated on how to get the best deal for itself. The focus was on trading off oranges and lemons, Riesling and Chianti. With their mind still on the grocery list, it was not surprising that the EEC countries attached thirty footnotes listing their reservations to twenty-three pages of the committee's report.[23] Britain, Denmark, and West Germany expressed reservations about the committee's insistence on moving toward greater integration. Ireland, a neutral, objected to defense aspects of the plan. But without a common defense policy a European political community was meaningless.

Nevertheless, the European movement may yet pick up new momentum because of two external influences on the community. One influence is the slow growth of the European nations' economies and the continuing high unemployment rate as Japan and, to a lesser extent, the United States continue to increase the technology gap in such critical areas as computers and semi-conductors. Spurred by the facts, the Europeans have set 1992 as the date for the final elimination of all the internal nontariff barriers to trade that took the place of tariffs after they were abolished. Trade (goods and services), capital, and labor will be able to move anywhere within the EEC after 1992. This, as noted earlier, requires "harmonization" of social and economics policy throughout the community to prevent favoritism or protection for selected industries. The goal is to reinvigorate the EEC, create a truly common market as originally envisaged, and transform Europe into an economic superpower as companies expand beyond their national frontiers. With the world's largest domestic market of about 325 million people, European industries would merge and organize on a European-wide basis and become more competitive at home with the United States and Japan, as well as in the international market, thereby accelerating European economic growth. In short, European integration is now viewed as a prerequisite for competing in the global economy.

To help matters along, studies are being prepared to furnish a blueprint for creating a European central bank and European currency, a key step toward European economic—and political—integration, but that may not be done until after 1992. Britain, the only country still clinging to British sovereignty and identity, is the main opposition, and it could stall the momentum for a European federation. If everything goes according to plan, however, after 1992 Europe will gain exceptional leverage in world trade and world affairs. Austria, a neutral state in the cold war, has already asked for membership, and

Turkey, Norway, Iceland, Sweden, and Finland are considering membership, although the latter two are neutrals as well. Thus, the EEC may be a "Europe of 18" by the next century.[24] Even the Communist states such as Czechoslovakia and Hungary have concluded trade arrangements; East Germany, because of its duty-free relationship with West Germany, already has access. In 1988 the EEC signed a recognition agreement with COMECON, its Eastern-bloc counterpart. The EEC is also likely to play a key role in helping East European states such as Poland and Hungary economically in their efforts to transform themselves into more politically pluralistic societies. Such states are drawing closer to the West and are experimenting with free markets; they may even seek some kind of membership eventually. They are trying not to alienate the Soviet Union, however, by remaining members of the Soviet-led Warsaw Pact alliance.

The other external influence on the EEC is Europe's defense and how much longer Europeans, forty-five years after World War II, feel they will be able to count on the United States. The 1980s saw increasing disharmony in the alliance as (1) Europe became economically more competitive, often underselling American agriculture; (2) Europeans and Americans differed on what policies to pursue toward Moscow; (3) the United States spent more on Europe's defense as a percentage of gross national product than the Europeans; (4) pacificism and neutralism became very visible in European protest movements against the deployment of U.S. intermediate-range missiles to counter those of the Soviet Union; (4) Asia, the Persian Gulf, and Central America increased in importance; (5) the huge U.S. deficit, required large cost cuts; and (6) the capability of the United States to sustain its growing commitments declined. Thus, if not a disengagement, an increasing devolution of Europe's defense to the Europeans seemed inevitable, even before the cold war receded. In an age of nuclear parity, the United States was hardly likely to risk commiting suicide in the defense of its allies. And in a period of improved East-West relations, with the possible erosion of the image of the Soviet Union as an enemy, the internal "de-Communization" of the states of Eastern Europe (while remaining members of the Warsaw Treaty Organization), the possible restructuring of Soviet forces and military doctrine to a more defensive posture, if not ultimately their withdrawal back to the Soviet Union, would encourage the "Europeanization" of NATO.

With the possibility in mind that some, if not most, American troops might be withdrawn in the 1990s as part of a redistribution of responsibilities (if WTO and NATO are not in fact dismantled), the Europeans have already made some initial moves. France and West Germany plan to form a joint defense council that would be open to other European states. France and Britain have announced that they are studying the joint production of air-launched cruise missiles that would carry nuclear warheads. And France, which withdrew from NATO's integrated command structure in 1966, declared in 1987 that it would automatically come to West Germany's defense if it were attacked. Thus, economic competition and security considerations may yet provide a new impetus for European integration. With a 1988 population of 325 million, a collective gross national product of $3.36 trillion, and a per capita gross national product of $10,106, there should be no material reason why the EEC could not basically defend itself against a disappearing threat *and* thrive economically.

INTERDEPENDENCE AND A MORE HARMONIOUS WORLD

Clearly, the transformation of the state system to a global system is not likely to occur soon. A world government cannot be established by a new constitutional convention, nor, even if the European experiment of transcending the nation-state should be successful in the next decade or two, can a world state be built on regional building blocs—"peace by pieces"—in the foreseeable future. The process is simply too time-consuming, and the conditions for supranational integration are clearly not present in the nonindustrialized and nondemocratic areas of the world. Speed has been an important ingredient in this process, however, because the constant fear of a nuclear war and catastrophe (at least until the current détente) made transformation of the state system a matter of great urgency. Forty years of avoiding that ultimate disaster was no guarantee, it was argued, that it could be successfully deterred another four decades.

It was in this context that interdependence appeared so promising a solution in the post-Vietnam late 1970s as the cold war resumed after détente I. *Interdependence was to be a sort of halfway house between the anarchy of the contemporary state system and the promise of a world-state in the future.*[25] Believers in the promise of interdependence expected the state system to continue but with the fangs of national interest drawn. Even before a world government comes into existence, they expected some of its benefits— greater cooperation, less emphasis on violent resolution of conflict, more emphasis on joint, peacefully negotiated solutions—to become common. States may remain the principal actors and a world-state only the ultimate objective, but interdependence increasingly will bind all states together, catch them in its web, and make their individual security, especially their economic fortunes, dependent on one another. Whatever the problems confronting a single state, solutions will no longer be national solutions achieved at the cost of other states. Instead, they will be reached collectively and will benefit all. The maxim of the historic state system, "Your gain is my loss," is to be replaced by the maxim "We shall all lose or gain together" in the new interdependent state system—that is, the emphasis of the "new politics" is on cooperation, not conflict. Interdependence within this context was seen as a replacement for an increasingly outdated power-politics approach and analysis of international politics. The actual evolution of economic interdependence demonstrated, however, as it did for the earlier functionalist version, the limits of the changes that could be expected in the character of international politics. But it was the assumptions underlying the theory of interdependence that led to such optimistic conclusions.

The first assumption was the priority of low-politics goals. The switch from high-politics foreign policy goals to low-politics goals stemmed from modernization. As traditional societies became industrialized, modernization resulted in increased standards of living, first in Europe in the nineteenth century and then in North America; they are now being extended to the rest of the world. For citizens of most countries concerned with their standard of living, low-politics issues are more important than high-politics issues. In democratic countries, where the "revolution of rising expectations" began, electoral pressures ensured governmental attention and commitment to improving people's lives. Their example has led the developing countries and Communist states to seek the same goals and, indeed, to do so by the same free-market practices that were so successful in the West. In short, since the Industrial Revolution, states have been able to create prosperity at home and no longer need to seek new territory, as they did when land was the source of wealth. Governments therefore must increasingly be responsive to low-politics issues. Their success is judged by the level of social services provided and the rate of growth of the gross national product. Management of the economy—even a free-enterprise economy—by government is politically necessary to ensure high employment, rapid economic growth, economic stability, and an equitable distribution of income. Governmental incompetence in economic management is not easily forgotten or forgiven at election time.

The second assumption underlying independence was that states are no longer self-sufficient. The days of autarky, when the great powers at least had or controlled the resources they needed and were in charge of their own economic destinies, are gone. No longer able to satisfy their people's demands for greater prosperity, governments increasingly have had to enter into the international economy. To fail to do so would be too costly politically because economic growth would be slow. Governments thus are drawn further and further into interdependence, even if they do not want to be. Foreign policy becomes thoroughly enmeshed with such issues as trade, aid, development, monetary stability, exchange rates, and debt problems, and the division between foreign and domestic policy becomes blurred, if not nonexistent.

The third assumption providing the basis of interdependence was that low politics involves cooperation, whereas high politics involves conflict. Nations have become so interdependent on bread-and-butter issues that they have no choice but to cooperate if they wish to promote their own prosperity. On security issues, states still operate as separate political units. A single nation's gain in power and security is still usually seen by a potential adversary as a loss of power and security for itself and as something to be opposed. But a gain in welfare for the same nation depends on gains in welfare for other nations as well. In the new socioeconomic game, states gain or lose together. An interdependent world is a world of exchange and sharing; war would disrupt this mutually beneficial relationship.

The fourth assumption was the irrelevance of force to low-politics issues. Interdependent states must cooperate over a long period; the use or threat of force is counterproductive in a game of coordination. Coercion or violence may pay off on a single issue, but, given the need for long-term collaboration, the resulting anger and resentment may lead to some sort of economic retaliation. If another nation possesses a much-needed commodity, it is hardly helpless, even if it is inferior militarily. The gains from force would therefore be few if any, and the costs probably quite high. In brief, the very meaning of power has changed. Given the uselessness of force, the need for cooperative behavior if common problems are to be solved, and the complexity of such issues as population control, increased food production, development of alternative energy sources, monetary stability, and economic growth, power has become a matter of technical expertise and persuasive skills so that states can find collective solutions.[26]

The final assumption underlying interdependence was the equality of states. In a world of many states, many issues, many games played simultaneously, and the nonuse of force, the historical hierarchy has been eroded. All states are essentially equal on welfare issues. The dominance of the superpowers and traditional power politics are said to have disappeared. Security is basically a given, and the primary objective of states is welfare.

The envisioned interdependent world, then, was one in which states will still exist, but they will not be the kinds of states studied here so far. Interdependence will have "tamed" them, drawing in the "sharp teeth of sovereignty." It will also have dissolved selfish national interests and bonds of national loyalty.[27] Genuinely equal states will live together in greater harmony and mutual understanding; at the very least, they will be disposed toward resolving conflicts peacefully. Economic and technological forces will bind them together, and national frontiers will become increasingly irrelevant, for economic cooperation will cross borders. Geopolitics and security conflicts will become anachronistic. Interdependence may not engender world government, but it will make the nation-state and power politics irrelevant in a world without frontiers. Nations will no longer be able to adequately solve their own problems and serve their people's desire for better lives. Global problems such as insufficient natural resources and energy, overpopulation, poverty, and shortages of food, as well as the potential revolutionary situations created by the division between rich and poor nations, will be solvable only at the global level. National solutions will no longer be possible.

This view, prevalent in the 1970s and 1980s, embodied an international system that is radically different from the one described earlier. While the structure of the state system remains, the power hierarchy has been replaced by a new egalitarianism. Force is no longer thinkable, and the key values of national security, prestige, and power have been replaced by economic welfare, consumerism, social justice, and environmental concerns. If there is one word that sums up the distinction, it is *cooperation*. Cooperation replaces conflict, the hallmark of the old system. This cooperation has been institutionalized in *regimes*, a set of rules or decision-making procedures used to resolve disputes about and encourage cooperation on a particular issue.[28] In a world in which population growth, pollution, poverty, and nuclear proliferation all have transnational consequences, and in which social and economic forces, whether oil prices or the "debt bomb," affect many if not all nations, international regimes became the new focus of studies. Regime members were not only individual states but also international governmental organizations and nongovernmental organizations. Regimes spanned everything from high-politics issues such as U.S.-Soviet arms control and nuclear diffusion to the more usual low-politics issues such as international trade, monetary systems, management of the seas, population, and health. These are all areas in which states find it to their benefit to have a set of rules to guide them and inform them about the multilateral problem-solving procedures. Regimes, indeed, became the prototype of a more ordered, peaceful, and cooperative world short of world government—and in the long run, perhaps, a transition toward it. Table 17-1 sums up the basic distinctions between the old security game and the new socioeconomic game.

INTERDEPENDENCE AND AMERICAN NORMS

The fundamental assumption underlying both supranational integration and interdependence is that *technological, economic, and social forces operating transnationally will inevitably drive all nations toward greater cooperation*. With a faith in the determinism of economic forces reminiscent of Marxism, proponents of this view are ready to abandon the troublesome world of politics. Perhaps their emphasis on economic necessities should not be surprising. Americans are especially prone to see economics as the universal palliative for the human condition. The basic assumption of *laissez-faire* capitalism is that people are motivated economically; the laws of supply and demand will thus transform individual economic selfishness into social benefits, "the greatest good for the greatest number." The role of the government is to stay out of the market. The best government is the one that governs least because political interference with economic laws will upset the results those laws are said to produce.

Not surprisingly, when the logic of the free market is projected internationally, it is possible to conclude that a peaceful international society will be created by free trade. People all over the world will gain a vested interest in peace if they carry on their economic relations. War and trade are

Table 17-1 Distinctions Between Power Politics and Interdependence

	Power Politics	*Interdependence*
Issues	High politics: security, balance of power, spheres of influence	Low politics: natural resources, energy, food and population, environment
Actors	States (primarily in the First and Second Worlds)	States (primarily in the First and Third Worlds), multinational corporations
State relationships	Conflicting national interests	Interdependence, common interests, and transnational cooperation
Rule	Conflict: "Your gain is my loss" (balance of power)	Cooperation: "We shall all lose or gain together" (community building)
Management	Bilateral	Multilateral
Role of power	Coercion	Rewards
Role of force	High	Low, if not obsolete
Organization	Hierarchical (bipolar or multipolar)	More nearly egalitarian
Future	Basic continuity	Radical change

supposedly incompatible. War impoverishes and destroys, creating ill will among nations, whereas commerce benefits all participating states. Commerce is thus nationally and individually profitable and creates a common interest in the preservation of peace. War, by contrast, is economically unprofitable and therefore obsolete. Free trade and peace are one and the same cause. This version of the argument for interdependence was already quite popular at the time the United States was born.

> This feeling that one civilization now encompassed the whole world was reinforced by the astounding growth of economic interdependence. The [national political] barriers that existed seemed artificial and ephemeral in comparison with the fine net by which the merchants tied the individuals of the different nations together like "threads of silk." . . . [T]he merchants—whether they are English, Dutch, Russian, or Chinese—do not serve a single nation; they serve everyone and are citizens of the whole world. Commerce was believed to bind the nations together and to create not only a community of interests but also a distribution of labor among them—a new comprehensive principle placing the isolated sovereign nations in a higher political unit. In the eighteenth century, writers were likely to say that the various nations belonged to "one society"; it was stated that all states together formed "a family of nations," and the whole globe a "general and unbreakable confederation." [29]

Implicit in this view is the notion that economics is good and politics bad—economics binds people together; politics drives them apart. Yet the current degree of interdependence has not yet replaced the security game or transferred the habits of cooperation from the economic to the political sphere. The "trading state" has not yet replaced the "warrior state," however lamentable that may be. But, as recent trade wars suggest (Chapter 16), the economic sphere, like the political one, can arouse conflict.

That criticism notwithstanding, the argument for interdependence largely reflects an attempt to escape from power politics into a calmer, more decent and humane world.[30] For many disillusioned supporters of U.S. cold war policies, the Vietnam War intensified this urge to escape from the wicked world of power politics. Having previously supported a policy that they believed was a crusade in defense of democracy against totalitarianism, they now sought both forgiveness for past errors and a new way to achieve the same goal of a more just and peaceful world. Economics—which was good and healing—not power—which was bad and divisive—would achieve this objective.

They also argued—in a characteristically American fashion—that it was the responsibility of the United States to lead the world into the new era. They remained crusaders for the moral cause. Thus, only a few years after the United States was widely criticized—often by the current proponents of interdependence—for pursuing a global foreign policy and extending American commitments beyond the nation's alleged capacities, including the costly adventure in Vietnam, globalism reappeared in a new form. Only the agenda had changed. Because the new welfare issues could not be managed by single nations, it was asserted, "foreign policy leaders schooled in the old arithmetic of national security will have to learn the formula of economic interdependence, the advanced calculus of planetary bargains and global welfare."[31] More than just a reaction to Vietnam, interdependence represented a deeply felt utopian streak—usually left implicit—in American thinking on international politics. The state system, conflict, and war remained unacceptable. If the United States could no longer abstain from power politics by isolating itself, or abolish power politics by democratizing its wicked practitioners, then it would dissolve the nature of international politics in the *bonhomie* of interdependence.

This critique does not deny the existence of economic interdependence, its significance, or the requirement for greater cooperation among states to assure their economic well-being (Chapter 15). What it does deny is the conclusions so often drawn: that the agenda of international politics has radically shifted from a priority on high-politics objectives to low-politics goals, and that states will transfer their new habit of cooperation from the socioeconomic realm to the political-military one. Interdependence, according to some of its more original and enthusiastic proponents, was a plea for establishing a world beyond the contemporary nation-state; for changing international behavior and building a better, more cooperative, and more harmonious world order; for subordinating power politics to welfare politics and national interests to planetary interests; and for recognizing before it is too late that humanity shares a common destiny. *Advocacy of interdependence thus became a prescription for a strategy of placing constraints on the national egotism and assertiveness of states by catching them in a "web of interdependence" in which they will become so deeply enmeshed that they will be unable to extricate themselves without suffering great harm, thereby compelling them to cooperate for the "good of humanity."* An argument based on description of the facts of interdependence, whether in security or in economics, thus shifts almost imperceptibly to advocacy of a course of policy intended to abolish conflict in the state system in favor of a focus on the welfare of all people.

Yet, as British economist Susan Strange has reminded us, the state system is basically characterized

> not by discipline and authority, but by the absence of government, by the precariousness of peace and order, by the dispersion not the concentration of authority, by the weakness of law, and by the large number of unresolved conflicts over what should be done, how it should be done, and who should do it.
>
> Above all, a single, recognized focus of power over time is the one attribute that the international system conspicuously lacks.[32]

That the term *regime* is used so often to describe cooperation between states in these circumstances suggests the special meaning with which the term has been vested: the collective management by the "international community" *in the absence of world government* of what is now commonly called the transnational or global agenda (population, food, resources, ocean management, and so forth). Regimes composed of agreements—treaties plus associated international machinery—are viewed as an essential ingredient of a spreading "global political process" or expanding "politics of global problem solving."[33] According to Strange,

> All these international arrangements dignified by the label *regimes* are only too easily upset when either the balance of bargaining power or the perception of national interests (or both together) change among those states who negotiated them. In general, moreover, *all the areas in which regimes in a national context exercise the central attributes of political discipline are precisely those in which corresponding international arrangements that might conceivably be dignified with the title are conspicuous by their absence.*[34]

Strange then succinctly concludes that regime theory "gives the false impression ... that international regimes are indeed advancing against the forces of disorder and anarchy."[35]

For Review

1. If anarchy is the basic cause of conflict, how can states overcome their differences in order to create a world-state?
2. Why is the American experience of building a federal system not a model for the world today?
3. How was functionalism supposed to overcome national differences and contribute toward building a greater "security community"?
4. What were the original expectations about interdependence and why?
5. What common assumption underlies both supranational integration and interdependence?

Notes

1. For example, Dennis Pirages, *Global Ecopolitics* (North Scituate, Mass.: Duxbury Press, 1978); and Pirages, *Global Technopolitics* (Pacific Grove, Calif.: Brooks/Cole, 1980). A popular summary is *Time's* January 2, 1989, issue, entitled "Planet of the New Year: Endangered Earth." Also see Lester R. Brown et al., *State of the World 1988* (New York: Norton, 1988); and Mel Gurtov, *Global Politics in the Human Interest* (Boulder, Colo.: Lynne Rienner, 1988).
2. Richard W. Sterling, *Macropolitics* (New York: Knopf, 1974), 5-6. Also see Jonathan Schell, *The Fate of the Earth* (New York: Avon Books, 1982), 218-231.
3. Emery Reves, *The Anatomy of Peace* (New York: Harper & Row, 1945), 253-270. Also see Carl Van Doren, *The Great Rehearsal* (New York: Viking, 1948), for a discussion of American constitutional nation building as an example for the world.
4. Inis L. Claude, Jr., *Power and International Relations* (New York: Random House, 1962), 260-261.
5. Hans J. Morgenthau, *Politics among Nations*, 4th ed. (New York: Knopf, 1967), 498, 499. Also see Crane Brinton, *From Many One* (Cambridge, Mass.: Harvard University Press, 1948).
6. Karl Deutsch et al., *Political Community and the North Atlantic Area* (Princeton, N.J.: Princeton University Press, 1957), 5.
7. Amitai Etzioni, *Political Unification* (New York: Holt, Rinehart & Winston, 1965), 4.
8. Deutsch et al., *Political Community*, 3-21.
9. On the process of "learning" and of defining national interests (and how these definitions change), see Joseph S. Nye, Jr., "Neorealism and Neoliberalism," *World Politics*, January 1988, 235-251; and for a case study, see Nye, "Nuclear Learning and U.S.-Soviet Security Regimes," *International Organization* (Summer 1987): 371-402.
10. Deutsch et al., *Political Community*, 46-58.
11. David Mitrany, *A Working Peace System* (London: National Peace Council, 1946).
12. Quoted by Inis L. Claude, Jr., *Swords into Plowshares* (New York: Random House, 1956), 376.
13. Mitrany, *Working Peace System*, 7.
14. Two of the better early discussions of the expected harmonizing of national

policies are Michael Shanks and John Lambert, *The Common Market Today—and Tomorrow* (New York: Holt, Rinehart & Winston, 1962), 56-105; and U. W. Kitzinger, *The Politics and Economics of European Integration* (New York: Holt, Rinehart & Winston, 1963), 21-59. Also see Emile Benoit, *Europe at Sixes and Sevens* (New York: Columbia University Press, 1961).

15. Kitzinger, *Politics and Economics of European Integration*, 60-61.

16. Ernst B. Haas, *The Uniting of Europe* (Stanford, Calif.: Stanford University Press, 1958), 12-13.

17. Ibid., xiii.

18. Ibid., 13-14.

19. Claude, *Swords into Plowshares*, 385.

20. This result is explained by the concept of "equilibrium": see Leon N. Lindberg and Stuart A. Scheingold, *Europe's Would-Be Polity* (Englewood Cliffs, N.J.: Prentice-Hall, 1970). Also see Joseph S. Nye, Jr., *Peace in Parts* (Boston: Little, Brown, 1972).

21. Ron Inglehart, "An End to European Integration?" *American Political Science Review* (March 1967): 91-105; and Inglehart, "The Silent Revolution in Europe: Intergenerational Change in Post-Industrial Societies," *American Political Science Review* (December 1971): 991-1017.

22. *New York Times*, Dec. 4, 1984.

23. *New York Times*, Dec. 9, 1984.

24. Steven Greenhouse, "As Europe Unites, Outsiders Line up to Join the Club," *New York Times*, Sept. 4, 1988.

25. For some of the basic books and articles on the nature of interdependence and the role of power, see Seyom Brown, *New Forces in World Politics* (Washington, D.C.: Brookings, 1974); Brown, *New Forces, Old Forces, and the Future of World Politics* (Glenview, Ill.: Scott, Foresman, 1988); Robert O. Keohane and Joseph S. Nye, *Power and Interdependence*, 2d ed. (Boston: Little, Brown, 1977); Andrew M. Scott, *The Dynamics of Interdependence* (Chapel Hill: University of North Carolina Press, 1982); and Stanley Hoffmann, "Choices," *Foreign Policy*, Fall 1973, 3-42. More popular treatments can be found in Lester R. Brown, *World Without Borders* (New York: Vintage, 1973); and Pirages, *Global Ecopolitics*. Excellent critiques may be found in Kal J. Holsti, "A New International Politics? Diplomacy in Complex Interdependence," *International Organization* (Spring 1978): 513-531; and Stanley J. Michalck, Jr., "Theoretical Perspective for Understanding International Interdependence," *World Politics*, October 1979, 136-150.

26. James N. Rosenau, "Capabilities and Control in an Interdependent World," *International Security*, Fall 1976, 44.

27. For a critique of the theory of interdependence as applied to relations between the First and Third Worlds, see Robert W. Tucker, *The Inequality of Nations* (New York: Basic Books, 1977). For a suggestion that the United States make world order, rather than the balance of power, the focus of its policy, see Stanley Hoffmann, *Primacy of World Order* (New York: McGraw-Hill, 1978).

28. Keohane and Nye, *Power and Interdependence*; and the Spring 1982 issue of *International Organization*, which was completely devoted to regimes.

29. Felix Gilbert, *To the Farewell Address* (Princeton, N.J.: Princeton University Press, 1961), 57.

30. For the contrasting and conflicting views on whether interdependence is utopian or not, see Ray Maghoori and Bennett Ramsberg, eds., *Globalism vs. Realism* (Boulder, Colo.: Westview Press, 1982).

31. Robert L. Paarlberg, "Domesticating Global Management," *Foreign Affairs* (April 1976): 576.

32. Susan Strange, "Cave! Hic Dragones: A Critique of Regime Analysis," *International Organization* (Spring 1982): 487.

33. Frederic S. Pearson and J. Martin Rochester; *International Relations* (Reading, Mass.: Addison-Wesley, 1984), Part IV, 395.

34. Strange, "Cave! Hic Dragones," 487 (emphasis added).

35. Ibid., 491. For an interesting critique of integration and regime theory, see Yale H. Ferguson and Richard W. Mansbach, *The Elusive Quest* (Columbia: University of South Carolina Press, 1988), 198-211.

C H A P T E R 18

Violence in a Multipolar Future

The state system remains fundamentally intact. For all the enormous changes in the post-World War II system—decolonization and the birth of many new states, the conflict between rich and poor nations, the nuclear revolution, the global American-Soviet rivalry, the growing economic interdependence, and the moves toward an integrated Western Europe—the continuities of international politics persist. Even the new environmental issues and calls for "global solutions to global problems" do not mean that observers of ancient conflicts would not quickly recognize the fundamental character of the contemporary "game." [1]

In a world of nation-states, national solutions retain priority over global solutions; indeed, they are a prerequisite for a broader international effort. Fertility, for example, has not been very amenable to agreement among states. The problem of rapidly growing populations is still primarily a national responsibility. What can foreign governments do in the absence of a domestic will to manage this issue? Similarly, emergency food shipments or worldwide food reserves to cope with famine and malnutrition are no substitute for national policies emphasizing agricultural development. These problems require, however, greater national commitments and shifts of internal priorities and resources than most developing countries have been willing to make in the past. For many, painful and difficult structural reforms in landowning patterns also will be necessary. "Global welfare cannot be properly managed abroad until it has been tolerably managed at home. Without a prior exercise of domestic political authority, the global welfare crisis will not admit to efficient interstate control." [2] States remain the most effective means for resolving nations' internal problems. Like charity, global welfare management must begin at home.

The fact is that the structure of the state system remains decentralized;

given its anarchical character and its emphasis on self-help to protect national security and independence, nations remain trapped by the security dilemma as each nation's effort to enhance its own security turns into a prime cause for insecurity. Even the shift from international anarchy to a security community in Western Europe stems fundamentally from America's security guarantee. By protecting Western Europe against the Soviet Union, the United States also protected the European states against one another and laid the foundation for European cooperation among them. By extending its deterrence to its North Atlantic Treaty Organization (NATO) allies, and by making a long-term commitment to their individual and collective security, the United States removed the self-help imperative, which, for example, had not allowed the victors after World War I to collaborate against the German threat in the 1930s. Specifically, it was the American security guarantee that removed the principal cause of conflict among the European states: the search for a national defense policy in which all states in an anarchical system trapped by the "security dilemma" must engage. In the absence of a U.S. protective shield, would West Germany, France, Italy, and Britain have moved toward European integration in response to the Soviet threat? During the alliance-building period of the 1950s,

> neither the Soviet challenge nor the destruction of the European balance during World War II were powerful enough to prompt the West Europeans to transcend their history.... By promising to protect Western Europe against others *and against itself,* the United States swept aside the rules of the self-help game that had governed and regularly brought grief to Europe in centuries past.[3]

Indeed, as the postwar European status quo dissolves, will the states of Western Europe once more fall to quarrelling with one another, or will their integration into the larger European Community and their postwar security community survive? As the states of Eastern Europe become more politically pluralistic and free market oriented domestically, the problem of Germany arises once again. East Germany has no rationale for existence except as a self-styled socialist state. Thus, as it liberalizes itself domestically, the possibility of a reunified Germany looms larger. Will such a Germany be integrated into Western Europe or will a neutralized Germany play off East against West, destabilizing Europe and once more arousing fears as Germany did from 1870 to 1945, when it was divided and East and West Germany became part of the Soviet- and United States-led alliances, respectively?

The socioeconomic game is played within the larger framework of the security game. Instead of economic interdependence generating a new kind of international order that weakens the traditional reliance on forcible means of conflict resolution, the historical and ever-present security problems are more likely to continue conditioning the character of interdependence. It was the United States' postwar security policy and its alliance with Europe that established the conditions for the high degree of interdependence that exists today not only within the European Economic Community (EEC) but also between its members and the United States. Multiple public and private links in trade, investment, production, and finance bind these highly industrialized states together. But for the U.S.-Soviet security conflict, the U.S. protection of Europe, and the European integration movement, the present high degree of interdependence probably would not exist.

The same is even truer for Japan. It is often said to be the model of the new "trading state" which increasingly will replace the historic territorial-military state because of, first, the increasing priority of low-politics objectives and the ability of industrial economies to satisfy the popular demand for economic prosperity, and, second, the decreasing need of states to conquer territory as a means of enhancing their wealth and power. In a "trading world" these economic gains could be realized by domestic development; external expansion and war would no longer be necessary. Thus, Japan is the wave of the future because it has demonstrated that the benefits of peaceful economic development and trading with other nations are considerably greater than military competition and territorial aggrandizement. Japan today is not a "smaller edition" of the United States—that is, a future great power once it has converted its economic and financial capabilities into military power and defined a political role for itself. "It is not the American model that Japan will ultimately follow. Rather, it is the Japanese model that America may ultimately follow." [4]

Japan too has been largely able to ignore high-politics considerations since World War II. Instead, it has concentrated on its economic development and an export strategy. This is not because Japan has had no security problem, but, rather, because the United States has extended deterrence to that country. In nearby Korea, American troops fought a war to keep hostile power distant. Without the U.S. protection of South Korea and the U.S.-Japan security treaty, Japan would have had a security problem, just as the European states did. Instead of devoting less than 1 percent of its gross national product to military spending for most of the postwar period (only in the 1980s did it exceed that level by a small amount), Japan would have had to devote the 3-4 percent common among NATO allies. One could therefore conclude that

> if major conflagration between the superpowers is avoided, if lesser conflicts are kept from spreading, if indeed governments are able to devote their energies to solving those planet-wide economic, social, and ecological problems which undeniably call for universal cooperation, it will be *because* of successful management of the strategic relationships between the superpowers. [5]

If the immediate future is unlikely to witness a transformation of the state system, it will, however, witness three significant changes in the characteristics of the system: (1) more awareness of the global ecological disasters facing humankind, requiring the cooperation of all states (for example, the twelve EEC states and the United States promised in 1989 to ban chemicals harmful to the ozone layer by the year 2000—although Washington later refused to commit itself to stabilizing emissions of carbon dioxide, the main contributor to the greenhouse effect, by that date until the matter receives "further study"); (2) the greater prominence of economic and financial issues in international politics; and (3) a new strategic environment. The first issue was cited briefly earlier (Chapter 17), but the time for "political ecology"—governmental action especially by the Western industrial states— appears at hand. The second issue has received much attention in this text, and additional comments will be relatively brief. The last issue, however, is central to this chapter because this book is concerned mainly with the issue of war and peace.

NEW PROMINENCE OF ECONOMIC ISSUES

The postwar bipolar distribution of power was always somewhat artificial, reflecting not just the great power of the United States and the Soviet Union, but the postwar economic collapse of the other great powers. That structure is about to change as both the United States and the Soviet Union are poised to take a more natural place in the international order. The relative decline of both superpowers—of the two, that of the Soviet Union is by far the worst because it faces a systemic crisis—and the recovery of both the vanquished (West Germany, Italy, and especially Japan) and the victors (Britain and France) of World War II are diffusing power on the international scene once more. This diffusion is occurring mainly within the American alliance framework. In 1992 the Europeans are initiating the final drive toward greater political integration and economic dynamism, a more prominent role in their own defense, and a common foreign policy independent of the United States. Japan too is likely to play a more visible political, perhaps even military, and certainly an economic and financial role. By contrast, the Soviet Union, with its far weaker allies (most of whom are now in the process of "de-Communizing" themselves domestically), appears to be recognizing the costliness of facing a capitalist alliance composed of the United States, Western Europe, and Japan (informally aligned with Communist China). By defusing the enemy image that has held the Western states together; substituting a more outgoing, humane, and friendly Soviet Union; and acquiescing in the vast internal changes transforming Eastern Europe, Moscow may be able to both promote the erosion of the U.S. alliances and attract the enormous credits and trade it needs from the West to make the Soviet economy more efficient and bring it into the twenty-first century.

While the expectations of the original proponents of interdependence are not likely to be met, there can, however, be little doubt of the contradictory trends among the Western allies. Increasingly tied together economically, as they have been politically and militarily, the Western states may, on the one hand, be well on the road to a greater confederation or security community of North America and Western Europe, together with the Pacific Rim countries. With the possible exception of Western Europe, supranational integration is not the wave of the future; yet among the democracies, economic progress may now be possible within a broader and more perfect international union forged by close cooperation and a mutual willingness to compromise. On the other hand, the Europeans, Japanese, and Americans are increasingly divided by trade issues, and there is great concern about the possibility of more trade wars and, worse, the formation of three large, feuding, mercantilist blocs. With its mercantilist outlook—that is, tenaciously exporting goods while allowing virtually no imports of either food or manufactured products—Japan was a major factor in the organization of the U.S.-Canada free-trade agreement and, more significantly, the 1992 European push to fully integrate the EEC. Both the United States and the European countries are increasingly fearful of Japan's increasing market shares for its exports and especially of Japanese dominance in such high-tech areas as semiconductors, telecommunications, robotics, and new materials. Thus "adversarial trade," as it has been called, may replace what has been, for most of the postwar period, essentially a free-trade regime. The political fallout, as well as the economic one, are likely to be serious as the allies of the United States, no longer faced by an overwhelmingly and commonly perceived external threat, are turning inward and giving national economic interests, no longer subordinated to common security concerns, a new priority. This may well split the United States from its alliances and add momentum to their eventual disappearance.

Indeed, one immediate concern has to be the possibility of the mismanagement—and collapse—of the international economy. This could result from a plunge of the U.S. dollar; foreigners dumping their U.S. Treasury bonds (which cover America's $3 trillion federal deficit) as the value of their holdings declines sharply; Japan's refusal to import substantial goods and services from its debtors while it continues to accumulate trade surpluses; the developing countries' persistent debt problems; and the growing protectionist pressures in the United States, the entry to whose market is essential not only for Japan, the newly industrialized countries, and many developing countries, but for the entire global economy and its healthy growth as well. As if these problems were not enough, the current nuclear bipolycentric system faces three other threatening trends: (1) the proliferation of nuclear arms, (2) the diffusion of conventional arms, and (3) the use of terrorism as warfare.

NEW STRATEGIC ENVIRONMENT: PROLIFERATION OF NUCLEAR ARMS

Hovering over the entire state system is the threat of the proliferation of nuclear weapons.[6] Why do states seek nuclear arms?

Why Seek 'the Bomb' ?

Do potential nuclear states not know that a few bombs or missiles constitute neither an effective deterrent nor a credible retaliatory force? Are they unaware that the extremely high cost of the special delivery system needed for these weapons adds enormously to the estimated cost of obtaining a minimal nuclear strike force? The United States was able to afford five stages of nuclear force development—from subsonic bombers to supersonic bombers to stationary missiles (powered by liquid and solid fuels) to mobile missiles with single warheads to those with multiple warheads. But Britain could not. Perhaps the cost could be reduced if national deterrents could be based on missiles from the start and if the rate of technological change in delivery systems could be slowed or stabilized by agreement among the major powers. The costs, nevertheless, would remain immense. But, more important, are the potential aspirants not aware that the costs of such weapons far outweigh their potential benefits because they are not usable without staking one's very existence on them and they are not accompanied by the influence one might expect? Why seek such dangerous and expensive power?

National Security.   One answer is that, despite the costs and the sacrifice of other needs, national security considerations remain foremost. Allies of the United States have become increasingly concerned about the credibility of American defense commitments that were made in a period when the United States had an atomic monopoly and vast strategic superiority but that now have to be carried out in an era of parity. The United States could easily honor its pledge of protection when it was essentially immune from destruction, but can it afford to do so now when keeping its word may spell its own destruction? First Britain and then France acquired nuclear capabilities because they were uncertain, in view of the growing number of Soviet intercontinental ballistic missiles (ICBMs), that the United States would always and in all circumstances come unhesitatingly to their defense.

One need only ask: What would West Germany, South Korea, and Israel do if they felt unprotected? The first two are U.S. allies, and West Germany was forbidden to produce and deploy nuclear arms in the treaty admitting it to NATO. Yet if West Germany or South Korea had felt isolated or vulnerable to external pressures from a hostile state (the Soviet Union or North Korea), would not either country have been tempted to seek nuclear arms? And can it be doubted that had it not had American diplomatic support and extensive military assistance, Israel might already have declared itself a nuclear power? It is widely believed that Israel already has such arms, perhaps as many as 100-200, although most estimates are around a dozen. A state such as Israel, increasingly isolated politically and pressured by friends to settle conflicts with its neighbors, is particularly likely to try to enhance its security by acquiring nuclear arms. Another such state is Taiwan; the United States dropped its security treaty with the Nationalist Chinese government when it recognized the Beijing government in 1979.

More broadly, if during the cold war other countries had felt that the United States was reducing its role in the world, the possibility of nuclear diffusion would have increased. The United States could not have it both ways: it could not have reduced its global security role and at the same time expect its allies and friends to accept nonproliferation of nuclear arms. There is a political cost to be paid, whatever the choice, and the choice is basically political. Should the U.S.-Japan security treaty lose credibility in Tokyo, will Japan not cast off the "nuclear allergy" that has characterized it since the bombing of Hiroshima? Since India exploded its first nuclear device in 1974, Pakistan, its bitterest enemy on the subcontinent, has reportedly moved closer to acquiring the bomb. It is estimated that it would take Pakistan only a few days or weeks to assemble a bomb, likely based on a reliable, tested bomb design given it by China.

Indeed, quests for the bomb often appear to come in pairs. For example, the United States and the Soviet Union both exploded their first bombs during the 1940s. As the Sino-Soviet split grew, China exploded its bomb in 1964, and India's rivalry and past border conflicts with China undoubtedly were as influential in leading to India's 1974 detonation as its bitter quarrel with Pakistan.

Prestige.   "Nukes" have become status symbols. Just as a great power once demonstrated its primacy by acquiring colonies and a strong navy, so after World War II it had to acquire nuclear weapons. For nations that were once great powers and that continue to harbor the great-power syndrome and for nations determined to become great powers, nuclear weapons are symbols of strength. In their view, not to possess such weapons is to retreat from greatness and to abandon power and international respect—and therefore self-respect. In the nuclear age, is a nation not impotent if it does not own such arms? Can a nation still claim the authority to make its own decisions on vital issues if it is dependent on another power's nuclear protection? National pride and self-recognition have been powerful incentives to the development of national nuclear deterrents.

For Great Britain, nukes became a desperate matter of keeping the *great* in its name, despite its rapid decline in power after 1945. These weapons also fitted its image of itself as the United States' junior partner. For France, defeated during World War II, then suffering the loss of Indochina in 1954, humiliation at Suez in 1956, the loss of the war in Algeria in 1962, and enduring a status in Europe second to Britain and later to West Germany as well, the nuclear bomb became a means of seeking to regain international respect and self-respect. China, carved up during the nineteenth century by the European powers, including Russia, regards the bomb as a symbol of great-power status and national dignity, as well as a weapon for protection against first the United States, and then the Soviet Union. It is indeed difficult not to associate such status and influence with possession of nuclear weapons because the United States, Soviet Union, Britain, France, and China are also all permanent members of the UN Security Council. The bomb seems to be the admission fee to a rather exclusive club that discriminates against nonnuclear states.

India, China's rival and its competitor for leadership in Asia, is also the leading power on the subcontinent. And it was the first nation to break the nuclear membership barrier in 1974. Brazil, which is poor in coal but rich in uranium, has sought both abundant energy and political greatness as the number-one power in Latin America. In the past, Brazil and Argentina were jealous rivals, and after its defeat by Britain in the Falkland Islands, a humiliated Argentina had an even stronger reason to seek nuclear arms. But in 1986 Brazil and Argentina's new democratic civilian leaders, both succeeding military governments, dampened this rivalry, at least momentarily. If states such as these, should acquire nuclear arms, can countries such as West Germany and Italy forego them?

Domestic Politics.   A final reason states seek nuclear arms is related to domestic politics. In fact, such considerations may reinforce the other two reasons. A nation beset by economic and social problems and low morale may—if it possesses the technological capability—seek the bomb to boost morale, restore national confidence, divert attention from domestic problems, and, of course, mobilize popular support for the government. Great powers traditionally have held military parades to stimulate patriotic feelings, and Charles de Gaulle in France and Indira Gandhi in India benefited politically from national pride in the first French and Indian nuclear explosions, respectively. Although such a benefit may be only temporary, because it does not alter the domestic conditions that may underlie political unpopularity, that possibility does not lessen the incentive to join the nuclear club.

Role of Nuclear Reactors.   Security, status, and domestic politics are three major reasons for the proliferation of nuclear arms. The possible use of nuclear energy as an alternative to oil will provide those nations that want such arms with the opportunity to acquire them. The United States is no longer the only nation exporting nuclear reactors to produce energy. Such plants are very expensive, which means sizable profits, jobs, and an improved balance of payments for the exporting nation. The United States had 109 nuclear power plants in 1988; 272 plants were operating in the rest of the world. But since the late 1970s, the United States and such countries as Sweden have halted or slowed plans for domestic nuclear expansion. The Soviet nuclear power rupture in Chernobyl in 1986, which sent radioactivity across Scandinavia and Western Europe, intensified fears and concern about nuclear power. In the United States, opponents of nuclear power have resorted to referendums to try to close nuclear plants. The fear of a catastrophic accident is widespread. Another fear is that radioactive emissions will cause cancer and other health problems. In 1988 several U.S. nuclear plants making bombs were shut down after it was discovered that they were, in emphasizing weapons production, neglecting the health of employees and of those living near the plants, as well as the surrounding environment.[7] Sweden has decided to phase out nuclear energy, which had provided 42 percent of its electricity. The Soviet program may also slow as well. Other countries, such as France, which receives 65 percent of its energy from nuclear reactors, have continued to invest in nuclear energy.

The problem is that reactors that produce the energy to meet legitimate economic and industrial needs also yield the byproduct from which bombs can be built. This material can be recovered in three ways. First, the spent fuel from a nuclear power plant can be reprocessed and the critical plutonium extracted. Second, the uranium burned in these power plants can be enriched. And third, a plutonium-fueled breeder reactor, which produces more fuel than it consumes, can be used. Multiplying the number of reprocessing and enrichment facilities thus greatly enhances the prospects of raising the number of nuclear states:

> Civilian nuclear energy programs now under way assure that many new countries will have travelled a long distance down the path leading to a nuclear weapons capability. The distance remaining will be shorter, less arduous, and much more rapidly covered. It need take only a smaller impulse to carry them the rest of the way. There is a kind of Damoclean overhang of countries increasingly near the edge of making bombs.[8]

Likely Results of Diffusion

The diffusion of nuclear power may thus endanger the peace achieved with such difficulty and diligence by the United States and the Soviet Union. Admittedly, the possibility that more nations may acquire reactors does not mean that they will necessarily seek nuclear weapons. Whether they do so involves *political* decisions and depends on each particular nation's political circumstances and objectives. There is no technological momentum that automatically requires nuclear reactors to be followed by nuclear bombs. Several European states, as well as Japan and Canada, have both the reactors and the requisite nuclear skills but have decided not to build bombs.

Nor would diffusion have an equal impact throughout the world. A Japanese decision to go nuclear would have profound effects, a Swedish decision little. A small Indian nuclear force may frighten Pakistan, but it is not likely to intimidate China. An Israeli nuclear force may overwhelm Israel's neighbors, but it would not be effective against the Soviet Union. Indeed, one nuclear explosion does not turn a country into a nuclear power. A token nuclear force does not constitute a militarily significant force, which requires a credible delivery system and for many countries a much larger investment of economic and technological resources than for conventional military forces.[9]

Nonetheless, in a system of nearly 170 nations, the diffusion of nuclear weapons to perhaps twenty or thirty nations will raise considerably the statistical odds of nuclear conflict. It may be unfair to think of non-Western nuclear states as juvenile delinquents of some sort, but such thoughts are generated by the instability of some governments and the fanaticism of some leaders, which raise the specter of irresponsible behavior. Imagine what might have happened had Fidel Castro been in charge of Soviet missiles in 1962 or what Muammar al-Qaddafi might do with a few nuclear bombs. But, even if all leaders were stable, wise, and careful in their calculations, would they be able to avoid accidents or miscalculations in every single confrontation that might occur? Will some states that have acquired a few bombs not feel compelled to exploit this advantage and attack potential adversaries before the latter acquire their bombs? Will even the superpowers be safe? The relatively tiny forces that most potential nuclear states might muster do not appear to threaten the superpowers. Yet could not some of them perhaps "rip off an arm," to use de Gaulle's vivid term for what he thought his small French force could do to the Soviet Union? Would they not gain leverage even with a capability of destroying one or two of the superpowers' cities?

Strategies to Slow Proliferation

Technological Strategy.   One possible way to halt or slow nuclear proliferation is use of a technological strategy. The United States now refuses to export plutonium reprocessing and uranium enrichment facilities. To set an example for other nations, President Jimmy Carter announced in 1977 that within its own boundaries the United States would not use plutonium as a commercial reactor fuel. Congress, in fact, has approved a law banning economic or military aid to any country that sells or receives such facilities not subjected to adequate safeguards.[10] West Germany and France have sold nuclear fuel cycles in the past, though both have declared that they will not export reprocessing plants in the future.[11] The pressure to sell remains, however, because it is a profitable business. But there are other reasons besides profits. For example, France and especially Italy provided nuclear assistance to Iraq— a radical and militant anti-American and anti-Israeli state—until its war with Iran in 1979. Italy, which imported one-third of its oil from Iraq during the 1970s, was seeking to ensure long-term access to Iraqi oil.[12]

The basic approach, however, has been multilateral. The United States, Soviet Union, Britain, West Germany, France, Japan, and Canada have jointly devised a series of principles for regulating their nuclear exports. The seven original members of this Suppliers' Club (Belgium, the Netherlands, Sweden, Italy, Switzerland, East Germany, Poland, and Czechoslovakia have since joined) agreed that recipients of nuclear technology must apply internationally accepted safeguards drawn up by the International Atomic Energy Agency (IAEA) and that they must give assurances that they will not use these imports for making nuclear explosives, even for peaceful purposes such as excavation.[13] President Carter was particularly insistent on tighter safeguards and controls. He proposed that the IAEA inspect "all nuclear materials and equipment" of countries receiving nuclear fuel from the United States for their reactors so that closer supervision could be exercised over their nuclear energy programs. (India has been a major exception).[14]

But the IAEA is grossly understaffed; it can report violations but cannot apply sanctions. Indeed, it is questionable whether the agency is capable of detecting all diversions of nuclear weapons. For plutonium reprocessing and uranium enrichment plants, inspectors in residence are probably needed. Whether IAEA inspectors visit nuclear plants from time to time (after giving advance notice of their visit) or are stationed there all the time, the implementation of safeguards to ensure against the diversion of nuclear materials requires the cooperation of the nations possessing the nuclear reactors. Iran, for example, has forbidden any IAEA inspection of its nuclear facilities since the 1979 revolution. In addition, the IAEA is powerless to act even if it detects diversion. International indifference and inaction were the responses when the IAEA raised the likelihood that Pakistan might have diverted spent fuel to extract plutonium. The technological strategy may in fact be deficient even if all members of the Suppliers' Club cooperate. The club may find itself outflanked by the club of "nuclear outcasts," composed of states that are very insecure—such as Israel and South Africa. These states can help one another while evading international restrictions. In return for uranium from South Africa, Israel reportedly has shared its nuclear expertise. Other potential suppliers are Argentina, Brazil, India, and China.

Thus, it may be too late to turn back the technological clock. In 1980 the nuclear experts from sixty-six countries who had participated in the International Nuclear Fuel Cycle Evaluation concluded after two years of study that the U.S. strategy for curbing the diffusion of nuclear weapons' by banning the manufacture and use of plutonium was too late. A country could not be stopped from building a bomb by outlawing plutonium-based technology; too much scientific knowledge and explosive material were already available.

Legal Strategy.   In addition to a technological strategy, there is a legal one. For example, under the Treaty on the Nonproliferation of Nuclear Weapons (NPT), which expires in 1995, the almost 130 current signatories agree that if they are already nuclear powers, they will not provide nuclear weapons to other countries; if they are not nuclear powers, they will not try to manufacture nuclear devices. They will also accept IAEA-administered safeguards for their peaceful nuclear activities. This will ensure that nuclear materials are not diverted into weapons making. The legal strategy for halting proliferation involves gaining maximum adherence to the treaty. All Warsaw Pact countries are treaty signatories, reflecting Soviet concern about nuclear diffusion. The weakness of this approach is that any country can terminate its adherence to the treaty with only ninety days' notice. Furthermore, Argentina, Brazil, China, Cuba, France, India, Israel, Pakistan, and South Africa have not signed the pact. The majority of NPT members would not be able to build nuclear weapons anyway; of those capable of eventually producing such weapons, only a small number have signed.

It is worth reemphasizing in this context that IAEA serves only as a monitoring agency for verifying national accounting systems for nuclear materials. It is also an agency very dependent upon the good will of the nations whose facilities it is inspecting. A nation bent on cheating can probably do so. Some experts have suggested either a multilateral agreement banning the export of enrichment a᾽ ᵤ reprocessing plants or a market-sharing agreement guaranteeing each supplier country a minimum number of reactor sales a year as a solution.[15] This approach might at least reduce commercial competition and permit greater control by Western suppliers.

Political Strategy. Finally, there is a political strategy, based on ensuring the security of nonnuclear states. The question asked by such states is, "If we forego becoming nuclear states, who will defend us against possible nuclear threat or attack by neighboring states?" The answer is, "We [the United States or the Soviet Union] will." But neither superpower is in fact willing to make such a definite commitment. Vague pledges at the time the nonproliferation treaty was signed have not been convincing enough. American and Soviet reluctance to tie their futures to states they do not control and over which they may have little influence is understandable. But, as already stressed, so is the motivation of very insecure states to acquire nuclear arms.

The choices remain fundamentally political, rather than technical, as in the refusal to sell nuclear power facilities, and they are agonizing political choices because conflicting values and consequences are at stake.[16] A number of policy options are available. One is to protect the security interests of potential nuclear states by supplying them with conventional arms or giving them a sense of security through an alliance relationship with the United States. For example, the United States can reduce South Korea's or Pakistan's insecurity in these ways (although providing conventional weapons may risk starting a local conventional arms race). A second option is for potential rival states to try to settle some of their differences and perhaps even cooperate on specific nuclear programs. In recent years political talks between Argentina and Brazil have shown some promise. India and Pakistan have talked as well, but theirs is a long and bitter rivalry. The Nationalists on Taiwan and Chinese Communists on the mainland are also seeking to improve their relationship. In the Middle East, progress in the peace talks between Israel and the Arab states would help relieve regional insecurities, but the prospects for a resolution of Israeli-Arab-Palestinian differences do not look promising for the near future. A third option is pressure, which the United States applied to South Korea and Taiwan; it forced the latter to shut down its largest civilian reactor. In 1988 the United States urged the Saudis to sign the nonproliferation treaty as evidence that they had no intention of acquiring nuclear warheads for the medium-range missiles they had purchased from China. Americans were concerned that this might spark off a new Middle East arms race. The Saudis signed.

Thus, with the present state system, its anarchical nature, and the security problem that it poses for all member states, "there are no simple solutions that are feasible, no feasible solutions that are simple, and no solutions at all that are applicable across the board." [17] Or, as two physicists and one political scientist wrote:

> In the final analysis, it would be illusory to think that nuclear weapons proliferation could be severely limited by imposing controls on the sale of nuclear power facilities. The fundamental problem remains: minimizing the motivation nations have to acquire nuclear weapons altogether. This involves issues far beyond the realm of a nation's interests and involvement in the development of nuclear power to generate electricity. [18]

One hopeful sign in this respect is the nonproliferation treaty. It has become a politically powerful symbolic norm. Whether nations acquire nuclear weapons depends on their leaders' calculations of the gains and costs. If the strong international approval of the nuclear nonproliferation treaty is any evidence, they must take into account the increasing international disapproval for states with nuclear ambitions. Thus, security, prestige, and domestic motivations for seeking nuclear weapons must be balanced not just against financial costs and military advantage, but also against the widespread belief among nonnuclear states that states wanting such weapons are a threat to peace. The widespread global support for the nonproliferation treaty has raised the political price for acquiring nuclear arms, thereby perhaps lowering the incentive to do so, at least for some nations. It also maintains the pressure on the nonsignatories. Nevertheless, in the final analysis, as the states who have already acquired nuclear weapons have shown, the decision to have—or not to have—the bomb is very much a national decision, at best only marginally influenced by external pressures to forego it.

Will Proliferation Upset Superpower Arms Control?

Despite this important psychological barrier, the real issue is not so much whether nuclear proliferation can be halted but whether a world with multiple nuclear states is manageable. Today, it is possible to pursue the requisite technologies *covertly*, leaving the world guessing about a state's nuclear status. Pakistan and Israel are examples of this situation. And if the most that can be expected is the slowing of proliferation, can the nations acquiring nuclear weapons be stopped from using them?

The critical question is whether the deterrence that has restrained the superpowers can be replicated among the new nuclear states at the regional level. This seems, as already noted, dubious. It is unrealistic to assume that all future nuclear state governments will be stable and unsusceptible to civil wars, strong ideological passions, territorial designs, or "crazy" leaders; that they will be able to resist any temptation to preempt when either their missiles/bombers or their adversary's nuclear delivery systems are vulnerable to a first strike; and that accidental war or unauthorized use can be prevented. Indeed, rather than increasing a nation's security, the acquisition of nuclear weapons may result in the opposite. This was demonstrated in 1981 when Israel, fearing that Iraq might produce nuclear bombs to be dropped on Israel once a French-built reactor was constructed, attacked preventively. [19]

And not given the attention it deserves is the impact of nuclear diffusion on superpower arms control agreements. The Soviets have long expressed their concern over British and French nuclear forces; the latter particularly is being expanded rapidly. At some point, these forces will have to become part of a larger East-West agreement. While the Soviets have until now not allowed this issue to block U.S.-Soviet arms agreements, this may not be true in the future if the United States and Soviet Union agree on major reductions in their strategic forces. China's growing nuclear forces may also have an upsetting impact on the bipolar balance; if China's economic growth should continue, how large will its nuclear arsenal be? No regime complying with the Strategic Arms Reduction Treaty (START) can long ignore other nuclear powers, if only because the British, French, and Chinese missiles are aimed at Moscow, not Washington. Their buildups and superpower reductions will alter significantly the ratio between their nuclear arms and those of the United States and Soviet Union. In the absence of arms agreements among all the principal nuclear powers, if one of the two superpowers feels it must add nuclear weapons to maintain equality with all its potential adversaries, thereby upsetting the bipolar balance, the other superpower may feel compelled to increase its arsenal. This could upset the superpowers' arms control regime, even in a period in which the superpower rivalry may be fading.

DIFFUSION OF CONVENTIONAL ARMS

The possible spread of nuclear arms is still largely in the future. The spread of conventional arms, however, is a reality. The arms trade has been growing rapidly, symptomatic of the diffusion of power in the state system from the Western industrial states to the developing countries. During the 1970s, it also reflected the need of the Western states to earn money to pay for oil, as well as the continuing competition of the superpowers for influence in the Third World. Arms have become not only big business (for the Soviets as well as the West) but also a key instrument of contemporary diplomacy. Both the United States and the Soviet Union use arms sales to gain influence and compete for the allegiance of certain developing countries. Sales have also, in a sense, become a substitute for the traditional means of seeking these goals, such as alliances and the deployment of forces in other countries for their protection:

> Arms sales ... have become a key instrument of diplomacy for the weapons suppliers, in some cases the best one available to them. There has been a decline in the traditional instruments of reassurance and diplomacy, such as formal alliances, the stationing of forces abroad, and the threat of direct intervention. At a time when the major powers are less likely to intervene with their own armed forces, they are more prone to shore up friendly states through the provision of arms or to play out their own competition through the arming of their proxies. *A contributing factor has been the reduction of other instruments of diplomacy, such as*

> *developmental aid. Both the United States and the Soviet Union now give less in economic than in military assistance.*[20]

Size of Arms Sales

Several features about these arms sales are worth noting. The first is their sheer magnitude. Arms sales totalled more than $20 billion in 1980 (in constant 1977 dollars). The United States and the Soviet Union were the largest suppliers; in 1978 each sold about 40 percent of the total. French and British sales quadrupled during the 1970s. In fact, by the end of the decade arms sales accounted for more than half of their trade surpluses.[21] For the Soviet Union, arms sales became a major means of earning dollars with which to buy Western technology and food. From 1979 to 1983, the United States and the Soviet Union were responsible for 57 percent of the world total of arms exports. American exports of $40 billion were 28 percent less than Soviet exports of $56 billion; the Soviets accounted for one-third of all arms exported during this period. During the closing years of the 1970s, the Soviet Union exported more tanks, self-propelled guns, surface-to-air missiles, and super-sonic aircraft to the Third World than did the United States.[22] The 1985 shares of arms exports among the leading Western powers and Soviet-bloc states are shown in Figure 18-1. The sharp increase of American arms sales in 1988, almost equalling those of the Soviet Union, meant that the two powers accounted for two-thirds of all arms sold to the Third World. But China was the fastest growing arms supplier. Perhaps the only good sign is that the overall value of all arms by all suppliers had declined from $37 billion in 1987 to $30 billion by 1988, partly because the developing countries were still absorbing the tanks and planes bought earlier, partly because the Iran-Iraq War had come to an end, and partly because of declining oil prices.[23]

Expansion of the Arms Market and Suppliers

A second important feature of arms sales is the expansion of the arms market. Earlier arms transfers went from the superpowers to their NATO and Warsaw Pact allies. In the 1970s, members of OPEC with large trade surpluses, such as Saudi Arabia and Iran under the shah, bought arms from the United States and other Western states. Iraq and Libya bought their arms from the Soviet Union and the Eastern-bloc nations. Israel and Syria too received large arms shipments from the United States and the Soviet Union, respectively. By 1979 about 35 percent of all arms shipped to the Third World went to the Middle East. In 1983 the Middle East received 42 percent of the world's arms imports. Later, imports declined as oil prices fell. But in 1988 the United States, still concerned about the security of the Persian Gulf countries during the Iran-Iraq War, targeted them for advanced arms and equipment to counter the threat from Iran.

Other developing countries in Africa, Asia, and Latin America were also increasing their arms purchases during this period.[24] India, for example, signed a $1.6 billion arms deal with Moscow; Ethiopia, a very poor country,

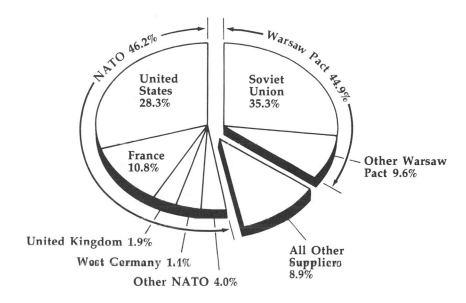

Figure 18-1   Shares of World Arms Exports, 1985

bought more than $1 billion in arms from the Soviet Union. All in all, more than three-quarters of the global arms trade now goes to the Third World. From 1977 to 1981, $128 billion in arms were delivered to the developing countries. By 1986, the developing countries were importing $180 billion in arms, a 40 percent increase in five years, although, as noted, there has been some decline recently.[25] Simultaneously, the developing countries have expanded their own arms production and sales dramatically. China, Brazil, Israel, and India, for example, have all become arms manufacturers, virtually doubling the size of their arms industries between 1981 and 1986. In the Third World, China and Brazil are in a class by themselves. China is a large-scale provider, in addition to missiles, of improved clones of Soviet-designed weapons of the late 1950s, and mid-1960s—simple, reliable weapons for developing countries armed forces. And Brazil is now the world's fifth largest arms exporter, producing such varied weapons as light tanks, armored cars and personnel carriers, trainer aircraft, and missiles. Communist Vietnam and North Korea are arms suppliers as well. Thus, the superpowers appear to be losing any control they may have had over arms distribution as the number of suppliers multiplies.[26]

'Conventional' Weapons

A third feature of arms sales is the character of the weapons. In many instances these weapons can hardly be described as conventional. If the adjective *conventional* meant *nonnuclear*, it was accurate; if it meant just *ordinary* arms—that is, surplus arms or obsolete arms—it was not always accurate. The arms sales of the 1970s, for example, often included quite sophisticated weapons, the same ones that were in the arsenals of the Western suppliers and the Soviet Union (for example, F-15 fighters and AWACS surveillance planes from the United States and MIG-23 fighters and T-72 tanks from the Soviet Union).

More and more frequently, conventional weapons have become anything but conventional. Many are precision-guided munitions or missiles (PGMs), which operate surface to air, surface to surface, and air to surface. Unlike the older generations of arms, which needed many rounds to hit the target, these new weapons usually require only one or two shots. They are guided to their targets by television, laser beams, or heat (infrared) rays. Also referred to as "smart bombs," they are becoming commonplace despite their technological sophistication. By modern standards, many of these weapons are reasonably priced, light, and ignitable by a small team. Because the weapons are highly accurate and not too expensive, they can make an attack very costly for the victim. When a $100,000 surface-to-air missile can shoot down a $35 million fighter, or a surface-to-surface missile costing a few hundred thousand dollars can hit a multi-hundred million dollar warship, the costs can be prohibitive, even for a major power, and will probably deter it from efforts to coerce smaller countries. For example, during the fighting in the Falkland Islands, $200,000 French Exocet missiles fired from French-built fighters, piloted by Argentinians, hit and destroyed a couple of British ships—one of which was a $50 million destroyer—from twenty miles away.

PGMs tend to favor the defense and make any military engagement costly because they destroy so much war materiel very quickly. Thus, the diffusion of modern arms should not be regarded lightly because they are conventional. In the 1973 Arab-Israeli war, the highly trained Israeli army and air force suffered enormous initial losses and were driven back by Egyptian and Syrian forces equipped by the Soviet Union with electronic warfare capability. Israel had none at the start of hostilities but later received the means for electronic countermeasures from the United States and reversed the early defeats. Nevertheless, the 1973 war was a dramatic turning point in modern warfare.

Given the prevalence of regional rivalries, this diffusion of modern weapons may tempt states to use force to resolve their differences or attain their ambitions. Examples include Argentina's 1982 invasion of the Falkland Islands and the subsequent war with Britain; the eight-year-long Iran-Iraq War; the war between India and Pakistan in 1971; and Syria's "assistance" in Lebanon in the early 1980s against Israel and the United States.

Proliferation of Missile Technology

One particularly worrisome matter in this respect is the recent ballistic missile race. In the Iran-Iraq War, Iraq used such missiles extensively to attack Iranian cities and to demoralize their people. China has exported missiles not only to Saudi Arabia but also to Iran, where they threatened U.S. warships in the

Persian Gulf. It has also supplied much of the technology for Brazil's missiles as well. Brazil's traditional rival, Argentina, was reportedly working with Italian and West German rocket experts. In fact, because the superpowers have eliminated their short- and intermediate-range missiles, China has a near monopoly on ballistic missiles with a range of 300-3,000 miles.[27] The missile used in India's space program, however, has been converted into an intermediate-range one. Israel too may have missiles to deliver warheads and it has reportedly helped South Africa develop its own.

In 1987 the United States, Canada, Britain, France, Italy, West Germany, and Japan, after four years of negotiations, adopted an important common policy to limit the export of all technology that might assist other countries in building missiles.[28] The fear, of course, was the mating of nuclear warheads and missile technology as more nations master missile technology. To the degree that nuclear materials and technological diffusion cannot be prevented, only slowed down, control of the means of delivering warheads is a second line of defense. Soon, however, it may no longer be true that a few simple bombs constitute a credible nuclear force; acquisition of missiles from China, for example, may create "instant" nuclear powers.

But a policy to limit the export of missile technology may already be too late, since the signatories, which do not include the Soviet Union and China, have no monopoly on missile production and states such as Libya and Syria may already have acquired missiles, in addition to Iraq and Iran. Even if Third World nations do not yet place nuclear warheads on their missiles, these warheads can carry poisonous gases. Such gases can be easily manufactured or bought in the international arms market. Iraq used chemical warfare regularly against Iran on the battlefield; in fact, Iraq was the first nation to do so on such a scale since World War I. According to U.S. observers, twenty nations are seeking to develop or already possess chemical weapons, and ten are thought to be moving toward biological warfare. What is disturbing about all this is that while Iran responded to Iraq with its own occasional use of gas (showing that such countries will use gas if they think it necessary) Iraq, the initiator and more frequent user, was not widely condemned by other states despite the fact that the use of chemical warfare had been outlawed by the signers of the 1925 Geneva Protocol. In short, the speed of missile technology, the availability of chemical weapons, and the apparent willingness to use them, are spreading to the underdeveloped countries, creating a dangerous world. In the Middle East, for example, the use of chemical warfare by such states as Iraq, Libya (said to have created the largest chemical weapons complex in the Third World), and Syria could seriously affect the regional balance of power.[29]

Like the spread of nuclear weapons, the diffusion of these "conventional" arms also has profound effects on the new strategic environment. First, the great powers must think twice about intervening against lesser states. Not only can the lesser states mobilize popular resistance but with PGMs they can destroy—at relatively low cost to themselves but at a prohibitive cost to the great powers—the latter's more sophisticated and expensive equipment, especially fighter planes and aircraft carriers. In short, the diffusion of PGMs contributes to the inversion of what used to be called the natural order of things—that is, a hierarchy with the great powers on top and all the others below.

Second, many of these smaller states are not only less powerful but also politically unstable and reckless. In any event, their acquisition of missiles is very dangerous. Perhaps someday packed with nuclear warheads, these missiles today can be packed with what has been called the poor state's bomb—poison gas. Iraq did not hesitate to use it against Iran (although neither of them was exactly poor, given their oil revenues). Given the lack of protest and sanctions against this usage, why should any country fear violating any possible future production ban? It is useful to remember here that in 1981 Israel bombed Iraq's almost completed nuclear reactor because of its fear that Iraq, despite its adherence to the nuclear nonproliferation treaty, might produce the bomb and use it against Israel. Given Iraq's prompt use of poison gas in what it initially saw as a desperate situation in the war against Iran, can it be doubted that but for Israel's peculiar policy of nonproliferation (a nonproliferation strategy that the United States considered using against the purported Libyan chemical plant in 1988 and 1989), Iraq might well have used a nuclear bomb against its enemy in the gulf? All this does not augur well for future regional conflicts.

Third, a longer-range and potentially more dangerous prospect is that the increasing diffusion of missile technology (or medium-range planes with air-refueling capacity, as Libya received from the Soviet Union in 1989) will give smaller states not only an enhanced capability to deal with neighbors and relatively close rivals but also a greater capability to deal with far more distant great powers. In the future small states possessing missiles and poison gas, and a real or perceived set of intense grievances, may be able to menace world peace as never before. An additional weapon, of course, available to such states and nongovernmental organizations with grievances is terrorism.

TERRORISM AS WARFARE

Concern about the diffusion of nuclear and conventional arms is matched by that about the widespread use of terrorism. Terrorism stems from the number of "just" causes and people determined to achieve their objectives, even at the cost of their own lives, in the contemporary world. And, in a world of multiplying ethnic and religious divisions, such causes seem to be increasing. As long as there are "just" causes, there will be groups who resort to terrorism because they believe that there are no legitimate ways to redress their grievances and realize their aspirations. Stemming from the Latin *terrere,* meaning "to frighten," terrorism seeks to achieve its goals by frightening those who appear to be standing in its way.[30]

Categories of Nonstate Terrorists

Nonstate terrorists fall into three categories. The first is the national liberation group or the so-called state-in-waiting. Most such groups resort primarily to guerrilla warfare. Examples are plentiful: the Communists in China; the Vietminh and Viet Cong in Vietnam; Castro's rebels in Cuba; the Sandinistas in Nicaragua; the former Patriotic Front, which sought majority rule in white-dominated Rhodesia and is now the government of Zimbabwe; the Afghan resistance to the Soviet Union; the Southwest African People's Organization, which in 1989 achieved power in a Namibia finally freed from South African control; and the Polisario, which wants to establish its own state in the western Sahara independent from Morocco. But some national liberation movements resort mainly to terror—for example, the Palestine Liberation Organization (PLO), which seeks a Palestinian state (although in the late 1988 it forswore the use of terror in words, if not in action); the Irish Republican Army, which wants a united Ireland; and several Puerto Rican groups, which are working toward an independent Puerto Rico.

The second category of nonstate terrorist is the revolutionary group, many of which exist within Western societies. Such groups proclaim their goals as the overthrow of capitalism because it is unjust domestically and aggressive internationally. They include the Italian Red Brigade, the German Red Army Faction, the Japanese Red Army, and the French Direct Action. Since late 1984, some of these groups and others have cooperated in attacks on NATO targets ranging from U.S. airbases to European arms manufacturers and bankers. Many of these terrorist groups have international links and do not limit themselves to actions only in their own countries.

The third category is ethnic or religious groups seeking either redress for past injuries or greater autonomy within a state, if not independence. Examples are the Basques in Spain; the Armenians, who have carried on their campaign against Turkey in both the United States and Europe; and the Sikhs in India, who have assassinated both its prime minister and, later, one of its moderate leaders. Sikhs are also suspected of blowing up an Air India 727 over the Atlantic Ocean in 1985 and of attempting to do the same with another plane. In the latter incident, the bomb went off after the passengers had deplaned in Tokyo.

Terrorism as Television Theater

To carry out their missions, terrorists resort to various means: assassination, seizure of embassies, hijacking of airplanes (even one ocean liner), kidnapping, and bombing. Although these acts are criminal in character, the groups' political aims make such terrorism a form of political violence. Fundamentally, terrorism is a weapon of the weak; the terrorists would lose a straight test of strength with the forces of "law and order." Terrorism—like guerrilla warfare—is consistent with Carl von Clausewitz's definition of war as the continuation of politics by other means.

As weak as they may be, terrorists wage their "war" by attracting publicity for their cause through their acts. Whether it is the seizure of an airliner or ship, the kidnapping of government officials or nongovernmental personnel, including tourists, or the murder of one or more individuals, these dramatic acts are viewed by millions on television and are covered by all the media. Television coverage especially provides an incentive for the performance of such acts. It offers a world stage on which the terrorists play and draw global attention, and the jet airplane allows them to strike quickly anywhere in the world and then fly to safety.

Terrorism is public theater in which there are no innocent bystanders. For the terrorists, everyone is a player; there are no distinctions between soldiers with rifles and tourists carrying Michelin guides. The audience may condemn their acts as senseless and brutal and decry these acts all the more when the victims are educators, clergy, and tourists. But these actions, while brutal, are not senseless or random; rather, they are the actions of fanatical advocates of a cause—not madmen—who know what they want and are often willing to kill themselves and others for this cause.

If the terrorists believe, rightly or wrongly, that a particular country—for example, the United States—is the cause of their grievances or blocks them from achieving their goal, they will consider *all* Americans guilty. Therefore, attacks on U.S. embassies or the seizure of diplomats or just "plain Americans" publicize their anti-Americanism. They are also intended to exact a cost, show the impotence of the United States because it cannot prevent such attacks, and undermine the legitimacy of the pro-American governments of countries such as Kuwait where such acts occur. Terrorists want people to feel helpless and defenseless and to lose faith in the government's ability to protect them. In the name of their cause, the ends justify all means.

Differences Between Terrorism and Guerrilla Warfare

While both terrorism and guerrilla warfare are the weapons of the weak, they are also very different. One need but list some of the leaders of guerrilla movements: Tito, Mao Zedong, Ho Chi Minh, and Fidel Castro. All were charismatic leaders. And all, except Tito, successfully organized the people in the countryside and by means of guerrilla warfare overthrew governments in power to become the heads of those governments themselves. Tito did it by waging war against German occupation forces in World War II. All became *national* leaders and symbols of their countries. They organized political discontent in their countries and pursued a long-term sociopolitical strategy, not just a military strategy, to capture power. Both in their own countries and widely outside their own countries, their cause was considered morally and socially just, the opposite of the government's position.

By contrast, terrorists are basically urban-based. Among the reasons for this are the anonymity of cities, the concentration of the media in cities, and, in the wake of their acts, the many hiding places found in cities. Terrorist leaders are seldom charismatic, and they do not pursue a broad-based strategy to arouse and organize the masses because in most cases their cause does not attract popular support. In fact, terrorists often wear hoods to cover their faces at television press conferences or when filmed in some act. Intimidation is the terrorist's stock in trade. For the guerrilla leader, terror may be used as an instrument as well, but it is not the basic reason for success. Indiscriminate terror as distinct from selective terror against government officials may alienate the mass support the guerrilla needs.

State Terrorism and Undeclared Wars

A new phenomenon appeared in the 1980s—terrorism by states.[31] The smaller states, with their relatively weak military forces, or their relative dependence upon external supplies of arms, find terrorism an attractive alternative to war. Terrorism expert Brian Jenkins has called terrorism a form of "surrogate warfare." He has also said:

> Finding modern conventional war an increasingly unattractive mode of conflict, some nations may try to exploit the demonstrated possibilities and greater potential of terrorist groups, and employ them as a means of *surrogate warfare against another nation*. A government could subsidize an existing terrorist group or create its own band of terrorists to disrupt, cause alarm, and create political and economic instability in another country. It requires only a small investment, certainly far less than what it costs to wage a conventional war, it is debilitating to the enemy, and it is deniable. . . .
>
> We are likely to see more examples of war being waged by groups that do not openly represent the government of a recognized state: revolutionaries, political extremists, lunatics, or criminals professing political aims, those we call terrorists, perhaps the surrogate soldiers of another state. Increasingly, there will be *war without declaration, war without authorization or even admission by any national government, war without invasions by armies as we now know them, war without front lines, war waged without regard to national borders or neutral countries, war without civilians, war without innocent bystanders.*[32]

Terror, then, shrinks the power differential between the United States and such countries as Iran, Syria, and Libya. Terrorists can do things governments cannot; moreover, the beauty is that governments that use terrorists as proxies can disavow them. Thus, through its support of radical Shiite Muslim groups such as the Islamic Jihad (Holy War) or Hezbullah (Party of God), Iran can seek to weaken, indeed eliminate, U.S. power from the Middle East-West Asia areas. Syria (an ally of Iran against Iraq), in seeking to bring Lebanon within its sphere of influence, can use such groups to undermine

American support for Lebanon's former pro-Western and pro-Israeli Christian-dominated government.* Or the Hezbullah can threaten to kill the American hostages it has seized if the United States takes some action that Iran does not like, such as sending warships into the Persian Gulf. Iran can officially repudiate such a threat, but obviously it would also benefit from U.S. restraint stemming from successful intimidation.

To the radical Shiite groups, the United States, the West's leading country, represents a secular civilization that has achieved great political, economic, and military power. It is also democratic, liberal, culturally preeminent, and dynamic, and it is spreading its influence to the Islamic world, which is weak, poor, and less developed. The 1979 seizure of the U.S. embassy in Tehran, and, during the 1980s, the bombing of the embassy in Kuwait (4 killed), the two bombings of the embassy in Lebanon (63 and 14 killed), the suicide bombing of the U.S. Marine compound in Beirut (241 killed), the attempt to blow up the U.S. embassy in Rome (foiled by the Italian police), and the kidnappings in Beirut of American citizens (only one of whom worked for the U.S. government and he was murdered) all testify to the fact that these Muslim radicals have seen themselves as waging an undeclared war against the United States. This anti-American pattern was practiced especially by those who followed the Ayatollah Ruhollah Khomeini. As the graffiti on a Beirut wall said, "We are all Khomeini." [33] To them, the United States was the "Great Satan," the devil to be exorcised. (None of this is intended to suggest that other Western states and friends were not targets; French and Israeli soldiers in Lebanon were also attacked.) Simultaneously, the Iranians wanted not only to revive but also to spread Islamic—and especially Shiite—civilization.

Many reasons are usually given for terrorist acts, such as U.S. support of Israel, revenge of a victim of retaliation (Israel's usual reason), and, not unexpectedly in a world of terrorists, the release of comrades who were captured and jailed. In the 1985 TWA hijacking, for example, the hijackers demanded that the Israelis return the Lebanese taken by them as they withdrew from Lebanon. The Israelis claimed that these Lebanese had been involved in acts of terror against their forces; whether or not the taking of such civilians was legal, the Israelis wanted to protect their soldiers as they withdrew. The Islamic Amal, whose leader was Lebanon's minister of justice and which took over the U.S. hostages when the TWA plane landed in Beirut, sought to equate the seized Americans with the Lebanese taken by Israel. The

---

*Because the United States intervened militarily in Lebanon's civil war, Syria supported the Sunni and Shiite Muslims and Druze factions, all pro-Arab. The 1983 attack on the American marine barracks with 12,000 tons of gas-enhanced explosives was organized in Syrian-controlled territory in Lebanon. It was either agreed to by the Syrians or, more likely, assisted by them, for this attack took careful planning and was carried out with military precision. Only an organization skilled with explosives could have assembled the bomb.

Americans were hostages, as the Lebanese were, and Amal demanded the release of the approximately 700 Lebanese for the Americans. This demand was obviously a rationalization for the seizure, not the reason for it. The Israelis had already begun releasing the Lebanese and had announced a quick release for the remaining prisoners.

There are literally thousands of reasons for terrorist acts; if it were not one, it would be another. The TWA hostage-taking was simply another blow to the United States, a humiliation all the more painful because it occurred at the same airport where U.S. Marines had been attacked, finally causing the United States to pull out of Lebanon in 1984. And once seized, the American hostages became central in a domestic struggle. The Shiite Muslims, represented by the Amal, are the largest population group in Lebanon, but long subservient to the Christians and Sunni Muslims. The hostage crisis thus offered the Amal the opportunity to enhance its influence. Neither Israel nor the United States was responsible for the Shiites' long oppression and backwardness. Nevertheless, they came to play a role in Lebanon's domestic power struggle.

Or, on December 21, 1988, a PanAm 747 with 259 persons aboard, most going home for the holidays, blew up over Scotland. According to ABC and Frontline public television investigations, this was an act of pure vengeance, instigated by Iran's former interior minister, for the U.S.S. *Vincennes'* mistaken shooting down of an Air Iran airbus carrying 290 passengers earlier that year. The act was carried out by the Popular Front for the Liberation of Palestine-General Command, an extremist anti-American group committed to the destruction of Israel. An additional motivation may have been that both the Front and Syria, where it was based and whose government it cooperated with in terrorist acts, also vehemently opposed the opening of diplomatic relations between the PLO and the United States.

State terrorism is not limited to the Middle East-West Asia areas. The North Koreans blew up most of South Korea's cabinet officers on a 1983 visit to Burma, and over the years that Qaddafi has been in power his gunmen have shot a number of exiled Libyan critics. President Ronald Reagan in fact accused Cuba, Iran, Libya, North Korea, and Nicaragua of sponsoring terrorism. Because Syria had just helped (for reasons of its own) to secure the release of the TWA passengers, Reagan diplomatically omitted naming Syria, although it cannot be excluded from such lists. South Yemen, a radical left-wing state aligned closely with Moscow, probably should be on such a list as well. Iraq, before its war with Iran, was also on the list.

Reprisals Against Terrorists

In 1984 Secretary of State George Shultz expressed the anger and frustration of most Americans when he said that the United States must not allow itself to become "the Hamlet of nations, worrying endlessly over whether and how to respond" to terrorist attacks. After the assault on the marine barracks in

1983, the United States, despite talk of retaliation, did not act. By contrast, the Israelis and French, who had also been attacked, did strike back.

The dilemma is obvious. On the one hand, if terrorists can carry out attacks and their victims remain passive, they are incited to further attacks to demonstrate their strength and the target's impotence. Only by exacting a heavy price can a nation discourage such attacks. On the other hand, punishment depends on knowing who and where the members of a terrorist group are, and then having the right means with which to retaliate. Even if one has that information, such as the whereabouts of the Iranian-controlled radical fundamentalist Muslims, how does one punish an enemy who deliberately surrounds himself with innocent civilians? Should this be allowed to discourage retaliation? A country such as the United States is restricted—and should be—by its standards of morality. The problem of retaliation is especially problematic when terrorists operate on another state's territory. Lebanon was too weak to expel the PLO; constant Israeli air attacks and an invasion to drive the PLO out left Lebanon in shambles. Its former pro-Western government collapsed; the civil war intensified among all its religious and ethnic factions; Syria gained dominant influence; and millions of formerly friendly Lebanese, especially the Shiites living in southern Lebanon on Israel's border, grew to detest Israel. This proved fertile ground for pro-Iranian terrorist groups.

In the case of state-sponsored terrorism, is the alternative to strike at the source? Does the United States really want to retaliate against an Iran or Syria? Obviously, the Reagan administration decided for political or military reasons not to do so during its tenure. It was willing, however, to attack a small country, Libya. Retaliation is not as easy as it appears; each act reverberates, sometimes in ways that cannot be controlled. Repercussions may range from violating one's own moral standards, to endangering relations with friendly states, to driving an unfriendly state into Soviet arms with even more damaging consequences. There are no easy solutions, and each case must be decided on its own merit. Moreover, there is no agreement among states about what to do. After the TWA hijacking, the Arab world protested against and the Europeans refused to go along with a U.S. plan to close Beirut's airport. For one party, a terrorist may be a freedom fighter; for another, inaction is at least unprovocative. Why act and buy trouble? When the leading TWA hijacker was caught in West Germany and the U.S. government asked for his extradition to stand trial in the United States, his friends in Beirut seized two German businessmen. Although the hijacker was not extradited, the West Germans did put him on trial. But even without such seizures, Europeans have preferred not to provoke terrorists, as was evident in 1986 when the United States struck Libya for its sponsorship of terrorism. Most U.S. allies refused to allow American bombers from England to fly over their territory. Because the British government gave its permission to use bombers based in Britain, it was widely condemned and may not grant such permission again. America's moderate Arab friends also protested.

Nevertheless, one of the ironies of this situation was its aftermath. Previous efforts by the United States to forge a common policy against Libya had been rejected. The Europeans had refused weak actions, such as reducing the personnel at Libyan "people's bureaus" or closing the embassies that were also being used to support terrorism, as well as stronger actions such as economic sanctions. Only after the United States, frustrated by this lack of cooperation, acted unilaterally, did the allies denounce Libya and restrict the numbers and mobility of Libyan "diplomatic" personnel in their countries. They felt they had to do these things to prevent those "crazy Americans" from using force again!

There are only three broad prescriptions on how to deal with terrorists: the incorrect way, the correct way, and the unlikely, if not impossible, way. An example of the incorrect way was the 1986 Reagan arms-for-hostages deal with Iran. The president had taken a tough public position that the United States would never deal with hostage takers because to reward terrorists would only encourage them to undertake further acts of terrorism, a position he had successfully pursued in several cases. He neglected to do so, however, in the case of the hostages seized by pro-Iranian groups in Beirut. Moved by their plight and the constant public pleas from the hostages' families, the president unsuccessfully sought their release by bartering with Iran. The successful way was demonstrated in 1988 when hijackers seized a Kuwaiti airliner to demand the release of fifteen terrorists jailed in that country—the same terrorists whose freedom was part of the price during the Iran affair. The Kuwaitis refused to capitulate even though the terrorists killed two Kuwaitis, dumped their bodies on the tarmac, and threatened to kill themselves and all their passengers. The hijackers finally released the latter in return for their own freedom.

The best but most unlikely prescription for dealing with terrorists is for the victim states to cooperate with all the economic and diplomatic means at their disposal against the states that sponsor or harbor terrorist groups. In 1989 the Israelis, tired of futile bargaining to get back three soldiers held captive by Hezbullah, kidnapped one of its major religious leaders and organizers, a man who among his accomplishments had seized an American marine colonel working for the United Nations in Lebanon. The terrorists demanded his immediate release. When Israel refused, the terrorists killed the colonel and provided the news media a gruesome video tape, which they claimed showed the hanging of the colonel. What could the United States do? Where in Beirut could special forces find Hezbullah leaders? Should U.S. aircraft just bomb entire areas where they might be hiding, killing hundreds or perhaps more innocent civilians living there? What would happen to the other hostages? Or should the United States attack Iran, jeopardizing the possibility of improving its relations with Khomeini's more pragmatic, less ideological successor? Obviously, a complete great-power economic boycott, a total ban on air travel to and from Iran, and political isolation by withdrawing recognition of Iran and by closing embassies would be effective means of pressuring Iran to end its sponsorship of terrorism. And if these measures fail, there are such steps as blockading harbors and attacking military and economic targets (oil storage and loading facilities, for example) to inflict severe economic damage. But such collective action against Iran (or another state sponsor) is not likely because of the fear of retaliation and business losses. Should the United States therefore act unilaterally? It did once against Libya, a tiny state, but not without condemnation by both allies and Third World nations. It has not been willing to take on a Syria or Iran, nations that might exact a higher price for an attack and are more capable of retaliatory action.

Future of Terrorism

Six factors favor continued international terrorism. The first is that present conditions in the world encourage terrorist tactics. These conditions include: the political fragmentation of states or unstable regimes in all areas and of groups holding grievances against the established order; commercial jets that provide both hostages and the means to transport them and their captors; states that are sympathetic to the terrorists and provide them training, money, and sanctuary; and mass media, especially television, that provide instant coverage and publicity for the terrorists' demands and causes.

The second is the trend toward smaller, lighter, more portable, more accurate, and cheaper weapons. Today, a small number of people can inflict the same kind of damage that earlier could have been inflicted only by large military units. These arms can be acquired relatively easily by terrorists. What is especially frightening is that some fanatical group may in the future steal or divert nuclear materials, sabotage a nuclear reactor, or threaten to blow up a city. One expert wrote:

> Sometime in the 1980s an organization that is not a national government may acquire a few nuclear weapons. If not in the 1980s then in the 1990s. . . . By "organization" I mean a political movement, a government in exile, a separatist or secessionist party, a military rebellion, adventurers from the underground or the underworld, or even some group of people merely bent on showing that it can be done.[34]

A fear that is almost as great is the use of chemical weapons, perhaps supplied by a state such as Libya to various terrorist groups. Even biological weapons may some day be used.

Third, modern industrial society is very complex and integrated, its fragile technology susceptible to breakdown and failure. If "natural" failures (such as the widespread power blackout in the northeastern United States in 1965 or the breakdowns caused by severe winter weather in 1977), labor strikes, or even peaceful demonstrations can cause major disruptions, the potential for sabotage and terrorism—bombs in buildings; destruction of industrial plants, hydroelectric stations, and nuclear reactors; or poisoning of urban water supplies—is frightening.

Fourth, terrorism is relatively easy to carry out against free societies. It is not surprising that terrorism is not heard of in totalitarian states. Their control of society is too pervasive and, even if a terrorist action occurred, control of the news media would prevent a leak. By contrast, terrorism flourishes in the environment of free Western societies with their ease of coming and going (aided frequently by lax airport security) and accessibility to the mass media. Moreover, the high regard for individual lives in Western countries eliminates the option of ignoring a terrorist's threat to murder hostages.

Fifth, state-sponsored terrorism may become used more widely by weaker states, allowing them to achieve objectives that before were attainable only by regular armed forces. This is particularly true against stronger adversaries. This kind of terrorism falls within the classical definition of war as a continuation of political activity by other means. The new battlefields—embassies, aircraft, city streets, power plants, and other vulnerable targets in a complex modern society—are novel and give the advantage to the attackers; they pick the target and time. Not everything can be defended at all times.

Sixth, terrorists have a vested interest in continued terrorism. On the one hand, terrorists genuinely hate their enemies, whom they see as the embodiment of evil. This makes it extremely difficult for their enemies to meet their stated grievances. On the other hand, within their own communities, those who wear the mantle of terrorism possess status and prestige and by their acts gain money for the organization. Given these conditions, terrorism is not likely to end soon.[35]

SUPERPOWERS AND REGIONAL CONFLICTS

The great powers have always been responsible for maintaining some kind of order in the international system through their bilateral and multilateral relationships, as well as through such organizations as the United Nations.[36] As the twentieth century ends, their responsibility for this task remains. Their own relationship in their adversary partnership has shifted, for the time being at least, from conflict and competition to cooperation and crisis-avoidance. The great powers have learned to cooperate with one another in more fully realizing their mutual security through arms control negotiations in both the nuclear and, increasingly, the conventional arms areas. Their overwhelming conventional power and their bipolar confrontation have made them cautious since the beginning of their conflict, and their additional huge nuclear arsenals have intensified this caution and have seemingly abolished war as a means of resolving their geopolitical and ideological differences. Both have realized that a nuclear war cannot be won and must not be fought. Thus, a great-power war—between them or their respective alliances—in the industrialized world is unlikely. Today, the problem of war lies in the Third World.

Causes of Conflict

There remain basically three causes of conflict in the Third World. The first is the historic competition among states. States in each region seek to become more influential than others and in the process generate friction. The Arab states, for example—especially Egypt, Syria, and Iraq—have long jockeyed for leadership of the Arab people, arousing intense rivalry among them. Because of the conflict with Israel, for about twenty-five years this rivalry revolved around who was the most militantly anti-Israeli and could lead the "holy war" to eliminate this alien entity from the Arab world. When Egypt, after four wars (all of which the Arabs lost), made its peace with Israel in 1978, it was shunned by the other Arab states. With Egypt isolated, Syria seemed to have inherited Egypt's status as the strongest Arab state.

But in the wake of the ayatollah's seizure of power in Iran, Iraq thought its moment had come. Before 1979, the shah's Iran had been pro-Western and had served as the protector of the Persian Gulf for the United States as American power declined after Vietnam. After the shah's overthrow, however, Iran was in turmoil; the Islamic republic had to consolidate its power against internal rivals. Its distrust of the officer corps, which had served the shah, was immense, and widespread purges were the result. In these circumstances, Saddam Hussein, Iraq's leader and a ruthless dictator, thought he could launch a war against Iran, defeat it, establish his control over the oil kingdoms fronting the gulf, and—with Syria supporting Iran against an Arab state—establish his claim to Arab leadership.

The second and third causes of conflict in the Third World lie in the ethnic, religious, racial, and linguistic divisions within so many of the new ex-colonial states. These internal schisms have given rise to two phenomena: irredentism and separatism. *Irredentism* is the movement by one state to incorporate within its boundaries the portion of its predominant ethnic group that has been separated from it as well as the territory on which that portion lives. Political borders, it is claimed, should coincide with ethnic entities. In the drive to reunite divided "peoples," frontiers become objects of conflict among the developing countries. For example, Somalia claimed portions of Ethiopia and Kenya. The claim against Ethiopia led to an undeclared war in which Soviet and Cuban intervention prevented Somalia from incorporating part of Ethiopia.

Separatism is a movement for self-determination. The new developing countries invoked this principle to legitimate their claims to independence from colonial rulers. But now it is being invoked against them by ethnic groups in their own populations, which could lead to national disintegration. An attempt to secede may lead to civil war as the government resists—as in Zaire after it became independent from Belgium (see Chapter 16). It can even lead to international war if another state becomes involved. For example, when East Pakistan sought to secede from Pakistan in the 1970s, its people were dealt with brutally by the Pakistani army; millions fled to India. The cost of feeding and caring for all these refugees was so high that war seemed cheaper. India therefore fought and defeated Pakistan and established the state of Bangladesh in what formerly had been East Pakistan. This move also weakened Pakistan so that it could no longer seriously rival India on the subcontinent. Some secessionist movements are successful, as in the case of Bangladesh. Others, however, such as those in Zaire, have failed. Some smolder and flare up once in a while or just continue year in and year out, like that of the Eritreans, who have sought to secede from Ethiopia for almost three decades, although negotiations to end the conflict began in 1989.

These three causes of conflict give rise to two types of war among the developing countries. One is the traditional interstate hostility; the other revolves around organizing the various ethnic groups into a new unified nation. Indeed, "the territorial integrity of many states, new and old, is now more threatened by separatist violence within their frontiers than by violence from the outside." [37] Most post-World War II wars have stemmed mainly from internal causes. This includes two wars that Americans have usually thought of as "international" wars: Korea and Vietnam. In the contemporary system, such civil wars include those fought in Afghanistan, Angola, Cambodia, El Salvador, Ethiopia, Lebanon, Nicaragua, Sri Lanka, and the Sudan. Interventions in these intrastate or internal wars have been twofold. One has been by mainly neighboring states: South Africa in Angola; Syria, Israel, and Iran (by means of terrorist groups) in Lebanon; and China in Vietnam. On occasion, the intervention has been by a more distant medium-size power such as Cuba in Angola and Ethiopia. The other kind of far more dangerous intervention has been by one or both of the superpowers.

In the postwar system their rivalry extended to all regional subsystems—such as the Middle East, Southwest Asia (Persian Gulf), or southern Africa—intersecting with regional interstate and national intrastate wars. As noted in the earlier discussion of preventive diplomacy (see Chapter 16), the superpowers have sought to exploit events in the various subsystems to expand their own influence or contain that of their rival. On occasion, one intervened preemptively in anticipation of the other doing so. Neither one knew that the other one would intervene, but, given the bipolar structure of the system, it was considered wise to try to beat the opponent to the draw. Repeatedly, especially in the Middle East, the United States and the Soviet Union internationalized local and civil wars. At some of the more dangerous moments, the United Nations played a critical role in terminating conflicts before they could escalate, although the international organization usually could not resolve the problem that precipitated these conflicts. The superpowers, by their support of rival states or factions in domestic quarrels, made settlements impossible and prolonged the stalemate among the parties to the conflict. A direct war between the superpowers and allies, then, may have become a diminishing danger, but war in the Third World clearly had not. In this context, the superpowers' history of competitive intervention posed an acute danger to the entire system. It was this realization that led them initially to cooperate in the United Nations' crucial preventive diplomacy. And they have both increasingly resorted to the United Nations in recent years to help them defuse their conflicts and differences.

Superpower Cooperation

Now that the danger of war has receded, opportunities for American-Soviet cooperation to make the Third World less combustible have arisen. The reasons are multiple. First, the nuclear balance appears to be stable. A START agreement could go a long way toward reducing the dangers of counterforce weapons and strategies, as could the deployment of mobile, single-warheaded missiles. One could even say with growing confidence that among the great powers there has been a "retreat from doomsday." Second, both superpowers face serious domestic economic problems. The United States must become more competitive with Japan and, increasingly, the European Economic Community. The Soviet Union faces an even worse crisis: communism as an economic system has been a failure. It will take time for both states to cope with these critical problems. Third, both superpowers have suffered severe setbacks, one in Vietnam, the other in Afghanistan. In the heyday of their global rivalry, the superpowers saw Third World conflicts largely as opportunities for increasing their power and administering a defeat to the opponent. Now both, having fought long, costly, and losing wars, are more skeptical about such interventions and are selective about where to become involved, especially with military force. They are bound to ask themselves more questions about the utility of military interventions in the Third World when it has become clear, contrary to all common-sense notions of power relationships, that all too often "great powers lose small wars." Thus, both American and Soviet habits are changing as they see few gains from such interventions and high costs in terms of lives lost, money spent, and loss of domestic and international support.

As the superpowers' confidence in the efficacy of force has been shaken and their internal problems have come to the fore, the saliency of Third World conflicts may be declining as their priorities change—although involvement in Third World issues that will affect them critically cannot be written off. But to the degree that each superpower has reduced its involvement in Third World subsystem conflicts, it has reduced the chances of the adversary's reactive or anticipatory intervention. Indeed, because each superpower's clients have become so costly and potentially dangerous, they have disengaged. The Soviet Union has done so in Afghanistan, and has pressured the Cubans to do so in Angola and the Vietnamese to pull out of Cambodia. Other settlements—for example, the Bush administration has been withdrawing from support of the contras in Nicaragua—may be forthcoming. If détente is to last, political resolutions of these regional quarrels must follow. Past interventions not only drained resources but also undermined détente I and progress on arms control.

The United States and the Soviet Union thus must reaffirm their special responsibility as the keepers of international order. But it remains to be seen whether they can achieve this by supplementing their current trend toward disengagement with cooperation on such central problems to the security of the entire system as the proliferation of nuclear weapons, missile technology, poison gas, terrorism, and regional rivalries in the Third World. They certainly cannot do it all by themselves. The United Nations, major regional actors (such as India), regional and subregional organizations, and secondary powers (such as the EEC members, China, and Japan)—described by one authority as "by definition their major potential rivals" but simultaneously also their potential "junior partners in their system of global management" [38]—all need to participate. To some degree they already do, as in the Suppliers' Club on nuclear proliferation and the recent missile technology regime, but this involvement needs to be expanded (for example, China should be brought into the latter regime). The changing superpower relationship may make it possible, at least for the moment, to advance toward greater international cooperation on systemic security. It is a hopeful sign that interstate and intrastate conflicts in the Third World are less likely to result in global nuclear conflagration. Nevertheless, even an end to the cold war, or a long respite from it, is not likely to end the potential combustibility of the contemporary world.

OBSOLESCENCE OF WAR?

The world may yet look back on the postwar nuclear bipolarity with nostalgia. In retrospect, it was a time of relative stability and peace. The nuclear superpowers learned to live together and through trial and error worked out the rules of coexistence. Moreover, they avoided war with one another, and in the center of Europe, the key front during the cold war and where they opposed one another with sizable armies, not a shot was fired. It is hard to believe that in the absence of the clear division of Europe and of nuclear weapons, none of the crises or the often tense situation in Europe would not have erupted in war. Although a World War III fought with conventional arms would not have been a desirable means of resolving the cold war, an even more costly repeat of World War II would presumably have been survivable. An all-out nuclear war, however, would have jeopardized the very existence and survival of the participants. Nuclear bipolarity imposed restraint and discipline on the foreign policies of the United States and the Soviet Union to a degree unknown to policy makers before World War I and German and Japanese leaders before World War II.

The changing strategic environment is therefore potentially dangerous. There are, however, two counterforces at work. One is the current détente between the superpowers which may last for a long time; indeed, the cold war, if not over, is certainly in remission. This, in turn may lead to closer

American-Soviet cooperation on such important issues as avoiding or resolving regional conflicts, which might in an earlier era have led to clashes, and preventing the proliferation of nuclear weapons, as well as the spread of dangerous conventional technologies such as missiles.

The other counterforce is probably even more potent and long-lasting: the growing rejection by the Western public of the use of force, at least for purposes requiring lengthy military involvements and heavy casualties. World War I forever changed the pre-1914 outlook that war was a natural, inevitable, and legitimate instrument for the resolution of key disputes between countries. Because this attitudinal change did not occur everywhere to the same degree, another global war was unavoidable, despite the bitter experiences of the Great War. It may well be true that democracies were not, as some have contended, more peaceful than undemocratic states in the nineteenth and early twentieth centuries. But since World War I, they have come to regard war as less legitimate; purposes other than self-defense are no longer considered grounds for resorting to war. And while the meaning of what constitutes self-defense may be stretched at times, if not occasionally ignored, the increasing scrutiny and questioning of Western elected governments make it difficult to use force for purposes that do not have widespread popular and legislative support. Not only were Britain and France reluctant to fight in the 1930s when they should have fought, but the United States was clearly unenthusiastic in both world wars to enter the fray against its enemies. This reluctance to resort to violence has manifested itself even more urgently since Vietnam (see Chapter 13). It is probably fair to add that among democratic countries today war is inconceivable. These nations include not only the members of the European security community, but also Canada, the United States, Japan, Australia, and New Zealand.

But perhaps "developed countries" should be substituted for "democratic countries." The Soviet Union suffered enormously in World War II, and the experience of Afghanistan is not likely to make it more eager to send its own forces, as distinct from proxy forces, into battle. Nor is the current economic crisis likely to add to its eagerness. This crisis, indeed, raises the question of how well the Soviet Union could sustain a protracted war against a major belligerent if the initial offensive strike fails to bring victory. The revulsion against war after World War I has become a general loss of appeal of war in the developed world:

> As a form of activity, war in the developed world may be following once fashionable dueling into obsolescence: the perceived wisdom, value, and efficacy of war may have moved gradually toward terminal disrepute. Where war was once casually seen as beneficial, virtuous, progressive, and glorious, or at least as necessary or inevitable, the conviction has now become widespread that war in the developed world would be intolerably costly, unwise, futile, and debased.[39]

Most of the wars since 1945 have occurred in the Third World. After the long, costly Iran-Iraq war, will the Third World follow the course of the developed world? Is there, as John Mueller, author of the above quotation, contends, a possibility that war will become obsolete? If the problem is seen as one mainly of wars among the developing countries, and if it is correct that many if not most of these wars originated in civil war, then perhaps democracy is the ultimate solution to war. As noted earlier (Chapter 9), one of the principal reasons for the frequency of civil war in the developing countries is the lack of alternative and legitimate ways to effect peaceful change. Force then appears to be the best means of attaining change and remedying perceived grievances. Thus the spread of democracy, where such change is feasible and governments are freely elected and responsible to public opinion, is likely to diminish one of the main causes of such civil disorder. Discontent is less likely to be so widespread and intense that it will threaten public order. But even if democracy is the "correct solution," what are the chances that it might prevail in the near future? At best, surely, this is a very long-term solution, if it comes to be a solution at all. In the meantime, a more urgent question is what can or will the large states, especially the United States, do to prevent smaller states—very possibly radical ones—from acquiring weapons of mass destruction and the means to deliver them?

Such a concern, however, should not detract from the most fundamental question: Is war really approaching obsolescence in a decentralized state system in which there exists no international organization with power superior to that of the member states, there are no agreed-upon and universally acceptable means for political change, and humanity continues to be divided into national entities rather than united by a common set of political values and emotional symbols? While the increasing cost of war in this century has led the democratic states at least to be reluctant to engage in major wars, it has been the U.S. alliances with Europe and Japan and nuclear armaments that were mainly responsible for the superpower peace of the post-World War II period. In any event, given the trends analyzed in this chapter, is a resort to violence any less likely in the future than in the past? As the cold war fades and as America hopes that the abnormality of international conflict will once more give way to harmony and peace among nations, it is well to remember that the history of the great powers when they were not actually engaged in fighting one another has been one of engagement in cold wars.

For Review

1. Can the proliferation of nuclear weapons be halted or slowed?
2. How will the diffusion of nuclear weapons affect the superpower arms control negotiations?
3. What will be the effects of the spread of conventional weapons, especially

missiles and chemical warfare, to more and more states?

4. What are the chances that the great powers will be drawn into the increasingly likely regional conflicts?

5. What is terrorism's role on the world scene?

6. Is war less likely in the future?

Notes

1. Robert Gilpin, *War and Change in World Politics* (New York: Cambridge University Press, 1983), 7; and Michael Howard, *The Causes of Wars*, 2d ed. (Cambridge, Mass.: Harvard University Press, 1983), 16-21.

2. Robert L. Paarlberg, "Domesticating Global Management," *Foreign Affairs* (April 1976): 571.

3. Josef Joffe, "Europe's American Pacifier," *Foreign Policy*, Spring 1984, 72 (emphasis added).

4. Richard Rosecrance, *Rise of the Trading State* (New York: Basic Books, 1986), xi.

5. John J. Weltman, "On the Obsolescence of War," *International Studies Quarterly* (December 1974): 413-414 (emphasis added).

6. See Leonard Beaton and John Maddox, *The Spread of Nuclear Weapons* (New York: Holt, Rinehart & Winston, 1962); Beaton, *Must the Bomb Spread?* (Baltimore: Penguin, 1966); Raymond Aron, "Spread of Nuclear Weapons," *Atlantic Monthly*, January 1965, 44-50; George H. Quester, *The Politics of Nuclear Proliferation* (Baltimore: Johns Hopkins University Press, 1973); Quester, "Can Proliferation Now Be Stopped?" *Foreign Affairs* (October 1974): 77-97; Lincoln Bloomfield, "Nuclear Spread and World Order," *Foreign Affairs* (July 1975): 743-755; Daniel Yergin, "Terrifying Prospect: Atomic Bombs Everywhere," *Atlantic Monthly*, April 1977, 47-65; Richard K. Betts, "Paranoids, Pygmies, Pariahs and Nonproliferation," *Foreign Policy*, Spring 1977, 157-183; Lewis A. Dunn, "Half Past India's Bang," *Foreign Policy*, Fall 1979, 71-88; Dunn, *Controlling the Bomb* (New Haven, Conn.: Yale University Press, 1981); Dunn and William H. Overholt, "The Next Phase in Nuclear Proliferation Research," *Orbis*, Summer 1976, 497-524; Ernest W. Lefever, *Nuclear Arms in the Third World* (Washington, D.C.: Brookings, 1979); Jed C. Snyder and Samuel F. Wells, Jr., *Limiting Nuclear Proliferation* (Cambridge, Mass.: Ballinger, 1985); Leonard S. Spector, *Going Nuclear* (Cambridge, Mass.: Ballinger, 1987); Spector, *The Undeclared Bomb* (Cambridge, Mass.: Ballinger, 1988); and McGeorge Bundy, *Disaster and Survival* (New York: Random House, 1988), 463-516, 525-535; Mitchell Reiss, *Without the Bomb* (New York: Columbia University Press, 1989).

7. Keith Scheider, "Chronic Failures at Atomic Plant Disclosed by the U.S." and "Seeking Victims of Radiation Near Weapons Plant," *New York Times*, Oct. 6 and 17, 1988, respectively.

8. Albert Wolhstetter, "Spreading the Bomb Without Quite Breaking the Rules," *Foreign Policy*, Winter 1976-77, 148-149.

9. Lefever, *Nuclear Arms in the Third World*, 9-11.

10. In 1979 it appeared that the United States might be relaxing its opposition to the use of plutonium by its principal allies (*New York Times*, Oct. 25, 1979). Also see Michael Brenner, "Carter's Bungled Promise," *Foreign Policy*, Fall 1979, 89ff.

11. On West Germany's plan, see Norman Gall, "Atoms for Brazil, Dangers for All," *Foreign Policy*, Summer 1976, 155-201; and Steven J. Baker, "Monopoly or Cartel?" *Foreign Policy*, Summer 1976, 202-220. On how the United States helped France develop its nuclear capability, see Richard H. Ullman, "The Covert French Connection," *Foreign Policy*, Summer 1989, 3-33.

12. *New York Times*, March 18, 1980.

13. *New York Times*, Feb. 24, 1976.

14. *New York Times*, April 28, 1977.

15. Abraham A. Ribicoff, "A Market-Sharing Approach to the Nuclear Sales Problems," *Foreign Affairs* (July 1976): 763-787.

16. Betts, "Paranoids, Pygmies"; and Lefever, *Nuclear Arms in the Third World*.

17. Betts, "Paranoids, Pygmies," 178.

18. Ted Greenwood, George W. Rathjens, and Jack Ruina, *Nuclear Power and Weapons Proliferation* (London: International Institute for Strategic Studies, 1977), 32. Also see Lewis A. Dunn, "Building on Success: The NPT at Fifteen," *Survival*, May/June 1986, 221-233.

19. Shari Feldman, "The Bombing of Osirag—Revisited," *International Security*, Fall 1982, 114-142.

20. Andrew J. Pierre, "Arms Sales: The New Diplomacy," *Foreign Affairs* (Winter 1981/82): 269 (emphasis added). Also see Pierre, *The Global Politics of Arms Sales* (Princeton, N.J.: Princeton University Press, 1982).

21. Richard W. Stevenson, "No Longer the Only Game in Town," *New York Times* (Business section), Dec. 4, 1988. On France, see Edward A. Kolodziej, ed., *Making and Marketing Arms* (Princeton, N.J.: Princeton University Press, 1987).

22. Arms Control and Disarmament Agency, *World Military Expenditures and Arms Transfers, 1984* (Washington, D.C.: Government Printing Office, 1985), 18.

23. Robert Pear, "U.S. Weapons Sales to Third World Increase by 66%," *New York Times*, Aug. 1, 1989.

24. Kolodziej, *Making and Marketing Arms*, 8. Also see Morton S. Miller, "Conventional Arms Trade in the Developing World, 1976-1986: Reflections on a Decade," in ibid., 20-22.

25. George P. Shultz, "Proliferation and the Third World," in Arms Control and Disarmament Agency, *Arms Control Update* (Washington, D.C.: Government Printing Office, 1988), 2.

26. Stephanie G. Neuman, "Arms, Aid and the Superpowers," *Foreign Affairs* (Summer 1988): 1044-1066, for the view that military aid is a potent tool for the superpowers in enhancing their control over the developing countries.

27. James L. Tyson, "U.S. Tries Again to Staunch China Arms Flow," *Christian Science Monitor*, Aug. 4, 1988.

28. Frederic J. Hollinger, "The Missile Technology Control Regime: A Major New Arms Control Achievement," in Arms Control and Disarmament Agency, *Arms Control Update*, 25-27.

29. David B. Ottaway, "Middle East Weapons Proliferate," *Washington Post*, Dec. 19, 1988; and Bernard E. Trainor, "Chemical Warfare: Specter Looms Around the World," *New York Times*, Aug. 5, 1988.

30. Walter Laqueur, *Terrorism* (Boston: Little, Brown, 1977). Also see Claire Sterling, *The Terror Network* (New York: Holt, Rinehart & Winston, 1981); Yonah Alexander, *International Terrorism*, rev. ed. (New York: Praeger, 1981); Benjamin Netanyahu, *Terrorism* (New York: Farrar, Straus, Giroux, 1986); and Donna M. Schlagheck,

International Terrorism (Lexington, Mass.: Lexington Books, 1988).

31. Ronald Reagan, "The New Network of Terrorist States" and Robert B. Oakley, "Terrorism: Overview and Developments," Current Policy No. 721 and 744, respectively (Washington, D.C.: Department of State, 1985).

32. Brian M. Jenkins, "High Technology Terrorism and Surrogate War: The Impact of New Technology on Low-Level Violence," in *The Other Arms Race,* ed. Geoffrey Kemp, Robert L. Pfaltzgraff, Jr., and Uri Ra'anan (Lexington, Mass.: Lexington Books, 1975), 102 (emphasis added).

33. Daniel Pipes, "Undeclared War," *New Republic,* January 7 and 14, 1985, 12-14; and Pipes, "Fundamentalist Muslims," *Foreign Affairs* (Summer 1986): 939-959. For a recent "inside story of America's war against terrorism," see David C. Martin and John Walcott, *Best Laid Plans* (New York: Harper & Row, 1988).

34. Thomas C. Schelling, "Thinking About Nuclear Terrorism," *International Security,* Spring 1982, 61.

35. Conor Cruise O'Brien, "Thinking About Terrorism" *Atlantic Monthly,* June 1986, 62-66.

36. Very helpful for this section were Robert S. Lutwak and Samuel F. Wells, Jr., eds., *Superpower Competition and Security in the Third World* (Cambridge, Mass.: Ballinger, 1988); Evan Luard, "Superpowers and Regional Conflicts," *Foreign Affairs* (Summer 1986): 1006-1025; Shahram Chubin, "The Superpowers, Regional Conflicts and World Order," in Adelphi Papers 237, *The Changing Strategic Landscape,* part III, 74-93; and Hedley Bull, *The Anarchical Society* (New York: Columbia University Press, 1977).

37. Bull, *Anarchical Society,* 197.

38. Bull, *Anarchical Society,* 229.

39. John Mueller, "The Essential Irrelevance of Nuclear Weapons: Stability in the Postwar World," *International Security,* Fall 1988, 78.

CHAPTER 19

The Primacy
of Realism

It is hardly surprising that theories about international politics have centered on the problem of war, the most traumatic event a nation can experience.[1] Thus, the causes and consequences of war, its possible elimination, or at least the reduction of its frequency have dominated these theories. The increasing horrors and costs of war in the twentieth century have accentuated this trend, which began in the nineteenth century with greater citizen participation in politics, the growth of nationalism and industrialization, and the invention of ever more efficient and destructive weapons. The birth of the nuclear age in 1945 intensified the search for solutions to the problem of war; without such a solution, the human race faced the very real possibility that it might not survive. Despite the contemporary optimism, stemming from the real possibility that the cold war may be fading fast and that war among the great powers is obsolete, can one really believe that the future will be radically different from the past? Will international politics in fact be so transformed that for the first time in history the issue of war and peace will no longer be the central issue among states?

FIRST LEVEL REVISITED

At the first, or state-system, level of analysis of international politics, war is explained by the anarchical environment in which states live. In the absence of a world government to settle disputes, each state must rely on its own capabilities to protect its national interests and remain secure. States seek to enhance their security by increasing their power, or, more accurately, they try to reduce their sense of vulnerability to the potential actions of other states. They may not succeed in this enterprise, however, because other states are also seeking security in the same ways. The result is a "security dilemma" in which one state's activities give the others no choice but to follow suit, perhaps leaving all of them less secure. The security dilemma describes succinctly the trap created by the anarchical structure of the state system. War is embedded in this structure.

Some scholars of international politics attempt to resolve the problem of war by transcending the state system and creating a world government. Others, who recognize that this prescription may be theoretically correct but unachievable in the real world, try to find cures within the framework of the state system. Among these cures are declawing states through disarmament, denationalizing them through cooperation within a universal organization, and, more recently, according to the logic of interdependence, taming states "from which the sharp teeth of sovereignty have at last been drawn" and "the parochial interests of the past have been replaced by the planetary interests." [2]

As states moved from functionalism, with its expectation of an automatic process in which separate countries would be politically integrated into larger security communities (first on a regional level, then on a global level), to interdependence, it was expected that economic and technological forces would override political, cultural, and national differences. Instead, the state system persists, and state behavior has not essentially changed. So far, none of the various political or economic prescriptions has proved capable of solving the recurring problem of war. In the anarchical environment that persists, the truth is that conflict and the possibility of war cannot be abolished. *The best that can be achieved is management of the system to minimize the possibilities of outbreaks of the most violent forms of war.* Such management is an ongoing process that promises no end to the problem of war.

This conclusion has never been accepted by liberal intellectuals, however. Michael Howard, a renowned British military historian, has commented that since the eighteenth century, liberal intellectuals have blamed war upon either the stupidity or self-interest of governing elites. War was obviously "a pathological aberration from the norm, at best a ghastly mistake, at worst a crime." [3] Inherent in this view was the notion that if sensible people controlled governments, war could be abolished. This idea implied a shift in emphasis from the environment in which states exist to the character of the states themselves and of the people who govern them—that is, to the second and third levels of analysis. A reluctance to accept the inevitability of war— or that the best states can do is to manage the system skillfully enough to prevent all-out war—led to the countereffort to eliminate war by thinking about it at the second or third levels. Bad states and bad leaders were to blame. Eliminate them and the problem of war would go away; reason and peace would prevail. Kenneth Waltz has called this method of resolving problems *reductionism.* [4]

There has been no shortage of states whose internal political systems were thought to cause war. During the eighteenth century, kings and the aristocracy were responsible, and war benefited only them. The French Revolution posed a solution to war: eliminate the warmongers, and reason, not force, would resolve interstate conflicts. The rule of monarchs and aristocrats was to be replaced by democracy in which the people would elect their rulers and then hold them accountable. Because ordinary people pay for wars with their lives and their tax money, they would be interested in preserving the peace. Democracy was by nature peaceful.

Liberal thinkers also recommended that all nationalities live within their own natural boundaries because, they asserted, it is unnatural for human beings to be organized on any basis except national identity. The map would have to be redrawn so that people could live in political units based on the principle of nationality. If the nature of the internal political system was the cause for war, then democracy and national self-determination would abolish war.

Marxist thinkers did not agree with these remedies. War could not be eradicated by establishing so-called democratic governments, for behind democracy's facade ruled a small class of capitalists or bourgeoisie who exploited their fellow citizens. For true democracy to bloom, according to the Marxists, the proletariat must gain control of the state, and this could be achieved only through revolution. Many non-Marxist thinkers, not sharing the belief that capitalism is inherently warlike, focused on political control of the "merchants of death."

AMERICAN EXPERIENCE AND THE ELIMINATION OF WAR

Marxist thinking on the elimination of war did not have much appeal for Americans, but liberal thought found a congenial reception. The belief that war was a permanent feature of existence was simply unacceptable; most Americans considered conflict and war abnormal, temporary, and avoidable. Balance-of-power thinking was generally considered "un-American," when it was not ignored altogether. This was not surprising. The United States had long been isolated from Europe, and its own domestic experiences and values shaped American thinking about international politics. The United States was a liberal society that placed value on individualism, private enterprise, and political democracy. This contrasted strongly to Europe, which had not only a liberal tradition but also conservative and socialist traditions. Liberalism therefore never established its supremacy; balance-of-power thinking retained its influence, especially among policy makers.[5]

Furthermore, once the United States was forced to give up its isolationism, the American experience in international politics confirmed the nation's liberal assumption about war. The countries that provoked or attacked the United States were led by authoritarian and antidemocratic men: the kaiser in World War I, Hitler and Tojo in World War II, and Stalin during the cold war. In war the goal of the United States was first the total defeat of the enemy and then the establishment of democratic governments, trusting the good sense of the citizens to avoid future wars. "Power politics" was to be banished once and for all; the world would be made peaceful by democratizing it.

Indeed, the Treaty of Versailles, drawn up at the close of World War I, embodied liberal thinking on international politics. National self-determination and the establishment of democracy were the basic principles underlying the treaty. The result was a redrawing of the map of central and southeastern Europe, leading to the rise of a number of new nations from the ruins of Austria-Hungary. Moreover, because the Allies insisted that they would deal only with a democratic Germany, the kaiser abdicated and a new democratic government was formed. Many Germans believed that democracy itself, in the form of the Allies, was responsible for imposing upon them a punitive peace treaty and a new form of government, which they were forced to accept.

National self-determination and democracy came together in the establishment of the League of Nations. "Open covenants of peace, openly arrived at" was President Woodrow Wilson's slogan. The peoples of all nations could watch their governments at work on the world stage and could hold them accountable. They would know what their leaders and diplomats were doing and have all the information necessary to determine who was the aggressor in any situation; the days of irresponsible elites and secret diplomacy were over. Democracy and peace were to be the wave of the future, as a pacific and informed world public opinion would prevail. The league, and later the United Nations, would deter aggression, punish any transgressors, and maintain law and order among the community of nations.

All the liberal assumptions about how to preserve the peace proved to be wrong. Indeed, experiences prior to World War I had already shown how flimsy these assumptions were. From 1815 to 1914 Europe had suffered no total wars; wars in the nineteenth century were limited in objectives, casualties, and duration. Diplomacy, largely secret, minimized the effects of public opinion. Negotiations were conducted by an aristocratic elite, which, because they spoke a common language, shared a code of conduct, mixed socially, and intermarried, also avoided misunderstandings. The assumption underlying the nineteenth-century European system was that the great powers were responsible for maintaining peace because they had the power to do so. No single great power tried to conquer or destroy another; the overall pattern was one of cooperation and restraint. For most of the century, the memory of Napoleon and his unleashing of a total war that had lasted twenty-five years cautioned all the principal European powers to compromise and to limit the purposes and intensity of force, if force was used.

In the late nineteenth century, however, public opinion began to increasingly affect the conduct of foreign policy. Popular involvement in foreign policy encouraged jingoism and bellicosity, not pacifism, and, once aroused, nationalistic enthusiasm made it more difficult for governments to practice restraint. This was as true for the European democracies as for the great autocracies of Russia, Austria-Hungary, and Germany. Moreover, the rise in popularity of a moderate social democratic party in Germany aroused the fear of revolution in the aristocracy as well as among the industrialists and bankers, whose answer was a "strong" foreign policy in Europe and colonialism overseas. By encouraging nationalism, the upper classes sought to avoid what they regarded as a dangerous domestic situation. The fear of revolution had a similar effect on the rulers of Russia and Austria-Hungary. Even in the United States at the turn of the century, jingoism, aroused by William Randolph Hearst's newspaper chain, was basically responsible for the Spanish-American War. President William McKinley had tried to avoid war with Spain, but an aroused public and Congress forced his hand.

Nor did national self-determination play the peace-keeping role envisaged for it. Although World War I had been precipitated by the nationalist aspirations of many of the ethnic groups in the Balkans and was fought in part to remedy these boundaries and unite nationalities, the wisdom of this solution was soon subject to doubt. The unification of Germany proved to be a disaster for all of Europe. Nationalism in Germany, as well as the nationalism of its neighbors, confounded even the Marxists. Having claimed that the working classes had no interest in supporting the nationalist causes of the capitalists and that working-class loyalty was to the workers of other lands, the Marxists were shocked when the social democratic parties everywhere voted funds for a war.

Once World War I was over, it was public opinion in the democracies that destroyed any chance of a lasting peace. French and British public opinion insisted on a punitive peace treaty that included a German "war guilt" clause and the imposition of astronomic economic reparations. By imposing this treaty on the new and fragile German democracy, the Allies ensured that Germans would associate democracy with defeat, and they provided Hitler with a means to condemn German democracy and to keep alive hostile feelings toward the Allies. Having exacted revenge, Allied opinion then turned pacifist. It was the hideousness of the war that transformed the democracies' attitude. Germany, a fascist state, did not share its neighbors' doubts about the continued legitimacy of modern warfare; it exploited their fears and doubts. Hitler, too, had a popular following.

Postwar Realism

Failure of the democracies to maintain peace was the main reason that realism gained intellectual respectability in the United States. World War II offered proof that the dream of subordinating national conflicts to the broader interests of humanity was not shared by all states. The power struggle among nations was all too evident, and democracies, if they wished to defend themselves, had to play power politics too. The wartime dream that the United Nations, the embodiment of hopes for a world community, would preserve the peace better than the League of Nations had faded quickly as the cold war began.

The United States, however, could tell itself that it was not behaving as states historically have behaved and thus keep its conscience clear. The postwar bipolar struggle involved both power and ideology, and the United States could practice *Realpolitik* while disguising it as another moral crusade. This was also the period of liberal Democratic administrations, "cold war liberals" as they were called. Liberals in the executive and legislative branches were quite willing to assert U.S. power and to use force, precisely because they were liberals. Committed to the freedom and dignity of the individual and social justice at home, they were equally committed to the defense of liberty against totalitarianism overseas. To be a "hardliner" and support the containment of Soviet or Chinese power was not considered a betrayal but an affirmation of liberal values. Only after the Vietnam War did domestic liberalism disassociate itself from a strong anti-Soviet interventionist stance. But it did not take long for the American penchant to crusade—to moralize international politics—to find a new outlet in interdependence and the building of a new world order beyond the balance of power.

In academic circles, the reaction to realism came earlier, in part because Hans Morgenthau, who had presented the realist position so articulately in his 1948 book *Politics among Nations,* was an easy target. His critics charged, among other things, that to Morgenthau power appeared to be an end, not just a means, and that his use of the term *national interest* suggested that there was always an objective, discoverable, and "correct" policy. He was said to subordinate morality to power, and his prescription of a balance of power, diplomacy, and prudence was said to hold no greater promise of avoiding a future war than it had in the past. Only the next war would be a nuclear war. In part, the criticism of realism also reflected the desire to try new approaches as older ones became familiar and perhaps boring, but in large part it was moral. Realism's tolerance of continued conflict and war was simply unacceptable. Postrealism's multiple perspectives once more reflected liberal ideas of the causes and cures for war.

In a liberal society it is not really surprising that liberal assumptions should be *implicit* in the study of politics, whether domestic or international, even if researchers appear unaware of the influence of these assumptions and believe that they are carrying on objective and scientific work.[6] To be sure, studies of international politics claim to be scientific. But no matter how carefully researchers assemble and quantify the data, the researchers' purposes will affect their conclusions. Purpose and analysis are inseparable. Data can be explained in a number of different ways; in themselves they have no meaning. But how they are selected, the importance assigned to them, and how they are organized and interpreted depend on the perspectives brought to a particular study.

Reaction to Realism

Two of the postrealist approaches consisted of examining the decision making practiced by leaders and trying to understand their perceptions. Both approaches were concerned with states' domestic policy processes, and in both the state system played a very subordinate role. Decision making, or bureaucratic politics, was essentially a resurrection of the group approach to explain American domestic politics and a reflection of the American pluralist tradition. When this was placed in the context of the foreign policy arena, policy was seen as evolving from the interactions among the various institutions, each with its own policy preferences. This shift of focus in the study of international politics from the external arena to the policy process within the state meant that if a policy were judged "defective," the necessary changes in organization or procedure could be introduced. For example, if there were a tendency among top policy makers to "groupthink," a devil's advocate might be brought in to challenge the assumptions underlying official policy. Policy problems could be resolved by organizational reforms.[7] The second reaction to realism, the emphasis on perception, meant that "wrong" policies could be attributed to misperceptions and, therefore, to misunderstandings. Policy should not be dominated by "diabolical enemy images," mirror images, or other forms of distortion. Rational—that is, correct—perceptions should govern policy makers if conflict is to be avoided. A solution to the problem of war would be found in domestic politics, psychology, and classical economies in their contemporary form—interdependence and regimes.

After its brief fling with *Realpolitik*, then, the American study of international politics once more embraced the reductionist orientation embodied in the traditional perceptions known as "national style." As political scientist John Weltman has perceptively remarked about some of the contemporary debate:

> Great contemporary controversy revolves around that complex of questions relating to: the survival and viability of the nation-state; the interdependence of nations; the role of force; the importance of the "high political" or strategic, as opposed to "low-political" or welfare concepts and issues; the significance of economic matters; the dominance of "North-South" concerns as opposed to "East-West" issues. *Empirical investigation is only superficially useful in answering this complex of questions.* When examined carefully, the positions of the participants in these controversies resolve themselves into modern versions of ancient outlooks.[8]

Those who emphasize the obsolescence of high politics basically represent the old utopian or idealist camp in its continuing quarrel with realism.

The fact that all the issues Weltman lists are often debated suggests that realism is still under siege. For many American scholars, international politics has become the politics of world order. The primacy of the state is rapidly disappearing in a welter of transnational nongovernmental organizations and intergovernmental organizations. The national interest, with its egotism and selfishness, has been (or must be) restrained by the new interdependence and regimes. And the self-help of states has been replaced by the search for a more moral and just world through disarmament, the abolition of world poverty, and the fulfillment of universal human rights. Military power has lost its crucial role as security issues have become subordinated to welfare issues and conflict between states has given way to cooperation for the collective interests of all humankind. Indeed, to many scholars and commentators, an emphasis on the lay role of military power in international politics in any context other than arms control, especially in East-West relations, is a mark of not only a lack of sophistication but also a misunderstanding of international politics. Nuclear technology has, in any event, made great-power wars a thing of the past.

Economic Peace or Pax Atomici?

That power politics and war are obsolete is hardly a novel conclusion in the age of economic interdependence. In 1910 Norman Angell's best seller, *The Great Illusion*, argued that war between modern industrial states had become an anachronism because it would be economically ruinous. Four years later, Germany was at war with two of its most important trading partners, Russia and Britain. The war proved Angell correct about the enormous cost in lives and economic resources. But the thesis that war and an industrialized society are incompatible is more than a mere reflection of the cost of war; the thesis rests on the conviction that uninterrupted commerce will realize what is the true interest of all states: the peaceful enjoyment of material progress. It is this economic enrichment that benefits all states and makes war obsolete. The eighteenth-century French philosophers (whose views were reflected in the institutions of the young United States) and the nineteenth-century British utilitarians had argued that modernization was playing the same role that war had played in preindustrial society.[9] This identical faith that human reason will give primacy to the common interest of humankind persists today.

How ironic it is then that "the bomb" is the foundation for the contemporary abstinence from war of the great powers. Because Americans regard war as an aberration, once provoked they fight to eliminate war itself, as in the two world wars. Aggressors must be punished so severely that they would never dare attack the United States again. Deterrence fits this approach exactly. Its purpose is to prevent war, but, should that fail, the United States is prepared to retaliate so that the enemy's industries and population will be utterly destroyed. The bomb carries the American concept of war to its logical conclusion: total elimination of the enemy. The irony is all the greater because the bomb may be the means *par excellence* to finally realize the American dream of abolishing war for all time.

CONTINUING NEED FOR REALISM

Reductionist approaches to international politics are very appealing for one reason: namely, they allow proponents to project their own solutions upon a rather intractable world. Systemic explanations offer far more understanding. This is not to belittle explanations at the second and third levels, merely to place them in context. The behavior of states—as well as of nonstate actors—can be analyzed and understood only in terms of the system or environment in which they live. A focus on the nature of states obviously concentrates on the individual member of the system, not on the system as a whole. Such factors as political systems, national and elite styles, class structures, and the process of decision making should not be neglected in any analysis of how states behave. *But any theory of international politics will be inadequate if it ignores the dominant influence of the state system and the security dilemma.* States have no choice about their concern for security and, indeed, survival. The system may not determine their behavior, but it does condition it. And from the anarchical nature of the state system everything else flows: the need for states to pay attention to their power, to maintain an equilibrium, and to be aware of the ever-present dangers of conflict and war. It is easy to understand why all this is condemned as immoral power politics, a denial of all civilized values, but it does not eliminate the need for states to "play the game."

Power politics is not some passing phase of international politics, a relic left over from the 1940s and 1950s. The Founders, notably Alexander Hamilton, were realists. More recently, realism was brought to America's shores by refugee scholars from Europe. Hans Morgenthau and Henry Kissinger, both from Germany, are the best-known proponents from the academic and diplomatic worlds, respectively. Kissinger once said that when he hears the phrase "balance of power" in the United States, it is usually preceded by such words as *old-fashioned* and *former*, as if the balance were irrelevant, of historic interest only. To be sure, these and other refugee scholars, as well as American scholars, emphasized the role of power, including military power, in international politics—an emphasis alien to an American tradition rooted in legal and moral concepts of law, human rights, and justice. Nevertheless, the United States learned to play power politics, even if reluctantly, after its long isolationism and during its deep involvement in the post–World War II world. Many American scholars, however, have refused to accept the role of force and have sought, using mathematical techniques and other social science methods, to eliminate it through peace research, conflict resolution studies, and world order modeling. More broadly, the hope today is that the problem of war has been eliminated because the American-Soviet conflict appears to be ending and nuclear weapons have neutralized each superpower.

The primacy of the state system should make any observer wary about the future abolition of violence and war. Nevertheless, the emphasis on the importance of contemporary economic interdependence should not blind one to the real limits to any possible reforms of the system and behavior of states. The proponents of interdependence are not so much wrong about its existence as they are wrong in concluding that its existence implies that security issues and the use of force no longer count. The fact is that economic interdependence and conflict, even war, coexist; one is not incompatible with the other elements. Drawing unsound conclusions about a gradual but fundamental transformation of the state system in which international harmony and peace will reign brings to mind Rudyard Kipling's words:

> Here we sit in a branchy row,
> Thinking of beautiful things we know,
> Dreaming of deeds that we mean to do,
> All complete, in a minute or two—
> Something noble and wise and good,
> Done by merely wishing we could.[10]

It is no contribution to any theory of international politics to forget what is fundamental to the subject: survival, security, and influence.[11] Or, to put it more frankly, international politics is about power, however ambiguous, imprecise, or unfashionable that concept may be. But power itself is about more than physical survival and physical security. It is also about the survival and security of the values that states embody. For Americans, the strength of American power and the willingness to assert that power is intimately related to the political, social, and economic freedoms that American society cherishes. Power remains a means to an end. The purpose of power politics is to preserve the security of a democratic America. The relative power and influence of other states are therefore of critical importance to the United States, as they are to other states equally determined to defend their "way of life."

Thus, while there are numerous approaches to understanding international politics (many more than included in this text), the only approach that permits one to appreciate the *essence* of the field is *realism* or the state system, the first level of analysis. Decision making, transnational relations, class structures, and all the other approaches contribute to the understanding of international politics, and each is valuable in its own right. But this does not mean that all approaches are equally valuable. Realism reveals the critical features of international politics. Without it, an understanding of the subject is impossible.

For Review

1. Why do analysts interested in the elimination of war focus on the second and third levels of explanation rather than the first level?
2. What were American expectations about the abolition of war in the past, and why were these expectations disappointed?
3. Why has realism not generally found a congenial reception in the United

States, unlike in Europe, except for a brief period after World War II?
4. Why should realism be central to any analysis and explanation of international politics?

Notes

1. In this chapter I am strongly indebted to John Weltman and his writings, especially "The American Tradition in International Thought: Science as Therapy" (Paper delivered at a Colorado College symposium, April 9, 1981); "Interpretation of International Thought," *Review of Politics* (January 1982): 27-41; and "On the Obsolescence of War," *International Studies Quarterly* (December 1974): 395-416.
2. Robert W. Tucker, "Egalitarianism and International Politics," *Commentary*, September 1975, 35.
3. Michael Howard, *The Causes of War* (Cambridge, Mass.: Harvard University Press, 1983), 10 11.
4. Kenneth N. Waltz, *Theory of International Politics* (Reading, Mass.: Addison-Wesley, 1979), 18ff.
5. Louis Hartz, *The Liberal Tradition* (New York: Harvest Books, 1955).
6. Bernard Crick, *The American Science of Politics* (London: Routledge & Kegan Paul, 1959).
7. See Alexander L. George, *Presidential Decisionmaking in Foreign Policy* (Boulder, Colo.: Westview Press, 1980), especially 169-174, 191-208; George, "The Case for Multiple Advocacy in Making Foreign Policy," *American Political Science Review* (September 1972): 751-785; Robert Jervis, *Perception and Misperception in International Politics* (Princeton, N.J.: Princeton University Press, 1976), 415-418; and, for a variation on this theme—that policy makers must not use historical analogies carelessly but should examine their relevance, if any—see Richard E. Neustadt and Ernest R. May, *Thinking in Time* (New York: Free Press, 1986).
8. Weltman, "Interpretation of International Thought," 34 (emphasis added).
9. Robert E. Osgood and Robert W. Tucker, *Force, Order, and Justice* (Baltimore: Johns Hopkins University Press, 1967), 16-18.
10. Rudyard Kipling, *Road-Song of the Bandar-Log*, in *Kipling*, vol. 1, ed. John Beecroft (Garden City, N.Y.: Doubleday, 1956), 248.
11. Colin Gray, *The Geopolitics of the Nuclear Era* (New York: Crane, Russak, 1977), 2-5. For different perspectives on the future, see Dennis Pirages, *Global Ecopolitics* (North Scituate, Mass.: Duxbury Press, 1978); Barry B. Hughes, *World Futures* (Baltimore: Johns Hopkins University Press, 1985); the pessimistic *The Global 2000 Report to the President*, vols. I and II (Washington, D.C.: Government Printing Office, 1980), and the optimistic Julian L. Simon, *The Ultimate Resource* (Princeton, N.J.: Princeton University Press, 1981); and Herman Kahn, *The Next 200 Years* (New York: Morrow, 1976).

Glossary

ABM Antiballistic missile, designed to "knock down" incoming missiles or their warheads (nuclear bombs) before designated targets are struck.

alliances Agreements among states to support each other militarily in case of attack or to enhance their mutual interests. Alliances supplement national power and clarify spheres of interest. (Examples: North Atlantic Treaty Organization and Warsaw Pact.)

anticolonialism Rejection of the former "father" or "mother" country by a Third World state.

appeasement In contemporary usage, a term of shame meaning one-sided concessions to an adversary. Prior to the Munich Conference of 1938, the term was respectable because it referred to the settlement of legitimate grievances and the consequent avoidance of war.

arms control Process of securing agreements that place restrictions upon numbers, types, and performance characteristics of strategic weapons. In the U.S.-Soviet context the process has aimed at stabilizing mutual deterrence and avoiding nuclear war by eliminating the incentive to strike first at the other side.

arms race Arms acquisitions by a nation or alliance, through increases in the production of weapons or technological breakthroughs, to compete with its adversaries. Arms races often are characterized by an action-reaction pattern among nations that are either trying to stay ahead of, or at least not fall behind, their adversaries.

balance of power Relationship in which nations strive to achieve security through establishment of an approximate power equilibrium in the state system, thus reducing the probability of warfare or domination. In short, power checks power.

balance of trade Difference between the value of a nation's exports and its imports. The balance will be either a surplus or deficit.

behavioral approach School of thought that developed in reaction to idealism and realism. Behaviorism claimed to have no *a priori* assumptions about state behavior and emphasized the need for empirical research. How to study, especially by means of value-free quantitative methods, often appeared to be its preoccupation rather than the key substantive issues in the "real world."

bilateral Between two states.

bipolar system International system dominated by *two* superpowers or coalitions. This system is characterized by a high degree of insecurity, clear distinctions between friend and foe, sensitivity to power shifts, arms races, and cohesiveness of each coalition.

bipolycentrism State system characterized by the loosening of rival bipolar blocs into less cohesive alliances and the simultaneous rise of influential Third World actors. Although the dominant military powers remain the United States and the Soviet Union (bi), the growing influence of other (poly) centers of influence marks the possible transition to future multipolarity.

boycott   Economic weapon used to pressure another nation by cutting off its imports.

bureaucratic politics   See **governmental politics model.**

capitalism   Economic system based on the private ownership of property, a free market based on the laws of supply and demand, a general absence of governmental interference, and the pursuit of individual profit.

Carter Doctrine   U.S. guarantee of protection extended to the Persian Gulf oil kingdoms after the Soviet invasion of Afghanistan.

cold war   Relationship characterized by conflict and competition, often accompanied by tension and hostility, that evolved between the United States (the West) and the Soviet Union (Communist bloc) after World War II.

COMECON   Council for Mutual Economic Assistance, founded in 1949 by the Soviet Union as a means of integrating the economies of the East European states and asserting Soviet control over them. Mongolia, Cuba, and Vietnam were allowed to join later.

Common Market   See **EEC.**

communism   Revolutionary ideology and political movement that seeks the destruction of capitalism and its replacement by a collectivist society in which private ownership of property is no longer necessary. Subsequently, both social and economic classes and the state will cease to exist.

containment   Post-World War II American foreign policy aimed at blocking Soviet expansion through countervailing American economic and military power. It was expected that the Soviet leadership would eventually mellow, abandon its expansionist drive, and accept the international status quo.

counterforce strategy   Strategic weapons targeted at the adversary's military capabilities such as bomber bases, ICBM silos, and air defense installations.

countervalue (countercity) strategy   Strategic weapons targeted at the adversary's population centers and industries, targets which it presumably values and does not want to lose.

credible commitment   Nation's stated obligation to defend an ally or friendly state that is *believed* by adversaries.

crises   Intense, relatively brief superpower confrontations that have become substitutes for war in the nuclear era. Crises involve threats to vital national interests, an increased perception of the possible use of force, and each party's reputation for power.

cruise missile   Nuclear missile, resembling a pilotless aircraft, that operates entirely within the earth's atmosphere and is launched from the air or sea.

crusade   Policy characterized by an unshakable missionary zeal to eliminate evil from the world. It tends to be transformed into total wars to utterly destroy adversaries.

Cuban missile crisis   Thirteen tense days in October 1962 when the United States and the Soviet Union clashed over the issue of Soviet missiles emplaced in Cuba. The crisis ended with Khrushchev's promise to remove the missiles in exchange for Kennedy's pledge not to invade Cuba.

decision-making approach   Level of analysis that focuses primarily on the specific policy makers and bureaucracy officially responsible for the conduct and implementation of foreign policy.

delivery vehicles or launchers   ICBMs (land-based intercontinental ballistic missiles), SLBMs (sea-launched ballistic missiles), and intercontinental bombers, all capable of delivering nuclear warheads or bombs.

dependency   Analytical perspective that views the state system and international economy as divided between the *core* First World (industrial capitalist states), which is rich because it dominates the global economy, and the *peripheral* Third World, which is poor because it is exploited.

détente In general, a relaxation of previously tenser relations between two or more countries. Specifically, in the United States détente means that U.S.-Soviet global conflict and competition can be moderated and restrained by cooperation in such areas as arms control, trade, and technology.

deterrence (nuclear) In the bipolar nuclear context, the assumption that total war is synonymous with mutual destruction because both superpowers possess effective second-strike capabilities. The resulting standoff, if perceived as credible by rational policy makers on both sides, prevents the outbreak of war.

developing country Less-developed countries of the international system, usually categorized as belonging to the Third World. Economic backwardness or ineffective, weak political institutions are typical of these states.

diplomacy International negotiations or bargaining to compromise conflicts among states over such issues as territorial divisions, arms ratios, and trade imbalances.

disarmament Agreement to reduce (or abolish) existing military forces or weapons.

divide-and-rule Balance-of-power technique in which nation A attempts to exploit existing differences among nation B and its allies to gain an advantage.

domino theory Belief that if one country falls to the enemy, that country's neighboring nations will also fall, upsetting the balance of power.

East Term encompassing the Communist states of Eastern Europe as well as the Soviet Union.

East-West conflict Another term for cold war or the American-Soviet conflict and competition for influence in the world.

EC European Community, composed of the European Coal and Steel Community, European Economic Community, and Euratom.

EEC European Economic Community (also known earlier as the Common Market), founded in 1958 to create unified national economic policies (such as a uniform external tariff wall and mobile labor and capital) among its original members (Belgium, France, Italy, Luxembourg, the Netherlands, and West Germany). The original members were joined by Britain, Denmark, and Ireland in 1973, Greece in 1981, and Portugal and Spain in 1986, for a total membership of twelve states.

embargo Economic weapon used by one nation to prevent its goods from being sold to the targeted nation.

first strike See ***counterforce strategy.***

First World Advanced urban-industrial economies and political democracies of Western Europe, North America (Canada and the United States), and Japan.

foreign policy Nation's efforts to realize its objectives or national interests in the state system.

free trade International movement of goods unhampered by tariff and nontariff restrictions.

functionalism Theory that envisions economic and social cooperation among nations in various fields and eventually a new international political community.

games nations play Games analogy is used in this book to refer to the need for states in the international system to pursue a strategy—a set of moves to be made in a competitive and conflictual situation—to advance their interests.

GATT General Agreement on Tariffs and Trade, organized in 1947 by the Western industrialized states. GATT, which now has over ninety members, including several Communist states, has become the key global arena for negotiating tariff and other reductions to stimulate trade.

General Assembly Body of the United Nations in which all its members are represented. Intended originally to be an advisory organ to the Security Council, its influence has grown with the addition of many Third World nations, which now constitute the majority.

glasnost Term referring to current Soviet efforts to allow more openness or freedom to express viewpoints different than officially sanctioned ones and to reexamine Soviet history.

GNP Gross national product or the sum market value of all consumer and capital goods and services produced in a year. It is one indicator or index used in calculating power rankings among nations.

governmental politics model Pluralistic decision-making approach that stresses the bargaining between the executive/legislative branches, nongovernmental interest groups, and executive agencies participating in the making of foreign policy.

great power See ***pole.***

greenhouse effect General warming of the planet, resulting in rising sea levels, shifting agricultural zones, and other problems, caused by a buildup of gases, especially carbon dioxide, that trap heat in the earth's atmosphere.

Group of 77 (G-77) Founded in 1976 by 77 developing countries and with a present membership of 120, a group that has been called the "poor nations' trade-union" in North-South negotiations.

groupthink Term coined by Irving L. Janis to indicate the tendency of the members of a decision making group to conform to the group's apparent views rather than ask awkward questions. Policy is therefore made on the basis of insufficient information and the failure to consider all available options.

guerrilla warfare See ***revolutionary warfare.***

guns versus butter Competition between objectives that many states confront—that is, security (military-defense) needs compete for priority with welfare needs (such as schools, hospitals, education, and housing).

hegemony Superiority or dominance of one state over other states.

high politics Term used to describe security and prestige issues, which usually involve military power.

human rights policy Moral and political commitment to individual freedoms and opposition to governments that flagrantly violate these principles.

ICBM Land-based intercontinental ballistic missile, which can be launched at targets 6,000 miles away. (Example: U.S. Minuteman III.)

idealist approach School of thinking that focuses on how nations *ought* to behave to eliminate international conflict and create greater international cooperation and peace.

ideology Comprehensive set of beliefs that critically describes and explains contemporary reality while prescribing a better state of affairs in the future.

IGOs Intergovernmental organizations, which may be classified as global (United Nations) or regional (Organization of American States, League of Arab States). Political, military, social, and economic functions can also distinguish IGOs (North Atlantic Treaty Organization and World Health Organization).

imports Products shipped into a nation from another nation.

incrementalism Tendency of policy makers to move forward step by step on a specific course of policy while concentrating on momentary, short-run aims rather than on comprehensive, long-range planning.

intangible components of power Components that do not lend themselves to accurate calculations or quantifications such as a state's national morale, quality of leadership, or the effectiveness of its political system.

integration Creation within a territory of a "sense of community" and of legitimate institutions and practices, leading to an expectation of "peaceful change" among its population.

intentions versus capabilities A state's goals or objectives, versus its power to achieve them.

interdependence Argument that the nations of the world have become *mutually sensitive* and *vulnerable* through an interrelationship of socioeconomic and techno logical issues and that their future behavior will be oriented toward long-term collaboration rather than toward conflict over security issues.

international system See **state system.**

intervention State or alliance involving itself either overtly or covertly in the affairs of another state to influence policy and events.

irredentism Desire of state A to annex territory of state B that contains people who possess linguistic, racial, or ethnic backgrounds similar to those of state A's citizenry.

isolationism In general, noninvolvement of a state in the affairs of the international system, although the degree of disinterest can vary considerably.

kiloton weapon Nuclear weapon, the yield of which is measured in thousands of tons of TNT. A 10-kiloton weapon is equal to the explosive power of 10,000 tons of TNT.

Kto, kovo? In Soviet ideological parlance, "Who will destroy whom?" Signifies the belief in the irreconcilable struggle between capitalism and communism.

levels of analysis Different explanatory levels, such as the state system (balance of power), the nation state (its internal nature), and decision making (leadership elites), used to explain and describe how and why nations play the games they do.

limited war Armed conflict fought for limited political objectives and with definite restrictions upon the use of force.

low politics Term used to describe welfare or socioeconomic issues.

macropolitics View that the *international interest* of humankind should be given priority over the traditional national interests of states in an increasingly interdependent world.

MAD Mutual assured destruction, a doctrine that is at the heart of strategic deterrence and is aimed at preventing all-out war between the United States and the Soviet Union. Because both sides would be destroyed regardless of who strikes first, nuclear war is prevented.

Marshall Plan Massive program of American economic aid ($15 billion) aimed at rebuilding war-torn Western Europe from 1948 to 1952.

Marxism Doctrine developed during the nineteenth century by Karl Marx and Friedrich Engels, which explained historical developments as a series of economic class struggles. Capitalism would eventually be overthrown by a proletarian (workers) revolution against the bourgeoisie (propertied, exploiting class), ushering in a classless, nonpropertied, nonexploitive utopia.

megaton weapon Nuclear weapon whose yield is explosively equivalent to 1 million tons of TNT. For example, a 5-megaton missile warhead would equal the explosive power of 5 million tons of TNT.

mercantilism Political philosophy that proposes the use of economic means to increase the prosperity and power of one's own state at the cost of other states.

microstates States with populations of less than 1 million (such as Grenada or the Seychelles) which are often unable to defend or economically sustain themselves.

MIRV Multiple independently targeted reentry vehicle or a single ballistic missile that carries a cluster of warheads with each warhead capable of hitting a separate target.

misperception Belief that wars occur because decision makers have good and evil or black-and-white images of the world that filter out any incoming information that conflicts with their preconceived cognitive maps. But for these maps, international harmony and peace would prevail.

MNCs Multinational corporations or business enterprises that conduct their operations across international boundaries and in multiple markets, in effect creating a global shopping center. American MNCs include Exxon, Pepsi-Cola, and General Motors.

modernization Long, complex, and often painful transformation of a state from an agrarian, politically fragmented entity to a urban-industrialized, politically unified society. Modernization involves fundamental changes in the population's values and expectations.

multilateral   Between more than two states.

multipolar system   System that has at least four approximately equal powers. In contrast to simple and rigid bipolarity, multipolarity is complex and flexible. Frequent alliance realignment and lowered sensitivities to changes in the balance of power are characteristic of this international structure.

national interests   Ordering of priorities in accordance with national goals.

national morale   Intangible component of power that refers to a population's patriotism, national loyalty, and willingness to sacrifice during times of war or international tension.

national style   Each state's particular approach to foreign policy based on its historical experience, political and social values, economic status, and cultural perspective.

NATO   North Atlantic Treaty Organization, the alliance between the United States and Western Europe, established in 1949.

neocolonial   Pejorative term used to describe the status of developing countries that, while politically independent, are said to be still economically controlled and exploited by the developed Western capitalist states.

neutralization   Balance-of-power technique or hands-off policy toward a strategically important country lying between two major powers.

NGO   Nongovernmental organization, such as a multinational corporation; national liberation, terrorist, religious, and humanitarian organizations; and other groups such as the Catholic church and the Red Cross.

NICs   Newly industrialized countries, a term used to describe the Pacific Rim nations (Hong Kong, Singapore, South Korea, and Taiwan), as well as other developing states such as Malaysia and Brazil.

NIEO   New international economic order, which is the more equitable distribution of the world's wealth demanded by the developing countries because the present order favors the rich Western industrial nations who allegedly exploited them in the past and continue to do so.

nonalignment   Policy of not aligning formally (particularly evident in the Third World) with either the Communist or free world alliances, mainly during the bipolar cold war period.

nontariff barriers   Informal barriers to free trade designed to make imports of foreign products very difficult.

North   Term usually referring to the Western democratic industrialized states (including Japan).

nuclear nonproliferation treaty   Treaty that forbids the transfer of nuclear weapons to nonnuclear states, which, if they are signatories, are obligated to forego the acquisition of nuclear weapons.

nuclear proliferation   Acquisition of nuclear capabilities by a significant number of middle- and lower-rank states.

nuclear winter   Scenario devised in 1983 by scientists in which the smoke and soot created by a full-scale superpower nuclear war would block out the sunlight for months, if not years, causing extensive freezing of the earth's surface and extermination of most of its plant and animal (including human) life.

OPEC   Organization of Petroleum Exporting Countries (Algeria, Ecuador, Gabon, Indonesia, Iran, Iraq, Kuwait, Libya, Nigeria, Qatar, Saudi Arabia, United Arab Emirates, and Venezuela), a producer-cartel whose purpose is collectively to fix the levels of production and the price of crude oil on the world market.

peace   Complex, multifaceted concept, which, in its most general sense, refers to the absence of major warfare in the international system.

peaceful coexistence   Soviet term, which, while acknowledging the dangers of nuclear war, asserts that the Communist-capitalist struggle can be channeled into nonmilitary areas of competition.

peace-keeping forces   Nonfighting UN forces inserted between Third World belligerents to provide a buffer zone and halt fighting that might escalate by involving the two superpowers, thereby transforming a regional conflict into a global conflagration.

perestroika   Term referring to Soviet leader Gorbachev's efforts to restructure the Soviet economic and political system.

petrodollars   Money paid by the industrialized states to OPEC for oil.

PGMs   Precision-guided munitions, more often known as smart bombs, which can hit their intended targets with great accuracy.

pole   Major actor or state in the international system, more often referred to as a great power.

political community   Community that effectively controls the means of violence, possesses a set of political institutions that peacefully allocates resources, and has a population that shares a common political identification.

political idealism   See *idealist approach.*

population explosion   Term reflecting concern that the rapid increase in the world's population, stemming from the high birthrates in the Third World, will overwhelm the earth's resources.

power (among states)   Capacity of one state to influence others in accordance with its own objectives—that is, to change the behavior of the others or prevent them from taking a particular action.

power politics   Term frequently used pejoratively to condemn international politics for its concern with power, conflict, and war. Its standard definition, originating in Europe, is a state's use of military or economic coercion to increase its own power or interests.

preemptive strike   Defensive attack to forestall what is believed to be an imminent first strike by the opponent. Differs from preventive strike, which is motivated by the offensive aim of eliminating the enemy and is independent of a perception that it is about to strike.

prestige   Nation's reputation for power among its fellow states and the degree of respect that it is subsequently accorded.

preventive diplomacy   UN peace-keeping function whereby multinational forces are injected into a conflict to separate the combatants and prevent the escalation of that conflict by the possible intervention of the superpowers.

preventive strike   Aggressor's unprovoked, carefully calculated attack upon an opponent with the expectation of defeating it.

proxy wars   Use of surrogates by the superpowers to advance their interests when they wanted to avoid a direct confrontation with its danger of nuclear war.

quota   Numerical limit on imports.

rapprochement   Reconciliation of two nations that were adversaries.

rational actor model   Decision-making approach that stresses a clear definition of policy goals and an examination of the alternative means of attaining those goals.

Reagan Doctrine   American support of guerrilla forces trying to overthrow the governments of countries in which the Soviet Union had directly or through proxies established Marxist regimes in the 1970s.

realist approach   School of thinking that focuses on the conflicts and rivalries among nations in an anarchical system. Balance of power plays a central role in this analysis, and war remains a continuing characteristic of international politics, to be avoided or limited through prudent management. War cannot be erased, however.

revisionist state   State that is dissatisfied with the contemporary distribution of power in the system and tries to change it in its favor.

revolutionary state   State whose leadership condemns the existing order as oppressive and exploitive and seeks to liberate humankind, bringing it freedom, justice, and peace. (Examples: late eighteenth-century France and the twentieth-century Soviet Union.)

revolutionary warfare (guerrilla warfare)   Lengthy conflicts fought by a band of insurgents (or self-proclaimed liberators) whose primary goal is to capture state power as a means of transforming the nation's sociopolitical structure and economy.

SALT   Strategic Arms Limitation Talks, negotiations between the United States and the Soviet Union, which began in 1969. The 1972 SALT I consisted of two agreements: a limit on ABMs and a five-year freeze on ICBMs and SLBMs. The 1979 SALT II agreement, not ratified by the United States, set ceilings on offensive missiles and bombers.

SDI   Strategic Defense Initiative, a proposal for a primarily space-based defense to destroy incoming missiles and protect America's population. More frequently called Star Wars because its technological feasibility is still very questionable, SDI may become operational at some future date as a limited defense of ICBMs, thus strengthening deterrence rather than replacing it as envisioned in 1983 by President Reagan.

search and destroy   Primary U.S. ground strategy in the Vietnam War in which American forces in helicopters searched for Communist guerrillas in the countryside to destroy them.

second-strike capability   Ability, after absorbing a nuclear first strike from the enemy, to deliver a retaliatory blow with sufficient remaining force (missiles and bombers) to destroy the enemy.

Second World   Soviet Union and the Communist states of Eastern Europe.

Security Council   Primary organ in the United Nations responsible for the preservation of peace and security. The fifteen-member council can take enforcement action against international aggression, provided one of the five great powers—United States, Soviet Union, Britain, France, and China, which are permanent members—does not veto it.

security dilemma   In an anarchical state system, follows from a state's attempt to ensure its security by increasing its power. As its potential adversary does the same, the first state's sense of insecurity recurs, leading it to increase its power once more, and so on.

security policy   Basic policy of a noncrisis nature. (Examples: defense spending, foreign aid, and arms control policy.)

Sino-Soviet split   Conflict between Communist China (People's Republic of China) and the Soviet Union over ideological interpretations, leadership of the international Communist movement, disputed territories, and major policy issues

SLBM   Submarine-launched (long-range) ballistic missile. (Examples: U.S. Poseidon and Trident.)

South   Term encompassing the developing countries.

sovereign state   Primary political actor in the international system. Each of the almost 170 states in this system is characterized by a territorial base, jurisdiction over its internal and external affairs, and, to varying degrees, a concept of self-identity (nationalism) and unity.

sphere of influence   Geographic areas under the influence or domination of a great power. (Example: Eastern Europe for the Soviet Union.)

stable deterrence   American-Soviet strategic nuclear balance in which the deterrent forces of both sides are invulnerable to the opponent's first strike.

stable state system   International system characterized by minimal violence and the peaceful settlement of national differences.

stagflation Simultaneous occurrence of recession and inflation.

stalemate Form of conflict resolution in which victory for either side is rejected as a result of *mutual* battlefield exhaustion, reluctance to invest further resources, or unwillingness to escalate due to the risks involved.

START Strategic Arms Reduction Treaty, the Reagan administration's term for the SALT negotiations. START's purpose was to emphasize strategic arms *reductions* rather than the arms limitations or ceilings on the numbers of weapons each side could have allegedly emphasized in the SALT bargaining.

state-centric Analysis focusing on the behavior of nation-states as the principal actors in international politics.

state system Regular and observable interactions of political actors (primarily nations) within a basically anarchical global context.

status quo state State that is satisfied with the current distribution of power in the system (or at least not sufficiently dissatisfied that it seeks to change it).

strategic balance Balance of power between the two nuclear superpowers. Parity is another term often used to describe this balance.

superpowers Nations that possess an extraordinary amount of power (military, economic, diplomatic) allowing them to pursue an independent role in global affairs or states whose actions have a substantial effect upon the policies of other political actors throughout the entire state system. Term generally refers to the United States and Soviet Union in the period since World War II.

supranational actor Best exemplified by the European Economic Community (EEC), in which twelve sovereign states have transferred a degree of their sovereign authority on economic issues to a superior decision-making body. (See *EEC*.)

tacit negotiations Informal, indirect bargaining among states as opposed to traditional, face-to-face diplomacy.

tangible components of power Usually, components that can be measured or quantified such as a nation's population, size, military strength, and economic productivity.

tariff Tax imposed on imports.

terrorism Use of political violence by nonstate actors (although some are state-supported) to intimidate their enemies and gain publicity for their causes.

Third World Non-Western, largely economically underdeveloped countries.

totalitarianism Political system that attempts to control every aspect of a citizen's life.

total war War in which the political objectives of complete victory over the enemy are matched by the full mobilization of a nation's military, economic, and social resources. (Example: World War II.)

transnational actor Nongovernmental organization characterized by having its headquarters in one country but conducting its centrally directed operations in two or more countries. (Example: multinational corporation.)

triad Strategic deterrent composed of bombers, submarines, and ICBMs.

Truman Doctrine The 1947 presidential pronouncement that "it must be the policy of the United States to support free peoples who are resisting subjugation by armed minorities or outside pressures." Originally directed at Greece and Turkey, the doctrine actually marked the beginning of the containment era and the U.S. role in preserving the balance of power in a bipolar world.

UNCTAD United Nations Conference on Trade and Development, usually equated with a Third World coalition strategy focusing on North-South economic issues.

unilateral One-sided.

unipolarity Situation in which a single state dominates and organizes the international system.

United Nations International organization with virtually global membership, founded after World War II as a successor to the defunct League of Nations to preserve international peace.

Uniting for Peace resolution   U.S.-sponsored UN resolution passed in November 1950. It transferred the authority to preserve peace from the Security Council to the General Assembly so that support for American anti-Communist policies in Korea would not be blocked by Soviet vetoes.

unstable deterrence   U.S.-Soviet nuclear balance in which one or both of the deterrent forces has become vulnerable, thereby tempting the other side to strike preemptively, especially during a crisis.

unstable state system   International system prone to the outbreak of major wars.

utopianism   See ***idealist approach.***

war   Hostilities between states that are conducted by armed force.

warhead   Part of a missile that contains the explosive material.

Warsaw Treaty Organization   Soviet alliance with the states of Eastern Europe organized in 1955. Also known as the Warsaw Pact.

West   Same as ***North***.

world government   Idealistic concept of a supreme global authority that would make wars among states impossible.

yield   Explosive force of a warhead.

zero-sum   What one nation gains (for example, security), another loses. International politics is often said to be a zero-sum game, underlining its conflictual character.

Select Bibliography
of Books

International Politics and the State System

Aron, Raymond. *Peace and War.** Garden City, N.Y.: Doubleday, 1966. Paperback ed. Melbourne, Fla.: Krieger, 1981.

Bull, Hedley. *The Anarchical Society.** New York: Columbia University Press, 1977.

Carr, Edward H. *Twenty Years' Crisis, 1919-1939.** New York: Macmillan, 1951.

Claude, Inis L., Jr. *Power and International Relations.* New York: Random House, 1962.

Dougherty, James E., and Robert L. Pfaltzgraff. *Contending Theories of International Relations.** Philadelphia: Lippincott, 1971. 2d ed. New York: Harper & Row, 1980.

Duchacek, Ivo D. *Territorial Dimension of Politics.* Boulder, Colo.: Westview Press, 1986.

Ferguson, Yale H., and Richard W. Mansbach. *The Elusive Quest.* Columbia: University of South Carolina Press, 1988.

Fromkin, David. *The Independence of Nations.** New York: Praeger, 1981.

Gilpin, Robert. *War and Change in World Politics.* New York: Cambridge University Press, 1983.

Herz, John H. *Political Realism and Political Idealism.* Chicago: University of Chicago Press, 1951.

Kennedy, Paul M. *The Rise and Fall of British Naval Mastery.* Atlantic Highlands, N.J.: Humanities, 1986.

———. *The Rise and Fall of the Great Powers.* New York: Random House, 1987.

Keohane, Robert O., ed. *Neorealism and Its Critics.* New York: Columbia University Press, 1986.

Knorr, Klaus, and James N. Rosenau, eds. *Contending Approaches to International Politics.** Princeton, N.J.: Princeton University Press, 1969.

Krasner, Stephen D. *Defending the National Interest.** Princeton, N.J.: Princeton University Press, 1978.

Mandelbaum, Michael. *The Fate of Nations.* New York: Cambridge University Press, 1988.

Morgan, Patrick M. *Theories and Approaches to International Politics.** 3d ed. New Brunswick, N.J.: Transaction Books, 1981. 4th ed., 1986.

Note: *See chapter notes for additional books and articles.*

* Indicates paperback.

Morgenthau, Hans J. *Politics Among Nations.* 5th ed. New York: Knopf, 1973. 6th rev. ed., edited by Kenneth W. Thompson, 1985.

Rosenau, James N., ed. *International Politics and Foreign Policy.* 2d ed. New York: Free Press, 1969.

Singer, J. David. *Quantitative International Politics.* New York: Free Press, 1968.

Smith, Michael Joseph. *Realist Thought from Weber to Kissinger.* Baton Rouge: Louisiana University Press, 1987.

Waltz, Kenneth N. *Man, the State, and War.** New York: Columbia University Press, 1959.

——. *Theory of International Politics.** Reading, Mass.: Addison-Wesley, 1979.

Wight, Martin. *Power Politics.* Edited by Hedley Bull and Carsten Holbraad. New York: Holmes & Meier, 1978.

Wolfers, Arnold. *Discord and Collaboration.** Baltimore: Johns Hopkins University Press, 1962.

Peace and War

Beer, Francis A. *Peace Against War.** San Francisco: W. H. Freeman, 1981.

Blainey, Geoffrey. *The Causes of War.** 2d ed. New York: Free Press, 1973. 3d ed., 1988.

Bueno de Mesquita, Bruce. *The War Trap.* New Haven, Conn.: Yale University Press, 1981.

Clausewitz, Carl von. *On War.* Edited and translated by Michael Howard and Peter Paret. Princeton, N.J.: Princeton University Press, 1976.

Harvard Nuclear Study Group. *Living with Nuclear Weapons.** New York: Bantam Books, 1983.

Howard, Michael. *The Causes of War.** Cambridge, Mass.: Harvard University Press, 1983.

Midlansky, Manus. *The Onset of War.* Winchester, Mass.: Unwin Hyman, 1988.

Preston, Richard A., and Sydney F. Wise. *Men in Arms.* Rev. ed. New York: Praeger, 1962. 4th ed. New York: Holt, Rinehart & Winston, 1979.

Ropp, Theodore. *War in the Modern World.* 2d ed. New York: Collier, 1962.

Small, Melvin, and J. David Singer. *Resort to Arms.* Beverly Hills, Calif.: Sage Publications, 1982.

Wright, Quincy. *A Study of War.* Abridged ed. Chicago: University of Chicago Press, 1964. Paperback ed., 1983.

American Foreign Policy

Almond, Gabriel. *The American People and Foreign Policy.** New York: Holt, Rinehart & Winston, 1960.

Bowker, Mike, and Phil Williams. *Superpower Détente.* Newbury Park, Calif.: Sage Publications, 1988.

Brzezinski, Zbigniew. *Game Plan.* Boston: Atlantic Monthly Press, 1986.

Gaddis, John L. *The Long Peace.* New York: Oxford University Press, 1987.

——. *Strategies of Containment.** New York: Oxford University Press, 1982.

——. *Russia, the Soviet Union, and the United States.* New York: Random House, 1978.

Gati, Charles, ed. *Caging the Bear.** New York: Bobbs-Merrill, 1973.

George, Alexander L., ed. *Managing U.S.-Soviet Rivalry.** Boulder, Colo.: Westview Press, 1983.

Gilbert, Felix. *To the Farewell Address.** Princeton, N.J.: Princeton University Press, 1961.

Halle, Louis J. *The Cold War as History.** New York: Harper & Row, 1967. Paperback ed., 1971.

Hoffmann, Stanley. *Primacy or World Order.** New York: McGraw-Hill, 1978. Paperback ed., 1980.

Hyland, William G. *Mortal Rivals.* New York: Random House, 1987.

Jones, Joseph M. *The Fifteen Weeks.** New York: Viking, 1955. Paperback ed. New York: Harcourt, Brace, 1965.

Kennan, George F. *American Diplomacy 1900-1950.** Chicago: University of Chicago Press, 1951. Enlarged ed., 1985.

Larson, Deborah. *Origins of Containment.* Princeton, N.J.: Princeton University Press, 1985.

Mandelbaum, Michael, and Strobe Talbott. *Reagan and Gorbachev.** New York: Vintage Books, 1987.

Morgenthau, Hans J. *In Defense of the National Interest.* New York: Knopf, 1951. Paperback ed. Lanham, Md.: University Press of America, 1983.

———. *A New Foreign Policy for the United States.** New York: Holt, Rinehart & Winston, 1969.

Mueller, John E. *War, Presidents, and Public Opinion.** New York: Wiley, 1973. Paperback ed. Lanham, Md.: University Press of America, 1985.

Osgood, Robert E. *Ideals and Self-Interest in America's Foreign Relations.** Chicago: University of Chicago Press, 1953.

Pastor, Robert. *Condemned to Repetition.* Princeton, N.J.: Princeton University Press, 1987.

Quester, George H. *American Foreign Policy.** New York: Praeger, 1982.

Schraeder, Peter J., ed. *Intervention in the 1980s.* Boulder, Colo.: Lynne Rienner, 1989.

Smith, Gaddis. *American Diplomacy During the Second World War.** New York: Wiley, 1966. Paperback ed. New York: Random House, 1985.

Spanier, John. *American Foreign Policy Since World War II.** 11th ed. Washington, D.C.: CQ Press, 1988.

Thomas, Hugh. *Armed Truce.* New York: Atheneum, 1987.

Tsou, Tang. *America's Failure in China.** Chicago: University of Chicago Press, 1963.

Tucker, Robert W. *The Purposes of American Power.** New York: Praeger, 1981.

———. *The Radical Left and American Foreign Policy.** Baltimore: Johns Hopkins University Press, 1971.

Weintraub, Sidney, ed. *Economic Coercion and U.S. Foreign Policy.* Boulder, Colo.: Westview Press, 1982.

Memoirs and Biographies of American Statesmen and Administrations

Acheson, Dean. *Present at the Creation.** New York: Norton, 1969.

Ambrose, Stephen E. *Eisenhower.* Vols. I and II. New York: Simon & Schuster, 1983 and 1984, respectively.

———. *Nixon.* Vols. I and II. New York: Simon & Schuster, 1987 and 1989, respectively.

Brown, Seyom. *The Crises of Power.* New York: Columbia University Press, 1979.

Brzezinski, Zbigniew. *Power and Principle.* New York: Farrar, Straus, Giroux, 1983.

Byrnes, James F. *Speaking Frankly.* New York: Harper & Brothers, 1947.

Eisenhower, David. *Eisenhower at War: 1943-1945.* New York: Random House, 1986.

Eisenhower, Dwight D. *White House Years: Mandate for Change.** Garden City, N.Y.: Doubleday, 1963.

———. *White House Years: Waging Peace.* Garden City, N.Y.: Doubleday, 1965.

Gerson, Louis L. *John Foster Dulles.* New York: Cooper Square, 1967.

Haig, Alexander M., Jr. *Caveat.* New York: Macmillan, 1984.

Hoopes, Townsend. *The Devil and John Foster Dulles.* Boston: Little, Brown, 1973.

Kissinger, Henry. *The White House Years.* Boston: Little, Brown, 1979.

———. *Years of Upheaval.* Boston: Little, Brown, 1982.

Nixon, Richard. *RN.** New York: Grosset & Dunlap, 1978.

Schulzinger, Robert D. *Henry Kissinger.* New York: Columbia University Press, 1989.

Truman, Harry S. *Memoirs.** 2 vols. Garden City, N.Y.: Doubleday, 1958.

Soviet Foreign and Military Policy

Adomeit, Hannes. *Soviet Risk Taking and Crisis Behavior.* Winchester, Mass.: Allen Unwin, 1982.

Aspaturian, Vernon V., ed. *Process and Power on Soviet Foreign Policy.* Boston: Little, Brown, 1971.

Berman, Robert P., and John C. Baker. *Soviet Strategic Forces.** Washington, D.C.: Brookings, 1982.

Bialer, Seweryn. *The Soviet Paradox.* New York: Knopf, 1986.

Bialer, Seweryn, ed. *The Domestic Context of Soviet Foreign Policy.* Boulder, Colo.: Westview Press, 1981.

Bialer, Seweryn, and Michael Mandelbaum, eds. *Gorbachev's Russia and American Foreign Policy.* Boulder, Colo.: Westview Press, 1988.

Brzezinski, Zbigniew K. *The Grand Failure.* New York: Scribner's, 1989.

_____. *Ideology and Power in Soviet Politics.** Rev. ed. New York: Holt, Rinehart & Winston, 1967.

Dallin, David J. *Soviet Foreign Policy After Stalin.* Philadelphia: Lippincott, 1961.

Deibel, T. L., ed. *Containing the Soviet Union.* McLean, Va.: Pergamon-Brassey, 1987.

Dinerstein, Herbert S. *War and the Soviet Union.** Rev. ed. New York: Holt, Rinehart & Winston, 1962.

Donaldson, Robert H., ed. *The Soviet Union in the Third World.* Boulder, Colo.: Westview Press, 1980.

Douglas, Joseph D., Jr., and Amoretta M. Hoeber. *Soviet Strategy for Nuclear War.** Stanford, Calif.: Hoover Press, 1979.

Garthoff, Raymond L. *Détente and Confrontation.** Washington, D.C.: Brookings, 1985.

_____. *Soviet Strategy in the Nuclear Age.** Rev. ed. New York: Holt, Rinehart & Winston, 1962.

Hammond, Thomas T. *Red Flag over Afghanistan.** Boulder, Colo.: Westview Press, 1984.

Holloway, David. *The Soviet Union and the Arms Race.** 2d ed. New Haven, Conn.: Yale University Press, 1984.

Horelick, Arnold L., and Myron Rush. *Strategic Power and Soviet Foreign Policy.* Chicago: University of Chicago Press, 1966.

Kennan, George F. *Russia and the West Under Lenin and Stalin.** Boston: Little, Brown, 1961. Paperback ed. New York: New American Library, 1961.

Korbonski, Andrzej, and Francis Fukuyama, eds. *The Soviet Union and the Third World.* Ithaca, N.Y.: Cornell University Press, 1987.

Leites, Nathan. *The Operational Code of the Politburo.* New York: McGraw-Hill, 1951.

_____. *A Study of Bolshevism.* New York: Free Press, 1953.

Lynch, Allen. *The Soviet Study of International Relations.* New York: Cambridge University Press, 1987.

Mackintosh, J. M. *Strategy and Tactics of Soviet Foreign Policy.* London: Oxford University Press, 1962.

Nogee, Joseph L., and Robert H. Donaldson. *Soviet Foreign Policy Since World War II.** 2d ed. New York: Pergamon Press, 1984. 3d ed., 1988.

Papp, Daniel S. *Soviet Policies Toward the Developing World During the 1980s.* Maxwell Air Force Base, Ala.: Air University Press, 1986.

Pipes, Richard. *Survival Is Not Enough.** Rev. ed. New York: Simon & Schuster, 1986.

Rubinstein, Alvin Z. *Moscow's Third World Strategy.* Princeton, N.J.: Princeton University Press, 1988.

Scott, Harriet F., and William F. Scott. *The Armed Forces of the USSR.* Boulder, Colo.: Westview Press, 1978.

Sherr, Alan B. *The Other Side of Arms Control.* Winchester, Mass.: Unwin Hyman, 1988.

Shulman, Marshall D. *Stalin's Foreign Policy Reappraised.* Cambridge, Mass.: Harvard University Press, 1963.

Taubman, William. *Stalin's American Policy.* New York: Norton, 1982.

Triska, Jan F., and David D. Finley. *Soviet Foreign Policy.* New York: Macmillan, 1968.

Ulam, Adam B. *Dangerous Relations.** New York: Oxford University Press, 1983.

_____. *Expansion and Coexistence.** 2d ed. New York: Holt, Rinehart & Winston, 1974.

Valkenier, Elizabeth K. *The Soviet Union and the Third World.* New York: Praeger, 1985.

Von Laue, Theodore H. *Why Lenin, Why Stalin?** Philadelphia: Lippincott, 1964.

Whetten, Lawrence L., ed. *The Future of Soviet Military Power.* New York: Crane, Russak, 1976.

Wolfe, Thomas W. *Soviet Power and Europe, 1945-1970.** Baltimore: Johns Hopkins University Press, 1970.

_____. *Soviet Strategy at the Crossroads.* Cambridge, Mass.: Harvard University Press, 1964.

Zimmerman, William. *Soviet Perspectives on International Relations, 1956-1967.* Princeton, N.J.: Princeton University Press, 1969.

Developing Countries and Modernization

Berger, Peter I. *The Capitalist Revolution.** New York: Basic Books, 1986.

Berliner, Joseph S. *Soviet Economic Aid.* New York: Holt, Rinehart & Winston, 1958.

Black, C. E. *The Dynamics of Modernization.** New York: Harper & Row, 1966.

Black, Eugene R. *The Diplomacy of Economic Development.** New York: Atheneum, 1963.

Bodenheimer, Susanne J. *The Ideology of Developmentalism.* Beverly Hills, Calif.: Sage Publications, 1971.

Brandt Commission. *North-South.* Cambridge, Mass.: M.I.T. Press, 1980.

Crabb, Cecil V., Jr. *The Elephants and the Grass.** New York: Holt, Rinehart & Winston, 1965.

Ehrlich, Paul R. *The Population Bomb.** New York: Ballantine, 1968.

Emerson, Rupert. *From Empire to Nation.* Cambridge, Mass.: Harvard University Press, 1960.

Faaland, J., and J. R. Parkinson. *The Political Economy of the Development.* New York: St. Martin's Press, 1986.

Gupte, Pranay. *The Crowded Earth.* New York: Norton, 1984.

Hansen, Roger D. *Beyond the North-South Stalemate.* New York: McGraw-Hill (for the Council on Foreign Relations/1980s Project), 1979.

Heilbroner, Robert L. *The Great Ascent.* New York: Harper & Row, 1963.

Higgins, Benjamin, and Jean Downing Higgins. *Economic Development of a Small Planet.* New York: Norton, 1979.

Hunter, Robert E., and John E. Rielly, eds. *Development Today.* New York: Holt, Rinehart & Winston, 1972.

Huntington, Samuel P. *Political Order in Changing Societies.** New Haven, Conn.: Yale University Press, 1968. Paperback ed., 1969.

Janowitz, Morris. *The Military in the Political Development of New Nations.** Chicago: University of Chicago Press, 1964.

Johnson, John J., ed. *The Role of the Military in Underdeveloped Countries.* Princeton, N.J.: Princeton University Press, 1962.

Krasner, Stephen D. *Structural Conflict.* Berkeley, Calif.: University of California Press, 1985.

Lewis, W. Arthur. *The Evolution of the International Economic Order.** Princeton, N.J.: Princeton University Press, 1978.

Martin, Laurence W., ed. *Neutralism and Nonalignment.** New York: Holt, Rinehart & Winston, 1962.

Meken, Jane, ed. *World Population and U.S. Policy.* New York: Norton, 1986.

Millikan, Max F., and Donald L. M. Blackmer, eds. *The Emerging Nations.** Boston: Little, Brown, 1961.

Moran, Theodore H. *Multinational Corporation and the Politics of Dependence.** Princeton, N.J.: Princeton University Press, 1974.

Mortimer, Robert A. *The Third World Coalition in International Politics.* 2d ed. Boulder, Colo.: Westview Press, 1984.

Myrdal, Gunnar. *The Challenge of World Poverty.* New York: Pantheon, 1970.

_____. *Rich Lands and Poor.* New York: Harper & Row, 1957.

Nordlinger, Eric A. *Soldiers in Politics.** Englewood Cliffs, N.J.: Prentice-Hall, 1977.

Nossiter, Bernard D. *The Global Struggle for More.* New York: Harper & Row, 1987.

Organski, A. F. K. *The Stages of Political Development.* New York: Knopf, 1965.

Rostow, W. W. *Stages of Economic Growth.** New York: Cambridge University Press, 1960.

Rothstein, Robert L. *Global Bargaining.* Princeton, N.J.: Princeton University Press, 1979.

_____. *The Third World and U.S. Foreign Policy.* Boulder, Colo.: Westview Press, 1981.

_____. *The Weak in the World of the Strong.* New York: Columbia University Press, 1977.

Salas, Rafael. *Reflections on Population.* 2d ed. New York: Pergamon Press, 1985.

Singer, Hans, and Javed A. Ansari. *Rich and Poor Countries.* 4th ed. London: Unwin Hyman, 1988.

Staley, Eugene. *The Future of Underdeveloped Countries.** Rev. ed. New York: Holt, Rinehart & Winston, 1961.

Tapinos, Georges, and Phyllis T. Piotrow. *Six Billion People.* New York: McGraw-Hill (for the Council on Foreign Relations/1980s Project), 1978.

Tinbergen, Jan. *Reshaping the International Order.* New York: Dutton, 1976.

Tucker, Robert W. *The Inequality of Nations.* New York: Basic Books, 1977. Paperback ed., 1979.

Ward, Barbara. *Rich Nations and the Poor Nations.** New York: Norton, 1962.

Wattenberg, Ben J. *The Birth Dearth.* New York: Pharos Books, 1987.

Wriggins, W. Howard, and Gunnar Adler-Karlsson. *Reducing Global Inequities.* New York: McGraw-Hill (for the Council on Foreign Relations/1980s Project), 1978.

Wright, Robin. *Sacred Rage.* New York: Linden Press, 1985.

Foreign Policy Decision Making

Abel, Elie. *The Missile Crisis.* Philadelphia: Lippincott, 1966.

Allison, Graham T. *Essence of Decision.* Glenview, Ill.: Scott, Foresman, 1971.

Barnet, Richard J. *The Roots of War.** Baltimore: Penguin, 1973.

Betts, Richard K. *Soldiers, Statesmen, and Cold War Crises.* Cambridge, Mass.: Harvard University Press, 1978.

Blight, James, and David A. Welch. *On the Brink.* New York: Hill and Wang, 1989.

Builder, Carl H. *The Masks of War.* Baltimore: Johns Hopkins University Press, 1989.

Destler, I. M. *Making Foreign Economic Policy.* Washington, D.C.: Brookings, 1980.

Gelb, Leslie H., and Richard K. Betts. *The Irony of Vietnam.** Washington, D.C.: Brookings, 1979.

George, Alexander L. *Presidential Decisionmaking in Foreign Policy.** Boulder, Colo.: Westview Press, 1980.

Graber, Doris. *Public Opinion, the President, and Foreign Policy.** New York: Holt, Rinehart & Winston, 1968.

Halperin, Morton. *Bureaucratic Politics and Foreign Policy.** Washington, D.C.: Brookings, 1974.

Head, Richard G., Frisco W. Short, and Robert C. McFarlane. *Crisis Resolution.* Boulder, Colo.: Westview Press, 1978.

Hilsman, Roger. *The Politics of Policy Making in Defense and Foreign Affairs.** New York: Harper & Row, 1971. Reissued. Englewood Cliffs, N.J.: Prentice-Hall, 1987.

Janis, Irving L. *Victims of Groupthink.** 2d ed. Boston: Houghton Mifflin, 1982.

Kennedy, Robert F. *Thirteen Days.** New York: Norton, 1967.

Levering, Ralph B. *The Public and American Foreign Policy, 1918-1978.* New York: William Morrow, 1978.

Purvis, Hoyt, and Steven J. Baker, eds. *Legislating Foreign Policy.* Boulder, Colo.: Westview Press, 1984.

Rourke, John T. *Congress and the Presidency in U.S. Foreign Policymaking.* Boulder, Colo.: Westview Press, 1983.

Spanier, John, and Eric M. Uslaner. *American Foreign Policy Making and the Democratic Dilemmas.** 5th ed. Pacific Grove, Calif.: Brooks/Cole, 1989.

Spanier, John, and Joseph L. Nogee, eds. *Congress, the Presidency and American Foreign Policy.** Elmsford, N.Y.: Pergamon, 1981.

Perception and Psychology

De Rivera, Joseph H. *The Psychological Dimension of Foreign Policy.* Columbus, Ohio: Merrill, 1968.

Holsti, Ole R., and James N. Rosenau. *American Leadership in World Affairs.* Boston: Allen & Unwin, 1984.

Jervis, Robert. *Perception and Misperception in International Politics.** Princeton, N.J.: Princeton University Press, 1976.

Kelman, Herbert C., ed. *International Behavior.* New York: Holt, Rinehart & Winston, 1965.

Klineberg, Otto. *The Human Dimension in International Relations.** New York: Holt, Rinehart & Winston, 1964.

Stagner, Ross. *Psychological Aspects of International Conflict.** Belmont, Calif.: Brooks/Cole, 1967.

Stoessinger, John G. *Nations in Darkness.** 3d ed. New York: Random House, 1982. 4th ed., 1986.

———. *Why Nations Go to War.* 5th ed. New York: St. Martin's Press, 1989.

White, Ralph K. *Nobody Wanted War.** Garden City, N.Y.: Doubleday, 1968.

Deterrence and Arms Control

Allison, Graham T., Albert Carnesale, and Joseph S. Nye, Jr., eds. *Hawks, Doves, and Owls.** New York: Norton, 1985.

Berkowitz, Bruce D. *Calculated Risks.* New York: Simon & Schuster, 1987.

Boffey, Philip J., et al. *Claiming the Heavens.* New York: Times Books, 1988.

Brodie, Bernard. *Strategy in the Missile Age.** Princeton, N.J.: Princeton University Press, 1959.

Bull, Hedley. *The Control of the Arms Race.** 2d ed. New York: Holt, Rinehart & Winston, 1965.

Bundy, McGeorge. *Danger and Survival.* New York: Random House, 1989.

Carnesale, Albert, and Richard N. Haass, eds. *Superpower Arms Control.* Cambridge, Mass.: Ballinger, 1987.

Collins, John M. *American and Soviet Military Trends Since the Cuban Missile Crisis.** Washington, D.C.: Georgetown University, Center for Strategic and International Studies, 1978.

Freedman, Lawrence. *The Evolution of Nuclear Strategy.* New York: St. Martin's Press, 1981.

George, Alexander L., et al. *The Limits of Coercive Diplomacy.** Boston: Little, Brown, 1971.

George, Alexander L., and Richard Smoke. *Deterrence in American Foreign Policy.** New York: Columbia University Press, 1974.

George, Alexander L., Philip J. Farley, and Alexander Dallin, eds. *U.S.-Soviet Security Cooperation.* New York: Oxford University Press, 1988.

Herken, Gregg. *Counsels of War*. Enlarged ed. New York: Oxford University Press, 1987.

International Institute for Strategic Studies. *The Military Balance*.* Published annually.

Jervis, Robert. *The Illogic of American Nuclear Strategy*.* Ithaca, N.Y.: Cornell University Press, 1984. Paperback ed., 1985.

_____. *The Meaning of the Nuclear Revolution*. Ithaca, N.Y.: Cornell University Press, 1989.

Jervis, Robert, et al. *Psychology and Deterrence*.* Baltimore: Johns Hopkins University Press, 1985.

Kahan, Jerome H. *Security in the Nuclear Age*.* Washington, D.C.: Brookings, 1975.

Katz, Arthur M. *Life After Nuclear War*.* Cambridge, Mass.: Ballinger, 1981.

Krepon, Michael. *Strategic Stalemate*. New York: St. Martin's Press, 1985. Paperback ed., 1986.

Levine, Robert A. *Arms Debate*. Cambridge, Mass.: Harvard University Press, 1963.

Mandelbaum, Michael. *The Nuclear Revolution*. Cambridge, Mass.: Cambridge University Press, 1981.

Martin, Laurence, ed. *Strategic Thought in the Nuclear Age*. Baltimore: Johns Hopkins University Press, 1980.

McNamara, Robert. *Blundering into Disaster*. New York: Pantheon, 1986.

Morgan, Patrick M. *Deterrence*.* Beverly Hills, Calif.: Sage Publications, 1977. 2d ed., 1983.

Mueller, John E. *Retreat from Doomsday*. New York: Basic Books, 1989.

Nacht, Michael. *The Age of Vulnerability*.* Washington, D.C.: Brookings, 1985.

Newhouse, John. *Cold Dawn*. New York: Holt, Rinehart & Winston, 1973.

Office of Technology Assessment. *The Effects of Nuclear War*.* Washington, D.C.: Government Printing Office, 1980.

Payne, Keith B. *Nuclear Deterrence in U.S.-Soviet Relations*. Boulder, Colo.: Westview Press, 1982.

_____. *Strategic Defense*.* Lanham, Md.: University Press of America, 1986.

Quester, George H. *The Future of Nuclear Deterrence*. Lexington, Mass.: Lexington Books, 1986.

Ranger, Robin. *Arms and Politics 1958-1978*. Boulder, Colo.: Westview Press, 1979.

Schell, Jonathan. *The Fate of the Earth*. New York: Knopf, 1982.

Schelling, Thomas C. *Strategy of Conflict*. Cambridge, Mass.: Harvard University Press, 1960.

Schelling, Thomas C., and Morton H. Halperin. *Strategy and Arms Control*.* Elmsford, N.Y.: Pergamon-Brassey, 1985.

Scoville, Herbert, Jr. *The MX*. Cambridge, Mass.: M.I.T. Press, 1981.

Smoke, Richard. *National Security and the Nuclear Dilemma*. 2d ed. New York: Random House, 1987.

Talbott, Strobe. *Endgame*.* New York: Harper & Row, 1979.

_____. *The Master of the Game*. New York: Knopf, 1988.

Tucker, Robert W. *The Nuclear Debate*.* New York: Holmes & Meier, 1985.

Wolfe, Thomas W. *The SALT Experience*. Cambridge, Mass.: Ballinger, 1979.

Limited War (Conventional and Revolutionary)

Blaufarb, Douglas S. *The Counterinsurgency Era*. New York: Free Press, 1977.

Blechman, Barry M., and Stephen S. Kaplan. *Force Without War*. Washington, D.C.: Brookings, 1978.

Gabriel, Richard A. *Military Incompetence*. New York: Hill and Wang, 1985.

Galula, David. *Counterinsurgency Warfare*. New York: Holt, Rinehart & Winston, 1964.

Greene, T. N., ed. *The Guerrilla—and How to Fight Him*.* New York: Holt, Rinehart & Winston, 1962.

Hadley, Arthur. *The Straw Giant*. New York: Random House, 1986.

Heilbrunn, Otto. *Partisan Warfare*. New York: Holt, Rinehart & Winston, 1962.

Kissinger, Henry A. *Nuclear Weapons and Foreign Policy.* * New York: Harper & Row, 1957. Abridged ed. New York: Norton, 1969.

Lebow, Richard Ned. *Between Peace and War.* Baltimore: Johns Hopkins University Press, 1981. Paperback ed. 1984.

———. *Nuclear Crisis Management.* Ithaca, N.Y.: Cornell University Press, 1987.

Mao Tse-tung on Guerrilla Warfare. Translated and with an Introduction by Samuel B. Griffith. New York: Holt, Rinehart & Winston, 1961.

Osgood, Robert E. *Limited War.* Chicago: University of Chicago Press, 1957.

———. *Limited War Revisited.* Boulder, Colo.: Westview Press, 1979.

Paret, Peter, and John W. Shy. *Guerrillas in the 1960's.* * Rev. ed. New York: Holt, Rinehart & Winston, 1962.

Smoke, Richard. *War: Controlling Escalation.* Cambridge, Mass.: Harvard University Press, 1978.

Snyder, Glenn H., and Paul Diesing. *Conflict Among Nations.* * Princeton, N.J.: Princeton University Press, 1977.

Spanier, John W. *The Truman-MacArthur Controversy and the Korean War.* * Cambridge, Mass.: Harvard University Press, 1959. Rev. paperback ed. New York: Norton, 1965.

Stern, Ellen P., ed. *The Limits of Military Intervention.* Bethesda, Md.: Seven Locks Press, 1977.

Thayer, Charles W. *Guerrilla.* * New York: Harper & Row, 1963.

Vietnam War

Berman, Larry. *Planning a Tragedy.* * New York: Norton, 1982.

———. *Lyndon Johnson's War.* New York: Norton, 1989.

Draper, Theodore. *Abuse of Power.* * New York: Viking, 1967.

Fall, Bernard B. *The Two Viet-Nams.* 2d rev. ed. New York: Holt, Rinehart & Winston, 1967. Paperback ed. Boulder, Colo.: Westview Press, 1985.

———. *Viet-Nam Witness, 1953-66.* New York: Holt, Rinehart & Winston, 1966.

Herring, George C. *America's Longest War.* * New York: Wiley, 1979. 2d ed. Philadelphia: Temple University Press, 1986.

Hoopes, Townsend. *The Limits of Intervention.* * New York: McKay, 1969.

Karnow, Stanley. *Vietnam.* New York: Viking, 1983.

Kattenburg, Paul M. *The Vietnam Trauma in American Foreign Policy, 1945-1975.* New Brunswick, N.J.: Transaction Books, 1980.

Krepinevich, Andrew F. *The Army and Vietnam.* * Baltimore: Johns Hopkins University Press, 1986.

Lewy, Guenter. *America in Vietnam.* * New York: Oxford University Press, 1978.

Lomperis, Timothy J. *The War Everyone Lost—And Won.* * Baton Rouge: Louisiana State University Press, 1984. Paperback ed. Washington, D.C.: CQ Press, 1987.

Oberdorfer, Don. *Tet.* Garden City, N.Y.: Doubleday, 1971.

Palmer, Bruce, Jr. *The Twenty-Five-Year War.* Paperback ed. New York: Simon & Schuster, 1985.

The Pentagon Papers. * Chicago: Quadrangle, 1971.

Pike, Douglas. *Viet Cong.* * Cambridge, Mass.: M.I.T. Press, 1966.

Rotter, Andrew J. *The Path to Vietnam.* Ithaca, N.Y.: Cornell University Press, 1987.

Sheehan, Neil. *A Bright Shining Light.* * New York: Random House, 1988.

Summers, Harry G., Jr. *On Strategy.* * New York: Dell, 1984.

Thompson, Sir Robert. *No Exit from Vietnam.* New York: McKay, 1969.

Nuclear and Nonnuclear Proliferation

Dunn, Lewis A. *Controlling the Bomb.* * New Haven, Conn.: Yale University Press, 1982.

Gompert, David C., et al. *Nuclear Weapons and World Politics.* * New York:

McGraw-Hill (for the Council on Foreign Relations/1980s Project), 1977.

Greenwood, Ted, Harold A. Feiveson, and Theodore B. Taylor. *Nuclear Proliferation.** New York: McGraw-Hill (for the Council on Foreign Relations/1980s Project), 1977.

Lefever, Ernest W. *Nuclear Arms in the Third World.** Washington, D.C.: Brookings, 1979.

Pierre, Andrew J. *The Global Politics of Arms Sales.** Princeton, N.J.: Princeton University Press, 1981.

Spector, Leonard S. *Going Nuclear.* Cambridge, Mass.: Ballinger, 1987.

_____. *The Undeclared Bomb.* Cambridge, Mass.: Ballinger, 1988.

Economics and Trade

Bhagwati, Jagdish N. *Protectionism.* Cambridge, Mass.: M.I.T. Press, 1988.

Blake, David H., and Robert S. Walters. *The Politics of Global Economic Relations.** 3d ed. Englewood Cliffs, N.J.: Prentice-Hall, 1987.

Dertouzos, Michael L., et al. *Made in America.* Cambridge, Mass.: M.I.T. Press, 1989.

Gilpin, Robert. *The Political Economy of International Relations.* Princeton, N.J.: Princeton University Press, 1987.

Hofheinz, Roy, Jr., and Kent E. Calder. *The East Asia Edge.* New York: Basic Books, 1982. Paperback ed., 1983.

Phillips, Kevin T. *Staying on Top.* New York: Random House, 1985.

Prestowitz, Clyde V., Jr. *Trading Places.* New York: Basic Books, 1988.

Rustow, Dankwart A. *Oil and Turmoil.* New York: Norton, 1982.

Spero, Joan E. *The Politics of International Economic Relations.** 3d ed. New York: St. Martin's Press, 1985.

Tolchin, Martin, and Susan Tolchin. *Buying into America.* New York: Times Books, 1988.

United Nations

Bailey, Sidney D. *The United Nations.** New York: Holt, Rinehart & Winston, 1963.

Bloomfield, Lincoln P., et al. *International Military Forces.* Boston: Little, Brown, 1964.

Boyd, Andrew. *United Nations.** Baltimore: Penguin, 1963.

Burns, Arthur Lee, and Nina Heathcote. *Peace-keeping by U.N. Forces.* New York: Holt, Rinehart & Winston, 1963.

Calvocoressi, Peter. *World Order and New States.* New York: Holt, Rinehart & Winston, 1962.

Claude, Inis L., Jr. *The Changing United Nations.** New York: Random House, 1967.

_____. *Swords into Plowshares.* 4th ed. New York: Random House, 1971.

Dallin, Alexander. *The Soviet Union at the United Nations.** New York: Holt, Rinehart & Winston, 1962.

Franck, Thomas M. *Nation Against Nation.* New York: Oxford University Press, 1985.

Goodrich, Leland M. *The United Nations in a Changing World.* New York: Columbia University Press, 1976.

Haas, Ernst B. *Why We Still Need the United Nations.* Berkeley, Calif.: Institute of International Studies, University of California, Berkeley, 1986.

Miller, Linda B. *World Order and Local Disorder.* Princeton, N.J.: Princeton University Press, 1967.

Miller, Lynn H. *Organizing Mankind.** Boston: Holbrook Press, 1972.

Nye, Joseph S., Jr. *Peace in Parts.** Boston: Little, Brown, 1971. Paperback ed. Lanham, Md.: University Press of America, 1987.

Roberts, Adam, and Benedict Kinsgbury. *United Nations, Divided World.* Oxford, England: Clarendon Press, 1988.

Stoessinger, John G. *The United Nations and the Superpowers.** New York: Random House, 1966. 4th ed., 1977.

International Law

Bozeman, Adda B. *The Future of Law in a Multicultural World.* Princeton, N.J.: Princeton University Press, 1971.

Brierly, James L. *The Law of Nations.* 6th ed. New York: Oxford University Press, 1963.

Corbett, Percy E. *Law and Society in the Relation of States.* New York: Harcourt, 1951.

Deutsch, Karl W., and Stanley Hoffman, eds. *The Relevance of International Law.* Garden City, N.Y.: Doubleday, 1971.

Henkin, Louis. *How Nations Behave.** New York: Holt, Rinehart & Winston, 1968.

Kaplan, Morton A., and Nicholas DeB. Katzenbach. *The Political Foundations of International Law.* New York: Wiley, 1961.

International Morality

Butterfield, Herbert. *International Conflict in the Twentieth Century: A Christian View.* New York: Harper & Row, 1960.

Davidson, Donald L. *Nuclear War and the American Churches.* Boulder, Colo.: Westview Press, 1983.

Dougherty, James E. *The Bishops and Nuclear Weapons.* Hamden, Conn.: Archon Books, 1984.

Herz, John H. *Political Realism and Political Idealism.* Chicago: University of Chicago Press, 1951.

Johnson, James Turner. *Just War Tradition and the Restraint of War.* Princeton, N.J.: Princeton University Press, 1981.

Lefever, Ernest W., ed. *Ethics and World Politics.** Baltimore: Johns Hopkins University Press, 1972.

National Conference of Catholic Bishops. *The Challenge of Peace.* Washington, D.C.: United States Catholic Conference, 1983.

Niebuhr, Reinhold. *The Children of Light and the Children of Darkness.* New York: Scribner, 1944.

_____. *The Irony of American History.** New York: Scribner, 1952.

_____. *Moral Man and Immoral Society.** New York: Scribner, 1932.

Nye, Joseph S., Jr. *Nuclear Ethics.* New York: Free Press, 1986.

Thompson, Kenneth W. *Political Realism and the Crisis of World Politics.* Princeton, N.J.: Princeton University Press, 1960.

Wolfers, Arnold, and Laurence W. Martin, eds. *The Anglo-American Tradition in Foreign Affairs.* Northford, Conn.: Elliot's Books, 1956.

Functionalism and Community Building

Deutsch, Karl, et al. *Political Community and the North Atlantic Area.* Princeton, N.J.: Princeton University Press, 1957.

Etzioni, Amitai. *Political Unification.** New York: Holt, Rinehart & Winston, 1965.

Haas, Ernst B. *The Uniting of Europe.* Rev. ed. Stanford, Calif.: Stanford University Press, 1968.

Kerr, Anthony J. *The Common Market and How It Works.* Oxford, England: Pergamon Press, 1983.

Lieber, Robert J. *British Politics and European Unity.* Berkeley, Calif.: University of California Press, 1970.

Lindberg, Leon N., and Stuart A. Scheingold. *Europe's Would-Be Polity.** Englewood Cliffs, N.J.: Prentice-Hall, 1970.

Transnationalism, World Order, and Socioeconomic Issues

Barnet, Richard J., and Ronald E. Müller. *Global Reach.** New York: Simon & Schuster, 1975.

Bergsten, C. Fred, Thomas Holst, and Theodore H. Moran. *American Multinationals and American Interests.** Washington, D.C.: Brookings, 1978.

Brown, Lester R. *In the Human Interest.** New York: Norton, 1974.

_____. *State of the World 1988*. New York: Norton, 1988.

_____. *World Without Borders.** New York: Vintage, 1973.

Brown, Seyom. *New Forces, Old Forces, and the Future of World Politics*. Glenview, Ill.: Scott, Foresman, 1988.

Falk, Richard A. *A Study of Future Worlds*. New York: Free Press, 1975.

Gilpin, Robert. *U.S. Power and the Multinational Corporation*. New York: Basic Books, 1975.

Hanson, Eric. *The Catholic Church in World Politics*. Princeton, N.J.: Princeton University Press, 1987.

Hopkins, Raymond F., Robert L. Paarlberg, and Mitchel B. Wallerstein. *Food in the Global Arena*. New York: Holt, Rinehart & Winston, 1982.

Johansen, Robert. *The National Interest and the Human Interest.** Princeton, N.J.: Princeton University Press, 1980.

Keohane, Robert O. *After Hegemony*. Princeton, N.J.: Princeton University Press, 1984.

Keohane, Robert O., and Joseph S. Nye. *Power and Interdependence.** 2d ed. Glenview, Ill.: Scott, Foresman, 1988.

Keohane, Robert O., and Joseph S. Nye, eds. *Transnational Relations and World Politics*. Cambridge, Mass.: Harvard University Press, 1972.

Kim, Samuel S. *The Quest for a Just World Order*. Boulder, Colo.: Westview Press, 1983.

Kindleberger, Charles P., ed. *The International Corporation*. Cambridge, Mass.: M.I.T. Press, 1970.

Laqueur, Walter. *Terrorism*. Boston: Little, Brown, 1977.

Maghoori, Ray, and Bennett Ramberg, eds. *Globalism vs. Realism.** Boulder, Colo.: Westview Press, 1982.

Mansbach, Richard W., Yale H. Ferguson, and Donald E. Lampert. *The Web of World Politics.** Englewood Cliffs, N.J.: Prentice-Hall, 1976.

Mendlovitz, Saul H., ed. *On the Creation of a Just World Order*. New York: Free Press, 1975. Paperback ed., 1977.

Miller, Lynn H. *Global Order*. Boulder, Colo.: Westview Press, 1985.

Pirages, Dennis. *Global Ecopolitics.** North Scituate, Mass.: Duxbury, 1978.

_____. *Global Technopolitics.** Pacific Grove, Calif.: Brooks/Cole, 1988.

Rosecrance, Richard. *The Rise of the Trading State*. New York: Basic Books, 1986.

Said, Abdul, and Lutz R. Simons, eds. *The New Sovereigns.** Englewood Cliffs, N.J.: Prentice-Hall, 1975.

Scott, Andrew N. *The Dynamics of Interdependence*. Chapel Hill, N.C.: University of North Carolina Press, 1982.

Sorous, Marvin S. *Beyond Sovereignty*. Columbia: University of South Carolina Press, 1986.

Stanley, C. Maxwell. *Managing Global Problems.** Iowa City: University of Iowa (for the Stanley Foundation), 1979.

Sterling, Claire. *The Terror Network*. New York: Holt, Rinehart & Winston, 1981. Paperback ed. New York: Berkley Publishing, 1984.

Taylor, Philip. *Nonstate Actors in International Politics*. Boulder, Colo.: Westview Press, 1982.

Vernon, Raymond. *Sovereignty at Bay*. New York: Basic Books, 1971.

Vernon, Raymond, ed. *The Oil Crisis.** New York: Norton, 1976.

Willetts, Peter, ed. *Pressure Groups in the Global System*. New York: St. Martin's Press, 1982.

World Commission on Environment and Development. *Our Common Future*. New York: Oxford University Press, 1987.

Index

ABM. *See* Antiballistic missiles
Abortion, 243
Abrahamson, James, 299
Acheson, Dean, 314
Acquired immune deficiency syndrome (AIDS), 417
Afghanistan, 126, 130, 194, 195, 205, 216, 246, 312, 376-378, 379, 472, 475
Africa. *See also* South Africa
  civil war in, 460-461
  debt of, 409
  ethnic issues in, 237-238
  famines in, 245-246
  government in, 255
  overpopulation in, 239
  Planned Parenthood in, 243
  poverty in, 232-233
  racial issues in, 236
  United Nations and, 467, 472-473, 476
Agriculture
  developing countries, in, 243-246, 440
  role of, 149-150
  subsidies of, 440, 443-444
Aid, 393-394, 400, 402-406, 410, 465-466
AIDS. *See* Acquired immune deficiency syndrome
al-Assad, Hafez, 68
Algeria, 373
Allende, Salvador, 397-398, 399-400
Alliance, 121-122, 127-132. *See also* Soviet Union, foreign policies, alliances; United States, foreign policies, alliances
Alliance for Progress, 286, 380
Allison, Graham, 276
America. *See* United States

Amin, Idi, 165, 167, 476
Anarchical systems, 92, 102, 105, 109, 111-112, 115, 478, 480, 483-484, 494, 499, 558
Angell, Norman, 564
Angola, 195, 216, 238, 473
Antiballistic missiles (ABMs)
  controversy surrounding, 290-294
  Johnson decisions regarding (1960s), 289, 291-294, 300
  Soviet, 296, 346
Antiballistic Missile Treaty 297, 298, 299-300, 350, 351
Appeasement, 314. *See also* Hitler, appeasement of
Aquino, Corazon, 400
Arab-Israeli War. *See also* Israel; Middle East
  1967, 459
  1973, 536
Arafat, Yasir
  Israel and, 543
  Palestine Liberation Organization (PLO) and, 52, 68
  United Nations and, 466-467
Argentina, 62-63, 381-382, 408, 527, 537
Armenia, 49
Arms control. *See also* Strategic Arms Limitation Talks
  nuclear proliferation and, 532-533
  Soviet Union and, 318, 330, 342
  Strategic Defense Initiative and, 297
  United States and, 196, 216, 318, 342, 344-352
Arms races, 121, 123-124, 216, 276, 279, 290-291, 292, 295-296, 331, 344, 347,

349-350, 352-359, 487
Arms sales, 533-536
Art, Robert, 301
Articles of Confederation, 496
ASEAN. *See* Association of Southeast
    Asian Nations
Asia, 166-169. *See also* individual coun-
    tries
Association of East Caribbean States, 63
Association of Southeast Asian Nations
    (ASEAN), 64
Assured destruction, 332, 344
Athens, 120
Atom bomb. *See* Nuclear weapons
Austria-Hungary, 48, 53, 142-143
Automatism, theory of, 102
Automobile production, 426, 427

Baker, James, 408
Balance of power. *See also* International
    politics; State system; Superpowers
    arms races and, 352-353
    China and, 26-27
    Cold war and, 21-24, 25, 38, 276, 279,
        293
    definition/status of, 20, 140, 200
    games analogy of, 104-105, 112
    international politics and, 16, 20, 102-
        105, 136, 193, 195, 197
    nuclear power and, 339-340, 341, 344-
        345, 533
    polarity and, 112-114, 119-121
    role of, 103-104, 118, 200-201
    Vietnam and, 26-27
    wars and, 20-22, 24-25, 119, 352, 366
Ball, George, 419, 430, 472
Bangladesh, 237, 246, 548-549
Barnet, Richard, 249
Battle of Britain (1940), 156
Bay of Pigs invasion (1961), 279
Behavioralism, 12-14, 16, 112
Beirut. *See* Lebanon
Belgium, 460
Benes, Eduard, 207-208
Bentsen, Lloyd, 81
Berlin Wall, 48, 219
Biafra, 465
Birth control, 241-243. *See also* Over-
    population
Bismarck, Otto von, 33, 314
Blake, David, 437
Boeing Corporation, 428
Bolivia, 76
Brady, Nicholas, 409

Brady Plan, 409
Brazil, 408, 410, 527, 537
Brezhnev, Leonid, 192-193, 209, 305,
    312, 391-392
Bridgestone, 427
Brierly, J. L., 480
Britain. *See also* Falkland Islands
    agriculture in, 149, 390
    balance of power and, 20-21, 83, 119
    Battle of Britain (1940), 156
    Battle of the Atlantic, 391
    European Economic Community and,
        508
    foreign intervention of, 56-57, 62-63
    Malaya and, 372
    Marshall Plan (1947), 393-394
    navy of, 21, 106, 390-391
    nuclear power and, 525, 526
    per capita income, 148
    political process, 305-306
    policies, 1930s, 24-25, 27-28, 36-37,
        313, 319, 353
    power of, 141-142, 153-154, 160, 161
    World War I, 4-5, 106-107
    World War II, 21, 24-25, 89, 100, 390-
        391
Brown, Lester, 66
Brzezinski, Zbigniew, 107, 164, 166, 169,
    170, 179, 202, 434-435
Bull, Hedley, 114, 166
Bundy, McGeorge, 357-358
Bureaucratic politics, 275-276
Burundi, 237-238
Bush, George
    defense spending and, 87
    drugs, war on, 77
    election of, 80
    Nicaragua and, 399, 550
    Strategic Defense Initiative and, 299-
        300
    United Nations and, 469

Calvin, John, 252
Cambodia, 465, 473, 475, 476
Capability analysis, 104-105
Capitalism
    Calvinism and, 252
    Catholic church and, 67
    developing countries and, 262-264
    international politics and, 14-15, 265
    laissez-faire capitalism, 252
    Marxism-Leninism and, 199-200
    Soviet Union and, 31-32, 198-207, 212-
        213, 316, 405, 511

Carnegie, Andrew, 5
Carr, E. H., 333, 417, 420
Carter Doctrine (1979), 126, 147, 194
Carter, Jimmy
  defense spending and, 87
  détente and, 193, 194, 392
  Iranian oil embargo, 402
  nuclear power and, 529
  Soviet grain embargo, 392, 400
  Strategic Arms Limitation Talks II
    (SALT II) (1979), 109
Castro, Fidel, 68, 69, 281, 372, 396-397,
  399, 408, 540
Catholic church, 67, 70
Central America. *See* Latin America
Central Intelligence Agency (CIA), 88
Chamberlain, Neville, 25, 28, 33, 36-37,
  274-275, 316, 484
Chemical warfare, 483, 537, 546
Chiang Kai-shek, 188, 372
Chile, 397-398, 399-400, 407
China, Communist
  antiballistic missiles and, 293, 300
  arms sales of, 535, 536-537
  economy of, 269
  food production in, 244-245, 246
  Korea and, 456. *See also* Korean War
  nuclear power and, 526, 533
  population of, 143
  Soviet Union and, 26, 59, 75, 127, 129,
    208-210, 366
  Third World nation, as, 59, 128, 166,
    169, 250
  United States and, 26, 30, 51, 52, 125,
    129, 188, 303, 312, 357, 366, 381, 457
  Vietnam and, 26-27
China, Nationalist
  collapse of, 26, 68-69, 125, 188-189
  United States and, 129, 525
Chinese, in Southeast Asia, 236
Christian Democrats, 500-501
Churchill, Winston
  civilization, end of, 3
  Hitler, perceptions of, 33-34, 36, 322
  law and, 482-483
  prime minister, as, 37, 319
  Soviet Union and, 89, 316
  World War II, 11
CIA. *See* Central Intelligence Agency
Civil war. *See* Wars, civil
Claude, Inis, 20, 497, 505
Clausewitz, Carl von, 100, 136, 152, 540
Clemenceau, Georges, 10
Coal, 143, 411, 503

Cocaine, 77
Coercion, economic. *See* Economic coercion; Sanctions
Cold war
  abatement of, 130-132, 192, 216, 218-
    220
  antiballistic missile agreements and,
    290-294
  balance of power and, 124-127, 131,
    258, 456
  development of, 21-24, 31-32, 38, 311-
    312, 319
  effects of, 87-88, 187-190
  multinational corporations and, 432
  political economy during, 391-393
  Soviet Union and, 21-24, 32, 35, 51,
    105, 182, 212-214, 216-220
  United Nations and, 457-459
  United States and, 21-24, 35, 87-88, 89,
    181, 194-196, 211-212, 215,
    455-457
  Vietnam War and, 322
Colombia
  coffee exports, 247
  drugs and, 45-46, 77, 247
  poverty in, 232
Colonialism, 233-234, 257
COMECON. *See* Council for Mutual
  Economic Assistance
Commodities, prices of, 406
Common Market, 503, 504, 506. *See also*
  European Economic Community
Communism. *See also* Soviet Union
  policy making and, 287-288
  United States and, 187-190
  Soviet Union and, 219-220
Communist bloc, 34. *See also* China,
  Communist; Soviet Union
Communist Party, 30. *See also* Soviet
  Union
Community, supranational, 499-507. *See*
  also European Economic Community
Competition, international, 106-107,
  121-122, 162, 163, 168, 311, 321, 351-
  352, 440-443, 508
Concert of Europe, 54, 61, 110
Conflict. *See also* Decision making, conflict in; State system, conflict in; War
  developing nations and, 547-550
  economic factors and, 438, 440-441
  interdependence and, 513, 521
  multinational corporations and, 432-
    433
  nuclear, 528-529

resolution of, 329-333, 456-459, 463,
    468, 487, 498, 502, 558
superpowers and, 547-551
Confrontation. *See* Polarity, bipolarity
Congo, Republic of, 460-461, 463, 464.
    See also Zaire
Congress of Vienna (1815), 4, 334
Congress, United States. *See also* Governmental institutions, legislative
    policy making, 35-36, 302-304, 322
    Strategic Defense Initiative and, 298
Conservation of enemies, principle of,
    27
Containment. *See* Soviet Union, expansionism
Conventional war. *See* War
Conventional weapons, 535-536
Council for Mutual Economic Assistance (COMECON), 62, 395-396, 508
Council on Competitiveness, 162
Covert operations, 383-384
Crisis management, 120-132, 277-281,
    285-286, 320, 342, 358, 379
Cuba
    economic pressures on, 397, 399
    government of, 255
    missile crisis, 63, 128, 153, 276, 278-
        281, 305, 332, 481, 492n6
    powers of, 57-58
    Soviet Union and, 126, 396-397
    United Nations and, 492n6
    United States, invasion by (1961), 55
Cultural imperialism, 432
Cyprus, 473
Czechoslovakia
    European Economic Community and,
        509
    Soviet Union and, 23, 207-208

Debt
    developing countries, 257, 406-409
    Eastern Europe, 396
    United States, 47-48, 79-80, 130, 163,
        428-429, 435
Decision making. *See also* Policy making
    coalitions in, 285-286
    conflict in, 284-285, 322
    crises, in, 277-281, 285-286
    policy makers and, 33-36, 275-276,
        282-283, 287-288
    political process and, 300-304, 563
    presidents and, 291-292
de Cuéllar, Javier Pérez, 472, 473
Defection, 94-95

de Gaulle, Charles, 527, 529
de Jouvenel, Bertrand, 334
Democratic party
    antiballistic missiles and, 290-291
    cold war and, 322, 562
    Communist China and, 30, 189, 302
    social, 560, 561
    Strategic Defense Initiative and, 299
Democratic states. *See also* Western democracies
    geography and, 140-141
    morale in, 155-156
    negotiation by, 329
    patterns of behavior, 27-30, 313, 317,
        319, 321, 488-489
    political independence of, 76
    political processes of, 152-153, 288-289
    security and, 87-90
    undemocratic states and, 89, 180
    war and, 333-334, 551-553, 561-562
Deng Xiaoping, 269
Détente
    détente I, 192-194, 210, 212, 216, 220,
        312-313
    détente II, 195-196, 210-211, 220, 312-
        313, 318-319, 550-552
    foreign policies and, 210-220, 315
    national economy and, 82, 131, 437-
        438
    nonaligned countries and, 83
    political economy and, 391-393
    role of, 129, 165, 203, 204
    U.S. attitudes toward, 217-218
Deterrence
    antiballistic missiles and, 295-296, 346
    arms race and, 354-355, 358
    conflict resolution and, 332
    role of, 11, 340
    nuclear war and, 340, 341, 342-349,
        487-488, 532-533
    United States and, 289-290, 295, 340-
        342
Deutch, Karl, 499
Developing countries. *See also* Third
    World countries; individual countries
    aid for, 402-406, 465-466
    civil war in, 93
    debt of, 257, 406-409
    domestic policies of, 149, 229-230, 241,
        243, 267-268
    economic policies of, 263-269, 416-417
    foreign policies of, 229-230, 257-261,
        265-266, 385-386, 485, 537-538
    health in, 230-231

modernization of, 82-83, 235-257, 261-264, 465, 511

multinational companies and, 248, 249, 428, 432, 434

per capita income, 148-149, 230, 261

politics in, 254-257

poverty in, 230-233, 239-240, 485

resources of, 230, 246-248, 263

ruling elites in, 264

self-determination of, 235, 262

Third World countries, as, 59, 82-83, 147, 225-227, 233, 436

trade with, 249-250, 409-410, 534-535

Westernization of, 233-235

Development loans, 404

Dictatorships. *See* Totalitarian government

Diplomacy

arms sales and, 533-534

force and, 98, 99

preventive, 457-465, 475, 549-550

United States, of, 184-185

war and, 99-100, 560

Disarmament, 105-106, 487-488. *See also* Arms control

Disarmament conferences, 10

Dollar, U.S., 407, 408, 429, 443, 444

Domestic policies

foreign policy making, compared with, 282-283

human rights, 46-47

Domestic politics. *See also* International politics; States, objectives of

conflicts in, 92-93, 95-96, 110, 292

force and, 95, 374-376, 380-382, 383

games analogy of, 95, 96

governmental institutions and, 93-95

nuclear power and, 427

political culture, role of, 95-96

political system in, 94

role of, 322

Domino effect, 120, 129, 188

Drucker, Peter, 430

Drugs

Colombian cartels and, 45-46

internal threats, as, 76-77

Nicaragua and, 398

war on, 76-77

Dukakis, Michael, 299

Dulles, John Foster, 314, 315

EC. *See* European Community

Ecological issues. *See* Environmental issues

Economic coercion, 397-402, 418-420, 446-447, 545-546. *See also* Sanctions

Economic development

developing countries, in, 254, 417-418

globalism, 426-427, 445

Economic leverage, 391-393, 397-406, 414-420, 508

Economic nationalism, 437, 445

Economic security. *See* Security, economic

Economics. *See also* Political economy

free market and, 417-418, 511, 513-514

interdependence, 435, 445, 446, 510-512

international aid and, 402-406

international politics and, 389-402, 443, 503-504, 511

laissez-faire, 389, 513

mercantilism, 438-445

multinational corporations and, 425-436

spillover in, 503, 507

Economies. *See also* Soviet Union, economy; United States, economy

industrial, 431

international, 264-269, 321, 417-418, 434-445, 524

power and, 138, 143, 147-150, 160-169, 418

social policies and, 81-83, 86, 504-505

world, 48, 85, 265, 411, 415

ECSC. *See* European Coal and Steel Community

Education

developing countries, in, 234-235

EEC. *See* European Economic Community

Egypt. *See also* Middle East

alignment of, 260-261, 459

Israel and, 76, 548

population of, 241

Soviet Union and, 126, 214, 260, 460

United States and, 260, 405

Eisenhower, David D., 304, 397, 400

El Salvador, 304, 467, 483

Embargoes, 391, 402. *See also* Sanctions

Emerson, Ralph Waldo, 186-187

Emigration, 242, 303, 401

Employment, blue-collar, 428

England. *See* Britain

Environmental issues, 495, 522-523

Estonia, 49-50

Ethiopia

Eritreans in, 549

famine in, 245-246
Italy and (1935), 481
Somalia and, 76, 237, 465, 548
Ethnic issues, developing countries, in, 237-238
Etzioni, Amitai, 499
Europe
  decline of, 203
  Eastern, 130, 157, 210, 218-220, 395-396, 521
  multinational corporations in, 426
  peace in, 142, 157
  population of, 242
  Western, 148, 166, 179, 330, 384, 394-395, 439-441, 442-443, 521
European Atomic Energy Community (Euratom), 64, 503
European Coal and Steel Community (ECSC) (1950), 62, 64, 394-395, 500, 503
European Community (EC), 64-65
European Economic Community (EEC) (1958)
  cooperation in, 108, 109, 169, 431, 500, 501-502
  defense and, 509-510
  development of, 62, 64, 395, 500-502, 506, 507-510
  Inner Six, 500, 501-502, 503, 506
  members, 508-509
  multinational corporations and, 431, 433
  role of, 166, 506
  rules of, 503-504
  success of, 506-507
  sugar exports of, 443
  United States and, 429-430, 431
Euratom. *See* European Atomic Energy Community

Falkland Islands, 56-57, 62-63, 381-382, 383, 384, 473, 536
Firestone Rubber & Tire Company, 427
First strike force, 342, 344, 347, 355, 361n19
Food, 244. *See also* Hunger
Force
  developing countries and, 385-386
  domestic politics, role in, 95, 374-376, 380-382, 383
  governmental use of, 46, 48, 84, 93, 95, 378, 379-382, 414
  interdependence and, 512
  international politics, role in, 85, 93,

98, 100, 101, 138, 281, 387, 552
  limited warfare, 364-368
  power and, 138, 446-447, 488
  Reagan, Ronald, use of by, 157
  revolutionary warfare, 368-373
Ford, Gerald, 392
Ford Motor Company, 427
Foreign policies. *See also* International politics; individual countries
  decision making and, 300-304
  domestic policy, compared with, 282-283
  focus of, 16
  moralism and, 490-491
  national interests and, 319-325, 487
  perceptions, role of, 310-320, 419
  public opinion and, 560-561
  theories of, 19, 20, 177-178
Foreign policies, styles of. *See also* individual countries
  détente and, 196, 210-220
  elite, 196-210
  insular, 177-179
  national, 180-186
  United States, postwar, 186-196
France
  Algeria and, 373
  debt, African countries of, 409
  European Coal and Steel Community and, 506
  European Economic Community and, 394-395
  foreign intervention of, 57
  French-Soviet Treaty of Mutual Assistance (1944), 394
  Germany and, 58, 394, 500, 506, 509
  Napoleonic Wars, 103
  nuclear power and, 525, 526
  nuclear reactors, 528
  Revolution (1789), 31, 111, 334
  Vietnam and, 372
  world wars, 4, 24, 142, 161
Frederick the Great, 98
Free trade
  European Economic Community and, 507
  interdependence and, 513-514
  international economy and, 437-438, 443, 524
  international politics and, 14, 436, 444
Fullbright, William, 191
Fundamentalism, Islamic, 84-85
Functionalism, 14, 558

Galula, David, 368
Gandhi, Indira, 236, 260, 527
GATT. *See* General Agreement on Tariffs and Trade
General Agreement on Tariffs and Trade (GATT), 61, 109-110, 437
General Assembly. *See* United Nations
General Motors (GM), 427
Geneva Conference (1954), 376
Geneva Protocol (1925), 537
Geography, 140-141
George, Alexander, 198
Germany.
    1920s-1930s, 29-30, 58, 161
    Berlin Wall, 48, 219
    division of, 125, 131, 219
    East Germany, reforms in, 219
    European Coal and Steel Community and, 503
    European Economic Community and, 509
    France and, 53, 394, 500, 509
    postwar period, in, 394-395
    power of, 141-142, 161
    reunification of, 132, 521
    Soviet Union and, 316
    Treaty of Versailles (1919) and, 103-104, 482, 561
    unification of, 141, 142, 160-161, 219-220
    United States and, 444
    World War I, 4, 21, 106-107, 124, 156, 158, 159, 182
    World War II, 24-25, 152, 156, 158, 182, 390-391, 561
Giap, Vo Nguyen, 156, 372, 375
Gilpin, Robert, 149
Glasnost, 164, 166-167
Glassboro meeting (1967), 217, 292
GM. *See* General Motors
GNP. *See* Gross national product
Good, Robert, 258
Gorbachev, Mikhail. *See also* Soviet Union
    arms control and, 330
    Baltic Republics and, 75
    reforms of, 49, 84, 105, 164-165, 216-220, 269, 305, 318-319, 396
    secretary general/president, 47, 154-155
    Strategic Defense Initiative and, 297
    United States and, 206
Governmental institutions
    bureaucracy, 280-281, 284

executive branch, 93-94, 95-96, 275-276, 277, 278-280, 282-283, 284, 285, 286, 287, 291-294. *See also* Presidents
    judiciary, 95, 96
    legislative branch, 94-95, 96, 275-276, 281, 282, 284, 285, 287, 288-289
Governments
    authority of, 45-46, 95
    decision making, 281-289
    domestic affairs, 46-47
    force, use of. *See* Force
Grain, U.S. exports of, 440
Gramm-Rudman-Hollings bill, 405
Great powers. *See also* Western democracies
    competition among, 106-107, 121-122, 162, 168, 311, 321, 351-352, 440-443, 508
    domestic policies of, 401
    hierarchy of, 55-56, 148, 445-447
    oil and, 412-413
    power and, 103, 110, 118, 417-418, 446
    primacy of, 53-55, 445-446
    role of, 53, 54, 56-58, 111, 122
    superpowers. *See* Superpowers
    United Nations and, 454-455
    war and, 381-382, 560
Greece, 507
Green Revolution, 244, 246
Grenada (1983), 63, 380, 382-383
Grey, Sir Edward, 352
Gross national product (GNP), 66, 148, 169, 404-405
Group of 77, 466
Guerrilla war, 368-373, 375, 376-378, 380, 540-541
Gulf Cooperation Council, 62

Haas, Ernst, 502-503
Haig, Alexander, 129
Haiti, 255
Hamilton, Alexander, 565
Hammarskjöld, Dag, 461
HDTV. *See* Television, high definition
Hearst, William Randolph, 561
Heilbroner, Robert, 231-232
Herara, Omar Torrijos, 55
Herz, John, 116n8
Hezbullah (Party of God), 541, 542, 545
Hideki, Tojo, 487
Highjacking, 542-543, 544, 545
Hitler, Adolph. *See also* Germany
    appeasement of (1938), 6, 10, 11, 22,

33, 36, 104, 136, 158, 274-275, 314, 316, 317
  rise to power, 30, 104, 313
  World War II and, 158, 161
Hobbes, Thomas, 92, 98, 100, 484
Ho Chi Minh, 69, 372, 540
Hoffmann, Stanley, 37-38
Holsti, Ole, 315
Honda, 426
Hong Kong, 52, 231
Hopkins, Harry, 22
Hostages, 85, 88, 99, 194, 475, 481, 542-543, 545-546
Howard, Michael, 558
Hull, Cordell, 22
Human rights, 46-47, 467, 476
Hungary, 130, 395-396, 509
Hunger, developing countries, in, 243-246
Huntington, Samuel, 432-433
Hussein, Saddam, 548
Hyundai, 426

IAEA. *See* International Atomic Energy Agency
ICBMs. *See* Intercontinental ballistic missiles
Ideology
  protection of, 83-85
  Soviet Union, in, 197-204
  systemic model and, 112-113
  Third World and, 548-549
IGOs. *See* Intergovernmental organizations
Incrementalism, 285-286, 287, 306, 319. *See also* Decision making
India
  alignment of, 260
  children in, 241
  food production in, 244
  interventions by, 385, 465
  language of, 238
  nuclear power of, 526, 527
  Pakistan and, 548-549
  population in, 242
  poverty in, 231-232
  religious issues in, 236
  United Nations and, 465
Indochina, 190, 372, 376. *See also* Vietnam
Industrial integration, European, 394-395
Industrial revolution, 244
INF. *See* Intermediate nuclear forces

Intelligentsia, 271n8
Intercontinental ballistic missiles (ICBMs), 276, 293, 297, 343, 347-348
Interdependence, 510-516, 521-522, 558, 562, 565-566
Interest groups, role of, 282
Intergovernmental organizations, 60-65, 70
Intermediate nuclear forces (INF), 216, 329-331
International Atomic Energy Agency (IAEA), 529-531
International Court of Justice, 476, 481, 482, 483
International law, 478-483
International Nuclear Fuel Cycle Evaluation, 530
International politics. *See also* Domestic policies; Foreign policies; Negotiations; State system
  community building in, 496-505
  conflicts in, 92-93, 96, 97-98, 100, 292, 329-333
  crisis management in, 120-132, 277-281, 285-286, 320
  force in, 85, 100, 373, 376. *See also* Force; War
  games analogy of, 7-8, 15-17, 19, 92, 104, 111, 112, 275, 284, 300, 521
  global system and, 57
  ideology and, 83, 85, 112-113, 197-204
  legal aspects of, 10. *See also* International law
  morality and, 420, 483-491, 545
  nuclear power and, 531-532. *See also* Nuclear weapons
  power politics, as. *See* Power politics
  security and, 322
  strategies of, 7, 85, 107-108
  Western democracies and, 10, 93
  zero-sum character of, 124, 128, 129, 130, 131
International politics, study of. *See also* States, objectives of; State system
  decision-making level, 32-39, 274-289, 300. *See also* Decision making; Policy making
  high politics, 85-86, 101, 389, 401, 511
  low politics, 85-86, 101, 389, 401, 494-495, 511
  models of, 275-277, 300, 302, 306, 562-564
  nation-state level, 27-32, 36-39, 333-334, 430, 431-434, 506-507, 520

state-system level, 20-27, 36-39, 45-71, 112-114, 431, 499, 557-559
systems, 19-20, 57
International relations, theories of
behavioralism, 12-14
contemporary approaches, 14-17, 85-86, 499-507
historical approach, 8-9
interdependence, 510-516, 564
realism, 11-12, 562-566
reductionism, 558
regime, 513, 516
utopianism, 9-10
Investment, international, 79-80
Iran. *See also* Hostages
foreign policy, 19
Iran-Iraq war, 84, 384, 465, 472, 476, 536
Islamic revolution (1979), 84-85, 127, 253, 489-490, 548
nuclear inspections and, 530
oil embargo, 402
Shah of, 55, 489, 548
terrorists and, 76, 474, 481, 483, 542
Vincennes, 348
Iran-contra scandal, 88-89
Iraq
chemical warfare, use of, 483, 537, 538
Iran-Iraq war, 84, 384, 465, 472, 476, 536
Ireland, 508
Iron Curtain, 49-50, 500-501
Irredentism, 548
Islamic Amal, 542-543
Islamic fundamentalism, 252, 253
Islamic Jihad (Holy War), 541
Israel. *See also* Middle East
Arab states and, 75, 158-159, 542, 548
domestic policies, 50
Egypt and, 76
military strength of, 150, 151-152, 481, 525
nuclear power, 525, 532, 538
Palestinians and, 50, 155, 462
preemptive strikes by, 481, 532
recognition of, 51
small power, as a, 55, 57
terrorism and, 476, 542-543, 544, 545
United Nations and, 466-467
United States and, 303, 405
Italy, 481, 542

Jackson-Vanik amendment, 303
Janis, Irving, 277-278

Japan
agriculture in, 444
aid program of, 405
competitiveness of, 427, 428
economy of, 167-170, 268, 321, 425-426, 439, 522
industry of, 439
Ministry of International Trade and Industry, 439
per capita income, 148
political role of, 103, 125, 167-170
resources, import of, 144, 147
Russia, attack of, 26
technological development of, 168-169, 524
Tokyo, 242
trade in, 441-443
United States and, 365, 434-435, 522, 524, 526
World War II, 156
Jenkins, Brian, 541
Jews, 401
Jingoism, 561
John Paul II (Pope), 67
Johnson, Lyndon B.
antiballistic missiles and, 289, 291-294, 300
Vietnam and, 34, 190, 222n19, 302, 381
War on Poverty, 86

Katanga, 460, 463. *See also* Shaba
Kellogg-Briand Pact (1928), 10
Kennan, George
democracies, 28-29, 152-153
international politics, 11, 201-202, 205
Russian revolution, 201-202
Soviet Union, 311-312
Kennedy, Robert, 487
Kennedy, John F.
Cuba and, 276, 278-280, 281, 286, 304, 380, 487
president, as, 302
space race and, 135-136
Vietnam War and, 34, 189, 376
Kirkpatrick, Jeanne, 467-469
Kissinger, Henry
balance of power and, 565
China and, 38-39
détente and, 192
Egypt and, 260, 461
national security adviser, as, 301-302
Soviet Union and, 105, 275, 303, 307, 392

thermonuclear war and, 339
Khomeini, Ayatollah Ruhollah, 84-85, 542
Korea, 268, 426
Korean War, 30, 125, 187, 332, 357, 364-365, 366, 367, 455
Kosygin, A. N., 292
Khrushchev, Nikita, 209, 279, 305, 337
Kuwait
    embassy, bombing of, 542
    per capita income, 149
    ships, U.S. reflagging of, 384, 472
    terrorism and, 545

Language, 238
Lasswell, Harold, 94
Latin America. *See also* individual countries
    debt of, 406-409, 410
    military in, 255
    peace plan for, 473
    sovereignty of, 47
    United States and, 55, 320
Law, international, 478-483, 498
Law of the Sea Treaty (1982), 476, 478, 479
League of Nations
    great powers and, 54
    international politics and, 9-10, 110, 481, 560
Lebanon
    religious issues in, 237
    terrorism in, 383, 472, 542-544
    United Nations and, 462, 473-474
    war in, 46
Lee Kuan Yew, 253
Lenin, V. I., 32, 203, 204, 218
Less developed countries (LDCs), 409-410, 419. *See also* Developing countries; Third World countries
Leverage, economic. *See* Economic leverage
Levy, Jack, 53
Levy, Walter, 414
Libya, 380, 465, 466, 544-545
Lincoln, Abraham, 181
Lippmann, Walter, 40n16
Liska, George, 402-403
List, Friedrich, 418
Lovell, John, 7
Luard, Evan, 270
Lumumba, Patrice, 460-461

MacArthur, Douglas, 184

Mack, Andrew, 381
MAD. *See* Mutual assured destruction
Magsaysay, Ramón, 372
Mahan, Alfred Thayer, 106
Malaya, 372
Malnutrition. *See* Hunger
Malthus, Thomas, 239-240, 245
Mandelbaum, Michael, 19
Mao Zedong, 69, 101, 209, 269, 370, 372, 377, 540
Marcos, Ferdinand, 400
Marshall, George C., 125
Marshall Plan, 125, 153, 393-394, 404
Marxism-Leninism
    Catholic church and, 67
    dependency and, 14-15
    political analysis and, 202-203
    tenets of, 198-200, 405
    United States, in, 206
    war, causes of, 15, 559
Marx, Karl, 101, 204, 417
Mass production techniques, export of, 425-426
May, Michael, 355
Mazda, 427
McCarthy, Joseph, 189
McKinley, William, 561
McNamara, Robert, 106, 242, 280, 290-293, 302
Medellin drug cartel, 45-46, 398, 399
Media, role of, 289
Mercantilism, 438-445, 524
METO. *See* Middle East Treaty Organization
Mexico
    consumer nation, as, 410
    debt of, 409
    Mexico City, 241-242
    population of, 241
Middle East. *See also* Egypt; Israel; Palestine
    arms sales and, 534-535
    conflict in, 548
    superpowers and, 459-460
    terrorists in, 490
    United Nations and, 461-462, 463, 464-465, 466-467, 473
Middle East Treaty Organization (METO), 125-126, 127, 188
Midgetman missiles, 355
Military government, developing countries, in, 255-257
Military power
    perceptions of, 136, 150, 165-166, 281

role of, 98-100
threat/vulnerability analysis, 159-160
Military service, universal, 334
Minh, Ho Chi, 127
Minutemen III missiles, 347
MIRV. *See* Multiple independent reentry vehicle
Missiles. *See also* Antiballistic missiles; Intercontinental ballistic missiles; Strategic Defense Initiative; Submarine-launched ballistic missiles
  numbers of, 344-345, 347, 536-538
  precision-guided munitions, 380, 536, 537-538
  role of, 343-345, 347
  sales of, 536
  Soviet Union, 213, 276, 292-293, 294-300, 329-330, 343, 344-345, 346, 347
  technology control regime (1987), 537
  United States, 276, 293, 296, 343, 344-345, 347, 350-351, 354
Mitrany, David, 502
Mitsubishi, 426
MNCs. *See* Multinational corporations
Modelski, George, 119
Monnet, Jean, 503
Monroe Doctrine, 55
Morality, 420, 483-491, 515, 545-546
Morgenthau, Hans
  international politics, 11-12
  Politics Among Nations, 11, 562
  state behavior, 113
Morocco, 472-473
Mueller, John, 553
Mujahedeen, 377
Muller, Ronald, 249
Multinational corporations (MNCs)
  developing countries and, 248, 249, 428, 432, 434
  development of, 425, 429-431
  host countries and, 433, 434
  role of, 65-66, 69-70, 71, 430-431, 433-434
Multiple independent reentry vehicle (MIRV), 347, 350-351, 354
Munich Agreement (1938), 332. *See also* Hitler, Adolph, appeasement of
Muslims, 46, 49
  Afghanistan, in, 377
  Middle East, in, 489
  Shiite, 542, 543
  Sunni, 543
Mussolini, Benito, 136-137

Mutual assured destruction (MAD), 332, 347-349, 356-359
Mutual deterrence, 346
Mutual vulnerability, 356-359
MX missiles, 347

Namibia, 473
Napoleonic Wars, 103, 560
Nasser, 461, 463
Nationalism
  Israel, in, 50
  role of, 50-51, 96, 188, 257, 373, 379-380
  self-determination and, 414, 445, 487, 548, 560, 561
  Soviet satellites, in, 49-50, 395-396
National interests, 319-325, 480-483
National liberation
  revolutionary wars and, 368-373, 539
  Soviet Union and, 203
  terrorism and, 539
  United Nations and, 467
National Liberation Groups, 68-69
NATO. *See* North Atlantic Treaty Organization
Natural resources, 143-144, 147
Naval power, 21, 106, 119, 390-391
Negotiations
  conflict resolution, 329-333, 461, 482
  governmental politics and, 306-307
  tacit diplomacy in, 329, 331, 367-368
  trade, 443
Nelson, Lord Horatio, 98
Netherlands, The, 119
Newly Industrialized Countries (NICs)
  government in, 257
  Third World countries, as, 59, 147, 225-226, 249-250, 252
  United States, trade with, 249
New York City, 242
New York Times, 168, 474
Ngo Dinh Diem, 188, 376
NGOs. *See* Nongovernmental organizations
Nguyen Van Thieu, 188
Nicaragua
  contras, 63, 195
  peace plan (1989), 63, 473
  Reagan administration and, 88, 99, 289, 304
  Sandinista government, 51, 68, 126, 320, 322, 325
  Soviet Union and, 130
  United States and, 482

NICs. *See* Newly Industrialized
Countries
Niebuhr, Reinhold, 11
Nigeria
civil war in, 465
hunger in, 246
religious issues in, 237
Nixon, Richard M.
antiballistic missiles and, 293-
294
Arab-Israeli War and, 459-460
Chile and, 397-398
China and, 26, 38-39
defense spending and, 87
détente and, 192, 318
summit meetings and, 317
Vietnam War and, 381
Nomenklatura (USSR), 196-197
Nonaligned states, 59-60, 83, 259-261
Nongovernmental organizations
intergovernmental organizations,
compared with, 65
humanitarian/religious organizations, 67-68
liberation groups, 68-69, 70-71
multinational corporations, 65-67, 69-
70
role of, 70-71
terrorists, 69. *See also* Terrorism
Noriega, Manuel, 47, 63, 138, 398-399
North Atlantic Treaty Organization
(NATO)
changes in, 509-510
disagreements in, 130-131, 509
establishment of, 125, 394
membership of, 62
oil and, 144
role of, 59, 127, 130, 157, 188, 217
terrorism and, 539
United States and, 365-366, 509, 525
North/South countries, 225-227, 233
NPT. *See* Treaty on the Nonproliferation of Nuclear Weapons
Nuclear reactors, 527-528
Nuclear suppliers, 529-530
Nuclear weapons. *See also* Arms race;
Deterrence
costs of, 525
disarmament, 487-488
great powers and, 54, 55, 78-79, 107,
128, 150, 220, 318
polarity and, 132, 330, 336-337, 339-
340
power of, 335-337, 339, 356

proliferation of, 524-533
protests against, 487-488
Strategic Defense Initiative and, 78-
79, 294-300
war and, 119, 132, 294-295, 334-337,
339, 356-359, 367, 445-446, 494, 564
Nuclear winter, 337-338
Nunn, Sam, 298
Nyerere, Julius, 485

OAS. *See* Organization of American
States
OAU. *See* Organization for African
Unity
Oil. *See also* Organization of Petroleum
Exporting Countries
companies, 66
economic power of, 101, 143-144
embargo, Arab (1973), 108
glut, 415
prices, 66, 227, 229, 406, 411-415, 435
production, 109, 412, 415
production, non-OPEC, 411-412, 415-
416
United States, use and production,
411-412
Olson, Richard, 419
OPEC. *See* Organization of Petroleum
Exporting Countries
Organization for African Unity (OAU),
62, 467
Organization of American States (OAS)
Falkland Islands episode and, 62-63
Latin American issues and, 61-62, 63
Noriega, Manuel, and, 63-64
Organization of Front-Line States, 64
Organization of Petroleum Exporting
Countries (OPEC), 60, 82, 83, 101
developing countries and, 266, 416,
465
non-OPEC oil and, 415-416
oil embargo (1973), 108, 227, 411
oil prices and, 227, 229, 411, 412-415
oil production and, 109, 412, 415, 435
policies of, 415, 416, 419, 487
world economies and, 411, 416
Outsourcing, 428
Overpopulation, 239-246. *See also* Birth
control

Pakistan
East Pakistan and, 465, 548-549
food supplies in, 246
nuclear power and, 526, 530

regionalism in, 237
United Nations and, 465, 472
Palestine, 50, 155. *See also* Israel
Palestine Liberation Organization (PLO)
Israel and, 52-53, 539, 541, 542, 543, 544
nongovernmental organization, as, 68, 70
United Nations and, 462, 466-467
Panama
Noriega, Manuel, 47, 63, 138, 398-399
United States and, 398-399
Patriotic Front, 68, 70
Patriotism, 156
Peace, 100, 103. *See also* War
nuclear power and, 532
preservation of, 445-447, 453, 498
United Nations and, 453-465, 469-474
Uniting for Peace resolution (1950), 455
world government and, 497-498, 502
Peace of Westphalia (1648), 4, 45, 71
Pearl Harbor, 286, 314. *See also* World War II
Per capita income
developing countries, of, 148-149, 230, 261
standard of wealth, as, 148-149
Perestroika, 164, 166-167, 218, 219, 220
Perkins, Dexter, 215
Pershing II missile, 330
Peru, 408
PGMs. *See* Precision-guided munitions
Philippines, 400
Physicians for Social Responsibility, 487-488
Planned Parenthood, 243
PLO. *See* Palestine Liberation Organization
Plutonium, 529, 530
Poland
economy of, 395-396
government reform (1989), 47, 130, 210, 218-219
Solidarity, 67, 218
Polarity, international
bipolarity, 119-121, 122-130, 131-132, 161, 257-259, 507, 523, 551, 562
bipolicentricity, 170-171
multipolarity, 121-124, 127, 132, 170
unipolarity, 118-119
Policy makers
conformity of, 277-278

perceptions of, 310-311, 419
Policy making. *See also* Decision making
capabilities and, 104-105
domestic versus foreign, 282-283
models of, 275-289
processes, 34-36, 275-277, 287-289, 396
Political economy, 390, 505-506. *See also* Economics
Political science. *See also* International politics, study of
study of, 8-17, 19-39
Pol Pot, 465
Population
growth of, 239, 241-243
national loyalties and, 48-49
overpopulation, 239-246
power and, 139, 141-143
worldwide implications of, 495
Portugal, 119, 507
Poverty
developing countries, of, 230-233
worldwide implications of, 495
Power. *See also* Balance of power; Force; Military power; Polarity
classification of states and, 53-56, 57-60
components of, 139-157
definition of, 137
economic, 101, 160-169, 417-418
perceptions of, 135-137, 139-140, 321, 343, 419, 420, 445-447
policy making and, 285
prestige and, 77-79
projection of, 56-58
sanctions/rewards and, 100-101, 137-139. *See also* Sanctions
security and, 97-104
war and, 157-159
Power politics, 74-75, 124-125, 128-129, 137-139, 171, 183, 190-191, 193-195, 208, 213-214, 475, 515, 565-566
Precision-guided munitions (PGMs), 380, 536, 537-538
Presidents. *See also* Governmental institutions, executive branch; individual presidents
antiballistic missile decisions of, 291-294, 300-301
foreign policy and, 300-302
policy making and, 35, 36, 278-280, 283, 284, 289, 322
Prestige, 77-79, 99
Prussia, 53

al-Qaddafi, Muammar, 529

Racial issues, 235-236, 476
Radiation, nuclear explosions, of, 336
Reagan Doctrine, 378
Reagan, Ronald
  administration of, 78, 79, 157, 194-196,
    302, 405
  agricultural subsidies and, 443
  defense spending, 80, 86, 87, 163, 215,
    428-429
  drugs, war on, 76-77
  family planning, 243
  grain embargo, 392
  intermediate nuclear forces and, 329-
    331
  Kuwaiti tankers and, 126, 384
  Moscow Summit (1988), 47
  Nicaragua and, 88-89, 126, 289, 398,
    482-483
  Panama and, 398, 400
  Philippines and, 400
  Saudi Arabia and, 147
  South Africa and, 147, 402
  Soviet Union and, 215-216, 220, 321,
    483
  Strategic Defense Initiative (SDI) and,
  terrorism and, 543, 545
  United Nations and, 469
Realism, international politics and, 11-
  12, 562-566
Recognition, national, 51-53
Reductionism, 558
Regimes, 513, 516
Religious issues, 236-237
Renan, Ernest, 49
Republican party
  antiballistic missiles and, 291, 293
  cold war and, 322
  Communist China and, 30, 38-39, 189,
    302
  Soviet Union and, 192-193, 279
  Strategic Defense Initiative and, 299
Revisionists, 214-215
Revolutionary states. *See also* Terrorism
  agrarian reform in, 244
  international economies and, 265
  justice and, 110-111
  patterns of behavior, 30-32, 83-84,
    110-111
Richardson, Elliot, 472
Rio Pact, 127
Roman Empire, 118-119
Romania, 130

Roosevelt, Franklin D.
  postwar expectations of, 187
  prewar recommendations of, 322
  Soviet Union and, 22, 206, 316
  Stalin, Joseph, and, 316
  World War II and, 21, 76, 286, 316
Rosenau, James, 160
Rousseau, Jean Jacques, 95
Rubber, 417
Rusk, Dean, 290
Russia, czarist, 21, 26, 29, 32, 49, 159,
  161, 179, 311. *See also* Soviet Union
Russo-Japanese War (1904-1905), 365

SAC. *See* Strategic Air Command
Sadat, Anwar, 155, 260, 261, 463
SALT. *See* Strategic Arms Limitation
  Talks
Sanchez, Oscar Arias, 63
Sanctions, 392, 397-399, 400-402, 413-
  414, 419-420, 468, 475, 481. *See also*
  Economic coercion
Saudi Arabia
  oil production of, 109
Schelling, Thomas, 343, 356-357
Schilling, Warner, 292
Schlesinger, Arthur, Jr., 487
Schultz, George
  bomb attack of, 76
  secretary of state, as, 302
  terrorism and, 543-544
  world population growth, 243
Schuman, Frederick, 502
Schuman, Robert, 503
SDI. *See* Strategic Defense Initiative
SEATO. *See* Southeast Asia Treaty Organization
Second strike forces, 343, 344, 346-347
Security. *See also* Deterrence
  arms control and, 351-352, 357
  cold war and, 322, 436, 525-526
  community, 499-500, 510
  dilemma of, 97, 105, 113-114, 116n8,
    357, 494, 499-500, 557-558, 565
  economic, 79-81, 101, 390-393
  interdependence and, 511-512
  national security, 75-77
  power and, 97-104
  security politics, 74-75, 97-98, 216-217,
    318-319, 357, 521
Security Council (United Nations), 454,
  463, 473-474, 475-476, 477, 481, 526-
  527
Self-determination, 414, 445, 487, 548,

561
Separatism, 548-549
Shaba, 460
Shiite. *See* Muslims, Shiite
Sigmund, Paul, 400
Sikhs, 236, 237, 539
Singapore, 253, 268
Sino-Soviet alliance (1950), 125, 128-129
Sino-Soviet bloc. *See also* China, Communist; Soviet Union
    dissolution, 209-210
    formation, 26
    U.S. perception of, 187, 287, 312
Six Day War, 461
SLBM. *See* Submarine-launched ballistic missile
Small powers, 55. *See also* Great powers; Superpowers
Smith, Adam, 252
Smith, Gaddis, 314
Smith, Walter Bedell, 376
Social spillover, 504-505
Social strategies, 371
Solidarity, 67
Somalia, 76, 237, 465, 548
Somme, Battle of the, 4
Somoza Debayle, Anastasio, 193
South Africa. *See also* Africa
    apartheid, 147, 401
    Blacks, treatment of, 47
    natural resources of, 147
    sanctions against, 401-402
    United Nations and, 476, 486
Southeast Asia, Chinese in, 236
Southeast Asia Treaty Organization (SEATO), 126, 127, 188
Southwest African People's Organization (SWAPO), 68, 467
Sovereignty, state, 45-48
Soviet Union. *See also* Gorbachev, Mikhail; Russia, czarist; Superpowers
    armed forces, 24, 78-79, 87, 148, 154, 192, 193, 194, 213, 217, 321, 353
    capitalism, attitudes toward, 31-32, 198-207, 212-213, 316, 405, 511
    Communist party ideology in, 196-210, 268-269
    decision making in, 304-306
    domestic policies, 49-50, 82, 154, 163-165, 216, 219-220, 401, 440
    economy of, 78, 82, 87, 148, 163-165, 268-269, 391-392, 523, 534, 550
    internal conflicts, 49-50, 84
    political elite of, 196-197, 304

    prestige of, 78-79, 154
    Revolutions of 1917, 29, 83-84, 111, 200
Soviet Union, foreign policies, 19, 32, 112, 114. *See also* Strategic Arms Limitation Talks
    aid program, 403-404, 405-406
    alliances, 125-132, 523
    cold war and, 21-24, 32, 35, 51, 105, 182, 212-214, 216-220
    détente and, 192-193, 203, 204, 212-213
    expansionism, 22-24, 104, 119, 179-180, 202, 208, 214, 216, 268-269, 314-315
    international politics and, 11, 196-210, 214
    intervention, 204-205, 333, 382, 385
    Strategic Defense Initiative (SDI) and, 78, 107, 296, 299-300
    superpower as, 54, 55-56, 78, 163-166, 192, 213-214, 216
    trade, 392-393
    world wars and, 21, 22-24, 104, 206, 207
Soviet Union, and foreign countries
    Afghanistan, 126, 130, 194, 195, 205, 216, 246, 312, 376-378, 379
    Africa, 460-461
    China, 26, 59, 75, 127, 129, 208-210
    Cuba, 278-280, 396-397. *See also* Cuba, missile crisis
    Egypt, 126, 214, 260, 460
    Middle East, 459-460
    satellite countries, 47, 49-50, 55, 75, 130, 210, 218, 317, 385, 395-396, 523
    United States, 107, 108, 109, 126, 195-196, 205, 212-213, 311-312
Space, exploration of, 107, 135-136
Spanish-American War, 561
Sparta, 120
Sri Lanka, 238
Stability
    international systems and, 118-132
    superpowers and, 120, 121, 122-123, 127, 128, 129-130, 364-365, 366-367, 458-459, 549-551
Stalemates, 332
Stalin, Joseph
    China and, 26
    cold war and, 215
    Roosevelt, Franklin D., and, 206, 208, 316
    United States, perceptions of, 314

Western democracies and, 32
Yalta Conference, 22
Yugoslavia and, 401
START. *See* Strategic Arms Reduction Talks
Star Wars. *See* Strategic Defense Initiative
States, objectives of. *See also* Domestic politics; International politics
economic security, 79-81
ideology, promotion of, 78, 83-85, 87-90
national prestige, 77-79, 99, 106-107, 136, 138
national security, 75-77, 85-90, 96-97, 103, 110, 120
national welfare, 81-83, 85-87, 110-111
power, 74-75, 97-104, 120
self-determination, 414, 445, 487, 560
State system. *See also* Balance of power; Polarity; Supranation system
behavior patterns of, 104-109, 112-115, 118, 494-496, 558
characteristics of, 45-53, 95, 96, 101, 109-113, 115, 136, 340, 477, 499, 516, 520-523, 565
classifications in, 53-60, 111-112
conflict in, 86-90, 105-106, 120, 121, 122, 132, 520, 521
dependency in, 14-15, 108
interdependency and, 510-516
international politics and, 19-27
nuclear power in, 531-532
organizations in, 60-70, 71
power in, 102-104, 118-132
rules/laws of, 109-112, 342, 478-479
states, role of, 70-71, 96, 97, 258
structure of, 118-132, 496, 502, 510
United Nations and, 454
Steel industry, 320
Steel, Ronald, 191
Sterling, Richard, 496
Stoessinger, John, 312
Strange, Susan, 516
Strategic Air Command (SAC), 364
Strategic Arms Limitation Talks (SALT). *See also* Arms control
SALT I (1972), 193, 214, 217, 289, 293, 344-345, 346, 347, 349-352
SALT II (1979), 109, 214, 217, 320, 347, 349
SALT III, 347
Strategic Arms Reduction Talks (START), 300, 351, 355, 533

Strategic Defense Initiative (SDI) (1983)
impact of, 107, 195, 331
politics of, 289-300
Soviet Union and, 78-79
Submarine-launched ballistic missile (SLBM), 343, 356
Submarines, 390
Sudan, 237
Suez War (1956), 380, 486
Superpowers. *See also* Great powers
Central America and, 126, 397-400
decline of, 161-171, 440-441, 523
economic power and, 397-406
Europe as, 508
foreign aid and, 402-406
gross national product and, 148
interdependence of, 435-436, 444, 445
Middle East and, 460
military strength and, 150-151, 344-345, 346-349, 353-354, 532-533
relations between, 54, 55-56, 57, 78-79, 128, 131, 220, 259-261, 522, 547-551
space and, 107
stability and, 120, 121, 122-123, 127, 128, 129-130, 364-365, 366-367, 458-459, 549-551
summit meetings of, 317
United Nations and, 454, 457-465, 473, 475
war and, 378-379
Supranation system, 500-507
SWAPO. *See* Southwest African People's Organization
Sweden, 150, 528
Switzerland, 150
Syria, 459-460, 541-542, 548

Taiwan, 52, 268, 426. *See also* China, Nationalist
Tanzania, 465
Taylor, A. J. P., 142
Technology
electronics, 431
European Economic Community and, 508
multinational corporations and, 429, 431
power of, 149, 379-380
television, high definition (HDTV), 168-169
weapons and, 536
Television
high definition (HDTV), 168-169
terrorism and, 539-540

Teller, Edward, 294
Territorial interests
  integrity, 75-76
  state borders and, 48
Terrorism
  fighting against, 383
  national liberation movements, compared with, 69
  Party of God (Shiite), 69
  Red Brigade (Italy), 69
  retaliation, 543-546
  role of, 371
  warfare, as, 538-543, 546-547
Tito, Marshal, 23, 68-69, 208, 401, 540
Thatcher, Margaret, 385-386
Third World countries. *See also* Developing countries
  aid to, 404
  arms sales to, 534-535
  Castro, Fidel, and, 397
  conflict in, 547-550
  debt of, 409
  description of, 225-226
  development of, 59, 82-83, 443
  food supplies in, 243-246
  nationalism of, 379
  population of, 242
  resources, export of, 147
  stability of, 269-270
  United Nations and, 463, 465-469
Thirty Years' War, 4, 236
Threat analysis, 159
Thucydides, 120
Toshiba, 434
Totalitarian governments, 152, 153, 156
Toyota, 427
Trade. *See also* Free trade; Mercantilism
  adversarial trade, 524
  barriers, 441-442, 524
  deficits, 442
  dependency, 14-15, 264-267, 268
  developing countries, with, 249-250, 409-410, 436
  Eastern European, 396
  European Economic Community and, 501-502, 508
  General Agreement on Tariffs and Trade (GATT), 61, 109-110, 437
  political economy and, 391-392, 437, 523-524
  political lever, as, 392-393
  trade wars, 441, 524
Traditionalists, 12
Transnational organizations. *See* Nongovernmental organizations
Treaties. *See* Law, international
Treaty of Versailles (1919), 10, 103-104, 560
Treaty of Westphalia (1648), 4, 45, 71
Treaty on the Nonproliferation of Nuclear Weapons (NPT), 530, 531, 532
Trotsky, Leon, 83-84
Truman Doctrine (1947), 89, 124-125, 153, 182-183, 317
Truman, Harry S
  cold war, 83
  decision making and, 292
  demobilization and, 316
  international politics of, 89, 182-183, 188, 286, 365
  Soviet policies, 38, 317
Tshombe, Moise, 460
Tucker, Robert, 413-414

U-2 episode, 481
Uganda, 465
UNCTAD. *See* United Nations Conference on Trade and Development
UNDOF. *See* United Nations Disengagement Observer Force
UNEF. *See* United Nations Emergency Force
UNESCO. *See* United Nations Educational, Scientific, and Cultural Organization
United Kingdom. *See* Britain
United Nations
  budget, 468-469
  developing countries and, 465-469, 472-473, 476
  establishment of, 110
  functions of, 453-455, 456, 457-465, 467-477
  great/super powers and, 54, 150, 217, 454-455, 457-459, 468-469, 475, 549-550
  growth of, 457, 468
  human rights and, 467, 476
  nonaligned countries and, 456, 457, 463, 464, 466, 468
  Population Fund, 241
  Soviet Union and, 455-456, 457-459, 464, 466, 469-472, 474, 476
  troika plan, 464
  United States and, 454-456, 457-459, 464, 466, 467-469, 472, 475-476
  Uniting for Peace resolution (1950), 455

voting in, 468
war and, 456, 464-465
Zionism and, 467
United Nations Conference on Trade
    and Development (UNCTAD), 60, 61,
    416-417, 466
United Nations Disengagement Ob-
    server Force (UNDOF), 461
United Nations Educational, Scientific,
    and Cultural Organization
    (UNESCO), 467, 476
United Nations Emergency Force
    (UNEF), 461, 462-463
United States. *See also* Governmental
    institutions; Superpowers
agriculture in, 149-150, 439-440
competitiveness of, 428
dependency, political, and, 14-15, 264
economy, 47-48, 79-81, 86, 161-163,
    249, 407, 409-410, 435, 437-438, 534,
    550
geography and, 141
gross national product, 148, 438
industry of, 161-163, 527
national perceptions of, 181-182, 186-
    187, 188, 194, 196, 213, 428, 487,
    513-516, 562
natural resources of, 143-144, 147,
    411-412
per capita income, 148
political process in, 300-304, 498
postwar policies, 37-38, 314
power of, 142, 160, 161-163, 215, 565-
    566
public debate in, 288-289, 294, 314
sovereignty, 47-48
success in, 181
superpower, as, 53-54, 55-56, 79, 119,
    153-154, 161-163, 440-441
United States, domestic policies. *See also*
    individual presidents
defense spending, 80, 86-87, 148, 194,
    195, 353, 405
deficit, 47-48, 79-80, 130, 163, 407, 408
law and order, 115-116n4
military, 21, 24, 80, 107, 150, 161-162
nuclear power, 525-526, 527, 528, 529
politics and, 188
social spending, 86-87
steel industry, 320
Strategic Defense Initiative and, 78-
    79, 107, 195, 294-295, 299-300
technology and, 149, 168-169
trade, 434-444. *See also* Multinational

corporations
United States, foreign policies
aid program, 403, 404-405, 407, 410
alliances, 89-90, 124-132, 317-318, 437,
    440-441, 445, 489, 523
arms control, 195, 340-352. *See also*
    Strategic Arms Limitation Talks
burden sharing, 170
cold war and, 21-24, 35, 87-88, 89, 181,
    194-196, 211-212, 214-216, 303, 315,
    322, 562-566
deterrent policy, 289-290, 295, 340-
    342. *See also* Deterrence
developing countries and, 262, 407-
    410
diplomacy in, 184-185
interventions, 46-47, 109, 114, 129,
    142, 180-181, 182-184, 189-190, 304,
    383, 384-385
isolationism and, 20-21, 22, 83, 103,
    114, 142, 161, 177-178, 180-183, 314
peacetime, during, 181-182, 183-184,
    191-196, 207
terrorism, 540, 541-546
wars and, 20-21, 76, 142, 156, 161, 181-
    182, 183-185, 214-215, 286, 313-314,
    332, 375, 559-564
United States, and foreign
    countries. *See also* individual
    countries
Canada, 444-445
Chile, 397-398, 399-400
China, 26, 30, 129, 187-189, 303, 357,
    366
Cuba, 278-281, 396-397, 399
Dominican Republic, 382-384
Germany, 444
Iran, 76, 402, 474, 481, 483, 489, 542,
    548
Israel, 151, 303, 542
Japan, 167-170, 321, 365, 434-435, 441-
    442
Korea, 30, 332, 365-366
Lebanon, 383, 463
Nicaragua, 398-399, 482-483
Panama, 398-399, 400
South Africa, 147
Soviet Union, 104, 106, 107, 108, 109,
    129, 187-189, 195-196, 211-212, 312,
    314-315
Vietnam, 26-27, 30, 34, 51, 52, 78, 99,
    100, 156, 188, 189-191, 331
Uranium, 530
USSR. *See* Soviet Union

Utopianism, 9-11, 12

Vance, Cyrus, 105, 472
Van Dyke, Vernon, 96
Verdun, 4
Versailles peace treaty, 58, 482
Veto, United Nations, 454-455, 463, 464, 467, 469, 476, 477
Vietnam. *See also* Indochina
　　Cambodia and, 465, 473, 475
　　Chinese, expulsion of, 236
　　United States and, 51, 52, 100, 129, 331
　　Vietnamese-Chinese War (1979), 236
Vietnam War (1965-1973)
　　bombing during, 156, 159, 376, 381, 487
　　China and, 26-27
　　consequences of, 35, 38, 78, 303, 322, 374, 376
　　costs of, 379
　　public opinion of, 288-289, 376, 486-487
　　Soviet Union and, 78
　　Tet offensive, 374
　　United States and, 26-27, 30, 34, 78, 99, 126, 127, 152, 158, 189-190, 373-376
　　Viet Cong and, 68, 371, 372-373, 374
Vincennes, 348
Violence. *See* Force; War
Vulnerability analysis, 159

Walters, Robert, 437
Waltz, Kenneth, 71, 122-123, 124, 131, 132, 305-306, 417, 558
War. *See also* Civil war; Nuclear weapons; Peace; individual wars
　　bombing during, 156
　　definition of, 136
　　democracies and, 28-30, 40n16, 380-382
　　geography and, 140
　　industrial revolution and, 334
　　international politics and, 3-4, 6, 7, 10-12, 98-100, 514, 549
　　legal aspects of, 10
　　military strength and, 151, 334
　　power and, 157-159, 182-184
　　self-sufficiency and, 390-391
　　solutions to, 11, 270, 551-553, 557-566
　　stability, international, and, 118, 119, 120, 123
Wars
　　arms race as, 353

civil, 93-94, 269-270, 465
　　limited, 364-368, 379
　　proxy, 378-379, 385, 445-446
　　revolutionary, 368-373, 374, 375, 376-378, 397
　　strikes, preemptive/preventive, 342-343, 346, 347-349, 356, 371, 481, 532
　　terrorist, 539-543
　　undeclared, 541-543
Warheads. *See* Missiles
War Powers Act (1973), 303-304
Warsaw Treaty Organization (WTO), 47, 125, 130, 132, 217, 509
Washington Naval Conference (1921-1922), 10
Watergate scandal, 303
Weapons. *See also* Arms control; Arms races; Arms sales; Missiles
　　balances of, 151-152, 352-353
　　chemical, 483, 537, 546
　　conventional, 535-536
　　modern, 380
　　terrorism and, 546
　　World War I, 4
Weinberger, Caspar, 302, 383
Weltman, John, 563
Western democracies. *See also* Democratic states; Great powers
　　cold war and, 31-32, 208, 487
　　competition, international, and, 168-169, 438
　　decolonization and, 110
　　developing countries and, 252-253, 262-263, 266-267, 269-270, 417-418, 419, 466, 479
　　domestic policies of, 10, 180-181
　　economy and, 523-524
　　geography and, 140-141
　　interdependence and, 14, 434-436
　　oil embargo (1973) and, 411
　　postwar policies of, 207-208, 381-386
　　resources, import of, 147
　　United Nations and, 465-469
Westernization, 262. *See also* Developing countries
Wilhelm II, Kaiser, 182
Wilson, Woodrow, 9-10, 83, 182, 560
Wolfers, Arnold, 102, 104, 105
Wordsworth, William, 266
World Bank, 409
World Court. *See* International Court of Justice
World government, 496-499, 510-516
World War I

balance of power and, 20-21, 160-161
causes of, 11, 124, 142-143
impact of, 4-6, 9-10
losses in, 4-5, 6
strategy, 4, 21
Treaty of Versailles, 103-104
World War II. *See also* participating nations
balance of power and, 21, 24-25, 119
causes of, 11, 28-30, 33-34, 89, 316
firestorms during, 360n9

impact of, 6, 153
peace following, 100, 104, 119, 124-125. *See also* Cold war
WTO. *See* Warsaw Treaty Organization

Yalta Conference (1945), 22
Yom Kippur War (1973), 151, 214

Zaire, 460-461, 548, 549
Zionism, 467

8374